TEMPTATION

JÁNOS SZÉKELY (1901–1958) was a Hungarian novelist and screenwriter. At 18 he fled Budapest for Berlin, where he penned scripts for silent movie stars including Marlene Dietrich. In 1938 he emigrated to the United States and continued writing for films in Hollywood, winning an Academy Award for Best Story for *Arise, My Love* in 1940. His novel *Temptation* was initially published in English translation in 1946 under the pseudonym John Pen. Blacklisted during the McCarthy era, Székely spent several years in Mexico with his family before returning to Berlin in 1957.

Pushkin Press

TEMPTATION

JÁNOS SZÉKELY

Translated from the
Hungarian by Mark Baczoni

Pushkin Press
71–75 Shelton Street
London WC2H 9JQ

First published by Creative Age Press, Inc. New York, 1946

First published by Pushkin Press in 2020

1 3 5 7 9 8 6 4 2

ISBN 13: 978-1-78227-548-0

Designed and typeset by Tetragon, London

Printed and bound by
CPI Group (UK) Ltd, Croydon, CRO 4YY

www.pushkinpress.com

TEMPTATION

ONE

Me and the Fine Young Gentleman

1

M Y LIFE BEGAN LIKE A REAL THRILLER: people were trying to kill me. But since this happened five months before I was born, I didn't upset myself too much about it. Although, if what they say in the village is true, I had every right. My life dangled by the hair of a peasant's head even before the five fingers that now hold this pen had had a chance to form.

My mother was sixteen at the time, and if the indications are to be believed, neither her soul nor her body wanted, one day, to have me call her "mother". And fair enough—it's not a blessing widely looked for by sixteen-year-old girls. But what my mother got up to—they tell me—went beyond all bounds. She revolted against motherhood as if she'd had the very Devil inside her. She resorted to the most shameful means, all the while doing the rounds of the churches, by turns kneeling and praying, then cursing the saints out of heaven. She ranted and raved, determined, come what may, not to have to birth me.

"If I'd loved that lousy father of his!" she said. "But I only saw him the once. Ain't seen hide or hair of him since."

And that was, indeed, the case. She'd met Mihály T. on the feast of St Peter and St Paul, seeing him neither before nor after. But the damage was done, though my mother wasn't the sort of "slutty tramp", as they used to say where I come from, who didn't care, who would have gone with anything in trousers. But I don't want to sugar-coat the thing, so let me tell it the way one of the women in the village, old Rozi—more about her anon—told it to me some time later.

According to her, "poor Anna" was no worse than the other young village girls. She was a quiet, neat girl with pale skin and black hair; she was beautiful. I remember her eyes most of all. She had unusually deep-set, small, black eyes, the sort that were always a little suspicious, always a little askance; a peasant's eyes peeking sharply out at the world, and yet with something of an old, gentle sadness. She lived with her stepmother. Her father had died when she was young, and she'd never known her mother. They were crushingly poor and she worked the fields. As young as fifteen, she worked her fingers to the bone on the Count's estate. So she more than deserved the little feast given for the labourers at St Peter and St Paul, where she met Mihály T.

He was renowned, Mihály T.—Mishka for short. Among themselves, the girls used to call him Dappermishka, all in one word, the way I've spelt it. Dappermishka had been born in the village, but left some ten years or so before. He was a wild-blooded adventurer by nature, and had left home as a teenager to go and see the world, like a boy in a fairy tale. Exotic stories had been doing the rounds about him ever since. Some folk said he'd become a ship's captain, others a pirate on the high seas. In fact, he was neither ship's captain nor pirate, but it's true he was a sailor on an ocean steamer, which was in itself a great destiny in a peasant's eyes. So Dappermishka had come home after ten years to show himself to the village, to let them see what had become of him. He was dressed carefully, with a genuine English briar pipe between his strong, fine, porcelain-white teeth and a little green cap he wore at a jaunty angle that he had bought—as he showed everyone—in Buenos Aires. He was a hot-blooded lad, strong as an ox, who swaggered, quarrelled and swept the girls off their feet. He strutted down the village streets like a cock pheasant, and was to be seen out by the haystacks with a different girl each night.

Anna didn't know Dappermishka, but had nevertheless heard plenty about him. When on that memorable summer evening of St Peter and St Paul she finally set eyes on him, she was dismissive, to say the least.

"You're all head over heels about *that?*" she said, good and loud for everyone to hear. "You've no damn sense at all."

The other girls, loyal to a fault, lost no time at all repeating this to Dappermishka, but—as so often in life—this had the very opposite effect to what they'd wanted, obviously, to achieve. All of a sudden Dappermishka appeared, without a word, at Anna's side, grabbed her by the waist and swept her into a *csárdás*, dancing with her again and again. What happened as they danced we'll never really know. They say my mother swore afterwards she only danced with him for effect, so that all them slutty tramps would be green with envy. The fact remains, though, that she danced with Dappermishka till dawn and didn't so much as look at anyone else.

It was a good, plentiful summer, the summer of 1912, and there was great excitement on the feast of St Peter and St Paul. His Lordship had provided enough stew for the village to stuff itself to bursting, secret stashes of wine flowed, they had a Gypsy band to play the *csárdás*. They say it was so hot that night that even at dawn people were covered in sweat, though they danced outdoors, in the open air. There was a small breeze sometime after midnight, it's true, but it served only to set the tricolour paper lanterns on fire, and brought no relief. The wind itself was as hot as if it had come from a fiery oven. So they stamped the flaming lanterns out, leaving only the moon and the stars to light them from the sky. But that was enough for the young folk, or perhaps too much even, for couples began slipping off one after the other to secret corners.

Dappermishka asked my mother:

"Got a favourite song?"

"'Course. Everybody does."

"What is it?"

"An old one. The Gypsies don't play it now."

"Oh really?" Dappermishka replied roguishly. "Well, tonight they'll play nothin' else!"

With that, he drew out a ten-pengő note, spat on it lustily and, like a carousing nobleman, stuck it on the bandleader's forehead. The band struck up the tune right away. It was a corny old tune, my mother's song:

> *I walked in the quiet forest glade*
> *Saw a bird there in the shade*
> *And a nest made just for two—*
> *How I fell in love with you*

And it was just as Dappermishka had said: the band played nothing else till dawn. The leader had, once or twice, screwed up his courage and tried to play something a little faster, but Dappermishka was there in a flash, setting about the band like a pack of wild dogs. So what could they do but play that slow, melancholy song until the break of dawn; and at a certain point Dappermishka crooned into my mother's ear, so that the other girls all fairly burst:

"How I fell in love with you!"

It was a crazy night, and there was hardly a soul sober in the village. The free-flowing wine had had its effect, as had the all-too starry sky and the slow, steady music—and what generally happens under such circumstances happened that night too. All at once, Anna found herself lying on a haystack with Dappermishka. It was only for a few minutes, the poor girl recounted later, and she barely even knew what had happened when he was already reaching for his watch, crying out as if skinned alive:

"I'll miss my damn train!"

With that he was up and across the open country before she'd adjusted her dress. He sprang off the end of the platform and leapt onto the end of the final carriage, a sight painful to watch, as the stationmaster recounted the day after.

So that's how it happened. It was no great love affair, not by a long shot. It was just folly, and such things happen; stranger things having happened on St Peter and St Paul in years past. The next day, to hear old Rozi tell it, my mother shrugged it off. She had a headache from the wine and went round humming moodily. It wasn't that she thought ill of Dappermishka, but she didn't think well of him, either. She took the whole thing the way you usually take such foolish things. It had happened, and that was that. She was none the poorer for it.

And perhaps she had already forgotten Mihály T.'s famously beautiful eyes by the time she realized one day that she was in trouble. She ran straight to the wise women, of course, but by then it was too late. Old Rozi, who was one of these wise women, claims there was something not quite right with my mother's womanly affairs that had stopped her noticing sooner. And of course she was young, too, and inexperienced in such things. Suffice to say that I was past three months by then.

Under normal circumstances, village midwives wouldn't have shrunk from a three-month case, but there were good reasons for them to do so with me. About six months before, our chemist's assistant had bled to death at the hands of an old quack in the next parish. It had become a nationwide scandal and the gendarmes had arrested a dozen women in our own village. There was much weeping and wailing, excitement and even a trial—the newspapers were full of it. After that, much to Anna's dismay, the obscure but flourishing guild of angel-makers suddenly got very careful. There wasn't a single one in the village who would help her.

My mother tried everyone, driven almost from her wits with desperation. She hitched a lift on every cart headed for a neighbouring parish, she tried all the neighbourhood midwives, quacks and old women who specialized in this sort of thing. They didn't help her either; they just kept stringing her along. They gave her all sorts of mysterious creams, teas, pills and, of course, plenty of advice. They told her to take such scalding baths, poor thing, that her body was covered in blisters for weeks. Those didn't help. The silver-tongued old ladies merely took the poor farmhand's hard-earned savings and told her, always regretfully and somehow managing to keep a straight face, that they couldn't help her at all:

"You come too late, dear!"

So Dear took her Sunday shawl, for this was around Advent time, and threw herself in the river. There was snow, the river had big blocks of ice floating on it, and yet the little peasant girl didn't die. They dragged her out and she was absolutely fine—she hadn't caught even so much as a blessed cold.

It seems I was a tough customer even as a foetus. The icy river couldn't freeze me, the scalding baths couldn't kill me, and the various creams, teas and pills didn't do anything to hurt me. I was born, I lived, I was as healthy as can be. I was almost five and a half kilos at birth, the village had never seen anything like it. I bellowed so loud with my brand-new lungs, they say, that I put the herdsmen's bugles to shame.

"Hideous," my mother said succinctly when they showed me to her. With that, she turned to the wall and didn't look at me again.

Well, I thought, if I've survived the icy river and the scalding baths, I'll survive her judgement, too. And so I did. I grew, and gained weight, and developed muscles, though I don't fully know how myself. People paid more attention to stray dogs than they did to me. I grew like weeds and brambles, and was just as hard to get rid of, that's for sure.

They say the first word I uttered was *bugger*. I picked up *mother* much later. Unhappily, this was due not so much to my mischievous nature as a sad reflection of how often I must—even as an infant—have been called by that juicy epithet; and how little, by contrast, I must have heard that gentler word that people down our way had such a wonderfully sweet way of pronouncing: "muther".

My own muther took up as a wet nurse in Budapest two weeks after I was born. She visited me in the village at most four or five times a year. It's hard to say, after all this time, why she came so infrequently. She may not have been able to get more time off, or maybe she couldn't afford the rail fare, or perhaps she still thought me so abominably *hideous*. Most likely, it was a combination of all three. Suffice to say that I did have a mother and I didn't, and I mostly didn't rather than did. And that good, wholesome milk that the very law of nature had set aside for me was gobbled instead by the premature offspring of a Budapest textile merchant, coddled in swaddling like an ailing silkworm.

So much, then, for the law. It seems even the laws of nature, ancient though they are, exist for people to try and get round them whenever they can.

2

So I STAYED IN THE VILLAGE with old Rozi, who despite having such a charming name, was the most disreputable old woman there. When she'd got too old to pursue her original profession, she devoted herself to bringing up illegitimate boys like myself—if you could call what she did to us an upbringing.

They say she was once a great beauty, a blonde and blue-eyed Slovak girl. At the age of fifteen, she became a maid in the household of the Count; it was he who'd brought her here from the Slovak lands. Rozi served three years as a maid before giving birth to a bouncing baby boy. The child's father was almost a child himself: the Count's sixteen-year-old son. They kicked Rozi out the moment they saw her belly filling out, but they couldn't get rid of her that easily. She was cunning, the pretty little Slovak girl, and knew what she was doing. She kicked up such a fuss, quarrelling and wheedling, threatening them with lawyers and who knows what else, that her master eventually opened his wallet. With his money, she bought the little house at the edge of the village in which I, too, was later brought up.

Six months after her severance from the Count's household, Rozi's baby died. His death was very unexpected, and to this day, the rumour in the village is that she had helped along his demise. That may, of course, just be village gossip, but knowing old Rozi as I do, I wouldn't rule it out for a second.

By that time, she was receiving regular visits from some local potentate who would always drive in from the neighbouring parish in his trap. He was married and had a family and could only come on Saturdays; and since there is more than one day in the week, Rozi made sure over time that she had visitors those other days as well. In the end, she was measuring her love out for sale the way others measured out wheat.

She was a thrifty soul and saved the money she made from her embraces assiduously. Soon, she had the rickety house put in order, a new fence built around the yard, and later bought a good deal of land. She prospered so visibly that the entire village was eaten up with jealousy.

Then one day something that so often happens to women like her—who want men only for their money—happened to her too. She fell in love with a man who wanted nothing from her but her money.

He was a big, dim fellow with bovine eyes, and I could never understand why, of all the dozens of men she'd known, she fell for him specifically. When I was home last, I ended up asking her. She herself couldn't really explain it.

"Well, he never was what you might call handsome, you see," she reflected in her strange, slightly foreign accent, "but the girls, they mad about him!"

So he wasn't even handsome, that fellow, and I know from extensive first-hand experience that he certainly wasn't clever. Besides all that, as old Rozi told it, he was poor as a church mouse, so poor that when he first came to the village, you could see his backside through his trousers. He was a ragtag sort of wanderer, of the sort girls usually didn't give a second thought.

"I was consumed with curiosity, you see," old Rozi admitted, "as to what his secret could be, this nothing man."

But "secrets" like that tend to stay secret for ever. A nothing sort of man comes along, a ragtag sort, not bright, nor handsome, or even rich, and yet the local women tear themselves apart over him. Even though, if what old Rozi told me is true, he wasn't too bothered with the ladies, they all ran after him as if possessed.

He had only one real passion, and that was fishing. He had a beautiful fishing rod he'd made himself, and he would sit alone with it day in, day out, on the riverbank, saying not a word. He was absolutely convinced that fish knew human speech and if they heard it, wouldn't go anywhere near the hook. Woe betide anyone who raised their voice while he was waiting for the fish to bite.

Old Rozi was so consumed by "curiosity" that one day she went down to the river where the lonely fisherman sat. She paraded past him once or twice, but "he don't even look at me, you see. Not so much as glance sideways."

But old Rozi was not one to get discouraged and kept going back down to the river till one day the man took pity on her. Not that he said anything to her—like I say, he couldn't stand anyone talking while he was fishing—but instead nodded silently to say that she could sit down beside him. So Rozi sat down. She didn't dare say a thing, watching the river quietly. He didn't say anything either, just stuck out his left hand leisurely, so that he didn't upset the rod in his right, and placed it on her breast in total silence. They sat like that for a long time, not a word between them. Rozi was, in her words, "fit to burst" by the time the man finally deigned to tie his rod to the reeds and lay her down on the grassy bank.

"Don't you breathe a sound, though!" he whispered in her ear. "So's not to scare the fish."

This sounds like a made-up story, but it had such an impact on Rozi that from that day on she didn't let that man out of her sight. She put him in her house at the edge of the village and devoted everything she got from other men to the upkeep of this one.

He remained just as calm as he'd always been. There was nothing in the world that could upset him, certainly not Rozi's profession. As long as he got to spend his days fishing by the river and had a litre or two of wine with his fish *paprikás* at supper, the missus could do as she liked. He lived on the money Rozi made with her favours like a lazy, kept mistress. In the village, they called him Mr Rozi, and even we children used to call him that among ourselves.

Rozi was by then no longer in her first youth. She must have been around thirty, an advanced age for a peasant girl. Her more genteel clientele began to fade away and Rozi was forced to lower prices and try to make up the difference by increasing turnover.

Mr Rozi went on happily working his way through the young peasant girls. Not that he desperately wanted them, but to kill the boredom while he waited for the fish, he'd occasionally signal to one or another that they could sit down beside him. And they came and sat.

Rozi knew, and pretended not to. It wasn't as if she could say anything, so she just looked on and "agonized". She would spend nights tossing and turning next to her snoring man, suffering pins and needles around her heart and cold sweats. This dissolute slattern, who'd been selling herself since the age of fifteen, was suddenly so overcome with jealousy that it was like an incurable illness.

One day she couldn't take any more, so she got to thinking and called the tailor to have a new suit made for her man.

"What's that for, then?" he asked, not being in the least bit vain.

"What for? For wedding. You can't wear old one to wedding."

"What wedding? Who the hell's gettin' married?"

"You and me, of course!"

He just stood there silent for a bit, because it took him a while to understand. When he finally did, he broke quietly into a smile.

"You can tell you're Slovak," he said, "by how cunning you think."

But he wasn't against the idea. Marriage? Why not. If the missus wanted it, let her have her way. After all, she brought home the bacon. Fortunately, the weather was lousy on their wedding day and he couldn't have gone fishing anyway.

Rozi, on the other hand, took their marriage very seriously indeed. The ring, the marriage certificate and the priest's sermon revolutionized her life. From that day on, she drove her visitors away, every one.

"Husband won't have it!" she'd say haughtily, though she knew full well that her "husband" would have fallen off his chair laughing if he'd heard her.

Two weeks after the wedding, she got on the train and went to the county town. To learn to be a midwife, she said. The village roared with laughter. Show me the poor forsaken fool, they said, who's going to have an innocent babe brought into the world by the likes of her!

But Rozi knew what she was doing. She wasn't going to bring babies into the world. Far from it. From then on, she made her living stopping children from being born.

Her idea paid off. The village abortionists were outmoded, ignorant and dirty old women, and everyone preferred to go to Rozi when they got into trouble. And they got into trouble pretty often, especially in the winter, when people have time on their hands.

But old Rozi kept another, larger business, too. Peasant girls who got into trouble and whom it was too late to "help", like my mother, could do their lying-in at hers. She would even feed them till they were strong enough to go up to the city as wet nurses. Their children stayed with Rozi and the poor girls, who in this way dealt with all their troubles in one fell swoop, couldn't thank her enough. Then, of course, they got to send the better half of their already meagre salaries to their selfless saviour for more or less the rest of their days.

This woman, this indestructible woman, was like a cat—she always landed on her feet. She was now making a living from other people's love affairs as she had once done from her own. The house at the edge of the village underwent a veritable renaissance. She now had pigs, cows and chickens; she had a horse, a cart and a maid.

But whenever possible, she would go out fishing with her man by the river. She didn't like to leave Mr Rozi alone much, and looked after him like some precious heirloom, though Mr Rozi was hardly a gilded youth any more. He must have been the same age as Rozi, and Rozi must have been pushing forty.

At that time, she had eight little bastard boys living with her. Rozi could easily have retired. Eight young servant girls in various different cities throughout the country worked in her stead from sunup to sundown. She just kept raking in the money, so that eventually she was among the richest peasants in our desperately poor little village. People even stopped bringing up her past because, as they say, bygones should be bygones, and more to the point, dogs may bark, but money talks.

Rozi began putting on weight. On Sundays, she'd wear a black silk dress buttoned to the neck and a cross as big as a bishop's. She changed her way of talking, too. She was no longer playful and chatty, but considered every word she said. She would talk to the little peasant girls who came to her in the family way with sanctimonious condescension, making it clear that though she looked down on them, she would forgive them in the name of our merciful Lord. She was short with the poor and would brook no familiarity, scolding her maids all the livelong day; but if a wealthy farmer greeted her on the market square, she was all honeyed words and gestures. In a word, she'd started acting like a *lady*.

She became religious. Before, she'd never gone to church, but now she would kneel for hours like a nun. She hung a huge picture of the Virgin Mary over the tired old couch where previously she'd frolicked with her clients, with an eternal flame burning under it in a gold-rimmed red glass.

One day, she turned to Mr Rozi.

"Ever thought about death, Jóska?"

"The hell I have!"

"Watch your mouth, I'm serious. We can't leave all this to dogs!"

Mr Rozi shrugged. Money hadn't changed him; he still didn't care anything about anything as long as his belly was full and he was left alone. Not so Rozi. She was going for immortality.

"We ought to make child."

"Right here?" asked Mr Rozi, since they were out on the street at the time.

But he had no objection to this either. Children? Why not. If the missus wanted it, let her have her way. *He* wasn't going to have to give birth to it. And she brought home the bacon. It was the least he could do. You couldn't fish at night, anyway.

"It could be here by Christmas," old Rozi said.

But it wasn't. And it didn't come for Easter either—it never came at all. This woman—who had been pregnant God knows how often when she hadn't wanted to be—couldn't get pregnant now that it was her greatest wish. She ran from one doctor to the next, went to the county town and even the capital. She took baths, pills, home-made concoctions. Nothing worked. Maybe it's my man, she thought; she tried others. That didn't help either.

For the first time in her life, she lost her head. She came and went like a madwoman. She couldn't, she wouldn't accept it, and she was convinced that everything she owned would "go to dogs".

One day, she tore the picture of the Virgin Mary off the wall and hurled it in the corner, candle and all. There wasn't a man alive who could've cursed the way she swore then. She spent entire days under a dark cloud and beat the children. Then she grew eerily calm. She threw herself into a corner of the front room and just sat there motionless for hours with the shutters closed. She would occasionally mutter something to herself, her hollow mouth moving almost soundlessly, like a defunct mechanism falling to bits.

She started going grey. She lost weight, shrivelled, grew old overnight. She became a mean and crotchety old woman.

She had always been mean, but at least till then her meanness had had some purpose. She had turned it into money, silks, gold chains, the pigs in the sty and the cow in the shed. Now her meanness became as barren as her womb, and she took no profit from it any more. She was wicked for the sake of it. She derived a perverse, inhuman pleasure, a revolting, sick satisfaction from causing others pain. But it also happened, which never used to happen before, that she was good. Then she would give gifts to all and sundry, be charming to everyone she met, and shower the children with frantic kisses. But this was a macabre and dangerous kind of goodness, and once a fit of it had passed, she was a hundred times meaner than before.

3

S HE DETESTED ME from the moment I was born.
I know that sounds unlikely. It may be that a grown-up doesn't particularly like a child left to their care, or they suddenly lose their temper, but detest?… It sounds unlikely, and yet it's true: she hated me. Not with some passing flicker of hate, either, born of irritable folk rubbing each other the wrong way, fading as quickly as it had come. No, this was a grave and consistent—almost masculine—hatred, you might say. It was permanent war, with not so much as a single truce in the entire fourteen years I spent under her roof.

The roots of this hatred must have gone alarmingly deep. I was born at just around the time she learnt, once and for all, that she would never have children. Maybe that was why she hated me. I don't know, it's just a guess. "For what man knoweth the things of a man," as St Paul writes to the Corinthians, "save the spirit of man which is in him?"

I wasn't what you might call a loveable child. I should make that much clear right now. I was unusually unfriendly, almost standoffish, suspicious, stubborn, and always ready to strike. By the age of seven, I was utterly devoid of what is commonly called boyish charm.

I have a photograph from back then, a group photo one boy's mother had taken of us. I've seen few less likeable children than myself in that image. There's something scary and rough about my entire being. My shoulders look like I'd borrowed them from someone five years older, and my face is hard, mean and low. I'm distinctly hideous in this photo, though on closer examination, my looks are not unattractive. I had quite large, deep-grey eyes, a strong, straight nose, a fine, determined mouth, and black hair that fell neatly to my brow. My looks were so fully formed that they haven't changed much since, and that was probably the trouble. I had the face of a man, and the things that make a man's face masculine make a child's face ugly.

They say that at the age of five or six I was at daggers drawn with the grown-ups around me. I never opened my mouth if I wasn't spoken to, and when I was, I gave short, snappish answers. I faced them with my hands jammed in my pockets, legs spread wide apart and chin forced down to my neck; that's how I looked up at them, like a bull, head down, ready to charge.

"What face you make again!" old Rozi would yell at me half a dozen times a day. "You look like murderer."

Yes, I was probably not the most charming of children, but then how, pray tell, was I supposed to be? Life does not begin at the moment of birth. They say that the emotional shocks suffered by a woman with child will often leave physical traces on her baby. Is it far-fetched, then, for me to feel that the deep-seated hatred that filled my mother as she bore me has left its mark on my life ever since? I don't know. This, too, is just a guess. But I do clearly remember that I was perfectly aware of my situation by the age of seven. I knew that there wasn't a creature on God's green earth, my mother included, who truly cared about my miserable fate; that there was nothing but hunters and hunted in this poachers' world, and I was not a hunter.

I thought that was natural. I was absolutely convinced that people were only good when they had to be. Bastard children had to be; rich people did not. I envied Rozi, that she could afford to be bad. Anyone who could afford to be bad had made it.

I was surprised by people being good to me. I was suspicious when they were. Why would someone be good to a little bastard? What were they after? I wondered, suspecting the worst, and if I realized they didn't want anything, I looked at them as if they'd had two noses or three hands. I thought people like that a little mad. Unnatural. Grass is green, the sky is blue, and man is mean. At least, anyone with any brains. Only Mad Wilma was good, and she was the laughing stock of the village.

When I think about it, I didn't even really know what the grown-ups meant by *good*. I thought it was some hollow slogan they'd thought up to fool children with. A lot of words were like that. *Religion*, for example. There was the Sunday religion that people practised in church, and the everyday religion people practised in the village, and I didn't understand

23

what the two had to do with each other. Old Rozi was *religious* too. She'd kneel for hours in front of the picture of the Virgin, and when she was having one of her fits of kindness, she wouldn't shut up about "Christian charity". As for what her Christian charity actually meant, I had more than my fair share of chances to discover. They could pour their sanctimonious words on me by the bucket; they meant nothing to me, just like their threats about the bogeyman. I didn't believe in their bogeyman, and I didn't believe in their fine, sanctimonious words either. I only believed in what I saw.

There was a sort of mischievous squirrel bounding around inside me, snickering softly and pulling faces each time the grown-ups parroted these words. But I never actually said a thing. A skunk protects itself with its smell, the peasant with his stupidity. Faced with grown-ups, I adopted an expression so vacuous, I looked like a cow chewing the cud. I thought them dumb, dishonest, base creatures, and I wasn't going to stand around arguing with them. I just watched their hypocritical faces, looking up with my head down, my chin pressed against my neck and my legs spread wide, hands in my pockets, saying nothing. I was completely unapproachable.

Honour thy father and thy mother, they preached. Very well, I said to myself, you do that. The squirrel jumped, stuck out his tongue and snickered. I'd never seen my father in my life, and all I knew about my mother was that she didn't concern herself overly with me. Four or five times a year a peasant girl came, a total stranger, spent the afternoon with me, and left. They told me she was my mother.

Secretly, I was terrified of these visits. I was seized by an awkward, suffocating anxiety whenever I saw her. I remember I would get a bitter taste in my mouth, as if chewing something rotten. As to why that was, I couldn't have told you. My mother was kind to me, never beat me, never even quarrelled; on the contrary, she used to bring me five krajcárs' worth of potato sweets, and I would have done almost anything for those. There were other advantages to her visits. On those days, I got a good lunch and could eat as much as I wanted, something that never happened otherwise. "Coincidentally" we always had my favourite food for lunch: *székelygulyás* stew and noodles with cottage cheese and bacon. I would have forgone both, though, if that strange peasant girl had only changed her mind and stayed at home.

She would always send a postcard to say when she was coming, and I would be filled with anxiety days in advance. She used to come on Sundays in the early afternoon. I would hide from the others. I used regularly to lock myself in the wooden shed that was the privy, attached to the back wall of the house, and if I wasn't disturbed, I would sit for hours on the boards, shipshape and scrubbed white, staring dully at the fat green flies humming greedily as they feasted in the pit below. These were times of great, heavy silence. Old Rozi and Mr Rozi were having their afternoon sleep, the maid had the afternoon off, and the children had scattered. The summer sun beat down on the roof of the wooden privy, the air was suffocating with its heat and smells, and the sweat streamed off me as my eyelids grew heavier and heavier. I would sit and wait like that, my head drooping down onto my chest, drifting in and out of sleep, until the bell of the little gate would interrupt the Sunday silence.

"Béééla!" called my mother's voice. "Rozi!"

I stood up, spat heavily, and then with the slow, deliberate steps of an old peasant, ambled over to my mother.

We weren't in the habit of kissing ladies' hands by way of greeting. My mother kissed my face, I never kissed hers. I don't know if she ever noticed, but if she did, she never said anything. She was a hard-natured woman who couldn't stand artificial sweetness. The other mothers would clamour with effusive, sentimental nicknames for their offspring, but she just sat beside me quietly. You could tell she had her private opinion of them.

"What news, Béla?" she asked seriously, simply, as if talking to a grown-up.

"None," I said, thinking of the sweets.

And my mother really would reach into her battered handbag and take out a packet of potato sweets.

Meanwhile, the kitchen door sprang open in a distinctly melodramatic way and old Rozi came out, swishing imperiously in her black silks, with her big cross, like a village queen.

"How are you, how are you, dear?" she'd murmur as soon as she saw my mother. "Long time no see. How are you, precious?"

"Thank you, Rozi," my mother replied humbly. "I'm all right."

The old woman patted my mother's shoulder with condescension and a saccharine smile, looking her up and down with a hard, malicious eye the while.

"What lovely fine dress you have, precious," she noted with extraordinarily mean-spirited emphasis, a reminder of the money my mother owed her; her sickly-sweet smile never faded from her lips.

"This thing? It's five years old, Rozi," my mother replied awkwardly, and quickly changed the subject. All her clothes were exactly five years old, poor thing.

Like in a well-rehearsed play, that was how these conversations used to go, more or less word for word, visit after visit, year after year. And then came the second act: scolding me.

"That son of yours, precious!" jabbered the old woman, "Why, he biggest good-for-nothing ever born!"

"That son of yours, precious, he end up on gallows one day, on my soul!"

"That son of yours…"

It went on like that for half an hour or so. She listed all my sins of the last quarter, down to the littlest detail. She had an incredible memory, and never left anything out. Everything she said was true, but what she forgot to say was *why* I did all those things. At the end of the day, the root cause of almost all my misbehaviour was that she wasn't giving me enough to eat.

But I had learnt early that silence was golden. I neither accused her nor defended myself. I just stood there, my legs spread wide, hands in my pockets, and stared at the old woman's gap-toothed mouth as she spilt her verbal slop.

My mother, too, was silent. She shook her head in increasing irritation, and from time to time shot an angry look at me. When the old woman finally finished, she'd start up herself.

"That the earth don't swallow you for shame, you ungrateful boy! After all the kindness Rozi's shown you!"

That was what she always said, word for word. Well, I thought, you can keep running your pie-hole as much as you like. Just *you* try old Rozi's kindness! Then whoops! the squirrel did a little hop, sticking out his tongue. But I just stood there, silent.

"I'll see he gets what's comin' to him, the little good-for-nothing," she said menacingly. "Come on, you shameful creature."

I went. With heavy, deliberate steps. At the end of the garden, there was a peach tree with a decaying, backless little bench beneath. We sat down there. My mother's demeanour changed as if she'd become a different person the second we were out of range of the old woman. Instead of berating me again, she looked quickly around to make sure no one could overhear, and then softly asked:

"She givin' you enough to eat?"

"No she damn well ain't!" I replied. "Only when you come."

This, too, was a scene we'd play every time. My mother would knit her brow and stare silently in front of her for a while. Then she'd say:

"I'll have a word with her."

Even at the age of five, I knew that was a barefaced lie. Squirrel snickered away quietly. As if she really would *have a word* with the old woman, I thought to myself, like hell she would! I know now that the poor thing was always behind on her payments, and was in constant fear of Rozi putting me out on the street, or sending me up to live with her in Budapest. But I knew none of that back then. All I knew of the whole thing was that my mother was lying to me. Instead of taking the old woman to task, she was all sweetness and light with her; it was enough to make you sick.

But I never said a word about that, either. I just sat on the rickety bench under the old peach tree and held my tongue. The sun beat down on the tree, and little yellow latticed spots of light trembled in the shade. I stared at those. My mother, too, just stared with those small, black, deep-set eyes of hers into the distance, or drew meaningless shapes in the dirt with the point of her shoe.

Around us, the yard was full of life. All the young mothers were chattering away, all over their little boys, playing with them, running about and teasing them so you could hear their boisterous mothering all the way down the street.

My mother, I could see, didn't really know what to do with me. She was no good at endearments, either in word or deed, and she was generally in no mood to play. So she just sat there beside me as beside another grown-up with whom she had nothing particular to talk about.

I, too, was to blame for our not getting closer. My mother did, occasionally, experience a sort of strange and timid affection, but I—without meaning to—always trampled on these delicate buds of feeling. I remember she asked me once why I "looked so mean" all the time.

"Go on, have a laugh for once!" she said cheerfully, tickling me.

I was naturally ticklish, so I jumped up and she ran after me. When she caught up with me, she grabbed me, pulled me close, and kissed me again and again. I don't know why, but at that moment I was overcome with an indescribably awkward feeling, a vague but intense shame. I pulled away from her with something akin to revulsion. As if she'd felt it, she let go of me at once. She didn't say anything, just quietly adjusted her kerchief and went in to old Rozi to "settle up".

Settling up was always hard. The old woman must have kept on about her arrears, because you could hear the sound of loud and bitter arguing from the front room, and when my mother came back to the yard, you could always tell that she'd been crying.

"Come on, then," she said curtly, in a dry voice full of suppressed tension. "G'night."

That's what she'd always say in parting, "G'night", though the sun was still shining brightly. Her train left a few minutes after seven, but we were always at the station by six. That hour until the train departed seemed intolerably long. The station was always full of people, because down our way, going out to the railway station on a Sunday afternoon was one of the great, worldly pleasures of village life. Hardly anyone actually went anywhere; people just paraded up and down the platforms in their Sunday best, forming little groups, greeting one another, having a little walk. The gilded youth were all there, and there were plenty of colourful bright dresses on display. The lads were overcome with a mischievous cheer, the girls all giggled as if someone were tickling them. The two of us looked on, like an ageing couple, at all this happy youth, and sat in silence like before, beneath the peach tree. But this was a different kind of silence. Though I didn't know why my mother had been crying, and come to think of it, I wasn't too curious either, I was nonetheless all at once overcome with an endless, heart-wrenching pity for her.

Who can find their way in the impenetrable jungle that is a child's heart? I'll admit, even if you think me inhuman for it, that I never felt what you might call a son's love for my mother. But I was almost always sorry for her. I felt so sorry for her I sometimes felt a physical pain around my heart. As small and ragged a child as I was, I felt stronger, smarter, and more capable than my mother. I remember, even at the age of six, I could have sworn I could handle my affairs better than her. But what could my mother have known of all that? I sat beside her politely and tried to make my face as dumb as a lowing calf's.

The train arrived at last. The wheezing locomotive belched smoke and the sleepy little station filled with the exciting smell of farewells, distance and adventure. I was relieved when my mother had boarded, but my heart nonetheless still felt heavy somehow.

"God bless," she said.

"God bless," I replied.

Then the conductor blew his little horn and the train lurched forward. My mother never waved, but disappeared immediately behind the window.

4

ONCE, WHEN I WAS WATCHING her train depart, I was overcome by a strange and frightening excitement, a chilling, magical feeling that constricted my throat and that would for years and years come over me each time I smelt the smell of train smoke, so full of adventure.

I want to try and describe it as precisely as a medical diagnosis. I must have been six. It was a stifling early midsummer eve. I was standing barefoot by the rails, not thinking of anything, just watching the red lamp hanging on the back of the train vanish in the distance. All at once, for no reason whatsoever, I felt a heavy, dull, incomprehensible pressure in my chest, and my throat closed so convulsively that I could barely breathe. It only lasted a few minutes altogether, but those few minutes were so frightening and so desolate that I lost my head completely. My heart pounded at my ribs and I felt my tears flowing into my mouth. I felt a terrifying, sharp, shooting pain, an almost *physical* desire to… *leave.* Leave my mother, leave old Rozi, leave the village. Where to? I didn't know. Why? I didn't know. I had no rational goal in mind, no clear desire, only an idea. To go, go, go.

But I was a peasant boy, with a peasant's common sense, and half an hour later, I was saying to myself: "foolishness!"

But whenever I smelt the sharp, exciting odour of train smoke, I was overcome again by that strange and frightening desire, so that I began to scare myself.

My teenage father must have felt the same when he ran away from home. It may even have been just such a stifling midsummer eve when he was overcome by wanderlust, and perhaps he didn't know either where to or why, but just upped and went, like a sleepwalker, following his irresistible desire.

On these occasions, I would avoid the high street, which was always crowded on Sunday evenings in summer. Peasants, if they're not given to drink, don't really know what to do with their time on a Sunday evening. Those were long days, and by the afternoon, people had recovered from the week, done their share of this and that, and were bored of doing nothing. They stood around their garden gates, as if they'd been waiting for Monday to come by the evening train. That was how people spent their Sundays.

I made my way home with a big detour through the fields. Until I was out of the village, I paid meticulous attention, as always, to my "rep". I ambled along with heavy, deliberate steps, hands in pockets, chin pressed down onto my neck, like an old peasant. Now and then I would spit juicily out of the corner of my mouth, for I was absolutely convinced that that sort of thing enhanced one's reputation. But as soon as the last houses faded behind me, I broke into a sudden run as if I'd been possessed. I ran through fields, meadows and pastures for as long as my legs would carry me. Then I would throw myself face down in the grass, panting, and lay perfectly still. The total opposite of before. The whole day's confusion would evaporate from my head, and the dumb tension in my nerves would ease off. I felt, lying in the young grass, beneath the unexpectedly broad sky, like someone who, after travelling strange and dangerous shores, had finally come home.

Dusk was gathering, but only the early dusk, when it seems you're seeing the world through a pane of glass gently overspread with a pale fog of breath. The field was pouring out the sunlight it had absorbed and there was the smell of warm earth as the sun bled on the horizon. The sky was dappled like a wonderful, endless peasant shawl, and somewhere in the distance the cowbells of a herd returning home sounded dully. I was home.

I wended my way back to the village quietly, humming. By nature, I could never walk past even the dirtiest cow, the shabbiest horse or the mangiest dog without giving them a long, tender pat. I felt an odd, unbounded love for animals. There weren't many people for whom I felt as much affection as I felt for, say, dogs. I didn't love anyone, not even my own mother, but it seems that man must love something, and in my case, that was animals. I was on friendly terms with all of them. Even the most vicious dogs in the village liked me, and even the Count's haughty greyhounds made a fuss of me, though I had no food to give them.

Few dogs had it as bad as I did. I almost always left the table hungry. The old woman was not one for equality, and every child was looked after according to their mother's means. And yet there weren't really significant differences, except for me, because the mothers used to visit their children regularly, and they would complain about any injustices. Péter would protest that Pál was getting better food, while Pál would whine that Istvány was getting more to eat. The poor little servant girls felt sorry for them, and they always managed somehow to produce the requisite little sums, so that a week later Péter would be eating the same as Pál and Pál would be getting just as much as Istvány. But who was there to care for me?

My mother, when she visited, was always having to make excuses for being behind on her payments. The poor thing really was in no position so much as to bring up the matter of how the old woman was feeding me. Day after day, I had to watch children my own age get more, and better, food than me. Is it any wonder, then, that I turned out the way I did?

There were moments in my childhood when I would have been capable of doing *anything* for a good meal.

I stole, I confess. I was like a magpie. In vain did the old woman keep everything under lock and key from me; necessity and practice honed my thieving into a fine art. There was hell to pay, of course, when she found out, but I never once felt remorse—I remember that clearly. There are situations in life in which not stealing is downright perverse. I hold that to be true to this day.

Was I meant to waste away, emaciated and consumptive, just to protect that tired old whore's filthy, ill-gotten goods? Not me!

Gradually, I became as determined and cunning as a prowling fox. I realized, for example, that you could turn the human thirst for revenge to your advantage. For, it should be noted, children still live by the rule of the fist. The stronger is always right, and every boy wanted to be right. Not me. I was hungry, and didn't give a damn about Platonic truth. There is only one truth for the hungry: bread. I didn't fight out of amateur enthusiasm, like the other children. For me, fighting was a serious, breadwinning, affair. Whenever two boys would start to quarrel, I would go up to the weaker one and say:

"How much'll you give me to lay him out for you?"

I asked ten fillérs, but I was willing to take on anyone for two, though the business did have its risks. The children almost all belonged to gangs, and sometimes I found myself up against an entire band. I left the battlefield with a bloodied head more than once, but I didn't care. The coins tinkling in my pockets made the happiest sound in the world, and I could go to the shop and get myself some bread.

The great highwayman Sándor Rózsa was my hero. Other boys wanted to be priests or generals, but I longed to be an outlaw who robbed the rich and gave to the poor. I didn't actually distribute what I got, but then again, I would have been hard pressed to find anyone poorer in the village than myself.

5

I N THE AUTUMN OF 1919—I was six at the time—my mother lost her
position. Instead of postal orders, the poor thing now kept sending
begging letters to the old woman, one after the other, imploring her
for goodness' sake to wait, at least till the first of next month, she was
bound to find a new position by then. But she didn't.

One day, as I was innocently sitting down to eat with the other boys,
the old woman burst out of the kitchen and shrieked that there was to
be no lunch for me, because my mother hadn't paid a penny for my
keep in four months.

"And you not sort of dear child I keep for love!"

At first, I didn't understand. I just stood there with my legs spread
wide, my hands in my pockets, my chin down on my neck, and watched
the old woman rant, waving in her hand my mother's letter, which must
have just arrived.

"If your filthy mother don't owe so much," she screamed, "I throw
you out in street long ago, stinking gallows rat!"

I was still silent. The other children had begun to eat. My mouth
began to water as I watched them. I remember it was potato *paprikás* with
kolbász sausage, and I can still sense its pleasant, tickling aroma. I was
damnably hungry. My throat was constricted with sobs, but I wouldn't
have cried for all the world. I could see the children's sly expressions as
they leant low over their plates and shoved each other under the table,
waiting to see what came next. So I paid special attention to my rep.

"Muther'll send those few pengős soon enough," I said, trying to
reason with her, "please give me somethin' to eat, I'm so hungry."

"Sorry," the old woman said, shaking her head. "Why you not tell
whore mother not to make herself child if she not pay for it!"

I saw that the boys could barely contain their laughter. An incredible
anger took hold of me, I was trembling all over.

"You're the whore!" I screamed, beside myself, and ran off.

The old woman was not usually the generous type, but when I said that, she threw the whole dish of potatoes at me so hard that it shattered into pieces. Fortunately, it only hit my backside and didn't do any serious damage. I kept running, but even out in the street, I could feel the good, hot *paprikás* dripping off my rear.

I was filled with impotent rage. My first thought was to go round the back of the house and take the old woman's eye out with a slingshot. I believe I could have strangled her without blinking, but I had learnt that you can't eat rage, and so I turned my attention to more practical propositions. I looked around the village to see where I could steal something. I couldn't steal anything. I was beset by ill fortune; I couldn't pilfer so much as a piece of fruit. As soon as my old friends, the dogs, saw me, they broke into such a chorus of yaps in their excitement that the farmers' wives appeared straight away in their kitchen doors. I spent hours hunting around like that, in vain.

All of a sudden, I found myself in front of the school. It was teatime, and the children were chasing around in the yard outside. Most of them had thick slices of bread spread with lard or jam, but had forgotten about them, they were so deeply involved in their games. They were charging round like mad, and only stopped for a moment now and then so they could, panting and on the fly, quite casually take a bite or two of their bread. I, meanwhile, was almost faint with hunger.

What would Sándor Rózsa do? I wondered, and all at once, I knew what I had to do. I spat juicily from the side of my mouth so the children would know who they were dealing with, and with slow, dignified steps, made my way into the yard.

I was not yet going to school myself. The children must have thought I was looking for someone, and in a way, they were not wrong. I was looking for a victim. Not without a little nervousness, I must admit, for the boys were a good deal older than me, but beggars can't be choosers, and finally I made up my mind. My victim was standing in the far corner of the yard, leaning against a lone acacia tree, picking away at his bread and jam with a melancholy, bovine face. He must have been a year or two my senior, but his bread was big, while he was small, so

I said to myself: now or never, and headed towards him. When I got behind him, I snatched the bread from his hand, quick as anything, and was away. The clueless boy didn't even know what had happened to him. By the time he started bawling, I was back on the street, so he could bawl away for all I cared.

I tore out to the outskirts and started feasting in the shadow of a hawthorn bush. I liked the bread and jam, and I liked the excitement. This was more like it! I said to myself. This was a real, Sándor Rózsa-type adventure. I laughed, loud and full-throated. I was pleased with myself.

I decided never to go home again. I was afraid that the old woman might throw another dish at me, and my backside was still stinging from the first. But as it started to grow dark, so my spirits, too, began to wane. I may well have been a faithful follower of Sándor Rózsa's, but I was none too keen on the darkness. I headed home.

The house was already sleeping. The dog wasn't a problem; all it took was one nod and it heeled very nicely, like a low-level functionary. It was a pitch-black, moonless night, and all was still. I climbed noise-lessly over the fence. Luckily, the room in which we children slept had been built on to the house later, and, clearly for reasons of economy, the old woman hadn't made a connecting door. The entrance was from the yard. I pressed the handle down slowly, gingerly. The door opened silently, and I was inside.

The children were deep asleep. Eight children slept in that room, myself included, which was, at most, five metres long and four metres wide. Whenever I entered from outside, I was always forcefully struck by a stomach-churning stench that made your head hurt, and every night for fourteen years, it took me a few minutes to get accustomed to it. I can still smell that incredible scent now, a quite extraordinary and complex mix of people, food, the mouldy odour from the per-petually damp walls and the constant stink of the privy attached to the back wall.

There were no beds. We slept on straw on the beaten-earth floor, huddled close. I had no shoes, so I didn't have to bother with those. I lay down in the straw just as I was and pulled the heavy horsehair blanket over me. Now that I finally felt safe, I was once more tormented

36

by hunger, which—it seems—fear and the excitement of the evening's adventures had suppressed till now. I couldn't get to sleep.

As I was lying there like this, the straw suddenly stirred beside me.

"Béla," whispered a childish voice. "You asleep?"

It was Gergely, a boy in his second year of elementary school.

"What is it?" I asked.

"Nothing," he whispered. "Here."

He pressed a slice of bread and a bit of *kolbász* into my hand. My stomach almost sprang out of my body in joy, but I made sure Gergely didn't notice. I accepted his gift like the Treasury accepts taxes. I didn't so much as say thank you. I ate it all without a word, lay back in the straw and in a dry, businesslike voice, I asked:

"Who d'you want layin' out?"

The idea that someone might give me a crust of bread and a bit of *kolbász* just because they knew I was hungry hadn't even occurred to me.

This Gergely was almost two years older than me, but he still had me beat up his "enemies" for him. He was the capitalist among us. His mother came to see him every Sunday, since she was in service in the neighbouring parish, and always gave him a krajcár or two. Gergely was therefore rolling in money, and could afford to have others beat up his enemies for him. He was a lanky, very blond boy with a girlish face, and a famous liar. There were always blue semicircles under his eyes, and I knew why.

As to who he wanted me to beat up, he didn't tell me for some time. The question, it seems, had caught him unawares; he must have been expecting more elaborate negotiations. But eventually, he did pour out his heart after all.

"Adam," he grumbled. "That ginger beast got me from behind again."

"As if he had to get you from behind," I said, not so much out of disdain for Adam, but more out of business considerations. "He's enormous."

"He's big, but he ain't strong."

"Not strong? Why you scared of him, then?"

"All right… he's strong, but he ain't that strong."

37

"Strong or not so strong," I said, putting an end to the debate, "I ain't layin' him out for a bit of *kolbász*!"

"I'll get you more tomorrow. And there'll be money come Sunday."

I didn't reply. I'd been planning something since the outskirts, and it was on my mind again.

"Can you write?" I asked all of a sudden.

"'Course. What d'you want?"

"A letter."

"Who to?"

"My muther."

"On account of the old woman?"

"Yeah, the old witch."

"Hm…" grumbled Gergely. "Not so simple. Not easy, that, writing letters, not easy."

"Think it's easy thumping the ginger boy?"

"Writing a letter's harder. Thump two of 'em."

I could see he wanted to blackmail me, damn him.

"You'll be the second!" I said.

He thought about that for a bit.

"All right," he said at last. "I'll write your letter. Be out in the field midday tomorrow."

"Who? The old woman?"

"Nah, Adam! Always takes the little path along the hill."

"Just wait your turn with Adam!" I said. "Write the letter first. G'night!"

With that, I turned my back on him and, job well done, went straight to sleep.

The letter really did get written next day. Gergely brought a little third-year with him with a face like a turkey's egg, and they wrote it together, with much sweat and toil. I don't think I sweated as much laying out that "ginger dog" as those two boys sweated over that letter. Many years later, I found it among my mother's affairs. It must have made quite an impression on the poor thing for her to have kept it so carefully. It read:

Dear Misses Anna,

This is Gergely, second-year elementary student from old Rozi's, you may rimember me, and I'm righting now because Béla asked me to right, to tell you that your loving son, Béla, he's hungry. Cos the old woman dont give him to eat. Cos the old woman says Misses Anna ain't sent her munney. So please send the munney, Misses Anna. Please send it right now because the old witch wont give Béla to eat till then, and whats Béla to do if he ain't got nothing to eat, tell me that? Yours, with deep respect (your loving son also sends grate respects).

Patriotic Greetins,

Gergely
Second-Year Elementary Student

And so the letter was done; but letters need stamps and the stamp cost twenty fillérs. Only paltry, inflationary fillérs, but in those days I wasn't familiar with the finer points of economic theory. In my world, twenty fillérs was still twenty fillérs, and twenty fillérs was an inconceivable sum. It wasn't an amount I could have scraped together before, much less now, when I had to feed myself as well! The old woman wasn't playing around. I knew that if she saw me, she'd hurl the first thing that came to hand right at me, so I no longer showed up at meals.

The first day I managed to get by somehow. The boys, after I threatened them each individually, secretly sneaked me a bite or two of their lunch and supper. But the next day, the old woman discovered the scam and anyone she found with food in their pockets, she gave a good hiding.

"Ungrateful bastards!" she screamed as she did each time she was angry with them, and from then on would not leave the table till the boys had finished eating.

The boys, I think, weren't really sorry. Children don't like to share their food with others, especially when they're not getting all that much themselves. I didn't eat a thing for twenty-four hours, and when you're six that kind of thing is apt to make you dispirited.

I grew wilder. I stole whatever I could, I blackmailed whoever I could, and I fought whenever anyone paid me. But I still couldn't fill my belly, because there weren't fights every day, and how much can you steal in a village? It was no use going after poultry, so that left fruit. But down our way the peasants didn't leave the fruit to idle on the tree, so I ended up whacking it off the branch still green or picking it up, half rotten, from the dusty road. I was permanently hungry as a wolf, and money never stays in a hungry man's pocket. As soon as I got hold of a couple of fillérs, I ran straight to the shop to buy bread, and so that twenty fillérs just didn't seem to want to come together. Over and over I swore that when I got hold of some money I wouldn't spend it, but the second I got hold of any money, I did spend it, over and over. Meanwhile the letter, which I had buried in a little box, just lay in the ground like a corpse and couldn't get on its life-saving way.

Sunday was my last hope. After protracted negotiations, I had agreed with the boys that they would give me whatever krajcárs they managed to get out of their mothers, and I would work it off, like the serf works off his potatoes for winter. But even your guardian angel can't help you when your path's been crossed by a black cat. On Sunday, the entire country poured with rain and the mothers didn't come, only Gergely's, a little later, when the weather had cleared. Gergely told her why I needed the twenty fillérs, but his mother only gave me ten.

"I'd give you the whole twenty, so you could buy that measly stamp," she said, "but what can I do when I don't have that much myself?"

She said that with such warmth and kindness that I had to believe her, but I still searched her little Gergely after she left, just to be sure she hadn't slipped him something on the sly. She hadn't, worse luck.

I put the ten fillérs in a little matchbox, and so I wouldn't be tempted again, buried it beside the letter. I still needed another ten fillérs.

The next day, it looked like my luck was in. The old woman had herself driven to the neighbouring parish and Gergely immediately told me the good news. I sneaked home. I knew that Mr Rozi always had a sleep after lunch. He was that sort of a man. Even at harvest time when the other peasants were working every hour that God sent, he would, the moment the church bells rang noon, amble home, have his lunch, and have a good sleep.

So I hid behind the stables and waited. About half an hour later, Gergely appeared.

"The old man's snorin'," he whispered.

The old man was a famous snorer. He used to erupt with such enormous snorts in his sleep that unless you were deaf, you could hear him in the street.

I sneaked up to the open window and peeked cautiously in. It was a fine, warm autumn, and the old man wasn't wearing his jacket yet, only a waistcoat. It hung there, enticingly, on the back of a chair. Silent as a cat, I climbed through the window and, with my heart beating terribly, petrified by every noise, I searched it. I found six fillérs, pocketed them, and climbed back through the window as quick as I could.

"Just four to go!" I exclaimed victoriously to Gergely. "And that letter'll be off to Budapest."

I was feeling very confident. Those last four mangy krajcárs would be no problem, I thought, and decided to bury the six fillérs, so as to avoid any possible temptation. I was only waiting for Gergely to leave, because I didn't want anyone to know where the money was hidden— not even him. But Gergely was all wound up from the adventure, and in his excitable state he started blabbering so much, it took me a good hour to get rid of him.

It was about two by then and I hadn't eaten anything all day. All of a sudden, I was seized by such an overpowering animal hunger that, casting all better judgement aside, I ran to the shop and spent every last one of the six fillérs.

So I was back to square one.

What's going to become of me? I wondered bitterly. If I always ate the price of the stamp, the letter would never be sent, my mother would never send money, and I would never get anything to eat.

"Oh, for the…" I said, launching into an endless, filthy tirade of swearing, and burst loudly into tears.

One day, I got so hungry that I approached a Jewish peddler on the outskirts of the village.

"Pleeeease, mister," I said in a chanting, pleading voice, the way

I'd heard professional beggars do it, "pleeeease spare a bit of change, I'm sooooo hungry!"

I would never have dared risk this with someone from the village, but this was just a ragged Jew, and back then even a six-year-old knew that "that was different". The White Terror was in its heyday and this kind of wandering Jew could count himself lucky if he made it through a village without a beating. He was almost touched that I was asking him for money instead of shouting the usual "dirty Jew" at him. He didn't hesitate, but reached straight into his pocket, dragged out a fistful of change and, lifting his shaky hand to his myopic eyes—he had the drooping, perpetually teary eyes of an old dog—found me five fillérs.

"*Schlaaachte zaytn*," he intoned with a sigh. "*Schlaaachte zaytn*."

Then he patted my head and wandered on, the embodiment of sorrow.

I really did bury those five fillérs, though by that time I had got so weak with hunger that even on cool days I was bathed in sweat, my eyelids always felt heavy and whenever I sat down, I fell straight asleep.

In my desperate state, I had a wild idea. I waited for the maid to take the leftovers from lunch out for the dog, sneaked over to the doghouse, and made them mine. The dog was an old, loyal pal, and he never made so much as a sound when I snatched the dish away from him. He just watched me with his weak, bloodshot eyes full of incomprehension. I felt sorry for our Komondor, but I felt more sorry for myself. I went to the privy, locked the door, and ate everything on that plate that was edible.

From then on, I lived on the dog's dinners. I had a good stomach, but it wasn't made of iron. One night, I woke to an appalling grumbling in my bowels. I got the runs so badly that I hardly dared leave the privy for three days straight. That was the only place I felt safe, for in the yard I had the constant fear of the old woman spotting me, and in the street, the fear of getting caught short. So, unless someone chased me out, I would sit for hours in the outhouse, my head lolling down onto my chest, nodding off now and again. I was not doing well, to say the least. But, like everything in life, this state, too, had its advantages: a dubious advantage, but an advantage nonetheless. I wasn't hungry any more.

When my stomach improved, I decided to get hold of the missing five fillérs come hell or high water. I was in luck, and got a commission for a fight, my client promising me five fillérs. The boy I had to beat up was a scraggly little lad who didn't belong to any gang, so the money was as good as mine.

"That letter'll get to Muther soon enough!" I boasted to Gergely when I left home to wallop the scraggly little lad.

But I didn't end up walloping him. Something terrible, something unbelievable happened. That scraggly little lad ended up walloping me. Before, I could have laid him out with one hand, but now he wiped the floor with me, and how! I could kiss the five fillérs goodbye, of course; all I had got out of it was a good hiding.

The runs had been torture, I was unbearably hungry, but what was all that compared to my shame? So much for my rep, so much for the stamp, so much for everything. I ran out beyond the village, threw myself down into the grass and sobbed as if the sky had fallen in.

"What's to become of me?" I cried. "What's to become of me?"

6

S UDDENLY, I HAD A BOLD IDEA. I sneaked home, dug up the letter and the fifteen fillérs, and ran to the post office.

The blonde, moon-faced young lady who ran the post office was all alone in the sleepy room that smelt of mouse droppings. I stood to attention before her, but I was so nervous I couldn't speak. The young lady smiled.

"What d'you need, son?" she asked.

"Please, miss, please," I managed to say at last, "send this letter for me!"

She glanced at the letter and counted my little collection of krajcárs.

"You're five fillérs short," she said. "The stamp's twenty."

"I know, miss, I know," I said, determined to see it through no matter what, "but what can I do when I only got fifteen?"

"You went and spent the other five on sweets, didn't you?"

She said that in a very schoolmistress-like way, and at the word "sweets", she furrowed her brows. Dear, sweet God, I thought to myself, if I had five fillérs to spare, I'd spend it on a crust of bread.

"I ain't had no sweets, miss," I sighed, and felt my tears welling up.

"Oh, don't cry!" said the young lady, and smiled again. "Did you lose it, then?"

I thought if she liked that idea so much it made her smile, then it was best to leave her to it. So I nodded yes.

"They give you a hidin' at home?"

I nodded again. The young lady was still smiling. What on earth were these fancy young ladies smiling at all the bloody time, I thought to myself. I didn't see anything funny in the situation at all.

"Go on, miss, have a heart!" I begged, my voice faltering. "I don't know what'll become of me if that letter don't get sent."

44

The young lady just looked at me, smiling, and started shaking her head more and more. I didn't know what that meant, her shaking her head, and I didn't know what to make of her constant dumpy smiling, either. Is she making fun of me, or what? My heart was in my mouth; I watched her tiniest movements.

"All right, then," she said at last. "But you come and bring me the rest, you hear?"

I couldn't believe my ears.

"You mean you'll send it?"

"Yes."

I thought my heart would burst for joy. I grabbed the young lady's hand and kissed it all over.

"God bless your kindness, miss! I'll bring that money as soon as I'm better."

That perennial, incurable smile vanished from the young lady's face.

"Why, what's the matter with you?" she asked, surprised.

"Oh, miss!" I said, the pent-up grievance bursting out of me, but that was as far as I got. My voice failed me, salty tears started flowing from my eyes, and though I wanted to speak, all that came out was "oh, oh, oh!", and all the while I was thinking that this fine young lady who laughed at everything was going to laugh at me now, and I was terribly ashamed. I turned, without a word, and ran out into the street.

I ran down the street, sobbing loudly.

This was a new experience for me. I wasn't one to cry much, and even if now and then I felt like crying, I wouldn't have done so in front of others for all the world. I would think of my rep, and my eyes stayed dry. But recently, there had been nothing I could do. My nerves, like shredded reins, did not respond to my will, and rep or no rep, the salt water just kept flowing from my eyes.

"What's the matter, son?" an old woman called after me, but I just swore at her kindness and tore out into the fields so no one would see me.

As soon as I was alone, I felt so weak I almost collapsed. I didn't know what had got into me. I was sweating in rivulets, but I was still cold. My knees felt soft, and I could barely drag myself along. I had to keep stopping to rest over and over, and it took me a good hour to get home.

There was a huge commotion in the yard. The boys were playing capture the flag, which told me that the old woman wasn't home. The world was spinning around me, but as I stepped into the yard, I drew myself up ramrod straight. I didn't so much as look at the boys. I thought they already knew about my humiliation, but as it turned out later, they had no idea. I went straight to our room and collapsed into the straw. My teeth were chattering, I had the chills all over, my whole body was trembling.

I'd never been ill before, and now I was scared to death. I listened to the dull click of my chattering teeth, petrified. I'm going to die, I thought, and cried, and cried, and cried. Then, all at once, I was unaware of everything. I'd fallen asleep.

I woke to someone shaking my shoulder. It was Péter, one of the boys. He was standing in the straw before me, looking at me in alarm.

"What's the matter with you?" he asked.

"Nothing," I muttered dully. "I was sleepin'. What you starin' at?"

"You was yellin' in your sleep."

"Doing what?"

"Yellin'. You could hear it all the way out in the yard."

I felt myself blush. I was dreadfully ashamed of having yelled. What could I have been yelling about? I wanted to ask, but didn't dare.

"None of your business!" I shouted, resenting him for having heard me yell. "Get lost, I need my sleep."

With that, I turned to the wall and closed my eyes. But he just stood there, as if he had something more to say. I made a point of not asking him what. In the end, he couldn't stand it any longer and leant down over me.

"Hey… Béla…"

He'd dropped his voice, his face was conspiratorial. I knew at once he had something important to say.

"What is it?"

Péter waited a few moments more for effect. Then he told me:

"The old woman's havin' one of her praying fits!"

At that, I jumped up as if I were fit as a fiddle. If the old woman was having one of her "praying fits", anyone could get anything out of her they wanted. The boys all knew that and made good use of her fits of kindness. Not me. I lied, I stole, I beat people up for money, but two-faced I wasn't. I'd always looked down on the boys for going and wheedling her at times like this, and now I was judging myself a hundred times more harshly for wanting to do the same thing. But what else could I do? I said to myself. I was already sick, and if she didn't give me something to eat, I'd die.

"Go on, get in there, go!" Péter told me. "She's kneelin' in front of the Virgin."

"Should I?" I asked, though by then I'd already made up my mind to go.

"Yeah."

"What do I do in there?"

"You never done it before?"

"No."

"You're a fool. Want to starve? Just go in, calm as can be, and kneel down next to the old witch. Then say an Our Father, loud as you can."

"That's it?"

"That's it. Then she forgives you, all merciful and everything."

"Oh the hell with her!" I burst out. "I hate the damn sight of her."

"Me too," Péter said. "But just you go in there. Know what's for supper?"

"What?"

"Brawn and onions. Swear to God."

My mouth began to water. My God, brawn and onions! I would have been off at once, but there was still one thing gnawing at me inside.

"Do you *have* to say an Our Father?"

"You don't have to, but it's better if you do."

"Then I don't think I will."

"Why? Scared of him?"

This he asked with such an air of disdain that I felt ashamed. Péter was a third-year, and since he couldn't compete with me physically, he was always trying to lay me low with his spiritual prowess instead. I

47

didn't know what to say. I have to admit, I hadn't thought much about theological questions at six. Maybe they'd learnt about it in third year, I thought, and—being a careful sort of lad—didn't reply. Péter was obviously relishing his spiritual superiority. He looked at me with furrowed brows like a strict but kindly teacher and put his hand on my shoulder with a significant gesture.

"Listen," he said. "I ain't scared of him no more."

"Not scared of God?"

"Not a bit! He don't care about us boys anyway, not if we're poor. It's a load of rubbish, my friend. When did Jesus last get you something to eat? Never, that's when. Far as he cares, you can go starve to death, ain't that right?"

I didn't have an answer for that, either. Jesus really hadn't brought me any food, that was true, but what Péter had said still made me angry, though I couldn't exactly tell you why. It's possible that some instinctive sense of religiousness revolted within me, but it's also possible that I was angry because this uppity boy was so full of his own knowledge again.

"But it's still wrong to say an Our Father and not mean it," I grumbled.

"Don't be so scared, my friend," he said dismissively, "It's all a load of tripe. Just do what I do."

"What's that?"

"I walk right in the front room, kneel down next to the old witch, roll my eyes all saint-like, then trot out the prayers, keen as anything, like I was sorry for my sins. But in my head, I just say:

> *Our Father,*
> *who art in heaven*
> *Your old man's*
> *a big ol' melon*
> *Your mam's a pea,*
> *and you're a lemon!"*

I broke into loud, vicious laughter.

"Again!" I said, panting for breath. "How'd it go?"

By then, Péter too had got the giggles. We were laughing like a couple of lunatics, whooping, jumping up and down, and repeating the little ditty again and again:

> *Our Father,*
> *who art in heaven*
> *Your old man's*
> *a big ol' melon*
> *Your mam's a pea,*
> *and you're a lemon!*

We tottered with laughter for several minutes, like a pair of drunks. Then Péter put his hand on my shoulder again, and with the haughtiness of a schoolteacher asked me:

"Still scared, my friend?"

"The hell I am!" I replied cockily. "And you can stop calling me 'my friend' or I'll kick you up the arse!"

With that, I turned and went out into the yard. Everything was churning up inside me. I don't have to be scared of God, I've got to convince the old woman, my friend, it's all a load of rubbish anyway! I spat a juicy one out of the side of my mouth and, pressing my chin down onto my neck, headed for the old woman's room with heavy, angry, bull-like steps, as if getting ready to kill.

It was already getting quite dark. An eerie quiet had settled on the yard. Not a soul around. In the kitchen, the maid was humming something in a flat, throaty voice, but that only seemed to make the silence deeper. I was cold. I must have had a high fever.

The maid left off her humming when I came into the kitchen and stared at me with her dumb, bovine eyes.

"What's the matter with you?"

I didn't reply. Absolutely determined, like someone climbing the gallows steps, I entered the front room. The old woman was kneeling in front of the picture of the Virgin, grinding away at her rosary, head bowed. It was dark in the room, only the flicker of the eternal flame glowing in the red glass under the Virgin. The wind blew in through the

49

open window, causing the flame of the candle to gutter and scratch again and again. Long, lopsided shadows swayed on the wall. The old woman looked at me, but it was as if she hadn't seen me. Her eyes were hollow and fixed, like a blind man's. I knelt down beside her without a word and, following Péter's advice, started mechanically muttering to myself:

> *Our Father,*
> *who art in heaven*
> *Your old man's*
> *a big ol' melon*
> *Your mam's a pea,*
> *and you're a lemon!*

"Our Father, who art in heaven…"

I shuddered. My voice seemed as strange as if I were hearing it for the first time. My teeth were chattering, I could barely go on.

"Give us this day our daily bread," I heard the strange voice beseech, and I started sobbing terribly.

"And forgive us our trespasses," the old woman continued, "as we forgive those that trespass against us…"

She spread out her arms wildly and her voice was as deep and full as Péter's when he was imitating her. All at once I came to my senses. I saw myself as if the old, healthy Béla had peered in at the keyhole, rolling about sobbing beside the half-crazed old bat, and Squirrel piped up in a mocking grumble:

> *Our Father,*
> *who art in heaven*
> *Your old man's*
> *a big ol' melon*
> *Your mam's a pea,*
> *and you're a lemon!*

"Amen," the old woman mumbled in a saintly voice, because she'd come to the end of her prayers meanwhile; and then she turned to me and irritably, like a servant just carrying out the master's orders, crowed at me: "You get food from today. Now out!"

But I just stood there in front of her, immobile, as if her incredible mercy had rooted me to the spot. I don't know what I was waiting for. Perhaps a miracle, or to get up enough courage to throw her sainted alms back into her face. I hated her more than ever, and the thought that I had no right to hate her seemed absolutely intolerable.

"Give me work," I begged. "I'll work for my bread."

"Don't talk back!" she snapped at me. "I said out!"

With that, she crossed herself and went on with her prayers.

That night, I had supper with the other children again. I felt awful and can't have had much of an appetite, but you don't eat for your stomach alone. Even the thought that I could eat at last was dizzying, especially brawn and onions.

We had supper out in the yard, around a long table under the walnut tree. I stared stiff and silent at the smoky petroleum lamp and never looked at the children. It was a fine, warm autumn evening, the sky full of shooting stars, the boys crowing, making wishes one after the other. All I wanted was for my stomach to be full and for the devil to take the old witch and the whole godforsaken world to boot.

Ilona, the dull-eyed maid, was serving supper. She was not a clever girl—even as a six-year-old I had established as much—but incredibly kind-hearted. She gave me twice as much as the other boys. Hungry as a wolf, I ate it all up, but started burping right after. This, in itself, did not upset me. Down our way, burping was considered a fine and healthy thing, and no one would have dreamt of thinking it rude. Peasants are absolutely convinced that if you don't burp after a meal, you haven't really had your fill, so it's actually downright impolite for a guest *not* to burp at his host's table. I'm nice and full, I thought, and tried not to notice that the world was spinning around me.

I didn't last long, though. My stomach was so upset that I almost had to vomit right there. I jumped up and ran as fast as I could, but didn't even make it as far as the privy. In thirty seconds, round the corner of the house, I threw up the dinner I had been waiting for so long and so desperately.

The old Komondor greeted my foul luck like some kind of birthday present. He bounded around my legs wagging his tail and licked up the whole lot while it was still warm. It was only later that I learnt that a man's vomit is, for dogs, a delicacy, and that more generally, there is nothing bad that can happen to one of God's creatures that isn't good for another in some form or another. But I was hardly aware of that at the age of six, and so I thought to myself, in the narrow-minded way that anyone who's suffering will, that Péter had been right after all when he said that God doesn't care about the children of the poor.

I was sick for some time. I got a high fever from time to time, but I never missed a meal. I simply could not imagine someone not eating when they were given food, and it was, time and again, the dog that reaped the rewards.

My mother got my letter, but not the position she'd been hoping for. Instead of money, she just kept sending pleading letters. The old woman—no doubt thinking of the debt my mother had amassed—didn't put me out of doors, but one morning she called me in to see her in the front room.

"If you want to work, work!" she grunted. "And not just run filthy mouth, you hear?"

Yes, I'd heard that, all right. That was clear as day and needed no eternal flame to illuminate it. From then on she was once more so genuinely loathsome that I could hate her with a clear conscience. So, with time, my emotional balance was restored.

I worked so hard I almost burst. Not because the old woman had told me to; good luck to her if she'd tried. No, I worked for pride, for my humanity. I wanted to show the old bat that I didn't need her charity: I would "work for my bread".

With occasional breaks of varying lengths, I worked seven or eight hours a day. I fetched water from the well, fed the animals, swept up, and cleaned the house. I didn't stop working even when my mother managed to send a little money. I had lost faith in that source of income. I thought of motherly love as nothing more than hollow words that grown-ups made up to fool children. You couldn't put it on a plate and eat it, I said to myself, thinking of my wild days of hunger. I wanted to stand on my own two feet.

I was quite a useful little lad and so strong that even the peasants passing by would stop and watch me work.

"Well, I'll be..." they'd say, feeling my muscles. "How long did your muther suckle *you*?"

But I didn't stop to chit-chat with them. Even praise I greeted with suspicion. Why would anyone praise a little bastard boy? They just want to make fun of me, I thought, and pressed my chin to my neck and looked up at my kindly elders with my eyes down low, like a little bull ready to charge. No, I was no "dear child". I was a lawless mongrel in this dog-eat-dog world of ours, with all its strict rules of breeding.

7

I F DAYDREAMING IS THE ENEMY of real life, then my little old life was in no danger whatsoever. I was as sober as an aged peasant.

I lost my head only once—on account of a girl, of course. It was a strange, stunted little love affair, but I still paid for it so bitterly that for the next eight years I didn't want anything at all to do with love.

Sárika was her name. I don't remember her face any more, only her pretty reddish-blond hair, her milk-white skin and her many, many freckles; and that she had that fragile, thin-as-a-rake look I couldn't abide in boys.

She had a big doll she used to play with day in, day out, alone. She had no actual friends, but that wasn't her fault. Nationalist Jew-bashing was in its heyday then, and Sárika was Jewish. There was only one Jewish family in the village, Sárika's parents and grandparents. Her father owned the village shop and her grandfather the inn. They were quiet, decent folk, and before this wave of bare-breasted nationalism had reared its head, they had been well liked in the village. Now, the only people who went to see them were asking for a loan. Anyone who didn't get one started cursing the filthy Jews, the ones who did nodding quietly along, because who doesn't curse their creditors?

Children learnt to hate the Jews before they learnt to read or write. It was all they heard, and little wonder if they simplified things a little in their own way. Jews were the cause of all earthly ills, from headaches to hail, and so they hated Sárika, the only child representative of the detested race, like the Devil incarnate. That little girl was such a pariah in the village that even a self-respecting Gypsy child would have been ashamed to play with her.

As to what my thoughts were on the Jewish Question at the age of six, I have no idea. But I suspect that it wasn't pure heroism that led me to swim against the tide of public opinion. Everything must have been upside down and inside out in my heart, so much so that I even forgot about my precious reputation. I didn't care what the village would say. I was ready to be ostracized by everyone if only that little Jewish girl they all detested would be my friend. Because the truth is, we weren't even on speaking terms yet.

Every time I headed to the shop, I resolved that this time, today, I would speak to her, but I always lost my nerve. It's true that her parents were always there, too, and they didn't let her out on the street alone. Sárika's grandfather, the seventy-year-old innkeeper, had been beaten half to death one night, and since then not even the adult members of the family dared go out after dark. The non-Jewish bartender served at the inn at night, and they always drew the shutters of the shop before it grew dark, closing themselves up in the house. People in the village said they used to perform twisted rituals by candlelight, sacrificing to a wrathful Jehovah.

Sárika was a quiet, serious little girl. She came and went noiselessly, eyes discreetly lowered, and as soon as I stepped into the shop, she'd switch to German with her parents. It seems she didn't want me to understand, because otherwise she always spoke Hungarian.

Needless to say, I always spent what little money I had in Sárika's family's shop. I would choose slowly and carefully, occasionally even commenting on the quality of the goods, partly to emphasize that I was a serious and regular customer, and partly—mainly—so I could be in there longer. I kept looking at Sárika the whole time. But Sárika took no notice of me. I spent months mooning after her like this, but all I managed to accomplish was that once—just once—she smiled at me. And even then, it was by accident. What happened was that one day, I tripped a boy in front of their shop. The boy must have been on his way to some birthday party or other celebration, because he was wearing his Sunday clothes on a weekday. He was irritatingly preened, and he was walking past the houses as cockily as a rooster at mating time. I don't remember why I did it—if it was out of jealousy, or because of his pretty Sunday clothes, or just because his strutting annoyed me—but the fact is, I tripped him up. The street was muddy and the little dandy landed face first in a good-sized puddle. I heard a muffled snicker behind me.

I turned and was absolutely dumbstruck. Sárika was standing in the doorway of the shop, smiling. Smiling at me.

I knew this was the moment. I've got to say something, I said to myself, and… didn't. I spent days kicking myself for my cowardice and spent weeks, months, doing everything I could to try and get another smile out of her. I'd spend hours in front of the shop and trip every child that came that way, regardless of age or sex. In vain. Sárika never smiled at me again.

I had just about given up hope when something unexpected happened.

8

B UT FIRST, I HAVE A CONFESSION to make. I was not, in the way
that grown-ups tend to think about these things, strictly speaking
faithful to Sárika.

I say in the way that grown-ups think about these things, because I
in no way considered what I got up to with a maid called Borcsa while
I was hopelessly in love with Sárika to be infidelity in any way. I, like
most other children, considered physical and emotional love to be two
completely separate things. I'd never felt any kind of physical desire or
curiosity with Sárika, though I was much concerned with the mystery
of those things at the time.

I lived among servant girls and worked alongside them all day long,
and they were mostly young, lively peasant girls who, being unacquainted
with the gems of the Hungarian film industry of the time, had no idea
what a decent, socially respectable Hungarian peasant girl was meant
to be like. They simply *were* Hungarian peasant girls, who said what
they thought, and what they actually thought—why deny it?—didn't
tend to appear much in the aforementioned cinematic masterpieces.

The girls treated me like a newborn kitten whose eyes have not yet
opened. They talked freely in front of me, especially of things supremely
suited to unsettling a prepubescent boy.

On the hot summer days when we went bathing in the river secretly,
behind the old woman's back, most of the girls undressed in front of
me. My childish eyes were free to roam over the hills and valleys of
these grown women's bodies, seeking out timidly, awkwardly and with
predatory hunger the "differences" in the regions around the breasts
and elsewhere, where those wild, dark, exciting grasses grew, and where
for a child, all was secret.

I saw them flirting with the lads and heard their shy giggles, ticklish
laughs and sensual squeals; I saw the lads' wild eyes, and that great,

incomprehensible madness, like a contagious sickness, lit its first fires within me too.

Meanwhile, I came and went among the grown-ups with the most innocent expression in the world. I gave deliberately naive answers to sensitive questions and pretended not to understand the screams of laughter that greeted my sanctimonious responses. They must have been absolutely convinced that I didn't even know yet whether I was a boy or a girl, whereas in my imagination, the Devil's burning bush was already lit and I was waiting, on tenterhooks, for its revelation.

And this, at least in part, did come to pass not too long thereafter, thanks to Borcsa.

It happened around harvest time. One brutally hot afternoon, when all the household was out in the fields, the old woman told Borcsa to take me and clean out the attic. There was no one else besides us in the house, so we locked the garden gate and went up to the attic to clean.

Upstairs, the heat was even more unbearable. We set about our task sluggishly, with a great deal of faffing, and what we did manage to accomplish wasn't worth a damn. Borcsa didn't try to force the thing too long, throwing her broom down in the corner, and then—swearing bitterly—herself too, in last year's hay. I was no more diligent and immediately followed her example.

We lay immobile beside each other. It was so quiet, it seemed as if the whole village had succumbed to heatstroke. Only the fat, shameless flies flew about with their awful humming, settling again and again on our sweaty faces.

Borcsa drew her knees up as she lay, which made her short skirt slip high up her legs. She herself may not have noticed, since she was lying with her eyes closed, but I was all the more attentive. I took such a good look at her I still retain the image in my mind today. I can no longer remember her face, but I still recall the maddening beauty of her white thighs peeking out beneath her short skirt.

She was a shapely peasant girl, hair black as coal, forever hopping about like a flea. She talked all day long, explaining, recounting, gossiping, laughing, and—when she was alone—humming constantly. But she really lost her head when she got a whiff of a lad. Then she'd rush about as if her backside were full of hot peppers.

"I was no angel as youth, Borcsa," said the old woman, "but you, you a real witch, fit to burn!"

I shut the door. The attic had no windows, and only a strip or two of light filtered through the gaps in the rotten door, as if drawn on the floor with a ruler. We lay silently in the semi-darkness. Suddenly, Borcsa sat up.

"This damn heat!" she murmured, and removed her shirt.

My eyes almost popped out of their sockets. Her damp undershirt clung to her pointed little breasts, and that maddening black hair poked out from her armpits. That, in itself, would already have been enough to drive me wild, but then she also removed her overskirt. She was now wearing nothing but an underskirt, and it wasn't even starched. It draped itself, soft and revealing, over her graceful young body and promised rather than veiled.

"You ought to take them rags off, too!" she said, and I immediately removed my sticky shirt. That in itself wouldn't have meant anything, since I often ran around shirtless. But Borcsa asked:

"Why don't you take your trousers off an' all?"

"I ain't got pants on."

"Me neither," she giggled.

"Yeah, but drawers," I said knowledgeably.

"Nor them."

"What, then?"

"Nothin'."

"*Nothin'?*"

"That's right, nothin'!"

And she giggled as if I'd been tickling her.

"Come off it, Borcsa!" I laughed, but my heart was beating as if Beelzebub himself had been chasing me.

"I ain't in the habit of tellin' lies," Borcsa tittered.

"Go on and prove it, then…"

I reached for her skirt. Borcsa struck at my hand.

"Aw… just a little!" I pleaded.

"Stop it, you little worm!"

"There!" I shouted with feigned childish glee. "You *do* have panties on, you're lyin'!"

"No I ain't."

"Go on and show me, then!"

"No damn chance!"

"Aw… Borcsa… go on… just a little…"

I reached under her skirt. She pushed me roughly away.

"Look at you!!" she snapped at me angrily. "Ain't you ashamed of yourself? I'll tell the old woman on you!"

She was so het up, I thought she'd throw me right out of the attic and drag me to the old woman by my ear. But she didn't. She just lay beside me in the half-light and then lots of things happened that I don't remember, until all at once…

I don't know how it happened. All at once I was lying in her warm, naked lap and the world seemed more wonderful than ever before. This wasn't strictly speaking lovemaking, or lovemaking in any sense really, since I was merely a prepubescent, curious little boy. She did with me what girls like her tend to do with curious little boys like me, far more often than people think.

I felt like when you're falling slowly in a dream, very slowly, without hitting the ground for the longest time. My hands grabbed on to her flesh tight, and it felt like my fingernails were on fire. I was dazed by this frightening, never-before felt, unbelievable bliss. My eyes grew heavy and I fell into a deep, strange semi-sleep, but at the same time I was wonderfully awake. It was as if our bodies and the whole world with them had started to melt in the dark, airless heat—everything flowed apart, fell to pieces, grew dreamlike, and was gone.

I was roused with a start. Borcsa was moaning loudly. Crumbling, incomprehensible words came out of her mouth and her heart was thumping so hard I felt the pressure of every beat in my chest. I stared at her twisted face, horrified. Her mouth was half open, her eyelids went dark, she was breathing in short, sharp bursts as if suffocating. I was incredibly scared. I thought she was going to die right there in my arms. I wanted to shake her, to wake her and ask what was wrong, but somehow my instinct stopped me.

A few minutes later, of course, she was wonderfully calm. Her arm fell limply into the hay, and she didn't move at all for some time. She was lying there as faint as if she were on her deathbed. I was still a little scared. But then she opened her eyes and smiled at me.

"You little worm!" she whispered with a strange, ringing laugh, and gave me the sort of delicate little slap with the tips of her five fingers that men, however little they may be, never resent.

"Come on, then, chop-chop!" she said in a changed tone. "We have to get to it."

With that she jumped up and, as if nothing at all had happened, got to work, humming loudly.

From then on we used to go up to the attic often, till one day the old woman caught Borcsa with Mr Rozi and threw her out of the house.

All this happened during the time I was madly in love with Sárika. I was not only *not* in love with Borcsa, I didn't even care for her. I craved her like a hungry man craves his food, but her soul mattered to me just as little as the pig's whose meat I ate in my favourite stews. All day, I thought about Sárika. Secretly, I would call her my heart's love, and hold imagined conversations with her. She was the first person ever to inspire in me the sweet but slightly incredible suspicion that there was more to the human soul than selfishness, greed and animal urges; and that perhaps the grown-ups weren't lying when they talked of love and affection.

After Borcsa left us, I tried my luck with some of the other servant girls but, to my great disappointment, got absolutely nowhere. I started missing Borcsa, and thought more about her than ever. At those times, I would sneak up to the attic and, in the hay where we'd lain together so often, close my eyes and relive our thrilling encounters in luscious detail. I heard her strange, sensual moans, I saw her maddeningly beautiful white thighs, and I did what Gergely used to do. Soon enough, I too had rings under my eyes.

9

T HE FIRST TIME I TALKED to Sárika was around Easter. It was spring, just like in the best love stories, and I was walking home, minding my own business, from the fields in the snapdragon-hued dusk. When I got to the high street, though, I heard the rumble of feet and a terrific chorus of children's voices.

Cohen, Levi, Bruck
every Jew's a crook!

This sort of thing was so common at the time that I didn't even bother to quicken my pace. The Jewish peddler's arrived, I thought. Or maybe they're playing pogrom, which was very popular among the children that year. But when I got to the main square, I saw that this was no joke. A shower of stones and mud was raining down on a terrified, sobbing little girl—the little girl being Sárika.

I saw red. Trembling with fury, I took the rake off my shoulder and a moment later three of the little terrors of the Jews were rolling on the ground, weeping and wailing. The others, two or three of them, were running as fast as they could, and the fallen heroes were not much more heroic. They got to their feet, sniffling and crying, and amid the usual curses and threats, limped off the battlefield.

I stood there alone in the road, having swept the field, as the dispatches used to put it, and I really did feel like a victorious general. I could see Sárika standing on the corner, watching the developments. She didn't dare, it seemed, go back to the shop, for she had clearly gone out on the street without permission, and was scared to tell her parents what had happened. I wanted to throw myself at her feet like the shepherd in the fairy tale who won the princess's hand with his heroism, but I saw at once that that sort of thing wasn't very dignified for a victorious general.

So I drew myself up straight, stuck my hands in my pockets, pressed my chin down against my neck and approached my heart's love with slow, dignified steps. As I walked, I was desperately trying to come up with some punchy line with which I could fittingly start the conversation. I can't comment on the rhetorical prowess of other generals, but what I do know is that after this victorious encounter I couldn't think of a single blasted word. So I just stood in front of my sweetheart; she, too, was silent. We were still panting heavily—me from fighting, her from running. I looked at her pale, pretty face; she looked down at the point of her shoe. We stood there like that, in silence, for several minutes.

Finally, I had an inspiration that would save the day. I reached into my pockets and produced ten or fifteen coloured glass balls and, squatting down, started playing on the ground in front of her. I was a real master at marbles, so I was certain that—coupled with my performance on the battlefield just now—my gaming skills would only serve to heighten the effect. Sárika looked on in silence.

"Know how to play?" I said at last, almost offhand, playing on.

"No," she replied in a thin, frightened voice.

"Come on, I'll show you."

But Sárika didn't move.

"Nothin' to be afraid of," I said, with a little masculine hauteur. "I don't hit good little girls—I fight injustice, like Sándor Rózsa!"

That was a fine little sentence, and I liked it very well, but it was not, apparently, having any particular effect on Sárika. She just stood there, eyes on the ground, scratching the pavement with the point of her shoe. I stood up and went a step closer.

"Why won't you play with me?"

"I'm not allowed," she replied quickly, barely audible.

"Ain't allowed?" I asked in astonishment. "They told you not to?"

"Yes."

"Why?"

"Because."

"'Cause what?" I snapped irritably, "Come on, out with it!"

She didn't reply. She just stood there, looking at the ground and scratching away at the pavement.

"I saved your life, and you ain't even goin' to answer me?" I said, with the wounded pride of a victorious general. "Why ain't you allowed to play with me? Go on, tell me!"

Sárika shrugged gently and, her eyes still lowered, quickly, almost mumbling, she said:

"Because you're one of old Rozi's boys."

I felt myself blush. I know it wasn't ignorance that made her call me one of old Rozi's boys. That's what they called us illegitimate children in the village, and we knew it—oh, we knew it all right. This simple, unqualified label, "one of old Rozi's boys", was almost as hurtful and humiliating as that other unqualified label of "Jew". They branded us like cattle for market. More than once, when I was walking down the street minding my own business, I heard my peers pipe up mockingly, chanting from behind a fence or window:

"*Old Roz-ee's son, where's your faa-ther gone?*"

Oh, I knew that well enough, all right. But that this little girl should say it to me, and me having saved her life barely moments before...

"Dirty Jew!" I said, a dark and bottomless hatred bursting out of me, and I spat in her eye, the eye of the little girl for whom barely minutes before I would have gladly laid down my life.

10

O H, I'D KNOWN ALL ALONG there was something not right about my background, but in the end, you get used to anything—and you live through it all. Except your own death, of course. My peasant stomach digested the dog's dinner, and my peasant soul digested my dog's life. I will admit, I was upset from time to time when that mocking chorus started up from behind a fence, but that was nothing more than a sort of emotional scratch—the wound was never very deep and barely left a trace.

But that pale little Jewish girl cut me to the quick. There was no longer any need to call after me from behind windows and fences, now I heard that taunting question everywhere, and I could no longer run from the answer. The question ran along with me, like a shadow with its body, forever echoing in my ear: old Roz-ee's son, where's your faa-ther gone?

I developed a nasty, bitter hatred for my mother. I blamed her for everything. It was that unknown servant girl who'd ruined my life, it was because of her I'd become the village mongrel, with whom even a little Jewish girl refused to play. "Just you show that shifty mug of yours round here again!" I threatened her in my head. "You'll get what's coming to you from your loving son!"

I didn't have long to wait. Two or three days after the fight, the usual postcard arrived from the capital. At other times, I would be terrified days before one of my mother's visits, but now I could hardly wait for Sunday. I was reeling with hatred. Now we'll have it out, I told myself and waited, gnashing my teeth.

As soon as we were alone, without any kind of build-up, I asked:

"Why don't you ever tell me about my father?"

My mother looked at me as if she'd been paralysed. First she blushed, then she paled, which gave her face, usually an earthy shade, a strange yellowish-green tinge.

"Your father?" she asked blandly, and looked around as usual, to make sure no one could overhear us.

"Yeah," I answered stubbornly.

We were sitting under the old peach tree, on the rickety little bench. My mother shifted uncomfortably in her seat.

"What d'you want me to say?" she asked with feigned ease, but her voice was halting and uncertain.

"What's with him, and everything?" I replied mercilessly.

I could see that she didn't know what to say, and I was cruelly enjoying her discomfort. Her small black eyes blinked in alarm, a vein swelled on her forehead and she didn't know what to do with herself. Mechanically, she opened her battered little handbag, fished out her handkerchief, pressed it to her perfectly dry nose, and replaced it, closing the bag with a flourish. Finally, as if facing the inevitable, she gave a deep, old-womanly sigh, and said:

"Well, he died, poor thing."

"Died?" I asked, astounded, because I was ready for anything but this.

"That's right. God rest his soul."

A long, awkward silence followed. The yard was full of noise, the mothers on their Sunday visit chattering volubly with their offspring, but around us there was silence. The silence was so palpable it was as if it had come to sit between us on the little bench. I didn't know what to say. I had done nothing, from Friday to Sunday, but prepare mentally for this discussion. I had been ready for every possible, and impossible, response—except this one. Nonetheless, I didn't believe what my mother had said for a moment. I knew, I could feel, that she was lying.

"Ain't what they say in the village," I said, noticing that my voice was somewhat hoarse.

"What they sayin' in the village?"

"Somethin' else. Somethin' different."

My mother's voice trembled with indignation. She gave me such an angry look, it was as if it was all my fault that everything was the way it was. That just drove me even wilder.

"Oh!" the pent-up anger burst out of me. "You know full well!"

"What?! What do I know?" she screamed at me, suddenly not caring if the others heard or not. "How dare you talk to your muther that way?"

I didn't reply. I just stared stubbornly ahead of me and savoured my mother's anger. My feigned calm made her even angrier.

"You ungrateful dog!" she hurled at me, trying to keep her voice down, because it seems she'd remembered meanwhile that there were others besides us in the yard. "I work my fingers to the bone for you day and night, I slave and I toil, I send you all that precious money, and this is the thanks I get?"

I listened to her with a cold and unsympathetic heart. I hated her to death at that moment. I remembered the old woman's words, when she'd told me in front of the other children to "tell your whore mother not to make herself child if she not pay for it!"

"It's your job to pay for me, Muther," I replied insolently.

"That so?" she jumped up. "You've got a damn nerve!"

And she gave me such a slap that I fell right off the bench. My mother had big, bony hands, and the slap hurt like the devil. But I still wouldn't have cried for all the world. I didn't feel sorry at all—just the opposite! Just then, I *needed* to have it out, and maybe I needed the slap too. My overstrung nerves soaked up the electric atmosphere of the coming storm with perverse gluttony. I was no longer quite sober. My humiliated childish soul was dizzy with the heady intoxication of revenge. I longed for some apocalyptic cataclysm to blow everything sky high and turn the whole world upside down.

"Who was it told you that, you little brat?"

"The old woman said so!" I replied with devilish glee, as I clambered up off the ground. "An' she said plenty more besides!"

"Is that right? Plenty more? What'd she say, then?"

I almost took pleasure in saying what I said next:

"That you're a filthy whore."

"What?!" she cried with all her might. "What did that old whore say?"

"Just that!" I replied, and felt a hideous, animal satisfaction.

By then, we were surrounded by the mothers and their children gaping at us, and even Ilona, the maid with the bovine expression, had rushed out of the kitchen.

"What happened, dear?" they asked my mother. "What's the matter? Go on, tell us!"

My mother did not reply. She shoved the curious onlookers roughly aside and headed, eyes blazing, for the house.

"I'll wring the old tramp's neck!" she screamed. "Wring her neck!"

Everyone ran after her; they forgot all about me.

It was only now I realized what I'd done. I, too, started to run, but not towards the house with the others—no, I ran in the opposite direction. People started gathering in front of the garden gate when they heard all the shouting, and I could see that I could no longer get out into the street. There was a cart full of hay in front of the stables; I climbed up onto that, quick as a flash, and disappeared inside the hay like the proverbial needle.

There was an unholy racket in the yard. Screaming, cursing, the pounding of feet running about. I could hear them looking for me. I peeked out, holding my breath. I could see from behind the hay my mother, the old woman, the entire band of mothers running towards the stables.

"Where that lying gallows rat?" the old woman seethed. "I scratch his eyes out!"

"No use you shoutin' like that, the boy can't make up somethin' like that on his own!"

"No?" the old woman screeched, and stopped in front of my mother, hands on her hips. "You think I lie, that it? You shut filthy mouth, dear, or they carry you out of here in sheet! So you don't send money, but you call names, that so? What you shout before in yard, eh?"

"The boy can't make up somethin' like that all by himself," my mother repeated stubbornly.

"I say, what-you-shout? Un-der-stand?"

My mother didn't answer. Tears were running from her eyes and she was trembling with the chills.

"Now you not so loud, eh? You coward worm! Who whore here, eh?"

"Ain't me!" my mother faltered. "I never took money from a man. I work my fingers to the bone day and night for that boy."

"Oh no, no, no!" the old woman squawked, waving her index finger under my mother's nose. "Don't you go put on air, devil take you! I know all about you, dear. You can't come Virgin with me! You never want to birth mangy son of yours. Running like madwoman to get rid of him. You just want your bull, but not his calf! And you still don't pay proper, like other girls. Little bastard starve to death for all you care, whoring round Budapest!"

"*What* d'you say?" my mother asked hoarsely, suddenly scarily calm.

"I said what I said," replied the old woman, looking my mother in the eyes defiantly.

For a moment, there was deathly silence. Then my mother threw herself at the old woman's throat with a bestial scream.

"You dare say that to me, *you*?" she screamed loud enough to burst your eardrum, as she and the old woman collapsed onto the ground. "Old whore! Village slut!"

"Murder!" the old woman cried. "Muuurde…"

Her voice faltered and became a rattle instead.

Unconsciously, I shut my eyes. I wanted to stop my ears as well, but I couldn't move, and even if I could have, I may not have had the strength. I was trembling all over.

When I opened my eyes, the old woman was lying unconscious on the ground and my mother was nowhere to be seen. People were running around weirdly, in terrified, wailing confusion. Three of the mothers were trying to revive the old woman all at the same time. They were rubbing her with vinegar, putting cold compresses on her heart and sticking something under her nose. One of the girls ran to the inn to fetch Mr Rozi, another wanted to fetch the gendarme, but someone stopped her. My mother, it seemed, had scarpered in the confusion.

The old woman came round at last. The poor, wretched peasant girls, who hated her just as much as my mother did, now made good use of the occasion to ingratiate themselves with her.

"Dear old Rozi!… Poor old Rozi!… Where's it hurt, Rozi?"

They called her all sorts of endearing little names, they fussed over her and played up to her. Five of them helped her off the ground, dusting her off and comforting her, showing her endless sympathy, hobbling off towards the house with the limping old woman as if they were bearing the consecrated host.

Everything turned silent. The unexpected silence was frightening after all the shouting. Once, when I was five, I watched an old day labourer die in the fields. That was the first time I saw a man wrestling with death, but even his eyes as they glazed over, his twitching limbs and endless death rattle didn't scare me as much as that indescribable moment when the dying man's mouth tautened and there was sudden quiet. It was this silence I remembered now, and I lay on that hay cart as if it were a coffin.

I'd had plenty of frights in my childhood, but I'd never been afraid like this before. So far, I'd only had to fear beatings and hunger, but now I had the additional fear that the old woman would chase me out of the house and I would have to go and live with my mother in the capital. I couldn't imagine anything worse, though it'd be hard to say why. Life could hardly have been worse for me in Budapest, but even if my mother had promised me an earthly paradise where I could spend my days skating on a lake of lard in a golden suit, I would still have begged to be left alone in hell on dry bread and water.

"I'd rather die!" I grumbled, though ever since I'd seen that old day labourer expire, I'd been petrified of death.

I didn't dare move. Like raindrops through a leaky roof, the minutes dripped down onto me, deathly slow.

The yard was empty. No one was looking for me.

Soon it grew dark around me. I heard the loud farewells of the visitors, the melancholy moos of the cows coming home, the countless creaks of the garden gate, the muffled clink of the knives and forks at supper and the distant noises of the boys going off to bed. Then I was alone with the silence.

Nothing now was moving, but I still heard noises—scratching, mysterious, terrifying noises, possibly from some other world; noises that could neither be identified nor described, because only little children can hear them at night, when the moon is full and the shadows dance, and terror seems to ride across the rooftops on its broomstick. At times like that, I would sit up, hold my breath, and listen. Then the spell would be immediately broken. It was just silence—ordinary, everyday silence.

The world was dead, dead, dead. A cold and malevolent full moon grimaced in the sky. The garden was silver and black like the tomb.

I vomited with fright. I got the chills and started saying the Lord's Prayer, teeth chattering. Then it was as if I, too, had died.

I fell asleep.

11

I HID FROM THE OLD WOMAN for days. At dawn, before the house
woke up, I sneaked out of the gate and only sneaked back home
at night when everyone was in bed. I collapsed in the straw half dead
with fatigue, but couldn't sleep. I was tortured by fear and hunger, and
the night was full of ghosts. Two scary green eyes stared in through
the moon-drenched window and a hanged man patrolled the yard in
a billowing sheet. If a bat swished past beneath the trees or the wind
rustled the bushes, I thought the old woman was coming to chase me
out into the night. I waited with chattering teeth, but the days went
by and she didn't come. She would have sold the Holy Spirit itself for
money and my mother owed her a lot. So she didn't throw me out. She
kept me as collateral instead.

I was almost faint with hunger when one morning the boys reported
that the night before, the old woman had had Ilona serve dinner because
she was "havin' another of her prayin' fits". So I went to the front
room and knelt down beside her, and this time I, too, said my prayers
as dispassionately as a magistrate on the third reading of an ordinance
on grazing rights. The old woman forgave me again, but as it turned
out afterwards, not purely in the name of Christian charity. Ilona told
me, most confidentially, that a postal order had arrived from my mother
and the old woman had replied by letter that "the boy" could stay as
long as she paid on time each month, but that my mother was never to
set foot in her house again.

My mother, it seems, accepted this ultimatum and didn't seem too
put out by it, because from then on for the next eight years, she made
no attempt whatever to see me.

I still don't really understand why. It's a fact that she wasn't crazy
about me, but I was still her son after all, her flesh and blood, bound
to her by the laws of nature. But then, can one judge things according

to the laws of nature in a society where the social norms are—to put it mildly—unnatural?

I can neither accuse nor defend. She was my mother, and she was the way she was. She hadn't brought herself into this world, nor had she brought this world, in which she was constrained to live, into being. Who knows what went on in the soul of this poor, vulnerable peasant maid during those eight eerily long years, years of inflation and deflation, of political hysteria, wretched heartache, back-breaking work and the inhuman degradations of unemployment? And besides, "What man knoweth the things of a man, save the spirit of man which is in him?"

Eight years is a terribly long time in the life of a child. The years, which flowed innocuously past, erased the image of my mother in me, to the point where eventually I hardly remembered her at all.

The old woman had clearly noticed how terrified I was that she would throw me out, because she never missed an opportunity to threaten doing it.

"You keep that up, gallows rat!" she'd say. "I kick you right out and you go live with whore mother in Budapest."

And so my mother came to play roughly the same role in my life as the bogeyman or the wicked witch in the lives of other children: she was a threat. I ended up with little else to tie me to her emotionally, and as the years passed and the children, as they grew, began to doubt the existence of the bogeyman and the wicked witch, so I eventually developed the vague sense that perhaps I didn't even really *have* a mother, that she had died long ago and they just hadn't told me so they could carry on scaring me with her.

I never admitted to anyone, not even myself, that I, too, could have done with a bit of that—for me—still slightly alien, florescent feeling that grown-ups called motherly love. I'd noticed that, for a little while now, I'd been developing strange symptoms. On Sundays, when the other children's mothers would come, I just couldn't bear to be around the house any more. I was beset by some sick, inchoate frustration. I would sidle off immediately after lunch and come back only in time for supper, when the visitors had already left.

"Stinks of mothers," I would grumble in revulsion and give the boys who'd had a visit from their mothers a cutting look. The boys swallowed my asides along with their dinner, because they knew there'd be a fight otherwise, and they knew full well it wasn't a good idea to try my patience at times like that.

No, I just couldn't stand that "mother stench". In summer I fled from it, but in the winter I could hardly spend too long outdoors. My wardrobe, to put it mildly, was somewhat rudimentary. I wore my summer clothes in winter too, my soles always had holes in them, and as for an overcoat, that was something I had only heard about. What could I do? Like a snappish dog chained to the doghouse, I threw myself into a corner of the house and watched the touching family scenes in furious silence. Now and then, one of the mothers would take pity on me and come and try to talk to me, but I only gave them curt, dismissive answers before turning on my heels and leaving them cold. I hated them. Sometimes even to the point of nausea; my stomach would turn queasily. That "mother stench" made me want to vomit.

I detested those long, dark, winter Sundays. I remember that sometimes, in the course of the afternoon, I would already have picked a victim from among the boys showered with gifts and affection, and in the evening, as soon as their mother had left, I would give them, for no reason whatever, a good hiding.

"Aw, there, there, don't cry, sweetheart," I'd say between smacks. "Mummy'll come and change your nappy for you, little one!"

There was a boy called István whom I particularly liked to beat up on these long winter evenings. This István, or Istvány, as we liked to call him, was a quiet, good-hearted lad, and I was angry not at him, but at his mother. His mother was the craziest of all the mothers who came to call, though we had all sorts there. Some of them were the effusive sort who simply melted when they saw their little offspring, but Istvány's mother outdid them all. I've not met a woman since who was as crazy about her son as that little peasant serving girl. Secretly, Istvány, too, was mad about his mother, but the poor thing didn't dare show it in front of me. When he thought I wasn't looking, he would cover her in kisses and endearments like a lover. They made up the most impossible little

74

endearing nicknames for each other. *Istványkám, Pistuka my love, my dove, my darling blossom*, the little serving girl would blather constantly, and the boy—when he thought I couldn't hear him—used to call his mother Motherdarlingdear. I was disgusted by them. I could have just about forgiven Istvány, for he was only a child, after all, and she did give him lots of presents, but as for his grown-up, darling mother, I thought she was simply crazy—and not in a euphemistic way, but in the original, clinical sense of the word.

That darling mother was, by the by, no bigger than a medium-sized fifteen-year-old girl. She must have been very young. Sometimes she would laugh and play with her little Istvánka in such a way you thought she could have done with a bit of mothering herself. I can no longer remember her face, but I know I thought her very pretty, which would occasionally make me uneasy for, like the other children, I too thought about things in black and white, and believed that only good people were pretty, strong and healthy, while bad people were ugly, twisted and repugnant, like the old woman.

Motherdarlingdear was very popular in our house. The old woman used to call her Piroshkamydear and would simply ooze honey when Piroshkamydear appeared on Sundays. This outpouring of the milk of human kindness was not so much meant for her as for her wallet, which could easily be charmed open. Piroshkamydear wore her heart in her purse, and the old woman knew just how to prise its lips apart.

"He so thin and sad this days, the boy," she'd say, shaking her head. "I didn't want to write, dear, but I am worrying, yes, worrying."

That was enough to set tears welling in Piroshkamydear's eyes and, following a long and involved discussion, send her reaching for her purse. And from then on, Istvány got eggs for breakfast.

Though Piroshkamydear wasn't exactly heir to the royal fortune—she was a housemaid in Kaposvár, in the household of a Jewish lawyer—her little Istvány still lived among us like some kind of exalted creature. He was treated differently to an infuriating extent. He would get the tastiest morsels, and he was the only one among us to get elevenses and tea. Most of the boys had rough, horsehair blankets in winter as well as summer, but Istvány had a cosy eiderdown and three pillows, while I had none. Piroshkamydear paid for all of that, apparently to the complete exhaustion of her meagre funds. She came to visit for years on end in the same ragged little muslin dress, and when there was mud, she would hop about on her heels like a crow, for her soles perpetually had holes in them. Once, I remember she lost five krajcárs at the station and couldn't get back because she'd only had the exact cost of her fare and not a whisper more.

But she never came empty-handed on Sundays. She would always bring her Istvánka a little something; if nothing else, then some worthless little bauble she'd clearly fished out of her master's wastebasket. For winter, she'd knit him warm little undercoats, shawls for his neck, stockings and wrist-warmers. Istvánka even had gloves and a good, warm winter hat.

It was only much later that I realized just what lengths that half-pint of a mother of his would go to for her little Istvánka. Once, for example, just before the Easter break, if I remember rightly, the Schoolmaster told the children to read a children's book, and come back and write a summary of the story from memory. So Istvány told his mother on Sunday that he needed a book for the break.

"Oh, dear, oh dear!" Piroshkamydear lamented, the tears welling up at once in her eyes. "I don't have money for it, my little dove."

"That's all right," Istvány reassured her. "It can wait till next Sunday."

"How can I, my darling blossom, when it's two weeks till the first of the month?"

"So you bring it in two weeks' time, then. I'll talk to the teacher."

Istvány tried to reassure her, because he was a nice boy, but his mother just couldn't let it go. Her mouth drooped, she started crying quietly.

"It's a dog's life bein' poor, my love."

But next Sunday she brought her Istvánka a book after all, a nice thick one, stamped in golden letters: *Rules of Civil Litigation.* The poor thing apparently just couldn't bear the thought of her beloved boy not having anything to read over the Easter break when his teacher had told him to, so she simply lifted the *Rules of Civil Litigation* from her master, thinking there was plenty enough to read in that, and if it was good enough for a fine, educated gentleman like her employer, the Jewish lawyer, then it would surely be good enough for her little Istvánka.

That was what she was like, that mother. She would have filched the stars out of heaven if her little boy had needed them.

Once, as I came into the front room, I saw her cradling her little Istvány like a suckling baby. I must have made a face, because Istvány got pretty scared. He wanted to slip out of his mother's arms, but she wouldn't let him.

"What's got into you, Pistuka my love?"

"Lemme go, Mother!" he flailed. "They'll make fun of me."

"Who'll make fun of you?"

Istvány didn't dare say.

"Is it Béla?" asked Piroshkamydear, and since Istvány didn't answer, she called me over. "Come over here a minute, Béla!"

I went over moodily.

"Here," she said, still clutching the child on her knee, "why d'you make fun of Istvánka?"

I didn't answer, but I also didn't lower my gaze as children usually do on such occasions. I just stood there silently, pressing my chin to my neck, and stubbornly looked the girl straight in the eyes, so she'd see that I wasn't afraid, not even of a mother.

"You don't have to glower like that," said Piroshkamydear, "don't *your* mother call you some nice name?"

"No," I replied rudely and left.

Just you wait, Pistuka, I raged to myself, I'll give you what for tonight!

I went out into the kitchen, swearing, and slumped down next to the stove. The kitchen, too, was full of visitors, and I couldn't escape the "mother stench". All the little maids on their day off were chatting away and they were all being so infuriatingly refined and sweet to each other, it was as if they'd left their normal way of speaking in the bottom of the drawer with their work clothes. I hated these uppity grown-ups, and I hated their children too; I hated everyone and everything on that hateful Sunday afternoon.

I took out my pocketknife and started whittling something. I'd been trying to make myself a whistle for days now, without success.

I desperately wanted a whistle. At first, it had seemed just another unattainable dream, like everything else that cost money, but then I heard that you could whittle yourself one out of willow, and the idea wouldn't let me rest.

I sat drilling and whittling in the corner for a long time. The whistle just wouldn't make a sound, but the knife, however, slipped and sliced my left thumb so that blood came pouring out of it. I squeezed my thumb, terrified, to stop the bleeding, but to no avail. I didn't know what to do. I had no handkerchief to tie it with, and I didn't dare say anything. Once, when I had had a similar accident, I'd run to the old woman in fright, but she just gave me a slap so hard by way of comfort that I'd never forgotten it.

"Why you not cut throat instead, eh?" she shouted. "Do us all favour, good-for-nothing."

But that had been back in the ancient past, when I was four. Since then, I had learnt all about rep. I just kept squeezing my thumb and kept my mouth shut. I was covered in blood—hands, feet, all over, and my stomach began to churn and my head go funny. I leant dizzily against the wall.

All of a sudden, I heard Piroshka's voice.

"What's the matter with you, Béla?"

"Nothing," I growled.

"Let me see!"

Piroshka leant down to me and as soon as she saw me covered in blood in the dim light of the corner, she let out a scream.

"Good grief, how'd you do that?"

They all gathered round me. Piroshka started running to and fro as if the house were on fire. She brought some water in the washing basin, managed to get hold of a clean cloth from somewhere, dragged me out of the corner, washed and bound my finger, and then put her arms around me and took me into the front room. She chased the mothers off the daybed, laid me down, sat down next to me and cradled me the way she used to do her Istványka.

"That better, Bélushka?" she cooed. "Go on, let's have a smile out of you, Bélushka!"

No one had ever called me *Bélushka*, but I would have told them just where to get off if they'd tried. Now I didn't say anything. I put up with the cradling and the *Bélushka*, and to my shame I found that rep or no rep, it felt simply wonderful. And that evening I didn't beat Istványka at all.

Next Sunday was the first of the month. On the first, Piroshka would always come loaded down with packages. This time, she was clutching four or five small packets; she could easily have made one larger package out of them, but Piroshka was a cunning mother and knew what children were like. She made a separate little packet of each present, sometimes wrapping them in as many as three or four bits of paper for effect, and tying each with fancy twine.

Istvány set about unwrapping the packages excitedly as I looked on jealously from the corner. I couldn't be angry with him that day, but this made it harder. A vague, heavy melancholy settled on my chest, and my throat tightened. I looked at Piroshka as she watched her little son, all excitement, radiant, and all at once I knew that she wasn't crazy at all, and that hurt so much that I almost went crazy myself with the pain. I wanted to leave so I wouldn't have to see them, but when I started heading for the door, Piroshka called after me:

"Come over here a minute, Bélushka!"

I went.

"Here," she said with a smile and handed me a little packet.

I stared at it, astounded. I didn't understand. Why would anyone give a stranger's bastard son a present?

"Go on, open it! It's yours."

My hand shook so badly that I could hardly untie the string. Inside the package there was a box, and in the box there was cotton wool, and inside that was a lead whistle. I'd been longing achingly for a whistle just like it, and yet now I couldn't be pleased. I just kept looking at it and my heart grew so heavy, it was as if it, too, were made of lead.

"Don't you like it, Bélushka?" Piroshka asked. "You was after a whistle, weren't you?"

"Yes," I stammered, "it's lovely, miss."

"No point giving that one things!" scowled the old woman, casting me a dirty look. "Say thanks you to Piroshka!"

My heart was so full of gratitude that I would have liked to take Piroshka's hand and kiss it all over, but after the old woman had told me off, I couldn't squeeze out a simple thank you. I just stood there with the longed-for whistle in my hand and stared helplessly at the floor. Then I turned without a word and ran out into the yard.

It was snowing and there was a deep winter's Sunday silence, and it was going on for evening. I stopped in the middle of the yard and blew my whistle. It had a hell of a sound, not like my willow whistle. It made a proud, sharp, high-pitched note, the snowy trees trembling at its call. Then there was silence once more, and I sat down on a tree trunk and began, bitterly, to cry.

From then on, I didn't run off on Sunday afternoons any more. It's muddy outside, I told myself that first Sunday, and there's a hole in my shoe. But then summer came and brought with it such a drought that they were praying for rain in church and even then I didn't feel much like running away. Rain or shine I sat at home and waited, like the other children, though I never got another little package. But it wasn't the packages I was waiting for—it was the woman who'd thought of them in the first place.

I never would have gone up to her, though. I just sat in an abandoned corner of the yard and waited for her to have her fill of Istványka, so she'd finally remember me, too.

"Why don't you come over here a bit, Bélushka?" she'd say, and my heart started beating faster. I wanted to run—to fly!—over to her, but instead, I made my face all sleepy and ambled over slowly, leisurely, as if it didn't mean a thing to me. I settled down next to her with a yawn, and sat there, silent. She, too, once asked me why I "looked so mean", but at least she went and did something about it, not like my poor mother. She gave me a good, hard smack on my behind and ran off like a thief caught red-handed.

"You're it!" she cried and I, grave and moody Béla, with my precious reputation, found myself running around, shrieking and playing catch.

Another Sunday, she brought cards and taught me to play rummy. We spent the whole afternoon playing cards, the three of us. Istvány and I were both so nervous, it was as if our very souls were in the balance; but neither of us was as excited as Piroshka, the grown-up.

She knew every children's game and took them all seriously. She was the one who taught me twenty questions and charades. She was the fastest runner, the best at ball games, and even played "it" with us with great conviction.

She also had a game she'd made up herself: playing dentist. Istvány was the dentist and I was the nurse. Piroshka would chase everyone except us out of the front room, lock the door, and climb, face down, under the couch. Istvány put on the old woman's pince-nez and await his clients, a big pair of pliers in hand. I would open the door and, with a highly officious air, call out into the waiting room for the next patient.

The patient would enter and we sat them down on the couch.

"Which one hurts?" Istvány asked severely.

"This one, here," the boy would complain with feigned seriousness, because we'd told them beforehand that there was nothing to be afraid of, the whole thing was just a game.

"Looks like it's got to come out!" the spectacled doctor announced. "Ain't scared, are you, sir?"

"'Course I ain't!" the boy would reply manfully, because he had no idea what lay in store for him.

For the moment Istvány had snapped his massive pliers together ominously and put the cold steel to the child's mouth, Piroshka reached out from under the bed and gave the patient a good hard pinch, at which point the patient—in his confusion—thought they'd actually drawn his tooth and would let out a terrific scream.

Occasionally, it even happened that Piroshka would, nothing better having come to mind, grab my hand and play "this little piggy" with my fingers, as if I were an infant. The most amazing thing was not only that I tolerated this, but that I secretly liked this humiliating game, because I was the only one Piroshka played it with—not even Istvány could join in. That's how far I'd stooped. What use dwelling on the details? Eventually, I even ended up playing itsy-bitsy spider with Piroshka in public.

I would sometimes see the boys looking on mockingly, as if to say—you too, big man? and I'd grow ashamed. If this carries on, I thought, my rep will be completely done for. But it didn't end up carrying on.

One Sunday at the end of June, Piroshka brought with her a man with a huge handlebar moustache, and led him over, very seriously, to Istvány.

"This man is your father, Istványka," she announced, her face crimson with excitement. "Be a good boy an' say hello, my little dove."

Istvány stared at the man with the moustache, not knowing what to do. At first, the poor boy couldn't so much as move for fright, but he did eventually manage to pull himself together and timidly shook the man's hand. The large, greying man stroked Istvány's head clumsily.

"Fine boy," he said, nodding, and Piroshka smiled.

Piroshka took the man's large red hand breezily and held it up in front of Istvány's face.

"What's this?" she asked mysteriously, pointing to the man's finger.

"A ring," Istvány sniffled.

"What kind of ring?"

"A weddin' ring."

"What about this?" she asked, pointing to her own finger.

"That's a weddin' ring, too."

"Yes it is!" Piroshka exclaimed loudly for everyone to hear. "Your father's gone and married me, you see!"

Istvány didn't say anything. At other times, you couldn't shut him up on Sundays, but now he was as silent in front of his tiny little mother and his mountain of a father as if he'd soiled himself.

The moustachioed man sat down on the little bench and drew the boy between his knees.

"An' that means you're comin' to live with us, Istvány. Ain't that nice?"

Istvány nodded yes, that was nice. Then he just stood there silently between his father's two strong knees and you couldn't tell at all whether he was happy or sad.

Even the old woman came out of the house at the big news and started blabbering emotionally. She launched into an emotional ode to Piroshka's heart of gold and Christian virtues, though even the stupidest among us knew that what she was really mourning was Piroshka's purse. She embraced Istvány and told him, terribly grave:

"Give thanks to Lord Jesus, my boy, who takes pity on little boys like you!"

"Amen," Piroshka sighed happily, wiping her teary eyes.

She forgot all about me that Sunday. I hung around her in vain, trying to attract her attention, but she was so consumed with her brand-new, personal joy that she didn't so much as notice me. So much for our famous friendship. My God. I was as hopelessly alone again as before. The pain in my heart was so strong, it was as if that big old man were sitting not on the bench at all, but on my chest.

It was getting dark. The visitors started packing up, Ilona brought out Istvány's things. And then, in the midst of all the farewells, Piroshka finally remembered me, too.

"Bélushka," she said emotionally, "we're taking Istványka."

Yes, I nodded silently, I knew. I couldn't look at her. I stared straight ahead, my lips pressed tight together to stop me crying.

"You be good now, Bélushka," she added. "An' the Lord'll help you, too."

Then she hugged me and kissed me. Oh God, there was so much I wanted to say to her in that hurried moment. I wanted to thank her for being so good to me, for binding my finger, and getting me that whistle, and playing itsy-bitsy spider with me on Sunday afternoons, and hiding under the couch at the "dentist's". And a lot more things besides, things I couldn't say, but my heart was so full of tears that I was afraid that if I moved, all that salty water would come sloshing out of me.

"Th-thank you!" is all I could say to her.

"What for, Bélushka?" she asked, surprised.

"Th-the whistle, P-Piroshka," I stammered clumsily and ran off, because I could no longer contain my tears.

I hid, shamefaced, behind the hedge, but when I saw them going out of the gate, I sneaked after them. They didn't turn around, they didn't see me. It's not as if I wanted to talk to them—God knows why I followed them. I just watched them from afar as they walked down the high street, the three of them, the half-pint mother on the left, the massive father on the right, and the boy István in the middle, as they held his hands from either side.

That was the end of my little story with Piroshkamydear. I never saw them again, but there was a time they drove me once more to tears. One morning, the old postman with a limp brought us a postcard: *With best wishes, István K.*

That was all it said, but that was enough. I knew that Istvány's surname had been "Cs." before, and this was probably the first time he had written his new—his father's—name.

He was no longer illegitimate.

12

FOR THE SAKE OF THE HISTORICAL record, I won't disguise the fact that I had to get Gergely to read Istvány's postcard, because although I was by then nine years old, I couldn't read or write. When I was six and had marched proudly off with the other boys to go sign up for school, the old woman had grabbed me by the ear and dragged me back in off the street.

"What next, gallows rat?" she bawled angrily. "Your bitch mother not pay for two months again, nothing at all, and you want go to school? Aren't you ashame? Not enough my bread you eat, devil take your guts, you want go to school on my money too?"

I stood there in front of the frothing old woman as if she'd struck me a blow to the head. School was the biggest goal of my miserable childhood, and here I was being told I was a gallows rat for trying to go. The sobs were clutching at my throat, but my eyes stayed dry. I was a bastard child, I said nothing. What could I have said? That there was such a thing as compulsory education was totally unknown to me, but I did know that my mother was unemployed again, and I knew what that meant. I didn't yet know how to write, but I had learnt that poor children like me only got from life whatever they could grab from it by force, subterfuge or cunning. So I had to bow to a wisdom beyond my years and admit that despite everything, my attempt at grabbing on to some knowledge had failed—I had been caught red-handed.

Six months before I might have protested, but since my mother had thrown herself at the old woman's throat, I didn't dare utter a word. I was in constant fear of finding myself out on the street, and I was cowed like a dog beaten into the corner. The old woman must have thought I'd resigned myself to my fate, but oh no—I was made of harder stuff than that. I was merely thinking like a peasant. I could see that the enemy was stronger and I wasn't going to bang my head against a brick wall.

I dug in under the powerful cover of silence and waited. As to what for, I don't know. Perhaps a miracle.

I never talked to anyone about this. I told the boys, when they brought it up, that only sops went to school and I wasn't a sop. But secretly I was consumed with jealousy when they left the house laden down with books on an autumn morning, or when they would talk about school life at the dinner table in what was to my ears a mysterious and incomprehensible slang.

Meanwhile, I'd become a maid. Zsuzsa, my predecessor, had got married on the feast of the Nativity of Mary, and since then the old woman had had me take over her duties. I did them well, and cost her nothing, so why would she have stood for my idling around in school instead? I was an expert in every kind of domestic chore, from peeling potatoes to scrubbing floors, and knew so much about the animals, most adults would have been green with envy. I could ride a horse bareback and was such a steady driver that they let me out in the cart alone on shorter trips.

This was something I liked to do. When I was driving, there was no one to boss me about; I'd lean back regally on the box and as the one-eyed mare clattered dolefully along with the creaking dray, I lost myself in daydreams, in fantastical castles in mythical lands. Myriad incredible tales filled my head, and I was always the hero—the great, just, renowned Béla who punished the oppressors of the poor, gave bread to the starving, and generally made certain the last would be first and the first last. The one-eyed mare, meanwhile, was transformed into a haughty charger and the rickety cart a glorious carriage in which I rode into town as a triumphant general, to the roar of cheering crowds. Sometimes, I'd embroider a single tale for months on end, working away at its colourful peasant-weave. Soon I would get so lost in my story that I began to talk aloud to my imagined companions, or give fiery speeches damning my enemies.

Where had that old, sober Béla gone? I was lost in a mist, taking dream-tablets to fight reality. I'd got so used to this dangerous game that I even imagined myself as a prince from a fairy tale who only went around barefoot in rags to get to know all the many tricks his people played so that one day, later, he'd be able to dispense justice all the more wisely. I had great plans. I told myself that when I grew up, I would organize the poor into gangs, like the children's gangs that we had formed, and—like Sándor Rózsa—steal treasure from the rich and distribute it to the poor.

"I'll show you all who Béla is!" I declaimed with an ominous crack of the whip, which—in my imagination—stood in for my sword.

Yes, I think I really was waiting for a miracle. But there are no miracles, of course. The years plodded by like the old woman's cart, the first-years at school became second-years, the second-years third, and I became nothing at all. In vain did I imagine myself a fairy-tale prince; from time to time, I too—like the drunkard waking with a hangover—had to face the hopelessness of reality. I was nine and a half and couldn't so much as read and write. I'd have been a fourth-year by now, I thought to myself, and burst bitterly into tears. Dear God, what's to become of me?

I tried everything. When the boys were doing their homework, I would loiter around them like a dog to try and glean a little of their knowledge. I once lifted Péter's reading and writing book and studied it for days on the privy. But what use was the book and my determination when I couldn't distinguish an "A" from a "B"? Yes, I thought, if I could read, I could study all by myself. But like this… In these moments, I saw clearly that my fancy plans were nothing but childish daydreams. The fact was that I knew nothing, and gradually, I too would become like the one-eyed mare that just kept plodding along with the old woman's cart until it plodded its way into the grave.

Finally, in the autumn of 1922, my fate did pull itself together. One morning when I was weeding in the cornfield, the swineherd called over:

"An' when exactly are you in school, my boy?"

"Saint Never's Day's, at midnight!" I replied with my usual insolence.

"Ain't they fined you yet?"

"Fine me? Why would they *fine me*?"

"Not you, the old woman."

"Her? What would they fine her for?"

"For not sending you to school."

That got my attention.

"They fine you for that?"

"They do, they do. Children got to go to school."

"Even poor children?"

"Them too. Poor boys, rich boys, it's all the same in the eyes of the law."

I must say I'd never noticed that before.

"The same?" I asked, stunned. "Hand on heart, brother?"

The old man nodded.

"Look at you, how surprised you look!"

"I am!" I said, and my heart beat so hard it was as if it wanted to pound straight out of my chest. "Well, God bless, brother!"

With that I turned and was gone. I felt so lit up that anyone who'd seen me must have thought I was drunk. And I was. I was drunk on old János's words. I screamed for joy and ran, galloped through the fields, meadows and pastures as far as my legs would take me. Then I threw myself face down in the grass, panting, and lay perfectly still. There was a great, humming, autumn silence, the sun beat down and the air was full of gossamer. I stared at the sky and thought feverishly. I knew what I was going to do. I had come up with my great plan: I was going to go and talk to the Schoolmaster!

But I wasn't going to rush into anything head first. I spent three or four weeks preparing for the fateful meeting. I turned every eventuality over in my mind with a peasant's natural caution: what he might ask, what I should answer, and what I would do if… I made up long, impressive sentences that I repeated to myself till I'd learnt my part like the catechism.

I also had a lot of trouble deciding when to go. On a weekday, he might say he was busy and couldn't see me, while on Sunday, he might say it was his day off and I wasn't to bother him. You can always find an excuse to turn away a child of shame, but in the end I decided on a Sunday after all. But that wasn't so simple either. Sunday, all right, but when? I would be sure to find him at home early in the morning, but if I woke him from his sleep, he'd be bound to be upset and throw me out. I could have caught him after mass, too, outside church, but if he'd taken Communion, he wouldn't have eaten anything and God save us all from a powerful man with an empty stomach! They may very well have just received the body and the blood of Christ, but they've no compunction cussing and swearing at the poor. After lunch—now that was different. A gentleman was bound to have a square meal on Sunday. His belly full, all that fine food would make him sleepy and he'd be too lazy to stir up any trouble. But would he even be lunching at home? He was a bachelor, after all. He might have been invited out for lunch to a house with unmarried daughters, or the priest's, or the doctor's. No, I didn't fancy that, either. In the end, I decided to go and see him before church; that was the safest option.

I didn't sleep much the night before that Sunday. I kept waking from my dream, and was up at five. There was a dreary, ice-cold autumn rain, and it was still dark as midnight. Shivering, I retreated to the warmth of the barn, and repeated my high-blown speech over and over to myself. When it finally got light, I went out to the well and washed for a good half-hour in the pouring rain. I borrowed the scissors from Ilona and cut the nails on my hands and feet. Then I ceremoniously donned the clean shirt I'd secretly been keeping for the occasion for some two weeks now; usually, I only got a fresh shirt every three or four weeks.

The weather was lousy, a dreary October morning fit for suicide. The autumn rains had started some two weeks before and the roads were so soaked that you had the feeling you were clumping through raw, rising dough. I trudged barefoot in the rain, since I had no shoes, and by the time I reached the Schoolmaster's house, my legs, muddied to the knee, looked like a ham-fisted sculptor's clay travesty.

The Schoolmaster lived with his spinster sister, whom the boys called Scarecrow among themselves. It was she who answered the door when I rang.

"What do you want?" she asked in her strange, high-pitched nasal voice.

"In the name of Our Lord Jesus Christ!" I said, launching into my well-rehearsed litany, because I figured that Jesus, too, had been poor, and it was worth reminding the rich. "Begging your pardon, miss, I've come to speak with the Schoolmaster, it's very important."

I don't know why, but I was absolutely convinced that when addressing your social superiors, you had to start every sentence of any significance with "begging your pardon".

"The Schoolmaster is sleeping," she said curtly.

"Begging you pardon, I'll wait."

"There's no point," she said irritably and was already shutting the door. "The Schoolmaster does not receive on Sundays."

Well, I said to myself, that's off to a good start. But I wasn't going to leave just like that. I sat down on a stone in front of the fence, settling in for the long haul. He's bound to go to church, I thought, and since I couldn't go in, I'll catch him on his way out. Just to be on the safe side, I rehearsed my speech once more in my head, and since he still hadn't come out by the time I'd finished, I went over it again. As I was sitting there like that in the ungodly weather, the window suddenly opened behind me.

"What are you doing out there, boy?" Scarecrow called down.

I jumped up respectfully and stood to attention martially, the way I'd seen the young cadets do it.

"Begging you pardon, miss, I'm waiting."

"Didn't I tell you the Schoolmaster's not receiving today?"

"Yes, miss, you did."

"Then what are you waiting for?"

"The Schoolmaster, miss, begging you pardon."

"What a foolish young man you are." The old spinster shook her pointy bird-like face. "You'll catch your death in this rain."

"Perhaps, miss. But I'll keep waiting."

Scarecrow smiled. The devil take these fancy ladies and gentlemen, I thought to myself, you never knew what they were smiling at. What was so amusing about any of this?

"Is it really all that important, what you've got to say?" she asked, a little more friendly.

"Yes, miss, terribly."

"Come on in, then, but be quick about it!"

I clicked my heels together.

"Thank you very much, miss. Begging you pardon!"

I went to the door, but before I pushed down on the handle, I looked around to make sure no one could see, and crossed myself. I never usually did that, but this time I wasn't going to leave anything to chance.

Finally, I was standing before the "gentleman" himself, the Schoolmaster. He was sitting at the table in his shirtsleeves, no collar, laying, with great gusto, into a bit of bacon. He was a handsome man, almost the archetype of the provincial Hungarian man, the kind who'd never quite outgrown his peasant roots. He had a bony face, burnt dark brown by the sun, its skin cracked, the purplish blots of his tippling shining on his cheeks like delicate, well-tended flowers. He must have been about forty. He was a man extremely fond of his drink and easily swayed by the ladies; they used to tell all sorts of stories about him. But he was good with the children, as long as you didn't answer back too much, because he was quick to raise his hand, dispensing mighty cuffs. He had the torso of a wrestler and from what I could see of his great, thick, dark neck, I couldn't even begin to imagine how he could squeeze himself into a collar. There was something scarily oriental about this bear of a man, but his eyes as he looked me up and down and his big black moustache as he chewed his bacon were so friendly that I wasn't the least bit afraid of him.

"Well, what is it, my friend?" he asked politely and sent a little glass of *pálinka* after his bacon.

"Begging you pardon, sir," I began, my voice trembling slightly, "I've come to see you, sir, with something important to ask you."

"Well, go on, then, I'm listening."

With that, he bit the end off his cigar, lit it, and leant back comfortably in his battered grandfather chair.

"Well, begging you pardon, sir, what I've come to ask you is," I said, stiffening to attention, "to let me go to school, sir, please, sir."

The Schoolmaster was surprised.

"How old are you, boy?"

"Gone nine, sir."

"Well, by goodness, then why aren't you in school already?"

"Begging you pardon, I ain't allowed."

"Who's stopping you? Your pa?"

I felt myself blush. I hadn't been expecting that question. I stood there in awkward silence for a few moments, but then I found my footing again. I avoided the question:

"My muther's in service in Budapest, sir."

The Schoolmaster must have understood my meaning, because his next question was:

"Who're you with here?"

"Um… old Rozi."

"Hm. And why doesn't the old girl let you go to school?"

"'Cause she says, sir, that my muther don't pay on time, so I have to work off my board."

The Schoolmaster leant forward in his chair.

"What do you have to work off?"

"Well, what I eat, sir."

The Schoolmaster shook his head and cast a long, meaningful look at his sister, who was listening to the conversation propped against an old sideboard. I thought he'd looked at her, shaking his head, because he was angry with her for letting a beggar like me into the house. And now he's going to say what they always say at times like this, that nothing in life is for free, not even dying, oh no, my friend, someone has to pay the priest! But I'd prepared for that eventuality, too. I hadn't spent so long preparing for this meeting for nothing. I even had the sentence prepared, I just had to go ahead and say it. I did so quickly, before he'd even had a chance to reply.

"I may be poor, sir, but I ain't askin' you to teach me for free, sir."

"Well, I'll be…" smiled the Schoolmaster. "So you want to pay, do you, my boy?"

Well, well, I thought, he's all smiles when there's talk of money.

"Well, I ain't got money to pay you with, begging you pardon, sir, but I'm strong—here, sir, feel my arm—and I'll work off my schooling if you let me."

The Schoolmaster looked once more at his sister, smiling this time.

"What's that you'd do?"

"Work it off, if you let me, sir."

"What would you work off?"

"That bit of learning, sir."

Scarecrow burst into laughter at that. Oh, go drown yourself, I thought, because it made me incredibly angry that she was laughing at me. Of course, it was easy to take a poor boy's labour for nothing when their masters hardly paid full-grown adults anything at all. But I had a counter-argument to that, as well:

"If you won't let me work, sir, I'll get 'em to write me a letter to the Regent, sir, to Horthy himself, I've got it all in my head, sir, it's just a case of writing it out, and it's such a fine letter that it's bound to touch the Regent's heart, and he's bound to pay for my schooling, sir."

The Schoolmaster, too, burst into laughter. Oh, go drown yourself, too, I thought, but all I said, very humbly, was:

"Please, sir, I ain't expectin' him to give it to me for nothing, neither."

"Is that right?" the Schoolmaster guffawed. "And just how are you planning to pay the Regent, then?"

"Well," I explained, "by joining up later, or serving the country some other way, and then the Regent could take it out of my wages."

By now, both of them were in hysterics. Damn the pair of you! I said to myself, and something slipped out of my mouth in my anger that I hadn't rehearsed at all.

"Begging you pardon, sir, but surely no Christian can envy a poor boy like me a scrap of learning!"

But they just kept on laughing like a pair of lunatics. I burst into tears.

"Come here, my boy," said the Schoolmaster then and put me between his knees. "So you want to go to school, come what may, is that it?"

"Yes, sir!" I bleated between snivels. "Please, sir, have pity on a poor boy."

"All right, then, stop crying, will you!" he muttered kindly, patting my face. "Go tell the old woman to come see me tomorrow morning before school."

My heart skipped a beat.

"I can't tell her that, sir!"

"You can't?"

"No, sir, she'd flay the hide off me."

"Flay the hide off you?"

"Yes, sir!" I snivelled, the salty tears flowing into my mouth.

The Schoolmaster puffed at his cigar, which was drawing poorly, then made up his mind and stood up.

"Well, in that case, I'll go and see her," he said. "Wait here a minute, my boy."

With that, he went into the other room and put on his coat and hat, and a few minutes later, we were walking up the muddy high street together towards the outskirts of the village.

I walked along, sly and uncertain, beside the long-legged ox of a man. What sort of a man is he? I wondered. Why is he doing this? What's he up to? If he'd said, very well, you can work off your schooling, but you'd better work hard, like a dog, because in this life nothing comes for free, then I would have understood. But he asked for nothing. He was playing nice, as if he wasn't one of the upper classes at all, tramping all the way to the end of the village in the rain, in the mud, on account of a bastard child without so much as a proper shirt on his back. Why? I was afraid of this mysterious man. I decided that I'd best be on my guard.

Fortunately, the old woman hadn't gone to church because she'd been suffering from her rheumatism for days now and could hardly move her swollen joints.

"I want to talk to her in private," said the Schoolmaster when we reached the house. "Wait here in the yard."

I hid behind the hedge and waited. The rain had stopped and there were only the drops of water falling now and then from the branches of the bare trees, like weak-eyed tears from an old man's wilted lashes. There was a great, Sunday-morning silence in the yard. The house was sleeping like an enchanted castle in a fairy tale. It's possible that a hundred years had passed since the Schoolmaster went in, and it was possible I'd only see him again on Judgement Day. The minutes sped by, but time had stopped. I shivered.

All of a sudden, the house broke out in ear-splitting shouts. I listened with bated breath, but couldn't make out what the old woman was shrieking. All I could hear was the Schoolmaster swearing horribly.

Then the door sprang open and the giant of a man burst out into the yard, his head purple with rage.

"Now you listen here," he bawled at me. "If you're not in school at eight o'clock tomorrow morning, I'll tear you limb from limb. Understand?"

My God, did I? No kind word had ever meant as much to me as this threat. I clicked my muddy, bare heels together and shouted like a soldier: "Yes, sir!"

My eyes grew moist, like a young girl's freshly engaged to her secret love, and I really felt that happiness had come to claim me for her own. But then I got such a cuff from behind that it made my nose bleed. I knew the old woman's hand and didn't even turn around, running for the hills. I ran out into the field, springing about like a wild horse.

"I'm going to school!" I screamed. "I'm going to school!"

Yes, on that morning, I got engaged to happiness.

And how fine it was, charging along laden down with books on autumn mornings, debating the happenings in school at lunch in that mysterious slang that was no longer a mystery.

How fine it was to wake knowing that school awaited and to go to bed feeling that the day had not been wasted.

How fine it is when you're not mourning the passing of time! When you drive your days gently before you, as if hurrying to a wedding feast, and you wait with the tender impatience of the bride. In the autumn I said: if it were only winter now, I'd know my alphabet. In the winter, I said: if it were only spring, I'd know how to read and write! In the spring, I said: if it were only summer, I would have finished the first grade.

Perhaps no child has ever studied with greater, more passionate devotion. I pictured knowledge as a mythical horse that, if I could tame it, would fly me out of the abyss of my miserable existence into the magical land of fabled promises.

I even stopped spying on the girls undressing by the riverbank. My precocious agitation ceased, as if by magic. I cared only for school.

I was the best student, though I could hardly say I learnt easily. Mine was a stuffy, peasant brain, hard to open, but once I'd learnt something, it became so much a part of me, it was like a ring in the trunk of a tree.

I could only study at home on the sly. I had to work in the afternoons, because the old woman didn't let me off work even now, and in the evening, "children belonged in bed". Woe betide anyone she found awake after eight o'clock—and she particularly had it in for me. So I pretended to sleep until the house grew quiet and then I would sneak out, laden down with books and notebooks, to the outhouse. My little money I now spent not on bread but on candles, and sometimes I would study half the night in secret, like some lonely conspirator.

I remained suspicious of the Schoolmaster for a long time. I didn't understand why he was being good to me. Why would anybody be good to a little bastard? What could he be after? I wondered, suspecting something evil, and when I realized that he wasn't after anything at all, I was even more unsettled. I thought him slightly crazy, and at the same time, I was convinced that he was the wisest man in the world. I was mad about him, and yet I kept him at arm's length. I didn't understand why he did what he did, though, to be fair, neither did other people. People in the village either thought him a lunatic or a genius, and there are strange stories told about him there to this day.

He came to us from a tiny village in Zala county. His father was a landless peasant and he himself had never been out of the country, but he spoke four languages, took French and British journals, and taught us—in our godforsaken little village—in a way of which any model establishment in any capital in the world could justly have been proud. He ploughed, sowed and weeded our tiny, uncultivated minds with the same age-old patience and humble gravity with which his ancestors had ploughed and sowed other people's land. Even his poorest student was a match for the best in the neighbouring villages, but that was nowhere near enough for him.

"I want to educate you, you dunderheads, not just teach you things!" he used to say, and those were no hollow words. He knew every boy's joys and sorrows, their conditions at home, and if he smelt trouble with any of us, he would take that boy aside and quietly say:

"Come by my house this afternoon."

There, over coffee and a sweet loaf, he'd have a talk with us. Subtle as an examining judge and kindly as a confessor, he would tease out of us our insignificant secrets and, with a sure and gentle hand, he would right the disrupted balance of our tiny lives. But if he got angry, he forgot all about his educational principles and the old peasant came out in him. He'd beat us black and blue, cursing nineteen to the dozen. He always repented afterwards. Once, I remember, he smacked one of our classmates unjustly. We all knew that the boy was innocent, but none of us dared say a word. About six months later, when we'd forgotten all about the incident, the boy really did do something he shouldn't have, but the Schoolmaster didn't touch him. He asked him in front of the whole class:

"Do you know why I'm not going to smack you now?"

"No, sir, I don't," blubbered the boy.

"Because, my dear boy, the smack you deserve now you already got six months ago. So we're quits."

Once or twice a week, the Schoolmaster would organize "afternoon chats".

"Only come if you really want to," he would say then, but there weren't many of us who didn't want to go to his chats.

These "afternoon chats" had nothing to do with school; or at least, so we thought. We used to walk out to the edge of the village, humming and singing all the way, and then gather round to sit about the Schoolmaster and "chat". He always started with something funny. He told us such funny stories that the peasant boys would be simply bursting with bright, sparkling, youthful laughter. And then slowly, playfully, without our even noticing it, he turned to more serious things. He would ask what one or another of us thought about this or that topic, and he would listen to our opinions as if we'd been his peers. Everyone was free to say what he thought. He never cut anyone off, was interested in everyone's opinion and would tell us his own only once we'd said our piece. He liked to hear us argue. He was all for, and visibly enjoyed, our unsophisticated duels of opinion and made sure that everyone took part in the debate. He fired up and encouraged the more timid boys and would listen to even the most insipid truisms with grave seriousness.

He took us all seriously, and the result was that we could argue and not hold anything back. In school he was strict, but on these afternoons, he gave us free rein. We could be as loud as we wanted. He would wait patiently for the end of the debate and then give us his opinion calmly, in simple, clear sentences.

In this way, over time, he managed to instil in us his whole world view, which was just as strange and dualistic as he himself. He was of the most extreme nationalist bent, at the same time professing himself a disciple of György Dózsa—his beliefs were almost revolutionary. He despised the great capitalists and landowners, the Jewish bankers and media barons, the slippery Christian middle class, the political elites and the whole heel-clicking "you scratch my back, I'll scratch yours" system as a whole. I think he despised everyone who wasn't either a peasant or poor. The land belonged to those who worked it, power to those who owned it, and all the land from the Carpathians to the Adriatic belonged to Hungary: that was his philosophy. He managed to translate this into childspeak, and explained it with such wonderful simplicity that even the first-years understood it.

"Tell me, children," he'd ask, "have you ever thought about who owns the snow?"

Loud laughter.

"No one!" one boy shouted.

"God!" cried another.

"And if someone makes a snowman out of that snow, who owns the snowman?"

"Whoever made it."

"Hm," muttered the schoolmaster. "And if someone makes a wheat field out of unworked land, by ploughing it, and sowing it, and taking care of it, then who does that field belong to?"

"Whoever ploughed and sowed it."

"Really?" nodded the schoolmaster. "Say, Péter Balogh, your father ploughs and sows and harvests, doesn't he?"

"Yes, sir, he does."

"And how much land does he own?"

"None, sir."

"Really, now?" the Schoolmaster wondered, as if he hadn't known that all along. "Then there's something wrong there, isn't there, children?"

There was indeed, we realized, and listened in silence. The Schoolmaster pretended not to understand, either, looking quizzical and scratching his stubbly chin.

"What do you think, children?" he asked. "Is that right?"

"No!" we chorused, because even the dullest child knows that this isn't right.

"Well if it isn't, then shouldn't we change it?"

"Yes!" we said.

"But how?" wondered the Schoolmaster. "How is this going to change?"

About that, of course, we didn't have a clue. So the Schoolmaster raised his voice, and almost ceremonially said:

"The only way to change this, children, is for *you* to go out and change it when you grow up!"

These were the sort of things he taught us in the very heart of Horthy's Hungary, with its bellicose crowing of National Renewal and merciless gendarmes. The more genteel people in the village avoided him like the plague, but didn't dare pick a fight with him, because the nature of this ox of a man was such that if he got angry, he would have set about the Minister for Religious and Educational Affairs himself.

For the peasants, he was like the Trinity: they didn't understand him, but they worshipped him. They even nominated him for parliament once, and there are still legendary stories about that in the village. The Schoolmaster, they say, gave such a fiery speech in one of the neighbouring parishes that he ended up getting dragged off the hustings by the gendarmes. The governing party's candidate, a great nativist Hungarian—of Saxon origin—called him a Red rat, and in the end the gendarmes had to drag him off the hustings too, though in his case it was because the peasants were getting ready to lynch him. Despite that—because miracles like this did occur in our village—the governing party candidate ended up winning the election. They wanted to bring charges against the Schoolmaster, but in the end the gentlemen changed their minds because they were afraid that if he had nothing left to lose, he might open his mouth about their electoral miracle. That's how they tell it in the village: whether that's true or not, I don't know. The fact is, a few years later they stripped him of his job.

The day after the election, he told us:

"Not to worry, children. By the time you grow up, it'll be a different world in Hungary! True enough, I'll be a doddering old fool by then, and might even be tempted to stand for the governing party. If I do, you can all come and spit in my eye, so help me God!"

That was the Schoolmaster; at least, in part. On the other hand, when something came over him, he forgot all his morals and got so stinking drunk that sometimes he couldn't teach for three days straight. It happened that at eight in the morning, when we got to school, we could still hear the Gypsy music and revelling from his apartments. When that happened poor old Scarecrow tried to herd us into the classroom, eyes red from crying, and you could tell that she was ashamed even in front of six-year-old children. I heard her knock on her brother's door once.

"Sándor, dear," she begged, "it's morning, and the children are all waiting for you."

"There *is* no morning this morning, my dove! Horthy's cancelled it," the Schoolmaster called. "It's still night, a Royal Hungarian night! Send the children home to bed."

His poor, lanky old spinster sister burst into tears in front of me. But the Gypsy music had piped up again inside, and you could hear the Schoolmaster's wonderful, deep baritone. He was singing his favourite song, the one that goes:

> *I've got a purse, but no money in it,*
> *My throat's so parched and dried!*
> *I've got a horse, but no saddle for it,*
> *How I long to ride!*
> *A good horse needs no saddle,*
> *It still walks with pride.*
> *My sweetheart's married to another man,*
> *But still keeps me by her side.*

There was a story to go along with that song—as for how much of it is true, I'm not sure. They say in the village that the Schoolmaster, who detested the captains of industry and the landowners so thoroughly, was secretly in love with the wife of our Count, with his thirty-thousand acres. He watched her ride out each day, passing her as if there was nothing at all in it, but secretly staring after her like a besotted youth, because he didn't even know her to say hello. One day, it seems, he got fed up with this hopeless state of affairs and decided to act. He therefore proposed in the village Cultural Circle that they organize a "charity cultural benefit" in aid of the Regent's wife's anti-poverty drive, of which the Countess was to be the patron. The gentlemen liked the idea, and a delegation, led by the Schoolmaster, was despatched to the castle. The Countess agreed to be the patron and promised to attend. The Schoolmaster spent three whole months preparing for this fateful meeting. He went up to the county town and ordered himself evening clothes at the finest tailor's. There was no greater sacrifice he could have made, including laying down his life, since a village funeral was far cheaper than evening clothes in town, and a dead Schoolmaster doesn't need to worry about making the repayments.

But it seems that strokes of luck also come in pairs, like Siamese twins. This was at the same time that they nominated the Schoolmaster for parliament, and these two bits of luck simply couldn't live side by side. A few days before the benefit, when the costly evening clothes were already hanging in the Schoolmaster's closet, the Cultural Circle wrote him a terribly polite letter in which they asked him to resign from the organizing committee, because "the fact that" the Countess was the patron of the evening was not compatible with that other "fact that" he, the Schoolmaster, one of the evening's organizers, had attacked His Lordship the Count in his stump speech. The Schoolmaster resigned— what else could the poor man have done? But he nonetheless still donned his evening clothes that fateful night and went… to the inn.

It was winter, and it was snowing, but he took no notice. He had them set up a table and chair in front of the inn, and sat—bareheaded and in evening clothes—out in the street. After the first litre of wine, he had them send for musicians, too, to play for him in the snow.

This was a great occasion in the otherwise uneventful life of the village. There were people who jumped out of bed and ran to the high street half dressed so as not to miss this rare treat. No one dared approach him, because now even those who had thought him a genius were convinced that he was crazy. They just watched him from afar in darkened doorways, or sneaked along on the other side of the street like conspirators hurrying to some secret gathering. Everyone knew that the crazy Schoolmaster was getting ready for something, but as to what that was, no one had a clue.

The benefit ended at midnight and the ladies and gentlemen started filtering home along the high street. Even that didn't bother the Schoolmaster. He just sat there in his brand-new evening clothes, his patent leather shoes and white silk gloves, in the snowy street, calling the tunes one after the other.

When the Count's trap appeared, galloping along, he went and stood out in the middle of road and caught the galloping thoroughbreds. The horses stopped—snorting and rearing angrily, but they stopped. They stopped and stood absolutely still in the Schoolmaster's frenetic grip. Then he calmly approached the Countess and—though at that point he had about three litres of wine in him—with the utmost, impeccable politeness, asked her and her husband to do him the honour of joining him.

The Count, they say, was so flustered by this daredevil invitation, it was as if he'd been the one who was drunk, and not the Schoolmaster. He muttered something awkwardly about it being late, and him being tired, and so on, but in the end he accepted the invitation because he was afraid of the Schoolmaster and even more afraid of his wilful wife who, never once taking her eyes off the handsome man making his gallant gesture, said why not, one glass really couldn't hurt.

"Very well," nodded the Count. "But only one!"

"Only one!" promised the Schoolmaster, but he made sure that that glass found itself refilled and who knows how, but the little company found itself still drinking together at two in the morning, the musicians playing on.

By three the Count was so drunk that the Schoolmaster carried him in his arms to the innkeeper's bedroom. And then it was the two of them, alone.

The Gypsy violinist says that at this point, the Schoolmaster proposed that he and Her Ladyship have a little walk in the glorious snowfall, and Her Ladyship replied, why not, we'll never be this young again. The Schoolmaster swore by heaven and earth that that was so, but that nonetheless, we were going to be forever young, isn't that right, Your Ladyship? Her Ladyship agreed with the Schoolmaster once more, and they drank to that, as one ought, and then wandered off together into the night. More than one curious onlooker was still loitering by the inn and they, like bloodhounds, sneaked after the unsuspecting couple.

The next morning, the entire village knew that Her Ladyship the Countess had sneaked into the school with the Schoolmaster; not into his apartments, where Scarecrow was sleeping, but—and this was the principal source of amusement for the village—into the gymnasium. As to what kind of exercises they got up to in there, not even the most curious could tell, because though they tried to peek in through the window, the couple inside lit no lights. Suffice to say that from then on, whenever the Schoolmaster was drunk, he had them play:

> *A good horse needs no saddle,*
> *It still walks with pride.*
> *My sweetheart's married to another man,*
> *But still keeps me by her side.*

This midnight escapade apparently grew into a great and serious affair. Those in the know like to claim that the Schoolmaster even wanted to marry the Countess, who was, however, strangely unwilling to renounce her thirty thousand acres and nine-pointed crown to marry a provincial Schoolmaster. The Countess believed in the rational division of labour, so she kept the Count for her husband and assigned the Schoolmaster a different role in which, if the signs are to be believed, he gave full satisfaction; from then on Her Ladyship was often seen with the firebrand

Schoolmaster to whom, it seems, she was set on proving the open and giving nature of the nobility.

I was always gripped by a strange anxiety if, when we arrived at school in the morning, we could still hear Gypsy music from the Schoolmaster's apartments. I felt ashamed, and didn't know why. Till then, I had thought in simple, straightforward terms. X is good, Y bad. Every predicate had only one subject, every emotion only one marker. I loved or hated someone, respected or despised them. These feelings now became frighteningly confused, flowing and mixing into one another. I began to suspect, with a sense of unease, that good people can also be bad and bad people can also be good; and that man is neither perhaps all good or all bad, but is like the stream at the end of the village, which sometimes roars by frothily, and sometimes is so peaceful and clear that you could see all the way to the bottom. My God, I thought, these people have a thousand natures and a thousand faces, and how am I meant to know which is their real one when, it seems, taken separately, none of them are?

I was bothered by these thoughts for a long time, but I didn't dare discuss them with anyone. I could smell some strange, suspicious secret to which everyone was party but me, and I was ashamed of being such an ignorant peasant.

I didn't understand the Schoolmaster, but I understood myself even less. I was a level-headed peasant lad, outraged by the fact that his Schoolmaster was uproariously drunk at eight o'clock in the morning when he knew that his students could hear him in the yard, but despite that—and this was what bothered me most—I worshipped and adored him and was angry not at the Schoolmaster, but at his students.

I hated the sly little boys who didn't dare to so much as move a muscle when the Schoolmaster was sober but let loose the second they were unattended. They knew that the village was gossiping about the Schoolmaster they loved so well, and yet they still got up to the sort of antics on these mornings that had people crowding round the school. I wanted to grab them by the throat, or beg them to control themselves, but I just sat in the corner and said nothing because I was afraid they'd think me a brown-nose, thick as thieves with the upper classes.

I did lose my temper once. That morning, the gentlemen in the Schoolmaster's apartments were singing a dirty tune, and of course that was all the invitation the children needed. They roared along with the filthy chorus and thumbed their noses at the adults standing around the school railings shaking their heads disapprovingly.

Poor Scarecrow tried in vain to drive them into the classroom, but the wild horde of children didn't so much as glance at her.

"The shame of it!" someone commented outside the railings. "A fine little school this is! A fine schoolmaster, I'll say!"

Scarecrow, completely powerless, burst into tears. She leant against the wall and her slender shoulders were shaken by sobs.

At that moment, I was overcome with a frightening anger I'd never felt before. I jumped up and screamed so loud at the boys that I scared even myself.

"Inside, now!"

As if by miracle, a minute later the yard was empty. The boys fell over themselves scrambling into the school, and in the wink of an eye, everyone was sitting in their places in deathly silence. I stood before them and shuddered. What was that? What had come over them? What had come over *me*? *I didn't mean to shout, and yet I shouted.* I had the uncanny feeling that someone else had shouted using my throat and the children had obeyed him, not me. Or that they had run into the classroom only because they thought I'd seen the Schoolmaster, and now they were petrified he might come in at any moment.

I was flustered. I didn't know what to do next, and the children felt that in an instant. The spell was broken. People started fidgeting here and there, broke out in whispers. And since nothing bad had happened to them, a huge peasant lad in the last row stood up and, playing the big man, called out to me:

"Well, go on, then, what you going to do? What you standing there like a damn gendarme for?"

The boys started to giggle. I could feel my knees trembling. For a moment I was lost, but no longer. Then that frightening anger I'd never felt before took hold of me again, and the blood rushed to my head. I ran over to the boy and smacked him in the face so hard that he fell right over. I was no longer thinking—I probably didn't even know what I was doing—but I was nonetheless filled with a wonderful sense of certainty, that mysterious force and equanimity of the soul that guides sleepwalkers safely along rooftops at night. I climbed up on the pedestal and brought my fist down on the podium.

"Move, and I'll bash all your brains in!" I screamed. "Textbooks out! Recite your lessons. Alföldy, you first!"

And the miracle came once more: Alföldy stood up and obediently recited his lessons—and the others didn't dare make so much as a peep.

No, I didn't understand. Till then, I had measured power so simply: that boy is stronger than me, and I'm stronger than that other. But the class I was now facing off against was a hundred times stronger than me, and yet, God knows why, I was more powerful than all of them. For the first time in my life, I felt, vaguely, obtusely, and with awe, that mysterious forces are at play in this world, forces impossible to define or quantify.

These were wonderful moments. I was gripped by a sort of festive, almost sacred feeling. My God, how mysterious your world is, I thought, trembling.

From then on, whenever the Schoolmaster was drunk, Scarecrow would call me over and quietly say:

"Béla, keep order!"

Keep order I did, and how! For poachers make the best gamekeepers. If a boy got out of line, I gave him a lesson he wouldn't forget till his final day in school. No one dared tell on me to the Schoolmaster, because they were afraid that he, too, would give them what for. So, slowly but surely, they got accustomed to the new order of things, and there were no more crowds of onlookers outside the school gates.

The summer was well advanced—and it was almost the feast of St Peter and St Paul—when we got our annual reports. In other years, I had always steered clear of the house on St Peter and St Paul to avoid the gloating children. The first-years were fit to burst that they were now officially second-years, the second-years that they were third-years, and my heart would break when I reflected that I, I was nothing. But this year, all that was different. This year had not passed in vain. I had learnt to read and write and knew that my report would be all "outstandings".

But then there was a snag on the last day of school. The Schoolmaster told us to put on our Sunday best for St Peter and St Paul, and that was the first problem in school I was unable to solve. For how could I have put on my Sunday best for St Peter and St Paul when I'd never had Sunday clothes at all?

I sneaked into the gymnasium, decorated for the festive occasion, like a beggar afraid of getting barked at by the dogs. Primped-up ladies and gentlemen sat all around the speaker's dais, and even the children had made an effort. When anyone glanced at me, I immediately blushed, because I thought they were looking at my ragged clothes. When the reed organ piped up for the prayers, I almost burst into tears. What use all those *outstanding*s, I thought, when the notary's son still has the finest clothes, though it was only out of pity that the Schoolmaster didn't fail him.

The reed organ fell silent, and the speakers piped up instead. Speech followed sermon, sermon followed speech. The words spattered like autumn rain. I wasn't listening. I wanted to cry.

There was a parcel lying on the table on the dais tied up with a tricolour ribbon in the colours of the national flag. This was the traditional prize book. In our bitterly poor school, they gave only one book as a prize each year, and even that was bought by the teacher out of his meagre salary. He always gave it to the student in the final year who had been the best student over his six years. The boys had been arguing excitedly for weeks now over who would win this prize, and now I was trying to cheer myself up with the thought that in five years' time, it would surely be mine. It was a nice thought as it went, but cold comfort, because when you're ten, five years seems like fifty, and for a bastard child, each year counts double.

The shower of words finally came to an end, and the Schoolmaster picked up the parcel with the red-white-and-green ribbon.

"As long as I've been a master at this school," he said with unaccustomed formality, "a sixth-year has been awarded our annual prize. This year, I'm going to depart from this custom and give it to a first-year instead, because never, in all my years as a teacher, have I had such an outstanding student. They work this poor peasant boy like a serf at home, and he still outshines his fellows in school. With this gesture, I want to prove both to him and to the rest of you as well, children, that nothing is impossible: with learning and tireless effort, the last can indeed be first!"

He held the prize aloft.

"For Béla R.," he enunciated clearly in the ceremonial hush, "the pride of our school!"

I thought my heart was going to stop. I could feel everyone looking at me, but I couldn't move. I just sat there, eyes lowered, petrified, like a catatonic. In the end, my neighbour elbowed me in the ribs. I jumped up, but my legs were trembling so hard I could barely mount the dais.

"Never forget your worth, my boy," said the Schoolmaster as he presented me with the book, and I believe he, too, was a little moved.

"Th-thank you kindly, s-sir!" I mumbled, as the tears flowed into my mouth.

The Schoolmaster put his arm around my shoulders and led me over to the guests. They all smiled at me, they all shook hands with me, even the bullish old notary.

I was the man of the moment.

Who'd have thought it?

You can stare at my patched trousers all you like now! I thought, and would have liked to jump for joy, like a kid.

There is a point at which joy comes to resemble suffering. The human soul, it seems, can only be heated to a certain point, and beyond that, it doesn't matter whether it's the fires of heaven or the fires of hell that are heating it: if it's too much, it dies. No wonder Hungarians say "I almost died of joy."

And that was what happened to me. I went around in a fever. I had never in my life left a crumb of my meagre rations, but today I hardly touched my food. The old woman, who must have known what happened, looked at me mockingly, and when a child told her the big news "officially", her only derisive response was:

"Better he give him pair of trousers so arse don't stick out."

But today I couldn't be angry, even at her. Mad as a hatter, I thought indulgently, and smiled. Today, there was only goodness and love in my heart, as if this fiery joy had seared all else out of it. I was drunk with joy, and like a drunk, I wanted to embrace everybody.

After lunch, I got away from the children and walked out to the edge of the village with the prize under my arm. It was a feast day out there, too. There was no one on the land; only occasionally did I see a young lad and his sweetheart, pressed up close, disappearing into the thickets of the little forest, as if seeking shelter from some invisible foe. Nothing moved. The ripe fields basked sleepily in the calm, and the landscape seemed to have drawn its jaunty hat over its eyes and nodded off under its elegant sheepskin jacket. There was silence; that mature, buzzing, lukewarm early-summer silence that almost hung in the air like gossamer.

I settled down in the grass and began to read. I lay in my usual place, where I had previously cried so much alone. The grass was flattened here and trampled, as if under the weight of those past heavy hours, and perhaps my former sorrows were still crawling around here somewhere in the form of invisible worms. My God, how the world had changed for me, how the sun had come out over me! I wasn't much of a one for religion, but now I felt that God was looking down from his heaven and smiling at me.

I read aloud, syllable by syllable, like we used to in school. The book was *Fairy Tales* by Elek Benedek. It was a wonderful book, as wonderful as only one's first book of fairy tales can be. Later, I read it so often I knew it all by heart, and even today, I could recite more than one passage verbatim. I remember that my favourite story began:

"Once upon a time, in a land far, far away, a crooked mile beyond the great blue sea, where all the fleas were shod with brass to stop them tripping over every little wrinkle, there lived a young serving boy. When he'd served three years, he went to his old father and said:

'I won't serve no more, Father, I've had enough of eating others' bread. I have a hundred silver *forints* of my own, and I'm going to put them to some use…'"

Yes, I thought, I too would have a hundred forints one day, and I, too, would put them to some use—and maybe I, too, would find a beautiful fairy like Tündér Ilona waiting for me on my travels.

My God, how wonderful life is!

My God, how much I still have before me!

My God, you just have to want it, and the last shall be first and even a lowly servant can win Tündér Ilona's hand!

My God, my God, my God!

I could feel that if I didn't do something, I would go mad with joy on the spot. And then, as if I'd found the key to all the mysteries, I knelt down in the great empty field and called out to the deserted horizon:

"Praise be to the Lord, Jesus Christ, for ever and ever, Amen."

13

FROM THEN ON, I WON THE SCHOOL PRIZE every year on St Peter and St Paul. I was past fourteen and had five finely bound prize books, but not so much as a pair of shoes. In other years, I had always got some sort of footwear, even if it was on its last legs, but this year, Advent had come and I was still going around barefoot. My mother had been laid up in the Rókus hospital since the autumn, and our village, which had been desperately poor to begin with, had grown so impoverished in the last few years that even the farmers were glad if they had something to put on their feet. Back then, in those parts, there was no pair of boots ragged enough to convince their owner to part with them.

It was a dark winter, though we were knee-deep in snow. It snowed so hard that we were cut off from the world for months. For a while, even the train stopped coming, but that didn't cause much upset in the village, for who had the money to travel? The heady days of hyperinflation were behind us. Even the better-off farmers were struggling. Where were all the banknotes breeding zeroes like rabbits, all the furniture, pianos and gramophones bought up so hastily and haphazardly from the gentry? Farmers used to talk of those times like some legendary Canaan from a hundred years before.

"Oh, them good old days of infation!" they'd say, sighing wistfully.

The poor peasants had no such golden age to long for. For them, "infation" had meant nothing but trouble, too, as had the war and all those other upper-class escapades. The only difference was that during "infation" they could still wear the uniforms in which they'd come back from the war, but later they, too, became ragged and worn, like so much else in the last twenty years. The war had passed, and so had the monarchy, then the Republic, the Soviet, and the White Terror.

"Ah," shrugged the poor peasants. "They all go the way of the rest."

They had already, from the beginning, resigned themselves to it all, and already, from the beginning, believed in none of it. The only time anyone ever bothered with them was during the elections, anyway, and even then it was mostly the gendarmes. Though it wasn't as if they had much to do round our way. The poor never expressed an opinion, partly because it was wiser to speak no evil, and partly because: why bother? There were, it's true, secret religious peasant sects, but most of their adherents were people who had already been driven slightly mad by history. Most people didn't even bother to go to church, and if they still thought about anything at all, it was mostly about how to fill their stomachs. The next village was now in a foreign country, and in-laws, friends, sons and daughters who spoke not a blighted word of that country's language became foreigners from one day to the next. It grew so you couldn't so much as spit without a visa, because likely as not it would land over some frontier. But even this was discussed with nothing but shrugs, because along with everything else, even the irredentism had passed. Everything had passed in our blessed little village: the roads and people's souls were covered with snow, but come the spring, that, too, would pass.

There was peace and quiet, that much is true. An eternal-rest sort of peace and quiet. The peasants, like hibernating bears, withdrew into their little shelters with the family, and whoever didn't have to didn't set foot outside at all. What for? All that walking would only make you hungry. The stove and the oven stood empty in most houses, and there wasn't much to stop the children asking: what's that for, Muther? And that despite the fact that not a quarter of an hour's walk away the Count had such extensive forests that even a half of them would have been enough to keep the village chimneys smoking for a century. But those belonged to the Count, whose ancestors had got them for handing over the country to the Habsburgs, while the peasants' forefathers had gone off, in their simple-minded way, to die for it instead—without demanding anything in return.

In any case, when the first winds of autumn came, the peasants would stuff up the windows with newspaper and rags and not open them again till Easter. Because however amazing gas and electricity are these days as a source of heat, there is another, even more amazing: the emissions of humans. There was more than one house where they slept six or eight to a room, and in those houses they made so much of this wonderful heating source that they could have sold the excess to the Ministry of Public Health. The peasants couldn't even afford matches. If a chimney in one of the houses began to smoke, all the neighbours would immediately head over and borrow an ember or two. As for lighting lamps, that simply went out fashion. By five or six in the afternoon, the village was as dark and deserted as an enormous cemetery. The peasants slept through the winter like the seeds under the snow, but while the seeds would bring forth shoots in spring, the only people to benefit from the peasants' winter slumbers were the angel-makers.

Lady Luck forsook even the old woman. Now one, now another, of the boys' mothers lost their jobs and the little pink slips delivering their monthly postal orders started growing less and less regular. Her lands, too, barely brought in anything at all. The price of everything fell; only taxes rose. The old woman reduced our portions, though her pantry had never been more full than in that year, because she'd hardly found buyers in the autumn. But:

"This not those times!" she said, and in the end the tastiest morsels ended up going to the pigs, because everything went mouldy over that long winter in the damp pantry.

But the children didn't complain much when their mothers came to visit them on Sunday. They knew there was no point. They kept quiet, and whenever they could, filched something from the pantry.

All that was old news for me. I had already been through this school of misery in the "good old days", so now I just smiled like an old veteran as the children cursed the miserly old woman's unchaste ancestors.

I was not the only boy that year to be without shoes. But the others simply didn't go to school in winter. The peasants said that if the Minister didn't like it, then he should send their sons a pair of shoes, and that was that. There were days when there were only six or eight of us knocking around the schoolroom.

The old woman forbade me, too, from going to school, but I still went, no matter how cold it was. That I didn't die of pneumonia despite that was thanks to two things: my ironclad constitution and the Hungarian press. Not that the press took too much of an interest in the fate of poor children like me—I would never have expected that of the Hungarian press, for I had learnt in my first year in school that it was the upper classes that wrote the papers, and the upper classes were one thing, and peasants another; but every morning, I would wrap my feet in newspaper, and newspaper—no matter what's printed on it—is an excellent insulator. Under my soles, I put two pieces of wood whittled for this purpose and then tied the whole bundle with string—and that's how I set off for school in the metre-high snow.

The days went by as if they weren't going by at all. You got the feeling that time had stopped; that it had got stuck in the snow, along with the local train.

It was only around Christmas time that the apparently defunct village stirred a bit. There was a frail, timid expectation in the air, but maybe that was something only we children felt. In the mornings, we would watch excitedly for the postman, to see if he'd brought any presents from our mothers. When he did bring them, we never knew who they were for because he used to deliver the parcels to the old woman, who would then hand them over to their rightful owners. But we nonetheless gathered round the limping, grumpy postman each morning like a flock of crows, and tried to guess, at the top of our lungs, who the parcels were for and what was in them. Our excitement grew day by day. Once, I remember, a first-year shouted so loudly in his sleep that we all woke up.

"Don't touch my packet!" he screamed. "My ma sent me that!"

I was not nearly so convinced that my own "ma" would send me anything for Christmas. My "ma" was not beholden to such traditions. It had happened in the past, it's true, but that was a long time ago, and I thought of Christmas presents in the same way that peasants thought of snow in May: it might, they used to say, be possible, but it's hardly likely. I hadn't seen her in eight years, and her image had faded within me, like that of someone long departed. That was, in fact, the way I thought of her—as someone long dead. I expected nothing of her.

But the human soul works in mysterious ways. It doubts, like Thomas, while it can, but when push comes to shove, it starts believing even in the unbelievable, because—it seems—you have to believe in *something*. That must have been why, two or three weeks before Christmas, I wrote my mother a letter and asked her to send me a pair of shoes. It took me a while to commit to the undertaking, but I was in quite a bad way, and could see no other solution. Winter had come early, it was freezing by early October, and I was still walking to school barefoot and without long trousers, in the fraying clothes I had outgrown long before, through which the wind passed like water through a sieve. My poor diet didn't help. I felt cold even in our room, and my head was so blurry that I could hardly learn my lessons. I knew that if I didn't get a pair of shoes for Christmas I, too, would give up the fight and stay off school. I would hang around at home like the other barefoot peasant boys, growing dull in the bestial stench of our room.

So I tore two sheets out of my language notebook, designated one as letter paper, and folded the other into an envelope, sticking it together with flour paste. I got the flour and the stamp from Ilona, the dull-eyed maid whom I had—wisely and with foresight—"got into my debt". For I had noticed while studying in the outhouse at night that after the house had grown quiet, a male spectre appeared, climbing over the fence and sneaking into dumb little Ilona's room; it seemed she was not so dumb after all. When I told her I knew about all this, she winked at me with her watery blue eyes and told me meaningfully that if I could keep my mouth shut, I wouldn't regret it. I kept my mouth firmly shut. Meanwhile, the affair had passed, the lad hadn't been since the autumn, but the debt—as debts do—remained, and it cost dull-eyed little Ilona a twenty-fillér stamp.

Having thus seen to the technical aspects of the undertaking, I set about writing the letter. First, I made a draft, dividing my message into three parts, as we did in school: introduction, argument and conclusion, going on to expound my desperate situation in the longest and most complex sentences possible (any dunce could write short sentences). I explained, elaborately and with much beating around the bush, that I was not a shameless child wanting to force his mother into unnecessary expenditures, and that all I was asking was for her please to find me a pair of shoes, any shoes, in which I could keep going to school. It didn't matter if they were ragged, or too big, the main thing was that they be shoes. To lend my request weight, I even fibbed a little. I wrote that I had caught a devil of a cold in the bitter winter conditions and the doctor had forbidden me to go to school without shoes. As for what a pity it would be for me to neglect my studies, my *outstanding* half-term report was the proof. I went on to "take the liberty of attaching it here to support my request". By the time I'd finished, the whole thing was more like a formal request for a hardship grant than a young man's letter to his mother.

But I was terribly pleased with it. I thought it impossible for my mother to refuse me once she'd read it. Even if she was sick, even if she had no money, I was sure she could get her hands on some old pair of shoes in that great big city when she found out that her son was going around barefoot in winter. I had heard that she had lately become a washerwoman, and therefore assumed that she had access to the upper classes; and the upper classes did not wear ragged shoes, but gave them away, and why shouldn't they give them to their washerwoman? To cut a long story short, all seemed to augur well for the shoes. The closer we got to Christmas Eve, the more sure I became of getting them. So I too started sniffing round the postman with the other children and looking forward to Christmas like never before.

On the morning of 24th December, I did not wrap my feet in newspaper. I think I wanted to suffer in the bitter cold, even more brutally than usual, so that I could revel more fully in the wonder of my warm shoes that evening. After lunch, when Rozi and Mr Rozi locked themselves in the front room to decorate the Christmas tree, I ran out barefoot to the snow-covered edge of the village like a lunatic.

It was frightfully cold, so cold that the snow couldn't fall, with merely the odd flake or two floating in the air, so that you couldn't tell if it was falling from the sky or if the wind had just blown it off the branches. The cold marred my skin like acid. But I just thought of the sparkling Christmas tree, and I could see "my shoes" so clearly, so definitely, among the presents that I could almost touch them. My feet won't be cold any more this evening, I thought with emotion and knelt down, as I never otherwise did, before the snowy tin cross.

"Praise be to the Lord Jesus Christ," I said aloud, "who brings poor boys shoes at Christmas."

I went home singing. It was as if there had been a miracle in the windows of the houses, and the lights had all gone on tonight and the chimneys started smoking, woken from the dead.

"Silent night," I sang, and my eyes grew wet with joy.

When I got home, the other children were all crowding round the door of the front room. Whoever had Sunday clothes had put them on, and they had all made an effort to scrub up. The excitement, as they say, was at fever pitch. We could hear mysterious noises from the front room, the shuffling of feet, unintelligible speech, the shifting of a piece of furniture, something falling to the floor. Then the bell rang inside and the door opened.

My mouth was bitter with excitement. In the middle of the room, the candles on the Christmas tree guttered and spat in the swaying, pine-scented obscurity, illuminating suggestively the presents in their festive arrangement. They'd even lit the stove in honour of the festival. The high-legged miniature iron stove glowed red-hot in the darkened corner. It was stiflingly hot. The old couple were standing ceremoniously beside the tree. Mr Rozi wasn't wearing a tie, but he *had* donned a terribly high, and—it seemed—very tight, stiff collar, which made his face so red and puffy it looked like he had toothache. The old woman was top to toe in black like the dolled-up horse on a funeral cart. Her dress was of some heavy, stiff silk that rustled with each step like an autumnal shrub when the wind blows its desiccated leaves. You could see that she was in her element. She stood before us gracefully like a woman bishop, and, full of pompous self-importance, her eyes turned to heaven, struck up a sentimental carol. We all sang along, but secretly we were all constantly stealing glances at the presents, glittering mysteriously in the light of the flickering candles.

I saw immediately that there were two pairs of shoes among them. One was brand new and just the right size for me; I knew at once they weren't mine. But the others were down-at-heel, aged, massive great things; those are the ones my mother sent, I thought, and my heart skipped a beat. What a pair of shoes! I rejoiced. Their soles were as thick as my finger. Aren't they far better than those teeny-tiny children's shoes? As far as I was concerned, from now on it could freeze till Easter. I was perfectly happy. I looked upon those sad, wrinkled, shoes like a sentimental lover gazing upon his sweetheart.

We finished singing at last. The old woman went over to the table in her rustling silk dress and called the children to her one by one. Today, she called them not by their Christian, but their family names, evidently to underline the festive and significant nature of the occasion. I, since my name began with R, was last in the household alphabet, but the old woman would have called me last even if my name had begun with an A.

The new shoes really did go to another boy, who—amid triumphant whooping—sat down right there on the floor and tried them on. There was an appalling cacophony. The boys, as if drunk with joy, went off jumping and screaming with their presents. Just Demeter to go, I thought, since he was the last but one, and started heading for the table. But then something took my breath away. The old woman gave the shoes to Demeter. *My shoes!* I thought I'd pass out.

"You not get nothing," said the old woman, her tone a mix of mockery and gratification.

I couldn't move. I stood there, empty-handed, in front of the bare table, alone. Maybe I was waiting for a miracle, or for it to turn out that there had been some mistake and the shoes weren't really for Demeter, or maybe I was just waiting for someone to say a kind word, that it would all be all right somehow. I don't know. What is for certain is that nothing like that happened, and there was no miracle. The others didn't even notice when I sneaked out.

I closed the door quietly behind me and stood in the empty room. I was overcome with a strange weariness, the kind you feel in a dream when you're running desperately towards some distant goal, only to get there and realize you can't remember what you wanted to do there.

The carols started once more in the front room: "Silent night!…"

"Holy night?" I muttered. "You mother's holy you-know-what!"

And I saw myself kneeling before the tin cross and tearfully thanking the Lord for the pair of shoes… Demeter had got.

"Baby Jesus, it seems, also plays favourites," I grumbled. "Even though his precious little Demeter failed religion."

A perverse, nasty laugh was brewing in my throat. Grumbling, I felt my way out into the yard through the darkened kitchen. It was a windy, moonless night with a heavy frost. I ran barefoot through the snow and into our room, so cold and foetid it could have been a refrigerated latrine. They hadn't even cut a chimney in this room, lest someone—in a momentary fit of madness—took it into their heads to heat it. I threw myself down into the straw fully dressed and climbed shivering under the rough threadbare blanket that had absorbed the mouldy moistness of the floor so deeply, I shuddered whenever it touched me. My head burned, my teeth chattered. In the great silence, you could make out clearly the sound of their solemn singing: "O come, O come, Emmanuel".

"Drop dead!" I said aloud and started swearing once again. I cursed my mother, from whom I only learnt years later that she hadn't received my letter, because they'd discharged her from the hospital just before Christmas. I cursed the old woman, I cursed the boys, I cursed the entire world, and I cursed the angels out of heaven. And then, like pus from an angry wound, the tears and sobs burst out of me.

The next day, I woke as if I'd drunk too much the night before. The other children were still asleep. Beside each of them lay their much-anticipated packages from home. Some had more, some less, but everyone had got something. Sándor, the first-year who'd dreamt someone was going to steal his present, was sleeping in a brand-new woollen hat, and "my shoes" protruded from under Demeter's horsehair blanket. I started crying.

The children breathed steadily in the half-light. Sniffling, I wrapped my feet in newspaper, tied the bits of wood under them and shuffled out. The weather had grown a little milder, and it was snowing heavily. I was greeted by a white, scary silence. The house was still sleeping, and only Ilona was up, boiling the milk, in her underskirts. We had breakfast together at the kitchen table.

"I put your supper aside for you," she whispered, winking, as was her wont, with her watery blue eyes. "You ain't going to leave it for that old witch, are you?"

I didn't answer. I was too tired even to open my mouth. I had cursed and cried myself out, and there was nothing left in me save a great, purposeless emptiness.

"What's the matter?" she asked.

"Nothing," I answered testily, wrapping up my supper in newspaper.

I knew the other children would soon be up, and I instinctively fled their Christmas cheer. I put my wrapped-up supper in my pocket and headed off, purposeless, into the snow.

The village, slowly and sleepily, was starting to wake. The street was deserted and I was walking through virgin snow. I didn't think of anything, I didn't feel anything. I was as empty as a clock that's had its mechanism removed. Why am I walking, why am I breathing, why is my heart beating at all? I walked like a sleepwalker, not knowing where to or why. The priest peeked out of the window of the rectory, but I didn't say hello. I turned my head moodily away.

There was a group of ragged people standing in front of the village hall. They were so ragged that if a stranger had seen them, they would have been bound to think that all the habitual vagrants in the county had fixed a rendezvous. But not a single one of them was a beggar at all. They were massive, strong peasant men, almost all of them employed, working from sunup to sundown on the Count's estates throughout the summer. The fact that many of them were nonetheless standing around barefoot outside the village hall on Christmas Day was attributable to that well-known and generally accepted tenet of the Hungarian economy, whereby a pair of halfway decent boots cost twenty-five pengős, while the Count paid less than a pengő a day for fourteen hours' work.

I spotted old János in the group, the swineherd who'd told me five years before that there was such a thing as compulsory schooling. Him I said hello to right away, nice and loudly.

"Well, my boy," the old man asked, patting me affectionately on the shoulder. "What did the Baby Jesus bring you for Christmas? I can see it weren't a pair of shoes!"

"Brought me this here load of thin air," I replied, "and the eye of a needle, only with no needle, to save me doing myself an injury."

"Whoa there, whoa," the old man smiled. "You sound mighty bitter."

"That's all right, brother János," I said, "the Count's happy enough for both of us—he's got nice shiny boots on *his* feet."

"Well, per'aps, per'aps, but just because he does don't mean they'll get him very far!" János twirled his great, greying moustache, and his small, piggy eyes glittered slyly. "Question is, my boy, which of us gets the last laugh."

So we talked. I found out that people were waiting for Christmas charity parcels. They'd been standing in front of the village hall for a whole blessed week now, because the parcels hadn't arrived due to the heavy snow. The gentlemen tasked with distributing them had said they'd let everybody know when the delivery arrived, but the poor came every morning anyway, on the principle that it's better to be safe than sorry. Yesterday, they'd finally announced the parcels had arrived, and told the people they'd start distributing them at nine o'clock this morning. It was not yet seven, but there were already some fifty people gathered there, and more than a few had been waiting in the freezing cold since five.

"You just go and join the line, my boy," the old man counselled. "There might be a pair of shoes in it for you."

It was good of him to say. Some tiny kernel of hope sprouted once more inside me, and since I didn't have anything else to do anyway, I joined the queue. János's kind words had softened me and I felt at home among the ragged and poor. With them, I didn't have to feel ashamed. They, too, were ragged, and cold, and the Baby Jesus had left them, too, off his list. I had begun to think that I didn't belong anywhere at all, but now, with a sudden warmth in my heart, I felt that I did, after all, have a place.

It was still snowing. The newspaper on my feet had soaked through. The others, too, were cold, every one of us hopping about in a coach-man's dance. From time to time, for want of anything else to lift our spirits, someone made a joke, and we laughed, and swore and some-how passed the time. By nine, there were so many of us that we could barely fit into the square, but they only started distributing the parcels at eleven, two hours late. But the people weren't restless. They'd got used to waiting; they'd done nothing else for the last thousand years. They waited their turn calmly, and whoever had got their parcel hurried quickly off with it, so that their families, too, would have something to be happy about at Christmas.

But many people, for unknown reasons, got nothing at all. They did not, however, leave the square. They formed a group in front of the village hall and grumbled. Not too loud, just a little, and only under their breath, because by then, the gendarmes had turned up to patrol in front of the building, bayonets fixed.

"They're only handing 'em out to people that voted for the government," an old peasant next to me mumbled, and spat heavily.

The village had known for some time that that was how it went when they distributed the packages. There were similar abuses elsewhere, too; the opposition deputies kept making speeches about it in parliament, and each time, the Minister would very properly promise to initiate a thorough investigation, and each time, that thorough investigation would reveal that there had been no abuses. The house accepted the Minister's reply, the newspapers wrote three lines about the affair, the peasants just shrugged their shoulders and muttered under their breath, and everything went on as before.

The bells were ringing noon by the time it was my turn. Behind the parcel-laden table stood a blond young man, hair slicked back with pomade.

"What d'you need?" he snapped at me irritably, and yawned.

"Begging your pardon, sir," I began with the abject humility bred into the Hungarian peasant over the last thousand years, "I need some shoes, 'cause I can't go barefoot to school no more. Makes no difference if they're old or…"

"Name and address," the young man interrupted impatiently.

I gave him my name and address. The young man leafed through his book and then drily proclaimed:

"You're not in the book. Move along!"

After me came a fortyish, beefy peasant called, if I remember rightly, Balog. The youth with the pomaded hair told him, too, that he was "not in the book" and to "move along".

But then something happened; something that left its mark on the whole rest of my life.

This Balog, or whatever his name was, when told to "move along", didn't. He just stood there in front of the pomade-scented young man and with ominous calm asked why he wasn't "in the book" when he had five "little ones" and a wife "what's sick in the lung" at home, no criminal record, and had spent four years fighting for his country. At first, I thought he was drunk. When sober, peasants didn't usually ask gentlemen *why*; they just said, "begging your pardon, sir", and if they were told to move on, moved on quietly. Mostly, they just cursed once or twice out of earshot—the more fiery ones might go home and beat the wife. I had never seen anything like this Balog, and it looked like no one else in the room had, either.

A frightened hush fell over the stuffy, overcrowded room. All eyes were on Balog. They watched him, mouths agape, blinking, as if he were some freak of nature. The blond boy didn't know what to say, either. He tapped his pencil nervously on the table and kept huffing gutturally over and over:

"Move along! Move along!"

But the man didn't move. He stood there like an old, weather-beaten tree that could be cut down, but never moved. He had asked his question, he was waiting for an answer; you could tell that he wasn't going anywhere.

At this point the young man with the pomaded hair remembered that gentlemen, when they don't have answers, resort to shouting.

"You'll get answers from the gendarme in a minute!" he cried. "If you don't shut your mouth."

That didn't help, either. The man just stood there, immobile.

"I ain't some old woman who can't stop flappin' her mouth," he said, a little hoarse but calm. "And if I weren't scared of no Russians, young man, I ain't going to soil myself for no gendarme, neither."

At this point, someone giggled in the stony silence. Mocking laughter burst up from all around and barbed comments hummed like carrion flies. The order of the queue broke down, and everyone pressed excitedly towards the table. Only Balog remained miraculously calm.

"Just because you don't vote for the government, sir," he said dispassionately, "that don't mean you ain't a God-fearin' Hungarian."

This quiet, unassuming sentence was enough to prick the suppressed emotion in the room.

"That's right!" people cried from all around. "That's right!"

Eyes flashed, arms flailed, feet drummed and an unholy cacophony broke out. The blond young man's voice was lost in the tumultuous clamour, his mouth flapping as if he'd been shouting from behind a window.

In the great throng, I couldn't see what was happening in front, because the others were a good head taller than me. All I remember is that at a certain point the crowd surged forward, and people fell over each other and grew entangled, as if someone had stirred them with an enormous ladle. Then there was a scream, a second, a third, and the gendarmes' bayonets waving about in the crowd, twisted faces, people doubled over. A man with a gendarme's feather in his hat threw himself at Balog. Balog fell onto me, and I fell under the table, where I could see only legs: legs struggling, kicking and stepping all over each other, like the limbs of some horrific prehistoric monster.

I didn't even have time to feel scared. On all fours, like a cornered animal, I backed away under the table, and suddenly noticed that I was inside the ringed-off part of the room, where the blond young man had been standing moments before. The charity packages lay scattered on the floor around me: underwear, second-hand clothes, worn hats and… shoes! Shoes!

It's hard to explain what happened next with hindsight. In such moments of danger, you'd think that all you could think about is saving your skin, and would never notice that…

Well, I noticed. Who knows, perhaps the need for a pair of shoes had become an obsession with me, or perhaps I simply wasn't aware of the danger I was in. Suffice to say that all at once, I was clutching a pair of shoes and making my way to the exit.

At this point, a hand grabbed me. In the tangled crowd, I could only recognize it by its smell: it was the boy with the pomade. With a desperate, clumsy motion, I tore myself from his grasp and ran for the door.

"Thief!" he screamed. "Stop that thief!"

I recall the rest only like some jumbled dream. A gendarme marching me down the high street. People rushing out of their houses.

"What's goin' on, Sergeant?"

Much shaking of heads, sharp looks. Words that cut straight to the bone.

"Can't you see? One of Rozi's boys."

"What'd you expect of his sort…"

Then I was standing in the guardroom face to face with a mousta-chioed junior officer in the gendarmes.

At this point, my memory fails me completely. Did he ask me something? Did I reply? I don't know. All I remember is that at some point he shot up from behind his desk and gave me an almighty slap.

I no longer knew what I was doing. With all my pent-up bitterness, misery, humiliation, my whole oppressed little life, I hated this man, this hard-handed gendarme, as if he, and only he, were responsible for it all. There is no spirit that can make you as drunk as hate. Everything was swaying within me and I no longer cared about anything. I picked up the enormous inkpot from the desk and flung it with all my might into the junior officer's face. I could see him totter, his face covered in ink, and then there was a massive blow from behind—someone had hit me in the back of the head with the butt of a rifle; the world went black before me.

I came to in a small lock-up smelling of mice. The bells were ringing… or was it just my ears?… "Silent night…" Two pairs of shoes under the Christmas tree… The smell of burnt pine… Well, my boy, and what did the Baby Jesus bring *you*?… The junior officer tottering about, his face covered in ink…

I staggered to my feet uncertainly. A dull, aching pain shot through me. There was a strange, alien trembling in my guts. What had happened to me?

I looked around. The windows were barred. Then this must be…

Suddenly, I remembered everything. I'd been stealing. They'd caught me, locked me up.

"Appallin'!" I muttered aloud, but without all conviction. "Appallin'," I repeated, but Squirrel just started to laugh. I didn't understand.

I'd been stealing. They'd caught me. Locked me up. I knew that what I'd done was "shameful" according to the grown-ups, or even "wild". I felt not the slightest morsel of guilt. Instead, I saw the moustachioed junior officer totter, his face covered in ink, and a broad, complacent sense of satisfaction came over me. Squirrel twitched his tail triumphantly.

"He got his, all right!" I mumbled to myself and laughed softly.

Strange, I thought, they've put me in jail and here I am laughing.

But when it came down to it, I'd got my lumps too. I went over my body with my hands. I was pleased to find there was nothing really wrong. There was a goodly bump on my head, it's true, and my chest and back ached, but I knew that dull, deep ache well from my days as a hired fighter. My injuries were, so to speak, the usual ones, and after the unusual events of the day, I found that almost reassuring.

"It's all right," I said aloud.

Though there was… a lump on my back as well. It seems they'd kept on beating me while I was unconscious. Or was it merely from the fall?

As I was feeling myself like this, I suddenly discovered that the wrapped-up Christmas dinner I had pocketed in the morning was still with me. Then I was gripped by a great, soothing, wonderful feeling—after the worrying and incoherent monologue from the confused and shifting soul, the body, refreshingly succinct: I'm hungry! Of course you are, I thought simply, you haven't had anything since morning. I set about opening the package. There was a decent-sized piece of meat, cold potatoes, a thick hunk of bread, a slice each of poppy-seed and walnut loaf. A really fine Christmas dinner, the kind you only got once a year. I could almost taste it in my mouth. I bit into the meat hungry as a wolf, but nonetheless still with a sense of embarrassment and almost shame, like someone who knows that what they're doing is not appropriate to their current situation and that it is—in some vague and ill-defined way—against the rules.

But my stomach took no notice of all that. I was a healthy, sturdy peasant lad and loved to eat. My stomach now happily switched into gear, my teeth tore at the meat joyfully, and my jaws set to their favourite work with passionate devotion; various waves of exciting, powerful juices coursed through me, and my body was filled with the steady truth of flesh and blood, the powerful, sweet certitudes of pure physical being.

Strange, I thought, I'm sitting in jail, enjoying my meal.

And it was strange. I saw myself like an outsider. As if my body and soul had been split into two by some strange magic and there were now two of me sitting there, and I was conversing with myself. So... so now I'm a thief. A real, proper thief, the kind the newspapers and penny dreadfuls write about. And they're going to take me to the county town clapped in irons, like Kelemen last summer, and try me.

"They might even hang me!" I muttered to myself, and carried on munching the poppy-seed loaf; next thing I knew, I caught myself humming—yes humming aloud—that silly tune that goes:

> *If I die, I die*
> *Angels'll sing my lullaby*
> *If I croak, I croak*
> *The Devil take me in one stroke*

The sound of my voice frightened me.

Was I really a gallows rat, like the old woman used to say?

'Course I wasn't! Why would I be a gallows rat?

Because I stole? All right, so I stole! Berci didn't steal. He was a good little boy. He went around barefoot instead, oh yes. And he ended up coughing his lungs out last November. Well, I wasn't going to cough my lungs out! I wasn't going to croak. No sir!

And if that was a crime, then let it be a crime, and if poor boys had to croak anyway, then it was all the same whether they died from pneumonia or on the gallows.

At least I'd given that moustachioed officer something to think about, the devil take him and all his kind!

> *If I die, I die*
> *Angels'll sing my lullaby*
> *If I croak, I croak*
> *The Devil take me in one stroke*

I heard the sound of footsteps. I quickly pocketed my dinner and sharpened my ears, my heart thumping. Someone stopped in front of the door.

No, there were two of them. I could hear them talking, but I couldn't hear what they were saying. My heart skipped.

The key turned in the lock. At first, I saw only a gendarme with his cock's feather, but then behind him in the battered frame of the low door, like a vision, stood the Schoolmaster.

I stood carefully to attention. My heart was in my mouth. I had never seen the Schoolmaster like this. His handsome, Tatar face was so stiff and cold, it was as if all human emotion had frozen off it. He didn't say a word, just stood there with his ox-like build in the tiny door and looked at me. Then, after a seemingly endless silence, he turned to the gendarme and said hoarsely:

"Looks like you did quite a job on him."

The gendarme didn't reply. His face was as impassive as if no one had said a word.

The Schoolmaster looked at me angrily.

"Come!" he said curtly, and was off, without saying goodbye to the gendarme.

I followed him. What now? I wondered, and broke out in a sweat. Where was he taking me?

The Schoolmaster didn't say anything, just walked ahead of me angrily down the bare, dark corridor. He stopped at the gate and showed the gendarme on duty a document, then turned around and gestured for me to follow.

I didn't understand what had happened. Was I free?

Yes, I was free; I was in the street, I could taste the strong, snowy air and... I didn't understand. It seemed so unlikely, so unbelievable. Both the fact they'd locked me up and the fact they'd let me out. I felt like someone who'd jolted awake and doesn't quite know what they'd only dreamt and what they'd actually lived.

I trailed after the Schoolmaster sheepishly, in a daze. He just kept striding in front of me with his great long legs down the snowy street as if I wasn't even there.

We reached the school. The Schoolmaster opened the door to his apartments without a word and I followed him in.

My heart was beating like a mis-rung bell. I knew he had a fearsome hand, but right now it was not his hand I was afraid of, but his tongue. He was the only person I loved.

No, I had never seen him like this before. At other times, when he was angry, he hit us and bellowed, but now he didn't say a word, just paced up and down with broad, heavy steps, not so much as looking at me. The minutes swelled to hours in my mind. In the end, I wished he'd shout at me, at least.

But he didn't. He stopped calmly in front of me and drily said:

"I fixed it with the gentlemen that nothing should happen to you. But you have to leave the village for good. Understand?"

I shuddered all over, but I still stood as stiffly to attention as a soldier in front of his superior.

"Yes, sir!"

"I've wired your mother, and she's replied. She's coming to fetch you on the thirty-first and she's taking you with her to Budapest."

"Yes, sir!"

That was all I said, though it felt like they'd knocked the bottom of my world out from under me. What I'd been terrified of my entire childhood had now come to pass. My throat tightened up with sobs.

The Schoolmaster went over to the window and for a while stared silently out into the street. Then, as if he'd read my mind, he said:

"It's still better than if they'd put you in a reformatory."

He didn't even turn around, his voice was dry and neutral, and yet I still felt a comforting warmth pour out of him.

"Thank you for your kindness, sir."

As I said that, the Schoolmaster turned around, his face scarlet as a turkey's, and looked at me as if I'd said something unforgivably insolent.

"Don't think you're getting off that easy!" he roared. "I hope you know they've hanged people for less. And I promised the gentlemen I'd give you a good thrashing. You're to report to me tomorrow morning, when I'll see you get what's coming to you, got it? I can see they've given you enough to be getting on with for today."

They had, it was true. My whole body ached and yet I still felt that the gendarme's rifle butt hadn't done half as much damage as the Schoolmaster's words.

"If I hear another word of complaint about you," he bellowed, "I'll break you in half, so help me God! Got that?"

"Yes, sir!"

"Well, then."

With that, he tore open the wardrobe door so violently he almost sent the whole rickety affair toppling over, took out a pair of shoes, and slammed them angrily down in front of me.

"Put these on!"

I stared at him as if he'd gone mad. What had possessed him? First he tells me I'm fit to be hung, now he gives me a pair of shoes?

"Didn't you hear me?" he barked. "Put them on!"

A little more softly, he added:

"There's footwraps in there too."

My hands were trembling so hard I could hardly put on the shoes. They were huge, with room enough for my feet twice over, but never has anyone been happier with a pair of shoes. They were warm as a kind word, caressed me like a friendly hand. I started to cry.

"Come on now, you're a big boy," he growled at me. "Don't tell me you're weeping like an old maid. What's done is done. The world'll keep turning."

With that, he gave me a good hard smack on the rump. I'll never forget that smack. I caught his big, hairy hand, the one he'd smacked me with, and kissed it all over.

He pushed me angrily away.

"Get out of here," he shouted. "Or I'll give you such a kick up the backside that your children's children'll still be rubbing ointment on it."

With that, he grabbed me by the scruff of the neck and tossed me out into the yard. But before he closed the door, he said quietly:

"Wear them well."

14

A s I STEPPED OUT INTO THE STREET, I was overcome by a strange joy. If I hadn't feared for my manliness, I might have started jumping like a ram, and as it was I could only restrain myself till I got to the road at the outskirts of the village. There, I jumped into the deepest snow in my nice warm shoes, and ran about willy-nilly.

Like a drunk, I was singing at the top of my voice:

> *I'll be leaving your village very soon*
> *Now I'll be looking at a different moon*

My lungs burned with the rapid breaths of ice-cold air and my heart beat wildly. Panting, I propped myself against a telegraph pole.

I couldn't understand what had got into me. For it was true that I was glad about the shoes, and even gladder for those few kind words from the Schoolmaster, but I knew that in itself could not have caused this sweet delirium that was running through me. Half an hour ago, I was cursing the world and everything in it, and now it seemed so wonderful to me, it was as if God had made it anew, this time with no snakes, and out of candyfloss. No, I thought, that sort of thing isn't about a pair of shoes; but as to what it *was* about, I didn't have the foggiest.

I was perfectly happy, though I knew full well that I had no cause to be. I even ran through in my mind, leaning against the telegraph pole, all the terrible things that had happened to me that day, but that crazy haphazard happiness just kept on singing within me, refusing to listen to any kind of reason. In vain did I keep repeating to myself that I'd stolen, was caught, locked up, that I was being sent away like a pariah, and that what I had always feared was now about to happen: my mother was coming to take me with her to Budapest.

"Terrible," I said aloud, and was perfectly happy.

I was happy and I didn't know why.

I wandered around aimlessly. It was already dark and the village had drawn its eiderdown of snow up tight, sleeping under the twinkling stars. Great filigree snowflakes were falling, the road was virgin and white, as if no one had ever walked before me—as if God really had made the world anew, and I was the first person in this great white paradise.

All at once, I found myself at the station. I hadn't been this way since the last time I accompanied my mother here. I could no longer say if I had avoided the station consciously, but the fact is that I had avoided it, the way people tend to avoid things—whether consciously or not—spending half their lives, more or less, obsessively and stubbornly avoiding something that, in the end, they can't get away from anyway.

The evening train was puffing away in the station, getting ready to depart. The raw, adventure-filled smell of its steam struck my nostrils and I was once more overtaken by that old, tingling magic that had enchanted me as a little boy whenever I saw a train depart. But this time, it drove me not to tears, but indescribable joy. On the thirty-first I, too, will be on that train, I thought, as the wheezing little coffee-grinder puffed itself up to move, and all of a sudden, I knew why I was so happy.

"I'm going!" I said, but that word "going" didn't just mean that I was "moving", that my address and my destiny was changing: it meant something much more, something mysterious, some obscure, veiled and above all symbolic thing that I could not have put into words.

Something had ended, I felt, and something was about to begin.

But what?

"Life!" I answered grandiloquently, and it sounded to my fourteen-year-old ears as if I'd said: happiness.

The Great Adventure!

That was my father's blood talking, I now know. My father who had run away from home at fifteen and spent a lifetime wandering the great wide world. When, many years later, I asked him why, what he was after, what desires drove him on, he looked at me as if he didn't quite understand the question, and I could see that he'd never really given it any thought.

"Well, because," he said, and could hardly say any more. "There's people that sit quietly in one place till they come and put 'em in a coffin, and then there's people that can't sit still even in their mother's wombs. And them, even if you lock the door behind them, they'll fly out through the keyhole."

Was I that sort, too?

Yes, yes I was. I didn't even mind that I was going with my mother—all I could think about, trembling with joy—was that I was "going". It's also true that by now, I hated my mother more out of habit than anything else. That old, wild, unnatural hatred that I had felt as a small child had been decomposing in the cemetery of my consciousness for several years, and now that I brought it once more into the daylight, it simply crumbled to ashes like a mummy brought out of a pyramid. But I would have gone with her now even if I had hated her the way I'd hated her as a child. I would have gone with the Devil himself, I was so driven by my *wanderlust*.

I could hardly wait for the thirty-first. This impatience was partly because I still had my "reckoning" with the Schoolmaster to face, which he had so ominously promised. Manliness or not, I was terrified of this "reckoning" and, to tell the truth, my knees were trembling as I rang the Schoolmaster's bell.

It was Scarecrow who opened the door.

"The Schoolmaster has gone away," she said, "but he'll be back by the thirty-first. He says you're to come and see him then."

"Yes, miss," I replied and was off, relieved.

But in the afternoon, when I went past the school, I was shocked to see the Schoolmaster looking out of the window. I was stunned. I looked stiffly over his head, as if I hadn't seen him; he could always call after me if he wanted to. But the Schoolmaster did not call after me.

The Schoolmaster had lied, and today I know that I, too, would have lied in his place. He had promised the gentlemen that he would "reckon" with me, but in reality he knew full well who and what deserved to be "reckoned with", for forcing a barefoot peasant boy to steal a pair of shoes so he could go to school. I didn't understand any of that at the time, but needless to say, I accepted it easily. Looks like we've got out of that, then, I thought to myself happily, because of course I knew that any "reckoning" that came just a few hours before my departure wouldn't be too severe.

Packing was not hard. I could fit my entire wardrobe into my trouser pockets. It consisted of two ragged shirts I'd outgrown long ago; their collars had grown so tight I hadn't been able to button them in years, and their arms were so short they only came up to my elbows. And then there were, to account for my other assets, my five prize books, about six dozen marbles, a rag-ball I'd made myself and the treasured lead whistle, a present from Piroshkamydear.

I "sold" the marbles to a second-year for a needle and some thread, and the ball to a fourth-year for rags to patch my clothes with. Then I spent all day cleaning and patching my single set of clothes and the two fraying shirts.

The boys gathered round and stared at me like I was some minor miracle. Since my spell inside, my stock with them had risen and risen. They all tried to assist me somehow. They bustled about me, one of them trimming my nails, the other my hair, while the third stole some soap to wash with. Sándor even cut the buttons off his own clothes so that I could sew them onto mine. In return, I had to tell and retell my Christmas horror story, from the moment I stole the shoes to when I ended up in the cell at the gendarmerie. They listened, mouths agape, faces burning with excitement. The thought that one of them, a ragged bastard child, could take such revenge on their towering Olympian superiors was enough to make them altogether drunk.

"Béla showed 'em!" they went about saying nice and loud in the street for everyone to hear, and their eyes shone with pride.

The old woman didn't mention the affair at all. The boys told me that before they let me out of prison, the Schoolmaster had a long talk with her behind closed doors, and that must have been why she was being so considerate. Only when she saw that I was in a good mood would she look at me murderously, but she never said a word. She would mumble something under her downy moustache, and I would think: drop dead. Quite the pair we made.

I slept naked the night before the thirty-first because I had washed both my shirts and put them under me, along with my other clothes, to "iron" them. This slightly unusual mode of ironing was very much in vogue with us, but only in summer, because there was no way we could sleep without our clothes in the freezing room. And it's true that I didn't end up sleeping much that night. My thoughts galloped about like scattered horses and even if—after much tossing and turning—I did manage to fall asleep, I would wake up after a few minutes as if I'd been stabbed: I kept dreaming I'd miss the train.

I went to the school early in the morning to say goodbye to the Schoolmaster. But the Schoolmaster had organized another one of those "Royal Hungarian nights" this night too, and was unwilling to acknowledge that it was morning. The house peeped, shutters closed, out into the glaring snowy sunshine, and you could hear the Gypsy music and excited yells from inside. The door was wide open—you could have helped yourself to whatever you liked.

I stood in the entryway among the damp, steaming coats, unsure what to do. I knocked on the door in vain, got no reply. Finally, after much hesitation, I opened the door and went into the parlour. There was no one there, either. The company was revelling in the next-door room. The door was ajar, tobacco smoke pouring out of it.

I didn't dare enter. There were six or eight men in their shirtsleeves swaying in the sickly yellow light of the petroleum lamp, drunk as lords. Coming from the sober daylight, they seemed ghostly in this artificial night as they hollered with bloodshot eyes in the clouds of tobacco smoke like the devotees of some semi-savage sect. The sweating, exhausted Gypsies were playing the Schoolmaster's song.

A good horse needs no saddle,
It still walks with pride.
My sweetheart's married to another man,
But still keeps me by her side.

"A *csárdás*!" cried the Schoolmaster and sprang, glass in hand, onto the table, doing a frantic dance.

135

"Forever young!"

He downed his wine and hurled the glass so hard at the mirror that it broke, crashing, into pieces.

Nobody noticed. I stood in the darkened room alone and a deep, animal sadness gripped my heart. I knew that I would never get to say goodbye to the Schoolmaster, and I didn't know what I was still waiting for. I just stood there aimlessly a while, and then sneaked silently out of the house.

That was the last time I saw the Schoolmaster. Six months later, his sister died, and from then on, they say, he grew even wilder. One day they stripped him of his position, and even took his miserable pension. When I was last home, people in the village hardly remembered him at all. There were still some anecdotes about him doing the rounds, it's true, of the sort that are impossible to verify—like the one about the Countess—but as to what an outstandingly knowledgeable and instinctively excellent teacher he was, even his own former students no longer remembered. He had become a tall tale and faded like the snows of yesteryear.

The new schoolmaster was a big success. His superiors were very keen on him and he was very popular with the local gentry. The peasants didn't like him much, it's true, but they nonetheless gave him his due; and even they admitted that he was a decent sort. He performed his duties impeccably, never touched alcohol or cards, and on the rare occasions when he took a fancy to a girl, it was to the pleasure of the mothers eager to marry off their daughters. "A good catch," they said, and it was true. He was a modest, well-to-do, industrious young gentleman, and everyone knew his family. He was distantly related to a well-known grandee in Budapest who—a devoted racialist and Great Hungarian—was needless to say of *Schwäbisch* descent. He had this connection to thank for his position as village schoolmaster, in which he only spent three years, as the grandee meanwhile was put in charge of the country's schools, at which point the schoolmaster was moved up to Budapest.

This upstanding young gentleman did wonders for the school's reputation. His students knew their textbooks by heart and had no time at all to wonder about who owned the snow. And he was a fair-minded man, treating everyone the same. He punished the barefoot peasant boys and the young gentlemen in snow boots just the same if they didn't turn up for school. His character and his uprightness were beyond question. His philosophical and emotional values mirrored perfectly that of His Hungarian Majesty's Ministers of Education and Religion. He taught with Germanic precision, thoroughness and discipline. He went studiously through the prescribed curriculum, as laid out in the latest government decrees and guidelines. Anything that fell outside those decrees and guidelines he just as studiously left out. To cut a long story short, he was the sort of man of whom they're bound to write, if one day—at the very end of human history—he does ever actually die, that he was an "exemplary schoolmaster and a gentleman of irreproachable character." But in all seriousness, we should also add that our society has his sort of exemplary schoolmasters to thank for the fact that, despite the many millions of barefoot peasant children, it abides and, above all, remains exemplary.

As for the Schoolmaster, the village thought that his firing hadn't made much of an impact at first. He had to hand over the apartments on 1st September 1930, and on the evening of 31st August he had himself such a ball—Gypsy music and all—that it was all the village could talk about. The next morning, when the new schoolmaster showed up to move into his apartments, he was left ringing the bell in vain: no one answered. In the end, he had to fetch the gendarmes and have the locksmith open the door. They found the Schoolmaster on the couch amid shattered glasses, bottles and puddles of wine, his chest covered in blood. The district doctor, with whom he'd been revelling till five that morning, could do nothing for him. The Schoolmaster had been an outstanding shot, and had found his heart with the utmost accuracy.

15

B UT ON THE MORNING OF MY DEPARTURE, the Schoolmaster was still hollering loud enough to be heard out on the street. I stood in front of the school and didn't know what to do. I had taken care of everything else—all that was left was to board the train. But the train only left at two twenty, and at that moment it seemed unbelievable to me that it would ever be two twenty at all. My mother had written that she would arrive at eleven thirty, and that I was to wait for her at the station, because she wouldn't set foot in the old woman's house.

I looked up at the village clock. It was a quarter past eight. Another six hours, I thought, and life begins. I wandered around aimlessly to kill the time. A sentimental poem from my literature textbook kept ringing in my ears:

> *Farewell, village of my birth, way back when;*
> *I wonder: will I e'er see your streets again?*

I, too, am leaving the village now, I thought, and tried to be suitably moved, in the spirit of the National Treasure who'd written those lines; but I couldn't. Being a baser soul, I told myself that the whole thing was a lot of nonsense, because how on earth could you say farewell to "the" village? Was I meant to say farewell to the houses, perhaps, whose thresholds I'd never been allowed to cross, because little bastard boys weren't welcome? Or the shops in which I couldn't buy anything, because no one gave me money to buy things with? Or was I meant to knock on strangers' doors, those who didn't give a damn about me? Or was it the junior officer in the gendarmes I was meant to say farewell to?

Then I remembered Sárika. In some vague, complicated way, I still cared. Not that I was in love with her. Time had blown away even the ashes of my childhood love, but the embers of my earlier hatred still smouldered within me, because hate, it seems, is an even stronger bond than love. I wanted to see her one last time. As to why, I couldn't have said, because at fourteen you don't yet know that when it comes to taking stock in life, all that really matters are your experiences, and that it's better to have bad experiences than none at all.

So I walked to the high street and peeked into the shop. The anaemic winter sun shone through the glass door at an angle, flooding the bulging sacks on the floor with weak, sallow light. Sárika was standing behind the counter, fixing her hair in a little hand-held mirror. She'd grown a lot since I'd last seen her. She'd become a gaunt, lanky teenage girl, freckles crowding over her pale white face. I looked at her and knew I didn't hate her any more. I didn't hate her, and I didn't love her. She's nothing to do with me, I thought, and felt a pang in my heart. I didn't understand why—how could I have? It takes a long time until you understand that it's still better to hate than to feel nothing at all; that it's better if you have someone who hates you than if you belong to no one at all. All at once, I realized that there wasn't a single soul in this godforsaken village to whom I could now happily go and say, "I'm off now, brother, God bless you."

Who was there to care that I was leaving when no one had cared for fourteen years if I lived or died? If I were to drop down dead now, here in the snow, they might as well send the knacker for me because, God knows, no one but the Schoolmaster ever treated me like a human.

But I wasn't going to die that easily! I grumbled to myself. I'll show you who you're dealing with! I'll show you! I repeated, and my childhood daydreams were all of a sudden resurrected. I saw myself riding into the village on a fine horse, to the joyful acclaim of the villagers: the just, the famous Béla, who dispensed justice to the oppressors of poor children, bread to the needy, and made the last first.

"I'll show you!" I mumbled aloud and stared at the passers-by with my chin pressed down against my neck like a little bull, ready to charge.

As I passed the gendarmerie, I spat heavily out of the side of my mouth, and with that, I considered my fond farewell to "the" village over and done with.

My send-off at home was not much more emotional. The boys were jealous, and if there was some more tender emotion lurking in their breasts, they didn't show it. They were debating the practical details of my journey, where I would leave the local train and pick up the "big" train, which route that train would take and when it would get to Budapest, checking it all excitedly on their school map. Mr Rozi didn't lunch at home, so I didn't get to say goodbye to him. But he didn't matter anyway. He was just a moving piece of furniture; we were used to him, and didn't pay him much attention. He wasn't bad to us, though he wasn't good either. He wasn't any particular way. He only cared for the fish. The old woman acted as if she didn't even know that I was leaving, while I spent the whole time trying to disguise my burning excitement so that I could take my leave calmly and with dignity—as a serious young man should.

But there was still some strange flicker of emotion within me when, after lunch, with my things wrapped under my arm, I stood before the old woman, and it was as if she, too, were moved. Her eyes were strange, unusually clouded, and a shy, awkward little smile played in the troughs of the tangled wrinkles around her mouth. But in the end, all she said was:

"I hope you better behaved in future."

And that was how we took our leave, after fourteen years.

The boys all wanted to come and accompany me to the train, but I didn't want them to be there when I saw my mother. So I made my way to the station alone. I still had plenty of time, so I walked leisurely down the high street and thought about that far-off evening in late June when Istvány, too, had walked this way to catch the train—except that he had his father, with his heavy moustache, to hold one hand, and his tiny mother the other.

I stood beside the rails when the eleven-thirty came in, but I couldn't see my mother anywhere. I pushed helplessly through the throng of noisy passengers, my mouth dry with the excitement. It had been eight years since I saw her last, and it was now in vain that I tried to conjure up the image of her face—I couldn't. Maybe she hadn't recognized me either, I reassured myself, and sat down, a tightness pressing at my throat, on a bench. Once the passengers have gone, we're bound to find each other, I thought. But the station was unusually crowded because of the holidays. The gilded youth of the village were out in force, young, frost-bitten faces shining beside the railway line, the lads in mischievous high spirits and the girls giggling as if someone were tickling them. I just sat there all alone in this great collective good humour, examining the people, heart thumping, one after the other.

Which of them was my mother?

Whenever a woman who looked like she might be from the big city glanced at me, I instantly thought it was her, and my heart skipped a beat. But the women moved on, and I wondered, terrified, what would happen if I couldn't find my mother, and after all those farewells I would be faced with the humiliation of staying.

Around two, they backed the train into the station. There was a good deal of commotion, and the passengers rushed the carriages, as the rest gathered under the windows to blurt the usual idiocies up to the people setting out. A woman in a brown coat, with a black kerchief tied around her hair, moved agitatedly up and down through the crowd, and I suddenly knew that this woman was my mother.

I was seized by a terrific excitement. I could see her heading towards me, but I didn't move. I stared straight ahead, looking bored, as if I hadn't noticed her, though I could hear the sound of her footsteps as she approached as if each one had been a hammer blow. She was now standing before me, but I still didn't look up. I could only hear her voice, as if it came from another world.

"Are you Béla R., little boy?"

I jumped up and stood stiffly to attention, as you did when talking to your superiors.

"Yes, ma'am," I replied crisply.

The woman just stood there and looked at me.

"Don't you know your own mother?" she asked with a weak smile.

"You didn't know me neither," I replied, not looking up, and tried to smile, too.

The woman looked at her shoes silently. You could see her anger flaring, but in the end, all she said was:

"Well, you've grown a lot."

We didn't have much more to say to each other. We just stood there in silence. Now it seemed that I did remember her, yes, I definitely remembered her. How old she looked, I thought. An old woman. Now I know that she was thirty-one at the time.

"Let's get on, then," she said at last and headed for the train.

We boarded. Around us there was a cacophony of farewells, some people crying, others laughing, but we just sat impassively like an ageing couple, staring out of the window. It was snowing once more.

"Hard winter this year," said my mother.

"Yes," I replied. "Very."

That was the totality of our conversation. She didn't ask, and I didn't say, anything. We stared out of the window.

The conductor blew his trumpet and the train started. I was seized by such excitement that I forgot all about my mother. I pressed my face hard against the window and stared at the passing landscape, temples throbbing. These few streets, these few hundred houses that the train now sped past in a couple of minutes had been, for me, for fourteen years "the" world. In vain had I learnt about other villages, other towns and countries—they were no more real for me than the pictures out of the *Arabian Nights*. They were a fairy tale, a neverland. Where the land touched the sky at the edge of the village was for me, despite all the geography I had learnt, more or less the end of the world. Everything happened within that frontier, everything that represented palpable and verifiable reality, all joy and pain, everything beautiful and everything revolting, my whole childhood. And now, as I looked out of the carriage window, I could see how ridiculously small this village, that had been my entire world, was.

The Schoolmaster had told us a story about the "Easter Eggs of Happiness". God—so the story went—had hidden away people's happiness in scattered spots around the great wide world, the way you hid painted eggs at Easter, and people now ran from city to city, from country to country, by train and ship and aeroplane, searching incurably for their happiness. I thought of that story now, and it suddenly seemed incomprehensible, terrible and shameful that I had wasted fourteen years in this cursed little village, when I had so much urgent searching to do in that great wide world. I could see the school globe before me, on which the name of our village didn't even feature, on which even Hungary was just a tiny pink dot within Europe, and Europe itself was not so much bigger compared to the size of the world itself.

Where was my happiness hidden?

Where would I find it? In which city, which country, over which lands far, far away?

In the story, the poor boy at the beginning said: "Now or never, do or die, I'll go find it where it may lie." And I, too, made the same promise to myself.

Now I felt that Budapest, too, was to be just a station on the long road on which I had set out that day with the two-twenty local, and perhaps not even a much more important one than the station where we would change from the local to the "big" train.

I was seized by such sweet impatience and such deliciously painful curiosity at the same time that I would have liked to whip the train on, bawling like a drunken coachman. I felt I had not a minute to lose—happiness was waiting for me somewhere, and I had urgently to make up for those fourteen years that I had so unforgivably allowed to pass me by.

My mother woke me from my thoughts.

"Come on," she said. "We've got to change trains."

Something happened on that other train. Nothing big, and at the time, I paid it no attention, but today I know that in a certain sense it influenced the whole rest of my life.

As the train pulled out, a dumpy, broad-chested lady pressed her way through the crowded carriage, accompanied by a boy of about my age. When my mother saw her, she jumped out of her seat, ran over to her, grabbed her hand and kissed it zealously all over. The lady, too, pasted a benign smile onto her face, but I nonetheless got the impression that my mother's outpourings bored her. Later on, they called me over and my mother introduced me to the lady and her dolled-up little gentleman of a son.

"Look," she said breathlessly, "I was this fine young gentleman's nurse when you was born."

I looked the fine young gentleman over, but didn't find him very fine at all. He was such a lanky, dull sort of boy that you could have made two of him from me. So this was the boy who'd drunk my mother's milk away from me.

The lady looked around the carriage disapprovingly.

"Come over to second class for a minute, dear," she said. "It does *smell* so here in third, it's simply unbearable."

It definitely smelt better in second class, that's for sure. I couldn't believe my eyes when I set foot in the carriage. I'd never seen anything so beautiful in my life. The seats were covered in red plush, like the Schoolmaster's grandfather chair, and the walls were decorated with beautiful pictures.

"Well, then, have a seat, dear, and tell me all about yourself," the lady said graciously, and sat back so comfortably on the soft padding that her horrible great breasts almost popped out of her silk dress.

My mother, too, sat down, only she sat down so modestly at the very edge of the seat, it was as if she were afraid that the delicate upholstery would take it as a personal insult if she interloped too far with her lower-class behind.

We two boys remained outside in the corridor. The "fine" young gentleman was dolled up as if he were going to—at the very least— some kind of festivity. He was wearing a fur coat, like the Count, a red tie with white polka dots, and a green hunting cap with a tuft of wild boar fur on it. But the thing that awed me most was his shoes. They'd thrown me in jail for trying to get my hands on a pair of worn-out old shoes so I could go to school, while this little dunce was wearing *two* pairs of shoes, one inside the other. The inner ones were yellow, and the outer ones sort of polished patent-leather black. I found out later they were called galoshes.

It was only as I stood beside this fancy young man that I really felt what a ragged beggar I was. He must have thought the same, because the way he looked at me got my blood up. If he'd looked at me that way in the village, I would have smacked him in the mouth; but here, I just mumbled something, like an idiot. I smiled and the anger boiled up inside me, because when it came to my rep I was deadly serious. This "fine" young gentleman was annoying me, and since I couldn't smack him, I tried to deal with him by other means. I steered the conversation round to school, on the theory that even the finest hunting cap couldn't help you there; there, you had to *know* things, and know things I knew I did. I started quizzing him with that sly peasant craftiness that feigns stupidity that not even Galician Jews can outdo. By the end, I was more or less cross-examining the boy, because I wanted to know if they'd dolled him up as fine on the inside as they had on the out.

The results were shocking. He was in the fourth year of secondary school, but despite the fact that I was only in the sixth year of primary, and apart from a few scraps of Latin and other things you only learnt in secondary, I was better than him at everything. He barely knew a thing about geography, had no clue about history, and just kept shooting his mouth off, humming and hawing, saying that they taught things differently in secondary school. Two and two is still four, even in secondary school, I thought, since that was the sort of error the fine young gentleman kept making.

I had never been a great fan of the upper classes, but I had nonetheless thought that they were different from us poor people, the way expensive cloth is different from cheap. I could see the difference now, all right.

And these are the people, I thought, who take everything away from us, even our mothers' milk?

Why? Why? Why?

By what right?

My mind is keener, my knowledge greater, and my fist... I almost laughed out loud. If I started on this "fine" young gentleman, that painted, broad-chested mother of his would be picking up the pieces in a sheet.

I could compete with the likes of him any day, the devil take his kind.

If ever I'd been afraid, that fear now disappeared, like chaff blown by the wind.

What did I have to lose?

Nothing.

I had the world before me.

Aprés moi le déluge!

TWO

Me and Her Excellency's Dog

1

BUDA WAS AS WHITE AND UNREAL as a Christmas story. There was no wind in the snowy streets, they were stiflingly calm; it was as if the whole city was holding its breath. The great snowflakes, shimmering like diamonds, descended slowly, like in a dream in the yellow halos of the elaborate streetlamps, and my overjoyed imagination pictured incredible palaces in the twinkling fog. Mysterious vehicles swept by behind the glittering curtain of snow: silent, gleaming, aristocratic motor cars, noisy little taxis on the hunt, enormous, flat-footed buses and even a sleigh, with its silvery tinkle, straight out of a fairy tale. Light and music poured out of the cafés, and an old man dressed up like a general opened the doors of the motor cars, bent double, in front of a place covered in coloured lights.

"Happy New Year!" he intoned, though there was still some time to go till midnight. "Happy New Year!"

Porcelain-faced ladies in toothpick-heeled slippers tottered out of the cars on the arms of their elegant beaus. Snow glittered in their hair, diamonds in their ears, and smiles on their faces. They were as beautiful and unreal as the city itself and I thought of Elek Benedek's fairy tales, because I had never seen anything like it in real life.

The Danube was still and white, like a highway under snow. Only when we got closer did I see that sheets of ice floated in the middle, with pitch-black water roiling beneath. My mother stopped under the illuminated arch of a great bridge.

"Look at all that!" she said, as if the whole city were hers and she was trying to sell it to me at great profit. "They say," she said proudly, "even the Prince of Wales was speechless when he saw it."

I don't know about the Prince of Wales, but I really *was* speechless as I saw the two cities meet, their long, illuminated bridge-arms touching over the Danube. I turned my head this way and that, not knowing where to look first. On the sides of the hills, like a reclining woman, Buda presented itself from beneath a white eiderdown of snow, while on the other side, flat and sly, Pest winked like a man with its myriad lights. Mysterious rays glowed here and there in the milky fog, flooding a building or a statue in fantastic light. Up high, almost swimming in the clouds, a ruined castle glimmered above the city and a little way off, on top of another great hill, stood a dreamlike building with lots of turrets; I simply had no idea what it was.

"Fisherman's Bastion," my mother explained. "And that over there is the Royal Palace."

I stared in awe, mouth agape. In the fog and the beams of the spotlights, the snowy Royal Palace looked so unreal that I couldn't imagine at all that anyone lived inside. It reminded me much more of the icing of a fancy cake, as its snow-capped dome poked into the sky on top of the hill. I leant against the railing of the bridge, heart thumping, and my eyes were moist with happiness. How great, I thought, that I get to live here! How great to be alive! How great…

"What you doing loitering there?" croaked a harsh, hoarse voice.

I turned around in fright. A heavily moustachioed man in a black uniform and silver helmet stood before us. There was a sword hanging by his side, a holster on his belt, and icicles on his moustache. With his daintily gloved hands—like a little girl at First Communion—he roughly pushed my mother away from the railings.

"Move along, move along," he mumbled. "You can't loiter here."

My mother took off in fright, and I panted after her.

"Why'd the soldier chase you away?" I asked when we'd got out of range.

My mother smiled.

"That weren't no soldier. It was a policeman."

"Policeman, then!" I muttered angrily, because I felt my reputation had been damaged. "Why'd he chase you away?"

"Must have thought I was going to jump in the river."

"Why would you do that?"

"Same as all the rest. So many people are jumpin' in the river these days, they've taken to guardin' the bridges. The papers say ain't nowhere in the world with more suicides than us."

We were on the Pest bank by then, walking past the big hotels. Wealth flaunted itself here like a pheasant at mating time. Huge, illuminated motor cars thronged the red-carpeted hotel doorways. White shirts and jewels flashed in the night, silk dresses rustled beneath furs, and the generals who held the doors were bending double, bowing before the motor cars.

"Good evening, sir."

"Good evening, Your Excellency."

"Welcome, Your Ladyship."

"How do you do, Your Honour."

"At your service, Mr Chairman."

I had never in my wildest dreams imagined that there were so many ways of addressing someone, or so many furs and jewels. Clouds of scent filled the air and the porcelain-faced ladies tottered on their tiny legs like birds more used to flying. What did these people want to jump in the river for?

My mother slowed her pace, dawdling at the sight, and I thought we were home.

"You live here?" I asked.

My mother smiled again and I wondered irritably once more what my mistake could have been.

"*We* live in Újpest," she said.

I remember, I was very pleased by that. *Újpest*! I repeated to myself and was overcome by curiosity. If the old Pest was this beautiful, what could this new, *új* Pest be like?

We got on the tram. That sounds simple, but for anyone who's never ridden a tram before, it was anything but. I had heard of these contraptions, it's true, but it's one thing to have heard of something and another to have seen it, especially at fourteen. Picture a railway carriage that, no joke, went and separated itself from its locomotive to wander wherever it pleased; that, at least, was more or less how it seemed to me.

It took us quite a while to reach Újpest. The farther the tram went, the darker and more deserted the landscape became. The pretty upper-class houses quickly vanished, faded ugly apartment blocks lining the badly lit streets; and then for a good long time there was nothing but warehouses—plain, granary-like buildings—the odd lonely hovel, and finally nothing but snow and darkness, and the occasional jaundiced streetlamp.

"This is Újpest?" I asked, disappointed, when we got off the tram.

"Yes," nodded my mother.

We crossed the road. On the other side, next to a scrap metal yard, there was a lonely shack leaning heavily in the snow, like the great, uneven heel of a shoe. Inside, in front of a smoky petroleum lamp, a gaunt, dishevelled man with an odd face sat watch, a battered tin clock on the wall behind him. My mother glanced at the clock and swore fiercely.

"I lost all track of time," she mumbled. "Come on, or we'll never get home before they lock the gate."

"They lock up the houses here?" I gaped.

"Yeah, at ten."

"And they don't let you in after?"

"Only if you pay. Ten fillérs a head, twenty after midnight."

We crossed a bumpy empty plot where the snow stood a metre high. There was only a thin little trodden path across it, and it was so narrow that we had to walk in single file. It was only now I realized how cold I had got. All I needed was to have to spend the night out here. No, thanks!

"Ain't you got twenty fillérs?" I sallied.

"I do," she said and sighed briefly. "I was going to get you some milk with it in the mornin'."

"Let's run," I said.

My mother broke into a run, and I ran after her. At last we saw the house. It was a strange house, narrow and tall like a huge brick turned on its side. It stood there alone among the snowed-in vacant plots, in the white wilderness with just the chimneys of a few factories silhouetted in the dark, and even those far, far behind. There was a ragged little tavern on the ground floor, Gypsy music spilling out of it.

"Now if we meet Herr Hausmeister," my mother panted as she ran, "be polite to him, 'cause…" She broke off the sentence and cried excitedly: "The gate's still open!"

We sprinted. Before the gate, my mother grabbed my arm and sneaked me into the house like a thief. It was only on the first floor that she stopped to catch her breath. We lived on the third, because in Pest— my mother explained—the higher up you lived, the lower the rent, and we only lived on the third floor because there was no fourth to live on.

When we got up there, my mother stopped on the stairs.

"I'm going to go do my business," she said. "Wait for me, and you can do yours after."

There was only one toilet on our floor; I later found out it served twelve families. We only had one outhouse at Rozi's, too, but what was that compared to this? There, the old woman had me scrub the planks white every Saturday, but here archaeologists would have discovered layers of filth dating back to the Stone Age underneath all the encrustations of subsequent generations. The toilet opened onto the courtyard; the water had frozen, and the stench was so unbearable that it stunned even my hardened nose.

My mother, meanwhile, had gone into the flat. There were twelve flats on the floor and I couldn't find ours in the dark. In the end, I called out to my mother, and one of the doors finally opened.

"Stop yellin', will you!" my mother shouted at me. "You'll upset Herr Hausmeister."

Her voice sounded very angry, but on her face a smile played, and she indicated with her eyes that it was all just for Herr Hausmeister's benefit. Then in a strange, awkward voice, she said:

"Come on in then, son. Welcome."

That was on 31st December 1927, at ten o'clock at night, when they were locking the gate, three and a half months before my fifteenth birthday. It was the first time I crossed the threshold of what—in better circumstances—people call the family home.

The "family home" consisted of a single room and a kitchen. The kitchen was very narrow and very long, and I would have taken it for a windowless corridor but for the stove and dishes. My mother had lit the stove and a big metal pot was simmering away on top, filling the apartment with the heavy smell of cabbage.

We went into the room. The unvarnished floorboards, full of splinters, were still a little damp from a scrubbing and the entire room had obviously had a thorough clean. The flat was very neat and very sad, though I couldn't say exactly why. The room was quite large, at least by my standards, and I even liked the furniture when it came down to it. There was a bed in the middle of the room, which for me was already a sign of luxury, and above it, in a broad gold frame, there was a colour lithograph: the Virgin Mary with the infant Jesus. There was also a sink in the room, a pitted white tin sink that wobbled on two legs beside the bed, because its third did not reach down to the uneven floor. A little way over, a stern, dumpy wardrobe squatted, staring angrily at the battered, lopsided dresser huddled beside the door like a poor relation. Above it on a pale pink ribbon hung a gingerbread heart; someone must have bought it years ago at a fair, the icing had peeled off all over. In the middle of the room there was a table with a wax tablecloth and a petroleum lamp with a green shade.

"But there's electric, too!" My mother boasted, and to show me she was telling the truth, she put the light—hanging on a black wire—on for a moment. "It's a good invention," she noted practically, "but it ain't for us poor folk. It's very dear, we don't use it much."

I didn't understand why she was using the plural.

"Someone else live here?" I asked.

"Only Manci now," she replied. "Before, I had someone else rentin' a bed, too. Paid four pengős a month, imagine! Though he only slept in the kitchen on the camp bed. Good man, he was, Antal. That was his name. But, anyway," sighed my mother, "I had to send him away on account of you."

"Me? Why?"

"Where was you going to sleep? Manci rents the bed and Antal, like I says, slept in the kitchen."

"What about you?"

"On the floor here. Now I'll sleep in the kitchen, an' you can sleep here in the room."

"With Manci?"

I could feel myself blushing, but my mother didn't notice.

"She's a good girl, Manci. Got a good heart. She didn't mind. If she don't come by the last tram, you can have the bed."

"The bed?"

My heart beat faster. I had never slept in a bed before.

"It's New Year's Eve, she probably ain't comin' home."

"She stay out often?" I ventured.

"When she's got a late client. You know, she's one of *them* girls, but long as she pays, what business is that of mine? Now hang on, I'd better go before your supper burns. Know what I've made you?"

"What?"

My mother winked meaningfully.

"*Székelygulyás.*"

My mouth watered. If I hadn't feared for my rep, I might have yelled for joy. As it was, I merely said, manfully:

"Not bad."

But when my mother went out of the room, I did a handstand in joy, and not just metaphorically, but actually. Well blow me down, I said to myself, I'd never have thought it. I get to sleep in a bed and get *székelygulyás* for supper. If I wrote them at home, the boys would think I was telling tales.

The Gypsy music drifted up from the tavern. They were playing some sad, melancholy tune, but it seemed terribly cheerful to me. I could barely wait till my mother finally called:

"Come on then, Béla, your supper's ready."

The *székelygulyás* was already steaming away on the kitchen table in the big metal pot, and my mother put a portion in front of me so large it would have been enough for Mr Rozi—and there was pretty much no one on earth who could eat more than he could.

I started sweating, I ate so hard. My God, what a *székelygulyás* that was! Pools of soured cream floated on top, the soft tenderloin melted in my mouth, and the cabbage—Lord, what cabbage! You could tell my mother had cooked it that morning, or perhaps even the night before, because only when you cook it twice can cabbage be that good. I was moved: for the rich, food goes only to their stomachs, but for the poor—it goes to their hearts. I stole a glance at my mother. She can't be too bad, I thought. Here was that good old Antal and she sent him away from one day to the next so her jailbird son would have somewhere to rest his head. And she makes *székelygulyás* for supper when she has no more than twenty fillérs. I leant low over my plate so my mother wouldn't see my emotion.

"How much did this *székelygulyás* cost, then?" I asked matter-of-factly.

"How much?" My mother started calculating. "Well, I paid eighty fillérs for the meat, ten for the cabbage, sixteen for the cream, and then there's that bit of lard and herbs and so on. I don't know, probably one pengő ten for the lot."

"That's a lot," I noted.

My mother didn't reply, but I could see she enjoyed the acknowledgement. But that wasn't why I'd said it. I had a little diary that Scarecrow had given me to write down the names of anyone who was misbehaving in school. I took it out, pulled a little pencil from the side and started writing very seriously. I still have that little diary, and this is what I wrote under "Outgoings" in the "Owed to" column: "31 Dec. 1927. Mother, one portion *székelygulyás*, 55 fillérs."

"What you writin'?" my mother asked.

"The price of supper."

"What for?"

"To keep accounts. 'Cause I'm going to pay you back, down to the last fillér. You'll see, I'll be better than old Antal."

And I proceeded to add in my little notebook: "Mother, one month's rent 5 pengős."

The way my mother looked at me, I thought at first she didn't understand. But she did. Her eyes went all moist, and she turned away.

"It's nice of you to think of it," she said a little hoarsely, "but forget all that scribblin'. You ain't a stranger here."

I, too, turned away, because those few words "you ain't a stranger here" stuck in my throat like a bone. I thought of Istvány. Maybe one day he, too, would come up to Pest, and we'd meet in the street, and he'd ask: "Where you living, Béla?" "Where?" I'd say, "At my muther's." I'd say it offhand, as if it were the most natural thing in the world. "I ain't a stranger no more, Istvány."

My mother was studying her empty plate, and I the water pipe, from which a lethargic drop would—at regular intervals—fall into the crooked sink. You could still hear Gypsy music from below. They were playing a familiar tune, and it was good to hear it. My mother leant her head slightly to one side and hummed casually.

> *A little room—who needs more?*
> *Darling, we'll fit, I'm sure,*
> *Won't we? We'll never fear*
> *God'll bless our poor lives there.*

The violin wailed, the zither chuckled, the flute whispered, and the double bass grumbled away. It was warm in the kitchen, the excellent meal spread through me like a blessing and my eyelids grew heavy. I leant back, satisfied.

"I ain't a stranger no more, Istvány."

All of a sudden my mother said:

"There's somethin' important I want to say to you, Béla."

"Yes? Go on."

My mother crossed her hands over her belly, as poor women do when they have something important to say.

"I got you a position in a hotel."

"Hotel?" I looked at her in surprise. "What for?"

"To work," she replied. "It's a good position, we're very lucky. I know the head porter, been washing for him for years. Well, when I got that letter from the Schoolmaster, I went to him and said, read this, sir, read this. The Schoolmaster wrote about my son that he's going to be somebody, says it right there, look. And I thought, maybe, seeing as how he's coming to Pest, maybe you could get him a place at the hotel, sir. I ain't asking for no favours, sir, I said, I'd do your washing for free long as he's there. He liked that, the little man. He didn't show it, though, 'cause that's his way. He kept going on about this and that instead, how it ain't that simple, but in the end he said: all right, then, Anna, I'll take a look at him. So we're going to the hotel tomorrow for you to show off all your studyin', so you don't make a fool of me."

"Don't worry," I said curtly, manfully, and tried to look impassive, because the news had got me very excited.

And I was curious about this letter from the Schoolmaster, too. All he'd said to me was that he'd sent a telegram; he never said he'd sent my mother a letter as well. Did he really write that I'd be somebody? My palms sweated with pride.

"What'll I do there, in this hotel?"

"You'll be a boy."

"What's that, then?"

"It's a… boy. You know. That's what they call 'em. They got these red uniforms and the fancy people send 'em to and fro."

"And what's one of them paid, then?"

"Nothing," she explained. "'Cause you have to be apprenticed four years and the hotel don't pay apprentices. But there's some very fine ladies and gentlemen that live there, and the head porter says they tip like anything. Sometimes, he says, you can make two or three pengős a day, but maybe he was talking big on account of the free washing."

I started counting in my head. If the head porter said a boy like that earned two or three pengős a day, then he might actually make one or two, and that would be fifty pengős a month. That's a lot; too much, I thought warily. There must be something wrong about all this. I asked:

"What hours do you work at this hotel, then?"

"The usual," my mother said, "morning till night."

There, I said to myself. So that's it.

"Can't do it," I said.

"Can't do it?" my mother looked at me in shock. "Why not?"

"'Cause I have to go to school."

"The hell you do. You're gone fourteen, you've finished primary, the law says you're fine."

"The rich make the laws," I said knowingly. "And us poor stay poor if we don't learn."

"You've learnt enough. The Schoolmaster's very pleased with you."

"Oh," I shrugged, "that's nothing. Take world history. What did we learn of that? It was all Hungarian history we did. And that's good, too, don't get me wrong, but the real thing is world history; that's how you find out what goes on in the world and why, don't you? Then there's natural history. Never learnt that, neither. But that's what teaches you how the world is made, and without it you just sit there on the tram like an idiot, not knowing what makes it go with no engine. And languages! I'm going to learn lots of languages, 'cause the Schoolmaster says that with Hungarian, you only get as far as the border, and beyond that, it's no use speaking it, there ain't no one to understand."

"So what?" smiled my mother. "You don't want to go abroad."

"Don't I!" I blurted out. "I want to see the whole world! God didn't make it for people not to see it. You ever been abroad?"

"Me?" my mother laughed. "Why would I have been abroad?"

"Well, ain't you curious?"

"'Bout what?"

"The world. It's such an amazing place! D'you have any idea of all the things out there in the world? In Venice, they say, even them great marble palaces are built on piles."

"What?"

"Piles. Because, believe it or not, there's rivers in the streets, and you've got to take a boat just to go to the shops. And in Paris there's a tower as high as Gellért Hill. I forget what it's called but it's made of steel, and it's so big there's even inns on it. And America! You heard of them hundred-storey palaces? And them incredible countries where the *Arabian Nights* is set? And Africa? And the jungle, where they hunt tigers? Well, I want to see all that—all of it. I want to meet all the peoples, the yellow ones and the black ones, and the copper-skinned Indians. And the seas. The Black Sea that our Danube flows into, and the China Sea, where they got them wild typhoons. D'you know what that is, a typhoon?"

"Look here, Béla," my mother said, somewhat impatiently. "That's all very well and good, you bein' so um… what's the word, anyway you knowin' everythin' and wantin' to see everythin'. But your mother's poor, and… you get me."

"You think I don't want to work?" I protested. "I worked for the old woman like a slave. And I don't want nothing different now. All I'm saying is I want work that I can do and go to school besides."

"There ain't no work like that."

"'Course there is! There's all them newspaper boys. I saw them all over the street. Why couldn't I do that? I could go to school in the morning, and then I could sell papers till late at night."

"You'd starve."

"Well, I'd do something else, then."

"Like what, exactly?"

That I couldn't say. My mother smiled.

"That's all crazy talk," she said. "If you're so smart, why don't you use your head? You'll be in the best hotel in the country, and if you work hard, in fifteen or twenty years, you could be head porter."

"But I don't *want* to be head porter, don't you understand?"

"What *do* you want to be, then, prime minister?"

"I don't know yet," I replied hesitantly, like someone who's considered the question but hasn't yet come to a decision. "That depends on what sort of a government Hungary'll have. Because I'd never be prime minister for this lot, not if they paid me ten pengős a day. They're all a bunch of thieves, they are, a bunch of thieving gentlemen is how the Schoolmaster said it, and the poor folk won't stand for it much longer."

My mother looked at me, horrified.

"What you sayin', child?" she shook her head. "Was he a Commernist, that Schoolmaster of yours?"

All we village children knew about "commernists" was that they were mainly Jews whose primary occupation was betraying the fatherland.

"How could you say such a thing?" I snapped. "The Schoolmaster ain't a Jew."

"No, he ain't a Jew," my mother grumbled. "He's worse. He's a drunk, always was. And he leads all them poor dumb children astray, I don't know how the ground don't swallow him up. He's a Commernist, I'm tellin' you, and you're talking like one too. But there won't be no Commernism in my house. I make my livin' decently, and so will you, or I'll wring your neck. We're going to that hotel tomorrow, and I don't want to hear any more of that talk out of you."

With that, it seemed, she considered the subject closed. She stood up, cleared the table, and started doing the dishes.

I hated her again the way I had when I was a little child. The Schoolmaster was, for me, everything fine and good in life, and she, who had so belittled him, just the opposite. She didn't so much as look at me for eight years, I said to myself, didn't even send me a ragged pair of shoes so I wouldn't freeze my feet off, and now she wants me to waste my mind for the two or three pengős some bloody head porter had dangled in front of her.

"Well, I ain't going to that hotel," I declared with impertinent calm, determined not to show how het up I was.

My mother turned around so sharply the wet plate almost flew out of her hand.

"Well what *do* you mean to do, then?" she cried. "Steal?"

"I ain't no thief," I grumbled.

"Is that right?" she asked with a malicious smile. "Ain't me they locked up for stealing."

That was all I needed. I jumped up.

"Don't you go calling me a thief, or..."

My mother put the plate down and came over with menacing slowness. "Or what?" she said, and her deep-set, small black eyes fixed on me angrily.

The blood went to my head.

"You're one to go calling the Schoolmaster a Commernist!" I bawled. "He was better to me than my own mother. I could have dropped dead as far as *you* was concerned."

"If only," she barked, and her great bony hand caught my arm. I think she meant to strike me, but she merely pushed me away. "Go to your room," she screamed, "or I'll break your neck the first night!"

Well, I wasn't going to wait around for that. I went to the room, slamming the door good and hard behind me so she'd see that she was dealing with a man, who would retreat if he had to, but not shirk from a fight.

"Commernist!" she screamed after me, mumbling something else I didn't catch.

There was silence—a suffocating, hostile silence. I stood in the middle of the room in the "family home" and suddenly caught myself yearning to be back at that despicable old woman's with the seven other little bastard boys.

I swore horribly. I cursed my mother and the whole "thieving world" that conspired against the children of the poor, and my overheated imagination fabricated wild plans, each more extreme than the last. I decided to run away. As to where, I had no clue, and didn't care. I just had to get away from here, I told myself, and then whatever happened would happen.

"What you burning that expensive petroleum for?" my mother called in. "Go to bed!"

I started taking my clothes off. That sounds natural enough, but not for someone used to sleeping fully clothed in winter. With the exception of the night before my journey, I hadn't undressed in almost three months. I now took off everything, like we used to do during heatwaves in the village, and climbed, bare naked, under the good warm covers.

It was the first time in my life I'd lain in a bed. How often I'd dreamt of this on the long winter nights when I'd wake in the wet straw to the chattering of my teeth. But I couldn't enjoy it. Under the warm covers, I realized that I wasn't going to run away, because after all, where could I go, especially now, in winter, when I had no one and nothing in the world, not even a pair of damned trousers. Male pride or no male pride, the salt tears started flowing from my eyes, and I fell asleep like an infant crying himself slowly to sleep.

I woke to terrible swearing. A hysterical girl was pushing and shoving in the doorway, curses pouring out of her like brown filth from a broken sewer. Her hair was bright yellow, her face painted, and the lipstick on her flapping mouth all smeared. My mother was standing in front of her, barefoot and in pyjamas, trying to calm her down.

"Manci, dear," she kept repeating. "How was I supposed to know you'd be home on New Year's?"

"New Year's or no New Year's," bawled the girl, "the bed's mine and I ain't paying good money for you to lay your dirty son in it!"

She suddenly tottered and hiccoughed. Only now did I see she was drunk.

"Should I make some coffee?" my mother asked meekly.

"To hell with your coffee!" bellowed the girl. "That's it, I'm givin' notice."

"But look, Mancika," my mother tried again, but Mancika simply shoved her out into the kitchen and slammed the door in her face.

I would have jumped out of bed long before had I not been naked, but as it was, I didn't know what to do. So I closed my eyes and lay still as if I was sleeping. Then there was a whiff of stale alcohol and the girl grabbed me by the shoulders.

"Get the hell out of my bed," she shouted, "or you'll be sorry."

"But I ain't got no clothes on," I said dumbly.

"So? Nothing I ain't seen before."

There was nothing else I could do; I jumped out of bed. But in my fright, I couldn't find my clothes and ran about looking for them desperately.

I suddenly felt the drunk girl looking at me. She wasn't looking at me the way you look at a child, but… I didn't yet quite know how, myself. A strange, panicky anxiety came over me. I climbed quickly into my trousers and threw on my shirt and waistcoat and, with my back to the girl, stood before the window. It was dark outside, the glass mirrored the lighted room, and I could see her starting to undress. I was an excitable young man, and used to lose my cool if the wind so much as caught a girl's skirt, but now that I was watching this Manci undress I felt nothing but cold, frightened revulsion.

I turned away. I heard her climb into bed and later saw her take a big swig from a bottle of *pálinka*. Then she spread a newspaper out before her, though only she knew why, because she certainly wasn't reading it. She crossed her arms under her head and stared at the ceiling, immobile. You could still hear the Gypsy music from downstairs.

"Music ain't bad," she mused.

I didn't reply. There was silence for a while.

"Poor Gypsies," she piped up. "They've got it bad too. Before, people would go around stickin' banknotes on their foreheads, and now they're sleepin' in the park. And that old bitch that owns the bar comes to 'em and says, 'Why don't you come and play at my place, son?' 'Yes, ma'am!' says the poor Gypsy. 'How much do you pay?' 'Pay? How could I pay?' the old tart gasps. 'It's only a little tavern, son, it don't make any money. I just saw you there, sleeping on the bench and all, and thought you could come sleep in the bar. There'd be a bit of food in it for you.' That's how she gets her Gypsies, the slut. Then, if one of them turns out handsome, she pounces like a hawk and drags him into her bed. What you standing there like a mute for?" she snapped at me. "Cat got your tongue?"

"What's with your manners?" my mother called in from the kitchen, "Why don't you answer Manci when she's talkin' to you?"

But Manci was in a conciliatory mood.

"Let him be," she said. "Shakes 'em up, Pest, kid like him. I remember how frightened I was when I came up from my village. Oh well," she sighed. "Come in, then, Anna, there's still a bit left in the bottle."

My mother didn't need asking twice. She was in such a hurry that she was still tying her underskirts, which she'd thrown over her shirt in the dark, as she walked. Manci handed her the bottle of *pálinka*.

"Cheers!"

My mother lifted the bottle.

"Happy New Year, Manci dear!"

Manci looked at her watch.

"Ain't New Year's yet," she said. "And maybe there'll never be another happy one anyway. It's a dog's life, this, a dog's life."

"What's wrong?" enquired my mother. "Why you home on New Year's Eve?"

"What's wrong?" Manci shrugged. "You can't make a decent living from November on, on account of Christmas, 'cause anyone with money goes and spends it all on presents. So then you're waiting for New Year's like nothin' else. And then this happens!"

She laughed a nasty, sick laugh.

"Why, what's happened?"

"What?" Manci's laughter turned to tears. She buried her head in the pillow and sobbed: "It's my time of the month!"

My mother just stood there next to her, helpless, as if she knew that there was no comfort for a blow like this.

"It ain't no life, bein' poor," she said softly and she, too, started crying.

Then the bells rang out, the violin downstairs played a crescendo, and there was the sound of wild cries—crazy shrieks from the women and hoarse, wine-soaked laughter from the men.

"Happy New Year!" they croaked. "Happy New Year!"

Well—I thought—this year's off to a damn fine start!

2

IN THE MORNING, I WAS WOKEN by my mother shaking me by the shoulder.

"Get up, will you!" she said, "We've got to go."

As to where, she didn't say and I didn't ask. I knew, in any case. It was a cold, sober, winter morning and I was cold and sober too. I thought of my plans—now up in smoke—the way peasants think of hail; it's a shame, of course, but what can you do? I remembered that bitter autumn morning when the old woman had called me a gallows rat because I wanted to go to school. But I'd outsmarted her in the end, I consoled myself, and I'd outsmart my mother, too. Knowledge, like bread, was hard to come by for a poor boy. If you really wanted it, you had to steal it.

I clambered up. There was a liverish half-light in the room. Manci was still asleep. The noise she made as she slept sounded like she was sawing wood. As if she were trying to cut bits of wood out of her throat so she could exhale. Outside, it had stopped snowing. It ain't no life, bein' poor, I thought.

I went out into the kitchen and washed. My mother put a glass of milk and a thick slice of bread in front of me. The bread wasn't fresh, though she'd just cut it, but I wasn't surprised by that. I knew that the poor didn't buy fresh bread—it was too good, you ate it up too quickly. But I was surprised by the milk. Till then, I had only known milk you got from a cow or a goat. This was something else. It had been invented for us poor by the upper classes. It was called skimmed milk, but it should really have been called milkless milk instead. It was more grey in colour than white, and tasted more like water than milk. Before I drank it, I took out my little notebook and entered it—along with the bread—in the "Owed to" column. I deliberately wrote it in front of my mother, but not the way I had the stew the night before. That had been from the heart; this was nothing but bile. I wanted to show my mother that ours was a purely business relationship: and her food was merely an advance, not a gift.

My mother didn't say anything. She put on her faded brown coat, tied the threadbare black kerchief on her head and took the duvet and pillows off the camp bed, tying them up in the sheets. I had slept on the floor, but I too had had a duvet and some pillows. My mother took those and tied them up in a sheet, too. She brought the bundle out into the kitchen and handed it to me.

"Take this," she said. "I'll take the other."

I was curious as to why we were taking our bedclothes to the hotel, but I didn't ask in case she thought I was ready to make peace.

We descended the narrow twisting stairs in silence. The dirty walls, eaten away by saltpetre, were black with graffitied comments. These highly informative little musings were primarily concerned with the relations between men and women, with an especial focus on their private parts, which the authors would illustrate, mostly beside the text, to avoid any danger of misunderstandings. These inscriptions were very varied indeed, and even included some that were quite poetic. On the third floor, I recall, someone had written "18th May 1926—We were happy" under a heart with an arrow through it. But the residents also took an interest in politics. On the wall of the second-floor toilet, someone had made a somewhat indecent suggestion to our Regent. Beside that instruction, another like-minded visitor had written in large, scrappy letters: "Mine too!!!" But the most common were phrases like: "Down with the exploiters!" "Long live organized labour!" "Capitalists, we're coming for you!" One folksy lyricist had characterized the Prime Minister thus, between the first and second floors:

> Coach rumbling at a fair old whack
> István Bethlen sitting in the back,
> Thinks the people love him true
> Love him true, so true,
> But the hell we do, the hell we do.

When we got down to the ground floor, my mother speeded up. But as she was trying to sneak past Herr Hausmeister's flat, the door sprang open and a deep male voice called after her:

"Not so fast, miss."

My mother blushed scarlet.

"Happy New Year," she muttered awkwardly and gave my sleeve a jerk. "Say hello to Herr Hausmeister, like a good boy."

"Good morning," I said.

But Herr Hausmeister returned neither our "Happy New Year" nor the "Good morning". He just stood in the doorway like some wrathful god and stared at my mother. He was an enormous Schwab with gingery-blond hair and blue eyes. His hard, red, pitted face was covered with a spider's web of blue veins, and his large nose, with its taut nostrils, showed that he liked a drink or two. He must have been in the middle of breakfast, because his moustache was dripping coffee and he was digging around in his mouth with his beetroot-stained index finger. When he had finally unseated the little morsel of food, he said, just like that:

"Well? What about that rent, then?"

My mother pointed to our bundles.

"We're just off to the pawnshop now."

"Didn't ask where you were going," he grunted. "I asked about the rent."

"All them railway fares took it, you see," my mother lamented. "I had to fetch the boy and now we won't have nothin' to cover ourselves with in the cold, I'm just off to hock the covers, as you can see. I'm a good tenant, you know that, I always pay regular."

"Were!" Herr Hausmeister replied curtly. "You're two months behind."

"Is it my fault I was laid up in hospital for six weeks? I almost died of that pneumonia, and I ought to be restin' even now and eatin' well, the doctor said so. But I keep working from morning till night like a dog to pay that blessed rent. What more can I do? Tell me! You ain't lackin' all Christian feeling, are you?"

But Herr Hausmeister wasn't interested in religious debates. He started poking around his teeth again with his index finger. Then he merely said:

"There's always some excuse with you lot."

There was silence. My mother didn't respond. I could see that she really wanted to go, but she didn't dare, waiting for the all-powerful man to give her the go-ahead.

"All I'm saying is," he finally declared ominously, "bring me that money, otherwise I'll have you thrown out on your ear, like that! Understood?"

"Yes, sir," my mother replied humbly and pulled on the sleeve of my jacket. "Come on, Béla."

We had to walk a good three quarters of an hour to get to the pawnshop, because needless to say we didn't have money for the tram. It being a holiday, the pawnshop was closed, and I thought we'd dragged ourselves there in vain. But my mother went inside the building, cut across the yard and rang the bell of a ground-floor flat.

A fish-faced little old man opened the door. His eyes protruded like a carp's, and his big bald head nodded left and right as if he were constantly protesting against something.

"Good morning, sir," my mother said with a humility of which only poor Hungarian women are capable when addressing their social superiors.

Fish-face nodded, but didn't say anything. He acted like a deaf mute. He turned on his heels without a word as if we weren't even there and padded through the dark little entranceway that smelt of onions, towards a door. We followed him silently with our bundles.

The door opened into the pawnshop. It was a pathetic little pawnshop, no more than one room. The old man put on the light, popped a pair of pince-nez tied with string onto the tip of his nose and gestured, still not deigning to say a word to us, for us to open the bundles. He looked at the two eiderdowns and four pillows, feeling them for a good while before finally honouring us with a high, reedy whine:

"Three pengős."

"For the lot?" my mother asked in fright.

"No, for each feather individually."

My mother didn't reply, merely sighing. Then she took off her coat. "How much would you give me for that?"

"Nothing."

"Why?" my mother said in surprise. "It's a good warm coat, this."

"That's as may be," Fish-face replied, "but only the most elegant of society ladies could carry it off, and they don't much shop with me."

My mother put her coat on and then just stood there, pensive, not knowing what to do.

"Will there be anything else?" the old man asked impatiently.

My mother said neither yes or no; I could see she was debating heavily with herself. Finally, she turned around, took off the little cross on the thin gold chain from around her neck, and—as if she wanted merely to wipe her mouth—gave it a fleeting, awkward kiss. Then she laid it down before Fish-face.

"Two," he said. "Five in total."

My mother went up closer and, reluctantly, quietly, almost whispering, she said:

"I'm in a real bind. Please."

"Six," he shrugged, and dug around in his pockets for the silver pengős.

My mother only dared count them once we were out on the street.

"Six pengős!" she said more to herself than to me. "What am I supposed to do with that? The rent's twenty and we owe forty. Mother of God, what we going to do?"

That, of course, I couldn't say. We walked in silence towards the tram stop. It was bitterly cold and the snow crunched underfoot like glass.

"It'll be hard at night without the covers," my mother said. "That old crook only gave us a pengő each for 'em. And they was so good for sleeping in!"

"Yeah, very good," I assented quietly.

A few stray flakes of snow drifted in the air. The sky was low, the horizon milky white. My mother stared into the distance.

"Still, it's the cross I'm sorry about," she said. "Belonged to my grandmother, then my mother." She sighed. "Looks like even the Lord forsakes the poor."

She didn't look at me and I didn't look at her.

"It was a fine cross," I said.

I felt so sorry for her at that moment that I'd have complimented her overcoat, the one Fish-face had mocked. It felt almost good to catch her arm when she slipped on the icy road. But she, poor thing, was upset even with the weather.

"Filthy weather!" she grumbled. "Colder'n hell."

"It's warm in hell," I said, with a knowing air. "No need for covers there!"

My mother gave a weak smile.

"Who knows, maybe we'd be better off!"

The tram came, we got on. The car was almost empty. My mother sat by the window, looking down, staring at her shoes. I watched her in the cold morning light. Only now did I see how poorly she was. Of course, I thought, her pneumonia. It's what Berci had died of in the autumn. She ought to be eating well. Resting.

"Muther!" I said.

I hadn't said that word in eight years; it sounded strange. It caught my mother's ear as well.

"What is it?"

"If they take me at that hotel, then…" I wanted to stop, but I had no choice now but to continue. "Then," I stuttered, "then I'll get that cross back for you 'cause it ain't for no other woman to wear."

My mother gave me a strange look and went back to staring at her shoes. I could see her lips were trembling.

"It was your great-grandmother's," she said. "Then your grandmother's. They'll be prayin' for you up in heaven."

Now I, too, took to staring at my shoes. The tram sped on. We were silent for a long time.

"You ain't a bad kid," my mother said. "Life's bad. Bein' poor."

"Yeah, it is," I nodded, and that was the last thing we said.

The hotel was in Mária Valéria utca, where we'd seen all those motor cars, furs and jewels the night before. My mother looked upon this temple of the rich with an almost religious sense of awe.

"Pretty, ain't it?"

"Very pretty," I emphasized, to please her.

We were waiting around in front of the entrance because the porter was not at his post. Through the glass, I looked at the huge marble columns of the lobby, the carpets, chandeliers and enormous armchairs, and I couldn't help thinking once more of the *Fairy Tales*.

"What you loitering here for?" said a porter dressed like a general, who seemed to have appeared from nowhere. He had said the same thing as the policeman on the bridge, and even his voice was similar, or at least it seemed that way to me. He was a bony, clean-shaven man of around forty, very tall, very thin and very strict.

"Begging you pardon," my mother said with an awkward bow, "we've come to talk to the head porter."

"What's it regardin'?" he asked suspiciously.

"A job," my mother replied. "For the boy, sir."

The porter looked at me. I could see, or at least I thought I could, that he thought the idea ridiculous: such a ragged little boy in such a fine, grand hotel. But all he said was:

"He didn't say anything to me. Best write him about it."

"But, begging your pardon, sir," my mother said anxiously, "the head porter said…"

What the head porter had said the porter never found out. For at that moment a thickset little man appeared behind the glass door, at the sight of whom the porter's entire manner was completely transformed. His surly face was filled with a sickly-sweet smile, and he simply dripped goodwill as he yanked open the door. Meanwhile he quietly scolded my mother:

"On your way, then!"

The thickset little man came through the door, with a servant behind him carrying his luggage. The stern porter addressed the short, ugly, thick little man with the same humility with which my mother had recently addressed him.

"Yes, sir, I'll fetch the car," he mumbled and ran off, with the man's servant, for the car.

My mother stopped a few steps away.

"What do we do now?" she asked desperately, as if I had any advice to give her. She was on the verge of tears in her helplessness. "Oh, God," she moaned, "one of them black cats must've crossed my path. And we need the money so bad, you can see the state we're in."

Indeed I could. I saw the state we were in, all right! Everyone treated the poor thing like a rag. And why? Because she was poor? Had Our Lord been any richer? My hands clenched into fists.

"Come with me," I said with that inexplicable conviction I always had in moments of action.

"Where?" she asked in surprise.

"Just come along!"

I could see that the porter was occupied behind the car, strapping on the luggage with the servant. I grabbed my mother's arm and whisked her into the hotel. She looked left and right in alarm in the vast, brightly lit lobby.

"My God," she whispered. "How we goin' to find him here?"

"We'll ask around," I said, with that inexplicable conviction. "Look, here comes someone now."

A boy in a scarlet uniform rushed towards us. He was a blond boy with a girlish face; he couldn't have been much more than a year older than me.

"Where d'you think you're going?" he said in a voice that reminded me of the policeman's.

My mother smiled at him nicely.

"We'd like to talk to the head porter, if you please, young man."

"Here?"

The boy looked at us as if we'd wandered into a holy sanctuary which we were now desecrating with our presence.

"Where could we find him?" my mother asked, just as nicely.

"Not here," the boy said curtly. "Please leave."

My mother was all set to leave, but then I stepped forward. I couldn't restrain myself any longer. Was even this snotty little kid going to humiliate my mother? I looked him straight in the eye.

"We ain't going nowhere," I said, ready for a fight. "And don't you come so high and mighty with us on account of your fancy red trousers!"

The boy's face went redder than his trousers. Even his voice broke in anger as he barked:

"Get going, or—"

"What's going on?" said another boy in a red uniform behind us.

The boy with the girlish face pointed at me.

"He's being insolent," he said. "I was just going to report him!"

My mother was pulling at my sleeve, but by this point, I was no longer frightened of anything.

"We want to talk to the head porter," I said stubbornly. "And he was being uppity with my mother."

The other boy must have been about seventeen. He was prematurely aged, short, quiet, and grave. He listened to us attentively, without interrupting.

"Come this way," he said in a calm, matter-of-fact voice, and gestured to the first boy that he would take it from there. The first boy shrugged angrily and left. We followed the short, grave boy silently.

We didn't know where he was taking us. He cut across the lobby with us and took us down a set of stairs into some sort of basement.

"Where you takin' us?" my mother asked timidly.

"To the head porter," replied the boy. "Isn't that what you wanted?"

"Oh yes," my mother sighed, relieved, and her eyes filled with tears of thanks. "Thank you for your kindness, young man."

"You're welcome," said the boy, my mother's humility apparently making him uncomfortable. "I'm sorry," he added later. "I'm very sorry that snot-nosed…" He didn't finish the sentence, and just shrugged instead. "They're all like that. Bicyclists by nature, the lot of them."

"What?" asked my mother.

"Bicyclists," the boy repeated. "They bow up and stomp down. It's the old Hungarian way."

His voice was colourless and his face so expressionless as he talked it was as if he'd been carved out of wood. But his eyes were something else. He must have seen his share of troubles, I thought.

The fact that he treated us like human beings put my mother somewhat at her ease. She recounted, in a roundabout way, why we'd come. The boy listened to her seriously.

"There is an opening," he said at last. "They just let a boy go the other day. He was a fine boy, but one of the guests made a complaint about him." He turned to my mother. "An affair involving a lady. Her Excellency." He said "Her Excellency" with the same sense of disgust as if he'd bitten into a rotten egg. Then he looked at me and added quietly, "You've got to be very careful round here."

I didn't quite understand what he was talking about, but I didn't dare ask, because I was afraid he'd think me a yokel. Besides, the boy had now stopped before a door.

"I'll let him know," he said. "Please wait here."

A few minutes later, he emerged with the head porter. The head porter was like a giant baby someone had dressed in a Santa Claus costume for a laugh. His big belly was protuberant in his gold-fringed uniform, and he had a great, old man's beard, but his face was like an infant's. A pair of tiny, light-blue eyes peeked out of that face, and a tiny nose; his skin was as pink as if he'd been born that very day, not ten minutes before.

"Morning, Anna," he said. "What brings you here?"

"I've brought the boy, sir."

Santa Claus looked at me.

"Yes," he said. That was all he said.

There was an awkward silence.

"Will you show him to the gentlemen?" my mother asked anxiously at last.

The head porter pointed at me.

"Like *that*?"

I didn't understand what he meant by that "*that*", and clearly my mother didn't either.

"I don't understand, sir, I'm sorry," she admitted finally.

"Don't you?" said the head porter. "Just look at the boy. He's a bundle of rags. The office'd think I'd picked up a vagrant off the street. Buy him a suit and then we can talk."

"But sir," my mother blurted out, "where would I get the money for that?"

This, however, did not interest the head porter. He looked at his watch.

"I've got to go now," he said, and headed off. "Come and see me again sometime. God bless."

We looked at each other, but said nothing. We wandered silently around the basement. All of a sudden, we came face to face with the

second boy in the scarlet uniform. We must have looked pretty despond-
ent, because he immediately asked:

"Something wrong?"

"And how!" my mother complained. "The head porter says the boy's
ragged and he can't show him to the gentlemen like this."

"Doesn't he have any other clothes?"

"No," my mother sighed.

The boy took a good look at me and said:

"My clothes would fit him just fine. I'll lend them to you."

"You will?" my mother said.

"'Course," the boy said lightly. "I have to wear this thing, anyway,"
he said, pointing with revulsion to his uniform. "Wait for me here," he
said, and gestured to me to follow him.

He led me into a large changing room. The walls were lined with
grey tin lockers. He opened one of them and took out his civilian
clothes.

"You're very kind, sir," I said shyly, and I could feel myself blush.

"Don't call me sir," he replied. "I'm a proletarian just like you. Call
me Elemér."

"I'm Béla."

We shook hands. I was dying to know what a "proletarian" was, but
I didn't dare reveal my ignorance. I started undressing silently.

"Don't you have trousers, either?" he asked in surprise.

I shrugged.

"It ain't so cold."

Elemér didn't reply, but his eyes flashed strangely. He stood and
stared in silence for a while, and then said quietly:

"And that lot up there think things can go on like this?"

"Yes," I nodded, because now I *did* know what he was talking about.
Our eyes met. We would have been friends back home, I thought.

Elemér removed his waistcoat, then his shirt, and handed them to me.

"Put these on, too."

"What about you?"

"Can't see it under the uniform. Can you tie a tie?"

"Never had one," I admitted.

He took his tie out of the locker and tied it under my collar. Then he looked me over again.

"Those shoes won't do, either," he said.

This really did surprise me.

"They're very good shoes, those," I said, "they were the Schoolmaster's."

"So I see," said Elemér. "But you'd best put mine on anyway."

We swapped shoes, and he took me over to the mirror. I couldn't believe my eyes. In his nice blue suit, I looked like a young gentleman.

My mother, too, was surprised when she saw me.

"Whew!" she said, her eyes glittering beautifully. "Bless my soul, I'd never have known you!"

Even the head porter was pleased with me.

"So you knew them, eh?" he asked Elemér, when he found out I'd got the clothes from him.

"Never seen us before in his life," my mother replied and looked gratefully at Elemér. "He's a real gent, he is, to the bone."

"Very well," said the head porter. "I'll talk to the Major."

"The Major's the head of personnel," Elemér told us quietly once the head porter had left. "He's as White as the driven snow, if you get my drift. Prays to Mussolini every night before bed."

I didn't understand that, either, but I could have sworn it was true. This Elemér told it like it was.

We waited a long time for the head porter, at least an hour. It was only later I found out that this stern Santa Claus was as terrified of the Major as we were of him, and it was only the thought of the free washing that had steeled him to the task.

Finally, I too was introduced into the presence of the Major. He sat behind a big desk and looked at me in a way that gave me the impression that, just to be on the safe side, he was about to drill a hole in my skull. He was a dry, spare man, whose mouth curved down in constant revulsion. He wore a round glass in his right eye, the kind you found on pocket watches. Why? I wondered to myself. His hair, parted in the middle, stuck glittering to his scalp. It must once have been black, but now it looked more green from all the dye. His moustache, too, was also green, and his face, too—or at least it seemed that way to me.

I was standing to attention, my hands on the seams of my trousers as per regulation. The head porter was also standing to attention. All that was missing was the beating of drums.

The Major looked at me for what seemed like an eternity, like a coper looking over a horse. Then he took the watch glass off his eye and began to talk in bursts.

"Name?"

I told him my name.

"Date of birth?"

I told him that, too.

"Father's trade?"

That I couldn't tell him. I could feel myself blushing. There was an unbearable silence.

In the end, it was the head porter who saved the day.

"He's dead, sir," he said with an apologetic smile.

"Let the boy speak!" the Major rebuked him.

"Yes, sir!"

"How many years of schooling have you got?"

"Six."

"Do you have your reports?"

"Yes, sir."

I handed them over. The Major put the watch glass to his eye again and started studying my reports. To dispel all doubt, I said crisply:

"Never got a 'C' in my life, sir."

The Major smiled faintly. Drop dead, I thought to myself.

"Were you a cadet?"

"Yes, sir. Won a prize for marksmanship."

He liked that, I could tell. He turned to the head porter.

"So you know his mother well?"

"Yes, Major. She's poor, but respectable."

"I can see she dresses her son properly," the Major said, and then added cantankerously: "Different sort of people in the villages, say what you will, not like the rabble here in Budapest!" He looked at me. "Just watch out and make sure these Red dogs don't get to you."

"Yes, sir!" I replied, though I hadn't the faintest clue what he was talking about.

"Very well, then," he said. "Go see the Chamber of Commerce with your mother about signing up as an apprentice. Kálmán'll explain."

"Yes, Major!" said the head porter and clicked his heels.

I, too, clicked mine. Our audience was over.

When my mother heard they'd taken me, she started crying with joy.

"No one's ever washed the way I'll wash for you!" she sniffed, and kissed the head porter's hand.

I changed back into my own clothes and we left. Elemér had explained where the staff exit was, it's true, but we got lost, what with all the stairs, and found ourselves again in the marble-pillared lobby. My mother was zigzagging to and fro in panic on the frighteningly soft carpets and kept bumping into people.

"Oh God, just get me out of here," she whispered, "or we'll ruin everything."

We made it safely out of the lobby, but the poor woman had forgotten to include the front doors in her supplications. The porter recognized us.

"How dare you sneak inside!" he screamed. "Where were you?"

My mother, instead of responding, ran for it as if she'd been caught stealing, and I, of course, ran after her.

"Don't let me see you here again, you rabble!" the porter yelled, and the passers-by looked at us as if we really had been up to no good.

I would have liked to jump at them and scratch out their judgemental eyes. Were we nothing but mangy dogs, that everyone treated us this way? I was haunted by shame and fled into the rainforest of my childhood fantasies. I was still fixated on my old plan of organizing the poor folk into gangs of grown-ups, the way we'd organized ourselves into gangs of children, and the thought that when I grew up, I would rob the rich of their treasure, like Sándor Rózsa, and distribute it to the poor. You have no idea what I'm capable of! I said to myself. I'll show you who you're dealing with! Once, long before, the Schoolmaster had told us the story of the Trojan Horse, and this now came back to me. Yes—I, too, would smuggle myself into the bastions of the enemy now, donning their uniform and serving them impassively, but one day I'd come bursting out of the Trojan Horse and then God help that world of gentlemen thieves, because that, that would be the Day of Judgement. Then there'd be cannon in Mária Valéria utca, and I would come, sword in hand, riding...

My mother laughed quietly. I looked at her in alarm. We were in Vilmos Császár út by now, and my mother, in her happiness, had forgotten all about her fright of not long before.

"My son the head porter!" she said with a girlish giggle and slapped me merrily on the shoulder. "I can just see you now, with your waxed moustache and your fancy uniform, people hardly able to get in and see you, and you gettin' one over all them poor folk."

"The only folk I'll be gettin' one over on is the rich folk!" I answered gravely. "And I won't spare them one bit, you can bet your life on that!"

"Aw," my mother shrugged, "That's what you think. By the time you're head porter, you'll think different, too. The poor always forget the poor if they make it among the rich, it's the way of the world."

It wasn't with sadness that she said this, but with a pensive smile; she even laughed. But then her coughing got hold of her. It was a nasty cough—poor Berci had used to cough like that. I'll buy her bacon as soon as I have money, I thought, good, thick bacon, and litres and litres of milk, and not that strained kind, but proper milk, full-fat milk to help fix her lungs.

"Well, slap me on the back, then, go on!" she said, because her coughing just wouldn't stop.

So I slapped her back, though I wanted to stroke it instead. I slapped her back and thought of the guns that would one day ring out in Mária Valéria utca. Then I would take her work-calloused hands, lead her into the marble-columned lobby and say, loud enough for all the upper-class gentlemen to hear: "Your finest room for my darling *muther*."

3

S o IT WAS THAT I WAS TRANSPOSED, overnight, from among the poorest to among the richest people in the world. There was nothing in between these two extremes. Till then, I'd seen peasants working from dusk till dawn for less than a pengő a day; now I saw gentlemen spend three times that on a packet of Egyptian cigarettes. My mother got up at five, worked till late at night and didn't make the price of the breakfast that ladies at the hotel, still bleary-eyed, would have sent up to them in bed at eleven o'clock in the morning.

My baffled young spirit just couldn't accept it. At the sight of these two extreme polarities, my outrage burst out of me like an electric spark. In Újpest, people ended up in prison, hospital or the morgue over tiny, insignificant sums, while here the pounds, francs, dollars and pengős flowed for the smallest things. In the mornings, when I would arrive from Újpest and enter the marble-columned lobby, I really did feel as if they'd smuggled me behind enemy lines. I despised this refined international crowd numbed by *ennui*. I hated them for everything: for my mother getting thinner every day, for my not being able to go to school, for the world being the way it was.

But the truth is, I had it good. The head porter had assigned me to Elemér, and he treated me like a brother. The food was outstanding. I'd never eaten as well in my life. But I still felt lost. They'd treated me terribly in the village, but I had belonged somewhere. The peasants would beat you harshly if they caught you stealing their fruit, but ask you how you were doing next time they saw you. Here, no one beat you, either in word or deed. They simply didn't notice you. They looked through you like a pane of glass. They reminded me of the goldfish in the hotel conservatory—it was as if they, too, were walled off by a sheet of glass. I could see them, I lived side by side with them, but they were completely out of reach. If I were to drop dead right in front of them, I thought, they'd just keep on smiling, politely and uncomprehendingly, as if they were blind. Someone might, perhaps, remove his monocle, go over to the telephone with a look of utter dispassion and—in a careless, nasal tone—call down to reception. "I say... there's a stiff here. Send up the manager, I wish to make a complaint."

Even the other bellboys did not accept me as their own. They were big-city boys, and looked down on peasants. They found my accent, behaviour and outlook ridiculous; indeed, the very fact of my existence, too. They were dyed-in-the-wool, right-wing nationalists: "bicyclists". They kissed up and kicked down, like all the rest of "Royal Hungarian" society. The system in which they lived gave everyone a rank or title, and since there was no rank so low that there was no one lower, even the most miserable pariahs could console themselves in thinking that they, too, had someone beneath them to kick. This was the case in the hotel as well. Passing through, we would have Mr Chairman, Mr President, Mr Vice President, Mr Director, Mr Deputy Director, and various heads of departments; and in the same way, there was in the hotel Mr Head Porter, Mr Porter, and even Mr Assistant Porter, and God help you if you called them by their surnames instead of their titles.

"Oh the fools!" Elemér once said. "When someone higher up gives them a kick, they immediately kick someone below instead of getting together and in a body kicking out the people who invented the system in the first place."

But he only said things like that when we were alone. He was generally silent in front of the others, and on the rare occasions when he did say something, he thought twice about it first. The bellboys had a strange, almost unfathomable respect for him, but later I was surprised to learn that they didn't *like* him, and called him Pokerface behind his back.

They were a corrupted lot, those boys. They aped the elegant guests—some even took on their mannerisms when they spoke. They were constantly eavesdropping, sniffing around and gossiping, and they were only really happy when they could stick their noses into something morally dubious. They were like bruised young fruit; they hadn't even ripened yet and had already begun to rot.

The sweet smell of putrefaction filled the entire hotel. I could smell it through the French perfume, though I didn't know it myself at the time. All I knew was that I suspected—I could smell—something that from the very first moment was horribly repulsive and at the same time terrifyingly tempting.

It all seemed so mysterious. Take the boy with the girlish face who had been so rude to my mother when we'd first come to the hotel. His name was Ferenc, but after the first few days, I noticed that they all just called him "Franciska", like a girl, behind his back. I asked Elemér why, but he didn't answer. He was a prudish boy who blushed easily, and he blushed at the question.

"It's nothing," he mumbled awkwardly and shrugged.

If he hadn't behaved so mysteriously, I would simply have assumed that they called Ferenc Franciska because of his girlish looks, but as it was, I knew that there was something else going on, and I became more curious than ever.

Then one day something odd happened. The head porter asked me: "Where's Ferenc?"

"He'll be right back," I replied, because Franciska had said that he was going up to room 302, and I knew that in the hotel, we only got short commissions and then either went straight back to the lobby or reported where we'd been sent.

But when the head porter had left, Antal, one of the bellboys, snapped at me:

"You mad?"

"Why?"

"Telling him he'll be right back."

"He said he was just goin' to 302."

"Well, quite. Which means he won't be right back."

"Why not?" I gawped.

"Why not," Antal repeated mockingly and, instead of replying, gestured dismissively, as if to indicate that there was no point wasting his breath on a hopeless case like me.

But Franciska really wasn't back right away; he was more than an hour in room 302. I didn't understand. If there had been a woman, I could understand, I said to myself. But room 302 belonged to a man: a rich, older German, the Budapest representative of a chemical company from the Rhine. Fancy that.

Yes, it was all so mysterious. There was plenty of gossip about Elemér, too. I was consumed with curiosity, but the boys didn't let me in on their secret. I only caught the odd sentence here and there.

"Boys," Lajos declared one morning. "Listen to this: my old man bumped into Pokerface at three o'clock in the mornin'. Didn't I tell you he goes to underground meetings?"

And another time, when Elemér had given him a dressing-down for something, he grumbled to the other boys:

"Look at him, all high and mighty, the Communist!"

Needless to say, I didn't believe that. Elemér wasn't a Jew and, besides, I thought he was a decent boy. But I, too, didn't quite understand him. I was always suspicious that he was only saying half of what he thought. He was never happy, he was never sad. He was Pokerface. He talked as dispassionately as an old man, and he was as dry and fair as a rule book. I couldn't begin to imagine how he lived, what he did when he took off his uniform. He never talked about himself, and if I tried to ask, he dodged the question.

It wasn't as if he didn't like me. He watched over me and trained me like a cat does its young, though it can't have been easy for him. Understanding upper-class ways does not come easily to peasant boys, but it was as if he liked even that about me. Whenever I wanted to thank him for some kindness, he always just shrugged.

"Nonsense," he'd say. "We're proles, you and me, we've got to stick together, that's all there is to it."

This slang version of "proletarian" was the first foreign word I ever learnt. I still didn't know what it meant, but I thought it was the nicest word in the world. For me, it meant that Elemér considered me an equal, and that I, too, belonged somewhere.

Whenever I got home, my mother's first words were always:

"Did you bring any money?"

"No," I replied in shame, because for the moment I was only an apprentice and they hadn't yet given me any of the sort of work that came with tips. My mother didn't say anything, just stared straight ahead.

"Maybe tomorrow," I tried to reassure her, but the next day I would come home empty-handed again.

The weeks passed, 1st February was approaching, and my mother grew more and more anxious by the day. On 1st January she had only managed five pengős towards the rent and Herr Hausmeister had told her that if she didn't pay all of what she owed on 1st February, he'd have her evicted. She owed seventy-five pengős, but she'd only managed to scrape together twenty-two, and I have no idea how she even managed *that*. She made three pengős a day when she was working, but she didn't work much more than fifteen days a month. The rest of her time was taken up looking for work, and that cost a lot of money because "ladies" lived in Pest, and my mother wasn't up to walking. She was coughing more and more each night under her faded brown coat, which had now taken the place of the duvet. I slept in my clothes, but the poor thing just couldn't get used to it. She grew thinner every day and her small black eyes sank so far into her pale face, it was as if they were trying to hide from her troubles.

On 1st February, when I got home, she seemed so agitated that instead of saying hello, I said:

"We gettin' evicted?"

"Not yet," she replied. "But if I don't pay it all off by 1st March…" She didn't finish the sentence, but broke bitterly into tears. "Even if you're starving, if you're starving inside four walls, you're still human," she sniffled, "but if you lose that, there ain't nothing left but *that*," she said and pointed at the bottle of lye. People like us would often drink lye when they couldn't take any more of life.

I wanted to console her, but what did I have to console her with? I just sat beside her, helpless. We didn't say a word all night.

The next morning, when she woke me up, I looked at the clock in surprise.

"Why you waking me?" I asked. "It's only half past four!"

My mother looked at her shoes, as she always did when she was embarrassed.

"Béla," she said quietly, "I ain't got money for your tram."

"That's all right," I replied. "How long's the walk?"

"Three hours, if you hurry."

"All right, then," I said. "Ain't no one ever died of that."

But my mother just stood there, staring ever more intently at her shoes.

"There ain't milk, either," she said.

"So what?" I shrugged. "I hate that watery mush anyway. Give me some bread, I'll eat it on the way."

"There ain't no bread, neither!" she said, breaking down into tears. "We ain't got nothing but misery."

So I left the house on an empty stomach at half past four. It was pitch black, a nasty morning. The wind blew through my ragged clothes so hard my limbs went numb. I had to run at the end, but I made it in on time. In the evening, though, it was a slower process. I was unbelievably tired. I would rest now and then on a bench or the side of the road, my head sinking down onto my chest, and I would find myself dozing off. It was midnight by the time I got home.

That was how it went from then on. I walked six hours a day. I was tired all day, incredibly tired, but what was worse was the constant need to sleep. If my fairy godmother had asked me back then what my greatest wish was, I would have said: to sleep. I was perpetually sleepy. In the apprentices' institute, where I had to go twice a week, I would hide behind the back of the person sitting in front of me and sleep, sometimes through the entire lesson. And my favourite drill in cadets was also sleeping. Whenever possible, I would sneak off to the lavatory and sleep. And in the hotel, too, I would disappear whenever I could and secretly snatch a bit of sleep.

My mother could barely wake me in the mornings. It was with the jaw-grinding anger of the tired that I faced my three-hour walk in the mornings, shivering, my stomach rumbling. How I despised those dead, soulless Újpest streets, which on these pitch-black early mornings were peopled only by drunks, prostitutes and burglars. Even policemen didn't dare show their faces round there at that hour. I only met one the entire time, but it was a meeting I could have done without.

"What are you wandering round the streets for?" he shouted at me. "Children ought to be in bed at this hour!"

I didn't reply. What could I have said? I agreed with him wholeheartedly. But my silence just made him angrier.

"Where are you going?" he bellowed.

"To work," I replied.

"At this hour?"

"It'll be morning by the time I get in," I assured him.

"Don't you have money for the tram?"

"No."

"Show me your pockets."

He turned my pockets inside out and even frisked me.

"Well, if your mother and father don't mind," he mumbled at last and spat, by way of comment on their parenting.

We got a plentiful lunch and dinner in the hotel, but no breakfast. So I worked on an empty stomach till noon, and by ten o'clock I was faint with hunger. Around me, waiters came and went with silver platters of breakfasts fit for a lunch, and I watched the tantalizing food go by, my stomach rumbling; food I could never taste: fish, fruits and a tenderloin steak for the fascist English lord who 'most every morning would send it back, saying that it was either too rare or too dry.

I watched them, fists clenched. I had to walk six hours a day for want of forty-eight fillérs, but here in the hotel, I heard the foreigners saying they found Hungary *ridiculously* cheap. And for them, it was. They got twice as much for their money as they did at home, and lived twice as high on the hog. There was an endless flow of pounds, francs, dollars and marks, but for me, this didn't extend even to the price of a tram ticket.

"It looks like," I said to Elemér once, "Hungary's the poorest country on earth."

"Oh, there's a few more like it in the neighbourhood," he replied. "No one bothered about them before 1914, either. Even back then their thinking went, what's it got to do with us? Just let them bash each other's brains in. But then there was the war and the bullets started flying past their own heads. Remember room 108?"

I didn't understand what room 108 had to do with it.

"The one with appendicitis?"

"Him," he nodded. "Take him. He was rich, he was powerful, not a care in the world. So he thought. Then he got those cramps and three days later—finished." He came closer. "Do you know how big an appendix is? Like this. Well, Hungary's about this big, too, compared to the rest of the world, and the rest of the world pays it about as much mind as a healthy man pays his appendix. But if these appendix-countries get inflamed one day, you'll see, the whole world'll feel the cramps. D'you see what I'm getting at?"

I didn't fully understand, but I could have sworn that it was true. Elemér told the truth, and besides, he was a prole. My mouth was bitter with hunger.

"If only it were here already!" I grumbled. "This upper-class world could do with a bit of appendicitis."

4

THE BUILDING IN WHICH WE LIVED was like a terminus. This is where people who had nothing left ended up, and from where people who had nothing yet started out. There were, among us, young working-class couples who were more or less still children and who believed in miracles, and large, storm-tossed jobless families who no longer believed in anything. More than a few of the younger people were unemployed, but over forty, almost everyone was. As for what these jobless families lived off, they themselves often didn't know. Strong, capable working men spent entire days lounging inertly on the walkways in the courtyard, waiting to see if their fifteen-year-old apprentice sons or daughters could get their hands on some dinner. More than one family was supported by canny children like that. Apprentices, after all, did get a bit of work on the side or a tip now and then, and if they didn't, being unable to watch their little brothers and sisters starve, they'd go out and steal. There was no lack of employment in the juvenile courts and the police were also not short of men. Hardly a day went by that someone didn't come tapping on the glass of the kitchen door:

"Police!"

Or:

"The flatfoot's coming!"

"The coppers are comin'!"

That's what the younger generation called policemen. There were ordinary coppers and there were "double-deckers", which is to say mounted policemen. When the coppers took someone away, people would just say:

"Poor thing. He's for it now."

Not that this was some sort "nest of criminals" on the outskirts of town. Most of the residents were workers—upright, decent people whose only crime, more or less, was being alive and wanting to support their families.

Next door to us, there was an old carpenter the house knew simply as Old Gábor. Old Gábor was well respected in the house, though everybody knew he was "funny". He was a tall, handsome man, strict-faced and dignified. He walked so upright he looked like he'd swallowed a rod, and he was particular about his appearance. His faded trousers were always beautifully ironed, his patched shoes polished to a high shine, and you could tell just by looking at his big, white military moustache that he wore a moustache net at night to look after it. He was a widower, but lived with three others in his little one-room flat. He rented the room to three young female workers, and slept in the kitchen. Once, he'd had his own workshop near Budapest, with three apprentices. Old Gábor had made coffins, and anyone investing in death will never lose. He put together quite a little fortune for himself, and had eight thousand koronas in the cooperative. Then the war broke out, they conscripted him into a militia and he had to shut the workshop. Then the revolution came and the Reds declared the old currency worthless. This was followed by the counter-revolution, when the Whites declared the *new* money worthless. Then there was inflation, and suddenly *both* currencies were worthless. So there was Old Gábor, left with absolutely nothing in his old age, and suddenly all this history got to him. He became obsessed with the idea that today's mournful coffins were contrary to the Christian spirit that said, as we all know, that the next world would be better than this one, and so—went his thinking—what cause was there for sorrow? He began making cheerful coffins. But the mourners did not take to this innovation and Old Gábor got fed up with his town. He came up to Budapest to develop his ideas; but he couldn't open a workshop for want of money, and couldn't find a job, either. Thus he, too, ended up joining the populous camp of the unemployed.

Of this he simply took no notice. With his remaining tools, he set up a workshop in his kitchen and carried on working the way he had before. He rose at five on the dot, started work at six, downed tools at the stroke of noon, and went off to look for work in his "lunch break". He never found any, but he didn't let that discourage him. He went home, took off his good clothes and went on working till six precisely. What was he working on? Well, to begin with, he furnished the one-room flat beautifully. He painted the furniture in the national colours—for he was a great patriot and made no secret of it. There were three little beds in the room, each a little masterpiece. They were beautifully carved, and painted in red and green on a white ground. At the head, two red angels held up a white heart with the name of the person renting it in green: Sári, Bözsi or Borcsa. If Old Gábor spotted a scratch or a faded patch on any of the furniture, he ran straight for his tools and fixed it then and there, because as well as the cheerful coffins, he'd become obsessed with tidiness as well. The girls weren't allowed to move anything out of its place, not even the chairs, the correct position of whose legs were marked by four red-white-and-green little circles on the floor.

If someone in the neighbourhood needed furniture, they'd bring Old Gábor the wood and the other necessaries, and he would make it for them, quickly and with great care. People would pay him something, or not; more often not. But recently, even with these easy terms, he'd had trouble finding work because the people in our neighbourhood didn't even have enough for firewood, let alone anything else. But Old Gábor wasn't discouraged. He kept on working on his own account. As to what he was working on, he never said. You could hear him banging away all day, and when it fell silent, we knew it was six o'clock.

Once, my mother sent me over to borrow a hammer, and then I found out what he was working on. He was making a coffin. It was a cheerful coffin, with a little angel sticking out his tongue on each of the four sides, cocking a snook at the world.

"That's nothing!" Old Gábor assured me. "Just wait till it's finished. But that'll be a good few months yet."

"Months?" I asked. "Who's the coffin for, then?"

"Me," he replied.

"You're joking."

"Not a bit of it, son," he said, very seriously. "I don't have no work down here on earth, so I'm working for them up there."

That was the kind of man Old Gábor was. All the building liked him, but he had only one real friend: Áron, the Sabbatarian. The two men liked each other very much and were forever arguing. Old Gábor would have turned the whole world upside down to regain Hungary's lost territories, while Áron, the Sabbatarian, despised war and believed only in the Kingdom of God. The Sabbatarian was a strange, spare man. His thin, Christ-like face was topped by a mane of hair and covered with a thin, scraggly beard. His long, pointed nose was unbelievably thin and almost transparent, like vellum. He must have been about fifty-five or sixty, but he looked much older. He was a night guard at the scrapyard nearby, the one we'd passed with my mother on New Year's Eve. I still saw him there each night on my way home from work, muttering his way through the Bible in his shack.

"If it weren't for him," Old Gábor said once, "this house would've gone a long time ago."

"How d'you mean?" I asked. The old man explained.

That was how I found out why our big three-storey building stood all alone among the vacant plots all round. Once, he told me, this was all working-class housing, but during the inflationary period, a company had bought up all the buildings because they wanted to build a factory on the site. They demolished the buildings one by one, and the residents ended up on the street from one day to the next because at the time, there was such a shortage of housing that even the rich had trouble getting a roof over their heads. The residents in our building, too, got their notice, but Áron, the Sabbatarian, declared that he wasn't going to move. He had a contract, he said, and they couldn't evict him. The company took him to court, but the hard-headed Sabbatarian was in luck: the judge trying the case was a refugee from Kolozsvár. The judge had been chased out of Kolozsvár by the Romanians when they'd taken the city, and the old man had fled to Budapest with his sizeable family. There, he'd spent eight months living in a railway freight car, like so many other Hungarians from Transylvania. Those eight months, it seemed, had stuck in the old man's mind, and so the Sabbatarian won. Ever since, he'd been shrouded in myth and legend, and he was treated with respect by everyone in the neighbourhood.

The truth is, he'd been lucky. The company appealed, but then deflation hit and the inflationary company went bust. The planned factory came to nought and the building, with the rest of the liquidated company's assets, ended up in the hands of a big bank. Barely four or five of the bank's hundreds of employees knew that the building even existed, and of them only one had seen it, once, when he took possession of the liquidated assets on the bank's behalf. Herr Hausmeister took them the rent on the first of every month, and someone in the bank credited a number to an account. The building became an *item*—an insignificant little item, of no concern to anyone.

So Herr Hausmeister was master of all he surveyed. He was all-powerful, and could throw out whoever he wanted; and since you couldn't find a flat for love nor money, anyone he didn't like literally ended up on the street. Herr Hausmeister knew this and took no end of perverse pleasure in his position.

He treated the residents like galley slaves. He was a beefy, unbelievably rough man who could barely read and write. He had been a sergeant in the army, staying on for fifteen years after his compulsory national service; there, they had perfected his talent for torturing his fellow human beings. An army sergeant was not only a rank in Újpest at the time, but far more. When we said someone was a real "army sergeant", that didn't necessarily mean he was a soldier. There were people like that in every field of civilian life. These working-class men who no longer belonged to the working class, but had not yet joined the bourgeoisie, were far harsher with their fellows than the most bloodthirsty of capitalist exploiters.

It wasn't easy to get a position like Herr Hausmeister's. Applicants had to be deemed "absolutely reliable", which is to say cut from roughly the same cloth as Herr Hausmeister. In addition, though, and this was the rub, the owners of the buildings used to ask for a large deposit. Herr Hausmeister had his wife to thank for his, and she her money to thank for a husband. For she was a thoroughly repulsive woman; it was difficult even to look at her, let alone share a bed with her. She'd been cook to a priest in Vác for twenty-five years, and he'd left her his money when he died. She was a goggle-eyed, owl-faced bag of bones; I'd never seen a cook as thin as her.

"But she's got consumption," Herr Hausmeister would wink when he was drunk, to let people know he wasn't as stupid as he looked.

He looked forward to his wife's death the way other people do to winning the lottery. Whenever they argued, which was several times a day, we children would settle in outside Herr Hausmeister's flat and listen to them going at each other with great delight.

"I ain't givin' you the satisfaction of dyin'!" the woman would howl. "I'll outlive you, you filthy Kraut, just to watch you squirm!"

The "filthy Kraut", however, didn't squirm. He took from other people's wives what he didn't get—or didn't want—from his own. He liked the very young ones, and since the attraction wasn't mutual, he simply blackmailed them. If a young woman didn't pay the rent on time, he'd go up and see her when her husband wasn't home and, without beating about the bush, would say:

"Well, sweetheart, you either give me the rent, or…"

"The 'or' is coming!" the women would say when they saw him go up to a young woman's apartment when her husband wasn't home.

We children would say the same thing, and someone would run off to fetch the alarm clock from the kitchen so we could see "how long it lasted".

He must have been driven by some sick collector's need. When he'd had a woman, he usually never looked at her again and was immediately off after someone else. Down in the tavern, he would just shrug if someone mentioned them.

"Had her, too," he'd say, and to prove it, he'd give a detailed description of the young lady's sexual abilities.

But he did have a hopeless love as well. Her name was Mária, but everyone in the building called her Márika instead. She was a rosy-cheeked, full-bodied, pretty little brunette, unbelievably young. She blew through the courtyard's walkways like a tornado, bringing the latest news and stopping to chat with everyone. She shared everybody's tears, she shared their laughter. She laughed, she cried, she talked for hours and, despite Herr Hausmeister's strict prohibition, used to sing at the top of her lungs. The "filthy Kraut" didn't come bellowing at *her* to stop. Whenever he saw her, his blue eyes would go so misty the whole building fell about laughing at him. But he didn't get far with Márika. He couldn't blackmail her because she always paid on time, and besides, she despised Herr Hausmeister. Once, when he put his arms around her, she slapped him so hard that I not only saw it, but heard it from the third floor.

Márika was married and had eyes only for her husband. She loved him passionately; the whole house resounded with her love. The object of her affections was called Árpád; he was twenty and a typesetter at a printer's. He loved Márika back, but more quietly, in his own way. He was a quiet, pale, short boy with spectacles on his narrow, crooked nose which magnified his bloodshot eyes frighteningly. He was the brains of the building. Whenever someone had some complicated official affair or had to write an important letter or request, they'd come up to the third floor to see Árpád. Árpád used to come home late and spend his spare time either down at the working men's society or in the corner at home, reading. Márika looked up to him like other people look up to the sky, never expecting (and perhaps never envisioning) that she could rise to such exalted spiritual heights.

They both worked: Árpád at the printer's and Márika at a cleaning firm. They were as careful with money as the old folk. To save on the tram fare, they used to cycle into Újpest, which is to say that Árpád would cycle while Márika stood on the back wheel, clinging to her husband. Árpád was still an apprentice, because he had started in the profession very late. He was from Salgótarján, and they had sent him down the mines very young—it had been a long, difficult road to that printer's in Budapest.

"But once he gets an idea into his head!" Márika would boast, indicating with a broad gesture that nothing, nothing could stand in his way.

She was always dreaming of the day when Árpád would finish his apprenticeship.

"And then!" she would say, her eyes aglow, and would throw her head back dreamily.

We were sitting around the kitchen, the three of us, one Sunday afternoon. Márika had brought chestnuts—we were roasting them on the stove.

"You'll be stinkin' rich," my mother said, "and if there's a flat goin', you'll leave us like there's no tomorrow."

Márika's face turned all mysterious.

"No, we can't," she said.

"Why not?"

"On account of the baby."

"Well, I'll be!" my mother said, smacking the table. "You don't mean you're in the family way?"

"Not yet," Márika replied. "But when Árpád finishes his apprenticeship..."

And that was all she talked about all afternoon.

"That's why we're so busy savin' up," she said in barely more than a whisper, as if she were imparting secrets. "But I swear that child will want for nothing."

"So he will," my mother said. "So he will."

Márika was as devoted to my mother as if she had been her own, and my mother, too, cared for her very much.

"If they wasn't around," she joked, poking Márika playfully in the side, "I might not be around no more, either."

Márika laughed. I didn't see why.

"Here I was, with a forty-degree fever," my mother recounted. "And I had no money for the doctor, and the hospital wouldn't take me. We can see that you're sick, they said, but there ain't no room, what can we do, we can't stick you on the roof. And in the other place they said, if it was an urgent operation, maybe, but like this... Then in the third place, they didn't even say that, just showed me the door, sayin' there ain't no room, and off you go, and I was left wandering on, on foot, no less, 'cause I'd used up all my money on the tram already. I was shivering with the chills, I could barely stand up, I thought I was going to die. And then that genius Árpád thought of faintin'."

"What?" I asked.

"Faintin'," repeated my mother. "Árpád says: they'll pick up even the poorest person off the street, 'cause they'd get in the way of all them ladies and gentlemen. They'll send the dog catcher for the dogs and the ambulance for the people. Think about it, he says. Yes, I says, but what am I to do if it ain't in my nature to faint, even when I'm this damn weak? Just make like you fainted, he says and takes me by the arm, headin' for the water tower. By then I was so sick, it didn't take much for me to make out like I'd fainted, I can tell you that. The copper wanted to jab me awake like a tired horse, but Árpád had told me not to let him. If I could lie there till the ambulance came, they'd take me to the hospital. That's how smart he is, Árpád."

"That's right!" Márika concurred. "He's smart, he is, and people don't know the half of it, on account of him being the quiet type."

The chestnuts, meanwhile, were done, and we started eating. They were lovely chestnuts and would have pleased anyone, but they were especially delicious to mother and me, because they were the first things we'd eaten all that Sunday. But of course, we didn't tell Márika that.

"Oh!" my mother gushed. "That were the life! Hungry? the nurse would ask, and off she went to fetch the milk. And not the kind, mind you, *we* drink, but real, fine milk, that costs thirty-four fillérs a litre! Never had it so good, me, not even in my muther's belly!"

I thought a lot about that later, when I read about the appalling conditions in the Rókus hospital. Everything in the world, it seems, is relative.

"It were wonderful," my mother repeated. "I keep thinkin' how nice it would be to get another bit of that pneumonia."

"That's right," Márika chorused. "We were just talking with Árpád the other day about how good it would be to be in hospital for a few weeks. Just lyin' there in peace, drinkin' that good milk and never mindin' what it cost. And I hear serious cases even gets chicken now and then! Mmmmm, that's the life!" she enthused, and threw her head back dreamily, as always when she was enthralled.

Those were the dreams people dreamt in that building. This was where I started out from each morning to go to the hotel where the gentlemen—and I don't know why, but this was what always infuriated me the most—would pay two and a half pengős for a packet of cigarettes.

5

C OMING HOME ONE NIGHT, as I got to the third floor, I was surprised to see the light on in the kitchen. I couldn't begin to imagine what had happened. My mother was usually asleep at this hour and even if she was awake she never used to put the light on, because we couldn't very well afford such luxuries. I recognized Márika's voice, and I was even more baffled. What was Márika doing with my mother at this hour?

I opened the door. I saw my mother lying in bed, yellow as a candle, and though it was bitterly cold, there were beads of sweat on her forehead. Márika was sitting on the edge of the bed with a pot of soup in her lap, from which my mother was drowsily spooning. I watched them in silence.

"Don't look so scared," said my mother. "There ain't no gettin' rid of me that easy!"

"What's wrong?" I finally managed.

"She came over all faint, poor thing," Márika said. "She was washing for the head porter and she fainted beside the tub."

"But this time they didn't take me to the hospital!" joked my mother. "Looks like if you faint for real, they don't take you."

"You seen a doctor?"

"They fetched one. It was him that brought me round."

"And what did he say?"

"What they always say. Rest up, eat well." She shrugged. "So much for them."

She began once more to spoon her soup. There was silence, only the Gypsy music from the tavern filtering in. My mother's eyelids began to droop; she put her head down on the mattress and fell asleep, spoon in hand. Márika stood up quietly.

"She's weak, poor thing," she whispered, and pulled me away from the bed. "Tell me, Béla, she eating properly?"

Properly? I thought. Is she eating at all?

"I don't know," I mumbled, but then it occurred to me how ashamed my mother would be if other people knew she was starving, so I added: "Yeah, 'course she is, I'm sure she is."

My mother groaned in her sleep. I looked at her, and when I saw her stiff, bloodless face, I was struck by a sense of cold dread. What if she dies of starvation in the night? She was complaining just the other day that the diminutive head porter had taken her washing for them for free to mean they didn't have to give her lunch, either. Who knows when the poor thing last had anything to eat?

"Márika!" I called, and I was frightened to hear my voice tremble.

Márika looked at me in surprise.

"What is it, Béla?"

"Um…" I muttered, "I don't know how to say this. I'm so ashamed. Mother gave me money this morning for bread, but I…"

"Spent it?"

The dumpy postmistress had asked the same thing when I hadn't had enough money for the stamp. I knew now to say yes. I nodded.

"Could you lend us a bit?"

"'Course I will," Márika replied, and off she ran to get it.

They lived opposite us, so it wasn't long before she was back. She brought a whole loaf, and I could have kissed her. My God, I thought, the good it'll do mother!

"But don't tell her," I whispered, because I knew my mother.

"Like I would!" she said, and winked conspiratorially. "But next time don't you go spending that money. Well, g'night!"

"G'night, Márika. God bless you for your kindness."

The door closed behind her and a fearful silence fell. Down in the bar, the Gypsies were still playing. I remembered poor Berci. He'd fainted once too. It was during geography; the Schoolmaster was drawing the waterways of Hungary up on the board, and in the silence, we heard a dull thud. That was in the spring. He was dead by autumn.

"Muther!" I said, alarmed.

My mother trembled.

"What is it?"

"I've brought you some bread. Won't you have some?"

"Sure," she replied weakly, but by the time I took her the bread, she was asleep again.

I sat down on the edge of the bed and waited. She was sleeping so deeply that I didn't have the heart to wake her. I just sat there and looked at her thin, careworn face. The next thing I knew, I too had fallen asleep. I dreamt that I was an altar boy, ringing the bell at my mother's funeral. I woke to find myself sobbing loudly. My mother was asleep. She made hoarse, whistling noises in her sleep, and now and then would moan like a child. The lamp had run out of petroleum, the wick glowing smokily in the darkness. I put it out. It was only when I touched the warm lamp that I felt how cold I was. I struck a match and looked at the clock. It was half past three. I have to go in an hour and a half, I thought. I should sleep, otherwise there'd be trouble at the hotel.

I went into the room and lay down, but couldn't sleep. My teeth chattered from the cold and tiredness. Manci wasn't home, so I got up and walked around the room. I walked around till dawn, but by the time I left home, I knew what I would do.

I deliberately missed the communal lunch at noon, and only came to the kitchen when the others had already left. I stuffed my pockets with paper and, in an unsupervised moment, wrapped up all the food in it. I only ate what I couldn't pocket: the soup and the vegetable stew. I did the same thing in the evening with dinner. On the way home, I was so hungry that I could barely resist the temptation. But then I remembered my mother and all at once I lost my appetite.

She was asleep by the time I got home.

"Evenin'," I said, nice and loud.

She looked at me in surprise, because I never usually woke her.

"Something the matter?"

"Not at all," I replied. "Just wanted to know how you're doing."

She shrugged.

"Like a cat in a well, my boy."

It was true, I could see that for myself. I quickly diverted the conversation.

"Didn't that doctor give you some medicine?"

"No," she replied a little testily.

The conversation just didn't want to get going.

"Has Márika been?" I asked, just for something to say.

"Yes."

"Anyone else?"

"The Sabbatarian came by in the afternoon."

"What'd he want?"

"Nothin'. He heard I were sick. Read me a bit of the Bible."

I kept on asking her questions about this and that, and it was only ten minutes later that I remarked, as casually as possible:

"I brought you something to eat. Here."

I took the package out of my pocket. There were two slices of meat, a good deal of potatoes and two big slices of bread. My mouth watered, and I could see that my mother, too, swallowed heavily. But she pushed the food away.

"You eat it, my boy," she said. "Grown-ups can go hungry easier."

"Hungry? Who's hungry?" I boasted. "They give us so much to eat at the hotel it's enough to spoil your stomach. I always end up leavin' half of it."

My mother gave me a funny look.

"Leavin' half of it?"

She sounded doubtful, but there was also a little indignation in her voice. I realized I'd gone too far. I wouldn't have believed her, either, if she told me she used to leave half her food. So I added:

"You know, for the others."

"Yes, 'course," she nodded, because this she could understand. The poor don't advertise their troubles.

"But I'm smarter than that now. I've figured out a way."

"Just mind you don't get yourself in trouble, son."

"I wasn't born yesterday. I've got my wits about me."

"Yes," she replied seriously. "You're a smart lad, no denying." She gazed pensively for a while, and then said without looking up, "You ought to be going to school."

I didn't reply. It grew silent; there was only the dripping of the water pipe.

My mother glanced again and again at the food.

"Sure you won't eat?"

"Told you I ain't hungry."

"Go on, have half!"

"Want me to spoil me stomach?"

That did the trick.

"All right, then," she said with a reluctant smile and bit into the thick, juicy pork chop.

I had to sit down, because I was faint with hunger. It was a two-faced moment. One of the finest of my youth. I had fed my starving mother.

From then on, I smuggled my food home every day. The lack of food and the distances I had to walk made me so weak that by the evening, I could barely stand up. I couldn't wait for the moment my shift ended, and at the same time I was terrified of it, because that was when the hardest part began: the walk to Újpest. I would drag myself along like a sick animal, and by the time I got home, I was often on the edge of fainting. And then something else happened, as well.

The Major, it seemed, couldn't live without the army, playing soldiers with us instead. Every morning, he'd line us up in ranks like privates and hold a strict "inspection". The brass buttons on our red bellboys' uniforms had to be gleaming, and God help whoever didn't have a perfect crease in their trousers. We had to comb our hair in the "regulation" manner, too: down flat, parted to the left. He "inspected" our fingernails, ears, and necks, and would sometimes even sniff us like a dog; and there was hell to pay if someone smelt of sweat.

During one of these inspections, he barked at me:

"What kind of shoes do you call those?"

I didn't know what to say. Should I have said that they were the Schoolmaster's shoes, and I'd been to hell and back to get them? That I had been thrown in jail because of them, beaten with the stock of a rifle and chased out of my village? That they were the reason I couldn't go to school any more? What was I supposed to say?

There was an awkward silence. I thought the world had ended. And then Elemér unexpectedly piped up:

"Sir, he's damaged his foot, sir. It's bandaged, and that's why he's wearing this… this great big pair of battered old shoes."

But the Major wasn't interested in the state of my foot. He snapped curtly:

"Don't let me see you wearing them again!"

"Yessir!"

"Not 'yessir', but yes, sir."

"Yes, sir."

"Dismissed."

When the Major had left, Elemér came over.

"You should buy a pair of shoes," he whispered.

"I know," I nodded.

"D'you have the money?"

"No."

"So what are you going to do?"

"What can I do?" I said with a shrug. "They'll fire me. And it couldn't have come at a worse time."

"Why?"

"My muther's sick. Very sick."

Elemér didn't say anything, just looked straight ahead. We were silent for some time.

"I ain't got money either," he said apologetically, and came closer. "He mustn't see you," he whispered. "Make yourself scarce if you see him."

"What's the point?" I replied. "I have to turn up for inspection."

"I'll say they've sent you off somewhere. You're in my section, I'm responsible for you."

"Sure," I shrugged, "but how long can we keep that up?"

"We'll think of something!" he said, but he didn't sound too confident.

I didn't say anything to my mother. She had enough trouble as it was. As soon as she could stand, she was up, and as soon as she was up, she went to work. And so it all started over.

But one evening, she was very cheerful when I got home.

"Guess what," she said with a smile.

"What?"

"Your apprenticeship's over. You're gettin' a position!"

"How d'you know?"

"The head porter told me. He says the rest is up to you. If you're good, you can make two or three pengős a day."

Her face radiated hope. There was nothing for it, I had to tell her.

"Muther, I'm afraid this post won't come to nothin'."

"Why?"

"There's something wrong. The Major don't like my shoes."

"What's wrong with 'em?"

"I don't know. They were good enough for the Schoolmaster, and his little finger was worth more than the whole Major, monocle and all. Sorry to spoil your mood."

But to my great surprise, my mother said:

"Well, if there's no other way, we'll just buy a pair."

I couldn't believe my ears.

"What about the rent?"

"If what the head porter says is true, you'll make the price of them shoes in three or four days."

"That's true," I said, relieved. "Hadn't thought of that."

I "skipped" an hour of the apprentices' institute and went with my mother to buy a pair of shoes. It was quite the occasion. This is how I recorded it on one of the "Owed to" pages of my old diary: "18th February 1928. Mother, one pair shoes, 7 pengős 20 fillérs." Then, below, in brackets, I put "Not worn, but brand new!" Indeed: I had a "brand-new" pair of shoes. They were beautiful shoes. People must have wondered why I was constantly staring at my feet. What I liked best about them was the way they squeaked good and loud. That may sound strange, but it isn't at all. Only shoes someone hasn't already worn in squeak, and I had never had such a pair of shoes before. So I was proud of them, very proud.

I did end up getting the post, but much good did it do me. They put me in one of the lifts, and I'm sure you've noticed that no one tips lift boys in hotels. So there I stood in my fine, squeaky shoes, beaming at the guests, and all for nought. The most I ever got out of it is that the truly generous ones—occasionally—smiled back.

The look my mother gave me when she found out, I thought she was going to faint again.

"Jesus," she said, white as a sheet. "And I spent seven pengős of the rent!"

I'd never heard her complain when she didn't have enough to eat, but she was constantly sighing about the rent. No one wants to end up on the street, obviously, but her constant terror of it was almost pathological.

"While you're starving inside four walls," she used to say, "you're still human. But if you ain't got that, there's nothing left but *this*," she said, pointing at the bottle of lye.

How many times I heard that, my God! I used to get cold chills down my back whenever I looked at the lye bottle.

But we made it through 1st March somehow. My mother promised Herr Hausmeister she'd do his washing for free, and the great man gave us a stay of execution till 1st April.

"But what'll we do then?" my mother asked, and I had no answer.

The 1st of April was my fifteenth birthday. Apart from me, of course, no one noticed at all, and even my mother forgot. The poor thing was preoccupied with the rent, rather than my birthday. She had ninety pengős to pay, the little diary tells me, but she could only scrape together thirty. It wasn't a very happy birthday. All day, I was wondering what would happen if they evicted us, and every time I remembered the bottle of lye, my heart skipped a beat.

The hotel was unusually cheerful that day: people were playing April Fool's jokes on each other. I was born on a fool's day, I thought to myself, so no wonder life was making a fool of me. The lift and I sped up and down, up and down, but all I could think about was that my mother might already be dead. I kept getting the wrong floor, and guests kept shouting at me—sometimes, I was afraid I'd strangle them. I could barely control myself by evening. I had to know what had been going on at home at all costs, and at the same time, I was scared of finding out.

I ambled home slower than ever before. It was a cold, foggy night, and it was spotting with rain. I walked the deserted streets with my collar turned up and my hands in my pockets, and wherever I looked,

I saw my mother lying on the metal bed, her eyes rolled up into her head, the empty bottle of lye beside her.

It was getting on for midnight. The rain had seeped through my clothes and I felt like it was seeping through my skin as well, turning my bones to mush. I leant against a lamppost, my head dipped down onto my chest, and my eyelids drooped closed. The rain dripped in beneath my collar and ran, ice-cold, down my back. I let it. I simply couldn't keep my head up.

"Quite the birthday," I mumbled aloud, and noticed that I was talking to myself, like Mad Wilma. But I just kept on talking: "Born on a crazy day, God knows that's true. April Fool! They really made a fool of you…"

Funny, I thought, but that rhymes. Did I read that somewhere? No, or rather… No, no, I hadn't. Odd. I was talking in verse. I felt dizzy. I felt the way you do when you're still half asleep, when reality turns fluid and melts into your dreams. It was some kind of sober drunkenness, some waking ecstasy.

I remember these moments very clearly, the way epileptics must recall their first seizure, or madmen in moments of clarity, the first time they saw the Vision. That was when it started.

I kept repeating these four lines, the way you keep humming four bars of an old tune you've long forgotten, or perhaps never even heard. These were mysterious moments, the moments of miracles and accidents, the victim of which can only recall them haltingly. It's like sitting in front of the radio, twisting the dial blankly, looking for something, you're not sure what, and all of a sudden you hear beautiful music. It's familiar, frighteningly so, and yet you've never heard it before. What is this? you ask. Where is it coming from? Who sent it? It only lasts a few seconds, four bars, that's it. The music disappears into the cacophony of the ether, and you hunt for it in vain. You keep turning the dial ever more anxiously, but all you get is a confusion of voices, strange incomprehensible signals, sent almost from some other world—a short, a long, a short, a long—and you have no idea what they mean. And then suddenly, there it is again. This time, you hear the tune distinctly, and you know what it means, yes, you know exactly what it means. But you still don't know where it's coming from, and you never will.

I grabbed the diary from my pocket excitedly and started writing with the thin little pencil in the spitting rain. The paper still bears the traces of the rain, like the faded tears of women's love letters. It was my first poem. I'm going to reproduce it here just as I wrote it.

APRIL FOOL

Born on a crazy day,
God knows it's true.
April Fool!
They made a fool of you.

They told you you'd get mother's milk
Told you it was your due.
April Fool!
A rich man's son drank it all away from you.

They told you you'd get mercy
Like every Christian child.
April Fool!
Even this, the poor will be denied.

The rich take from the poor
The milk, the mercy the Lord God sends.
April Fool!
Who knows how all this ends.

Young masters, do you really think
it will always be this way?
April Fools!
You'll see, there'll be hell to pay!

I later deleted the last line. It seems I scared myself with my forthright-ness, which was hardly surprising, since the officially sanctioned poetry I'd read in school hadn't had anything of this sort in it. I rewrote the sentence, but then crossed out the new version as well and put a dotted line under the original to indicate that it should stay as it was. Underneath the poem is the following, heavily underlined:

I am not an upper-class poet, and I don't want to be. There'll be hell to pay!

That's what I wrote underneath my first poem. It's what I'll write under the last. Looks like I haven't changed very much at all.

There was some good news when I got home: Herr Hausmeister had given us an extension till 1st May. It hadn't been free: he wasn't the generous type. My mother was now washing for free for three of the great man's "friends", which meant an extra nine pengős a month for Herr Hausmeister, or twelve, along with his own washing. But my mother didn't care. She greeted me as if we'd won the lottery.

It was St Hugo's day, and since Árpád's younger brother was called Hugo, they were celebrating. Márika had brought us a big piece of poppy-seed loaf and my mother put it aside for me. We sat down at the table, she eating my food and I her poppy-seed loaf. We sat there eating in the light of the good news like partners in crime who had just dodged the gallows.

In the morning, when I left, my mother gave me a kiss, which she never did. In the evening, however, when I got home, she didn't so much as reply to my hello.

"Give me the money!" she snapped at me, just like that.

"What money?" I asked.

"You know full well," she replied menacingly. "The money you made."

I looked at her astounded.

"You joking?"

My mother stood up and came over to me, her face flushed crimson.

"So you lying to my face now?"

"Who's lying?" I shouted angrily.

"You!" she screamed. "Ain't you ashamed of yourself? I were wash-ing at the head porter's today, and there's all sorts of bloodstains on the clothes. Well, the old woman's past that age, so I say, madam, I say, you ain't havin' me wash for other people now, are you? So she starts screaming at me, all how dare I, and how ungrateful I am, and how my son makes plenty at the hotel!"

"Lyin' old witch," I screamed, beside myself. "That dirty, lyin' tramp."

"It's you that's lyin'!" she yelled. "She wouldn't dare make up somethin' like that. She'd have to be as cold-blooded as you are."

That was all I needed. I said terrible things to my mother. I don't know what, exactly, and I think I didn't even know at the time. We screamed at each other like sworn enemies. All that suppressed hatred that couldn't find its rightful target now came bursting out of us. We were unpredictable, like hungry, cornered beasts of prey.

"Shut your filthy mouths or I'll fetch a policeman!" Herr Hausmeister called up.

That sobered my mother up right away.

"Get yourself in the room," she said hoarsely, "before I wring your neck!"

We didn't speak to each other for weeks. At night, when I came home, my mother was already sleeping, or at least pretending to sleep. I still brought my food home and put it silently down on the kitchen table before going into the room to sleep. In the mornings I regularly woke to find my mother going through my pockets. Good luck to her. I pretended to be asleep and didn't open my eyes till she growled at me:

"It's four. Get up."

Then I washed quickly and left without saying goodbye.

That was how I lived in the "family home". As if that weren't enough, they moved Elemér to the night shift. There was no longer a soul with whom I could exchange a friendly word. I was once more as lonely as when I was young, and once more fled from reality into the world of daydreams. I made up friends to accompany me on the dark, frightening streets of Újpest, and I told them everything I couldn't tell anyone else. Wild, rambling tales were born in this period, of which I was always the hero, the great, just and famous Béla who punished the oppressors of the poor, and like Sándor Rózsa robbed the rich to give to the poor. I've long forgotten these tales of adventure, but I do still remember a very bourgeois little tale, not in the least adventurous, which featured again and again among my daydreams. The "story" went that I was grown up, with a wife and children, and we lived happily in a three-room apartment. The "action" would usually begin with it being the dead of night and me coming home, tired, from work.

My wife (her name was Erzsike and she was, of course, very beautiful) ran to meet me in the doorway and threw herself, sobbing, around my neck.

"Oh, my sweet darling," she'd say, half laughing, half crying, "we thought some harm had come to you! Don't you know how much we've been expecting you? It's past midnight, where have you been all this time?"

"I walked," I would reply, taking a little puff of my handsome porcelain pipe.

"Walked?" my wife says, shocked. "In this weather? We're not doing so badly that you should have to walk six hours a day!"

"Not at all!" I reply proudly. "But I'm saving up for the family."

"But what good is money, darling one, if you run yourself flat? You can't keep this up for very long. Swear to me, darling love, that you're not going to do it any more."

"Life's hard," I would reply seriously. "A man has to think of his family."

On that final word, "family", our children appear: five, to be precise. Three boys and two girls. They're all legitimate children, breastfed for a full year. They all have fine, squeaky shoes, and wear galoshes even in the house so they'll never catch cold. The boys all have the same suit as the "fine" young gentleman my mother nursed, and I've even bought them green hunting caps with tufts of wild boar bristle. As for the girls—they're a sight to behold! They're like little princesses. They both have little gold crosses round their necks and they catch a beating if they ever try and pawn them.

So anyway, these five children now rush over and kiss me, begging me not to walk any more as well. Then the whole family accompanies me into the living room. It's a beautiful room. There's a crackling fire with a grandfather chair before it, the kind the Schoolmaster used to have, and I now settle comfortably into it. My eldest son pulls off my right shoe, the younger one my left, while their little brother runs to the bedroom for my slippers, because my feet have got very wet indeed in the rain (for I, unlike my children, do not have galoshes). The two girls, meanwhile, rub my numbed hands, the elder the right, the younger the left, so neither is neglected. Finally, Erzsike shoos them away.

"Leave your father be," she says, "he must be starving, poor dear."

"So I am," I say. "What's for dinner?"

"*Székelygulyás*," she says, naturally.

"Not bad," I say, just as naturally.

"But that's not all, darling!"

"You're joking."

"Not at all. Why would I be? Anyone that works as hard as you has to eat well. I made cottage cheese noodles as well."

"Well," I say, "this makes all that work worthwhile. Now come on, everyone, let's gather round and say grace. For the food we're about to eat…"

The old Hungarian saying is right: *when you've got no dog to bark at night, you'll end up barking in its stead.*

6

O NE OF THE PAGES of the little old diary bears this mysterious
inscription:

3rd July 1928, 8.42 a.m. P.—First time!

I remember this "first time" very clearly. When the two new guests got
in the lift, I was immediately seized by a strange excitement.

"What are you staring at?" the manager accompanying the guests
whispered angrily. "Third floor, hurry up!"

I started the lift. British, I thought, or American, for I knew that this
particular manager tended to deal with British and American clients. He
oozed such charm with our Anglo-Saxon guests that the boys used to call
him Mister Saccharine. He was a pale, ginger, fattish young man, like a
sugar-coated spider. He was a constant pest to anyone beneath him, but
the way he talked to rich foreigners, you'd have thought he was trying to
trap them in a web of sweet syrup. The boys had a term for this as well.

"He's working the geezer," they'd say.

This was what Mister Saccharine was doing now. The "geezer" in
this case was a tall, blond man of around forty, but he was not what
had caught my attention. I was looking at his daughter, the prettiest
girl ever to get in the lift in the history of the world, or at least, as far as
I was concerned. She must have been one or two years younger than
me. She had shoulder-length, gold-blond hair, big, playful, dark eyes, a
fleshy mouth that curved upwards, and the prettiest nose I'd ever seen.
I watched her out of the corner of one eye, carefully, as if operating the
lift were taking up all of my attention. That was how I always examined
the "interesting" guests; it was a tried and tested method, and no one
ever noticed. This time, however, something unprecedented happened.

The girl smiled at me. At first, I thought she'd spotted something strange in my appearance, or had seen me staring. But when they got out, she smiled at me again, and this time I was sure it wasn't out of mockery. It was a warm, friendly smile, a conspiratorial smile. I got so excited I forgot to close the door. I could hear the buzzer going, I knew people were waiting for the lift, but I just stood there and stared at the corridor. The corridor was empty, not a soul, only a lonely clock ticking on the wall as if to commemorate the historic moment. It was 8.42.

In the next hour and a quarter, I must have got the wrong floor half a dozen times. Then they finally came again. The girl had changed meanwhile. She was wearing a light, colourful flower-patterned dress, and was waving a bag full of bathing things in one hand. When she got in the lift, she smiled at me, and to my greatest surprise, said hello in Hungarian.

"Goomorning," she said in her dreadful, endearing accent.

But after that, she didn't look at me again, and that sobered me up a little. Who knows, perhaps foreign girls smile at every boy. But it stayed with me. I was waiting for something—I did not know what.

Nothing happened till five. I was beginning to think she'd gone up with the other lift when all at once I spotted her at the end of the corridor. I got so excited I could barely close the lift door. We were alone.

"Say," she said, "was father mine here?"

"I haven't seen the gentleman yet," I replied. "That was what you meant, wasn't it?"

"Yes," she laughed. "I again forget Hungarian. Every year I come and forget. Though I know when I little like this," she said, indicating with her hand how "little" she'd been back then.

"Are you Hungarian, then, miss?" I asked in surprise.

"Oh no!" she laughed again. "I American. But father mine he bring every year when he come branch here… how you say? Wait." She drew a tiny dictionary out of her bag. "Inspect," she read. "Ours branch here. American company, see? Oil. Understand when I speak Hungarian?"

"You speak very nicely, miss," I complimented her, even as I heard the buzzer sound angrily. The lift had stopped some time ago, but the girl did not get out. "I'm sorry, miss, but they want the lift, I have to go down."

"I go too," she replied cheerfully. "I wait for father mine. Is boring by self, you know?"

"Yes," I replied dimly, because nothing better came to mind.

Downstairs, an old man was waiting angrily.

"Were you asleep?" he yelled at me. "I've been waiting five minutes!"

I wanted to excuse myself, the way one does in these situations, but I didn't dare open my mouth because the girl was making such faces behind the old man's back that I was afraid I'd start laughing the second I did.

"Monkey!" she said when the old man had got out. "Say, you like this work?"

"I don't know," I replied noncommittally. I didn't want to lie, but I didn't dare tell her the truth, either.

"Boring, no?" she asked. "Up-down, up-down, all the day. And lots of old monkeys. What you want to do?"

"Study," I replied.

"What?"

"Everything."

She laughed.

"Everything? All everything? You want to be wise man?"

"Yes," I admitted, and felt myself blush.

Meanwhile, the lift had come to a halt. I opened the door, but the girl just kept on talking.

"I see that on you right away," she said.

"What did you see, miss?"

"That you are…" She couldn't find the word, she started thinking. "That you have plenty here," she said finally, making it simple, and pointed to her head.

"Ah," I muttered awkwardly, and blushed even deeper.

The girl took out a bag of sweets and offered me one. We chewed in silence for a while. I don't know about her, but I couldn't taste the sweet at all.

"How much old you are?" she asked.

"Just gone fifteen, miss."

"I think you were more," she noted. "Because of size. I thirteen."

"I thought you were older, too," I said, returning the compliment. "I thought you were *much* older."

"Oh, here in Budapest, everybody thinks. Because I paint mouth. I hear if girl paints mouth here, they throw her out of school. Silly, no?"

I wanted to reply, but the words stuck in my throat. Her father was coming. Well, I thought, there'll be hell to pay now. The old man must have noticed that his daughter was cosying up to the lift boy.

But to my great surprise, nothing happened. The "old man" smiled at me kindly, while his daughter had absolutely no intention of being embarrassed. She pointed to me cheerfully and explained something to her father, who didn't speak a word of Hungarian. Her father smiled at me again, and when he got out, he pressed a pengő into my hand.

This was my first income. That night, when I got home, I put that pengő on the kitchen table along with the packet of food and didn't say a word. My mother didn't say anything, either—we were still not on speaking terms—but the next morning, I think, she didn't go through my pockets. Or maybe it was just that I didn't notice. I slept very deeply that morning, because I'd spent half the night awake. I kept seeing those playful eyes in the darkness and that upturned little nose, and they kept me tossing and turning as if in a fever.

I'd been in the hotel six months now, but nothing like this had ever happened. The ladies either didn't talk to me or addressed me from such lofty heights, it was like a muezzin calling down to the people from his minaret. I had become so used to not being treated like a human being that I simply couldn't understand what had got into this American girl. Is she in love with me? I wondered excitedly. But in the morning, I realized that was ridiculous.

She came home from the lido at five the next day as well. Again she waited for "father mine", who arrived well after six. She came up and down with me in the lift, and when there weren't any guests, we talked. Once, she said:

"Why you say me always 'Miss'? I have name. Patsy. Spell like this. You have pencil?" I gave her my diary with the thin little pencil. She wrote her name down; I still have it. "See?" she pointed. "Now write name you." I did so. "B-é-l-a," she spelt it out. "No English name like this. But I like. Nice name."

"There's no Patsy in Hungarian, either," I told her. "But that's a nice name, too."

She laughed.

"We have two nice name, yes?"

I laughed as well. We laughed for several minutes at that. Later, she asked:

"How much money you make, Béla?"

"Nothing," I replied awkwardly.

She didn't want to believe it.

"Then why you in lift?"

"Because later I might make some money."

"How much?"

"That depends. Some boys make forty to fifty pengős a month."

That did not satisfy Patsy at all.

"In America," she said, "lift boy make more in dollars. And dollars worth five times pengő. And can study, too, if they wants."

"Really?" I said, surprised.

"Of course," she said. "You know, your country pretty, but not good."

I felt a little hurt that she'd said that about Hungary.

"It's not so bad," I said. "The people are decent, believe me. The problem is the way the ruling class treats them."

"Why people put up with?"

I smiled. The question seemed terribly childish.

"What else could they do?"

"Throw out government!"

This time, I laughed out loud. She's still a child, I thought.

"You can't do that," I replied like an indulgent schoolmaster. "The government is in the hands of the ruling class, the people have no say."

"There problem!" Patsy replied passionately. "In America, if people not like government, they kick out!"

"Kick them out?" I asked, enthusiastically.

"Of course. They choose new. Why not? We are free country."

"And are there no poor people?"

"There are."

"And why don't you help them, then?"

"Oh," Patsy smiled, "poor have always been and poor will always be."

That sobered me up somewhat. That's not what the Schoolmaster had said. Or Elemér. But I didn't say anything about that to Patsy.

From then on, she waited for "father mine" every afternoon, and I spent the whole day preparing for the hour that she spent with me in the lift. Later, she'd come home from the lido at four thirty instead of five, and sometimes she'd even come at four. Then she rode the lift with me.

The boys, of course, noticed this unusual friendship. They began to make remarks, mock us and spy on us. They thought me a dumb peasant and couldn't understand what a "lady" would want with me.

"Still waters run deep!" Antal once commented pointedly, and the nickname stuck.

From then on, I was Mr Still Waters.

Once, when she came back from the lido, Patsy said:

"Why not you come swimming with me once?"

I was so unprepared for the question, I didn't know what to say. I thought she was joking.

"Don't you want?"

"Of course I want to."

"Then come."

We knew each other quite well by then, and I was confident enough to joke with her. I said:

"All right. When?"

"Tomorrow."

"All right."

Patsy poked me in the ribs.

"Why you laugh? I talk to manager, and he let you go. You don't believe?"

"Of course I do."

"Let's make bet."

"All right," I said, because I still thought she was joking.

But the next morning, the Major wanted to see me.

"Do you know the city?" he asked.

"Yes, sir!" I lied instinctively.

"Then you will now take the American girl and show her around."

"Yes, Major."

I could feel myself blushing. Fortunately, the Major didn't look at me, because he was in the process of polishing his monocle.

"I don't want any complaints about you," he snapped. "Be respectful, understand? No overfamiliarity!"

"Yes, Major."

"If you have any expenses, write them down. Do you have cash?"

"No, sir, I don't."

The Major scribbled something on a piece of paper and handed it to me.

"Take this to the cashier. They'll give you ten pengős. Tomorrow, you account for every fillér." He inserted his monocle and looked at me severely. "E-ve-ry *fill-ér*!" he repeated menacingly. "Am I understood?"

"Yes, sir, Major."

"Dismissed."

The cashier gave me a ten-pengő note. I'd heard that such things existed, but had never seen one first-hand. It was a tantalizing sight. I didn't know which pocket to put it in; I was petrified of losing it.

Patsy was already waiting for me in front of the lift.

"You see!" she said, and her big, playful eyes seemed even more playful now.

Out on the street, I asked her:

"What do you want to see, Patsy?"

"Yours silly face," she replied cheerfully.

But I was serious.

"The Major said you wanted to see the town."

"Really?" she said, surprised. "Who could have tell him that?"

We both laughed. We were wheezing with laughter and couldn't stop.

"But where we going, actually?" she said, stopping suddenly.

"I don't know," I admitted. "Wherever you want."

"You like beach Margit Island?"

"I've never been to Margit Island."

"My God!" she said, shocked. "You live Budapest and you never go Margit Island? And I come from other end of world to see it. Most beautiful place on earth, trust me."

And indeed, there was no reason to doubt that when I saw it—though to be truthful, I didn't see all that much of it. The old traditional mansions and the luxurious new hotels, the hundred-year-old trees and the modern sports facilities, the ruins of the legendary monastery and the flashy pomp of the nightclub, the wild shrubs growing among the ruins and the artistic finesse of the flowerbeds, the endless lawn of the polo field and the rose garden fit for a fairy tale: the whole of this little paradise beside the Danube flowed into one for me like the blurred background of a clear portrait. I saw only *her*; the world was but a blurred and unreal background.

It must have been the end of August. The bloated summer, like a sated *roué*, snoozed in the gold-flecked shade of the portly trees. There was a warm breeze off the Danube carrying the scent of flowers and scraps of distant, dreamlike music. It was all a little surreal, as if the world had cocked its hat jauntily to one side.

We didn't know what to do with our good mood. We'd break into a run for no reason at all, then drag our heels like a couple of lame caterpillars. Sometimes, we'd shout over one another, so desperately urgent was what we had to say; at others, we stayed silent for fifteen minutes at a time.

Patsy took my arm, but I didn't even dare take her hand. At night, when I couldn't sleep because of her, I pictured all sorts of things, but in the morning I was so ashamed of these thoughts, it was as if I'd been planning to murder someone. You could imagine doing *that* with Borcsa and other girls like her, but with Patsy... never! My blood was hotter than many eighteen-year-old boys', but when it came to things like this, I was more innocent than most thirteen-year-old girls. I still considered physical and emotional love two completely different things. There were Borcsas and there were Patsys, I thought, and that was the way of the world. Patsy was my heart's love, and the heart's love was sacred and untouchable.

"What you thinking?" asked Patsy.

"Nothing," I replied. "Margit Island really is the most beautiful place on earth."

It was only when we got to the lido that I realized I didn't have bathing trunks.

You get over there," she said, pointing to one of the buildings. "Change and we meet that bench. There, see?"

"Yes."

But when I'd got some trunks and started heading for the changing rooms, Patsy was still standing where I'd left her. She was talking to a boy about my age. He was dressed all in white with white shoes and a white straw hat, a red carnation in his buttonhole. All at once, I was sorry I'd come. I can't compete with this lot, I thought, deflated, and tried to sneak off. But Patsy saw me and introduced me to the boy.

"Count B——" she said. "Miki."

I knew the name well: we'd learnt it in history at school. Not even our Count had come from such an old and hallowed family, though where I came from people had thought he was the Lord God Almighty. I got terribly flustered.

"This is my friend," Patsy said, introducing me.

The Count looked at me and smiled condescendingly. He must have thought I'd brought some message from the hotel, and Patsy saying "my friend" was just some sort of American exaggeration. But when he realized that Patsy was serious, some strange, forced expression came over his features.

"How do you do," he said. He said it in such a way that I would have given ten years of my life to be able to smack him.

He did not extend his hand. He exchanged a few words with Patsy and then left.

"You can't do that sort of thing in Hungary!" I said.

"What sort?"

"Introducing me to a Count and saying I'm your friend."

"You are not my friend?"

"Yes, but…"

"But?"

I drew myself up straight.

"I'm not a gentleman," I said, almost antagonistically, and though I still didn't know what it meant, I added: "I'm a prole."

"And?" Patsy laughed. "You are too my friend. Forget Count. Now go change, silly!"

It was the first time in my life I'd worn bathing trunks. When I stepped out of the changing rooms, I felt completely naked. I thought everyone was staring at me.

Patsy was sunbathing in the sand. When I saw her in her bathing suit, I got so embarrassed I didn't know what to do with myself. I could feel her looking at me, too, though I couldn't see her eyes because they were covered by her dark sunglasses. There was an awkward silence. We couldn't break it for several minutes.

"Warm," she said at last.

"Yes," I said. "Very."

Then we fell silent again. The sun blazed down fearfully, the bathers thronged around us noisily. I closed my eyes and suddenly I was surrounded by a strange silence, as if I were lying on the bottom of the sea with warm waves breaking over my head. It'd be good to kiss her, I thought. At least her hand.

Patsy sat up. Not far from us, half a dozen or so boys were lying on their stomachs in the sand.

"Say," she began quietly. "Which one of them is Count?"

I didn't see what she was getting at. I looked at her in surprise.

"I don't know."

"You know why not?" she asked. "I tell. Because naked Count is just like other people. Or not even. Look at you. You are bigger than him. Stronger. You have more brain than three such counts. You see, silly?"

Oh yes, this I understood, and how! I drank in her every word like the earth drinks in water in a drought. But then… why doesn't she talk the same way about the poor? If she thought about counts what she thought about the poor, then she should have said: "Counts have always been and counts will always be." Why was it that she understood *that* so well? Was it only that they, too, weren't counts? Yes, it was "only" that, I told myself, and all at once I understood something whose significance I would only fully realize later. But I didn't say a word about that to Patsy.

She drew closer to me.

"It's not good for you here," she said softly. "Learn English and come America. There you have *shot*."

"What?"

"*A shot.* Oh! How you say in Hungarian?"

She couldn't think of the word. She dug around in her bathing satchel, but the little dictionary was not in it. She called over to the Count.

"Miki!"

"Yes?"

The boy came over.

"Say, how you say Hungarian *a shot*?"

"Opportunity," he replied.

"Now you see?" Patsy said to me. "In America, you have opportunity. Not here."

"Why not?" asked the Count, who clearly thought Patsy had wanted to draw him into the conversation.

"Because this not free country."

"Why isn't it a free country?"

"Because it isn't. No democracy. Or are you democrat, Miki?"

"I am a Hungarian," came the Count's spirited reply. "And proud of it."

"Why?" Patsy asked provocatively.

"Aren't you proud to be American?"

"No. Why would I be? Where you born is chance, but to America people go because they don't like where they born."

"Don't you like where you were born?"

"I do, but not because I was born there by chance."

"Why, then?"

"Because is best for me there. Here in Yoorop, I see same everywhere. French man proud because French and hates German because is German. German proud because German and hates French because is French. You, Miki, proud because you Hungarian, and hate Romanian, Serb and I don't know. Is all like that, Yoorop."

"Nonetheless, I am still proud to be a Hungarian," repeated the Count, this time a little angrily.

"Proud," shrugged Patsy. "Look at that old man over there sweeping sand. I respect him, because I respect all work. But if he came here and told is proud because is street-sweeper and hates porter, because porter not street-sweeper, I would say street-sweeper mad. You just as mad, Miki. All Yoorop just as mad."

And it went on like this for half an hour. I didn't take part in this debate, only listened in awe. My God, I thought, the way she's talking to a Count! It must be good to be American. A rich American. Though it's also true that being rich was probably a good thing anywhere, even in hell.

These days went by as quickly as only days of pure happiness can. August became September, and the leaves of the chestnut outside the hotel turned a rusty brown. The days were still intensely hot, but summer was blowing out its hot breath the way a runner pants before collapsing at the finish line. Autumn was climbing into the Buda hills.

One morning, Patsy said:

"One week today we leave, Béla."

My throat constricted, but I said nothing. Neither did she. We didn't mention her leaving again. And yet it was as if we were forever saying goodbye.

One day, she said:

"Give me photograph, Béla."

"I don't have one," I said, ashamed.

"Old one?"

"No."

The next morning, she brought a camera with her and took a photo of me. So then I steeled myself and asked her for a picture too. It seems she'd been expecting this, because she took one out of her bag right away.

"Old," she said apologetically. "Still look like little girl."

"When's it from?"

"Oh, I don't know. Maybe a year."

I pinched a piece of letter paper and an envelope from the drawing room and wrapped the photo in them carefully, lest it come to any harm. From then on, I had it with me always, in my left-hand pocket, above my heart.

Another time, she pointed at her hand.

"How you like mine ring?"

"It's lovely," I gushed.

She pulled it off her finger and gave it to me.

"To remember," she said, blushing slightly.

I could feel the warmth of her hand in the ring. I examined it, deeply touched. It was a thin, braided little thing, like a sort of round golden thread. There were three small stones in it, two little rubies and in the middle an even smaller diamond. I hadn't a clue about the value of such things. I thought it cost a fortune.

"Thank you, Patsy," I said, moved, "I'd really like to, but I can't take this."

"Why not?" she asked in surprise.

"Because I have no ring. I have nothing to give you."

"Did I ask?"

"No, but…"

"Don't be so silly! This no value."

She kept insisting, but I held firm. Oh, but how I would have liked something to remember her by! It ain't good to be poor, I thought.

They left on 21st September. That was a Monday and on the Sunday I had the day off. On Saturday, Patsy suggested we took a day-trip to Visegrád.

"Is beautiful!" she enthused. "Is old castle. Solomon Tower and everything. And the boat ride… oh God! I love Danube. You come?"

"Of course!" I said happily, because the thought of spending Sunday with her was delicious.

But when we parted, I came back down to earth. My God, I said to myself, I've taken leave of my senses! I can't put on my hotel uniform on my day off, and I can hardly be seen in my rags. And anyway, where was I supposed to get the money for the outing?

I spent the whole day wondering what to do. Finally, I wrote her a letter that evening in which I told her I'd caught a cold, had a fever, and couldn't go to Visegrád with her. I left the letter at reception.

"Someone just brought it," I lied, and quickly left the hotel so I wouldn't be there when Patsy got it.

I had a dreary Sunday. Cadet practice was cancelled and I could finally have had a lie-in, but I had become so accustomed to getting up early that I started awake at dawn. I was alone in the flat. Manci hadn't come home and my mother had gone to do the washing at the head porter's because she didn't want the work she did for free to interfere with her weekdays. The house was still asleep. It was so quiet, I could hear the dripping of the water pipe in the kitchen. She's off tomorrow—was my first thought, and I lay in bed as if her train had already run over my heart.

Time refused to pass though I did everything I could to kill it. I tidied up the flat, patched my clothes, washed and ironed my shirts. And it was still only nine a.m. For want of anything better to do, I started making lunch. I made potato soup, with dry crusts to go with it—good and filling. By eleven, I had even finished the washing-up and was at a definite loss what to do.

I went and sat on the walkway in front of our door and waited for someone to come and talk to me. The kids were playing football on a vacant plot next door. I could have gone and joined them, but I couldn't quite face it. When you work all week on an empty stomach and walk six hours a day to boot, you don't feel like kicking a ball about on Sunday, even if you have absolutely nothing else to do. But adults didn't come and chat to children where we lived, or at most Old Gábor, but he had recently given up treating Sunday as a day of rest. He was terribly busy. They had evicted a jobless family from the second floor and a very young locksmith had moved in in their place with his even younger wife. It had been three months since they'd come, but their flat was still as empty as the day they'd rented it. They slept on the bare floor and had two old chests and nothing else besides. So Old Gábor took pity on them. He promised to furnish the apartment on spec, if they got the raw materials together, and the locksmith got them all right. The whole thing cost him twenty fillérs, at least that's what they said in the house. For there was a lumber yard nearby, and on the yard there was a night guard. The locksmith got friendly with this night guard and spent every night for a full week playing cards with him. He lost no more than twenty fillérs, and that only out of courtesy. Meanwhile, his little lady dragged home the wood they needed, finding it easier not to bother the owners of the yard with the details.

So Old Gábor was working at full capacity. His weekdays were taken up with the young couple's furniture, and it was only on Sundays that he could work on his coffin. The magnum opus still wasn't ready. Or rather, it had been ready several times already, but Old Gábor kept starting again from scratch because he was never satisfied with it.

"You want to do your best for them up there in heaven," he told me once, "but it'd be nice if people down here understood it too. That's the artist's difficulty, my boy."

I listened to his hammering and all at once felt jealous. It's good when you get to work on something you like, even if that's making your own coffin. It's good to believe in something, even if that something's nonsense.

The building was beset by dreary Sunday boredom, the open windows looked like they were yawning. You could hear Márika singing from the typesetter's apartment:

> By the river singing, a canary
> You've lost your head now, young Mary
> Broke away from your true rose
> Like a dove from her partner does

Well, I couldn't take too much of that. I went into the room and lay down on the bed. I thought the same thing as so many millions of the poor: oh, I wish it wasn't Sunday! At least on weekdays you get by somehow. Someone's constantly breathing down your neck, you don't have time to think. But on Sunday you're left alone with your troubles, loneliness caging you with them like with a wild animal. It's a bad pairing, a dangerous combination, and anything can happen. There's no one—only the bottle of lye watching over you from beneath the sink.

And Márika kept on singing and singing:

> Silk scarf, string of pearls,
> Oh Mary, you'll be like those girls,
> The orphan birds that hop
> From branch to branch and never stop.

It was only now that I got the meaning of this old song. Márika still doesn't get it, I reflected. Good for her.

Suddenly, there was a knock. I opened the door, and I thought I was seeing things. It was Patsy.

"What are you doing here?" I asked, stunned.

"I ask your address," she smiled. "Come on, let's see. You have still fever?"

"No," I muttered awkwardly, and led her into the room.

I was wearing my shorts, which were very much on their last legs, my shirt that was several sizes too small and patched to death, and the Schoolmaster's enormous, mended shoes. It was only now that Patsy noticed, and it seemed that it had all become clear to her. She didn't ask me about my illness any more. We sat down.

"Your parents not home?" she asked.

"My mother's gone to work," I replied evasively.

"On Sunday?" she asked, surprised. "What kind shop she has?"

"She doesn't have a shop," I said, avoiding answering again, and went from one blush to another.

I was horribly ashamed. At first, I was ashamed only of our poverty, but then I was even more ashamed of being ashamed of it.

"My mother's a washerwoman," I blurted out, "and we're so poor that sometimes we can't afford bread. That's why I didn't come today, the rest was lies. I don't even have money for the tram, I walk six hours a day. These are my only clothes—look at them! Would you have gone to Visegrád with me looking like this?"

Patsy did not reply. She was looking at the picture of the Virgin above the bed, as if that were the only thing she was interested in. But her face was white as a sheet.

She took my hand. She didn't say anything, just looked at me. Her hand was warm—it almost melted my heart.

"I would have really liked to go to Visegrád," I said. "You do believe me?"

She nodded. We sat in silence.

"Béla, I have taxi waiting. Come."

"Where?"

"Doesn't matter. Wherever you want."

"I can't go like this, Patsy. I don't have any other clothes."

"We go somewhere they don't see. Hűvösvölgy, OK? Nice big forest there."

She stood up, took me by the arm, and I didn't protest any more.

The taxi caused quite a commotion in the house. This was probably the first one ever to have drawn up here. People's mouths hung open when they saw me getting into it. I didn't know what to do, I was so flustered.

It was the first time I'd ever sat in a car. My God, I thought, sitting there on the cushioned seat, if only I could do something for her, too! Something. Anything! If, say, we were attacked by bandits, and I could protect her. You don't need money for that. Or if the driver turned around and held her up at gunpoint, and I sacrificed my life to save her. But the driver did not turn around, only at the edge of the forest where we'd stopped. Then he thanked her politely for the tip and we were left alone, without any obvious peril in sight.

We walked slowly through the forest. Few people came here, mostly the poor, and I forgot about my ragged clothes. Patsy produced some peanuts and we munched them in silence. It was warm, it was calm, the birds above were singing.

Deep in the forest, we lay down in a clearing. Here, there was no one. We were alone, and it was as if the world had closed its eyes. We lay in silence. Burnt leaves lay on the grass, the forest was turning slowly to autumn.

"Autumn soon," Patsy said, but her mind seemed to be somewhere else.

"Yes," I said, my mind somewhere else, too.

Where would she be this time tomorrow? That's what I was wondering. My God, if I could only kiss her hand, I thought, but I avoided even her gaze, like a murderer his victim's. I lay motionless in the grass and stared at the sky. The sky was blue, a herd of white clouds grazing upon it. I want to die for her, I thought.

A squirrel ran across the path. Patsy tried to tempt it over with peanuts, but to no avail. The squirrel ran up a tree and didn't go for the peanuts even when Patsy threw them far away.

"Funny squirrel," she said, shaking her head.

"Why funny?"

"Because he no want to eat peanut."

"He does," I explained expertly, "but he's afraid. All squirrels are like that."

"Oh no!" Patsy protested. "In New York, squirrels eat from people hands in park. That's difference between America and Yoorop, you see. Here, Yoorop, everyone afraid. Though always big trouble from fear, always. You know what happen to me once?"

"What?"

"I was then eight and went to see friend mine to do math homework. I was always bad math, but homework was so hard that even friend mine could hardly do. We think and think long time and suddenly I see is ten o'clock night. I very afraid because friend mine live not good neighbourhood, out, far, you know. And suddenly, when I walking desert little street, man calls to me. I no say anything, just run, but then man grabs me and I scream: help! help! Then other man come grab him and say: you not ashamed chasing little girl? Don't be stupid, first man replies, I know this girl and if you don't let go right now, you regret. Then they fight and fall in puddle both and policeman come and take us all police station and call father mine. And then turns out—you know what? Man who call to me is friend father mine, only I no dare look at him in street because I afraid. And other man good man too. Two good men almost beat each other to death because silly little girl afraid. You know what father mine said when we see Berlin, Paris, and everywhere, how Yooropeans afraid each other? He say: all this Europe will finish like those two good men. Only with no police to make order."

Later, when this tale had turned into history, I thought a lot about those two good men. But even then I had no idea that Patsy's father, who had so eerily prophesied our future, would—two decades later, when he left his oil company for a senior position in the US government—act just as rashly as the two "Yooropean" good men. It seems that fear can pop even American corn. Or maybe it wasn't corn with Patsy's father at all, but oil; who knows? He was a good man, and always tipped me.

*

The next morning they left. They came down late and were in a big hurry. Patsy's father kept looking at his watch. Patsy kept staring at her shoes. She didn't look at me except when the lift stopped.

"See you next summer," she said, and got out quickly. But then she cried, "Oh! I forget something up in room!"

She explained this to her father in English, and got back in the lift. Halfway between the second and third floors she said:

"*Stop* the lift!" she said, half in English.

I didn't understand what she wanted.

"Stop it!" she said impatiently, this time in Hungarian.

I stopped the lift.

"I just wanted say goodbye," she said quietly.

"Yes," I muttered, and I felt my throat clenching up with sadness.

We didn't look at each other. We stood there for several minutes in silence, not looking up. All at once, she threw her arms around me and kissed me quickly on the lips.

"Come on," she whispered and I started the lift again.

Neither of us could speak. The lift stopped and Patsy ran out. A minute later the whole thing seemed so unreal, it was as if I'd dreamt it all.

The next morning, I woke to my mother's screaming.

"You stealing again? Ain't you ashamed?"

I looked at her blankly. She was holding Patsy's ring.

"How d'you get this?" she screamed.

"I don't know," I said and told her the story of the ring, stuttering and embarrassed.

"Is it that girl whose photo you carry in your pocket?" she asked.

"Yes," I admitted.

It seemed to me that something like a smile crossed her face. But she didn't say anything and went quickly out into the kitchen.

I've lost many things since then, but that little child's ring I still have. As I look at it, I have to say, the things that come to mind aren't terribly original. That's life, I think. If someone hadn't got into a lift in Budapest at 8.42 on the morning of 3rd July 1928, I might never have ended up in America.

7

A FEW DAYS LATER, ON A RAINY October night, I suddenly stopped the lift halfway between the second and third floors, where Patsy had kissed me, and said aloud:

"I'm going to America."

Later, even *I* thought the idea childish. How was I going to get to America when I couldn't even arrange a passage to Újpest? But reason only went so far. The idea had taken root, and I couldn't, didn't want to, kill it.

The backdrop to my stories now became American, and of course they always featured Patsy. But I could dream only at night, on the way home from work—during the day I was occupied with sober, practical planning. First of all, I'd decided to learn English as a matter of urgency. Yes, but how? How was a poor boy supposed to buy knowledge of the English language? A school was an impossible dream, and I immediately excluded it from my calculations. I'll learn on my own, I said to myself—all I need is a textbook. Well yes, but where do I get one? How much can they cost? I had no idea.

I started looking into it. I was meticulous. On my days off, instead of getting rested, I traipsed into the city for noon and spent the rest of the day, till nightfall, examining the windows of the bookshops. I didn't dare go in, because I had learnt that it wasn't a good idea to show yourself in the company of gentlemen in the kind of clothes that I was wearing. They might have refused to talk to me. Maybe they'd even have thrown me out. Slowly, I realized there were shops that sold used books as well, and I began concentrating on these. I went to one after the other, and one day I found what I was looking for.

It was lying there, biding its time in the window of a bookshop on Vilmos Császár út, as if waiting specially for me. My heart fluttered when I saw it. It was a nice thick book with a colourful cover and a big band around it:

LEARN ENGLISH PERFECTLY
IN ONLY SIX MONTHS WITH THIS BOOK
NO TEACHER REQUIRED, IN THE COMFORT
OF YOUR OWN HOME

Beneath it was a piece of white cardboard that said:

USED COPY, GOOD CONDITION, 2.20.

I'd never in my life had two pengős and twenty fillérs, but the thought that if I did have it, I could buy this book with it reassured me no end. I swore right then and there that I would get my hands on that two pengős and twenty fillérs if it was the last thing I did. The only thing that worried me was: what if they sold the book meanwhile?

The next day after work I hurried out to Vilmos Császár út to check if it was still in the window. It was. I was relieved. And from then on, I took a detour on my way home every night to visit the English book. I made eyes at it through the glass like a poor boy at his secret love, surrounded by rich suitors—to one of whom her evil father has probably already promised her.

One day, I saw the head porter looking something up in a Hungarian-English dictionary. That dictionary stayed in my thoughts all day, and the next day I decided to take the plunge. I went to the head porter.

"Sir," I said excitedly, "could you please lend me that Hungarian-English dictionary for ten minutes?"

"What for?" he asked. "You're not learning English?"

"Yes," I said. "Could I please have it? Ten minutes, I promise."

"All right," he said. "But bring it back in ten minutes, I might need it."

"Yes, sir! Thank you very much, sir."

I quickly purloined a bit of writing paper from a writing desk and copied out as many words as I could in ten minutes from the dictionary. It wasn't many, since I was constantly interrupted by the arrival of guests and had to stop writing each time. Ten minutes later, I returned the dictionary and started learning the copied words. It wasn't easy. I'd only known Hungarian words all my life, I'd heard no others before I came to the hotel. But whatever I managed to learn, I never forgot. I still, to this day, sometimes mispronounce the words I copied out of the head porter's dictionary: that's how well I mis-learnt them.

From then on, I borrowed the dictionary every day. I never dared keep it more than ten or fifteen minutes, because I was afraid I wouldn't get it again the next day. But if the head porter went off to lunch or dinner and there happened to be no one else around, I quickly sneaked the dictionary and copied out as many words as I could. I kept raiding the dictionary the way other children raid the jam jars in the pantry, and the more I had, the greater grew my appetite. I was insatiable.

One evening, the boy who was relieving me said:

"There's a letter for you at reception."

At first I thought he was joking. Who would write to me, especially at the hotel? But then my heart fluttered. Patsy! I thought, and ran all the way to reception.

It wasn't a letter, just a postcard. It was from Paris; I remember, it had the Arc de Triomphe on it. She only wrote a few words, but what I read into them would have filled a hundred postcards. I was so happy I wanted to turn cartwheels.

From then on, I was constantly waiting for a letter. I had to wait a long time. The next postcard was from New York. She wrote that they'd arrived safely and that she couldn't wait for next summer to see me again, but that I should write to her meanwhile "much and many detail". That was all well and good; this card made me even happier than the one from Paris. But then I realized that the post office had stuck the stamp over her address in such a way that it was now impossible to make out. So I waited for the next card; what else could I do? But I waited in vain. It didn't come. Tomorrow! I reassured myself, and the next day I again said: tomorrow!

In the meantime, I tried to learn as much as I could about America. If I found a newspaper, the first thing I read was the American news. I devoured the stories from across the pond as if each one had featured a close personal friend. Once, I recall, one of the Sunday papers printed a biography of a famous American millionaire who had come to America as a pauper when he was a child. I cut that article out of the paper and from then on kept it always on me, in between the photograph of Patsy and the two postcards. When life was mean to me, I would comfort myself with the thought that it would all be different in America. Whenever I saw something to make my blood boil, I would say: that could never happen in America. America for me became the Promised Land, and Patsy the Sleeping Beauty awaiting my arrival across the sea.

I was very grateful to her. One afternoon at the apprentices' institute, they taught us how to fill out a receipt. That night, I wrote the following poem:

RECEIPT

A receipt, this my tune
Made out for
Immense good fortune.

Thanks be to those up high
For the few weeks' lease of
The finest star in all the sky.

They called in their loan apace
But, like Moses did with God,
At least I got to see her face.

Though the memory now stings
I follow that star,
Like the three Wise Kings.

I see now how dreams are made,
And what I must fight for,
Like a Knight of the Crusade.

This receipt, first of all
I give to the heavenly
Office responsible.

A receipt is this, my tune
Humble proof
Of a poor boy's great boon.

*

Slowly, I started writing poems. It began like pneumonia—with light, pleasant bouts of fever, subtle, almost unnoticed. Instead of daydreamt stories, I now made up poems going home, and I ascribed no more importance to them than I had to my stories previously. I wrote the way a dog barks. There were weeks when I wrote a couple of poems a day. I didn't care if they were good or bad. I liked them, but if someone had told me they were awful, I would almost certainly have believed them and would not have lost much sleep over it. I had nothing to compare them to: I only knew the few poems we'd learnt in school. The truth is, I had never even been all that interested in poems. I'd always been more "academically" minded and was interested especially in history and geography. I wanted to learn languages, lots of languages. But poems... what for? I thought.

Now all at once I got a taste for them and I devoured rhymes voraciously—there were plenty of literary journals lying about in the hotel. I cut the poems out of the back issues and read them all. I had a strange feeling about them. They were good, very good, but still... Who knows? They reminded me of the dolled-up, porcelain-faced ladies who floated into the lift on a cloud of perfume in their toothpick stilettos. I was in awe of them, but I didn't like them. Not that I thought my own poems superior. Not at all. I knew that the porcelain-faced ladies were finely bred and I was just a filthy peasant; and I was completely convinced that what I was reading was literature and what I was writing was nothing more than idle scribbling. I wasn't upset about it; I merely noted the fact. I liked writing poems, and what's more, it was free—so I kept writing them.

But all at once, I was beset by worrying symptoms. I fell in love with my own writings and would curse "upper-class poetry", as I called it at the time. They're like pastries, I said to myself. They're for jaded gentlemen who no longer know what to do with their stomachs and their souls. But I was a sensible peasant boy and soon got over this superiority complex. I told myself: it's a case of sour grapes, you filthy peasant. I started to doubt, I lost faith; but I paid just as little attention to my feelings of doubt as I had to my feelings of superiority. I was torn between extremes and couldn't find my place. One day I had an idea.

At first, I was frightened by my plan, but eventually I said, why not? I cut the address off some hotel writing paper and carefully copied out my poems. There were already thirty or forty by that time. I gave the "collection" the title *When You've Got No Dog to Bark at Night, You'll End Up Barking in Its Stead*. Then I put them in an envelope and addressed it to the biggest daily in Budapest. The problem was that the postal service back then did not deliver poetry, no matter how good, without a stamp, and I had no stamp, nor money with which to buy one. I waited a few days for some spark of inspiration, and then had an idea that saved the day. I took the letter into the newspaper's offices and gave it to the first office boy I saw.

"A gentleman sent it," I lied. "Told me to deliver it here."

With that, and without waiting for a response, I turned and fled out into the street.

From then on, I no longer opened the newspapers at the front, but at the back, at the "Messages from the Editor" section, waiting anxiously for the fateful judgement. I don't know how long I waited—all I remember was that it seemed an unbearably long time; which of course doesn't mean anything, because when you're fifteen and have your whole life ahead of you, oddly enough you're far more impatient than later, when your years are already numbered.

One day, when I opened the newspaper, my heart skipped a beat. Among the messages from the editor was the following:

Béla R. His poems signal the emergence of a tumultuous, raw, but astoundingly original talent. We will be printing "My

236

Harmonica" in this Sunday's issue. Please come see us at the offices between five and seven p.m.

Fireworks went off inside me. I didn't know what to do with myself. I ran to the toilets, locked the door, gratitude overflowing within me—to the extent that it poured out of my eyes as tears.

"Thank you, Lord!" I whispered, my hands clenched together in prayer. For want of a more fitting altar, I fell to my knees right there before the porcelain bowl; I hope no one in heaven took that amiss.

The next day was my day off. I spent the morning in a state of tremendous excitement. I prepared for my visit to the editors like a young man going off to find himself a bride. And this was, indeed, a betrothal—a lifelong and serious betrothal—only I didn't know it at the time. I was getting betrothed to my destiny.

I left home at noon so I'd be at the offices by five on the dot. It was the end of November, but the weather was still amazingly clement. I ambled slowly towards Pest. I was gripped by an inchoate fear, and my mouth was bitter with excitement. I tried to imagine the conversation, the editor's questions, my responses, and generally every possible and impossible eventuality. Whether they would pay for printing a poem, I didn't know, and as to how much, I was even more uncertain. My God, I thought, if they gave me two pengős for it, I'd run straight to the pawnshop and get back my mother's cross.

By the time I made it to the offices, my stomach was grumbling anxiously. There was only an office boy in the lobby, licking envelopes at a desk. He was a stocky, thirtyish man with the face of a sergeant-major, a louche blond Germanic moustache above a harsh mouth. I could see, when he looked me up and down with his liquid blue eyes, that in his mind, he'd already thrown me out.

"Well, what is it?" he demanded.

"I'd like to speak to the editor, please."

"Which one?" he mumbled. "They're nineteen to the dozen here."

That threw me. I hadn't anticipated the question. The front page of the newspaper just said "editor", like that, in the singular, so I had thought there was only one editor. And since the section in which they'd written to me was called messages from the editor, I had assumed that my message came from *the* editor. I didn't know what to say.

"Whoever," I got out at last, and to show him that I wasn't trying to be cheeky, I added: "Whoever's free."

"You can't talk to *whoever*," he replied acerbically, "Mr Whoever is out to lunch. You'd best write to him instead."

"But please," I said anxiously, and was about to explain that they had asked me to come, when one of the doors opened and a gentleman called out:

"Bence!"

Bence left me standing there and hurried into the room. I was alone. I spotted myself in the mirror.

It was a frightening moment. In our little mirror at home, I saw only my face, and the mirrors in the hotel showed a well-proportioned, scarlet-uniformed, quite handsome lad. Now I saw a frightened, ragged beggar in impossibly shabby clothes and shorts with no stockings. My God, I thought, if the editor sees me like this, he may not even print my poem on Sunday! He must have imagined some fine gentleman when he wrote that I was an "astoundingly original talent", and now...

I heard the door opening and jumped quickly away from the mirror.

"Yes, sir," I heard Bence saying. "I'll call the print room right away."

I made up my mind then and there. By the time Bence had come back into the lobby, I was out in the corridor, running for the stairs. I never did find out which editor had written that wonderful *message*, and the editor never found out who he'd been writing to, because I never again set foot in those offices.

This happened on Monday or Tuesday; I wanted to retreat to a cave, like a bear, and sleep the week away till Sunday.

I don't know what I was expecting from that Sunday. A life-changing event, a celestial sign, a miracle? You only wait like this once in your life: when you're waiting for your first poem to appear in print. These were days full of wonder and terror. Sometimes, I was seized by superstitious fear that I would die before Sunday and wouldn't get to see my poem in print. I would start awake at night and recite the poem for hours, rejoicing over a line I found good, despairing over a sub-par adjective. It was enough for me to spot a guest reading *that* newspaper for my heart to skip a beat. You don't so much as notice me now, I said to myself, but on Sunday you too will be reading my poem, yes, *my* poem! You're a gentleman, sure, and I'm only a filthy peasant, but this filthy peasant can write poems, unlike you, despite your manicured nails.

The whole world revolved around my poem. My God, I thought, if I could only send it to Patsy! What would she make of it? Next summer, when she came back, we'd go out to Margit Island again one day and sit among the ruins where no one ever goes, and I would hand it to her without a word. How did you write something so beautiful? she'd ask, overcome, and I would reply: I had you for a muse! Then she would embrace me and kiss me like she did in the lift before they left, and this time I would kiss her back, and that would be our betrothal. And when they asked her in America who her fiancé was, she would say: a poet. A real poet.

These were my daydreams, night and day. By Saturday, I was sick with anticipation. I had a splitting headache and stomach cramps—my throat kept clenching up with stress. All day long, I couldn't wait for it to be evening, but when evening finally came and my shift ended, I was seized by a strange emptiness, an inexplicable disappointment.

I couldn't go home. I wandered the streets and suddenly found myself in front of the newspaper's offices. They must be printing it by now, I thought, and walked round the building, my heart thumping, like a murderer stalking the scene of his crime. The print room was in the basement, and its windows opened onto a quiet little side street. I stopped in front of the open door and looked in. I was struck by the bitter, exciting smell of printer's ink, fatal perfume of the muses. That was the first time I'd smelt it. It was a great moment. Down in the basement, the printing presses clattered on, the paper rushing on the rollers. *They're printing my poem*, I told myself, and my eyes welled up. Only young poets can feel this way when their first poem is being printed, or ageing fathers helping their daughters into their bridal gowns.

I didn't sleep till dawn. In the morning, when I was going to cadet practice, the Sunday paper had already hit the streets. But despite it being right there, I couldn't buy it—where would I have got the sixteen

239

fillérs for it? I asked every boy at practice whether they had the paper, but even if they did, it wasn't the one I was after. In the end, I was forced to turn to my mother.

"Muther," I said clumsily, awkwardly. "Could you give me sixteen fillérs?"

"What for?" she asked in surprise, because I had never before asked her for money.

"I want to buy the paper."

"You gone mad? You don't really mean to spend our hard-earned money on a *newspaper*?"

I reddened. My writing poetry was the biggest secret of my life, one I guarded with an almost obsessive jealousy. I had never told anyone about it, least of all my mother. Now, however, I was forced to reveal it.

"I… wrote something in the paper," I mumbled.

My mother looked at me, astounded.

"I did."

"What?"

"A poem."

"And they printed it?"

"Yes."

"Why?"

"Because… well, they liked it."

"How d'you know?"

"They said so. Here, look."

I took out my little diary into which I had pasted—just to be safe— the *message from the editor* so that I wouldn't end up somehow losing it. My mother read it, looked at me and—as if she couldn't believe her eyes—read it again. Then she was silent for a space.

"Where d'you learn to write poems?" she asked at last.

"I didn't, Muther."

"Then… how d'you do it?"

"I don't know. It just *came*."

"It just *comes*?"

"Sometimes. Not always."

"What's it depend on?"

"I don't know. Maybe it's from God."

"Hm."

My mother stared at her shoes as she always did when she was nervous.

"Well, that I *would* pay sixteen fillérs to see!" she said eventually, without looking up.

"But you don't have it?"

"No. Yesterday was the first."

I didn't say anything. What was there to say? My mother stood there for a little while and then went out into the kitchen without a word. I swore horribly to myself, but that didn't help much. I took out my English notes and tried to learn some words. I couldn't. My head was full of the poem. Everyone could read it except me!

You could hear Márika singing from the walkway. I threw aside my notes and walked out.

"Where you going?" my mother asked.

"To Márika's."

"For the paper?"

"Yes."

My mother shrugged.

"Don't bother. They get the other one."

"Then maybe someone else'll have it."

"They don't."

"How do you know?"

My mother blushed, as if caught in the act.

"I asked," she confessed, then turned around and pretended to have something very important to do.

So I went back into the room. I tried to study but still couldn't. A few minutes later my mother came in.

"Here," she said, "I wash for a woman that has a newsagent's, she might let us get a look at that paper."

"You think?" I asked hopefully.

"Yes," she replied. "If the old lady's in, we won't have no trouble. I don't know her daughter so well. Come on, it's worth a try."

She didn't have to ask *me* twice.

"Where is this newsagent lady, then?" I asked in the street.

"In Buda. On Margit körút."

"Margit körút?"

"Yes. Why you so surprised?"

"Won't that be a bit much for you? Three hours there, three back? It'll be evening by the time we're home."

My mother shrugged.

"It's Sunday, I ain't got nothing better to do," she replied with forced levity. "I've brought the bread with us. There ain't nothing else for lunch, anyhow."

"Thank you, Muther."

"What for?" she joked. "Keepin' you on bread and water?"

"It's the thought that counts," I said, it being my turn for forced levity. "It's good of you to come with me."

My mother gave a little laugh.

"Anyone can go to the cinema that's got the money, but not everyone gets to read her son's poem, ain't that right? Come on, then, let's step on it, or we'll never get there."

The church bells had tolled three by the time we got to Margit körút. My mother went ahead to check the lay of the land.

"It's her!" she reported excitedly. "Come on."

The lady who owned the store was talking to an elderly gentleman when we came in. She was a dumpy, brown-haired woman with twinkling eyes. She was nice to my mother, as nice as if she'd been her favourite dog.

"Well, what's up, my girl?"

My mother just stood there for a few moments and stared at her shoes. It seems she was embarrassed in front of the old man.

"Please, madam," she said very timidly, "could we have a little look at one of the papers?"

"Sure," she nodded. "They're over there, go help yourself, my girl."

And with that, she went back to chatting with the old man.

My mother went over to the counter but didn't dare lift the paper off it. She bent over to leaf through it, while I looked on over her shoulders on tiptoe, heart beating wildly. Suddenly, my heart skipped a beat altogether.

"There it is!" I whispered and broke out in a sweat.

My mother leant over the paper and I leant, stretching, over her to read in this borrowed newspaper my first published poem. It went like this:

MY HARMONICA

My hands are peasant's hands. They can't play violin,
Can't pluck the strings of a fancy mandolin.
They have no place in a grand philharmonica
All they have is this cheap harmonica.

A humble thing, no decoration north or south.
Only wood and tin, as naked as my mouth.
A plain wooden cradle, a plain wooden coffin
Is the song of this simple piece of wood and tin.

So easily a violin will break its strings
Like all those delicate and fancy things.
Naked you go out, as naked you came in
Is the song of this simple piece of wood and tin.

Its song a song of poverty, of life and death,
And how my mother coughs out all her breath.
Perhaps the only way of taking all this in
Is softly, by night, on this piece of wood and tin.

There is a carpenter. A poor man, so I hear.
And to this my song, he may sometime lend an ear.
Perhaps one day his father, too, will listen in,
To the song of this simple wood and tin.

"How is it?" I whispered.

"I don't know," my mother replied. "If they printed it, it must be good."

But when the old man left, she handed the paper to the newsagent.

"Here, madam, have you read this poem yet?"

The lady glanced at the paper.

"Look at the name," she said.

"Some relation?" the lady asked.

"My son!" my mother said and swallowed heavily. Her face flushed a deep red, her eyes glittered. "It's by my boy!"

The newsagent was very surprised.

"How old are you, my boy?"

"Just gone fifteen, ma'am."

"And you're writing in the paper?" she asked, shaking her head from side to side. "Well, Anna, this is quite something," she said in congratulatory tones. "Let me read that poem, then."

She put on her spectacles and started reading. I watched her face, but in vain. It was exactly the same as when she'd been talking to the old man.

"It's good," she said at last. "A little modern, but good."

I would have liked to ask what "a little modern" meant, but I thought it best to keep quiet, since a poet should obviously know that kind of thing already. In any case, it can't have been anything good. I swore right then and there never to show my poems to anyone else again. Maybe Patsy, I added later, softening.

The newsagent turned to my mother.

"You're not sick, are you, Anna?"

"Not me," replied my mother. "Why d'you ask, madam?"

"Because your son says you keep coughing."

My mother became horribly embarrassed.

"Um," she muttered, "he just meant… um… you know."

"For the rhyme," smiled the lady, with a professional air.

"That's right," my mother said, seizing on the word, and looked at me. "Ain't it, Béla?"

"Yes," I said, and was horribly ashamed of myself.

My mother, having thanked the newsagent profusely, was getting ready to go when the lady asked me:

"Don't you want to take the paper?"

Didn't I! These ladies and their questions! I glanced over at my mother out of the corner of my eye.

"I forgot my purse, madam," she said.

"That's all right," the lady replied, "I'll take it out of next week's washing."

"Thank you so much."

"Yes, thank you, ma'am."

I walked triumphantly out with the paper. My mother didn't say anything for a while, and then she said reproachfully:

"You oughtn't to have written that."

I said nothing. My mother dropped her voice, as if she was afraid of being overheard.

"Ladies don't like poor people that cough," she said. "They're afraid of 'em. Won't employ 'em. I think it's best if we don't show that poem to anyone."

"I wouldn't have shown it to anyone, anyway," I muttered.

"Why not?"

"Well… it's best to keep your mouth shut."

"Yeah," my mother nodded empathetically. "Best for the likes of us to keep our mouths shut. Now, you as hungry as I am?"

I nodded.

"Then let's sit ourselves down on a bench and have our bread," she said, what with our being just on the square at Pálffy tér.

We sat down. My mother broke the bread, handed one half to me, and bit greedily into the other. Then she opened the newspaper. She treated it differently than she had in the newsagent's. Every one of her gestures showed that this was *her* newspaper, that she would work for it, and that she could do with it as she pleased. She smoothed the page on which they'd printed my poem flat on her knee, folded it double and began to read. She read differently than she had at the newsagent's. She made her way through the words slowly, ponderously, her mouth moving a little as she read. When she'd got to the end, she said:

"It's really somethin'." But then, it seems, she got embarrassed, because she quickly added: "The newsagent lady said so. Did you hear her?"

"Yes."

She looked out towards the Danube. There was fog over the river, and a ship's horn sounded somewhere in the distance. We sat in silence for a long time. Suddenly, she said:

"He'll be sorry for not taking an interest in you yet, your pa. Could have been *his* name they printed in the paper."

"Your name's good enough for me," I said.

"Yes… it ain't nothin' to be ashamed of. It's a pretty common name, I'll admit, but decent Christian folk have worn it."

"You'll be proud of it someday!"

"Proud? Why?"

"Because I'm going to make that name of yours famous. They'll know it everywhere, even in America. Would you believe that?"

"Maybe," she said pensively. "Because if a poor kid as miserable as you can have his poem printed in the paper at fifteen, then it seems to me that nothing's quite impossible in this world." She said nothing for a while and just stared at the Danube. "Who knows," she said, munching on her bread, "you may really be famous someday, and then you'll deny your poor mother."

"I damn well won't!"

"Why shouldn't you?" she said softly, without a trace of bitterness. "You go ahead, if you think it'll help. That's the way of the world. Ain't nothin' to write home about, a mother like yours. And besides," she shrugged, "where I'll be by then, Lord knows!"

"Stop talking like that!" I snapped. "What do you mean where'll you be? I'll tell you where. You know where you'll be?"

"Where?"

"In America!"

She smiled.

"Why there?"

"'Cause I'll take you there. More than one poor boy has made his fortune there. And I'm going to as well, you'll see. And when we get hungry, like now, I'll take you to the finest restaurant, and you can eat so much you'll have to take that white powder afterwards, like the fancy gentlemen do."

"Oh let them drink that stuff, much good may it do 'em!" laughed my mother. "*Székelygulyás* is good enough for me."

"And noodles with cottage cheese!" I added severely.

"And maybe some bean soup before?" she enquired, giggling.

"Very well," I agreed magnanimously. "But only if it's got smoked ham in it!"

"Yeah!" she said, laughing out loud. "We ain't never had it so good! So when we off to America, then?"

"You think I'm joking? I've got it all worked out. And you know, I'm going to make a lot of money in America, that's for sure. And I'll get a flat for us the likes of which you've never seen. A real millionaire's flat. Three rooms, central heatin', a lavatory and everything, so we won't have to freeze to the planks in winter. And you'll have the finest room, I've got that all planned out too. And you'll have a sofa in it like the one Márika and Árpád have, for you to lie around on all day. And I'll even get a washerwoman in every month."

"Washerwoman?" my mother laughed and her eyes suddenly brimmed with tears. "Washerwoman?" she repeated and put her arm around my shoulder. "You're still a little boy, poems or no poems. But your heart," she added more softly, "your heart, my boy, is as if the Lord Jesus had touched it with his hand."

Then she opened her battered little bag and took out her handkerchief, because by now she was no longer laughing, but crying bitter tears.

8

WINTER TIPTOED INTO THE CITY LIKE a thief. In the morning, the sun was still shining and the asters paraded unsuspecting in the gardens of Buda. Gentlemen walked by the riverside with their jackets open. But in the afternoon, the sky unexpectedly clouded over, an angry north wind swept the streets, and a strange sort of precipitation beat down that was neither snow nor rain. I woke in the night to find that I was cold. There was an icy draught in the room, the window rattled, the doors creaked, and there was a mysterious banging from the roof. The wind howled so you'd have thought people were being massacred in the dark outside. In the morning, when I went out into the street, the city was so quiet it was as if everyone were at home in mourning. The wind stopped. There were sheets of ice on the river. It snowed.

It was on that day that it happened. In the afternoon, the lift broke down, and since they couldn't fix it till morning, they let me go home early. It must have been around ten when I got back to the apartment. It was dark in the kitchen. I felt my way, with well-practised movements, to the table, put the packet of food down, and went into the room. But when I wanted to go to bed, something didn't feel right. I went back into the kitchen and lit a match. My mother wasn't in her bed. I looked in the room as well, but she wasn't there either. I'd been living with my mother for more or less a year now, but this had never happened before, though it was true that I usually got home a good two hours later. Was she usually out at this time? I wondered. I was gripped by a vague sense of unease. I decided that I wouldn't go to sleep till my mother got home, but I was so tired that the second I lay down I was overcome by sleep.

I woke to the opening of the front door. I wanted to say something, but then I heard a man's voice in the kitchen. It was saying things to my mother. They were whispering. My mother's voice was so strange that at first I thought it might not be her at all. She was giggling like a schoolgirl.

"You shouldn't have made me drink all that wine," she said. "I'm as dizzy as a merry-go-round."

"D'you deny you had a good time?" the man asked tipsily.

"No, I don't," my mother said, before making some little, wordless noise. I didn't know if she was yawning or sighing. "How long it's been since I drunk wine. How long since I heard the Gypsies play! Oh dear, oh dear... What time is it?"

I heard the striking of a match. They lit the petroleum lamp in the kitchen.

"The clock's stopped," the man said.

My mother found that quite amusing.

"It's on strike," she giggled. "I usually wind it at eight. Must be angry that I ain't payin' it no attention. How does that song go again?"

"Which one?"

"The one you had 'em play me all the time."

The man started humming softly in a fine baritone. He hummed a melancholy tune, and my mother joined him.

I felt an unpleasant pressure in my gut. What was going on? Was my mother drinking in secret? And bringing home men? Had she brought home other men before, and was it just that I hadn't noticed in the dark? I was overcome by revulsion and anger. My mother laughed.

"What you laughing at?" the man asked.

"Makes me laugh to remember."

"What?"

"You not recognizin' me. I'd never have thought it!"

"But then I did remember you."

"Then! It's easy to remember after. You looked at me like you'd never seen me before in your life. What I'd like to know is, if that's so, why you came over and talked to me."

"Why? 'Cause you were lookin' at me. Weren't you lookin' at me?"

"'Course I was lookin' at you!"

"There you are, then. When a lady as pretty as yourself looks at me, I'm going to go over and talk to her. It's the way I am."

"Oh, you can sweet-talk, all right, you sweet-talker!" my mother laughed again. "You should have seen your face when I said your name!"

"Well… it's been a while since we saw each other."

"Yes indeed," my mother replied, and this time, I clearly heard her sigh.

So they're old friends, I thought, who haven't seen each other for a long time. That reassured me a little. But then the man said:

"Listen, Anna, couldn't I sleep here tonight?"

"You've got a nerve! You lost your mind?"

"All right, all right, no need to bite my head off. I could sleep in the other room, if you didn't want me sleeping in here."

"I told you already I've got someone that rents the bed. Why d'you want to sleep here anyway?"

The man was quiet for a moment. Then he said:

"I'll tell you like it is, Anna, I've got nowhere to stay."

"But you said you lived on Váci út!"

"Oh, I was just saying that, you know how it is. Truth is, I'd only just arrived in Pest when I saw you at the station."

"You mean you don't live here?"

"Well, yes, usually."

"Then why don't you have a flat?"

"I was down in the countryside for a while."

"Where?"

"All around."

"What for?"

"Business."

"You're in business now?"

"Mostly."

"What sort of business?"

"All sorts."

They went on like this for a while. My mother asking this and that and the man giving her evasive answers. I had an uneasy feeling. Something isn't right with this man, I said to myself. God knows who my mother had picked up!

"So, can I sleep here, then?" he asked again.

"I already told you you can't. But if you've got nowhere to stay, I could put in a word for you with the Bognárs. They live downstairs. They might still be up. You want me to come down with you?"

"No, it's all right."

"Why not?"

"It's not important. Let's leave it."

A few moments of silence followed.

"Here," said my mother. "You didn't go and spend all your money at the inn, did you?"

The man did not reply.

"My God," said my mother, "you really are the biggest spendthrift I ever saw. You take me to dinner, wine flowin' like there's no tomorrow, throwin' all that precious money at the fiddler; and then you ain't got nothin' left to find a bed with!"

"It's the way I am," the man said, not without a touch of pride. "When I take a woman out, I don't think about what comes after. I've never been cheap with a woman. It's just my nature."

"You've not changed a bit, d'you know that?"

"Not much, no," he admitted, "though I'm fifteen years older."

"Don't you go making yourself younger than you are. It's been more than sixteen years, it has. I should know."

I was struck by a shocking thought. It couldn't be… My throat clenched up.

There was silence in the kitchen for a while. Then my mother said:

"Well, if Manci don't come home with the last tram, then I don't mind, you can go sleep in the bed. If only I knew what time it was."

"The last tram left ages ago."

"How d'you know? You ain't got a watch."

"I don't need a watch to tell me that," he boasted. "A sailor can feel the time in his bones!"

Sailor! I repeated to myself. *It's been more than sixteen years, it has… I should know…* I felt a cold sweat coming over me.

"I'd rather sleep with you out here," he whispered tenderly, and then there came the sounds of a quiet struggle.

"Oh, come on… you mad? You'll wake the boy!"

"So what? I can't hardly wait to meet him anyway."

"You've not been so impatient these fifteen years!"

"How could I have been when I didn't know he existed!" And then, more softly: "Come on, Anna, don't be like that… You're the mother of my child, and all!"

Something metallic fell loudly onto the stone floor.

"You see!" he whispered. "It'll be *you* that ends up waking him!"

There was silence.

"Go get yourself in the other room, there's a good boy," said my mother. "And don't you strike a match! The bed's at the back, by the wall."

"A dark soul'll find his way in the dark, my dear. Well, g'night. Not even a kiss good night?"

"G'night," my mother replied, curt and impatient.

The door opened quietly and closed again. Slow, careful steps, someone feeling their way. Suddenly, the bed creaked. More feeling of the way, then the soft sounds of someone undressing. The dull thud of a shoe on the floor.

My heart was in my mouth. I could hear my mother opening up her folding bed and climbing into it. A few minutes later, the bed in the room also gave a groan. Then silence. Silence, silence, silence.

The minutes liquefied and dispersed into time unbearably slowly, a calm, steady breathing coming from the bed, and not a bit of noise from outside. They were both asleep. Chunks of snow sometimes fell softly off the roof, rattling the window frames and spattering loudly on the stone of the walkway outside—you could hear the dripping of the pipe in the kitchen. My father, I thought, and stuffed my hand to my mouth so they wouldn't hear me crying.

I had just dropped off when the door sprang open. A yellow shaft of light filtered into the room and lit up my mother's white underskirts. She tiptoed over to the bed and started trying to wake my father.

"Get up, Manci's here," she whispered.

"Oh damn it all!" my father grumbled sleepily, but then jumped out of bed, climbed into his clothes, and went out into the kitchen.

A long discussion followed, during which my father referred to Manci as a "pretty lady", too—more than once—and Manci—as far as I could tell from her voice—was strangely enough not at all upset that he'd been sleeping in her bed.

"He's warmed it up for me," she giggled, and her voice sounded different than usual.

Finally, she bid them good night and came into the room.

"You asleep?" she asked quietly.

She asked that every night, though I had never once replied. I always pretended to be asleep when she came into the room. I felt a strange revulsion for her, a revulsion mixed with a hatred that was hard to define, and tingling curiosity; and though I never actually admitted it to myself, I was also slightly afraid of her. I couldn't forget the way she'd looked at me when she was drunk, how her gaze had moved over me on New Year's Eve, when I'd clambered out of her bed. Yes, I was a little scared of her.

I heard her light the lamp and begin to undress. I knew the process of her undressing so intimately that I could have told you even with my eyes closed when she was taking off her stockings, when she was undoing the elastic of her bra, and so on. I was also familiar with the noises that came after she had undressed—the creaking of the bed as she climbed in, the rustling of the paper as she laid it out before her, the clink and swish of the *pálinka* bottle as she took a swig and the dull, searing sound of the petroleum lamp as she blew it out. Then there was a short pause, followed by that deep, scary snoring that sounded in the dark like she was having to saw bits of wood out of her throat to be able to exhale.

But tonight, I was only half aware of all that. I was constantly trying to hear what was going on in the kitchen. It was so quiet, it was as if there hadn't been anyone in there at all, though my father had not yet left. Or had he left without me hearing him? I even held my breath now and then to hear each little noise, but in vain. There was silence—mysterious, unbearable silence. I don't know how long I lay there listening: five minutes, half an hour, or an eternity. I'd lost my sense of time completely.

Suddenly, I heard whispering from the kitchen.

"Don't, Mishka… they'll hear!"

"'Course they won't. Listen to her snorin'."

"No, Mishka, really…"

"Aw, don't be so… come on."

"Mishka…"

The bed gave an enormous creak, and then all I could hear was unintelligible muttering. Their words were aflame and floated darkly, vaguely, in the silence like burning ash. Till then, I'd thought only the dying groan, moan and pant like that. I wanted to go deaf so I wouldn't hear, but at the same time I listened to every noise like a doctor examining the symptoms of an unknown illness.

When there was silence again at last, I, too, nodded off. I don't know how long I slept. It was still pitch black when I started awake. There was a heavy fog inside my head; I remember thinking I'd dreamt the whole thing. And then reality and dreams really did get all mixed up: I fell into a slumber. When I jolted awake again, I'd sweated through my shirt. It must be late, I thought, my mother might come in at any moment. I was gripped by some inexplicable fear at the thought. I didn't want to see her. Not her, nor that man. Never, ever again.

I jumped up. The floor creaked with the sudden movement. I listened in fear to see if anyone had heard. No one had. Manci was snoring away and there was steady breathing from the kitchen. I tiptoed to the window and opened it slowly, carefully. The sharp, snowy air struck my face. Outside, nothing was moving. The house was still asleep. I perched up on the windowsill, pulled up my legs, swung silently around and stepped out onto the walkway. Then I raced down the stairs like a man possessed. I felt so relieved when I got out into the street, it was as if I'd just managed to escape a brush with evil.

I didn't want to go home again. I spent the whole day dreaming up plans for escape, most of them fit for a thriller, of course, but I knew, with my peasant's common sense, that I would end up going home after all, because what else was there to do? But I was simply unable to imagine what would happen when I saw my mother, not to mention… that man. I tried to reassure myself by saying that my mother would be asleep by the time I got home anyway, and that tomorrow I could once more climb out of the window.

I had decided on this course of action as I headed home. But as I was passing the scrapyard, I heard my mother's voice behind my back.

"Béla!"

I turned in surprise. My mother was in the Sabbatarian's hut and had called after me from the door.

"Yes?" I muttered, my mouth dry, trying to avoid her gaze.

My mother came out after me but didn't say a thing. We walked in silence across the vacant plot. I noticed she was clutching the little satchel with which she used to go to work in the morning; she hadn't been home. *She's been lying in wait,* I told myself, and waited, suspiciously, to see what happened next.

It was long gone midnight. There was a cold winter moon in the sky, the snow sparkled on the empty plot, and a silvery-blue fog hung in the distance.

"There was no need for you to go climbin' out the window like a thief," she said all at once, without any introduction.

I didn't reply. The snow crunched under our feet, unnaturally loudly.

"He is your father, after all," she added. It had been intended as a reproach, but had ended up more of an apology. "Ain't you curious to meet him?"

"No."

The word burst out of me like a deadly bullet and it silenced my mother for good. She didn't say a word all the rest of the way.

When we got to the building, we were greeted by an unbelievable racket. A party of drunks was yelling and singing in one of the upstairs flats.

We exchanged a look, despite ourselves. We knew that the almighty Herr Hausmeister didn't stand for people so much as talking loudly, and we couldn't understand what was going on. There was no way he hadn't heard the noise.

"He must be out," my mother said. "There'll be hell to pay when he gets back. Where's it comin' from?"

"The second or third," I guessed.

"It ain't us, is it?"

"Who'd be making that kind of racket at ours?"

My mother didn't reply, but grew increasingly uneasy as we got farther and farther up the stairs. By the time we got up to the third, I could see why. All that noise *was* coming from our flat.

"Mother of God!" she whispered, petrified, and quickly crossed herself.

No one heard us open the door amid all the noise. The kitchen was empty. We stopped in the dark and stared, astounded, into the room through the half-open door.

It was a dreadful sight. A large man, worker's cap drawn down over his eyes, was drowsing in Manci's bed, my mother's gingerbread heart was now hanging around some tottering drunk's neck, and there were broken glasses, overturned bottles and cigarette butts everywhere. The freshly scrubbed floor was stained with puddles of red wine like little lakes of blood. The room was full of tobacco smoke and the furniture seemed to be swaying amid clouds—stormy and unbearably smelly clouds—in which the smell of sweat and alcohol had mixed with the nauseating stench of drunken burping. The lights, too, were on, the precious electric lights that not even Manci was allowed to touch. The table lamp was flat out atop the wardrobe, dripping petroleum, as if it, too, had been blind drunk.

The drunks were falling over each other. They were a strange bunch, a strange bunch indeed; I, at any rate, had never seen the likes of them before.

I'd known peasants, workers and gentlemen, but these men were neither one nor the other of those things. Their exteriors were far too humble for gentlemen, and far too gentlemanly for the poor. They dressed with hell-raising carelessness, but there was something very studied in their carelessness. They wore loud ties with bright, multi-coloured handkerchiefs hanging out of their breast pockets, and their speech was even more bizarre than their dress. They spoke in a casual slang, the words tumbling out of their mouths with limbs mangled and broken; I could barely understand them. They were now standing, or to be precise, tottering, in a circle around the table, shoulder to shoulder, bawling at the top of their lungs that uplifting and—at the time—very popular little ditty that went:

> *And they say Budapest has no whores.*
> *Then what are those fine ladies for?*
> *Their eyes are blue, can't ask for more,*
> *It's what the Good Lord made them for!*

In the middle of this group stood a huge, handsome man. He was waving an empty wine bottle above his head, conducting the drunken chorus. His rich baritone fluttered over the voices of the rest like a flag, his soft, coal-black hair dancing on his forehead, his strong, fine teeth almost glowing. I stared at this unknown face that was more familiar than any I'd ever seen and felt a frightening trembling in my heart. Those grey, daredevil eyes with their heavy lids, the strong, meaty, sensual lips, that nose, that brow, that determined, angular chin… where did I know them from? I shuddered. I suddenly realized I knew them from the mirror. That face, which I was seeing for the first time, was my face. That man, with whom I'd never exchanged a word, was my father. I wanted to run away, but I just stood there and gawped. I couldn't take my eyes off him.

Suddenly, as if he'd felt my gaze upon him, he turned around. His mouth fell open when he saw me, and a total silence fell. I can still hear the silence in that room. It was as if that silence—like the drunks—was tottering too, as if it had leant against me, trying to tip me over. My father came over to me, took my chin in his hand, and looked me in the eyes. Then he smiled. There was nothing of his former nonchalance in that smile; it was a gentle smile, almost emotional. It broke across his face like clear water, and washed off it—almost before my eyes—the muddy fug of drunkenness. He didn't say a word, just looked at me and smiled. He smiled, but he was serious.

Suddenly, though, he seemed to grow embarrassed. Or was it just his drunkenness coming back? Then he gave a great cry, picked me up with one hand and, like a glass of wine, light as air, stood me on the table.

"*Gentle*men!" he yelled, like a circus crier. "Behold Dappermishka's son!"

I couldn't define what I felt at that moment. Nothing, I think. Patients under local anaesthetic must feel this way: seeing, hearing they're being operated on, and not feeling a thing. I stared, vacant and dull, at the puffy-faced drunks who stood gawping at me like some two-headed freak of nature.

"Three cheers for Dappermishka's son!" someone shouted, and from every corner of the room came deafening cries:

"Hip-hip hooray!"

"Hip-hip hooray!"

"Hip-hip hooray!"

My father propped himself against the wall and examined me, like a sculptor his latest masterpiece.

"Oh yes," he said, satisfied. "We did a good job with him, Anna. Well, what do you say to that, then, boys? A genuine, large as life poet!"

"But does he know it?"

"'Course he does, he's a *real* poet!" my father boasted, and produced the newspaper in which my poem had been published from his pocket. "Look, look here! He writes for the finest papers. Come see for yourselves!"

One of the drunks snatched the paper out of his hand and started reading my poem aloud. I felt an unpleasant pressure in my gut. I wanted to strangle him, though the poor man was gushing.

"Rhymes damn well!" he noted when he'd finished his performance. "Is he really just fifteen?"

"Just so, my friend, just so!" my father answered lightly. "Hell of a kid, this one. A real boy wonder. He's going to be bigger than Petőfi! And look at his muscles!" he said suddenly, because meanwhile, he'd been feeling my biceps. "Takes after his old man. Go on, have a feel!"

They started feeling my muscles as if I were a horse at auction. My mother, meanwhile, just stood in the door, saying nothing.

"Get down from there!" she screamed at me suddenly, as if she had only just awoken to what was going on. With that, she was beside the table in the blink of an eye and yanked me down. "Mishka!" she yelled at my father. "You mad? What is all this?"

"This?" my father replied jovially. "It's a christening! It ain't every day a man has a fifteen-year-old son born to him. I brought my friends

258

to see him. This deserves a celebration. We waited for you, but you didn't come, so... we thought we'd start rehearsing."

"So's not to disappoint!" someone called.

"Will you stop yellin', for the love of God!" my mother begged, on the verge of tears. "Herr Hausmeister'll be up, and..."

"Oh, he's been up already!" my father said cheerfully, and the others—I didn't know why—started laughing uproariously.

My mother went white as a sheet.

"He's been up?" she asked, petrified. "What happened?"

"Well... in he comes and starts throwing his weight around... Telling us to do this and do that, and how we should shut our traps or..."

"Tell me what *happened*!" my mother interrupted.

"What happened?" my father winked. "I grabbed him by his lapel like this," he said, and immediately demonstrated on one of the drunks, "and I said to him: friend, I says, people don't talk to Dappermishka that way. Either you drink this wine and take my hand, the way friends should, or you can say your prayers. 'Cause with me, one punch is enough. A second would be mutilatin' a corpse!"

"Don't go on so," my mother begged. "What'd he do?"

"What could he do? He drank! Not just that one glass, either. Or two, for that matter. He's just popped out to be sick."

"I was only havin' a piss!" Herr Hausmeister protested indignantly, having timed his entrance perfectly.

"No shame in being sick!" my father reassured him. "What's it matter if it comes out up top or down below? Makes no difference. Now, are we friends or are we not?"

"We are," Herr Hausmeister reassured him. "So get on with the story."

"Hear! hear!" several others chorused. "Go on, Mishka."

"All right," said my father and sat down on the table. "Where was I?"

"The Italians had just torpedoed the boat!" Herr Hausmeister prompted.

"No, we've heard that!" interrupted a man with scars on his face. "What happened when you were on your own in the lifeboat?"

"That's just it!" my father replied. "Nothing happened at all. Spent two damn weeks tossing about in that lifeboat, and nothing happened.

Not a single boat on the horizon, not a soul anywhere. No food, no water, nothing. Just the ocean, and me, and the sharks. Lived off raw fish, like a seal, whatever I could catch. Well, Mishka, I says to myself, if you get out of this alive, you'll know what it's like to be livin' on borrowed time."

"How'd they fish you out, then?" asked Herr Hausmeister.

"I can hardly recall," my father said. "I was completely round the bend by that point. Cruiser picked me up and I slept for thirty-six hours straight. And that was when the real fun started!"

"How d'you mean?" asked Scar-face.

"I mean, my friend, that was when the revolution broke out, because all this was in October 1918. It was the sailors that started it, they were the first to revolt. One day, they just stopped obeying orders, took the ship into port and went off up to Budapest to make a revolution. What a fine time that was, oh yes, what a time! The people were drunk on that brand-new peace, they were hugging each other in the streets, and everyone was sayin' new times were coming, better times. And what did we get? Damn all. They carved up Hungary like a slaughterhouse carcass. The Italians took the sea, and where there ain't a sea, there ain't a navy, neither. There were no more Hungarian ships, and they didn't take me on the foreign ones. Told me they had plenty of people of their own out of work. So I came on up to Budapest, but things here were even stranger. Here was our Admiral, that Horthy, acting like he was Lord God Almighty. But he was a funny sort of Almighty. During the war, he'd been telling us to go out and kill the Ities and die for the King, and now here he was kickin' out the King and thick as thieves with the Ities. That fat-head Mussolini was his new best friend and no one mentioned our sea any more. Well, I says to myself, that was worth it! The poor were even poorer, the rich were even richer than before. They just sat on all their money and didn't put it to work at all—why would they? The stock markets paid far better! Even skilled workers couldn't get jobs, so what chance did I have, not knowing anything about anything other than sailing? It was just like being back in that lifeboat: no food, no water, nothin'—nothin' but three medals, and they don't give you nothin' for *them* down the pawnshop!"

"So what d'you do?" Scar-face asked.

My father shrugged.

"What could I do? I did the same thing I did on that lifeboat: tried to stay afloat. Couldn't find work, so I tried to get by without it. I had a very good pal, Menyhért was his name, he'd been in the navy, too. Then he became a big revolutionary. And this Menyhért, he says to me, he says, Mishka, he says, in a world like ours, there's only two things a man can be: a revolutionary or a crook. Well, I wasn't going to turn to revolution. Ain't in my nature. And I'd promised myself on that lifeboat that if I got out of this alive, I'd never be miserable again. And I never was. If my food weren't good, I thought of the raw fish, and when I had nowhere to sleep, I thought of that little boat. That's how I got so cheerful. I ate when I could, I kissed girls when there were girls to kiss, and I never asked who they belonged to. I stayed alive any way I could, and it wasn't anybody's business but mine. Gentlemen, the main thing is to remain cheerful. We're all alone, all of us are out at sea, and you do what you have to do to survive. That's the truth, and everything else is just rubbish. You have to stay afloat, the rest don't matter. Everybody's right, because everybody wants to stay alive, so if you think about it, no one's right at all. But that don't matter, either. It's the same thing as war. Some people win, others lose."

"And some people get taken prisoner!" Scar-face added knowingly, and the others fell about laughing.

"This kind of talk ain't fit for you," my mother said, loud enough for the others to hear, and shooed me out into the kitchen.

It must have been about two. I was dead tired. As soon as I sat down, I was overcome with sleep, but the yelling kept waking me up again and again. My mother kept pacing to and fro in the kitchen, muttering angrily.

"Damn their bellies!" she snapped at length. "They've gone and had Manci's bacon!"

At first, I couldn't believe it. Manci's bacon was sacred and inviolable, and we never touched it, even when we were starving. And now this lot had gone and eaten it all? They had. My mother pointed to the nail on which the bacon had been hanging. All that was left on it was a bare piece of string.

"Bunch of crooks," she muttered, and tore open the door violently. "It's two o'clock!" she shouted. "The boy has to get to bed!"

They simply took no notice of her.

"You deaf?" she screamed at the top of her lungs. "Mishka! Get over here."

My father went over to her, but I couldn't hear what they were saying with all the noise. Suddenly, he jumped up on the table.

"Closin' time!" he called jauntily. "We're shutting up shop. Time to go, gentlemen!"

But the "gentlemen" had no intention of leaving. They broke into a rousing chorus of:

> *No, no, no! No, we just won't go!*
> *We're staying, and there's no doubt,*
> *Till the owner, yes! the owner,*
> *gets a stick and throws us out.*

"Well, I may not have a stick," my father remarked and jumped, laughing, off the table. "But I'll chase you out with my bare hands, if it comes to it."

With that, he grabbed two of them by the scruff of the neck and hurled them out the door. Then he did the same with all the others till the flat was empty.

"A fine evening," he said, happily. "Come on, Anna, let's drink the boy's health."

But my mother didn't drink.

"Where'd you get the wine?" she asked suspiciously.

"It ain't from the pharmacy, if that's what you're thinking. Won't kill you."

My father extended a glass, but my mother pushed it away.

"Yesterday you said you had no money."

"Who needs money when you've got credit?"

"People round here don't give credit."

"Maybe not to you!" laughed my father.

"D'you get it downstairs?"

"Yeah."

My mother went beetroot red.

"Ain't you ashamed of yourself?" she said hoarsely. "Shacking up on your first day with that whore of a barmaid who'll take anythin' in trousers!"

My father just smiled.

"Who's shacking up with who?" he asked calmly.

"You with that whore!" my mother replied. "Don't play the fool with me. You ain't that smart. That tramp don't give *me* credit!"

My father winked mischievously.

"You ain't Dappermishka."

"Dappermishka be damned!" my mother burst out bitterly. "We're starvin' and you go eat all of Manci's bacon. Ain't you ashamed? Dogs take more care of their children than you do! Not so much as a word for sixteen years and now you make yourself at home? You ain't comin' here to live off me, you hear? If you can get yourself wine, you can find yourself a room. I never want to see you again. Get your things and clear off!"

But even that failed to ruffle my father's calm. He finished his wine, pocketed his cigarettes, had a stretch and stood comfortably up.

"Well, so long, my boy," he said, and clapped me cheerfully on the shoulder. "We'll talk tomorrow. No use trying now, your mother's in a mood. G'night, then."

"G'night."

I was left alone in the room. Out in the kitchen, they continued to argue. Every insult in the Hungarian language, my mother treated my father to them all. She was blaming him for all the ills, wrongs, and sufferings of the last seventeen years, and she cursed the day she ever met him.

I could barely stand up any more. I lay down and fell straight asleep. Strangely enough, my mother's shouting didn't bother me at all, but the second she fell silent, I woke up. I could hear the same whispering and panting and creaking of the bed as last night, but this time, I was even more surprised. I didn't understand them at all. I'd gone to sleep to the sound of my mother cursing my father, and had woken to find her whispering sweet nothings in his ear. I was disgusted by her, I was disgusted by him, I was disgusted by life.

Nonetheless, the next morning I did not climb out of the window. I went out into the kitchen as always, and washed at the tap. My father was shaving, shirtless, in front of the little scrap of mirror. There was a woman tattooed on his wide, hairy chest, a naked woman, hair billowing in the wind, legs apart. The area around the tattoo was shaved, but not all over: the naked woman had real hair, and not just on her head. It was an amusing sight, but I was not at all amused. Well, I said to myself, you chose yourself a hell of a father!

But he didn't have any idea about all that.

"A fine good mornin'!" he boomed, and went on shaving, whistling all the while.

But my mother blushed beetroot. She started poking at the fire furiously, though there was absolutely no need, and didn't so much as turn around while I was in the kitchen.

That night, Manci came back with the last tram and my father now slept "officially" beside my mother. I felt it, I knew it as soon as I entered the darkened kitchen, but to dispel all doubt, my father wished me a loud good night.

"You shouldn't have," I heard my mother whisper as I closed the door behind me.

"Why not? I'm his father, after all, or somethin'!"

"Still. Must be strange for him."

"So? He'll get used to it."

He was right. I got used to this, too, with time. There was someone sharing my mother's bed at night, and in the morning he would shave, bare-chested, in the kitchen. They told me this stranger was my father.

Yes, I got used to that too, because there is nothing in life that you don't—with time—get accustomed to, and you survive everything that doesn't actually kill you. As for death, that doesn't come so easy.

9

I WAS A TOUGH LITTLE MAN, but a man nonetheless, and man—it seems—was not made to work morning till night on an empty stomach at fifteen, walking six hours a day on top of it. I got so weak that on the way home I had to keep stopping to sit down on the kerb because my legs, stubborn as they were, simply refused to carry me. One wintry Advent night I fell asleep as I sat and if a streetwalker hadn't woken me, I might have frozen to death right there on the pavement.

The spectre of accidental sleep was constantly haunting me at the hotel, too. It sometimes happened that I nodded off standing right in the middle of the lobby. I knew that if they caught me, it would cost me my job and I fought sleep bitterly, but in vain. Sleep haunted me permanently, the way apoplexy haunts the corpulent.

I couldn't stand the cold the way I had before, either. I'd gone without a coat in winters before, and in shorts instead of trousers and had never been the worse for it. This year, the frost ate away at my whole lower body.

"What's with you, you got lice?" the head porter snapped at me once. "You'd best be careful—if they see you scratching, you'll be out of here so fast your feet won't touch the ground."

In any case, I knew that scratching didn't help, but the knowledge that I wasn't allowed to scratch now and then almost drove me mad. And all the while, I had to be careful not to let my face show the torture, because the Major wouldn't stand for long faces: bellboys had always to smile, like ballet dancers. Sometimes, when there weren't any passengers, I stopped the lift in between two floors and whined like a wounded animal. But only rarely did I let myself go like that and, even then, never for long. A few minutes later, I was back, standing to attention for the guests, and smiling my regulation smile.

It was willpower, like an iron beam, that held me together. Learning English was harder than before, but I kept at it, angrily, out of spite. I visited the *Teach Yourself English* book faithfully every night. It was still there in the window, and that reassured me no end. Two pengős twenty wasn't the end of the world, I told myself, and one day it would be mine. Then I would learn English in six months, and leave for America. The papers at the time made a lot of a thirteen-year-old stowaway who'd hidden himself so well aboard an ocean liner they'd only found him in New York when the passengers were disembarking. Ever since I'd read that, I'd stopped worrying about my fare. If I can just get as far as the harbour, I told myself... and get there I would, even if I had to go on foot.

On summer evenings, I would stand around beside the Danube, watching the boat to Vienna preparing to set off. In the morning, it'll be in Austria, I thought to myself, and Austria is that much closer to America. One day, I too would smuggle myself on board a boat like that, and I was bound to figure out some way of continuing on from Vienna. When the boat left, and I saw the blue light on its stern, I was seized once more by that old, trembling wonder I had felt as a child watching the red light on the back of a retreating train. "Go, go, go!" the old desire piped up within me. Go look for the Easter egg of happiness, and don't stop till you've found it.

I thought about the New World the way believers think about the next world. I was absolutely convinced that all I had to do was make it out to America and everything would be all right. That there were poor people there as well and according to Patsy "poor will always be", I didn't think about. America grew ever finer in my mind, eventually becoming a sort of earthly paradise. All I had to do was get there, I told myself, and get there I would—if it was the last thing I did.

But one day, I caught a chill and started coughing terribly. The chill passed, but the coughing did not. It was a dry, nasty cough, the sort of cough poor Berci had had. Each time I was gripped by a heavy fit, I thought of that morning in early autumn when we buried Berci.

"It was poverty that killed him," the Schoolmaster said beside the open grave, "and I say we show the killers no mercy. The coughing of a poor child is a cry for help, and anyone who doesn't want to hear it is an accomplice to the killers."

The truth is that back then, we children hadn't really heard it much, either. Berci's coughing was as much a part of our dark winter mornings as the lamplight or the ringing of the bell for school. I myself only really heard it when he stopped, poor thing. There was an unbearable silence then in class, and now I always thought of that silence whenever I was woken by my own coughing in the night. My God, I said to myself, what's going to become of me? Yes, my coughing, too, was a cry for help, and there was no one to hear it in my case, either. I was as alone as the very first man, and I knew that my rib would become not a helpmeet, but just so much rubbish in the operating room where they cut it out, like they did Berci's.

I knew that, yes I knew it, but I refused to accept it. Bitterly, stubbornly, I tried to resist. I had the most extraordinary ideas. For example, I stole a roll of toilet paper from the hotel and wrapped it, instead of trousers, around my chilblained thighs. I packed my shirt, front and back, with newspaper and pressed my palms to my mouth to "warm" the air. When I got very cold, I started to run, breathing carefully through my nose. I took less food home for my mother; but the little I took for myself didn't help my stomach very much, while it hurt my conscience all the more. I knew that my father was out of work and I knew also what that meant. My mother was in a bad way, even worse than me, and I felt sorry every time I looked at her. As for her, she didn't notice any difference in me, or if she did, she never said anything. I would never have complained to her anyway; the poor thing had enough trouble as it was. I knew that there was no one I could count on.

And Patsy didn't write. I couldn't blame her: how could I? I was the one who hadn't replied. But how was I supposed to reply if I didn't know her address? And even if I *did* know her address, I added bitterly, where was I supposed to get the money for a stamp?

It all seemed so hopeless. The days passed and nothing happened, except that my strength got a little less and my coughing got a little worse. I was powerless, observing this ominous process. I was now

JÁNOS SZÉKELY

covered in sweat in even the severest cold, and there was a heavy fug in my head—I was constantly afraid that I would faint.

One evening, I became unwell on Vilmos Császár út. I had strength enough only to sit down on the steps of the Basilica, and then I passed out. I came to a few minutes later, but I could feel I didn't have the strength to move on. I dragged myself inside. In the incense-filled semi-darkness I saw only a few figures kneeling; the draught fluttered the candles, and it seemed to me that the whole church was swaying. I slumped down on the first pew and fell asleep straight away.

I woke to words humming round my head: strange, magic words, as if otherworldly bees were bringing their bittersweet honey home, into me. I could barely keep my eyes open, but my mind worked with unnatural clarity. I took the diary out of my pocket, pulled the little pencil out of the side and quickly began to write. It was a poem. I reproduce it here:

CONVERSATION WITH A CARPENTER

I don't know if you really lived,
Or how you made it through,
But if you didn't, then God bless
The man who invented you.

What a great invention,
If that is what you are,
Either way, you should know
From my heart you're never far.
It beats so weakly now,
For lack of food to drive it,
But you and your cross
Will always live inside it.

It's good to know you lived,
And if not, that you might have done,
That miracles for the poor you made,
And more than just the one.

268

I've no more prayers,
All my strength now freezes,
But still it's good to say:
O! My good Lord Jesus.

O! My good Lord Jesus,
I am not bad inside, down deep,
All I need's some daily bread,
Or a crumb of sleep.

Or a crumb of sleep.

That was my last poem. From then on, I couldn't even write. The magic stopped, the font of inspiration dried up. I still copied the English words out of the dictionary, but I could no longer commit them to memory. My mind was no longer sharp. I was still alive, but only just *alive*. The stubborn flame of my will to live flickered in unwilling flesh; my mind was burned out like an empty saucepan on the stove. One night, I found myself saying aloud in the street:

"I'm going to die. I'll never see America."

And that is clearly what would have happened, if at this point luck had not stooped to pick me up. It was a dubious sort of luck, and it cost me dear, but nonetheless it saved my life.

It was all thanks to a dog. The dog was called Cesar, and he was a very elegant dog indeed. He came and went in the hotel like a haughty diplomat with extraterritorial rights who didn't give a damn about anyone. He was a fine, large, long-haired animal, an impossibly white Russian wolfhound. Everyone turned to look at him when he passed through the lobby, but he didn't so much as glance at his admirers. His aristocratic features spoke of boredom and disdain. When anyone asked who he belonged to, the bellboy who happened to be taking him for his walk would reply, ceremoniously and *sotto voce*:

"This is Her Excellency's dog."

I didn't know Her Excellency, because she'd been in Paris for some

269

time. Her husband, His Excellency, known to the bellboys as Exfix, used to bring the dog down in the lift. Exfix, as I later found out, was short for "Excellency" and "fixer". I don't know if it was the bellboys who'd come up with this nickname, or others, too, called him by it behind his back, but the fact remains that for us, he was Exfix.

Exfix must have been around fifty. He was a stocky, thickset man with a fat neck; his head resembled an outsized billiard ball. He was bald all over, and shaved the little patches of hair remaining on his head as smooth as he shaved his cheeks. He had small, piggy eyes and a big, meaty nose, beneath which languished a thick, pointed moustache. It was a carefully groomed, studiously "casual" aristocratic moustache that was always, since it was dyed a little too often, a shade blacker than the blackest of black moustaches. He was a rosy-cheeked, full-of-life character, and you could tell that he loved his bloody steaks and good rich sauces. The strange thing was that this big, scrappy man, strong as an ox, did everything he could to affect the manner of a degenerate aristocrat. He imitated their sleepy, arrogant speech, their lazy, slightly swaying walk, and generally did his best to appear as dull and eccentric as any peer with a propensity for early-onset senility. But everyone knew, of course, that he was of painfully middle-class origin. His father had been a smallholder near Debrecen who'd done well for himself. Apparently he'd been illiterate, and if Exfix hadn't worn such fine English suits, you'd have thought that he, too, was some well-to-do provincial farmer who'd come up to the sinful capital to deal with some troublesome administrative affair, and was trying to imitate the gentlemen he'd found there.

Elemér once pointedly said that Exfix was only an excellency because an absent-minded prime minister had once made him a cabinet minister by mistake. He was a minister without portfolio for about seven or eight months. That was many years before, but in those days if someone had been a minister for a day and a half, they still got to put "Cabinet Minister (ret'd)" on their calling cards for the rest of their lives, and those calling cards were gold in Hungary at the time. A cabinet minister (ret'd), especially one as sharp as Exfix, could arrange almost anything, and anything he couldn't arrange, he could find others to arrange for him—people he'd arranged things for in the past. Eventually, Exfix attained almost everything you could attain in Hungary in those days. He was a member of parliament, a privy counsellor, a member of the Vitéz order, the recipient of the Corvin Medal and more or less every other civilian decoration in existence; president, secretary or treasurer of the most exclusive social and cultural institutions; second to the finest gentlemen in their duels; guest of honour, patron, honorary citizen, and just generally everything that could possibly feature on a pillar of the Hungarian community's calling card and in their obituary. But that was not what got him his twenty-thousand-acre estate. Exfix, whom newspapers and masters of ceremonies always called "a distinguished statesman" was, in actual fact, a fixer.

"Fixer" did not feature in the dictionary of the Hungarian language as a profession, but it was all the more a feature of Hungarian public life. The Horthyist state stuck its slimy fingers so far into every pie that in the end, you could barely breathe without some form of official permission. And anyone who didn't want to wait till Judgement Day for their official requests to be approved, if they were approved at all, turned to a fixer, who would fix whatever needed to be fixed. "Fixer" was a collective term like, for example, money, and in just the same way as there were single-figure notes and six-figure notes, there were single-figure fixers and six-figure fixers. A single-figure fixer was a dirty, hungry little man in fraying trousers who made a living because he knew three clerks in the ministry or in some other department, who would—if adequately compensated—take the relevant forms and move them from the bottom to the top of the pile on the departmental secretary's desk—or if it wasn't in the pile at all, would slip it in. A double-figure fixer knew the departmental secretary himself, who would do the same thing with his boss's desk. A triple-figure fixer was a close personal friend of the boss, while a four-figure fixer was friends with the ministerial advisor, the five-figure fixer with the Secretary of State, and so on, right up to the Minister himself.

Exfix, needless to say, was a six-figure fixer. In keeping with his rank, he bribed only the highest echelons of society, and no one dreamt of calling him a fixer. Only single-, double-, and triple-figure fixers actually went and "fixed" anything. Four-figure fixers were said to "intercede", five-figure fixers "lent their support", while six-figure fixers "worked for the public good".

Exfix's work was made easier not only by his own rank, but the fact that his late father-in-law had been, in his time, one of the most influential men in the country. Exfix's ascent began the day he married his father-in-law's daughter. Those in the know also claimed to have insights as to why and how he did that, but that does not belong in these pages.

Exfix was apparently still aping his father-in-law. For the old man had been a real aristocrat, a Count and an honest-to-goodness peer who sat, on festive occasions, at Lord God Almighty Horthy's right hand; and all that separated him from Christ himself was that this seat was down here on earth and not in heaven, and in Hungary what's more—which at the time was hardly an earthly paradise.

The dowager Countess was still a regular feature of the society pages. She had once been a famous beauty, and for the gossip columnists, she still was. She was a good thirty years younger than her husband and rumour had it that she had been cuckolding him since their wedding day with a man from the Foreign Office, a fact of which everybody was aware except the Count himself, although some claimed that even he knew. As to how much of that is true, I don't know, but the fact remains that after the Count's death the man from the Foreign Office married the lady and her forty thousand acres. In my time, he was a leading light of the Hungarian mission in Paris, where Mrs Exfix, Her Excellency, was now paying him a visit.

Mrs Exfix's dog was the first animal in my life for which I had felt a marked disdain. Every time I saw it, I was seized by a strange anger. His bored aristocratic features annoyed me, as did his slow, dignified, diplomat's gait, and everything about him just generally. The dislike was mutual, manifesting itself with Cesar in the fact that he never took any notice of me. He looked right through me, just like the two-legged guests of the hotel. His dislike of me made perfect sense in both human and dog terms. The other bellboys constantly sucked up to him, partly because he was Her Excellency's dog, and partly because whoever took him for his walk always got a tip. I did not make nice with him, and of course, I could hardly have taken him for his walk anyway, because I couldn't leave the lift.

In the mornings, when Exfix got out of the lift, he would throw the dog's lead to the first bellboy he saw and, with aristocratic nonchalance, say:

"You... boy... what's your name again? Take Cesar for a walk."

One morning, he couldn't find any bellboys in the lobby and he brought the dog back to me.

"You... boy... what's your name again?" he asked, and without waiting for an answer, as usual, he said: "Look after Cesar till they pick him up."

So we were left alone. Reception, it seems, had forgotten about Cesar, because it was a good two hours till they came for him.

We were both acutely embarrassed. At first, we tried to ignore one another, but after a while, this proved impossible. Whenever a guest came, I had to usher Cesar into the lift, and if he took an undue interest in a skirted female guest's silk-stockinged leg, I was forced to intervene. His presence made me strangely uncomfortable. The dog, too, was restless. We watched each other testily.

Around noon, I pulled the lever a second sooner than I should have and Cesar's tail got caught in the door. After that I stroked him, but that was all.

From then on, however, our relationship changed. We still kept our distance, but were no longer enemies. Cesar began to take notice of my presence. He was hardly friendly, but he occasionally turned his aristocratic face towards me and looked at me with cool politeness, the way you do at a vague acquaintance who is no friend, but tolerable company nonetheless, and socially respectable.

Then one day, something unusual happened. Exfix used to feed the dog chocolate, something I, as a country boy, considered utterly ridiculous. Exfix, who also came from the countryside, must have felt that, for he once said to me, almost apologetically:

"Her Excellency got him into the habit."

One morning, when he left me with Cesar once more, he gave me a handful of chocolate.

"Give him those," he said. "They're from Gerbeaud. His favourite."

That was around eleven a.m. I had last eaten at seven the night before, and had hardly had my fill even then. Long story short, as soon as Exfix had left, I took the chocolate and the dog into the lift and stopped in between two floors, where there was no danger of my being surprised, and devoured the chocolate.

Cesar looked at me angrily, or at least it seemed so at the time.

"Don't be stingy," I said, my mouth full. "You get plenty to eat and I'm starving to death."

Cesar, however, was not moved by this argument. He stood up on his hind legs and demanded his chocolate. If I had given him a piece, he would probably have calmed down, but just then the lift's buzzer rang, and in my haste, I stuffed the last of the chocolate into my mouth. Cesar started barking at the top of his voice. I was afraid that someone would hear and give me a ticking off for hanging around between two floors when there were people waiting for the lift. But I wanted to finish the chocolate, and even if I hadn't wanted to, I could hardly show myself before the guests with my mouth full. But Cesar was barking more and more wildly, and finally, the buzzer rang again. This was enough to cause my already frayed nerves to hand in their notice. I burst into tears.

That was when the unusual thing happened. When Cesar saw that I was crying, he sidled up to me and started whining. I knew a lot about dogs, and was aware that this sort of thing did happen, but I had never imagined that this jaded, disdainful beast would be capable of it.

When Lajos came to collect him to take him for his walk, I asked him to cover the lift for a few minutes, hurried down to the kitchen and asked them for a bone "for Her Excellency's dog".

Cesar broke into barks of joy when I gave it to him. It was the first time I'd seen him happy. His whole being changed. He was no longer an aristocratic dog, but just a dog plain and simple, a dog happy with his bone.

The next morning he came up to me and dropped the chocolate Exfix had given him at my feet. I was absolutely convinced he did it out of gratitude, though it's possible—or even likely—that he was simply bored of sweets. Suffice to say that from then on, I liked him far better than the hotel's two-legged guests.

Whenever Exfix gave him to me to look after, I went and got him a nice big bone. Eventually, Exfix noticed.

"You're giving the dog bones?" he asked in horror.

I looked at him uncomprehendingly.

"They're very good bones, Your Excellency," I said. "See how Cesar likes them."

"That may be," Exfix agreed, clearly remembering his provincial childhood. "But if Her Excellency sees you, she'll have your guts for garters."

It seems he, too, was a little scared of Her Excellency. It seemed to me *everyone* was a little afraid of her.

Her Excellency was a legendary figure in the hotel. The most out-landish tales circulated about her. Once, for example, she had slapped the second-floor maid—the kind and obliging Eszter—so hard she bled because her new evening dress had proved too tight at the last moment and the poor girl had been unable to do it up. Then she gave her the 250-pengő dress.

"She's not a bad person," said Eszter, "she's just crazy. You never know what she's going to do next."

"But what a woman!" Gyula noted expertly. "Those tits, my friend… phew! Like that!" he said, demonstrating. "And they're the real deal. Never wears a bra. I swear, she's the finest thing I ever saw."

Generally, whenever her name cropped up, there was always a superlative attached to it. She had the "sweetest tits". She had the "best legs". She had the "finest little rear". She had the "cutest red hair". She gave the most generous tips. She was the nicest guest. She was the rudest guest. She "made the biggest spectacle" when she got drunk at the bar, which happened often. She had the dirtiest mouth. She was the most refined lady. Just generally, she was "the most" in everything.

If a new bellboy complained about a guest, the others just shrugged and said:

"That's nothing compared to Her Excellency!"

But if, on the other hand, they were raving about someone, the others would also say:

"That's nothing compared to Her Excellency!"

They insisted on this idea of Her Excellency being "the most" in an unfathomable and sometimes really quite ridiculous way. Once, I remember, there was a delivery of a two-metre-tall basket of flowers for someone, and one of the maids said it was the biggest bunch of flowers ever made. But the others couldn't let even that stand. Three of them chorused:

"You should have seen Her Excellency's flowers!"

Her Excellency was also the most irresistible woman. Apparently, she drove all the men mad. The boys had an entire roll call on hand, featuring the cream of Hungarian society.

"But she's just playing with 'em," Gyula said. "She plays 'em all for fools."

"Not András!" Antal interrupted. "She gave him the goods, all right."

"What do you know about it? Were you holding the candle?"

"No need for candles. You'd have had to be blind not to see it."

"Rubbish," Gyula grumbled, insisting—for reasons of his own—on Her Excellency's unapproachability. "Like she'd want András, of all people. She didn't want Horthy, no, but that useless sixteen-year-old bellboy, oh yes, that's just what she wanted. As if!"

"It's possible," Lajos intervened. "Likes 'em young. Bit of fresh meat."

"Then why did she get András fired, eh?" retorted Gyula angrily.

"'Cause she'd had enough of him," Lajos replied. "András must've been making a fuss, so she had him fired, that's all."

"Oh, you can all go shove it up your you-know-what," Gyula said furiously, putting an end to the argument. "You ought to wash your mouths out with soap and water!"

In that respect, Gyula was absolutely right. But from then on, I thought a lot about Her Excellency.

This was back when Elemér was still on the day shift. I remembered that when my mother had asked whether there were any vacancies, Elemér had mentioned a boy they'd just let go because of some Excellency. Later, I tried to get some details out of him, but he would always deflect the conversation, just like when I asked him why the boys called Ferenc Franciska. He blushed when I asked him.

"Nonsense," he shrugged awkwardly. "Dezső was just unlucky, that's all there is to it."

So his name was Dezső—at least I'd found out this much.

Once, when Antal was in a chatty mood, I asked him:

"Did Her Excellency have something to do with someone called Dezső, too?"

"Dezső?" Antal looked at me. "But that's András!"

"How's that?"

"Her Excellency started calling him András, and it stuck."

That sounds strange, but at the time it seemed perfectly natural to me. It was part of an old and venerable tradition to which our upper classes were very given. The highest members of society didn't bother to remember their servants' names. You inherited not only your predecessor's uniform, but also their name. The butler, maid or footman might change, but their names stayed the same. This was how their masters expressed, though perhaps not consciously, that they did not consider their servants people, but merely functional objects that were just as much a part of the furniture as, say, the dining-room table.

As I say, this did not strike me as outrageous. I only started feeling a bit uncomfortable one morning when Exfix said:

"You… boy… what's your name again?" and, unusually, actually waited for my response. After I had respectfully informed him that my given name was Béla, in the most natural tone in the world he said:

"Well, from now on, I'm going to call you András. I'm used to that."

"Yes, Your Excellency," I replied politely, and felt a cold shiver running down my spine, though I didn't quite know why.

I didn't even know Her Excellency at the time. She was nothing but a room number to me, like any other guest, and people are not generally afraid of room numbers.

But one morning, when I went into the changing room to put on my uniform, the boys were in a heated discussion over something.

"What is it?" I asked, because lately they'd started letting me in on their secrets.

"Ain't you heard?" asked Lajos. "Her Excellency's back."

*

I knew it was her as soon as she stepped into the lift. The boys had told me so much about her that when I set eyes on her, I felt like a little boy seeing a witch or a fairy in a dream, only I didn't know which. There was something in her that frightened me so that I could hardly look at her, and there was something spellbinding in her that meant I could hardly take my eyes off her.

Her Excellency really was "the most". I thought her twenty-eight or thirty at the time, but now I know that it is impossible to determine the age of women like her. She might have been ten years older, but she could equally have been ten years younger. The most striking things were her eyes. They were the greyest eyes I had ever seen, light grey like a winter sky when the sun glows through the clouds, dazzling you when you look up. They were slightly slanted and below them, as if her gaze had singed her skin, there was a darker, sooty little semicircle. She had shoulder-length red hair, a delicate, straight nose, and a strange, wide, highly arched mouth that wore an odd, dull pout, the sort little children have when they've been crying. She used a bitter, provocative perfume whose smell seemed to linger in the lift hours after she'd gone. And she really did never wear a bra.

I always got a strange little thrill when she stepped into the lift. She was usually buttoning her gloves at the time and went straight to the mirror, like women generally. She would adjust her hair, veil or hat, but this was clearly just a ruse, on which she didn't insist too strongly. Essentially, she was just looking at herself. It was what the other women, too, did when they were alone in the lift, but the way she looked at herself was different. There were women who were so in love with their reflections, I thought they were going to go over and start kissing the mirror. There were others who were angry with themselves, or at least with the night before, which had left its mark on their faces. They would feel the wrinkles around their eyes irritably and usually make a last-ditch effort with their powder puffs. There were some who were more dispassionate, who examined themselves as soberly and matter-of-factly as a shopkeeper examines his goods before putting them out in the window. Some had trouble with their stockings, some with their corsets, which would make quiet little popping noises as they pulled them to and fro on their midriffs.

Her Excellency belonged to none of these groups. She looked at herself the way a collector looks at his favourite painting, whose value and flaws he knows precisely. And she could hardly have adjusted her corset because, as I said, she didn't wear one. She had a black silk dress that hugged her figure so tight that every time I saw her I thought she was naked and had merely painted herself black. No, Her Excellency definitely did *not* wear a corset, and as I realized later, she didn't—unlike most women—wear a garter belt either. She wore her stockings doubled over at the top, and once, as she adjusted them with her back to me, I saw in the mirror that there was nothing above them for the longest way. I began to suspect that she didn't wear underwear, either.

She only rarely came down with her husband—most of the time, she came down with a girlfriend. The bellboys called her friend Whitewash, partly because she was as long and thin as the handle of a whitewashing brush, and partly because the make-up she used was so white, it was as if her greatest wish when applying it was for people to mistake her for a corpse. Only her thick lips, painted crimson, stuck out of this deadly pallor, accentuated even further by her smooth, shiny, coal-black hair. She was Her Excellency's best friend. If Exfix was away, which was often, Whitewash sometimes even spent the night at Her Excellency's. She was engaged to an oyster-faced Viennese arms manufacturer, who would stay with us whenever he was in Budapest. As to just how engaged they were, I don't know, but the boys all said "intimately".

At first, Her Excellency did not walk Cesar. She would get up at noon, when the dog had already been for his morning walk, and in the evening, when she got back, Cesar had been walked for the second time as well. But one day, she did bring him with her, and it was to this I owed my luck.

Cesar broke into barks of joy when he saw me. As always, he wanted to come over, but his owner, as usual, went straight to the mirror, dragging the dog with her. But Cesar wouldn't let it rest. He pulled at his leash to indicate he wanted to come over to me, and since his owner was taking no notice, started barking angrily. Finally, she turned around and snapped:

"What is it?"

I didn't know if she was talking to me or the dog, but I had no time to reply in any event, because just then Cesar gave his lead such a yank that Her Excellency almost toppled over.

I caught her at the last moment. She was in my arms only for a heartbeat, but I almost burst into flames at her touch. I felt myself blush.

Her Excellency looked at me. At first just briefly, in passing, but then her gaze returned and rested on me. She wasn't looking at me the way you usually look at a lift boy, but... I didn't quite know how myself. A vague memory flashed through me, but I wasn't sure what I was remembering. All I knew was that my knees were shaking.

Her Excellency smiled.

"What's your name?" she asked in a slightly sing-song voice.

"Béla," I replied, and it only occurred to me much later that I ought to have said András.

"How come I've never seen you before? Are you new?"

"I've been here over a year, Your Excellency."

"In the lift?"

"Yes, Your Excellency. I've served Your Excellency quite a lot."

"Really?" she asked in surprise, and looked at me in that strange way again.

I suddenly realized what that look reminded me of. It was the way Manci had looked at me when I got out of bed naked. I could feel myself blush again.

Cesar, meanwhile, was licking my hand.

"Quite the love affair, I see," she said with a smile. "Are you the one that walks him?"

"No, Your Excellency."

"Why not, since you're so close?"

"I can't leave the lift, ma'am."

"Would you like to walk him from now on?"

"Yes, Your Excellency."

"All right, then, I'll have a word."

With that, she left, but as she passed me she smiled again, brushing the tip of my nose playfully with her finger.

10

S O CESAR, THAT WELL-CONNECTED DOG, managed to arrange with a yank of his leash what my mother had spent a year begging the head porter for. The next day, I was moved to reception.

Her Excellency probably didn't even realize that she had taken on the role of fairy godmother in my life. She had clearly just gone to the manager, or whoever, and told them that from now on she wanted the lift boy Béla to walk her dog, and since lift boys couldn't walk dogs, they had moved me to reception.

Reception, for me, was a veritable gold mine. If I carried or fetched something for a guest, they would always tip me ten or twenty fillérs, sometimes more. Each assignment meant a tip, and each tip a little more bread, a little less coughing, half or three-quarters of a tram ticket, a slice of the rent and a great big dollop of hope.

The very first day, I made two pengős. When I had scraped together the first pengő, I decided to take the tram home that night. All day, I thought happily of my tram ride, but in the evening, I finally changed my mind. I walked, and with those two pengős, reclaimed my mother's gold cross on the way. I was indescribably proud. My great-grandmother had given this cross to my grandmother, who had given it to my mother. Now I had got it back.

I wanted to see my mother's face as she put it on, but it was dark in the kitchen by the time I got home. I opened the door louder than usual so the sound would wake her, but someone who washes twelve hours a day is not so easy to wake. So I felt my way to the kitchen table and, as always, put the packet of food down on the table, with the cross on top.

My mother's eyes shone strangely when she woke me next morning.

"Somethin' happen, son?" she asked, moved. When I told her the big news, she started crying.

I tried to appear calm, as befits a serious breadwinner, even attempting a very grown-up yawn. My mother held the cross in her hand and looked at it through her tears.

"It were your great-grandmother's, then your grandmother's," she whispered softly. "I told you they'd pray for you, didn't I?"

I didn't reply. I pretended to be very sleepy, because I was afraid that I, too, would burst into tears. My mother stroked my head.

"Should I have let you sleep in today?"

"Why? What time is it?"

"Half past four."

"Then I've got to get going."

"Ain't you got nothin' left for the tram?"

"I had two pengős. I spent it on the cross."

"Oh, Lord! That cross could have waited, you know."

"No it couldn't," I said with masculine pride. "I promised to get it back when I had money, and when you give your word on something, it's only right to keep it."

"Well, it were good of you, I will say that. You've a heart of gold, son, just like this cross." She wiped away her tears with the back of her hand, and then added more matter-of-factly, "But from now on, I want you to take the tram when you've got the money, because you've lost a lot of weight, only I didn't want to say before."

I didn't need telling twice. That evening, I took the tram home. It's a wonderful thing, the tram, ladies and gentlemen, and only people who've walked six hours a day for more than a year know just how wonderful it is. How wonderful to sit in one of those fine, well-lit carriages, looking out of the window at the streets you'd tramped so often on foot. How good to lean back in the comfortable seat, kicking your heels, not caring a damn for the weather; how good to look about, get lost in thought, dreaming of Patsy and America.

And how early you got home! Usually, you weren't even a quarter of the way at that hour, and now you could lounge about in a chair, read, study or hang about the house doing this and that, letting your thoughts graze in the pastures of inactivity, masticating happily on the sweet, lazy minutes. Later, your eyelids grow slowly heavy and start closing like a cat's beside the stove—but so what? Why stay awake? You kick off your shoes, arrange yourself leisurely on the floor, pull your cap over your eyes and sleep till six thirty, like the rich. The button of your cap will leave its mark on your face, just as you'll feel the sleep throughout your body. You're no longer tormented by the deadly frustration of the sleepless. You start enjoying the mornings, the cold water, you start enjoying being alive. There's no three-hour walk ahead of you; the tram does the walking for you, and you get to sit and watch the lights wither in the windows as the sky grows gently lighter and morning breaks over the city. Yes, the tram's a wonderful thing, ladies and gentlemen. An ode to the tram! A hymn to sleeping in, and a blessing on the suburban sun that now and again shines, even on the poor.

Every day, I brought my mother home a pengő or two.

I entered my earnings carefully in the "Credit" column of my little diary, because when it came to bookkeeping, I wasn't kidding around. I had recorded every fillér my mother had given me since the night I arrived and now set about paying her back energetically. How nice it was to be writing in the "Credit" column at last! What joy, what pride! In three weeks, I reclaimed our bedclothes as well, but I didn't put that into the "Credit" column, because only the rich take the "Credit" column so seriously—the poor use their hearts, even in their accounting.

One day, I said to my mother:

"Did you know I don't get breakfast at the hotel?"

"You don't? Since when?"

"Never did."

"You never said nothin'."

"I'm sayin' somethin' now. And, if you don't mind my sayin', my belly don't like it one bit."

"I don't mind givin' you breakfast money, not a bit. It ain't my fault you never said nothin' before."

"That's not what I meant. Horses eat by themselves, and I ain't a horse. I'm a man, and what I'd like, Muther, from now on, is for there to be bread and milk in the house and for us to have breakfast together like other families."

"Don't waste your money," she shrugged. "You go have breakfast by yourself—God knows you deserve it."

"And you don't? Every workin' man and woman deserves it. Only them useless layabouts don't."

"All right, all right," she cut me off. "You don't have to get all Commernist right away."

But she wasn't upset, even at my "Commernism". She flicked me playfully on the backside and went out into the kitchen, where I could hear her whispering excitedly with my father.

I will never forget our first breakfast together as a family. We were all three of us a little preoccupied as we sat down at the kitchen table and avoided each other's gaze. The smell of coffee and freshly warmed milk filled the flat; the one-room apartment was a home for the first time, and we were a family. My mother crossed herself before cutting the bread, her eyes full of tears.

"Praise the Lord Jesus Christ," she said as she cut into the bread, making us each a slice as thick as a prayer book.

Then she spread a good thick layer of lard over each slice and we began devouring them with our eyes even as she was doing it. The smell of the food hovered around us like the first dove after the flood. The smell of life had returned to the formerly dormant kitchen.

We began to eat and didn't say a word till we'd finished everything. Then my mother put her hand on mine.

"He's a good boy, our son," she said to my father. "Ain't that so, Mishka?"

My father decided to make a joke of it.

"Now don't you go makin' yourself younger!" he teased her. "This ain't no boy, not by a long shot." But then he added in a completely different tone: "Boys don't think the way he does. He's a man, I can tell you, and not just any kind of man, at that!" and he offered me a cigarette. "Go on, have a smoke, young man," he said, "it'll help you digest."

"Thank you," I replied, blushing, and lit up nervously.

It was my first cigarette. It did absolutely no good for my stomach or my lungs, but all the more for my vanity. I said a hurried goodbye so the people in the house would see me with my lit cigarette and know that I wasn't a boy, but a man, and not just any kind of man, at that!

So I started eating three meals a day: once at home and twice at the hotel. I didn't put anything aside for my mother, because I figured that she could buy herself food from my wages, of which I handed over every last fillér. But I quickly realized that I was wrong. Anyone who's been hungry as often as I have can recognize someone going without. Their face is different, and their speech, even their breath smells different; but most of all, they eat differently when they do finally get the chance. One day, I watched her at breakfast and suddenly knew that she was starving once more.

"Why ain't you eatin' properly?" I asked when we were alone.

"I am," she replied awkwardly.

"Don't look like it."

"What d'you want me to do? It's how I look."

I could see I wasn't going to get far like this, so I said:

"I can bring you food from the hotel again, if you want. Lord knows, there's enough of it."

"Well… yes, that would be good. Seein' as how your father ain't got no work, and… you know how it is. I couldn't make the rent last month, and well, it ain't easy, no use denyin'. Herr Hausmeister makes twelve pengős with me washing for him, but he's still got to pay the bank and they said they'd put us out if I don't pay by the first. That's how it is," she said, finishing her confession and staring at her shoes.

From then on, I took my lunch and dinner home once more. It was a deception, a kind deception; I bought myself other food instead. It was the cheapest I could get, that much is true: bread, lard, salami, brawn, but I bought lots and lots of it. I ate so much in those days I wouldn't be able to manage half of it today, though even now I have quite an appetite. I gobbled food like a life-saving drug and thanked my lucky stars that it gave me pleasure, too.

I felt the same about spiritual food as well. I devoured my English words like the brawn. Each one was a little mouthful of America for me, and I said to myself gratefully: how wonderful that they gave me pleasure, too.

"Muther," I said one day, "I want to start savin' up for an English textbook."

"English textbook?" she repeated hesitantly. "You thinkin' them strange thoughts again?"

I could see that the truth wasn't going to help, so I decided to lie.

"They told me to. There's lots of English guests and I can't talk to them."

My mother's expression, along with her whole viewpoint, changed at once.

"That's different," she said forgivingly. "How much is it?"

"Two twenty."

"That's a lot," she sighed, "but we'll get it together somehow."

I knew that was more than just talk. My mother was a dutiful member of her class and considered an order from her social superiors to be absolutely final, especially in such a "big job" as mine. The next day, I looked on the English book the way a groom looks at his bride-to-be after the engagement. A few more weeks, I thought, and you'll be mine. Decent food, it seems, will fatten up your hopes as well. At the time, I felt I would eventually get everything I wanted.

I put on weight, I gained in strength and eventually my cough, too, subsided. I would swing the heaviest suitcases, which three months previously I could barely move, onto my back so easily that the adults just stood and stared. The lanky porter who'd called us good-for-nothings when we'd first come to the hotel once said to me anxiously:

"Put that down, for goodness' sake, you'll break your back!"

"Not me!" I said, gave him a mischievous wink, and headed off cheerfully with the suitcase on my back.

"You're very strong," he said and felt my arm. "By God! Where d'you get them muscles?"

"Runs in the family. My father can lift a grown man with one hand."

"Your father?" the porter said, looking at me in surprise. "I thought your father was dead."

I blushed, but a moment later regained my balance because all that meat, it seems, helps your *sang froid* as well.

"'Course he isn't. We just thought that because we hadn't heard from him for so long."

"Where was he, then?"

"In America," I lied. "My old man's a sailor. He's seen quite a bit of the world."

"Looks like you're pretty proud of him."

As far as that went, I wasn't so desperately proud of him, but it was true enough that I did like to boast that I had a father at all.

"The way I see it," I said with pious condescension, "anyone that's got a father at all ought to be pleased about it."

"Too true," the porter nodded. "If only my own son saw it that way."

My strength soon became legendary in the hotel, and news of it even reached the Major. He once watched me heaving a wardrobe trunk onto my back, and his Fascist heart swelled with pride like a pig's bladder.

"A cadet!" he explained excitedly to the staff who'd gathered round to watch. "You can see for yourself the benefits of a military upbringing. That's the kind of young men we make in the cadets!"

Oh sure, I thought—as far as the cadets were concerned I could have coughed my lungs out long ago, but I didn't say anything, because poor children learn early on not to make a fuss. But I was pleased with the praise, because if you don't get praise very often, you'll take anything, even the praise of someone you despise.

Slowly, my confidence returned. I was once more jealous of my rep, and wouldn't stand for the bellboys being "uppity". If needs be I told them just where to get off and what they could go and do if they didn't like it. In the end, they got the message, because they realized that my fists were fast and I had no fear of going up against older boys as well. No one dared mess around with me, and I knew full well why: I was the old Béla again—a rooster perched atop his dust heap.

I hadn't seen Her Excellency since. She had appeared, like a fairy godmother, set my life on course, and disappeared back into the mysterious fairy-tale world that to me was the life of the rich.

In the morning, when I brought Cesar back, she was still sleeping, and in the afternoon when I went once more to fetch the dog, I found her already out. On these occasions, I would be alone in her suite and everything went smoothly. But the mornings were dangerous. Exfix had made me swear, for the love of God, not to wake Her Excellency, and I knew well enough from the horror stories the boys told what to expect if I did.

But that was not the only thing that made me uneasy in the mornings. There was something else besides. Something I couldn't quite put into words, something that lived for a very long time only in the depths of my unconscious. My heart always fluttered when I opened the door to the suite to let Cesar in. These were dark, adventurous moments. There, beyond the entranceway, everything was a mystery. A woman was sleeping inside, a beautiful and terrible woman, and I occasionally felt that waking her was not the only thing I was afraid of.

Yes, there was something else besides. In the afternoon, when we came back from our walks and there was no one home, I had to lock Cesar in the bathroom, and the bathroom opened off her bedroom. I was always seized by a strange excitement when I set foot in there. It was the same as all the other bedrooms in the hotel, and yet it was *completely* different. I didn't know why, but it reminded me of another bedroom, 508, where one night someone had strangled an old lady. I had been in that room a few hours after the act to bring the detectives paper and pens. They'd taken the body away by then, but had otherwise left everything just the way it was when the perpetrator had left the room. Despite that—and this was what surprised me most—the room showed absolutely no sign of the murder. It, too, was just the same as the other bedrooms in the hotel, and yet different, *completely* different. The sun shone through the window, but the room was heavy with the night before, the murder. The furnishings surrounded the detectives like silent, petrified accomplices who knew all but were saying nothing.

Her furniture looked at me the same way. The maid hadn't yet been and here, too, everything was just the same as when the perpetrator had left. The unmade bed shone white in the semi-darkness and on it, like a beautiful female cadaver, lay her nightgown. As soon as I entered, my eyes fell on the gown and from then on, I couldn't take them off it. I didn't dare touch it for the longest time. I looked at it as if I was afraid that it was only playing dead and might telephone the manager at any moment.

One day, however, I couldn't resist the temptation. I locked the front door, left the key in the lock, ran back into the bedroom and picked up the gown. It was a salmon-pink, lacy silk nightgown and it exuded a quite extraordinary scent. That bitter perfume I knew so well from the lift was mixed with an altogether *different* scent that drove me absolutely wild.

I reached under the gown. I could see my hand through the thin layer of silk as if I was seeing it through a layer of salmon-pink glass, a magical, enchanted glass whose touch was as soft and warm as her body itself. In the mornings, whenever I came into the suite, I seemed to see her in this gown through the closed doors, and it was an image I couldn't shake off the whole of the rest of the day—it sometimes even haunted me in my sleep.

One night, I dreamt that András, *the previous András*, whom I had never seen, sneaked into the suite before me as I was bringing Cesar home. I only saw his back as he disappeared in the darkened entrance hall, and he didn't notice me following him. We went through a great many rooms, up and down stairs, and then all at once we were in her bedroom. I couldn't see the room because it was completely dark, but I knew right away that it was her bedroom. András, *the previous András*, went straight over to the bed and they, too, began whispering, panting, and groaning like my mother and father on that first night together. I wanted to get closer, but I couldn't move: my whole body had turned to stone. I just stood there in the dark and listened tensely, with bated breath. I wanted to know *what* they were whispering, but I couldn't understand them at all. The words caught fire in their mouths and floated—black, unrecognizable in the silence—like falling ash. Then there was muffled laughter. It was her laughing in a strange, cooing voice, as if she were being tickled in a very unusual place, and I suddenly awoke to what sixteen-year-old boys generally find in such situations.

My fantasy began to pursue the beautiful, terrible woman's "secret" more and more wildly. I was looking for something in that suite, but as to what, I couldn't have said. I grew more daring by the day. I once

JÁNOS SZÉKELY

lay in her bed and, trembling, laid my head in the hollow of her own head on the pillow.

I looked through the other rooms as well. The most exciting was the bathroom. I was struck by the warm steam as I entered and her moist towel gave off that intoxicating smell. Not long before, she had been lying in that bath without so much as that thin silk gown on. A few drops of water glistened on the edge of it, and the walls were dewy with drops formed by the steam. That was what I saw, but as to what I *fantasized*, I'd best not say.

Then there was that mysterious bidet. For the longest time, I didn't know what it was for—I had only vague suspicions. I wanted to ask the boys, but I was afraid they'd laugh at me. In the end, I managed to solve the mystery with the help of my burgeoning English. I once overheard Mister Saccharine telling another clerk that they had no bidets in America, and that Americans—would you believe it—had no idea what they were for. Once, an American guest had asked him:

"Is that to wash the baby in?"

"No, madam," Mister Saccharine apparently replied, "it's to wash the baby *out*."

Yes, a boy learns quickly in a hotel like that. I now knew what it was for, and from then on I used to spend even longer in front of it. This, too, was like all the other bidets in the hotel, and yet different, *completely* different. It looked at me like that silent, petrified accomplice that knows everything and is saying nothing.

I was afraid of this "mysterious" woman. I wanted to know her "secret", but deep down, I was glad I didn't actually see her. To that instinctive, inexplicable fear I had felt the first time I saw her in the lift, was now added another kind of fear, a sober and not at all unreasonable one. I was afraid I would end up the same way as *the previous András*.

The boys, who were jealous of my privileged position, were forever making comments. Antal once said straight out:

"You'd better watch out, Mr Still Waters. The other András thought it was all a bed of roses, too."

"Sour grapes!" I said casually, but without much effect.

I was living in fear. My fear was heightened by seeing her at the beginning of February, and then not just once—as these things so often happen—but three times in the space of two weeks. It's not as though anything happened. Nothing did. Twice, she had company, and merely smiled at me in parting—I couldn't even have sworn that she actually recognized me. But when she was alone, she paused a moment.

"How are you?" she asked with a strange little smile, and touched the tip of my nose playfully with her finger.

That was all. After that, I didn't see her again for weeks.

But I only got *really* scared when Gyula was transferred to the night shift and Elemér took his place. He drew me aside in the changing room the very first morning.

"I hear you're the new András."

"Yes," I replied, avoiding his gaze.

Elemér looked around to make sure no one could hear, and quietly said:

"Be careful with that woman."

I could feel myself blush, but there was no way Elemér could have seen that, because I was just doing up my shoelaces.

"Why?" I asked, pretending not to know.

Elemér was silent for a space.

"Didn't you hear what happened to the previous András?"

"No," I lied. "What happened to him?"

It was now Elemér's turn to blush.

"Doesn't matter. How's she treat you?"

"Who?" I said, though I knew precisely who.

"That woman."

"She doesn't treat me one way or the other. I never see her."

Elemér gave me a searching glance.

"How's that?"

"Like I said. In the morning, when I take the dog back up, she's still asleep, and in the afternoons she's never in."

"A good thing, too," Elemér mumbled, and then added meaningfully: "The less you have to do with her, the better."

That was all I needed! I was now so terrified of the woman that I almost literally ran away from her. I thought of starving, and of the six-hour walks, and I repeated to myself what Elemér had said: "The less you have to do with her, the better."

And for a while, I did manage to avoid her. But then something happened and everything changed.

Exfix left one evening, and the following morning no one brought down the dog. Around noon, the head porter called me over.

"Go up to 205," he said. "Her Excellency phoned for you."

"Her Excellency?" I repeated dimly, and in my fright I just stood there in front of the Santa Claus-like head porter as if waiting for an explanation—or perhaps a miracle that would preclude me having to go up to 205.

"Well, what you waiting for?" he snapped. "Get going."

"Yes, sir."

My heart was in my mouth as I knocked. At first, I knocked softly, then louder, but there was no answer. I took out my key, as was the protocol, and opened the door. The entrance hall was dark, and it was as if the whole suite were still sleeping. I felt my way to the door of the salon, not daring to put on the lights, and knocked again. Still no answer. I knocked another two or three times, and then opened the door. There was no one in the salon either, but the door of the bedroom stood open. Soft sounds of conversation filtered out. I was unbelievably relieved: she wasn't alone. I was also incredibly disappointed.

She was talking to a woman. It must have been a private discussion, a personal, girls' chat. Occasionally, they would giggle like accomplices, mysteriously and ambiguously, the way these women sometimes would when they were alone. Apparently, they hadn't heard me come in. I didn't know what to do. I couldn't knock, since the door was open, but I didn't dare go in. Eventually, I gave a cough.

"András," she called, "is that you?"

"Yes, Your Excellency."

"Come in."

I went in, clicked my heels together smartly and, though it was well past noon, I said good morning, the way you're meant to.

The woman with her was Whitewash. The two women were still lying in bed—they were just having breakfast. The covers only came up to their waists, and it seemed to me, as my gaze moved over them, that you could see their breasts through their silk nightgowns. At that time, I didn't know that in Hungary, upper-class ladies took so little notice of their male servants as *men* that they sometimes walked around half naked in front of them. I thought it was just my imagination playing tricks on me, because I didn't dare have a proper look.

Cesar ran over to me as soon as I came in.

"Take him out," she said. "The poor thing's not been down since yesterday."

"Yes, ma'am," I replied, and leant down to the dog to attach his lead. When I was standing back up, my gaze accidentally fell on her. As she leant over her plate peeling her egg, her nightgown fell open at the front, and I could no longer delude myself—it was not just my imagination playing tricks on me. This was reality: a most wonderful, gorgeous reality. You could see her breasts through her nightgown as it fell forward, those legendary, beautiful breasts about which the boys had talked so much, and over which I had so often secretly lingered.

The blood rushed to my head. I grabbed Cesar's lead as a prelude to leaving the room, but she called after me.

"András!" she said in that high, slightly sing-song voice, a strange little half-smile playing around her lips.

I could tell she'd seen it all. My face must have been red as a beetroot and that was clearly not all she'd noticed. But she did not pull up the covers. She just looked at me with that strange little smile, and the way she was looking at me reminded me once more of Manci.

"Um…" she said lightly, absent-mindedly. "Hand me my purse. It's on the chest of drawers."

I handed it to her. I didn't dare so much as glance at her, but I could feel her watching me the while. She took a pengő from her purse and handed it to me. I don't know if I even thanked her in my confusion.

All I remember is that afterwards, she smiled at me once more and, as was her wont, brushed the tip of my nose with her finger.

When I turned to leave, I heard Whitewash's voice. She was speaking English, very softly. She said:

"What a handsome boy!"

"Isn't he?" the lady replied, and then said something else I didn't understand, and then they both laughed, like two partners in crime, mysteriously and ambiguously.

I emerged from the suite as if I'd been drunk. I stopped in front of the first mirror and looked at myself. *What a handsome boy!*—the phrase echoed inside me. And then the other voice, high and slightly sing-song. *Isn't he?*

I was blind drunk. When I reached Országház tér, I was suddenly struck by the thought that Whitewash might have left and she was lying there in bed alone, in her see-through nightgown, and then I no longer cared, no longer cared about anything at all. I grabbed Cesar's lead and ran back.

She wasn't at home. She must have just left—her cigarette was still smoking on the nightstand. The bathroom was warm and steamy, and you could see her footprint on the little pink carpet in front of the bath. The bedroom, with its closed shutters, was full of yellow half-light, and her nightgown lay, exposed, on the unmade bed. I threw myself upon it, half crazed, clutching and kissing it, and the bed as well, and what had happened before, in my sleep, now happened again.

The next day was my day off. I wandered the streets hazily and seemed forever to see her in her salmon-pink nightie with her breasts peeping through as she leant over her plate; she could see that I could see and just looked at me with that Manci-like look in her eyes, not pulling up the covers. I could barely wait for the next morning, but then I was in for a nasty surprise. Exfix had arrived in the evening, and it was he who brought down the dog.

I didn't see her again for weeks. Before, when I was running away from her, I kept bumping into her all the time, and now, when I sought her company every waking moment and did nothing but wait to see her again, I never did.

I grew more uneasy by the day. I was afraid of what I wanted, and I wanted what I was afraid of. I grew so bold that I started slamming the doors in the morning, though I knew full well what would happen to me if I woke her. But I didn't care. Yes, I wanted to wake her, wanted her to call out to me, wanted to be able to go in to her. I was no longer in my right mind—I was completely drunk.

In the end, I got what I wanted. One morning, when I had let Cesar into the suite, that high voice called out from the bedroom.

"András… is that you?"

I don't know what came over me at that moment. Instead of replying, instead of being happy, I turned on my heels in panic and ran all the way down the stairs.

"What's the matter with you?" asked the porter when I reached the lobby. "You look like you've seen a ghost."

"I don't know," I mumbled and wiped the perspiration off me.

"Go stretch your legs," he suggested. "A bit of fresh air'll do you good."

I went and walked to the Vigadó theatre. There, I suddenly stopped. She must have thought I hadn't heard her, it occurred to me, and I was dead sure that she was telephoning for me at that very moment. So I ran right back to the hotel to get what I had run away from a few minutes before, and—giving in once and for all to my fate—waited for her to call me. I waited for some time.

Almost four months, in fact.

11

S PRING SEEMED TO HAVE DRIVEN everybody wild. The boys came
in with circles under their eyes in the morning, whispering together
like conspirators. Their faces were full of mysteries and spots, they kept
showing each other letters and photos, and anyone who was anyone
at all carried a lock of a girl's hair in his wallet. Some of them really
did lose their hearts, like Antal, for example, who was "fatally" in love
with Flóra, the third-floor maid. There were others who got whatever
they could, like Gyula, who would "pick up" women on the street or
in the park, and announce triumphantly next day that they'd "given
up the goods". And there were some who got into serious trouble,
like Lajos, who only just avoided becoming a father: it being spring,
he could finally take his Ilus to the forests around Hűvösvölgy. In the
winter, they had to confine themselves to petting down at the cinema.
But lots of the boys were all mouth and no trousers. They would make
up all sorts of stories to deflect the terrible suspicion of virginity, though
in those crazy days, you could never tell if what you'd made up as a
story to tell in the morning wouldn't be true by sundown. Love rushed
at us in this early spring of our teenagerhood like the big, warm drops
of a summer storm you could see approaching from a distance. You
yourself were still dry, but you could see the dust rising off the ground
not far off as the raindrops hit, and you knew that—sooner or later—it
would reach you, too.

All the talk was of women. The boys exchanged their hard-won bits
of technical know-how in the field of love like stamps. Only raw recruits
in love and first-year medical students are capable of the level of detail
and insistent pedantry with which the boys discussed the secrets of the
female body. They talked very loudly, very dirtily and very haughtily,
but I still often had the impression that they were just as frightened and
confused as myself. Some mornings, they'd come into the changing

room brooding and grumpy, touchy and silent for days, only daring to ask one of their fellows for advice much, much later.

"Say, old man," they'd whisper in some quiet corner, "has it ever happened to you that…"

Yes indeed, all this was the fault of spring. Love was costly in winter and the boys couldn't afford it. Only Franciska had money, but he didn't spend it on women. The others, who were interested exclusively in the gentler sex, had their seven lean years of love in the winter. Their girlfriends didn't have flats of their own either—at most, they could have taken them to a cheap hotel, but they didn't have the means. That left petting in darkened doorways, on abandoned benches in snowy parks or under the exotic arcades of the Fisherman's Bastion in Buda, where people routinely smashed the light bulbs every night until the authorities eventually gave up replacing them. Then there was the cinema, of course, the cheap, suspicious little side-street fleapits of Pest. If you got an unexpectedly large tip, and things were relatively OK at home, you took "the little woman" to one of these fleapits. The next morning, the gushing reviews wouldn't be about the film, but about the lady's breasts, and to be perfectly honest, not just them. For some of the fleapits had very correctly understood the spirit of the age and adapted ingeniously to the needs of their clientele. In these establishments, lovers could get discreet little cages referred to as "boxes" on the price list outside, and in those boxes, as the boys used to say, "anything went". Before the lights came back on, they would ring a little bell, a tactful but obstinate bell that helped guide couples back down to earth from their respective paradises in time—you could thus feel completely at ease. But this, too, became a question of money, which is to say an intractable question, since these "boxes" cost a lot more than ordinary seats, and the boys barely had enough to cover even those.

But now, all that had changed. It was spring, and the boys would report enthusiastically in the morning:

"I took the little woman to the Mauthner Hotel last night."

The Mauthner Hotel was what paperback writers used to refer to as "the great outdoors". It was named after the largest supplier of seeds in Hungary, who used to put up little signs in the public parks advertising the fact that their lawns had been planted with Mauthner seeds. The Mauthner Hotel should, therefore, properly be plural, because there wasn't just one, but lots, a franchise—an entire chain in fact—that welcomed free of charge its impecunious and impatient guests.

Gyula was the most experienced Mauthnerite among us. We thought him a low, unscrupulous, heartbreaking skirt-chaser, and that of course made him highly respected. He was a freckled, lanky teenage boy, very nice and very dumb. He liked his women wholesale, so to speak, and would open up their letters, photos and occasionally items of intimate clothing to public display, as well as giving a detailed account of their skills and failings in the bedroom. He loved to gloat; so much so that he used not to go home at all after his exhausting late-night sessions, but would sleep in a corner of the basement just so he could get up and recount his latest conquest while the experience was still fresh.

This pocket Don Juan, this good-hearted, simple Lothario, turned out to be the first victim of spring. One morning, to our general amazement, he announced:

"Boys, I think my goose is cooked. I'm so in love it ain't true."

The boys, of course, started pressing him as to "what lady is that which doth enrich the hand of yonder knight?", to which Gyula admitted—to our great surprise—that he himself didn't actually know.

"Ain't got a clue," he said. "It all started on the tram. She wanted to close the window, and I of course helped her. We got talking, and then we ended up fooling around before going out to Hűvösvölgy. But get this: she wouldn't even tell me her name. She says: 'Don't ask questions, I won't either. It's springtime, and we're young.' What d'you say to that? I'd always thought this kind of thing only happened in the movies! Not that I'd swap her for one of them bottle-blonde Hollywood tarts, no way! Oooh, boys, if you only knew how fine she was!"

We, of course, wanted to know all about how fine she was, and Gyula did not need coaxing. He gave us a full physical description, the long and the short of which was that this woman was the prettiest, most elegant, most mysterious and just generally finest woman in the world.

"And?" Lajos asked. "What happened at the Mauthner?"

Gyula gave a low whistle.

"You ain't seen nothin' like it! There we are in the pitch-black forest and she won't let me so much as take her hand. She gave me such a slap when I tried to kiss her I thought my eye'd fall out. Well, I said to myself, this ain't going to end well, so I tell her my grandmother's sick. All right, she says, she's got to go as well. What about a farewell kiss, then, I ask. All right, she says, if I behave myself, she doesn't mind. But only a little one. That little kiss became a great big one, and now listen. She got so excited from all the kissing that she gave me the goods right there! Now tell me, you ever heard anything like that?"

No, no we hadn't, but that only made the story more exciting. The serialized stories in the movies, on radio and in the papers were so full at the time of thrilling sexual encounters that secretly we all longed for just this kind of Mysterious Woman. We kept up with further developments anxiously, but they, alas, did not turn out the way they used to in the serials. First of all, the woman did not show up to the next rendezvous, which in itself would not have been out of place, given the thriller-like mood of this mysterious liaison. What *was* more out of place was that Gyula did not grow downhearted, like the hero in a novel, but started chasing after the new kitchen maid. But all that was by the by. The surprising twist was yet to come.

About two or three weeks later, when we'd already started to forget the incident, we noticed odd changes in Gyula. He didn't boast about women any more; he wasn't interested in anything, and he even "ditched" the kitchen maid. He visibly lost weight, grew deathly pale, and walked among us like he was mourning something.

"He can't let her go," Antal—an expert in hopeless love thanks to Flóra—announced, and the others, too, were convinced that this failed affair was what was eating Gyula.

But one morning, Gyula spilt his secret. By the time I came into the changing room, he'd finished talking, and it was only by the boys' faces I could tell that important news had been imparted.

"I saw my brother's when he got it," Márton said a little while later. "If it's the same, I can tell you right off."

"Let's go to the toilets," Franciska, ever careful, said. "Anyone could walk in here."

They trooped into the lavatories, locked the door behind them, and when they came out, they all looked awkward and strangely scared.

"My brother's was nothing like that!" Márton declared. "You'd best show that to a doctor."

"Like I've got the money!"

"Then go down the Public Infirmary."

"Yeah, right," Gyula waved angrily. "I wouldn't let them touch my little finger, let alone my…" and he told them what.

Gyula was not alone in his opinion of the Infirmary. Whoever could, went to a "proper" doctor. The boys didn't insist. Besides, it was late, and everyone went off to their various duties.

Elemér, who had been in the changing room throughout, hadn't said anything. He combed his hair in silence, put on his uniform, and generally pretended not to care about the whole thing. But when Gyula made to leave with the others, he called after him to stay behind.

"If you want, I can get you in to see a doctor," he said. "He won't charge you."

"Won't charge me?" Gyula asked, giving Elemér a somewhat suspicious look. "What kind of doctor is he, then?"

"A very good one."

"Then why won't he charge me?"

"Workers' solidarity," Elemér replied, his prematurely aged eyes glittering. "He's a comrade," he said, more softly. "A Socialist."

"But I ain't in the Party," Gyula protested.

"If you were, you wouldn't have got yourself into this kind of mess," Elemér responded strictly. "You'd be enlightened. Not just a man, a *Mensch*. But that's not important right now." He shrugged. His voice was neutral as always, but very determined. "Go see him today, all right?"

"Yes," replied Gyula, and the huge boy stood there in front of Elemér—thin, spare, and half a head shorter than him—as if he'd been his father. "Yes," he repeated, "I'll go today."

But the next day he didn't show up in the changing room.

"Anybody seen him?" Elemér asked.

"No," replied Lajos. "Looks like there's something wrong."

We waited for him a little while longer, because we were all curious as to what the doctor had said, but in the end we had to get going. Elemér and I were the last to leave. When we, too, were getting ready to leave, the bathroom door opened suddenly and Gyula stood before us.

"You been here all this time?" Elemér asked in surprise.

Gyula did not reply. He just stood there, in front of the toilets, white as a sheet and immobile, as if he hadn't heard Elemér at all.

"Did you go and see the doctor?"

Gyula nodded, but still didn't say anything. There was an unbearable silence.

"And?" Elemér asked eventually.

Gyula came closer and slumped down on a bench. His mouth opened; he wanted to say something, but no sound came out of it. He lay down on the bench and started crying, wailing like a small boy.

"Sy-phi-lis!" he sobbed. "Sy-phi-lis!"

We didn't know what to say. We watched him wail with childish fright, lost and dumb. Then Elemér went and sat down next to him and put his hand on Gyula's shoulder.

"They can cure it," he said quietly.

"Not for sure," Gyula snivelled. "Yesterday, I read in a medical book that many times it comes back again. And even if it don't, you can go mad from it, and… what about Katica?" he exclaimed without any warning.

"Who's that?" Elemér asked in surprise.

"My… my… fiancée," Gyula sobbed. "I was goin' to marry her as soon as I was making a bit more, and…" He couldn't continue, descending into inarticulate noises.

We listened, shaken. This show-off, loud-mouthed teenage boy, who had told us all about his many adventures, had never—not once—mentioned Katica.

There was a long silence. Then Elemér said:

"You have to take her to the doctor too."

"Why?"

"Why?" Elemér repeated irritably. "She's bound to realize you gave it to her eventually."

"Katica?" Gyula looked at him in surprise. "You don't think?... I never laid a finger on her! I want to *marry* her... or, that is, I wanted to," he added bitterly and started sobbing once more.

That was sensational news, of course. Though the boys tried to discuss "the affair" like seasoned medical doctors, men who have seen something of the world and are no longer surprised by anything, you could see the terror in their eyes whenever they looked at Gyula. He was our first victim, and these carefree soldiers of love who had marched out to battle with whoops of joy, now looked on horrified and felt like hiding behind their mother's skirts. Some vowed eternal chastity, and no one so much as mentioned women... for three days. Then they slowly emerged from their terror and tried to convince themselves they'd never been scared. One morning, they were once more gathered round someone who, "Oooh, boys!", had had some extraordinary and amazing adventure, and were excitedly pressing him to tell them "what lady is that which doth enrich the hand of yonder knight", laughing a great deal, nervously, at the dirty details. No one mentioned Gyula if they didn't have to, in the same way that soldiers didn't talk of fallen comrades. They pretended nothing had happened, and it all started over again.

The hotel guests, of course, did not have to visit the Mauthner franchise, but they, too, had their own difficulties in love. It was strictly forbidden for guests to "take a woman up" to their rooms. This moral prohibition, to which all the finer hotels adhered, was just as immoral as the system to which it owed its existence. For, if you had a *suite*, you could take up as many women as you liked. And even for those who could only afford a room, there was nothing to prevent them renting another for the lady, who would "unexpectedly depart" a few hours later. The problem was that all new guests had to submit to certain formalities, and young ladies of good family—who guarded their reputations jealously—as well as respectable ladies anxious to preserve the sanctity of their marriages, did not want to take the risk. Among other things, they had to fill in a police registration card. This in itself may not have been a problem, because you can put whatever you like on one of these cards, but they were afraid that someone might spot them doing it and think ill of them, though they'd been motivated by nothing but good intentions when deciding to do it.

In such cases, the gentlemen would approach us confidentially and we would tactfully "take the woman up" to their rooms without any fuss. This smuggling of women was one of our primary sources of income. It's what brought the greatest tips, and it had other benefits besides. Thanks to this sideline, if there was a honeymoon, we always knew precisely where and when it would be, and if there was no one staying in the room next door, we'd take turns decamping there in groups of various sizes. The rooms were separated by doors, and those doors were thin enough to satisfy, at least in part, our limitless thirst for knowledge. If there was no key in the lock, and we'd make sure that there wasn't, then we could not only listen to, but also watch these romantic interludes, which—I hardly need tell you—were extremely instructive, given that you get all sorts in a hotel; and these various sorts of people had their various ways of practising the endlessly elaborate art of love.

I had been living like this for more than a year now. It was the hotel's swampy, feverish climate that had produced in me this venereal malaria from whose fever I'd been suffering for months. The other boys, no matter if they were lying or telling the truth, could at least expel the poison, or at least a part of it, through talk, but I was silent as the grave. I buried my secret and sometimes even I could believe that it had died. I was disgusted by the things I did and saw, and now and again I really did manage to snap out of it all. But this daytime sobriety was always interrupted at night by that high voice, and up to two or three times a week, I would wake to find that I had been trying to feel, up and down stairs, my way to her bedroom in my dream, before what used to happen at this juncture happened again.

I changed externally, too. I grew so fast my father said you could *hear* it. I was now one metre eighty, and with the spring my face—just like the bushes in the park—had also burst into new life. It was full of spots and overgrown with hairs like weeds.

"Why don't you shave?" the Major snapped at me one morning at inspection. "You look like a widowed monkey."

From then on, I shaved every day with my father's razor. By my six-teenth birthday, I was the proud proprietor of a moustache—a scrappy, thin little moustache, it's true, but black enough to disguise its flaws as far as others were concerned; generally, people took me for two years older than I actually was.

Women looked at me differently than six months before. The young chambermaids rarely passed me without comment—they teased, giggled and flirted with me; one or two even rubbed up against me, and they all looked at me as if they had a secret they were burning to tell. It's possible that my dangerous rep also attracted them, for I had a terrible reputation, though to this day I don't quite know why. Lajos once asked me, to the great amusement of the boys:

"Tell us, Mr Still Waters, are you taking the maids to the Mauthner alphabetically, or do you make them take turns and draw their names out of a hat?"

The truth is, nothing had happened with any of them. I would occa-sionally, it's true, feel them up a little if the opportunity presented itself, but I never went any further, not for a lack of enthusiasm on the part of the girls. They all thought I was seeing one of the others, whichever one they'd seen me with last, because of course it didn't occur to any of them that inside this big, devil-may-care young man was a scared and confused little boy who—despite his moustache, his strength and his venereal malaria—was still secretly dreaming of a fourteen-year-old American girl, and for whom the rest wasn't to be taken seriously at all, because it was only a symptom of his illness, all just fever-talk.

Yes, it seemed this spring was driving everyone wild. My parents were acting strange, too. Something changed at home. There was something in the air, something strange and unnerving. I could feel it the way a rheumatic feels a change in the weather, but I couldn't have told you what, exactly, it was. To tell the truth, I wasn't that bothered, either. You're so concerned with yourself, in the spring of your seventeenth year, that you don't have too much time to think about others. They're acting strange, I said to myself, and left it at that. But sometimes I thought something had happened to them.

My mother had changed externally. Her face was fuller and had some colour, and I only rarely heard her cough. Her body was more shapely now, her gait easier; she looked inexplicably younger. Her face lost that dreary bitterness, the apathetic, almost sleepy hopelessness that had made me so sad even as a child. Her eyes grew gentler, her lines grew softer, and she emanated a strange good cheer. She smiled a lot and, it seemed to me, with a bit of mystery—as if she knew something she wasn't telling anyone.

At first, I thought it was all down to better quality of life, but then I saw that I was wrong. It was her hair that gave it away. One day, I was surprised to see that she had a *hairstyle*. Until now, she'd always worn a kerchief which she only rarely took off, and only at home, like most poor women. Her greasy black hair stuck flatly to her scalp, ending in a shapeless straggle down the back of her neck. That straggle was now gone. Márika had cut it off, after lengthy and detailed consultation, and from then on, my mother had a *hairstyle*, like a lady. Her hair was no longer sticky and greasy; her blue-black locks curled gently around her head, and suddenly I became aware that she had nice hair.

Next, I discovered her legs. She started taking up her skirts, and all at once it turned out that she had nice legs, too. Whenever my father was out, she was constantly operating on her clothes. She would amputate the long, worn-out sleeves, cut valleys into shirts once buttoned to the collar, attaching new buttons and neat little home-made collars, and even add the occasional little playful flourish here and there. Her post-operative shirts showed off her fresh, surprisingly shapely breasts, which I had never before noticed—just like her legs or hair. Until now, I had considered her some genderless creature, but I was now forced to notice that she was a *woman*. That fact—I didn't know why—filled me with a strange disquiet. There were so many *women* out there; you only had one mother. I felt uncomfortable each time I looked at her. A mother shouldn't be a *woman*.

Before, when she got home from work, she'd grab a bite to eat and then go straight to bed. Now, it was as if this was the real start of her day. She locked herself in the kitchen and spent an unbelievably long time washing and dressing. She put on a clean dress, freshly washed and ironed, pulling her skirt up to the waist before she sat down so as not to crease it. It used to make me laugh, almost. I knew that if my father had happened to come home just then, my mother would have sat on her freshly ironed skirt without a second thought, trying generally to behave as if she, too, were just as untidy and devil-may-care as him.

I looked at these changes askance. My mother must have realized what was going on inside me, because she, too, felt uncomfortable when we were alone. We didn't talk much whenever that happened. I would study my English and she would sit, and sew, and wait. If my father wasn't home by ten, she used to start pestering me to go to bed.

"Look at your eyes, they're like pins," she said, and was visibly relieved if I replied:

"Yes, it's getting late."

Then she would go out into the kitchen and carry on sewing. I could see through the cracks in the door that she kept burning the lamp, which she had never used to do before. That, too, made me angry. If he wanted to see her, he should have come home earlier, and if he didn't want to see her, then why the hell was she waiting for him and burning all that precious petroleum? She should have been saving up for my English book instead.

My father would sometimes only come home at dawn. I would always wake with a start on these occasions, because he used to come in whistling and would talk loudly. My mother never asked him where he'd been. She made as if she'd been expecting him just at the hour he'd happened to arrive. They chatted happily, joked and laughed as if they were strangers altogether to trouble. In the end, they went to bed and then that blasted creaking would once more begin, growing wilder every day.

My father was forever cheerful. He left whistling in the morning and came home whistling at night. As to what he got up to in between, I think my mother had just as little notion as I did. He didn't work, but it appears he lived pretty well, for he was always in fine fettle, simply radiating health. He smoked Extra cigarettes, some forty or fifty a day. How he could afford all this was a mystery, known only to himself and his Maker.

I had a strange relationship with him. I liked his strength, his cheer, his determination, the way he took everything that happened to him in his stride—or rather the way he took no notice of it at all. He bit into life like an apple, the sweet juice almost spilling over out of his mouth; if there happened to be a worm in it, then—to hell with it!—he spat it out and kept on chewing. I liked his homespun peasant wisdom that had broadened and deepened during his many wanderings without losing its original shape and flavour. I liked that he was a man, and treated me like one too, and though I didn't dare admit it, my mood always soured when he didn't come home. I liked to spend the evenings with him, but the next morning I would usually find myself angrily judging his every word. The suspect charm of his being both attracted and repelled me so strongly that in the end I didn't know how I felt about him. He was irresistible. He was a charmer.

"Treats your mother like the apple of his eye," Márika noted once, and I had to admit that it was true.

People in Újpest treated their women the way my father treated my mother every day only in the headiest heyday of their wooing. He was always kind to her and never threw his weight around; and I was pleased about that, very pleased—on the one hand. On the other hand, I was seized by an anxious confusion when I saw him all over my mother. I would have liked him to behave the way other fathers did. A father shouldn't be all over your mother.

Everything had changed since he'd come to live with us, even the apartment. Before, it was neat and sad, like my mother, and nothing ever happened there. Its corners were webbed in by the grey spider of trouble and our days, like dead flies, hung in those webs. Now, it was as if there was a constant flow of air. There was something in the air, something strange and unnerving. As a young poet, the way I put it at the time was: *My father brought the scent of life with him.* I liked this phrase, but not the way my father lived, because back then I had only very vague ideas about the "scent of life". I didn't know—or I didn't want to know—that the earth gives off not only the warmth of the sun and the freshness of the winds, but also the smell of dung and putrefaction, and that the strange mystery I felt around my father was, in part, the mystery of fertility, and in part the mystery of life itself.

I wanted to find the solution to this mystery at all costs, and couldn't understand my mother, who acquiesced to everything without asking any questions. This isn't going to end well, I thought, and when there really was trouble, I told myself she deserved it, because at sixteen you don't yet know that it's better for a woman to have to pay for her happiness than not to have happiness in her life at all.

The first scandal erupted one evening in early spring. When I got home, the woman from the tavern downstairs was in the flat with my mother and I guessed it wasn't to bring her beer. She was a made-up suburban "lady", blonde, dumpy and attractive in a vulgar way. She must have been about thirty or thirty-five and talked with her mouth sucked in to sound refined. Her eyelids drooped down as she talked. They were sitting at the table, stiff and anxious, and when I arrived, they smiled stiffly.

"Go into the kitchen, son," my mother said, and I immediately suspected that it was something to do with my father and that there would be trouble.

I stopped in front of the door and, with the delicate artistry they had so perfected in me at the hotel, put my ear to the door to listen. At first, they talked so softly that I could hardly hear a thing, but then the proprietress of the bar got "carried away" as they say, and in a few minutes I knew that it really was about my father.

"And then that good-for-nothing says to me, Karolin, he says, you know I have a family, and we can't keep this up for ever. Well, 'course we can't, I knew that, but why didn't he tell me that before he goes turning my head? Because, like I say, he didn't say a word, I swear. The next morning, he told me, it's true, but by then…" The sentence remained unfinished, and there was the sound of someone crying softly in the room. "I swear," the woman sniffed, "and I confessed everything to the priest, and I prayed and I lit candles, but in vain. I couldn't leave him. I was bad, I'd sinned, I admit it, but what can I do? I'm just a helpless woman. He drives me wild. There's evil in that man, oh yes. He whips 'em on and drives 'em wild with his eyes. He's the Devil incarnate, he is. But it's you I feel sorry for, my dear. And when he left me, I went to church and swore to the Virgin Mary that I wouldn't rest till I'd atoned for my sins. I worked night and day, but I've done it, yes *this time I've done it.* Cost me eighty-five pengős, but strike me down if it isn't true."

"You gave the church eighty-five pengős?"

"Not the church. The detective."

"What detective?"

"The one that investigated him."

"Who?"

"Him! Don't you get it? The lying dirty pig told me ever so sincerely he was leaving me because he was a family man. Well, now the truth is out about this *family man.* And you know what that truth is, my dear?"

My dear said nothing, but the woman told her the truth anyway.

"He's shacked up with another woman," she hissed. "A nobody. Some little tramp. That the earth don't swallow him! She's all of eighteen, one of those little tarts with the button noses. A chambermaid with some baroness. I even know her name. Want me to tell you?"

"No," my mother replied firmly.

There was silence.

"Well… I understand," the woman said, more quietly. "The important thing is not who they're cheating on you with. The important thing is they're cheating on you. I just wanted to right my own wrongs. You know what it says in the Lord's Prayer: *and deliver us from evil.* Well, I'm going to deliver you from evil. I won't let him lie through his back teeth to you. I'm going to stay here and tell him the truth to his face. When's he usually come home?"

"Oh, it depends."

"Doesn't matter," the woman said encouragingly. "You can count on me, dear. I'll stay till dawn if I have to."

"Don't," my mother said curtly.

"Why not?"

My mother was silent for a few moments and then said a little hoarsely:

"Because, with respect, it ain't any of your business."

"Is that so?" she burst out as if someone had stepped on her corns, and I heard her stand up.

I quickly sneaked away from the door so they wouldn't notice I'd been listening. I sat down at the kitchen table and waited, but inside, the conversation started up again. I couldn't hear what they were saying from where I was, but I didn't dare go back to the door. I only caught the occasional, disjointed word. You could hear the Gypsy music drifting up from the tavern, it being Saturday night, and there always being Gypsy music down there on a Saturday night.

I don't know how long I waited like that. At the time, it seemed a very long while. Suddenly, there was shouting from within.

"How dare you!" the woman shouted. "I'm a respectable lady, who—"

"Who sleeps with other people's menfolk!" My mother finished the sentence for her. "You can talk to me about the priest and the Virgin all you like. What *you're* after you won't find in the Bible. Truth is, Mishka'd had enough of you and that's what all this is about—the rest is just hot air."

"Ha ha ha!" the woman cried, without actually laughing. "Ha ha ha. You make me laugh. You really think he's in love with you? Or he's with you for that pretty little face of yours? Ha ha! He's a pimp, my dear, nothing but a common pimp. He's with you because you keep him."

"Maybe that's what he's with *you* for," my mother retorted, "but he ain't never got money from me. I ain't never given him nothin' but a bed, which is what you wish you *could* give him!"

"Is that so?" the woman hissed again. "Now I see. You're in it together."

"What?! We're what?"

"You're in it together. You put up with him being with other women, and he gives you the cash. You probably robbed me too, and—"

She didn't make it further than that "and". A tremendous slap put an end to that sentence. Then there was screaming and bestial yelling, and by the time I tore open the door, they were at each other's throats.

I got between them. The barkeeper made a spirited attempt at murdering me, too, in her anger, but I caught both her hands with a quick movement and slung her out of the apartment.

Outside, she was greeted with raucous laughter. Every child in the building old enough to stand on their own two feet was gathered in front of our place, enjoying the show. The furious barkeeper stuck her tongue out at them and pulled her skirts up from behind.

"Higher!" the children shouted. "Higher!"

The adults didn't want to miss the fun, either; the walkway was full of them. Whoever had gone to bed had leapt back out and stood, half naked, staring out of their windows and doors. Everyone was desperate to know what had happened, they were all talking at once, and if you didn't know any better, you'd have thought you'd landed in the middle of a madhouse.

Áron, the Sabbatarian, was running to and fro, trying to bring the scandal-hungry people to their senses. But all his talk of loving thy neighbour and human dignity was in vain—the curious crowd paid him no attention at all.

Herr Hausmeister was screaming in the courtyard.

"Quiet down or I'll fetch the police!"

The barkeeper was screaming on the stairs.

"Other people's money, that's what they're living off, other women's money! Thieves! Murderers!"

But not even that was as unbearable as the silence when everything at last fell quiet and you could once more hear the Gypsy music from downstairs.

We hung around the flat in silence. What was there to say? My mother merely mumbled:

"That'll give 'em something to gossip about."

I replied:

"Don't pay 'em any mind."

And that was that.

My mother went out into the kitchen, washed, changed, came back, sat down and waited. This time, she didn't pull her skirt up before she sat down and she wasn't sewing, either. She just waited.

The door opened at last and in walked my father.

"Evenin'," he said, tossing his hat, as was his wont, across the room onto the hook.

"Evenin'," said my mother.

"Evenin'," I said.

Then we relapsed into silence. My mother went into the kitchen, and I pretended to study.

"English?" my father asked.

"Yes."

"How's it going?"

"All right."

He looked at my notes.

"Hard language, English."

"Yes," I said. "Quite hard."

And there our conversation dried up completely. We were silent. We waited.

My mother brought in the dinner and put it on the table. There was quite a lot on the plate, because as well as the food I got from the hotel, I always added a little bit of the food I bought for myself. My father and I didn't usually eat on these occasions, because we'd both had dinner before we got home, but my mother nonetheless laid out plates for us both every night. At other times, we would just have a bite or two for her sake, but tonight, neither of us dared refuse the food. We ate in silence, forcing each bite down, avoiding each other's eyes. We ate slowly, unbearably slowly. None of us dared to stop.

Suddenly, my father banged the table.

"Will you stop it with this ridiculous charade!" he shouted, and pushed his plate away.

"What charade?" my mother asked softly, without looking up.

"Oh, you know!" my father shouted at her, beetroot red. "Even the boy knows. The whole house knows! Stop beatin' around the bush! Out with it!"

My mother shrugged.

"What do you want me to say?"

"Whatever you want! Anything. Tell me to go to hell. Tell me I'm a bastard. Kick me out. Do what you want. Just don't sit there in silence like Christ on the Cross, 'cause I can't take it. Got it?" he screamed, and banged the table once more. "*I can't take it!*"

My mother looked at him. It was the first time she'd looked at him all evening.

312

"You want to go?" she asked drily, with incredible self-control.

"This is your flat!" my father shouted. "Only you can kick me out. So go on, do it, let's get it over with."

My mother once more avoided looking at him. She began rearranging the breadcrumbs on the table and didn't say anything for a long time.

"You ain't got to worry about me, Mishka," she said. "I ain't goin' to tell you to go to hell. I won't scream at you to get out, and I won't beg you to stay. You come by yourself, you go by yourself, and you stay by yourself. And let me ease your mind for you. You ain't never been bad to me—I'm tellin' you so in front of your son. You was always good to me, and ain't no one ever been good to me in my life. I ain't got so many good memories as to forget the ones I do have. You was kind to me, and I won't ever forget it. There, that's it. I ain't got nothin' more to say."

This was not, apparently, what my father had been expecting. I could see he didn't know what to do. He didn't look at my mother, but just kept blinking restlessly and shifting in his seat. Then he finally kicked his chair out from under him, stood up, paced to and fro, and hurriedly lit a cigarette. Then he stopped in front of my mother.

"D'you know what you're like?" he shouted. "You're like that strong-man game at the fairground people're always punching. You never hit back, either, goddamn it—people just end up wearing their fists out on you. For God's sake, woman, can't you see I'm bad?"

"P'raps," my mother said in a matter-of-fact, serious way. "P'raps you are. I don't know. And even if I did know, what good would it do me? What's that matter? Someone's either a part of you or they ain't. You don't cut off your hand no matter how much it hurts. If it falls off, that's different. Then it either kills you or you learn to live without it. But while it's there, what can you do with it? If it hurts, it hurts, you've got to deal with it. You've got to wait for it to get better, if it does get better. So I'm telling you, Mishka, you don't have to worry about me. I'm a strange sort. You can do with me what you want."

Then she was silent again and started, once more, rearranging the crumbs. She sat there, eyes downcast, like a defendant in court who's confessed all and is now waiting for their sentence. There was silence;

313

only my father's steps resounded as he kept pacing the room. Then he stopped.

"You got some paper and an envelope?" he asked me.

"Only hotel paper."

"That'll do," he said, and sat down at the table without looking at my mother.

I put the paper and envelope down before him. He took out a pencil, chewed it for a bit, then started writing. When the letter was finished, he said to my mother:

"Read it, Anna."

My mother read it and handed it back to him without a word. She acted as if there were nothing special in the letter, but I could see her lips were trembling. Then my father chucked her playfully in the side and my mother gave a weak, tired smile.

"You read it too," he said, and handed the letter to me.

The letter was addressed to a girl called Gizi, whom he apprised of the situation without beating around the bush, though not without a certain amount of regret. He wrote that it was all over because "a family man, after all, belongs to his family", but admitted that it had been good, very good, with her, that he would never forget it, and asked her not to be angry with him—life was suffering, that's how it was, everything came to an end.

My father leant over me and read the letter along with me—he seemed very pleased with it.

"Your old man can write too, eh?" he joked, and started whistling cheerfully. "Would you go out and post it? I want your mother to sleep easy."

I took the letter down, not knowing if I was happy or sad about the way things had turned out.

The flat was suspiciously quiet when I got back. I coughed before I opened the door to the room, but even so it was mistimed. I still caught them jumping apart. They were both flustered and soon said it was late, and time for bed.

So I went to bed, but couldn't fall asleep for the longest time because the bed outside kept creaking for at least two hours that night. I felt revulsion and hatred for them, but at the same time affection and pity, too. I couldn't understand myself, I couldn't understand them, I couldn't understand anything. I stared into the darkness, and life itself seemed all dark.

Patsy—I said to myself—tell me this doesn't happen in America?

From then on, my father spent his evenings at home. What he did during the day, however, remained a mystery. He left, whistling, in the morning, came home whistling at night, and never said so much as a word as to what had happened in between. He came through the door like a guest in a house where you could only talk about pleasant and entertaining things.

It would be hard to say who was more besotted with him: my mother or himself. He was a born actor, and you could see that he was excited by this demanding role so little suited to him—that of the *paterfamilias*—and that he was delighted with his performance. But sometimes I still felt he was bored of the whole thing, like someone who's been playing the same role too long and wants to try something new. Occasionally, I noticed, he was seized by a strange restlessness, especially on Saturday and Sunday nights when the Gypsy music would filter up from the tavern.

"Why you sittin' round at home?" my mother would ask with forced gaiety. "Go have yourself a good time, show 'em how it's done!"

But my father didn't take her up on it. He tried to turn the whole thing into a joke.

"I can't, my dear," he'd say. "The markets are down. Even the stockbrokers have gone home to their wives."

Then they'd laugh and not bring it up again. But the restlessness still hung in the air, like the smell of incense after mass, and my mother looked like those lonely poor women praying to St Antal in the empty church when someone in the family falls ill.

One evening, she asked my father:

"D'you like twenty-one?"

My father seemed to take the question badly, I didn't know why.

"Why?" he asked suspiciously.

315

"I was just wonderin'," my mother replied. "They say it's a fine game."

"It ain't bad."

"Is it hard?"

"'Course not. If we had the cards, I could teach you in ten minutes."

"We do have cards," my mother said unexpectedly.

"We do? Where d'you get 'em?"

"Never you mind," she replied mysteriously, and produced a brand-new pack of cards from the cupboard. "Will you teach me?"

My father had apparently not been expecting that.

"Why not?" he said, visibly relieved. "But what I want to know is, what's got into you?"

"The spirit of sin," my mother replied, and sat happily down at the table. "Go on, then, teach me this wonderful game."

My father explained the game, and from then on, we played so passionately night after night we'd have pawned our salvation for a good hand. My father was always the most excited among us because he was—myself included—the biggest child of all of us. He couldn't do anything by halves. He would whoop with joy when luck was with him and curse the stars out of the heaven if he got a bad hand.

One evening, my mother stood up mid-game, and to our great surprise, put a bottle of wine down on the table.

"Whose birthday is it?" asked my father.

My mother winked at him mischievously.

"The tooth fairy's," she said, and poured.

"Well, in that case, long live the tooth fairy!" my father cried, and we all drank the tooth fairy's good health.

From then on, every night was the tooth fairy's birthday at our house. There was always wine in the house and later on, my mother even managed to produce other "surprises". She would stand up suddenly mid-game, go out into the kitchen with a secretive expression and fetch rolls, cheese, pretzels and the like; once, we even got herrings. Yes, we were living high on the hog back then.

My father loved wine, cards and women, and my mother, it seems, wanted to show him that he could get all that at home. We ate, drank and made merry, we played cards and sometimes, when the music filtered up from the little tavern downstairs, we'd sing along with the Gypsies. They were fine, heartfelt nights, these, the best of my childhood nights.

Once, the band downstairs was playing:

I walked in the quiet forest glade
I saw a bird there in the shade
And a nest made just for two
How I fell in love with you

"Remember?" my mother asked softly, awkwardly, and turned aside, because her eyes had filled with tears.

"How could I forget!" replied my father, and took her hand. "What a fine night that was. What a wild night." He took my hand, too. "That was the night I met your mother," he said, and his rich baritone began accompanying the musicians:

"How I fell in love with you…"

*

The way he treated my mother in those weeks, I thought he could never look at another woman. But he could. Oh, how he could! I once had the opportunity of finding out for myself.

It happened on the boat to Margit Island. A guest had sent me off to the island to deliver a large bunch of flowers. It was a fine, warm spring afternoon, and I was wandering, unsuspecting, about the boat. I went down a set of stairs and when I got to the ship's belly, I was suddenly brought up short. There he was, in that little oval room they called a "salon" where there was generally no one when the weather was fine. He was sitting with a very young and very pretty girl in the semi-darkness, and I didn't have to wonder why. He saw me, too, there was no doubt about it, though I took off the second I spotted him. I fled as if he'd caught *me* in the act and was about to mete out some terrible punishment.

All day, I dreaded the moment I'd see him again. I was once more consumed with plans for escape, but in the end, of course, I went home, and it all turned out very differently to how I'd expected.

My father acted as if nothing at all had happened. He was nice to me, but not any nicer than usual, and between two games, when my mother was shuffling, he laughed and said:

"Never be afraid of women, Béla! It's only the ones like your mother you've got to watch out for."

I blushed to my roots, but my mother didn't notice, since—as I say—she was busy shuffling the cards. Besides, as far as she was concerned, what my father had said was a compliment.

"Why?" she said, almost flirtatiously.

"I'll tell you why!" my father replied. "There's plenty of women in the world. Some of them are sweet as honey, others peppery as steak. Some are this way, others that—there's all sorts. But women like *her*," he said, pointing to my mother, "they're like home-made bread. You never get tired of 'em. I'll admit, you need a bit of steak with your bread now and then, but so what? So nothin'," he answered himself, and looked at me. "Nothin' at all! Even the best food gets borin' in the end, but you always need bread. Steak is steak, just flesh and nothin' else—but bread can also be the body of Christ, and what do steak and bread have in common? Nothin'," he repeated, looking at me. "Nothin' at all, and one day you, too, will realize that, my boy."

"Fine things you're teaching him," my mother scolded him cheerfully. "Look to your cards instead. It's your turn."

That was it. My father continued to be all over my mother and it was no use me telling myself that he was a miserable, lying fraud, for in my heart of hearts I was strangely convinced that his kisses for my mother were just as sincere as his kisses for the pretty girl on the boat, and that was what confused me the most. Life's awful, I thought to myself, and could no longer enjoy our evenings together. My mother's "surprises" just infuriated me, and I wondered angrily where she got the money.

"Do we still not have the money for that English book?" I once asked her harshly.

My mother blushed like a thief caught in the act.

"Did they tell you off?" she asked in alarm.

"Yeah," I lied viciously.

"Good God," she muttered and stared at her shoes for some time. Then she said uncertainly: "Your father'll start working, too, and," she swallowed hard, "then we'll get you that book."

"You'd better get on with it," I said pointedly, and left.

"Béla!" she called after me.

"Yes?"

"Don't tell your father."

"Why not?" I asked combatively.

"'Cause… you know," my mother stared at her shoes again, "I don't like to bother him with these things."

There you go! I fumed to myself. *I don't like to bother him with these things.* That's a laugh! It was as strange coming out of her mouth as a fancy cigarette holder out of mine. Damned if I can understand them, I thought, but didn't say anything. I went huffily into the other room. This isn't going to end well, I noted, and unfortunately I was right once more.

One night, when we were well into our cards, there was a knock on the kitchen door. My mother went out, closed the door behind her—which she never did—and spent a long time talking to someone in the kitchen.

"Who is it?" my father asked after a while.

"Don't know," I replied. "I think it's Herr Hausmeister."

My father stood up and went out into the kitchen.

"Well, my friend, what is it?" he said to Herr Hausmeister, for it really was him. "You two keeping secrets?"

"We're done," my mother replied hurriedly, irritably, but Herr Hausmeister, it appeared, was of a different opinion.

"Not just yet," he said menacingly.

"In that case come in and have a drop," my father said cheerfully. "Wine loosens the tongue. So, what's the matter, then?"

Herr Hausmeister wiped his moustache with the back of his hand, because he had, in fact, just "had a drop", looked at my mother, shrugged regretfully and eventually said, portending doom:

"The bank won't wait any longer."

"Who told 'em to?" my father said with undiminished cheer.

Herr Hausmeister cleared his throat.

"You ain't paid rent in two months," he said gravely. "And then there's what you owe from before. And, well, they won't wait any longer."

My poor mother, I could see, was wishing the ground would swallow her up, and I wasn't feeling too good, either. But not even this could dent my father's good humour.

"How much is the outstanding?" he asked lightly.

"A lot," Herr Hausmeister said evasively. "But if you could put down fifty pengős, I think I could square it with 'em."

"You're talkin' like a Jew," my father said disparagingly. "I didn't ask you what you could square. I asked how much they're owed."

Herr Hausmeister glanced at my mother again, as if to say: what can I do, you can see for yourself it's not up to me. Then he finally came out with it:

"Eighty-seven pengős."

My father laughed.

"Well," he said, "you shouldn't have made all that fuss over nothing, then. Come and pick it up this time tomorrow."

We looked at him as if he'd hit us each individually on the head with a stick. All three of us were convinced that he was lying, but none of us dared say a word, not even Herr Hausmeister. He, too, had learnt that it was not a good idea to tangle with Dappermishka, so he took my father at his word and slinked off quietly.

When we were alone again, my mother wanted to say something, but my father hushed her.

"Leave it to me," he said with a wave of his arm, as if it were something hardly worth mentioning, and took up his cards once more.

My mother didn't dare ask about the eighty-seven pengős next evening either, and my father didn't mention it at all. There was a hard silence. We played cards quietly.

Herr Hausmeister knocked around ten. My mother stood up to let him in, but my father pushed her back into her chair.

"Come!" he called, and carried on with his cards.

Herr Hausmeister entered.

"Sit," said my father. "If you feel like watching." He most definitely didn't. He stood there in front of us like an executioner.

"I've got things to do," he said ominously, but failed to intimidate my father.

"Go do 'em, then," he said casually, and didn't so much as look up from his hand.

Herr Hausmeister did not go about his other business. He stood there and waited. Like a figure of fate, I thought poetically, and I could see the cards trembling in my mother's hand.

When we'd finished the hand, my father leant back in his chair and, with a distracted air, as if it had just occurred to him, said to Herr Hausmeister:

"Oh yes. You can start writin' out the receipt."

"For how much?"

"What do you mean, how much?" my father snapped. "I told you you'd get your eighty-seven pengős, and when I say something, I mean it. Got it?"

Herr Hausmeister didn't get it, you could tell, but he nonetheless wrote out the receipt and handed it to my father. My father reached into his waistcoat pocket and, with a casual motion, took out eighty-seven pengős and threw it down in front of Herr Hausmeister. He threw it down the way a card player throws down a packet of cigarettes if someone asks him for a smoke in the middle of a hand. Then he went right back to shuffling the cards.

Herr Hausmeister's eyes bulged like a carp's. He counted the money three times over, but you could tell that he still didn't understand what was going on.

"Will there be anythin' else?" my father asked pointedly.

"No," Herr Hausmeister answered awkwardly.

My father put down his cards.

"No more free washing?" he asked, raising an eyebrow.

Herr Hausmeister went red—and when a pock-marked man goes red, it's a sight to behold. Small, white, egg-shaped spots shone out on his face, as if they'd been painted on.

"I never asked her to do that!" he declared hastily. "She offered. It was just a little favour."

The man was clearly afraid that my father would now start asking for the monthly twelve pengős back, and really got his back up, as they say. His pock-marked face was like a cornered dog's, and he, too, wanted to bark and bite. But he was a cowardly old dog, so he kept quiet.

My father looked at him for a while, not without taking some pleasure in the situation. Then he laughed.

"You're a dirty dog!" he said, and patted him cheerfully on the shoulder. "But don't think I'm one to hold it against you. It was a low trick, no doubt about it, but it ain't your fault Anna fell for it. You'd have to be a fool not to take what's offered to you. That's not it, my friend. But see here: this woman is Dappermishka's woman now, and if you hold your life dear, you'll remember what that means. So listen here, my friend. I'm going to let the past be the past, but if you ever forget the present, I'll smash your face in. That's all. Now let's have a drink. We friends?"

"We are," Herr Hausmeister grinned, making a sweet enough face, but all the while surveying my father suspiciously, as if he were afraid there was some cunning ploy behind all this.

But there was no ploy. That's just how Dappermishka conducted his business. He was a determined man, a show-off, and terrible when angry. If someone angered him, he'd take care of him then and there, but he never held a grudge. I'm just as certain that all his anger towards Herr Hausmeister had already gone as I am that he really would have knocked his block off if he'd dared so much as look askance at my mother. Now, he was cheerful and plied this man, whom he'd just put through the wringer, with wine and dirty stories. Then, when he got bored, he simply came out and said:

"Off you go to bed, then."

As to where he'd got the eighty-seven pengős from, I never found out. My mother, instead of asking him, snatched up his hand the second Herr Hausmeister was out the door, and kissed it, right in front of me. My father put his arm around her waist and said it was late, and time for bed, and I got to lay there for hours listening to the creaking of their blasted bed.

As if everything was always and everywhere about *that*; as if nothing else in the world had existed. It was what the pimply bellboys were talking about in the changing room, what the naked couples we spied on were whispering about in the bedrooms, and it was what my parents were now mumbling about in the creaky bed, a few paces away from me, behind the worn-out door. That was what I saw in the hotel, that was what I saw at home. That was what I saw each evening on the park benches, behind the bushes in the woods and the woodpiles on the outskirts of town. It was what I saw beneath the darkened arcades of the Fisherman's Bastion, in the ruins of the monastery on Margit Island, down in the rowboats drifting gently along the Danube, up on the secretive slopes of the Buda hills, behind the windows of suspect little houses, in the depths of parked cars, in the semi-obscurity of doorways, at the dark ends of alleys and, at night, even in the cemeteries.

"This spring seems to have driven everybody wild!" I would say, and I said it mockingly, with a nervous laugh, never noticing—not wanting to notice—that I was the wildest of them all.

Sometimes I almost mewled with desire, like a tomcat stretching on a moonlit roof. I looked around me and sniffed the air in heat, but I never actually pursued the cats next door. I was a virgin. I knew nothing, though I'd seen everything. I had watched black masses through the keyholes, I had seen other people's sexual acrobatics, but I myself was a virgin—still just a virgin. I bore my virginity like some torturous growth that gave me fevers and chills, but I never spoke to anyone else about it; I was ashamed, the way people usually are ashamed of such diseases. I wanted to be free of it. Every day, I left home thinking yes, today was the day, but in the end, I always baulked at the operation.

I was clean of spirit and at the same time very much corrupted. I would lie, in secret, in Her Excellency's bed, I made love to her negligée, but when what usually happens in such circumstances came to pass, I was seized by a brutal guilt and a horrible hangover and felt like spitting in my own eye. I swore "never again" and thought only of Patsy… until I went wild again.

My mind was like a badly exposed photographic plate onto which some lunatic had exposed images over and over again. Individually, each one may have been all right, but all together they had no meaning. Once, a long, long time ago, a few months ago, everything had seemed so simple, with Elemér's talk of "workers' solidarity". I felt I belonged somewhere, and knew where it was that I belonged. Now, I felt a suffocating confusion and belonged nowhere. I saw that Elemér was right when he outlined his thinking, but I also saw Her Excellency was right, with her fine, easy life, the outspread wings of wealth spiriting her above all those things that seemed insoluble problems in my own life. And they were not the only ones I thought were right. There were all those papers, magazines and literary journals that I read cover to cover at the hotel. Those, too, were purveyors of "truths", truths that were tempting and fine like fake jewels in a bazaar, and I went through an enthusiasm of a few days or a few weeks for almost all of them. I was like a pregnant woman: I had cravings for everything which in the end nothing could actually satisfy. I wanted to be a "proletarian" and a "bourgeois" at the same time, a Sándor Rózsa robbing the rich to give to the poor and a magnate surrounded by scraping flunkeys, a rebellious György Dózsa to deliver the peasantry from their dire lot and a refined poet locked in his ivory tower.

My poems, too, became confused, like a river in flood. I was constantly writing about Love, like that, with a capital L, but my poems remained just as unconsummated as my loves. My notebook was full of half-finished poems and my heart was full of half-finished feelings. Everything was only half done within me, everything was vague and undefined. I dreamt of a girl and was kept awake by a woman. The girl was halfway across the world and the woman in a different firmament, while I floated, like Muhammad's coffin, between heaven and earth, in the void.

Yes, this spring seemed to have driven everybody wild.

12

O NE MORNING, A SCANDAL BROKE OUT in the changing room.
The subject of this scandal was the communal towel and the
participants Franciska and Gyula. Franciska seemed to be in the right.
Gyula had used the shared towel though he himself had said, when
he'd got ill, that he would only use his own from then on. Franciska was
not rude to him; this pretty boy with his girlish face was only rude to
people he knew were weaker than him. All he said was:

"Gyula, please don't use our towel."

So there was no real cause for scandal. Gyula was, in any case, far
too careful since he'd found out what was wrong with him, and there
was no question that he had only gone and used the towel by accident.
The poor boy had clearly forgotten his trouble, something that happened to him far too infrequently. You could see, or at least I always
thought I could see, that he thought of nothing else. He became so
closed off and silent that we couldn't understand why he still stayed in
the hotel till the morning just to see us. It seems he didn't have many
friends besides us, or at least not ones he could talk with about his
trouble. Not that he talked much about it with us, either. He mostly
just sat there, head bowed, smoking one cigarette after the other in
silence. He'd never been combative by nature, and since "it" had
happened to him, he had grown eerily quiet. None of us, therefore,
could comprehend his behaviour now. Instead of taking the warning
to heart, he continued defiantly towelling himself with the communal
towel, just for the sake of it.

"You got a problem with me usin' it?" he asked threateningly, going
up to Franciska belligerently. "Look here," he said, "I'll use whatever
towel I please."

We knew he wasn't right, of course we knew that, and yet we nonetheless, strangely enough, took his side.

"Stop buggering him about," Lajos told Franciska.

"*I'm* buggering *him* about?" Franciska protested. "Do you want us all to catch it from him?"

He was right about that, too, of course. He was right, and maintained a matter-of-fact, almost polite tone. Gyula was wrong, and was aggressive about it to boot. So why did we still take sides against Franciska? After all, it wasn't as if we were desperate to experience the joys of syphilis, either, and were exposed to the dangers just the same as him. I might have said of myself that I wanted to take revenge for his having been so rough with my mother, but the others had no personal axe to grind, and they *still* turned against him. There was something in his voice, his look or his manner, and I couldn't say exactly which, but there was something that made your hands curl into fists. There is a certain type of person from whom even the truth is infuriating and we, it seemed, had instinctively detected that Franciska was of that type.

"I know I'm wrong," Gyula said unexpectedly. "But it's still better to catch syphilis from a woman than to be kept by a man. Got it?" he shouted at Franciska, and grabbed him by the front of his shirt.

Franciska let out a scream like a hysterical spinster.

"Stop screaming," Elemér snapped at him. "They'll hear you."

"Then let them!" Franciska screamed, wheezing like a chicken. "At least everyone will know. And you can get your syphilitic hands off me."

Fortunately, Elemér jumped between them at this point.

"Let him go, Gyula," he cried. "And you, shut up."

Gyula pushed Franciska away.

"You're right, Elemér," he said. "It ain't right to hit a woman."

The "woman" didn't say a word, just gathered his uniform under his arm and left the changing room half dressed. But when he got out into the corridor, where he felt secure, he turned back.

"Ugh!" he cried, spitting heavily. "Syphilitic pig."

Gyula went after him, but Elemér blocked his way.

"D'you really want everyone to know and have that little creep laughing at you?"

Gyula saw the truth in that. He shrugged silently, as if to say: well, yes. What can you do? He reached absently, with a mechanical gesture, for his cigarettes, lit up distractedly, took his hat and left without saying goodbye.

We thought that was the end of it, but of course it wasn't. It had only just begun in earnest. As to what exactly happened, no one was sure. But the fact was, Gyula got fired the next day.

We were all convinced it was Franciska's doing and wanted to get revenge on him. We were just wondering *how* when Elemér entered the changing room and told us he did not agree.

"It looks bad for him, I admit," he said, "but that doesn't mean anything. Looks can be deceiving."

He was a strange boy, Elemér. I knew he didn't like Franciska. He had never, of course, admitted that to anyone, but I had noticed in the very first weeks of our acquaintance that he really kept his distance from Franciska, and if anyone could understand that, it was me. The strange thing was that he seemed to feel kind of guilty about it, and it appeared to me that this was behind what he said now, too.

"Where would we be if we all just followed our emotions?" he asked with unusual passion, and then signalled to us to come closer. He dropped his voice and said in a near-whisper: "Listen. In a few days, I'll find out what happened, and if what you say is true, I'll join you. All right?"

"How are you going to find out?" Antal asked.

"I'm going to ask a comrade," Elemér replied, but it seemed he regretted it at once, because he blushed to his roots.

That's how we learnt that he had a "comrade" among the senior management of the hotel, but as to who that was, he didn't say.

The boys eventually accepted his "motion" and we all went about our business. It was morning, an ordinary, normal weekday morning, the same as usual, the same as always, and the last thing that crossed my mind was that this incident would affect me, too, intimately, or that it would lead to a big change in my life.

But that was, in fact, what happened. In the afternoon, the Major sent for me and asked me kindly—*inexplicably kindly*—if I wanted to take Gyula's place. Naturally, I said yes, because poor children in Hungary in those days learnt early that there were certain questions from the upper classes to which you only answered yes. And since the Major knew this just as well as I did, I simply didn't understand why he was beating around the bush so much. He repeated several times that I didn't *have* to take the new shift if I didn't want to, and even if I did, he would only give me the position if my parents confirmed in writing that they had no objection to my being assigned to the night shift. Then he said something to the effect that he liked me and wanted me to make a bit more money. For in the bar, in case I didn't know, people tended to drink at night, and alcohol did wonderful things to both the heartstrings and wallets of gentlemen. Needless to say, I had no objection to that; it was just the Major's "paternal goodwill" that unnerved me a little, because among other things, I had also learnt that the poor had better have their wits about them when the rich start feeling "paternal goodwill" for them.

As to why he'd been so inexplicably kind, I only found out a year later, when I'd left the hotel far behind. That was when I first found out that there had apparently been some law or directive that prohibited children my age from working at night. I didn't get any further into it, and so I still don't know whether that law really existed or not; but that doesn't really matter anyway because even if it did exist, it did so in name only, like so many similar protections in Hungary.

The truth is, I wouldn't have been glad of a law like that at the time anyway. I was sixteen, and even more tempting than the fat tips was that mysterious "other"—night-time—world the boys talked so much about. So I wouldn't have needed much convincing. I didn't play hard to get. The next day, I reported happily to the Major that my parents had no objection to my working the night shift. So began a new chapter in my life.

For the first few days, I felt like I was living in foreign climes, in a new, exciting, adventurous world with new weather and new customs, and where everything was more or less back to front. I put on my uniform when the others were taking off theirs, and by the time the bar really got going, three-quarters of the city was fast asleep. When I woke up, I would say "good evening". When I went to bed, I said "good morning". I lived in the same city as the others, and yet I lived under different skies, somewhere where the sun rose at midnight and went down at dawn, in a country whose denizens lived for, or off, love, where there was nothing else besides.

That was what it was all for. The bars and the brothels, the fancy nightclubs and other "establishments", the run-down inns notorious for stabbings, the various dives in constant fear of police raids. *That* was what kept the fancy hotels along the riverbank awake, *that* was what sustained the bachelor pads rented together by friends, the rooms with their own "separate entrance" for those "visitors", all those clubs, meeting places and "massage parlours", not to mention the rooms at the Mauthner hotels. *That* was behind the smiles on the faces of the porcelain-skinned ladies, the streetwalkers on the corner and the tired waitresses on subsistence wages. *That* was why the porters dressed like generals bowed and scraped, as did the portly maître d's in the various "locales", the innkeepers, bartenders, the little old ladies selling flowers and the taxi drivers hunting for amorous couples. *That* was what made the evening-gowned *chanteuses* and the famished provincial crooners sing. *That* was what the "proles" and the "ladies and gentlemen" danced for. *That* was what the jazz bands, coat-tailed Gypsy violinists and amateur bands played for. *That* was what made the violins cry, the saxophones chortle, and *that* was what drove the drummers wild. *That* was why men bought roses and mournful, melancholy tunes full of longing for pretty women. *That* was what music, song and dance were for, what the whispering, champagne and semi-darkness were about. *That* was what hands and feet searched for under tables. And *that* was why the streets were so silvery on the moonlit nights when I would hold the door for exiting couples who all seemed to be going to the same place: to some mysterious Mecca of love.

Yes, *that* was what it was all for, and *that* was all I needed.

It "happened" the very first night.

There was an insalubrious little space bathed in obscurity between the bar and the cloakrooms from where the toilets and the telephone booths opened. That was where I was standing—or rather sitting—guard in my fancy, gold-trimmed uniform, between the ladies' toilets and one of the telephone booths. My responsibilities were just as obscure and dubious as the place I was haunting. I answered the phone, came and went with messages, and would stand in from time to time for the porter, the cloakroom girl and anyone else who needed standing in for. But I was also the one they sent out to the pharmacy for condoms at three in the morning, and I was the one calling up husbands and wives with their spouses' lame and pathetic lies. I was the clerk who telephoned home to the wife to say that the conference might stretch on till dawn, and I was the driver who informed husbands that their wives would not be home till morning because the car had broken down along the highway. I even "played" a policeman once in order to inform the district attorney's wife that the suspect still hadn't confessed, and it might be morning before he cracked.

The buzz of lies around this dark little space was as monotonously soporific as the buzzing of bees around a hive. Everybody whispered here, as people generally do behind the scenes. The bar was the stage where people would try and stick, as best they could, to the script demanded by society, but here, beside the bathrooms, was real life, and people talked in whispers. This was where husbands whose wives and wives whose husbands were inside on the dance floor made rendezvous. This was where impatient gentlemen conspired with the waiters who promised them, for a fee, to mix something into the hard-hearted lady's drink that, take my word for it, sir, will do the job. This was where gentlemen smoking nervously could make the acquaintance of ladies from someone else's party who they could never approach in the bar. This was where jealous men would come to blows, and this was where members of the Officers' Club playing at duels would exchange calling cards. This was where, one memorable night, that unknown man in the grey suit had the well-known banker called before flashing some official document and telling him, in a theatrical whisper, to "come with me, please, quietly."

Inside, meanwhile, they were doing the Charleston, which was all the rage at the time, and by dawn, the entire bar was shouting along with the singer that:

My baby's got dark tresses
Her eyes are black abysses
Her hair dark as the raven,
Her skin black as her race, and,
She makes the mirror smile
When she undresses

Couples pulsed about the little dance floor pressed against each other amid balloons and coloured lights that pierced the clouds of cigarette smoke, along with the flashes of jewellery and feminine whiteness, to the sound of the bass drum and the lingering flutes, and to me—who had never seen anything like it—it all seemed as beautiful and unreal as some gripping fairy tale.

I liked this nocturnal world, I liked this great, rococo debauchery—what sixteen-year-old boy wouldn't? I made good money, too—my pockets were full of tips—and I could eat and drink as much as I liked. A huge, active woman known to everyone simply as Iluci presided over the kitchen. Iluci had a heart of gold. She was well into her fifties, and must have weighed a hundred and fifty kilos, but despite her age and size, she kept a lover so young that the first time I saw him, I thought he was her son. She was a rosy-cheeked brunette with sparkling eyes who loved her drink, and song, and dirty jokes, but who went straight to church from work on Sundays, where she would faithfully confess and take Communion. She took to me at once and stuffed me like a goose. She fed me exotic-tasting and incredibly expensive hors d'oeuvres that three or four guests had already paid for anyway, and laughed at me on the first night when I asked her for some water.

"You don't want to catch cholera, do you?" she asked, pointing at the bottles of champagne that the waiters—by this time of night—used to bring back sometimes half full from the bar. "Whatever's left in the bottle, we pour down the drain," she said. "So I'd rather you drank it to my health instead."

I got used to these heavenly circumstances, but on that first night I simply couldn't control myself. I stuffed myself to bursting on the unfamiliar delights and washed them down with the best French champagne the way horses guzzle water when they've been ridden hard.

Suddenly I found myself in a hell of a good mood. The world had never seemed so safe a place as on this dawn. The only thing I didn't understand, as I ambled back to my post, was why my legs were so unsteady. Not that I was too concerned, though. On the contrary! Let the worriers worry—I wasn't going to any more, by God. I felt strange, that's true, but it was a *good* sort of strange, so I was all for the strangeness if it wanted to continue. The voice inside me was singing:

> *Why, Mr Stux, what's this,*
> *You know it's wrong—*
> *Have some patience, sir,*
> *The night's still long.*

I only noticed that I was singing along with the band when I felt a guest's gaze upon me. He seemed to have appeared from nowhere. Fortunately he, too, was thoroughly tipsy and, instead of telling me off, he gave me a rousing Hungarian chorus of:

"Forever young! Isn't that right, my friend?"

"'Course it is!" I replied. "Long as we keep off the water!"

At that, the guest threw me an Egyptian cigarette and, moved, I decided that this whole bourgeois–proletarian thing was a lot of stuff and nonsense. I mean, take this bourgeois for example. He was a good enough sort! What cause did I have to be angry at him? I liked all the upper-class gentlemen now, and liked the upper-class women even more. One or two of them smiled at me when they saw me so cheerful. "Oh, sweetheart," I sighed after the prettiest ones, once the bathroom door had closed behind them, "if only I could come with you! If only I could have a little feel of all that!"

> *Why, Mr Stux, you're so decadent!*
> *Why do I feel that you've been*
> *Heaven sent?*

From where I was sitting, I could only see a corner of the bar. It was inhabited by rather a funny couple—I'd been keeping an eye on them all evening. The funny thing about them was that when they'd come in, they'd been terribly measured with each other; the man had insisted on calling the lady "madam", and madam had behaved accordingly. And then they "warmed up to each other" so suddenly, and so passionately, that I couldn't take my eyes off them. I would have liked to know how these gentlemen did this. I watched them like a dog its quarry. The man was a handsome, "forceful" sort of Transylvanian squire, greying at the temples, with something of the Gypsy to his face. He'd been staying some three weeks, but I hadn't seen the woman once. I liked the look of her, and why deny it? I was just as excited as her partner. She was a thin woman with mischievous eyes, all soft and blonde and—ooh, yes please. By the time I went out to the kitchen, they were thoroughly entangled, but what was that compared to what I was seeing now! The woman was almost lying down tipsily beside the man, whose hand... No, I told myself, you're seeing things. Am I really that drunk? Because it looked as if one of the gentleman's hands were feeling about beneath the woman's skirt, while the other held his cigarette so steady I was forced to wonder if these two hands were controlled by the same body at all.

In the end, I couldn't resist the temptation, so I got up and went closer. No, I wasn't imagining things. There was definitely something moving beneath her skirt.

But I was brought up short. For the man whispered something to the lady and then suddenly stood up and made his way straight towards me. There's going to be trouble, I told myself, this geezer's really going to give me hell for spying on them.

But the "geezer" did no such thing. He handed me his cloakroom ticket and gave me a friendly smile.

"Right away, sir," I said, relieved, but when I made to leave, he put his hand on my shoulder.

"Wait," he said softly, and slipped five pengős into my hand as he glanced briefly but meaningfully at the girl and then back at me again.

That was all an experienced woman-smuggler needed. I immediately understood the situation.

"Yes, sir, I see, sir," I replied in that refined, decadent voice that is close but not familiar. "Right away?"

"Yes," he replied. "But be careful. The lady's had a lot to drink. You understand?"

"Of course."

When I came back from the cloakroom, they were both waiting for me in the doorway. The lady really *had* had a lot to drink, more than a lot, actually, but that just made her all the more desirable. Her eyes said "take me to bed" so strongly that it made me, too, hot all over. When I helped her into her mink stole, I inadvertently touched her shoulder, and she must have felt the excitement inside me, because she turned around and smiled.

I rushed out into the lobby to see if the way was clear, and I was pleased to see it was. They'd turned off the big chandeliers long before and only a few soporific lamps twinkled in the half-light; there was no one on the horizon. I went back to fetch them, or rather, I opened the door and signalled them to come.

The lady was worryingly unsteady on her feet, but fortunately we didn't meet anyone and I took them up in the lift, the daytime lift, which no one used at night. They stood there pressed against one another, pressed very tight, as the man hummed and the woman closed her eyes, while I couldn't take my drunken mind off what these two were about to get up to in their room.

They got off at the third floor, and I was about to head back down when I saw the woman totter. She leant against the wall, pressed her hand to her forehead, and swallowed heavily, as if there were something stuck in her throat.

"What's the matter?" the man asked, a little frightened.

"I don't know," she replied, barely audibly. "I'm dizzy."

The man called me over.

"Could you bring us up a strong black coffee?"

"Yes, sir, right away."

"Hurry."

Despite my best efforts, it was a half an hour before I managed to take them the coffee, because I had to stand in for the cloakroom girl meanwhile. When I finally got up there, no one replied to my knocking. I assumed the gentleman had thought it best to take the lady home, but since they had already been charged for the coffee, I opened the door with my key to deposit the coffee with its rightful owner.

The entrance hall was dark, but the doors were wide open and I was brought up short so suddenly the tray almost fell out of my hands. Across the darkened salon, I could see that back there, in the illuminated bedroom… What *was* that? I wondered. Am I drunk? At first, it seemed as if I were looking at a statue, a seated female nude, but… how did that statue get onto the bed… and…

I don't know how long I stood there watching them. It could have been moments, it could have been minutes, or it might well have been much longer. At a certain moment, the hot coffee spilt onto my hand and that made me snap out of it. I put the tray down on the table in the salon and then I felt my way, dizzily and drowsily, out through the darkened entrance hall.

I managed to make my way to the lift, but start it I could not. It had been too much for one night, this and the French champagne.

There was a fiery breeze blowing through my breast, blasting, singeing my heart. I sat dizzily down on the velvet seat and fell into a sort of semi-dream state. My mouth was dry, my tongue felt swollen, and I was unbearably thirsty.

I observed myself dully, uncomprehending. What was this? What had happened to me? But then the dizziness passed and I was a big lad once more.

"Forever young!" I muttered to myself. "I'm thirsty, that's all."

And since I didn't intend to catch cholera, I went down to the kitchen and had a glass of champagne.

As to how I got home, I don't know. I suspect that I didn't know even at the time. My parents weren't home, and that had a very good effect on my mood, which had already been pretty good to begin with. I was pleased with my parents.

"Well done!" I said aloud, and immediately noted that I was now talking to myself, which is to say that I was drunk, or rather not that I was drunk, because if I were drunk, then I wouldn't know that I was drunk. "Well done, anyway," I said aloud once more, and went into the room.

The shutters were closed, and that also drew my approbation. Look at that—the old folks had thought of that, too! "Well done. Very well done." After all, isn't that what parents were for?

I started to undress. It was so dark that I couldn't see my own hands, but I didn't open the shutters. The hell with all that blasted light! Really kills the mood. The world was so ugly in the morning, filthy, smelly and nauseating. The streets were full of week-old corpses dragging themselves along, a bunch of grumpy sourpusses. And the looks they gave you! Idiots. What did they know?

> *Why, Mr Stux, what's this,*
> *You know it's wrong—*
> *Have some patience, sir,*
> *The night's still long.*

Oh, if that little blonde had been alone in that bed…

If… Well, and why not? It could happen. Doctors, for example, get called out at night all the time. Let's assume the man's a doctor, and…

What would she have thought if I'd suddenly walked in from the darkened salon? She'd given me a good once over when I'd helped her into her stole. She really had that look. Or was it just my imagination? And anyway, it's not like she could have said anything. I was just bringing the coffee. They'd asked for it. At worst, she would have pulled the covers up. But she might not have. Her Excellency hadn't.

Oh… but she was something else… That red hair… those sweet little breasts peeking out of her nightgown… oh yes. How amazing she must look naked, with all that red… Shame she shaves her armpits. It's so nice when you get a little flash of hair down there…

That little blonde shaved her armpits, too. She wasn't bad, either, the little blonde. Not a bit of it! I tell you, when I saw her there on the bed… whoooo!… Lying in bed with a woman like that, my God! Or rather, she was sitting. I wouldn't mind giving her something to sit on… oh yes… yes, yes… How am I ever going to get to sleep in this condition?

Why, Mr Stux, you're so decadent!
Why do I feel that you've been
Heaven sent?

I was buck naked by now, but it still didn't want to subside. I felt about in the dark till I found my father's cigarettes and matches. The flame flashed in my hand and I was chilled with horror.

There was someone else in the room.

Someone was laughing behind my back.

I turned around so fast the match burned my finger. It was Manci. She was lying in bed, giggling.

Of course. She, too, only came home in the morning. I'd forgotten she even existed. Why *did* she even exist?

"What you laughing at?" I snapped.

She didn't reply, she couldn't. She was laughing so hard she could only make inarticulate noises.

"What you laughing at?" I asked again, shouting this time, but she just kept on giggling hysterically.

"Give us a fag," she said at last, exhausted.

I felt my way to the bed in the dark. Manci lit the cigarette slowly, awkwardly, and never took her eyes off me.

"Where were you?" she giggled.

"With my girl," I replied angrily.

That just made her laugh even harder.

"Why are you still laughing? Don't you believe me?"

"No, sport, I don't. I don't buy it," she guffawed.

"Why not?"

"You fool! Who comes home like that from a girl?" she laughed, and I felt her hand upon me.

The inexplicable disgust I had felt for her from the very first moment took such powerful hold of me then that I pulled away with almost childish horror. I was behaving like a frightened little virgin, I thought in shame, and I didn't know what to do. Her warm, dirty touch felt good, shamefully good, infuriatingly good, and yet I wanted to run away. Yes, I was once more a little scared of her.

There was silence. Our two cigarettes glowed sharply in the dark.

"Tell me," she said then, "you ever been with a woman?"

"'Course I have!" I snapped indignantly, and to show her how experienced I was, I added cockily: "Who hasn't?"

"What woman?"

"All sorts."

"You go to brothels?"

"No."

"Where, then?"

"To hers."

"She got a flat?"

"And how!"

I accompanied this with sweeping hand gestures, suggesting great, terrible secrets, because now I wanted more than anything to pique her curiosity. I wanted her to be curious, to ask, so I could answer. I no longer felt fear and revulsion—the desire to talk overrode everything.

Manci sat up.

"She rich?"

"Like you wouldn't believe."

"Some man give her the dough?"

"Nah."

"Well, then?"

"She's a lady. Married."

"What's her husband do?"

I hesitated. Back then, I still hesitated.

"Why don't you answer me?"

"Promise not to tell anyone?"

"Oh, my dear," she laughed, "if I told you the half the things I've heard from men…"

I liked her treating me like a man like that. Yes, here was a woman you could talk to.

"All right, I'll tell you," I said graciously, and leant in closer. "He's a minister," I whispered. "An ex-minister."

Manci gave a whistle.

"Well, I'll be… only an excellency good enough for you, eh?"

I pulled on my cigarette, almost hard enough to swallow it.

"Here, Manci," I asked excitedly, "have you… you ever heard anything about her sort?"

"'Course," she said. "Plenty. She likes 'em young, is all. She pick you up at the hotel?"

"What d'you mean picked me up? You can't pick *me* up just like that."

"Leave it out, dear. She give you money?"

"I don't need her money, I'm not a kept man!"

Her cigarette glowed. I could see her smiling.

"So she's just playin' with you."

"What d'you mean, playing with me?"

"Playin' hard to get. Not givin' it up."

"What d'you take me for?"

"Well, then, what you doing in this state all by yourself? You said you were at hers."

"Yes, but…"

"But?"

"Her husband was home. There. So now you know."

"Aha," said Manci, but I couldn't tell from her voice if she believed what I'd said or not. "She old?" she asked.

"Younger than you! And what a woman… ooh, brother!"

"You're pretty smitten, dear."

"Yeah," I admitted.

"And her?"

"Well, she isn't with me for my money."

"What, then?"

"For the carnation in my buttonhole."

"Well, she's got taste. I like your carnation, too."

She wasn't laughing now. We'd put the cigarettes out some time ago. It was completely dark.

"It's hot in here," she said, and I could hear her pushing her covers off in the dark.

I was struck by a smell. It wasn't a bad smell, but I was overcome again with disgust. It was a woman's smell, no better and no worse than that other, the one on the lacy, salmon-coloured slip, only that one drove

339

me crazy, and this one filled me with revulsion. But you don't really think too much about that when you're sixteen.

Besides, it only lasted a few minutes. After that, I smelt only that other smell, so close and so completely that it was as if it were that other woman lying in bed beside me, and then she really did appear, a gift of the borrowed reality of dreams; whether it lasted seconds or hours, I couldn't have said.

Then I heard Manci's voice.

"You asleep?"

"'Course not."

"Come… lie down over here…"

"…"

"No… you just lie there… I'll do it… Like that…"

"…"

"Is that nice?… Does it feel nice?… Say something!"

"Shut up!" I snapped, because when she talked, I could no longer hear her voice, that high, slightly sing-song voice that was now quite close to my ear, whispering indescribable secrets.

13

THAT EVENING, WHEN I ENTERED the hotel, I could feel that something had happened. There was an undefined uneasiness in my overstretched nerves, though I couldn't say why. Nothing had changed in the hotel; the shift moved silently in its normal course like an elegant alien star to whom mere earthly laws did not apply. The hotel's thick carpets might have muffled even death's heavy footsteps; everything was so quiet, cool and elegant that you got the feeling that nothing out of the ordinary could ever happen here. And yet there seemed to be something in the air, something that—like the air itself—was impossible to see or touch.

I paid heightened attention. My head was still blurry from my drunken night, and Manci and the hors d'oeuvres had unsettled my stomach; I was beginning to think whatever was wrong was wrong with me. But then two members of staff whispered together, or the draught slammed a door somewhere, and I was once more overcome with anxiety. Something had happened, I told myself.

I didn't see a familiar face anywhere. The boys had gone home, and the bar was empty. There was only an old, distracted waiter playing patience at one of the tables, scratching a spot on his bald head.

"Good evenin'," I said, and thought: maybe now I'll find out.

But the old man didn't even look up from his cards.

"Evening," he mumbled, and yawned.

"What's new? Anything going on?"

"Yes," he said, scratching his spot. "A cow jumped over the moon."

He yawned again, took out a pocket mirror and examined the spot sleepily.

"Broke a leg," he said.

"Who?"

"The cow."

He laughed, wheezing dozily, and his voice—like a cracked pot—reverberated in the empty space. The bar was like a corpse in an elegant dress. Yesterday, it had been a beautiful woman. You'd danced together and felt her warm, excited breath, her eyes, hair, shoulders driving you wild—and now here she was, lying inert before you in her fancy frippery, fake breasts on display.

I left and sat down in my place. There was a sleepy silence and a sleepy semi-darkness. I stared at the wall vacantly and without interest, watching a fly nap and scratch itself with its front leg. It was a very old and very tired fly, and maybe it, too, had a spot on its bald head.

Suddenly, I heard my own voice.

"Never again!" I mumbled, but I didn't quite know what I was referring to: Manci, or the whole female sex, drinking, or something completely different and much more important.

The fug in my mind was turning my stomach. I wanted to throw up on everything in the entire world, but most of all myself. I think I had never hated anyone as much as I hated this strange boy in the red uniform who bore my name. I wanted to wriggle out of my skin, like a snake, so that I could immediately start a new life in some temptation-free paradise.

It suddenly felt unbearable in the room; I had the feeling that all the air had been pumped out of it. I called in to the bar.

"Can I go stand by the door a bit?"

The old man shrugged.

"For all I care!" he said, scratching his spot.

The bar opened onto the riverfront. It was a fine, warm night, and the Buda hills were alive with the early signs of summer. Up there, on their peaks, the spotlights were just going on, flooding the Citadel, the Royal Palace, the Fisherman's Bastion and the lookout tower in faint illumination. The morning star was up too, examining itself in the Danube together with the waterfront lights, but the sky still hung opaquely, painting colourful scenes upon the river. You could hear music coming from the riverside places, the wind occasionally mixing the Gypsy and the jazz and wafting a strong smell of lilac from the park. The flood of passers-by rumbled colourfully past the throng of musical cafés on the promenade. The women were already wearing summer dresses under their expensive furs, and the gentlemen were mostly without their coats. Everything was full of colours, lights, scents and music; everything was full of spring, spring! I watched the walking rich and sighed. How wonderful this city was—*for them*!

A hoarse hooting shook the air, and I flushed hot. The boat to Vienna was just leaving. My God, to get on board one of those and to get out of here—out, out, out!

And then all of a sudden, with no transition, my heart was filled with a pure, childlike joy. I thought: it'll be summer soon, and summer meant Patsy, and Patsy meant happiness. Summer was coming, and happiness, and Patsy. I don't know why, but I was absolutely convinced that everything would be all right once Patsy was around. Everything! Life itself. I would confess to her about last night, I would confess to her about everything—you can't start a new life based on lies.

I was overcome with a lofty festive feeling, a great, clear sense of calm. I suddenly felt that my life so far had merely been some kind of phase, that I had been waiting for my train in some dusty little station, and maybe it didn't matter at all what I had spent my time doing as I waited: who I'd talked to, who I'd kissed. Life was only just beginning, and life was beautiful; life was full of wonder.

The door opened behind me. A young girl came out of the bar; she must have been fifteen or sixteen. She was a pretty, nondescript little thing, a working-class girl dressed up in her best. She was wearing a frilly, starched, light dress, white net stockings and black patent-leather shoes. Her smooth brown hair was gathered in two large ponytails on her shoulders, a pink ribbon in each, and she had a little gold cross around her neck. What was she doing in the bar? I thought.

The girl looked at me and stopped hesitantly.

"Are you Master Béla?" she asked.

"Yes," I replied in surprise.

"The waiter inside said you'd be here."

"Yes."

She stared ahead of her awkwardly. It was only now I saw how distraught she was.

Her face was ashen, her eyes red and puffy. She was silent for a space, then looked at me once more.

"Has Master Elemér gone home?"

"Yes, why?"

"I came to bring him greetings," she said in a strangely excited voice, and avoided my glance. "And for yourself as well."

I didn't understand a word of what was going on.

"From who?" I asked.

"From Gyula," she said, and I could see her lip was trembling.

"How is he?"

"How… how is he?" she said, looking at me in shock, and you could see that she was about to be overwhelmed by sobs. "Ain't you heard?"

"Heard what?"

"It's in the papers and everythin'. All the evening papers."

"I don't understand," I said anxiously. "What's in the papers?"

The girl started sobbing loudly. I could barely understand her.

"It's over! Over! He died at once."

"What?!" I panted. "Gyula's de—" I couldn't even bring myself to say it. "For God's sake, what happened?"

"They let him go, poor thing," she sniffed. "You know they let him go?"

"Yes," I said impatiently. "And?"

"And, well, he came to get his papers today, and… said goodbye to everyone and… he went down to the kitchen to say goodbye too, and… he grabbed the kitchen knife, the biggest knife, yes sir, and… he stabbed himself through the heart, and…" I didn't catch the rest—it was lost in a flood of tears.

So that's what's happened, I said to myself and stood, frozen, helpless, beside the weeping girl. We'd started to attract looks from the passers-by. I touched her arm.

"Come to the park with me," I said. "We can talk in peace there."

She followed obediently.

The park was dark and quiet, a heavy scent of lilac in the air. We sat down on a bench. That was when it occurred to me that I didn't even know who this girl was, or rather…

"You Katica, miss?" I asked.

344

"Oh! I'm sorry, sir, I didn't even introduce myself! I feel like I'm losin' my mind. Oh, God, who'd have thought it? Only just last night…" she suddenly left off the sentence and looked at me. "How d'you know who I was?"

"Gyula talked about you, miss."

That silly, sir-and-madam way of speaking the poor adopt when they want to sound "refined", the way they put on their Sunday best when going to a feast, had rubbed off on me, too.

She was silent for a bit.

"What'd he say about me?" she asked softly.

"That you were engaged."

"And… what else?"

She said this in such a pleading voice that I took pity on her.

"That he loved you very much, miss. That he'd never loved nobody else."

I hadn't actually heard Gyula say as much, but I still felt I was telling her the truth.

Katica started to cry.

"Then do you understand all this, sir?"

"What?"

"All *this*. What he did."

"My God!" I said, and sat looking out at the park, because I suddenly realized that there was nothing much more that I *could* say.

Katica, too, was silent for a bit. Then she turned to me.

"Do you know what was wrong with him?" she whispered.

"Yes," I nodded. "So you knew too, miss?"

"Not at all," she shrugged. "He only told me in the letter. You know, sir, the one in which he sent your greetings, too. And he wrote, even there he wrote, that he'd never loved nobody else, and…" She started crying again, "and that he'll be waiting for me in heaven, and… So how could he, then… tell me that!"

"Oh, miss!" I sighed, and felt very, very old all of a sudden. "Believe me, the two things have nothin' to do with each other. *That* in itself means nothing to men. Believe me, I speak from experience. You love someone, but you still go with someone you don't love at all. Why? I don't know.

You just have to. Or rather, you don't have to, and yet sometimes, you still do. It's hard to explain, miss. You're young still, miss. Believe me, Gyula had nothing to do with that woman, really."

"Nothing to do with her?" she looked at me. "Well you listen here, Master Béla. Gyula wrote that he'd only been with that," she swallowed hard, "that woman only once. But he'd known me since I was a little girl and apparently he loved me and I couldn't imagine my life without him, and I still can't, and I'll never be able to, but… but what was that all worth? He died of *that*. And then you go tellin' me he had nothing to do with her?"

I wanted to answer her, but the words stuck in my throat like a deadly fishbone. It was a suffocating thought. A murderous thought. That was the first time it occurred to me, and I couldn't be free of it again.

I broke out in a sweat. Yes, I thought I had nothing to do with Manci, and now it might turn out I had more to do with her than with anybody else. The seeds of death she'd sowed the night before might already be germinating in my blood, too. And then there will be no Patsy, no America, no nothing. It'll all be over before it's begun. Why, why, why? What did I have to do with her? One word from Patsy meant more to me than the whole of that *other* body, the whole of that other woman, than all that… hideousness. I had nothing, nothing, nothing to do with her! I was just waiting for my train in an insignificant little station, and someone had gone and poisoned me in the waiting room.

"Terrible!" I almost shouted. "Terrible!"

Katica sobbed, and then there was silence for a long time. The Gypsy music drifted in from the promenade, the colourful lilac bushes bowed gently in the wind, and everything was full of colour, scent and music—everything was full of spring, spring! And soon it would be summer, and… Suddenly, I felt Katica's hand on my arm.

"You crying too, sir?"

I was terribly ashamed.

"I have to go, miss," I said quickly, nervously. "They'll be looking for me. It's very late."

"Yes," Katica replied in her thin, obedient little voice. "I hope you don't mind my disturbin' you."

She stood up, I stood up too. But when I wanted to go, she came closer and looked at me like a frightened pup.

"Master Béla!" she whispered.

"Yes."

"Do you think I'm to blame as well?"

"Why would I think that?" I looked at her in surprise.

"That's what Böske said. Böske's my friend, you see."

"*What* did she say?"

"Well, that… If *I'd* been with Gyula in the same way as that woman… you see, Böske's that way with her fiancé, and…" she started sobbing. "Oh God, I think I'm goin' to go mad with all this!"

I didn't know what to say. Was it possible that what Böske said was true? Maybe. But then the devil take her and her truth!

"Böske's plain common," I said harshly, wildly, with genuine hatred. "A common slut. She's worthless! And you shouldn't be friends with people like her. Understand? Men *do* want clean and innocent women, women like you, miss."

"But then they go to someone else, who…" Here, she grabbed my arm and almost shouted: "Why? Tell me why? Why?"

"Because we're animals!" I burst out. "Understand? Animals! Filthy, dirty, ugly animals. Worse than animals, in fact."

I hadn't noticed till now that I was shouting, but I was unable to stop. I don't know what I said, I don't know how I took my leave of Katica, whether I even said goodbye. All I remember is that when I got to the hotel, I ran straight to the first toilet to check if you could already "see the symptoms". You couldn't. But then I remembered that Gyula had only noticed it two weeks after, and I spent so long in there alone, crying, that by the time I got back to the bar, the jazz band was already playing.

> *Why, Mr Stux, what's this,*
> *You know it's wrong—*
> *Have some patience, sir,*
> *The night's still long.*

*

I didn't dare go home after closing, because I was afraid of finding Manci there. So I slept in a nook in the basement, the way poor Gyula used to do, tossing and turning sleeplessly till the boys arrived. Then I went and joined them in the changing room, and listened—shuddering—to the tale of Gyula's suicide which, the way they told it, became a sort of cheap horror story.

The truth was, they didn't know anything either. None of them had seen it, and the few members of staff who really did know something decided it was best to keep their mouths shut, because the management was merciless in these matters. "Indiscretion", as they called it, was grounds for immediate dismissal. As for the papers, which in these cases were always paid off, all they wrote was a brief news item saying that in "one of the elegant riverside hotels" an apprentice (name, age, and address such-and-such), had committed suicide, and that the reasons for his actions were unknown. Despite that, or maybe precisely because of that, there was barely a boy in the changing room who didn't know some suspiciously dramatic detail of Gyula's death. Antal, for example, told us that Gyula, with the kitchen knife sticking out of his heart, staggered into the lobby and, covered in blood and in the midst of his death throes, screamed at the flabbergasted guests:

"The management's murdered me! Boycott this hotel!"

Lajos, on the other hand, had heard from the girl who washed the dishes—the one Gyula had once been keen on—that our late friend had bled out in the toilets beside the kitchen, where he had severed his artery with the pig knife.

"My blood is on his hands!" he was supposed to have said, and when they asked him who he meant, eyes rolling back in his head, he croaked: "Franciska!" and died.

These big-city smart guys, who'd seen it all before, and who in normal circumstances would have dismissed stories like these straight away with a simple wave of the hand, now listened to the contradictory, penny-dreadful details of these tales with grave and serious faces. No matter how corrupted they'd become, they were nevertheless partly children still and for most of them, this was their first experience of death; after what had happened, nothing seemed quite impossible. Poor Gyula was already on the road to reincarnation: he had become gossip, a thrilling old wives' tale.

That it had been Franciska who betrayed him to the management was now beyond doubt. Elemér had spoken to his "comrade", and when we asked him what he'd found out, all he'd said reluctantly was:

"Unfortunately, you were right."

So we determined to get our revenge on Franciska, but when it came to *how*, the boys grew uneasy. Gyula's case scared them: none of them dared take a stand; they were all afraid they'd get in trouble. They hummed and hawed and beat around the bush, talking in generalities.

"He should be beaten to death!" they called. "He should be driven to suicide himself!"

"What do you mean *should*?" I snapped finally. "We have to give him such a hiding, and before the day is out, that he never even thinks of doing something like this again till the day he dies."

"Yes," said Márton. "But how?"

"Leave that to me. I'll teach him a lesson, the little fag."

This was greeted with general approbation; only Elemér protested.

"That sort of thing isn't worthy of a conscious proletarian," he declared drily and didactically. "It goes against the Socialist world view."

"So go give him a pat on the back, then!" I burst out angrily.

"Hear! hear!" the boys chorused.

He didn't get far with his "Socialist world view" with them either. They, too, had only the vaguest notion of what it was. Everyone took my part, and I took advantage of the situation rather viciously.

"Socialist world view!" I muttered mockingly. "Where I come from, they call that cowardice."

The boys laughed, but Elemér still wasn't angry with me. His voice stayed calm and practical.

"Let's leave the demagoguery out of it," he said neutrally. "Think about it. The first thing Franciska would do is go tell on Béla, and then he'd be out on his ear like poor Gyula."

"That's my affair," I said. "Why are you always so worried about everybody else's problems?"

349

"Because this is collective action. No one person can take responsibility for this."

"You're all welcome to come and kick him up the backside, too, as far as I'm concerned," I said, somewhat less academically; I thought that had really put me over the top with the others.

But that wasn't the case; quite the opposite, in fact. The boys no longer dared support me openly, because they were afraid that if they did, they'd have to take part in the beating, too, and then Franciska would tell on all of them as well, and they would all go the way of Gyula.

Besides, another idea was then mooted.

"Let's do to him what he did to Gyula," Gábor suggested. "Let's tell 'em he's a fag, and then he'll be out on his ear, too."

That was effective and seemed to me completely risk-free, too. Everyone was delighted. Elemér waited for them to finish rejoicing, and then asked:

"Do you know about his family?"

There was silence. It suddenly turned out that we knew nothing at all about Franciska, except that he was a "fag".

"Well, then," Elemér continued. "Listen. Franciska's father is one of the finest men in the movement, an honest-to-God metalworker, a good old-fashioned Socialist. They blacklisted him for it years ago. Can't get a job and the whole family lives off what Franciska makes. D'you want them to starve to death?"

That settled the boys down a bit, but had just as little effect as the "Socialist world view".

"You can't always be so bloody considerate," Lajos said. "He can keep them with his fag-money!"

That resulted in another round of general laughter. Elemér waited till it had settled down and then tried a different tack.

"All right," he said, "but do you really think the management don't know why Franciska spends half the day in 302? If you're gone for half an hour, the sky falls in. Why do you think they turn a blind eye for him? Because his *friend* is connected up to here. He supplies the army with German chemicals, and that means more to your bourgeois than morality. You can rest assured that an anonymous tip-off will end up in the bin, and if one of us reports him in person, they'll end up carrying the can. So what's the point?"

That, of course, did the job. No one was laughing now. They hummed and hawed and beat around the bush again.

By that point, I had long withdrawn from the debate. I just sat there by myself, smoking one cigarette after the other in silence. Just like poor Gyula, I thought, and my mouth went dry.

The debate had well and truly petered out when Elemér laid out his plan.

"Let's boycott him," he proposed. "We won't speak to him any more. Let's say that from this moment on he's dead to us, and we'll boycott anyone that talks to him, too. Everyone in favour, raise your hands!"

Everybody but me put their hands up.

"What about you?" Elemér looked at me. "I want you to know, you have the right to make a counter-proposal if you want."

"Kiss my arse," I grunted. "That's my proposal."

With that I left, slamming the door behind me.

It was still only eight o'clock, and I didn't dare go home. I lay down again in the basement, but couldn't sleep. Eventually, I gave up the hopeless struggle, went into the changing room and changed. I checked in the bathroom, and still couldn't see anything—that reassured me a little. I'll go over to Buda and take a walk, I thought.

When I left the hotel, I found myself face to face with Franciska. He was pretty, he was fresh, he smelt good, his girlish baby-face was all smiles. Had he been smiling last night, as well?

I wanted to get going, but then I saw that Elemér was watching me through the window of the lobby, and—possessed by something—I said hello to Franciska.

"What's up?" I asked. "Where you headed?"

Franciska winked.

"Officially, I'm off to the Ministry of Defence."

"And less officially?"

"Guess."

"Skipping work?"

"Precisely. You off home?"

"Not yet. I'll hang around with you a bit."

"Let's go up to Gellérthegy, all right?"

"All right," I nodded and we left together.

Elemér was still watching from the window, and this filled me with a queer satisfaction. I started whistling.

"Did you see him?"

"Who?"

"Elemér. He was really looking at you."

"And?"

Franciska shot me an inquisitive glance. His blue, noncommittal eyes were cold as steel.

"They'll stop talking to you," he teased. "Aren't you scared?"

"Only of the Almighty. And not always of him, either."

So he knows, I thought. Or does he only suspect and is he trying to find out from me? Well, he's barking up the wrong tree if he is.

"Aren't you surprised?" he asked.

"About what?"

"That I know."

I deliberately didn't ask him what he knew. I whistled "Mr Stux".

"My sources are good, aren't they?" he laughed. "What a silly bunch, I ask you. *Boycott*. That's a laugh. Elemér must have been going on about the Socialist world view again."

I tried to smile. I'm not sure I succeeded.

It was a fine, sunny morning. We were walking across the bridge. What if I shoved him into the Danube? I wondered. I shivered unconsciously as we passed a policeman.

Franciska took my arm.

"Old man," he said confidentially, "I have to say I admire you."

"Why?"

"Because you couldn't care less about them. You know where to belong."

"I do?"

"'Course. Don't be so modest. I've had my eye on you for some time. First the Americans, then Their Excellencies, now the night shift.

You're the only one of the boys who knows how to make their luck." He sounded sincere now. I felt incredibly awkward. He liked me more and more every minute. "I don't know why we weren't friends sooner. We're going to make something of ourselves, you and I. Shall I tell you why?"

"Why?"

"Because we know where to belong. These idiots are never going to do more than pick up scraps, because they spend their whole lives chasing after an empty cart." He smiled. "But you and I know how to make our luck, don't we? Socialist world view!" He made a face. "Tell me, what do you think of that?"

"I don't know. I don't know anything about it."

"I do," he said disparagingly. "My old man's a Social Democrat. I get the Socialist world view for breakfast."

"And what do *you* think of it?"

"What do I think?" he shrugged. "That they're right. Poverty's bad. So? Death's bad, too. But you try fighting that. There's always been death, and there's always been poverty. The question is, do you like being poor?"

"No one likes being poor."

"Well, then. What about the conscious proletarian? Load of hooey. No one likes being poor. What's the cure for poverty? Money, isn't it? And where can you find money? Where there *is* money. And where is it? With the rich. There. Then why should I stick with the poor? You know, it's all a case of sour grapes. The only reason that lot complain about the bourgeoisie is 'cause they're too stupid to get into it. And then there's people like Elemér—they're worse."

"Why?"

"Because they're not stupid but still choose to live stupidly. Instead of trying to help themselves, they want to save the world. Just imagine— Elemér saving the world. They live eight to a room and three of his brothers've died of consumption, but he's got *principles*, don't you know."

"And you don't?"

"I do. But the difference is, I don't cling to them. Life isn't algebra, where every equation makes sense. My principle is: whatever works. Why should I cling to a principle if it does me no good?"

"But it would be good for you too if they put an end to poverty."

"*If* they did! Where have they ever? When have they ever?"

"That's what they're fighting for, though, isn't it? Maybe they'll get there eventually."

"Eventually. I like that. After I'm long gone, I'll bet. Well, my boy, you can keep that as far as I'm concerned. Just look at my old man. Spent his whole life fighting for that. And what's it got him? Damn all. He hasn't saved the world, and he's ruined his own life. Ever since I can remember, I've seen nothing at home except misery, strife, sickness and fear. Whenever a policeman enters the building, my ma has a heart attack. The old man's been inside four times, once for two years at a stretch. Had to have three of his ribs removed, he got beaten up by the police so bad. He's blacklisted, he can't get work; he's like a hunted animal, and that's how it's been forever. We've never had enough to eat, never had decent clothes, never had a good day. We've always lived like dogs. And why? For the future, says the old man. Aren't I, his son, the future? Tell me, please. You can tell me that, can't you?"

"'Course you are."

"There. And I don't give a damn that he's spent his whole life fighting. I don't want that world of his, he can keep it. So then what's he been fighting for? What was the point of it all?"

"Not everybody thinks like you."

"And not everybody thinks like him, either. How on earth does he know whether people in the future really will think the life he imagines for them right now is so good? Am I right or am I right? Why aren't you saying anything?"

"You're right," I said, and was shocked to find I meant it.

Yes, he was right—he was right about a lot of things, and that was the terrible thing.

We were already heading uphill. This was the hill the pagans had rolled Bishop Gellért off of into the river for trying to convert them. *What would happen if I took him and?...*

I took my arm out of his.

"Got a smoke?" I asked. My voice sounded very strange.

He didn't notice.

354

"Here you go," he said generously, extending a silver cigarette case.

It was full of Egyptian cigarettes, ten in each half. The peasants in our village had to work four full days for the price of those twenty cigarettes. Who was right now?

"Let's sit down," Franciska suggested.

We lay down in the shade of a lilac bush. There was a sweet, warm scent in the air, the meadow covered in colourful flowers, and a light, pleasant breeze tickled the tall grass. Up here, you could no longer hear the noise of the city. It was quiet, not a soul in sight, only a bird singing above us. It suddenly swooped, picked off a maggot and flew on, to carry on singing. It was all so peaceful here. The bigger animals ate the smaller ones, and down in the city, people did the same. We smoked on in silence.

All at once, Franciska turned to me.

"Did you know I keep my whole family?"

"Really?"

"Yes. And you know what thanks I get for it? Yesterday, my little brother called me a hooligan in front of the whole family, and a selfish pig. You'd have thought the old man would smack him, wouldn't you? Not a bit of it. He didn't say a word, but I know he thinks the same thing. The whole family does. What do you say to that? I'm the selfish pig that keeps them all, and the old man is so selfless, though we all would have starved to death long ago if it were up to him." He knocked the ash tetchily off his cigarette. "But it won't go on much longer," he added angrily. "I'm going to get the old man a job so they don't end up in the street, and then they'll have seen the last of me."

"*You're* going to get the old man a job?"

"Who else? The Socialist world view isn't!"

"But how can you get him a job in this day and age?"

Franciska was quiet for a moment.

"I can tell *you*," he said and dropped his voice somewhat. "I asked the German. It's easy for him."

"So the old man'll get a job."

Franciska furrowed his brows and stared pensively after the smoke from his cigarette.

355

"It's not quite as simple as that," he said eventually.

"Why?"

"You know, he's not a bad sort, the German, but he's got a fixation. Or rather, two. The Reds and the Jews. You've never heard anything like it, believe me. He says they're going to wipe them out in Germany, but not in the haphazard way our Whites do it, when they toss the editor of *Népszava* in the Danube, or massacre a couple of hundred Jews, and then nothing. He says that's *Sauwirtschaft*, a joke. They have to wipe them out in an organized way, he says, legally, openly, clean and proper—the German way."

"And he knows your old man's Red?"

"He does now. Problem is, he didn't hear it from me. You know, I should have fed it to him slowly, with some good sentimental yarn. But it's done now. I was stupid, I didn't tell him. They told him in the factory where he wanted them to take him."

"And?"

Franciska gave a whistle.

"Oh boy! You should have seen it. He was furious. How I've put him in an impossible position, and what was I thinking trying to get him to help someone like that. Someone like that can go starve to death, and so can his entire family, and so on, and so on."

"So what you going to do now?"

"Leave that to me!" he shrugged. "First of all, I'm going to starve him."

"How do you mean?"

"You know what I mean," he snapped. "They gossip enough about me in the hotel." He looked at me and added mysteriously: "But there's something they don't know."

"What?"

"That he's mad about me."

He said that as naturally as if his German had been a woman, or if he'd been a woman, and his German a besotted suitor. I must have made a very silly face, because he was almost confrontational when he asked:

"Well, what are you staring at?"

I was acutely embarrassed, but at the same time I was so curious that I couldn't let it go at that.

"It's just that," I stuttered slightly, "I've never... I've never known... one of *them*, and..." I dropped my voice unconsciously. "What's it really like? Can someone like that be in love with a man the same way that, say, I can with a girl?"

Franciska gave a dismissive wave of the arm.

"Of course! Much more so."

"And... are you in love with him?"

He laughed sharply.

"The hell I am!"

"But you're... like *that*, too, aren't you?"

"No."

"No?"

"Not at all. What are you looking at me like that for? Not everybody who does it is like that."

"Well, what then?"

"Some people are born that way, and some people just do it. I just do it."

"But how can you do it if you're not like *that*?"

"How? Don't be stupid. Didn't the boys in your school do it with each other?"

"Yeah, some."

"And were they all like *that*?"

"No, I don't think so."

"There you go, then. If I could do it with the boys in school, why couldn't I do it with him now?"

"Is that all you do? You don't do anything else?"

"We do other things, sure, but..." he smiled. "You know, that's not so bad either. And why shouldn't I do it, if it's to my advantage?"

"Is that the only reason you do it?"

Franciska thought about it.

"You know, I really don't know," he said. "You have to do something, and at the end of the day it's all the same, isn't it? The boys spend all their money on it and end up catching all sorts of diseases from those girls, to boot. And then they're the ones with the big mouths. Well, they can talk all they want, for all I care. Eventually, I'll get married, and not to just any woman, either!"

357

I looked at him in surprise.

"You got somebody?"

"Not yet. Once I'm in society."

"You want to marry for money?"

"'Course not. I'm going to love my wife. And I'm only going to marry someone very clever and very pretty. Or do you think only poor girls can be pretty and clever?"

"No. But what'll you do if you fall in love with a poor girl?"

"That's why I want to get into society. If I only know rich people, I won't end up falling in love with a poor girl, will I? Well, then. Yes, sir, I'm going to marry for love."

What can you say to that! Yes, he really would end up marrying for love. I felt very stupid compared to him. I just lay there in silence and stared at the sky. The sky was as blue and noncommittal as Franciska's eyes.

"Tell me," I said, "you an atheist?"

"Me?" he said, practically incensed. "What are you talking about? Only Reds and Jews are atheists. I render unto God what is God's, and to Caesar what is Caesar's."

"But your way of thinking, it's hardly religious."

"Why not? Because I'm realistic? I think like the society I live in. Society's Caesar, isn't it? And the Bible doesn't say you should render unto a *good* Caesar what is Caesar's, it just says render unto Caesar. And what the Caesars were like back in those days, you should know from school. Were they all so good? Come on, tell me."

"No."

"Well, then," he said. "So you see that I'm on firm religious ground."

How do you argue with that? He was right again. Yes, he knew how to make his luck. He was going to make something of himself. And Elemér thought a simple *boycott* would take care of him. Poor Elemér. Poor believers. I looked up at the sky because I didn't want him to see my face.

"Here," I said. "What d'you say about this thing with poor Gyula?"

"It's terrible," he said equivocally. "Poor boy."

"But do you think someone really did report him?"

"I don't know. But what difference does that make, anyway?"

"What difference? If they hadn't reported him, he wouldn't have committed suicide!"

"He didn't have to go committing suicide. Besides, as a Catholic, I don't agree with suicide. He was weak, that's why he died. It's a shame, but that's how it is. The weak fall by the wayside."

"But Gyula wasn't weak. He was stronger and healthier than you."

Franciska looked at me suspiciously.

"Looks like it takes more than that, my friend," he said, and I felt both mockery and glee in his voice.

"What does it take, then?"

He shrugged.

"The stronger come out on top. The rest doesn't matter."

I fell silent. Why hadn't Gyula managed to come out on top? Strong, healthy Gyula. Was it because he wasn't "strong" and "healthy" enough to snap other people's necks? Or because he dared to dream a little? Because he took that syphilitic tramp for the heroine of some great romance? Franciska didn't dream—no sir. Franciska was "realistic". He would have simply used a condom. Is that what life boiled down to?

"And the rest doesn't matter?"

"No."

"And is that all right?"

"I don't know," he said, and shrugged. "And to be honest, I don't care. The fact is that's the way it is, and I don't fight the facts. I'm realistic."

"And what if you were weaker?" I asked suddenly and crept closer to him. "Take us, for example. I'm stronger than you. What would you do if I tried to strangle you right now?"

The blue apathetic eyes surveyed me calmly.

"I'd shoot you," he said, completely naturally.

"You got a gun?"

"Sure. You don't?"

"No."

"There you go, then," he smiled. "It all comes down to things like that." He took a thin little black Browning out of his back pocket. "It's loaded," he said.

There was silence. I looked more closely at the pistol. It was a tiny, delicate, almost effeminate thing. Like a toy, I thought. But if he shoots me, I'm finished. Yes, it seemed life really did come down to things like that. My heart beat fast. I was gripped by mortal fear.

Franciska smiled.

"Let's go," he said lightly, but there was hidden menace in his voice. It was an order.

I stood up. The pistol was still in his hand. He was holding it in his left hand as he dusted himself off behind with his right. The glorious victor, I thought. I looked at his satisfied baby-face, his blue, non-committal eyes, his confident smile, and at that moment something happened within me.

It's hard to explain these things, perhaps impossible. I used to feel this in school when I was young, whenever I would stand up to my class, which could have torn me limb from limb like a wild beast, and come out stronger. The blood rushed to my head. I was no longer quite myself. Only sleepwalkers can feel so secure. It's ridiculous, I thought, even as I was doing it. You're an idiot. He'll shoot you. But then I could think no more. I was carried away by passion, blood, instinct or something else, for which there are no words.

"Go on and shoot me if you can," I said hoarsely.

Franciska went white.

"Are you mad?" he asked with a twisted, forced smile. "What's wrong with you?"

"I'm going to give you the beating of your life now," I said without raising my voice at all. "And you've got a gun. Let's see who comes out on top."

Franciska gave a nervous, dismissive wave.

"Go to hell," he said, and made to leave.

I gave him an almighty slap. Franciska raised his gun, but I smacked it out of his hand. He screamed.

"Heeeeel—"

That was as far as he got. I stuffed my handkerchief into his mouth and smacked him so hard on the head, he fell to the ground. I sat on his stomach.

"There," I said. "Now here we are, the two of us. Let's see who comes out on top. I could beat you to death, but I won't. You know why? 'Cause that would get me in trouble, too. You see? I learn quickly. I'm only going to beat you *half* to death, because that won't cause me any grief. And why not? Because you're not going to rat on me, the way you did with Gyula. And you know why, you realist? Because if you do, I'll tell them you were trying it on with me, and who wouldn't believe me? Everybody knows you're a fag. You think your German'll smooth things over for you? That he'll have me kicked out of the hotel? You're wrong. 'Cause if he does, I'll write the whole thing up for the papers. And if you bribe the papers, I'll report you to the police. And if you bribe the judge, so what? Because, meanwhile, I'll make up all sorts of things about you and that German and the upstanding gentlemen in the management who let things like that go on in the hotel. But there won't be any need for all that. You know why? Because you're all realists. You're scared. You're scared of the obvious, what you can feel—of this. You're not afraid of ghosts. But it's a ghost that's sitting on you now—Gyula's. Don't believe me, realist? Then listen up—this smack is from Gyula, the dead Gyula. How does it feel to *take* it, my friend? Did you really think that you, the weak, would always be on top, and we, the strong, would stay forever on the bottom? Did you think we had *qualms*? Just because we dared to dream? Well, you're out of luck, my friend, because even the likes of me have dreams. Not just the likes of Elemér. And some of us are filthy peasants who haven't forgotten how to use our fists. Get that into your head, you realist!"

I laid into him and didn't stop hitting him till he passed out. Then I took the handkerchief out of his mouth, pocketed the Browning and walked down to the river. It was only there I felt how tired I was. I sat down on the riverbank steps, right beside the water. The pistol clunked on the stone of the step.

I looked around. There was nobody about. I took out the gun and threw it into the Danube. Then I just sat and watched the river. There was a splash and concentric rings trembled on its surface; then it became so smooth I could see my face in it. I smiled.

"Dear Lord," I said, half aloud. "Thank you for filling my heart with noble dreams and for giving me rough, peasant hands to back them up with. I know they'll help us through. I know, with them, we'll get them in the end."

My head drooped down onto my chest, my eyelids grew heavy. I remembered old summer evenings when they had me reaping wheat from sunup till sundown at fourteen. That was when I'd last felt this tired and this satisfied. The moon shone onto the mowed field. I looked at it, and it was a pleasure to behold. I had done my work well. I would amble home with the other peasants, our heavy, tired steps resounding darkly under the moonlit poplars. At the Cultural Circle, the Gypsy music was playing for the upper classes, and we too were singing—but ours was a different tune:

> *I'm every bit as tough as you*
> *I can make order just like you*

14

A BOUT NINE O'CLOCK THAT EVENING, the telephone rang.
"Is that you, Béla?"

"Yes. Who's this?"

"Elemér."

I shuddered. What could he want? Maybe Franciska had snitched on me, and… I quickly closed the door of the booth so no one would overhear.

"Yes?" I said apprehensively.

"Could you wait for me in the morning?"

"Why?"

"I want to talk to you."

"Has something… happened?"

A small silence. Then:

"Yes."

"What?"

"I'll tell you in the morning. Meet me at the front door at eight thirty."

"All right."

I looked at the clock. It wasn't even nine thirty. I had to wait another eleven hours. Eleven hours is six hundred and sixty minutes, and those are minutes in which great ideals don't much count. I thought of the hard days of starvation, the six hours of walking, the nights filled with coughing. Of Berci, my mother, the bottle of lye. And I asked myself: was it really worth it?

A frightened silence took hold inside me. If I told myself yes, the voice inside me answered: no. If I told myself no, the voice inside me said: yes.

Yes. No. Yes. No. Who was right?

Was it Franciska yet again? Yes. Yet again. He wouldn't do something that stupid. He'd say: what does it get me? Only I could be that stupid, I scolded myself, but my heart was deeply proud of my "stupidity". I was proud that I wasn't as "smart" as he was. And I was indescribably jealous of him.

Elemér was punctual as always, "ridiculously punctual", as the boys used to say. He wasn't early and he wasn't late. He stepped out of the front door at precisely the moment the minute hand on the electric clock on the corner touched the six.

"Walk with me? I'm going to police headquarters."

I shuddered involuntarily when he said police headquarters.

"I'm dropping off the registration cards," he said, and pointed to the bundle he was carrying.

Of course, I thought, he goes there every morning. I'm really losing it.

"Let's go," I said, and we set off together.

We walked in silence beside one another. Elemér was clearly waiting for me to start the conversation, but I didn't say a word. I was focused only on my rep now. I walked along beside him, hands in my pockets, chin pressed down onto my neck, the way I did when I was a child.

Eventually, it was Elemér who broke the silence.

"You heard?"

"What?"

"Franciska's in hospital."

"What's wrong with him?" I asked with forced calm.

"Don't you know?"

"How would I?"

"You're the one who saw him last."

"There was nothing wrong with him then."

I didn't look up, but I could feel Elemér looking at me.

"Well, he's in a pretty sorry state now," he said. "The doctors are afraid he might have internal injuries."

"Oh really?"

"Yes."

No use denying it, it wasn't Franciska's internal injuries I was worried about. I was more concerned with my own potential injuries. I looked up, but Elemér's face didn't reveal a thing. It was expressionless as always. Pokerface, I thought to myself angrily.

"And what are they saying in the hotel?" I ventured.

"They say it was a car accident."

"A car accident?!"

"Yes."

I almost believed it. And why not? I thought, encouraged. Things like that do happen.

"You don't mean he was run over by a car?"

"No." Elemér was silent for a moment. "I think this whole car accident is nonsense."

There was something strange in his voice. I didn't dare look at him.

"How come?"

He didn't reply straight away. I could feel that he was looking at me again.

"I think somebody beat him up."

"What makes you say that?"

"I visited him in hospital."

"Despite the boycott?"

He pretended not to have noticed the ironic tone.

"Yes," he said. "I was afraid he might land someone in the same trouble he did Gyula."

He said it so simply, in such a straightforward way, it was as if he had been entrusted with the care of all our souls and he had to answer for us with his life. I was ashamed.

There was more silence. It took me a long time to summon the courage to ask:

"And what did he say?"

"Same thing."

"That it was a car accident?"

"Yes."

"And he didn't say anything else?"

"No."

"And is that what he told the management?"

"Probably."

"So you're not sure? I mean…" I fell suddenly silent, afraid I'd let something slip.

Elemér gave me an inquisitive look.

"You meant, did he snitch on anyone?"

"Yes," I admitted.

"I doubt it," he said, still looking at me hard.

I could feel myself blush. But I couldn't stop myself asking.

"How come?"

"Because whoever it was would no longer have a job. The management don't tend to stand for that sort of thing."

So it's all right, then, I thought, relieved. But then I asked myself in fright: then why does he want to talk to me?

We had come into view of the great yellow building that was police headquarters. I have to find out, I thought. Anything's better than this uncertainty. But how… how was I meant to ask without incriminating myself? I slowed down.

Elemér looked at me.

"Do you want to go down to the river for a few minutes?"

"Yes," I answered greedily.

We cut across the square and went down to the river. There were no passers-by here, only a few boatmen hanging around the empty quay. We sat down on the stone steps of the riverbank. It was a fine, calm morning, the sun sprinkling the Danube with fragments of silver, the water lolling sleepily.

"Did you beat him up?" Elemér asked out of nowhere.

He looked at me so openly with his cat's eyes—already growing wrinkled—that I couldn't lie to him.

"Yes," I nodded.

Elemér didn't say anything. He just looked out at the water pensively for a long while, and then asked with his typically matter-of-fact, almost scientific curiosity:

"Why d'you do it?"

I was annoyed by his incredible calm. I shrugged my shoulders testily.

"You know well enough."

"I do," he replied. "The question is do *you*?"

I looked at him, uncomprehending.

"If you get this upset, you'll never understand," he replied in his dry, professorial voice, but his cat's eyes, old before their time, were full of benevolence. "Look," he said, "I want to talk to you seriously. Tell me why you did it."

I shrugged again.

"You can see I was right."

"In what way?"

"He didn't dare report me."

"He didn't. And?"

"What do you mean 'and'?" I said, more and more agitated by the minute. "He just laughed at your precious boycott. It has no effect on him. *This* he won't forget in a hurry. The next time he's thinking of snitching on someone he'll remember his 'car accident'. He'll look twice before crossing the road."

"Maybe," nodded Elemér. "But that wasn't the only reason you did it, was it?"

"No," I replied, and I was seized by a vague, suffocating anxiety. "How did you know?" I asked with childlike wonder.

"That's how it started with me, too," he replied softly, simply. "That's how it starts with everyone. You come up against an insignificant little crook, and you think you've started a crusade against all the crooks in the world. You wouldn't have risked everything for Franciska. The feeling that made you act was great. The act itself was small. You can't take care of this with your fists."

"That's the only way to do it!" I replied heatedly. "I realized that just yesterday. Have you ever really talked to Franciska?"

"No."

"There you go, then. If you'd heard the things he was saying, you wouldn't be saying what you just said. You think you can convince his sort? 'Course you can't. You can't, and you know why you can't? Because..." I suddenly stopped. What I wanted to say seemed so harsh, so upsetting, that I didn't want to say it. But then my gaze met Elemér's, and when I saw in his eyes that awful, unshakeable calm, I was overcome with rage. I went ahead and told him, almost screaming: "Because they're right! Get it? *They're right!*"

"Well, of course," Elemér said without any surprise at all. "That's just it. If you want to get somewhere in today's world you more or less have to be like Franciska. You can't change these people. You have to change the world instead, Béla, that's the point. Then their truths will no longer be true and their depravity won't be necessary. You think Franciska's any worse than the rest of them? 'Course he isn't. Listen: today's world belongs to the Franciskas. Everybody has a Franciska inside them, but they don't always pin their colours to the mast right away. You'll find thousands of decent, upstanding people who—when push comes to shove—would be just the same. And then you get the bourgeoisie bemoaning how terrible people are. But that's all rubbish. People aren't good and people aren't bad. People are people. They want to live and they live how they can. There's only one way for them to live today, so they live like that. What else could they do? You have to run with the pack, the bourgeois will tell you, and in a way, they're right about that too. You have to run with the pack. Or stand up to it. There's no third option. You have to choose between the two. Do you see now what I'm getting at?"

"I do," I replied, and suddenly remembered what Menyhért, the sailor, had told my father. *In a world like ours you can only be two things. A revolutionary or a crook.*

Yes, it looked like you had to choose between the two. Don't get me wrong, there were fine, upstanding crooks too, like—for example—my father, just as there were prissy ones like Franciska, and the grand and glorious ones, like His Excellency. How were they different? In the end, it was all the same. When push came to shove, you were either a crook or a revolutionary. You either ran with the pack or you stood up to it.

"Yes," I said, and my voice was almost festive. "I think I've learnt a lesson for life."

Elemér put his hand on my shoulder.

"You'd make a good Socialist, Béla."

"Really?" I asked with childish greed.

"Yes," he nodded, and I felt like I had at the prize-giving at school when I'd been given my book.

Dear Lord, I thought, finally to belong somewhere! To pull myself out of this fog, this mess, to find myself and my place in the world!

"Tell me," I asked excitedly, "you're a member of the Party, right?"

"Yes. I work in the youth wing."

"Could you get me in, too?"

"Yes," he replied pensively. "But I'd wait a bit, if I were you."

"Why?"

"You don't know enough yet."

"But the others are just apprentices, too!" I rankled. "Do they all know more than me?"

"Not at all," Elemér said. "But they're not as talented as you. Talent can be dangerous, Béla. And what with you being a peasant, to top it all—the bourgeoisie keeps the peasants in complete darkness. I'm afraid the light might be too much for you all at once. Especially since even Franciska made you so angry you almost killed him. And that's nothing compared to what you'll see if you join the movement! Oh yes," he said, giving a wave of his arm. "Wait a bit, Béla. Study."

"How am I going to study if I'm not in the movement?"

"Read."

"As if I had money for books."

"I'll bring you the books," he said, and reached awkwardly into his pocket. "Here's the first one."

He pulled out a dog-eared book that had been read to death, entitled *The ABC of Socialism*.

Looking at the plain yellow paper covers, I felt discouraged. I remembered the English language book on Vilmos Császár út. That said anyone could learn English in six months with "no teacher required, in the comfort of your own home". This was only an ABC. Where was the rest? I wanted to ask how long it took to learn Socialism, but I didn't dare because I was afraid the learned Elemér would laugh at me. But I did decide that the second he left, I would start in on this book and not move from where I was till I'd finished it. I'd show him how quickly I could learn Socialism! And one day, I'd put even him to shame.

"If you want," he said, "you could always wait for me in the morning like this. We can skip out a bit and discuss your reading. All right?"

"Yes."

"But don't say anything to the others," he said. "Not about me visiting Franciska, or that... Anyway, just don't say anything. We maintain the boycott. From now on, you won't be talking to him much, either, will you?"

"No."

"Then I'll be off," he said, standing up.

He stood up like a good, conscientious employee who's managed to convince the client of the quality of his material and the firm's *bona fides*. There was something ridiculous about him, and something wonderful. I watched him, and I was suddenly so grateful I didn't know what to do. My God, I thought, how much I have to thank him for! First, he lent me his clothes, then his heart, and now his mind.

"Thank you, Elemér!" slipped out of me.

"What for?" he said in surprise.

His face was expressionless. He was Pokerface once more.

"The book," I said, and tried to remain expressionless too, the way a good Socialist should.

The two weeks were up, and there were still no signs. I started to relax. Everything around me went quiet, too. We sent a wreath for Gyula's funeral, and then quickly forgot all about him. A new boy came in his place, Boldizsár, and one day Franciska, too, came out of hospital. I watched him suspiciously for a while, but then realized I had nothing to fear from him. When we met, he made as if he'd never seen me before in his life, and I of course did not try to remind him. The boys really did boycott him, which was fine, but not at all difficult, because Franciska avoided us so fastidiously that we wouldn't have had a chance to talk to him, boycott or no boycott. There were no visible signs of his "car accident". He was as handsome, fresh and perfumed as before, and his effeminate baby-face was all smiles. Gyula's uniform fitted Boldizsár so perfectly that not even a button needed adjusting, and he settled into the post the same way—you could hardly notice the difference. He wasn't stupid, and he wasn't smart; he was as neutral as Switzerland. After a week, we no longer even noticed him—he was part of the furniture, part of the hotel. The shifts carried on in their prescribed way, and our days were grey as donkeys, trudging uneventfully along their beaten paths.

I had been avoiding Manci like the plague ever since. I didn't go home after closing for fear of meeting her. Around dawn, I would crash in some corner of the basement, sleep till eight thirty and then walk with Elemér to police headquarters. That was how it was, day after day. When Elemér was done, we would usually walk down to the river, or "play hookey" in Buda among the little one-storey gingerbread houses where Biedermeier and geraniums in the window were still the style, and the young ladies practised "Für Elise" on the piano.

They were lovely, those quiet morning walks. Elemér must have been eighteen at the time, I was sixteen, and it was summer. The lilac was blooming, the winding little streets were full of scents and piano music, and we talked of putting the world to rights.

It was a strange friendship, ours. We were together day after day, we were attached to each other in the way that you can be at that age and no other, but we never spoke of intimate things, not once. Elemér continued to be impersonal, never talked about his private affairs—even by accident—and never asked me about mine. He kept strictly to explanations of the "Socialist world view". He really did start with the *ABC* and guided me through the jungle of this strange science with the dispassionate care and precision of a professional big game hunter. He brought me the dog-eared books that had been read to death, and I devoured them like a wolf. There were weeks when I would read one almost every day.

I really did have a wolf's appetite. My unquenched thirst for knowledge threw itself on Marxism like a starving beast. I swallowed its heavy fare half chewed, and more than once had trouble digesting it. Gradually, I learnt the secret slang of its technical terms and began bandying foreign words when we would "discuss my reading" with Elemér, but internally, not to put too fine a point on it, I somewhat simplified Socialism for myself. The whole thing seemed so Sándor Rózsa-like to me—taking treasure from the rich and distributing it to the poor. Of course that was the thing to do, there could be no doubt about that. The thought did not seem novel at all. Sándor

Rózsa did the same thing, and I was an old disciple of the famous outlaw. As for helping the proletariat organize, I felt I had already got the key to that as a child when I wanted to organize the poor into gangs, the way we children had organized ourselves into gangs. The difference is just, I thought, that the Socialists didn't want to organize the poor of a single village, city or country into gangs, but the poor of all five continents, and that was quite right: workers of the world, unite!

That was all fine as far as it went. That was all good, it was all exciting, and I was passionately keen about that. But when it came down to the details, there were plenty of things I secretly despised. First of all, I couldn't understand what all that complicated intellectual mumbo-jumbo was for. Of the fact that poverty is a bad thing there was no need to convince the poor, and there was no chance of convincing the rich. The rich were behind the whole crooked enterprise and they'd have to be mad just to hand everything they'd stolen over centuries back to the poor when asked politely. Power had to be wrenched from their hands by force, like Marx said. By force—which is to say, the only way possible.

"So why don't they do that?" I asked Elemér.

"Because we can't yet," he replied. "The bourgeoisie's still too strong. The right historical moment hasn't come."

Initially, I more or less accepted that, but later, when I started reading the foreign affairs section of the newspapers more attentively, I started having alarming doubts. I could see that the Party (which for us always meant the Social Democrats) already held power in many countries—there were Social Democrat ministers and prime ministers, and yet everything remained the same.

"Why?" I asked Elemér.

"Because they haven't taken power yet," he replied.

"I don't understand," I said. "Why haven't they taken power, if they're in power?"

"Because the right historical moment hasn't come yet," came the eternal refrain.

No, I couldn't understand that at all. I suddenly dropped the scientific tone.

"Rubbish!" I said. "When's this historical moment goin' to come if not when they're in power?"

Elemér always avoided the question. He would say something like: "These are difficult questions. We're not there yet."

Or: "Don't bother with that for the moment. Get the basics straight first."

Well, basics or no basics, I just couldn't get this into my peasant's brain and I told him so. Elemér sometimes looked at me the way a doctor looks at a patient with worrying symptoms. At other times, I had the feeling that, deep down, he liked my questions, though for some reason he avoided them, and that confused me even more. You just can't tell with Pokerface, I thought.

I remember one debate we had in particular. He was talking about Mussolini, who was a demigod in Hungary at the time—even the democratically minded press kowtowed to him. Elemér said he was the arch-enemy of the workers' movement. He said he was a Judas who had betrayed the proletariat to the bourgeoisie, and that the Party had to focus all its energies on the fight against Fascism. I had just read how powerful the Party had been in Italy after the war, and I couldn't understand how they'd let Mussolini come to power.

"They didn't let him!" Elemér said. "The King appointed him, and they've got the guns."

That seemed clear enough; that I could understand. The argument only started when Germany came up. Elemér was saying that Hitler was even more dangerous than Mussolini, because if Fascism triumphed in Germany, then all Europe would turn Fascist and that was it for Socialism for the foreseeable future. Here was something else I couldn't understand at all.

"But there ain't no king in Prussia," I said. "The Party controls the police. Why don't they just take care of this Hitler?"

"Because Germany is a democracy," he replied, "and in a democracy, everyone's free to do as they like."

"But Hitler wants to do away with democracy, doesn't he?"

"Yes," he nodded.

"Well, then," I said, looking at him. "What are they waiting for? For him to go ahead and do away with them?"

Elemér grew a little tense.

"You've got to understand," he said, "that the rules of democracy guarantee full freedom for all political parties. It's not as simple as you think."

"'Course it is! Democracy or not, if someone wants to do away with my family, I shoot him like a dog. And whoever doesn't is either a coward, or stupid, or probably both."

Elemér wanted to avoid the question again, but I didn't let him. Finally, when I had really forced him into a corner, he said:

"Look, I don't agree with everything the Party says, either, but there isn't another workers' party in Hungary, and…" He suddenly left off, and I could see he was sorry about what he'd said.

Well, I thought, if that was all those wise gentlemen could come up with, I would stick to my peasant common sense, thank you very much. If they put me in charge of the Prussian police, I'd show them what to do with that Hitler and his movement.

I was back in the same place as when I had knocked the Browning out of Franciska's hand, but this time Elemér couldn't convince me he was right. All he'd accomplished was that I tried to avoid arguing with him, because I was afraid that if I proved too recalcitrant, he wouldn't bring me into the Party and that was more important to me than anything. For I was absolutely convinced that all I had to do was join the Party and I would soon take over leadership, the same way I had done at school.

That's how, over time, two distinct kinds of Socialism developed inside me. One of them was the one Elemér used to present to me, and the other the one I myself imagined. It was a strange sort of fantasy, chaotic and wonderful, crazy but beautiful. The childishly naive mixed with the instinct for good within me the way it only could in a sixteen-year-old peasant boy's imagination.

Elemér's moral doubts did not worry me at all. Power had to be seized, I told myself; as to how it was done, that didn't matter. War is war and all is fair in war. That there'd be blood? Yes, of course there would. In what war wasn't there? Thousands, tens of thousands, possibly hundreds of thousands would die, but millions had died in the wars the bourgeoisie had made. And for what? They told my father to kill the Italians because they were our worst enemies, and they told me to adore them, because they were our best friends. Sorry, patriots, there's been some mistake, forget what we told you before—all those bodies in Piave and Isonzo no longer count.

If you could send millions to the slaughter for "mistakes" like that, then why should I have moral doubts when we were fighting to ensure that "mistakes" like these were never made again? We were only at war with war in trying to topple this half-crazy world order that couldn't live without it. And when we won, we would create a classless society in which there would be no more rich and no more poor—only people who could at long last love their fellow human beings, because they won't have any more reason to hate them. Everyone would find their place in the world, every people and every person. There wouldn't be oppressors, and there wouldn't be oppressed, there wouldn't be luxury and there wouldn't be misery. We'd live simple, clean lives and pay for them with work instead of money. This obligatory daily work would take no more than five or six hours, and then—I told myself—everybody *can turn their attention to higher things*. There would still be competition—not to see who could be the most cunning in taking the bread out of the other's mouth, but rather who could do the best for the community. And there would still be wars, yes, but only against stupidity and evil, illness and death.

So why would I have had moral doubts? This end justified all means, even the most merciless. Anyone who shied away from *this* kind of war had no right to talk of morals. I thought of Petőfi:

> *And all of you are good for nought*
> *who won't die for your country, when you ought*

I would occasionally move myself to tears picturing my own death. I fell in the heat of battle, of course, beneath fluttering red flags on a dark and stormy night, just before the final victory. The whole city turned out for my funeral, the factory sirens hooted, traffic stopped.

"Pres-eeent arms!" came the order, and the red flags were lowered over my coffin.

I could see the workers' battalions standing to attention, I could hear the muffled mourning drums, I pictured my statue on the village square, and my grave, carved upon which were the words: *He died so liberty could live.*

But mostly I pictured myself alive. I could see Béla, the celebrated young soldier of the revolution; Béla, greying at the temples, a pillar of the classless society; and Béla the aged veteran wandering past old Rozi's house bending on his cane. The state would long since have taken over her house, the old woman having died well before of old age or revenge from the boys. But the boys there, the sons of this new world, would be standing at the gate, well fed in squeaky new shoes, whispering in awe as I passed.

"If it weren't for him," they'd say, "we'd still be little bastards—hungry, ragged, abandoned children that people called after on the street from behind the bushes."

No, no one would be calling after them from behind the bushes any more. Every single person in the world would be equal. That's how it'll be, and I'll make sure of it, I swore to myself. So help me God.

While this shameful world continued, humanity's true history could not begin. Humanity could not be humanity while it was fighting for such unworthy causes as its daily bread, its rent, its rags. Humanity's true history would begin when each person could "turn their attention to higher things", and their "eyes and their ears"—as I put it in one of my poems—"were opened to the miracles".

I was only interested in the class struggle and the revolution from this standpoint. I held both to be necessary evils that we had to have done with, the sooner the better. I'm not so young any more, I thought, I'm gone sixteen, how much longer did I have to deal with these anachronisms like, for example, capitalism? What would I say to my children? They would think of the period before the revolution the way we think of the heathens today, or prehistory. They'll be bored at school when they have to learn it, they'll find it ridiculous and unbelievable, and they'll look down on their ancestors who lived like this for centuries.

This imagined world now became for me reality. Reality itself seemed merely to be a kind of fleeting Carnival masquerade whose Ash Wednesday was just around the corner, when people would throw off their masks and costumes and head, finally, after the stars, like the Three Kings: towards the manger of peace, love and purity.

This was how "poetically" I pictured the future, this was how simple it all seemed to me. These were good days, and it's good to think back on them. I felt old, while the world was so young, barely past seventeen. The lilac bloomed in the winding streets of Buda, pianos played in the little single-storey houses, and the future seemed as fine and simple as "Für Elise".

15

MEANWHILE, MYSTERIOUS THINGS were happening at home. One night, when I came into the kitchen, my mother was standing in front of the mirror in a silk dress—yes, that's right, a *silk dress*, painting her mouth.

"Your father's taking me to the theatre!" she chirped. "You know, the one with the real live actors."

I don't know what I said to that, probably nothing. I knew that the theatre was an impossible dream even for well-paid workers, and that only ladies wore silk dresses. What had happened? Had they won the lottery? I wondered anxiously, because, to be honest, I had other suspicions.

I didn't dare ask any questions while my father was around, of course. Instead, I observed them in silence with a strange tightness in my stomach. My father, too, was dressed in brand-new clothes. He was wearing a beautiful blue suit, and you could see he hadn't bought it second-hand, the way people generally did in Újpest, or rather used to do, because they no longer had the money. Dressed like this, he looked even more handsome, even younger, even more attractive. He sat at the head of the table kicking his heels, and his fine, skirt-chasing blue eyes were filled with full-blooded good cheer. You could see he was pleased with both himself and the world. He was humming a fashionable little ditty and absently playing with his gold watch chain, because he was suddenly so well off he even had a gold chain for his watch.

My mother, it seems, must have guessed what I was thinking, because all at once she grew flustered. Recently, I always felt that she got flustered when we met, which was rarely enough. By the time I got home, they were out, and when they got back, I was deep asleep. Sometimes, half asleep, I could hear them coming and going in the room, but mostly they were just changing and would go out again soon after. Almost every evening they had an "engagement", as they put it, and that *was* how they put it, all fancy, though among ourselves we still spoke in our old peasant manner. And on the rare occasions they happened to be home, I hardly got a chance to talk to them because I would read for so long before going to sleep that I woke up late every evening and had to rush to make sure I wasn't late for work. Besides, we were all caught up with our own affairs. Me with the future and my mother with the present which—I now know—must have been as wonderful for her as the future was for me.

But at the time, I didn't think of that. When a child has to wear the kind of rags I did, he doesn't have too much compassion for his mother when she's in a silk dress. I was seized by an ugly, jealous rage. My own parents! I said to myself bitterly. There's a laugh. I looked like I could have been begging from them in the street.

Something similar must have occurred to my mother, too, for she now blushed.

"Mishka," she said suddenly, turning to my father, "could I take your brown suit and adjust it for the boy? You know, the one you don't wear no more."

"What the hell for?" my father asked chirpily. "I'll buy him a new one if he needs one." It was only now that he looked at me, and I could see that he was almost shocked. "Why you letting him go about looking like that?" he asked my mother indignantly, and I'm certain his outrage was genuine. But that was what he was like. He simply hadn't noticed until now how ragged his son looked. "You might've said something before!" he grumbled, and looked at my mother reproachfully.

"Before?" the word echoed inside me. Yes, it seems, this hadn't happened overnight. Looking back, I now realized that my mother hadn't mentioned the bottle of lye for some time, and that I had seen other signs of change, too, only… I hadn't noticed them. The future, that wonderful *Future* with its capital F, had occupied my thoughts so thoroughly that, like a horse with his blinkers, I could see only forward. As to the things that happened around me, I could see nothing; or if I did see it, I didn't take any notice.

I now started paying attention and grew more and more uneasy by the day. Where was all this money coming from? I wondered. My father's lifestyle hadn't changed, my mother was working less than before, and if they really had won the lottery, I'd have heard about that, by God!

One evening when my father wasn't home, I asked my mother straight out:

"Where's all this money coming from suddenly?"

"Where?" my mother looked at me. "Your father makes it."

"Doin' what?"

"Business."

"What sort of business?"

"Don't know. All sorts."

"Who's he working for?"

"No one. He does his own things."

"Does he keep a shop?"

"Oh, no, he ain't the type for that."

"An office, then?"

"'Course not."

"Then I don't understand," I said.

"What don't you understand?"

"The whole thing, to be honest. You either work for yourself or you work for other people. There's no third way."

My mother, it seems, had not considered that, because she looked somewhat taken aback. But then she shrugged and merely said:

"Well, this is how he does it. An' you can see for yourself he's doin' well."

That was the end of the conversation. It was past seven and I had to get to work. My mother was wearing yet another new dress. She was waiting for my father—they were off out.

I could feel that something wasn't right and tried to convince myself that everything was. Besides, I thought, what business was it of mine? They didn't spend too much time worrying about me.

I became as alienated from my mother as I had been when I was a little boy. I was sixteen and couldn't understand—how could I? I just watched with the mercilessness of youth, hostile and stunned. What had become of that sober, straightforward, decent woman? A few months ago, I used to laugh to myself whenever she tried to imitate my father's easy-going manner, but now, it was no longer a case of imitation. She learnt fast, scarily fast.

Once, I found her still in bed about noon, when I got home.

"You sick?"

"Not a bit of it!" my father replied for her. He himself was still only half dressed and just shaving. "We were out till dawn," he told me chirpily. "Only got home about six."

"And your father didn't let me go to work, either," my mother said, yawning, and sat up in bed. "Listen," she asked, "could you ring up that lady from the hotel?"

"Yes," I nodded. "What d'you want me to say?"

The lie she came up with was so complicated I was ashamed in advance of having to produce it. But in the end I didn't have to, because when the lady heard who was calling, she started screaming down the phone and didn't let me get a word in edgeways.

"That's the fourth time she's done this to me!" she yelled. "Well, there won't be a fifth. Understand? You can't treat me like that. That kind of woman isn't welcome in my house! You tell her that…"

I didn't hear the rest; I'd put the phone down.

When I told her about the conversation, my mother's expression changed for a few minutes and she was her old self again, the frightened, grave peasant woman I had known since my youth.

"You see!" she turned to my father. "Didn't I tell you?"

"So what?" laughed my father. "We had a good time. The hell with her, anyway!"

"Easy for you to say," complained my mother. "Soon I'll lose all my places."

"Don't worry about it." My father put down his razor and went, just as he was, half-shaved, and embraced my mother. "I won't have you working much longer, anyway," he said with a swagger, and started humming in her ear:

> *I'll build a room all in glass*
> *For my baby her time to pass*
> *On Friday, Saturday and Sunday.*

"Oh cut it out, you clown," said my mother, pushing him away, but as I went into the next room, I could hear her singing along.

Yes, she had completely lost her head. She was either singing or crying, and that is not poetic licence. If I didn't hear her singing in the kitchen, I would always notice afterwards that her eyes were red from crying. At first, I thought she was worried about the same things as me, but later I realized that there wasn't a bit of truth in that. She was wracked with jealousy. She had clearly realized something was going on—and who knows how many times these things had gone on before?

One evening, I woke to hear her sobbing, complaining to Márika in the kitchen. It must have been about a woman, because Márika kept comforting her that:

"He'll get bored of her too. He got bored of all the rest. You're the one he really loves, after all."

"Yes," muttered my mother bitterly. "Me and the whole rest of the female sex."

She said that, but you could hear in her voice that she didn't believe what she was saying, though there was a lot of truth in it. Fortunately, not even she realized just how much. Sometimes I had the feeling that my father really was, in the strictest sense, in love with the whole female sex, and as passionately, to boot, as most men love only a single woman. He couldn't pass a woman without making sure there was some physical contact, even if only the slightest. If he couldn't do better, he'd grab their hands on the pretext of shaking hands, but he grabbed plenty of other things, too—mostly other things, in fact, and he couldn't contain himself even in front of me. The extraordinary thing was that he was not only interested in the young and the beautiful. I saw him with women whom perhaps no one, aside from him, had ever wooed. Even if they were too young or too old, if they wore a skirt, Dappermishka wanted to know what was under it. To be fair, it wasn't too hard for him—women were crazy about him. He had, it seems, some overarching masculine charm that women found impossible to resist—especially my mother.

Now I understand her, of course I do. Dappermishka was the kind of man a woman would follow into the depths of hell if she was curious about heaven. How strange women are! I thought at the time, but now—past sixteen—I know that they're not so strange at all. Because like it or not, in life you have to know what you're doing, and it stands to reason that the only people who really know what they're doing when it comes to love are people like Dappermishka, for whom it's a full-time occupation. Other men can be perfectly wonderful, outstanding husbands and exemplary fathers, but when it comes to love they will forever remain amateurs, and wherever possible, of course, it's best to turn to a professional. It's a hard truth, I know, but it's true nonetheless and there's nothing I can do about it. I know it's the amateurs that shed the real tears, but it's not what the public's looking for. They need an actor, an honest-to-God actor, and a real actor always plays a part: they know the method and impact of their work. But it's still of them that people will say: "That's an evening I'll never forget."

Dappermishka was just such a player. Yet I can say, and I'd be lying if I said any different, that my mother couldn't have hoped for a better husband. "Husband" is, of course, an exaggeration in this case—and not only in a legal sense—since I for one have never seen a husband be as attentive, good and affectionate to his wife as Dappermishka was to my mother. Where he got to during the day, and what he got up to, I don't know, though it's more than likely that he was quite a long way off the straight and narrow, but it was always my mother he took out in the evening, and he took her out the way a lover takes his sweetheart. He showered her with compliments and gifts, treated her like the apple of his eye and demanded that others do the same. Is it any wonder, then, that this poor woman lost her head, this woman whom everyone, throughout her life, had always treated like a rag? Now they were handling her with kid gloves because everyone was scared of Dappermishka's famous fists; and they knew he pulled no punches when it came to his woman.

Once, I remember, my mother had complained in tears that an Andrássy út lawyer (a nobleman with two titles to his name) had called her a thief because his shirt had apparently gone missing in the wash. My father pretended not to have heard, but afterwards, he went over to Andrássy út and gave the aristocratic lawyer the beating of his life. My mother only found out about the whole thing when the summons came—because the lawyer was suing my father for grievous bodily harm.

I was at the hearing. I had a day off and my father told me he'd take me shopping for a suit afterwards.

"And besides," he said, "it don't hurt to know your way around these situations. In life, you have to know how to handle women and judges. Besides, it'll be a laugh, you won't be bored."

It was, indeed, a laugh. The lawyer wasn't doing too well in the way of witnesses because my father, it turned out, had staked him out early in the morning when there was no one in the office and thrashed him one-to-one. His assistant and the secretary, who arrived only after my father had left, could only state that the office was "in a terrible state", that there were signs of a struggle, and that the lawyer had shown them his injuries. As to where he'd got those injuries, of course, they couldn't say, and since the lawyer had no proof other than the doctor's report, my father could have easily won if he'd denied everything. Three out of four "respectable" people would have done so, but the roguish Dappermishka did not. Why not? It seems it wouldn't have been enough of a "laugh" for him; he was an actor through and through, and he wanted a chance to perform. You could see he was preparing for his role, and I have to say he gave a sterling performance. He stood before the judge the very figure of upstanding decency, the model citizen, the famous "simple, God-fearing Hungarian" you heard so much about back in those days. He gave a speech that went something like this:

"Your Honour! I'm a simple man, but even I know the law won't convict you without proof. But I hold justice even higher than the law, so I'll tell you plain and simple that I did give that man a beating, and a terrific one at that. I'm sorry that, in doing so, I was forced to break the law, but since—as I say—I hold justice even higher than the law, I'll tell you straight that if he was to go around insulting my wife again, I'd do the same all over. Because, Your Honour," he said, his voice hitting a sudden crescendo, "the kind of man that don't stand up for his woman is the kind of man that don't stand up for his country, and I'm the kind of man that stands up for both, and if you need proof, you have before you a plaintiff with a face full of bruises and these here medals." He laid out three medals for bravery (one of them gold) in front of the judge.

The lawyer interrupted sardonically:

"That woman isn't even your wife!"

"I'd stand up for your wife, and all!" my father retorted. "Because *I'm* a God-fearing Hungarian, and a God-fearing Hungarian will stand up for every woman. And anyone who won't," he shrugged with a smile, "is the kind of 'man' the plaintiff is."

The audience began to giggle, and the judge called them to order twice, but I deeply suspect he was tempted to laugh right along with them. Yes, Dappermishka was playing his part well—he had already made his opponent ridiculous.

But the best was still to come. The judge asked the lawyer if he really had called my mother a thief. The lawyer denied it furiously, but his maid, whom my father had called as a witness, swore that he had indeed called her a thief, though the shirt had later turned up. This the lawyer admitted, but continued to protest the word "thief".

"How do you know what I said to the laundrywoman?" he snapped at the maid. "You weren't even there when the whole thing happened."

"Weren't there?" said the pretty maid. "You trying to say I'm lying? You'd better watch it, sir, 'cause I've got a fiancé too!"

There was loud laughter.

"Silence!" cried the judge, but you could see he was on my father's side.

In the interests of historical accuracy, I should say that from a conversation I happened later to overhear, I found out that the maid really had *not* been present when the argument took place. As to why she swore to the opposite and sacrificed her position to do so, I don't know, but it's also best not to ask. The fact is that my father had "talked" with her ahead of time.

In the end, thanks to the "attenuating circumstances", he got off with a fine of just a few pengős, which made my father very angry, but not on account of the money. Something else was bothering him.

"If I'd known the whole thing was going to be this cheap," he told me when we were finally alone, "I'd have bashed his brains in, so help me God."

Then he did an impression of the judge, the lawyer, and above all himself in the role of the "God-fearing Hungarian" that had my mother and me in stitches. I've met a lot of people who could do impressions of other people since then, but no one, not anywhere, ever, who could do such a merciless impression of themselves.

As for the clothes shopping, it didn't happen. My father bumped into an old acquaintance on the way and was so pleased to see him he left me simply standing there. He merely called back to me from the corner and said:

"We'll get that suit on your next day off!"

But we didn't get it on my next day off, either; we never did. He had a good heart, but a terrible memory. When he was with me, I think he would have done anything for me, but when he wasn't, he may very well have forgotten that I existed at all. Besides, my next day off happened to be a Sunday, and then after that he had something to take care of, or I did, and somehow something always got in the way. When we did meet from time to time, he would ask:

"When we going to get that suit, then?"

"On my next day off," I'd reply, but on my next day off something would always come up.

In the end, he stopped bringing it up. To be fair, I was also partly to blame. I felt very alienated from him in those days, especially from his money. I dare say the suit, had he actually bought it, would have given me great pleasure, but when it came to saying something, to bringing it up, to *asking* for it, I wasn't going to go that far.

So, over time, we forgot about the whole thing. My mother who, God knows why, had also forgotten about it, one day really did "adjust" his old brown suit for me, and I felt elegant enough in that, though I must have looked quite ridiculous. For her "adjustments" consisted of taking up the sleeves and hems, which—of course—did not change the cut of the suit at all. You could have got two of me into it.

That said, my father loved to give, and did give plenty... when he didn't forget. Once, when my mother asked him for money, it turned out he didn't have a bean.

"I met poor Jóska on the stairs," he told my mother, "an' he told me the trouble he's in."

"How much did you give him?"

"Don't know. Whatever I had in my pockets."

"You didn't even check?"

"No, ma'am."

"You want your head examined, you do. Why d'you keep doing things like that?"

"Why?" my father shrugged, laughing. "It's just my nature."

I remember another occasion that was typical not only of my father, but of Hungary at the time.

One evening, my mother came up from the laundry room laughing.

"That Márika!" she said, but had to stop there, she was laughing so hard.

"What's happened to her now?" asked my father, because something was always happening to Márika.

"See for yourself!" my mother replied, pointing out of the window. "She's got quite an audience."

We all looked out. The "audience" was gathered on the first-floor walkway; about a dozen ladies were standing around Márika, who was talking away, nineteen to the dozen.

"Her and Rózsi havin' a fight?" my father asked, because that was how it looked from here.

"'Course not. She's bargaining."

"What for?"

"Rózsi's baby carriage."

"How come?" my father asked in surprise. "She in the family way?"

"'Course not," my mother said, with a dismissive wave of the arm, and laughed again. "But Árpád's finishing his apprenticeship on Saturday and she's going about tellin' the whole house how they're going to go and make a baby right away. They've got his birthday all planned out, and they've given him a name and everything. He's going to be Árpád, too."

"What'll they do if it's a girl?"

"That's just it!" giggled my mother. "She says it won't be a girl, because them scientists have figured out some way to make sure. Árpád got it from a book."

"And? How d'you make sure?"

My mother was embarrassed to say in front of me, but my father laughed at her for it.

387

"You don't have to worry about him," he said. "He don't believe in the stork any more, anyway. Out with it, what's this scientific method, then?"

"Well that you," my mother was flustered, she had to reach for the words, "you... she says you... um... that if in the *moment* it's better for the man, it'll be a girl, and if it's better for the woman, it'll be a boy. And that Saturday night, Árpád's going to do it so it's better for Márika."

"Easier said than done!" my father teased. "Judging by that slip of a man, my money's on it bein' a girl."

"Don't be so mean," my mother told him, but she, too, giggled to herself.

Downstairs, the "audience" was still around. Márika just wouldn't shut up.

"She hagglin' about the price?" asked my father.

"Nah, they'll have agreed on that by now. She'll pay in instalments, a pengő a month for nine months. Trouble is, Rózsi don't want to give it to her till she's put down five pengős. And Márika wants it now."

"What the hell for?"

"Just to look at, she says. She wants to picture little Árpád in it, 'cause she thinks it'll be easier then, poor thing. Because, you know, she's so crazy about that little boy that ain't even been conceived in her yet, the waiting's nearly killin' her."

My father didn't say anything for some time, just watched Márika with a smile. Then he said:

"Nine pengős is too much for that pram. I'll get her one for half that, and she can have it right away. Go tell her."

"No chance," my mother protested. "Don't you go doin' something crazy again. That poor woman is going crazy for that pram, and you'd forget about it in half an hour."

"I won't forget," insisted my father, and indeed, he didn't.

The next day, he brought Márika a baby carriage—as a present. It wasn't a used one like Rózsi's, and not a cheap baby carriage, either. It was a refined, upper-class little carriage, and it must have cost a fortune.

"Oh my God!" wailed my mother. "How much did you spend on that?"

"Six days," my father said. "The seventh was free."

We never found out how much it cost. It remained a secret, like everything about my father.

On Saturday night, we all went down to give it to Márika and Árpád. My mother and I went ahead while my father stayed back with the pram, for effect. We were expecting a great to-do, but what we saw when we got there had nothing festive about it at all. Márika's face was swollen with tears, and Árpád was blinking behind his thick glasses like a cat in a thunderstorm. We didn't ask what was going on out of politeness, and pretended not to have noticed anything.

"Evenin'," we said.

"Evenin'," they said.

Then there was silence. I thought they might have had a bit of a fight, as married couples sometimes do, but that the surprise would cheer them up. But when my father wheeled the pram in, neither of them so much as looked at it.

"You needn't've bothered," Márika said. "We don't need a pram."

"Don't need it?" my father looked at her, astounded. "Why not?"

Márika's eyes welled up with tears.

"What for, if there ain't no one to put in it?"

"What you talkin' about?" my mother asked, bewildered.

Márika threw herself onto the couch and started weeping and moaning.

"There ain't going to be no little Árpád!" she bawled. "No little Árpád!"

"Did the doctor say so?"

"'Course not."

"Well then?"

"The printer's!"

"What d'you mean, the printer's? Didn't Árpád finish his apprenticeship?"

"Yes, but they fired him the second he did, damn the lot of 'em."

"Why?"

"Because they'd have had to pay him a decent wage now, that's why. And they didn't want *that*, the bastards."

There was silence. What was there to say? We knew what this meant. My father looked at Árpád.

"But they liked you so well!"

"Liked me!" Árpád shrugged. "As if that means anything these days. Your bourgeois is just a bourgeois, all they care about is money. They took a kid on in my place, and gave my work to the oldest of the apprentices. That's how it is now, everywhere. I'm not the only one."

"And we'd decided on his birthday and everything!" Márika sniffed. "Oh God, what about his birthday?"

"He'll get a job elsewhere," my mother said, trying to console her. "Won't you, Árpád?"

"Of course," he nodded, but his voice lacked conviction.

"Get a job, in this day and age!" Márika grumbled, her bitterness bursting out of her. "I'm no Commernist, but as far as I'm concerned they can go and hang every last one of them bourgeois. Bunch of murderers, fit for hangin'! Murderers, murderers, murderers!"

"Stop shouting," Árpád scolded quietly. "You know Herr Hausmeister's a stooge."

"To hell with Herr Hausmeister!" Márika screamed at the top of her lungs. "To hell with the whole world!"

My mother sat beside her and put her arm around her shoulders.

"There, there," she said, comforting her like a child. "Calm down and think it over. It ain't the end of the world. Ain't you even going to have a look at the pram?"

She took her over to the pram, at the sight of which Márika's face transformed miraculously.

"It's brand new!" she cried. "And it's so beautiful! My God, I ain't never seen anything so pretty. And it's got brakes and everything…" Her voice suddenly grew sober. "How much is it?" she asked suspiciously.

"Free," replied my father. "It's a gift."

"Gift?"

Márika's mouth hung open, and then something happened that I've read a lot about but never believed existed: she started laughing and crying at the same time.

"Thank you!" she said, throwing herself around my mother's neck.

Then she started thanking my father and finally, she even came and hugged me.

"It's even got his name on it," my father pointed out.

"His name?" Márika asked, amazed. "Where?"

"There."

Márika had clearly never seen anything like it. She knelt down in front of the pram and read out the sparkling metal letters:

"Á-r-p-á-d." Suddenly, she was crying again. "Oh, little Árpád, what have they done to you? What about your birthday?"

She pressed her head frantically to little Árpád's pillow as we stood around the fine, melancholy pram the way people usually stand around the open grave at a funeral. I've never seen a sadder baby carriage than that one, with a young woman robbed of motherhood wailing in it instead of her baby.

Yes, that was what became of the festivities. The next day, I saw that Márika had pulled the little table away from the window and put the baby carriage in its place. There it stood in pride of place; I saw it every day when I walked past their window. Meanwhile, Árpád would ride into town every day, pedalling all day long, but all that did was wear out his tyres—work he did not find. One day they sold the fine old couch I had admired so often, and all the other furniture in turn. In the end, there was barely anything left besides the bed, but the baby carriage still stood there in the window. Márika would not hear of selling it.

She became obsessed with little Árpád. One day, when they no longer had so much as a crust to eat, she told Árpád that, come what may, she wanted that child—she didn't care about the rest. Árpád tried to make her see that she had no right, that she couldn't take responsibility for the child, but much good did it do him. It escalated into the hell of an argument. Márika was screaming so loud she roused the whole house. The next day, she did admit that Árpád was right, but the day after that, she found another reason to fight with him, and that's how it was from then on. The rosy peasant flush left her cheeks and she grew stiff and thin. She became common, vulgar and querulous.

One evening, when I was just getting ready to leave for the hotel, she came charging over to ours like a woman possessed.

"Look at him!" she screamed, pointing out of the window. "He's off to sell my baby carriage!"

Poor Árpád really was taking the carriage to sell it. I've never seen anyone pushing a pram so miserably.

"You've got to stop him!" Márika pleaded. "He's got no right! Thief!"

"Leave him alone," said my mother, trying to calm her. "It's hard enough for him as it is."

"I won't let him!" Márika screamed full force and made to run after Árpád. My mother held her back, dragged her into the kitchen and locked the door behind her.

Márika threw herself onto the floor and sobbed, kicked and screamed, shaking her fists as if she'd lost her mind.

"They're killin' my baby! Murderers! Murderers! Murderers!"

I could still hear her hysterical shouting in the bar, and my hands clenched into fists, like hers, whenever I saw the people dancing. Murderers! I echoed.

But then I grew ashamed. What right did I have to accuse them? Every day the papers wrote about the thousands of children dying in China, and what did I feel about that? Nothing. That was the truth. Dreadful, I'd say, and turn the page. If someone came and asked me whether it was forty or four hundred thousand children who'd starved to death in China, I wouldn't be able to say. It was all meaningless. Numbers that said nothing, that were as far from my heart as China itself and could never shock me as much as that single Hungarian child who'd never even been conceived.

Such is man. So limited, so miserable. That is what *they* build on, that's what makes them so strong and immovable. They're building on a solid bedrock: human stupidity. We ought to make gangs of these poor, miserable mothers, the Chinese and the Hungarian, and the others too, all of them, every one, so they could shout together into this deaf world's ears until everyone's hands clenched into fists:

"Murderers! Murderers! Murderers!"

16

THERE WAS ONE NIGHT OF THE WEEK that was unlike the others. It was a strange night, hard to describe. Even in the very moment of waking, I was seized by a physical sense of excitement at knowing that that night I was free, and could do whatever I wanted until tomorrow evening. Perhaps tonight, I thought obsessively, and stretched like a rooftop tomcat. I was naked, the summer evening was peeking in through the window, and the scent of the lilacs drifted up, even here to the third floor. At these moments, there was no one home. I would potter sleepily, move things to and fro, wash with needling scrupulousness and take a good look at myself in the mirror.

Everything was still so fine. I stood in front of the mirror and thought of those many thousands of women who were also standing before the mirror, prettying themselves up, getting ready; maybe one of them was doing it for me. What's she like? I wondered, staring into the mirror longingly, as if I could see her there. These were the finest moments of all. Everything was still possible then, and anything could happen.

I dressed like someone getting ready for a very special, very important event, though I didn't know myself *what*. I had no one in the world, not even a mangy dog out there waiting for me, and I had no idea where I was meant to go. I had a date with fortune; I was waiting for my Great Adventure, that particular Fateful Encounter.

I boarded the tram feeling that "something would happen". God knows what I had in mind. Maybe a *miracle* would get on at the next stop and "something would happen" that had never happened before. Needless to say, nothing happened. The suburban tram trundled sleepily along, peopled by the poor, not *miracles*. Tired working-class girls dozed on the hard wooden benches. They were coming home from work, and on their care-worn faces, you could see that at the very most they were dreaming of a square meal, if they dreamt at all. No, there are no miracles between Újpest and Nyugati railway station.

I got off at the last stop and wandered aimlessly around the city. I looked at the women as if I really *was* waiting for someone, a very specific someone, and was afraid of missing her among the crowd. Occasionally, I would stop in front of an advertising column, where young lovers would arrange to meet, and pretend that I, too, had a rendezvous—don't ask me why. I don't know. I just stood there and waited. There was an electric clock on top of the column and I watched the hand jumping ahead and tried to look impatient like those happy lovers who get to wait and agonize.

Sometimes I would spot a girl across the street and follow her. Something drew me like a magnet, something set my fantasy alight. Women are so beautiful from afar, and looking at them like that, from behind, the imagination runs wild. Maybe it's her, I thought. Yes, maybe she's the one. I would follow her for some time, and then… turn away; though some were pretty, and some even looked at me invitingly, but… I don't know. All of a sudden, I just didn't want them.

I was thinking of *her*. I imagined what it would be like if she came walking down the street, right now, and… Make-believe! I told myself. First of all, she never goes anywhere on foot. And even if she did, and we met, then what? Nothing. I would say hello, she'd say hello back, and then move on. I went through all that clearly, rationally, in my mind, and then I went back to daydreaming about what would happen if she *did* come walking down the street…

"Oh, is that you, András?" she'd say, flicking the end of my nose playfully with her gloved hand. "Where are you off to?"

"The cinema."

"Oh, really? That's where I'm going, too."

I'd say nothing. We'd be standing very close to one another, and I could smell that exotic, bitter perfume, her red hair glinting in the light.

"Would you care to come with me?" she'd ask. "I'm going to the UFA."

The UFA was the best cinema in Budapest at the time. That's where I would usually end up, though it was expensive, at least by my standards. The cheapest seats, in the first two rows, were eighty fillérs.

In a cinema in the suburbs, I could almost have got a box for the same money, but of course those were only little fleapits, whereas here I could, in principle, have even bumped into *her*, and people will do many things for their principles—even, sometimes, die for them.

Besides, the UFA was amazing. On warm summer nights like these, the roof of the cinema would slide open soundlessly so that you found yourself, suddenly, beneath the sky. I sat there underneath the stars and waited for the *miracle*. But you know how it goes. The pretty women always sit somewhere else. I would end up beside a fat old crone who smelt of mice and breathed heavily, or at best a very young girl pressed tightly to her beau. As if I didn't have enough trouble. The film was always some German mush—cheap, sickly, and affected—and often I would leave before the end. I thought of Elemér, who had explained more than once that the cinema was just another form of numbing opiate the bourgeoisie stuffed into the pipes of the proletariat so they would never wake up to reality. He's right, I would think guiltily then, and head angrily home to study Socialism.

But one time, I did indeed have an adventure. She came and sat beside me mid-performance. They were playing a woeful sentimental German melody. She came into my life to a musical accompaniment, if you will, like the prima donna in an opera. She was young, she was blonde, and she seemed beautiful in the dark. My arm began a careful conversation with hers, and by the end of the performance, I was holding her hand. God how exciting holding someone's hand in the dark can be when you're sixteen, and as passionate a sixteen-year-old as I was! There was music, there was darkness, they were kissing up on screen, and the stars winked above us. The whole thing was as unreal as the film they were showing, and so fine, so much finer!

Here was my Fateful Encounter, my long-awaited Great Adventure… until they put the lights on.

She wasn't ugly. She was quite a pretty girl, in fact, but… so different to the way I had imagined her in the dark. Suddenly, I didn't want her.

"Can I walk you home?" I asked.

"No," she replied with a blush, wobbling her head like a bird.

"Why not?"

"Because."

I started begging, but in vain.

"Anyway, I ain't going home," she said at last. She drew her mouth tight in an affected way and kept wobbling her head as she talked. "I'm meetin' someone."

That made me angry. That was women for you.

"I see. I shan't disturb you any longer, then," I said curtly.

She didn't move.

"It's a nice evenin'," she said. "Proper summer. I wonder what time it is?"

"Midnight."

"D'you want to get a coffee?"

"I thought you said you were meeting someone."

She started to giggle.

"Oh, I was just sayin' that."

"Why?"

"Because I don't let strangers take me out, if you must know."

"Am I really such a stranger?" I asked sentimentally, but all the while I was thinking of poor Gyula and his Mysterious Woman, whom he had met in much the same way one night. She must be quite a piece of work, too, I thought. Getting touchy-feely with strangers in the dark and going to cafés at midnight. "Why aren't you sayin' anything?" I continued, just as sentimentally.

"Don't ask so many questions," she said. "You'll get old before your time. So, you want to go to a caff or not?"

Caff! What a word. I bet she's got syphilis, too.

"I'm sorry, but I really *am* meeting someone," I said. "How about tomorrow?"

"I told you I don't let strangers take me out!"

There was an edge to her voice now, and she turned away moodily. I didn't say anything. We were still standing in front of the UFA. The crowd was starting to disperse, the lights had gone off in the cinema.

"You're a strange one," she said after a while.

"Why?"

"Because."

All this back and forth was irritating me.

"So when can I see you?"

She didn't reply; I could see she wanted me to keep asking. So I didn't. We were now alone in front of the darkened cinema. Workers came out from inside with ladders and tools to put up the advertisement for the latest film above the entrance. The girl looked at the big colourful poster.

"Looks good," she said. "I'm goin' to come and see it."

"When?"

"None of your business," she said, flashing her eyes at me flirtatiously, and looking back up at the poster. "Tomorrow, I think," she said, as if by the by.

"What time?"

"Ten."

"Here, in front of the cinema?"

"Oh, you're so pushy!" she snapped. Then she said, "Make it quarter to."

"All right," I nodded, though I knew, of course, that at quarter to ten I wouldn't be here at all—I'd be in the hotel's bar.

I was glad when I finally got rid of her, but by the time the tram got to Újpest, I was sorry I hadn't gone with her. The "caff" may not, after all, have cost very much, and afterwards we might have ended up in the Mauthner. Margit Island was not so far from the UFA, we could have walked out there, with "a little chat, a little food, a little this and that", and then there on the island, among the ruins... I wanted to hit myself. Who was I waiting for, anyway? The fairy queen? Now I had to go home all by myself. Damn it all!

I determined to buy a condom the very next day, and be wiser next time. But I didn't buy the condom next day and was no wiser the next time. I was waiting, once more, for my Great Adventure, that Fateful Encounter, and ended up skulking off home to study Socialism again.

I slept barely three or four hours at such times because Manci was usually home by seven and I didn't want to bump into her. It did happen, it's true, that she was out for days at a time, but you never knew when that would be, and I was still very much conscious of those two terrible weeks when I would check, trembling, every half-hour, if there were any "signs". So I went to the hotel instead and accompanied Elemér to police headquarters.

It went on like this for weeks. Then the time came when I could no longer even read. I would struggle over a book for hours, doggedly devouring the letters, but digest them I could not. In the end, I switched off the lamp, lay down and tried to sleep, but I would just end up tossing and turning in the dark, and needless to say my mind was not on Karl Marx. The images kept coming back again and again, like the chorus of a song: the dusky bedroom... the bed... the nightgown... the steamy bathroom. *Her* adjusting her stockings in the lift and there being nothing else above for a long, long way, save for that electrifying whiteness and the possibility that she wasn't wearing anything at all, not even drawers. Or her sitting in bed, leaning over breakfast with her breasts peeking whitely out of her nightgown as it fell forward, knowing I could see and not pulling up the covers.

"What a handsome boy!"

"Isn't he?"

And then the *previous* András again and again, with whom she'd apparently had an affair, only by the time it passed midnight, I'd dropped all pretence of "apparently". If she'd been with him, why not me? After all, she'd even called to me once; I could still hear her voice:

"András... is that you?"

Oh, if I hadn't been so foolish then, I would have gone in there, and...

That's how it always started and the most shameful thing was that by three in the morning, I was no longer thinking of *her* at all—anyone would have done, *anyone*, even Manci. I would decide to wait for *her* again and again, but by the time it grew light I'd sobered up. Surely I wasn't going to ruin my life for a single hour? Sleepily, my head pounding, I would scrape myself together and go talk Socialism with Elemér.

Then one morning, I didn't go. I dreamt that I was with Manci, but she had red hair and slightly slanted grey eyes, and then it was no longer Manci at all, but *her*, and then Manci after all, and everything happened the way it had that morning when I came home drunk. It was past seven when I started from my dream. It's too late to get up now, I thought. If she comes home, she'll find me here anyway, and if not, then what was the point of getting up? Besides, it was hardly likely she'd come home, it was past seven. But if she did come home, and if it happened to work out that way... After all, I hadn't caught anything last time.

She did come home, and it did work out that way. Afterwards, I was scared and revolted again and swore never again. But I didn't catch anything this time, either, and on my next day off, I waited for her again. I was scared and revolted, and then the week after... It started all over again.

And then one day I did buy the condom, and from then on I wasn't scared. I did feel revulsion, it's true, but it was a different kind of revulsion. It was a grown-up revulsion, a wise revulsion: I knew that by the end of the week, I would stop feeling it again.

There was an assistant porter at the hotel who'd got malaria in the war. His illness kept coming back from time to time, but the assistant porter was no longer scared—he'd got used to it, like a dog to barking.

"Oh dear," he'd say two days before, "here comes the fever!"

He went home, lay down, took his medication, and then a few days later he was back at his post as if nothing had happened.

It's the same with physical desire, I thought. It keeps coming back like malaria. And if, towards the end of the week, I couldn't get to sleep, I too could say to myself:

"Oh dear, here comes the fever!"

But I was no longer frightened of it now, either. I had got used to it and knew the cure. I was no longer a child. I was a man: I was wise and low-down. I slept with Manci once a week, and the next day I was back at my post as if nothing had happened.

The regularity of this life calmed me. I could read again, sleep again, and the misty sensation of guilt slowly evaporated out of me. I can still be a good Socialist, I reassured myself. After all, Manci, too, was working class, and, when you thought about it, a victim of the bourgeoisie.

Her Excellency, of course, did not fit so comfortably into the "Socialist world view". I tried not to think of her, and I more or less managed... for six days. On the seventh, lying in Manci's bed, what had happened that first, drunken morning always happened again, with frightening regularity. It began with Manci asking about her, but later I talked about her even when she didn't ask. She was always with us, and Manci looked more and more like her from week to week, after I'd turned out the lights. There were moments—dark, sick, insanely beautiful moments—when Manci no longer even existed: only her, her, *her*! Every week, once a week, I slept with a woman I hadn't seen in four months.

And then one night she came into the bar.

17

THERE WAS A HEATWAVE, it was the depths of low season, only a few people were still hanging around the bar. The jazz band took half-hour breaks, the waiters played blackjack in the kitchen. The porter, too, was playing blackjack; I was replacing him on the door. There was a warm, hazy rain, the air was suffocating. It must have been about two. I was listening dozily to the drumming of the rain, nodding off for minutes on end.

And then suddenly there was her car before the door. There were four people in it: her, Whitewash, the oyster-faced Viennese armaments manufacturer and a man I'd never seen before. They greeted me loudly, in a tipsy cheer, when I opened the door of the car. They must have been out partying already—they were all drunk.

She recognized me.

"Oh, is that you, András?" she said in that high voice of hers. "How are you?"

"Fine, thank you, Your Excellency."

She must have had a lot to drink, too. She was lounging sleepily in her seat, but in her eyes all the Devil's bastard children were at play. She was beautiful like this, with her hair loose, carefree, and excited from the alcohol. I had never seen her like this. My heart beat fast.

Scarecrow and the arms manufacturer got out first. I held the giant umbrella over them, took them to the door, and hurried back to the car. The unknown man was whispering a story into her ear, and she laughed a loud, trilling laugh.

I had to wait. The rain drummed on the umbrella, I could feel my knees trembling. Who was this man?

"Wait for the Deputy," she said to the driver, "and then you can go home."

They finally got out. She grabbed on to me under the umbrella, the parliamentarian on the other side of me. He was wearing a top hat, so I had to lift the umbrella high, but that meant that the rain fell on the lady.

"Hold it lower!" she said, and as I drew the umbrella down, I knocked off the Deputy's hat.

The wind caught the top hat and the Deputy had to run after it, because the lady was dragging me in towards the entrance. I was already opening the door for her when the man caught up with us, muddy top hat in hand.

"Idiot!" he snapped at me softly, and gave me an almighty slap.

It was so unexpected that by the time I realized what had happened, they were gone. I was furious. I was going to beat him to a pulp, right before her eyes, I decided, but at the same time, the sober peasant inside me said: No you won't. They'd kick you out, blacklist you, and in the end you couldn't even give him a real beating. The staff would intervene to protect him, and then the state, the law and the whole wide world, and who would be on your side? They'd drag you down to the police station, beat you unconscious again with the butt of their guns, throw you in a cell, send you to the reformatory, because you're just a penniless boy and they can do with you whatever they want. No they can't! rebelled my pride, but all the while I knew full well they could, and my helplessness just made me angrier. Then I felt something warm on my face.

I touched it—it was blood. At the sight of the blood, I lost what little common sense I still had left. It was my father's blood, a thick, dangerous blood, and my mother's peasant good sense was no good any more. I could feel that I was going to do something anyone in their right minds would never do, but as to what, I wasn't sure.

"I'll pay their price," I mumbled, the anger coursing inside me as if the Devil himself were spurring it on.

Suddenly, I heard someone calling my name. It was the head waiter. I went in. He looked at me as if I'd run away with the hotel funds. He was a butlerish, bald, stocky man, a real "bicyclist" by nature, as Elemér would say. He kicked down and kissed up, and I—of course—was beneath him, right down under the sole of his shoe. He grabbed my sleeve roughly and drew me aside into a corner.

"What happened?" he hissed.

I told him. He shook his head as he listened; that he wasn't shaking it on account of the slap was perfectly clear to me.

"I'll deal with you later," he said ominously. "But for now go have a wash and get yourself to the bar. The Deputy wants to see you."

I should have gone, but I didn't move. I wanted to say something, but I didn't know what. I was trembling with anger.

"Frightened?" he grinned, showing his false teeth.

"Not a bit," I snapped. "I'd have gone to see him even without his calling me. No one goes around slapping *me*."

"Cut it out!" he growled at me softly. "You'll be lucky if that slap is all you get. Or don't you know who it was that slapped you?"

No, I didn't know. The head waiter told me, and manliness or no manliness, when I heard the name, I trembled. It was a terrifying name, and not just for me. For the Deputy, before he became a member of parliament, had been a professional murderer: one of the most blood-thirsty ringleaders of the White Terror. He murdered—and had others murder—innocent people by the hundreds, with Miklós Horthy, the Regent, Admiral, Supreme Warlord and Royal Hungarian Lord God Almighty's highest blessing. He went after Communists and Jews, but as to who was a Communist or Jew, he himself decided; on the basis, what's more, of how people paid—at least, that's what they used to say in our village. For he'd been active down our way too: he'd made two hundred people dig their own graves in the nearby forest, and he'd buried more than one of them alive. We children had avoided the forest even eight years later, because the villagers said invisible ghosts inhabited the trees, though by then they had long cleared away those two hundred graves, and besides we had had our "consolidation", in case you didn't know, which—in less elevated language—meant simply that the country had grown so weak from the blood it had lost in the war and three subsequent revolutions that there was no more need for such extrajudicial killings. We became a fine and civilized country, where people—rare though they were—who dared open their mouths were killed *with* the full blessing of the law. Their trials were held in public, and so that they couldn't complain of mistreatment, our esteemed parliament had voted—both chambers—to legalize caning in such cases. With this judicially sanctioned caning, they could beat the accused until he signed a confession for which they could "legally" hang him. It was no empty boast of Horthy's, later, that Hitler and Mussolini had learnt at his knee. He really had been ahead of both, and the all-powerful British and French statesmen at the time who treated the representatives of democratic Hungary like mangy dogs were just as friendly with him as they later were with Hitler and Mussolini. And the murderers to whom he owed his position got, instead of the rope, cushy, comfortable jobs; that was how this man, too, had become a member of parliament. In a secret ballot, he'd never have got ten votes, but in our "consolidated" country, they used to write, beside each peasant's name, who they'd voted for and so even widows ended up "voting" for the man who'd murdered their husbands, for fear that if they didn't, the candidate might come and kill their children, too. To cut a long story short, I'd really gone and picked my man.

"What's he want from me?" I asked the head waiter.

"Well, I don't think he wants to whisper sweet nothings in your ear," he replied and flashed his false teeth once more. "All I'm saying is, keep your mouth shut if you know what's good for you, and do as he says. Well, go on, then!"

I went to the toilets and washed the blood off. As I was wiping my face before the sink, I suddenly saw my position completely clearly. Yes, the Deputy did not want to see me to whisper sweet nothings, and the Major would certainly not be on my side. Either way, then, my time here was up; but instead of getting downhearted, I felt strangely relieved. At least I had nothing left to lose. I was free as a bird, and could shit on whoever I wanted. I was almost glad that things had turned out this way. Come what may, I told myself, one thing's for certain: I'm going to give old Top-hat his comeuppance!

I could see in the mirror that my face was frighteningly pale. I pinched it till it reddened out and then I drew myself up straight, pressed my chin unconsciously down onto my neck, the way I had done when I was a child, and headed out of the toilets.

It felt like everyone was watching me, and the only thing I cared about any more was my rep. I walked slowly, with loping peasant steps, like on those old summer nights walking home from the fields with the adults after a long day's harvest. I could hear our tune, and it now rang in my ears like a battle song:

I'm every bit as tough as you
I can make order just like you

"Stop humming!" the head waiter hissed in my ear. "You really that cheerful?"

"Never been happier!" I replied impertinently and entered the bar.

I didn't pick up my pace even there, but merely lifted my head higher as I approached him.

I'm every bit as tough as you
I can make order just like you

I stopped in front of their table. I stood to attention because it had been beaten into us peasant children that you stood to attention when talking to your social superiors so hard that you stood to attention whether you wanted to or not.

"At your service," I said slowly, stretching out the syllables like an old peasant, and looked the Deputy right in the eye.

The Deputy was stirring his drink and said nothing for the moment. The alcohol was really showing on his face. His eyes were distracted, his face buttery and swollen. As if he'd been fished out of the river, I thought. Like a corpse from a river.

Her Excellency looked at him, and since he still wasn't saying anything, she turned to me.

"The Deputy is sorry he hit you, András," she said.

I could see that that wasn't true, though the Deputy did in fact nod curtly. It was obvious that he was only doing it for the lady's sake, which made me even happier. I had been expecting something so different, and now she herself had come and... My mouth hung open in wonder. I still don't really know why she did it. She did have a humane streak running through her madness, I don't deny it. Perhaps she genuinely felt sorry for me, perhaps she even liked me a little; but the "comedy" value of it, I think, excited her more. She was clearly taking pleasure in teaching the infamous wild-child a lesson, testing the limits of her influence with him. She looked at him provocatively, with an odd smile.

"Shake on it, then," she instructed him.

The Deputy extended his hand the way you open your mouth at the dentist's. I took it unsuspecting, but a moment later felt a terrible pain.

"I hope I am not shaking your hand too hard," he said viciously, with exaggerated politeness.

"Not at all," I replied. "Don't feel a thing."

"Not a thing, eh?"

An ugly, wet smile spread over the buttery yellow face and he gripped my hand even stronger.

The pain was almost unbearable now, but I could feel the lady's gaze on me, and I didn't make a sound. I can still recall, there was a triple candelabrum on the wall opposite, with little red shades, and I focused rigidly on that, my teeth gritted together.

The music fell quiet, and there was a ghostly silence in the bar. The candelabrum began to wobble before my eyes.

"Let him go!" she instructed him.

"No, please," I said. "Let him continue. It doesn't hurt at all."

"Not at all?"

The Deputy gave a short laugh and squeezed my hand even harder.

"Not at all," I repeated stubbornly.

My hand hurt so much by now that these subtle differences of degree really didn't count at all any more. Anger and hatred made me almost numb to pain. I turned away from the trembling candelabrum and looked him square in the face. His face was now like a slab of butter sweating in the heat. His forehead had big beads of sweat on it, his veins were protruding, and his eyes were bloodshot.

In the end, he couldn't keep it up; he let me go.

"What kind of hand is that?" he asked, shaking his head, and tried to smile.

I looked him in the eyes and said, hard and loud:

"A peasant hand, sir."

I could feel the lady watching me, and I stole a glance at her. Her gaze was now almost palpable and I felt it on me like a hand, a caressing hand. She smiled at me. Then she said to the Deputy:

"Now let András squeeze your hand."

"Mine?" He smiled in a superior way and extended it. "Oh, he can squeeze it till the cows come home!"

I looked at his hand. He had a nice hand, with long fingers—a fine, white, gentleman's hand.

"Well, come on," he goaded, and I took it.

I hesitated a moment and then squeezed it so hard my own hand hurt. The Deputy's face twisted.

"Does it hurt?" she asked provocatively.

"Not a bit," he said, gesturing dismissively with his other hand and giving me a tough look. "Go ahead, my boy, squeeze it harder if you can."

He didn't have to ask me twice. I gave it everything I had. All the anger I had inside of me, and Lord knows there was plenty of that, I squeezed into that fine, white murderous hand.

The drunken population of the bar looked on in suspense. They sat around their tables as still as waxwork figures in a museum. The head waiter, who was standing a few tables over, gestured angrily for me to stop, but I didn't stop, I wasn't going to stop; I just kept squeezing as hard as I could. The hell with you, I swore silently. Go teach your grandmother to suck eggs!

The Deputy was still trying to smile, but the smile on his face, distorted with pain, was like the grin of a death's head. I looked at him and suddenly saw a different face, the face of the mad, dishevelled peasant woman in the village we all called Mad Wilma. Wilma had turned into Mad Wilma when the Deputy buried her husband alive right before her eyes.

I don't know exactly what I did at that moment—all I remember is that the Deputy suddenly made a sort of creaking sound and snatched his hand away.

There was still silence, a deadly silence. I was standing to attention, waiting to see what would happen next.

"All right, András," I heard the lady say. "You can go now."

I looked at her. I had never seen her eyes this way. I didn't know what exactly it was that was in them, because you can't yet read a woman's eyes at sixteen, but whatever it was made me drunker—without a drop of alcohol—than the whole drunken company in the bar. I clicked my heels together crisply and said:

"Very good, ma'am. Good evening."

Now all eyes really *were* on me, but I didn't look back at anyone. I left the way I'd come in, with slow, unhurried peasant strides, though in my joy, I would have liked to cartwheel all the way.

> *I'm every bit as tough as you*
> *I can make order just like you*

When I left the bar, the head waiter caught my arm and dragged me furiously towards the kitchen.

"If he calls for the kid again," he whispered to one of the waiters, "tell him he's gone home."

With that, he tore open the kitchen door and shoved me roughly in.

"I'll see to you later," he growled, and slammed the door behind me.

In the kitchen, everyone was already up to speed with the "incident". Iluci examined my hand anxiously—you could still see the signs of the struggle.

"Did it hurt?"

"Yeah, him!" I replied drily, and said no more about it.

The waiters also quizzed me, but I didn't say much more to them, either. The truth is, it would have been good to talk about it, even boast a little, but I was a peasant lad and knew that that sort of thing wasn't on, and what's more wasn't advisable, either. If you do something praiseworthy, people will praise you for it, and if they don't, it's no use praising yourself. But I lit a cigarette, which I would not otherwise have dared to do, and the waiters didn't say a word. That was the best acknowledgement they could have given me: they saw me as a grown-up, entitled to a smoke.

Iluci put a big plate of food in front of me. It was full of the choicest cuts, and I wolfed it down hungrily, then had a glass of champagne and leant comfortably back in my chair. Life's good, I thought. They may very well fire me now, but... I had another glass of champagne and stopped thinking about it. Let someone else worry for a change!

Then I heard the head waiter's voice.

"Closing time," he said.

He stood there as if he'd appeared from thin air—I hadn't noticed him come in. The champagne seemed to be bubbling inside my head, tickling my thoughts. So they've gone home, I noted slightly tipsily. She'd be getting naked about now.

The waiters put down their cards and started getting their things together. The head waiter looked at me ominously and I could see that he was just waiting to get me alone. Old fool! I thought. You think I'm scared of you?

The telephone rang. Iluci picked it up.

"Yes, Your Excellency," she said. "A bottle of the usual. Yes. Who?" Her face changed suddenly. "Who, m'lady?" she repeated. "Yes, he's still here. As you wish, m'lady."

She replaced the receiver and looked anxiously at the head waiter.

"She says András is to take it up. What else do they want from this kid?"

"You didn't tell her he's still here, did you?"

"Yes."

"Oh, for..." the head waiter swore, and lit up nervously. "Well, it's done now," he said with a shrug after a while and looked at me. "Take the champagne up. Then..." He couldn't bring himself to say what he wanted to. "And then you can go home."

Then, without looking at me again, he quickly left.

Iluci was very agitated.

"You be careful!" she said with genuine concern. "You know who you're dealing with."

"I do," I shrugged. "I'm tough as boots, you don't have to worry about me."

Inside, though, I was far less self-assured. Of course, I thought to myself, the Deputy was never going to leave it at that. Now he'll have a far easier time of it. The hotel was asleep and there was no one but them in her quarters.

Iluci handed me a bottle of chilled champagne in a glass bucket and a silver tray with four glasses. It was French champagne in a big, heavy bottle. If he tries anything, I thought in the lift, I'll bash his brains in with it.

It must have been around three. The glasses clinked eerily in the dead, reverberating corridor as I made my way to her rooms. It was so quiet you could even hear my footsteps on the thick carpet. The great lift shaft yawned darkly behind its grille, the greasy cables hanging limply in the depths. Nothing was moving, the air itself seemed stilled. Yes, the hotel was asleep.

I stopped in front of the familiar door and knocked.

"András?" I heard her say.

"Yes, ma'am."

"Come in."

I was expecting to find a drunk, boisterous company inside, but the suite was so quiet, it seemed they'd all already gone to sleep. The silence almost struck me like a gust of wind when I entered. The entrance hall was dark, the doors wide open. I stopped, looked around. Inside, a greenish obscurity reigned, like in a thriller. In the depths of the room, in the tall Venetian mirror, I saw only myself and the furnishings. What is all this? I wondered. Where are they? I listened keenly, but could hear only the clinking of the glasses on the tray. In the mirror, I could see how pale I was.

I finally entered.

She was lying on the chaise longue, smoking. She was alone. A single low, green-shaded standing lamp illuminated the room, the wind blew in through the open balcony door, the curtains billowed in the semi-darkness. There was something theatrical and unreal about the whole thing. She was lying there so still it was as if she were smoking in her sleep. Her arm hung down like a catatonic's. Her heavy, painted blue eyelids half covered her eyes. She looked at me but said nothing. I stopped, clumsily, awkwardly, not knowing what to do. What was with her? Was she drunk? Or ill?

"I've brought the champagne," I practically whispered, as if she couldn't see for herself.

"Put it down there," she said at last, slowly and pensively, like someone who wasn't going to rush such a critical decision, pointing to the occasional table beside the chaise longue. She sounded like she had a swollen tongue, and her voice was a little hoarse from the alcohol. "Go ahead and pour," she added, knocking the ash from her cigarette onto the carpet like a somnambulist.

Outside, it was still raining. The windows occasionally rattled with the wind, as if someone were tapping on them softly, as if the night itself wanted to come inside, into her room. I opened the bottle and started pouring mechanically. When I put the neck of the bottle over the third glass, she said:

"Only two glasses."

My heart was in my mouth. So they're alone, I thought, and glanced automatically towards the bedroom. Its door was closed.

"Sit down," she said softly, hoarsely, and drew her mouth out slightly like someone trying to smile, forced to acknowledge that they won't succeed for lack of strength, and giving up on the whole thing.

I sat down on the edge of an armchair and waited anxiously to see what would happen next.

"Drink," she said, leaning forward unsteadily, as if still sleeping, for a glass.

I still had one eye on the bedroom. What was going on?

"To… to Your Excellency's health!" I stuttered, and in my embarrassment drained the glass in a single go.

She sipped her glass for a long while, thoughtfully, seriously, like a sommelier, watching me through her glass the entire time. She looked at me sleepily but curiously, the way you look out at a strange new landscape from a train window at night, your eyes heavy with sleep.

"You're not sitting comfortably," she said. Her voice was now strangely gentle and yet, in some indefinable way, still commanding. "I want you to enjoy yourself," she added, pointing at the table. "There's cigarettes there."

"Thank you," I mumbled, shifting slightly farther into the chair, but not touching the cigarettes.

Silence fell. It was still stiflingly hot. The air was so humid, it felt like there was hot water falling from the sky, not rain, and even the wind brought no relief. That, too, was hot and unnerving, like the breath of a woman aroused.

I kept waiting for the door to open.

The silent room was now full of noises. The curtains rustled in the wind, whispering together, something buzzed or rattled somewhere, you couldn't tell what, and sometimes, it seemed that the noises were coming from the bedroom.

"Why do you keep looking at the door?" she asked suddenly.

"I wasn't," I replied lamely and felt myself blush.

She leant forward, removed a cigarette from the box with two fingers, and put it between my lips.

"Go ahead and smoke," she said and flashed a curious smile. "We're alone."

The match trembled in my hand as I lit up, the blood rushed to my head. We're alone. I was alone with her.

I stole an unconscious glance at her, but she didn't say anything. She lay, immobile, on the chaise longue and looked at me like a strange landscape. She now seemed so alien it was as if she weren't the woman I knew at all. It was as if she merely reminded me of someone, another woman, another woman who was her, and yet not her, the way a portrait reminded you of a model the artist hadn't painted from life. Had I seen her like this in my dream? Or in the dark, with Manci? I don't know. It's hard to explain. There was something now in her face, in her whole being, that I had only vaguely suspected before. Something had taken on a physical reality that before had been invisible and impossible to define, like when the salt crystallizes from seawater, and water becomes solid and acquires volume and weight: a palpable body. She was so beautiful I wanted to scream or cry, or jump all over her to bite and strangle her, or to die right then, there, at her feet. I'm drunk, I thought. And then I thought once more: to die right there, at her feet!

"How old are you?" she asked.

"I'm turning seventeen."

"Seventeen!" she repeated pensively, and nodded like a doctor who's made a full diagnosis of the symptoms and knows that the patient's condition is serious, but won't say anything till later to the family. "Drink," she said, almost consolingly, like someone who's tried the cure themselves and knows it will work.

I poured and we drank. She looked at me through her glass again, seriously, attentively, with an almost professional eye, as if she really were a doctor sedating a patient, making sure not to begin the operation until their stupor had reached the necessary point.

I didn't dare look at her, I stared out of the open balcony door. The Danube glinted blackly in the humid night and in the rain it looked as if it were bubbling like hot tar. The whole world seemed to be like that: dark, foggy, about to boil over.

"Are you looking at the stars?" she asked.

I thought she was joking. I smiled.

"There are no stars tonight," I said a little haltingly, because by this time my own tongue felt a little swollen.

She leant forward a little; her face was mysterious.

"Oh, there are," she said softly, confidentially, like someone imparting news of a great discovery. "The stars are always in the sky, only we can't see them for the clouds." She thought about that for a little while, and then nodded slowly but very firmly. You could see that she'd thought it over and had once and for all approved her statement. "The sky is full of stars," she said, "only people can't see them." That made her sad. She sighed. "I've had a lot to drink," she noted. "Pour."

We drank. I now had the feeling that the champagne was going not to my stomach, but straight to my head. I was very dizzy. My head drooped back onto the chair, I couldn't support it any longer. It was heavy, wonderfully heavy, full of champagne and stars.

"That was nice," I mused.

"What?"

"What you said about the stars."

She sighed.

"You're tipsy too."

"Yes," I said melancholically, and nodded, as if to say I was aware of the gravity of the situation.

"Show me your hand," she said suddenly.

I was no longer surprised at anything, not even this. I extended my hand. She took it with two fingers like something fragile; my whole body stiffened with her touch as if her fingers had carried an electric charge, a strange, high-voltage charge.

She was completely occupied with my hand. She examined it, turned it this way and that, considered. Then she looked up.

"Did you know whose hand you were squeezing?"

"Yes."

"Weren't you frightened?"

"No," I replied, but then corrected myself: "*Not by then.*"

"Of course," she nodded. "Only the thought is frightening, always just the thought. The thing itself," she said with a grimace, "is nothing. Isn't that right? Life, really, is nothing at all, when you think about it." She shrugged. "You get over it, like an operation. It's just the *thought* of the operation," she said hoarsely and fell silent. She stared straight ahead of her, drew up her eyebrows and gave a little shiver. "That's terrib-le," she said, emphasizing each syllable, and leant closer, as if afraid of being overheard. "You've got to drink, understand?" she whispered. "Drink a lot. Or really believe in something." She suddenly laughed—a strange, hysterical laugh. "I drink," she said disdainfully and, as if that were the end of that, changed her tone completely. "Squeeze my hand."

I didn't understand.

"Squeeze it!" she said.

I took her hand. It was a delicate, white, shapely hand, warm and fragile like a baby bird. How could you squeeze *that*? I thought. But my hands and knees started trembling so hard that—to disguise it—I gave her hand such a squeeze in my fright that her face distorted with pain.

"You're not afraid of me, either?" she asked in a strange tone.

"A little," I admitted, and dropped her hand.

She looked at me quizzically.

"Why?"

Why?… Yes, why, after all? I thought about it for a long time.

414

"You're so beautiful," I said.

We were whispering like a pair of conspirators.

"Squeeze it," she said, "like you squeezed his."

"It'll hurt," I whispered.

"Don't worry about that," she said, with a wave of the hand. And then she said, barely audibly: "Sometimes that's good."

There was something frightening about her now. Her eyes grew strangely wide, her mouth opened a little, her lips were trembling. Then she threw herself back with that strange mixture of determination and fear with which one climbs on the operating table. She closed her eyes and gritted her teeth: she was waiting for the pain.

When I took her hand, she shivered slightly. She drew up her legs and her skirt fell above her knees. I could see she was pressing them hard together. The clips of her stockings showed through her skirt, now stretched tight, but there were no traces of anything else underneath—the skirt hugged her form revealingly. She's not wearing underwear! I thought, and I gave her hand a big squeeze, as if I'd been struck by lightning.

I could feel the pain flash through her. Her leg twitched, hiking up her skirt and revealing a white flash of thigh above her stockings—a tiny strip, but bright enough to blind.

I watched her, mesmerized. What if, I thought, I...

"More!" she panted in a whisper. "Harder!"

She's mad, I thought. She's gone mad. And now I really was a little afraid of her, and wanted to scream or cry, or jump on her and bite and strangle her, or die right there, on the spot, at her feet.

"More... More!..."

By turns she would almost beg, like a child, in a pitiful voice, out of breath, and then shout, and scream and order:

"More!... More!... More!"

I watched her, horrified and captivated. Pain and ecstasy as phenomena had been as opposed for me until now as fire and water, or birth and death, and now that I saw the two meld into one for the first time in my life, this freak child of the emotions shocked me so much I shivered. Her face was ghostly. It was beastly, hideous, and yet supernaturally beautiful. She reminded me a little of the saints in agony, a little of quiet, deceptive lunatics, and a little of something else, something inexpressible that lives only in the bloodthirsty underworld of dreams and which there are no words to describe.

I couldn't bear to watch her agony any more—I turned away. I stared, silent, petrified, into nothingness. Suddenly, she gave a soft cry, almost a scream. I looked at her and my heart skipped a beat. Her skirt had slipped all the way up and... she wasn't wearing underwear! the thought screamed within me. If I went and sat on the other side, opposite her, then...

All at once, I had the feeling she was watching me. I glanced at her furtively, out of the corner of my eye, and her eyes were, indeed, open. She was watching me watch her, but did not adjust her skirt. Our gazes met. *Now!* I thought, and leant in towards her mouth. Suddenly, she stood up.

"I'm terribly hot," she said. "I'm going to take a bath."

I've gone and ruined it all, I thought angrily, and clambered up myself.

"Good night," I spat, bitter and disappointed.

She turned around.

"Leaving so soon?" she asked with an air of surprise.

"N-no," I mumbled.

"In that case, wait for me," she said. "I'll only be a few minutes." Suddenly, she grabbed the back of my chair. "I'm so dizzy," she whispered, and pressed her hand to her forehead.

She stood like that for a few moments and then made her way unsteadily into the bedroom. She left the door half open, but from where I was standing I could see only the bed—the bathroom was on the other side. I could hear the bathroom door open, but not close. She hadn't left it open? I thought, excited. I listened for a long time, but the door didn't close. Then there was a terrifying sound.

A noise in Exfix's room.

I was bathed in cold sweat. What was that? Was Exfix home? Each moment felt like minutes, the minutes felt like hours, and an eternity passed.

Then I was relieved. A dog whined, that soft, childishly pleading and yet still slightly lascivious whine every dog lover knows. Cesar was dreaming. So Exfix was out of town, I established, because I knew that otherwise, Cesar slept in the entrance hall.

You could hear the sound of rushing water from the bathroom. She's undressing, I thought. Or is she naked already?

There was silence, then a splash, and you could clearly hear her climbing into the bath and settling in. I was now certain that the door was open. How many times I had fantasized about her like this in the bath when I was here alone with Cesar in the afternoons, and now I had but to take a few steps to… I stood up and headed to the bathroom. But then there was another noise from Exfix's room. I stopped, listened. Yes, it was Cesar, no doubt about it, but I still did not go on. I really will end up spoiling it all, I thought, and went quickly back to my seat.

A few minutes later, I heard her get out of the bath. Soon, she'll be here, and then… what then? I didn't understand anything any more. First she lets me look at her naked thighs, then she leaves when I try to kiss her, now she's bathing with the door open. I stared at the billowing curtains in a daze. The wind was picking up outside, the rain was battering the windows. She's mad, I thought. Maybe she really is mad.

"András!" I heard her say.

"Yes, ma'am."

"Come here."

The room was spinning, I went like a sleepwalker. She was sitting in front of her dressing table, her back to me, in a bathrobe.

"You should bathe too," she said with no preliminaries or explanation, without even turning round.

"Yes, ma'am," I replied vaguely, and went into the bathroom.

"Um…" she called after me, "András!"

"Yes, ma'am?"

"His Excellency's bathrobe is up on the hook. Do you see it?"

"Yes, ma'am."

"Put that on. It's so hot in here."

I thought I was hearing things. *Put that on… His Excellency's bathrobe…* It took me several minutes to comprehend what that meant, or at least until I managed to accept that it really did mean what I thought it meant.

But why do I need to bathe first? I wondered in the bath, because the water had sobered me up a little. Does she think I'm dirty? I hated her so much at that moment I could have strangled her, but a moment later I had forgotten all about it, and all I could think of was that… No, actually, I couldn't think at all. A crazed director was running amuck in my head, cutting my thoughts into frames like film reel and splicing them together all mixed up and topsy-turvy, then setting fire to the whole thing. As I was towelling, it occurred to me that I ought to be angry, but I couldn't remember why. *Now!*—that was the single, the only word thundering, flashing, singing inside me. *Now, now, now!*

As I put on Exfix's robe and placed my hand on the door handle to leave the bathroom, I was seized by a momentary doubt as to whether I really had understood correctly, but then the door was open and I was in the bedroom.

It was pitch black, I couldn't see a thing.

"I'm over here," she said, as if talking in her sleep, or as if I were dreaming the whole thing.

I felt my way haltingly towards the voice. I suddenly felt her out-stretched hand.

"Sit here," she said, and I obeyed dizzily.

I was sitting on the edge of the bed. There she is, lying next to me, I thought, trembling. *Now, now, now!* But suddenly I grew flustered. Yes, now, but… how do you begin? With a peasant girl, it would be easy, or a maid. But what are you supposed to make of a lady who shows you her naked thighs, then walks off in a huff? I didn't dare move; I was scared I would spoil it all. I sat, silent, trembling, on the edge of the bed, and was indescribably ashamed.

"Drink," she said. "There's cognac on the nightstand."

I started feeling around for it. I found the bottle, but not the glass.

"Can I put the light on?" I asked awkwardly.

"No," she replied, as if it amused her terribly.

I gathered all my courage.

"Why not?"

She laughed silently.

"Drink from the bottle."

I drank.

"More," she said.

And then, again:

"More."

Here, in the bedroom, with its windows and doors all closed, the heat was even more unbearable. The strong spirit caught fire within me. I burned, burned and shook with cold.

"Why can't I put the light on?" I repeated dimly. My voice trembled. She stroked my head.

"Are you a virgin?" she asked softly.

"No."

"You have a girl?"

"Yes."

She was silent for a space.

"What's her name?"

"Manci."

"Are you in love with her?"

"No."

"Then why are you with her?"

"I don't know. There isn't anyone else."

"How long have you been together?"

"Few months."

"Was she the first?"

"Yes."

"And before that?"

"Nothing."

"You didn't think about women?"

"I did."

"A lot?"

"Oh, boy!"

"Was it bad?"

"Very."

"And now? Is it better now?"

"No."

She reached for the bottle and took a swig.

"I was the same," she said pensively. "I'm often still the same. Real life is mostly made up of Mancis. You'll learn that. Are you still thinking of other women?"

"Yes."

"Even when you're with her?"

"Yes."

"What do you think about?"

"All sorts of things."

"Like what?… Go on, tell me!"

I couldn't. My teeth began to chatter; I gritted them together hard so she wouldn't hear.

"Drink," she told me, and I drank.

I couldn't keep my eyes open. I felt as if I were asleep, awake and dreaming at the same time. I could hear myself talking, but my voice sounded completely alien.

"I always think of you."

She drew closer, her voice aflame.

"Of me?"

"Of you."

"And what do you fantasize about me?"

"Everything. Absolutely everything. I've even lain in your bed."

"In my bed?… Here?"

"Yes."

"And what did you do?"

"I thought of you."

"You've said that already," she whispered impatiently. "What else?"

"I felt your gown."

"And?"

"I pictured you in it."

"*And?*" she squeezed my hand hard. "Tell me everything!"

"I can't," I moaned.

She was right up close now, I could feel her breath. Her breathing was heavy, staccato, her voice stifled with excitement.

"Will you tell me if I let you come over here?"

"Yes."

"Come on, then."

I finally touched her, but she pulled away, almost in disgust. I reached after her, but she jumped out of bed.

"You want me to call the manager?" she yelled, and I heard her pick up the phone.

I sat there, petrified, saying nothing. She didn't move either, and a frightened silence fell. It's all over now, I thought.

"Shall I come back?" she whispered.

"Yes," I pleaded.

"You promise not to touch me?"

"…"

"Say it."

"Y-yes."

"And you'll do exactly as I say?"

"Yes."

"And nothing else?"

"Yes."

She got back into bed, as far away from me as possible.

"Then talk."

"What about?"

"You know."

There she was, lying next to me, as far from me as the stars. My teeth once more began to chatter; I held my mouth shut.

"Why won't you say anything?" she asked, her voice gentle now, almost tender. "Are you embarrassed?"

"No."

"You want another drink?"

"No."

"What's wrong, then?"

"Nothing."

"Then why won't you say anything?"

"Because you drew away from me like I was a toad."

She was silent for a moment.

"You promise not to touch me?"

"Yes."

"Swear?"

"I swear! Stop torturing me."

"All right," she whispered, and I felt her hand on me.

She no longer had to ask. I talked and talked; the words poured out of me. I told her everything, but nothing was enough for her. She wouldn't tolerate allusions or half-sentences, I had to say everything just as it was, and the filthiest words were not filthy enough for her. Even now, by turns like before, when I was squeezing her hand, she begged like a child, and then yelled and demanded:

"More!… More!… More!"

Suddenly, she withdrew her hand.

"No!" I begged. "Your hand."

She leant over me, and for a moment I felt her breast.

"Now imagine I'm not here… Imagine you're alone again in my bed… Yes… That's it, yes… Yes!!"

She put the light on and looked at me.

"Good…" she panted feverishly. "Good!…"

"What are you doing?"

"Can't you see?"

I put my arms around her, but she pushed me away even harder and when I reached after her, jumped out of bed. This time, though, she didn't get a chance to lift the receiver, or even shout. I caught her, put my hand over her mouth and threw her on the bed. She kicked, bit and scratched, but I didn't care. I was an animal in heat—I pushed her down and threw myself upon her. The whole world seemed to explode, and then there was the silence of Judgement Day.

She fell asleep. She was breathing deep and steady in my arms. Outside, the wind seemed to have stopped and dawn crept in through the cracks in the blinds. Half asleep, I could still hear Cesar whining, but so softly it seemed like it was coming from a distant star.

Her Ladyship's dog was dreaming.

THREE

Me and the Smiling Machinist

1

S OMEONE WAS SHAKING ME by the shoulder.

"Get up!" I heard from somewhere very far away.

The voice seemed incredibly familiar. Could it be *her*? I wondered vaguely. Strange. I must be dreaming about her, people often dream they're dreaming. Or rather… wait a bit. No. Right now, I'm dreaming that I'm awake, or rather, I *am* awake and I'm dreaming that… Hey! Stop shaking me. Is it really that late?

"What time is it?"

"I don't know. Make sure they don't see you in the corridor."

I finally managed to open my eyes.

She was lying beside me so still that at first I thought she was asleep and had been talking in her sleep. Sunlight filtered through the gaps in the blinds—thin, lopsided golden shafts shimmering in the half-light. My mind was full of fog, my stomach of nausea, and I could barely keep my eyes open. I was dizzy. Horribly dizzy. I had to make sure they didn't see me in the corridor.

Her eyelashes gave a flutter; she opened her eyes with difficulty.

"It's over there on the dresser," she mumbled sleepily, and said something else I didn't understand.

"What is?"

"My purse," she repeated a little tersely. "Take some money."

"How much?"

"Whatever you want."

I obediently got out of bed, but when I put my foot on the floor, it wobbled under me. I grabbed the headboard of the bed, but the bed, too, was wobbling, the walls were shaking, and the room turned slowly, heavily, on its side. How unusual, I thought. Must get to the bottom of that. I thought about it for a long time, and finally realized. Aha! Of course. I'm drunk, that's all. All right, come on, where's that dresser?

The floor by the dresser slanted steeply. Hadn't noticed that before. Strange. I had to keep holding on to the furniture.

The purse really was on the dresser. I picked it up, looked at it, pondered. Then I suddenly realized I didn't understand at all.

"What am I supposed to do with the money?" I asked.

She did not reply. Was she sleeping? I felt my way to the bed, purse in hand.

"Here you go," I said, handing it to her.

"Let me sleep," she groaned, turning angrily away.

I looked at the purse, confused. What did she want with it? I wondered. What does she want with me? Here I was, and I didn't understand a thing.

But she's my lover! I thought suddenly, repeating the word to myself with the same obsessive effort with which you try and fix the memory of a dream at the moment of waking: my lover! It sounds impossible, I thought.

There she lay, naked, spreadeagled; I had slept with her last night, had just got up from beside her, and yet I still could not believe it. I watched her like someone spying on a woman in the building opposite through binoculars, a naked woman lying on the bed, her legs apart. She seems so close, and yet you know that she's so far away: *over there, over there.*

I was drunk, and sixteen, and couldn't let it rest. I leant closer to her, closer, ever closer. I could feel her breath, but it was as if the distance were still the same. It was in vain that I approached, I couldn't get close to her. I saw a mouth that was silent, two eyes that remained closed, I saw arms and legs, breasts and loins, pretty, indecipherable hieroglyphs that told me nothing. She was a woman, and she was beautiful. That's all I knew.

"Terrible!" I said, frightened by the sound of my own voice.

She didn't move a muscle. She was sleeping deeply, calmly, infuriatingly close. The light illuminated only half her body—her face remained in shadow. Her hair looked almost black on her head, but lower, where the light hit, it burned a golden red, like a fiery exclamation mark with no point beneath, a sweet, ominous warning. She's beautiful, I thought, with a shiver. Beautiful and terrible. I must make sure they don't see me in the corridor.

I felt my way to the bathroom. My face looked so alien when I spotted it in the mirror as I was dressing, I seemed to be seeing it for the very first time. I stared at my reflection in alarm. There was something I hadn't learnt, I thought anxiously, and something I had. Oh well, I shrugged, you could only say it in a poem anyhow. The important thing was that they didn't see me in the corridor.

No one saw me in the corridor. I did, however, bump into Franciska on the service staircase. Drop dead, I thought, but otherwise the incident made no impression. I knew Franciska's memory would serve, and he wouldn't forget his "car accident".

Just don't let Elemér see me like this! I prayed, because Franciska reminded me of Elemér and at the thought of meeting him, I trembled. I knew, even in the state I was in, that he was the only one I could trust completely, that he was the only one who would never—under any circumstances—rat on me, and yet I was still afraid of him, afraid only of *him* and no one else, and the strange thing about it was that I didn't find that strange at all.

I listened for a long time before I went into the changing room, because I was afraid I'd find him there. But there was no one in there. Little puddles glinted on the floor; I noted that the boys on the day shift had already washed and dressed, which is to say it was past eight o'clock. The problem was, I didn't know by how much. I usually met up with Elemér at half past eight, and I was afraid he was waiting for me at the front door. I dressed incredibly slowly to kill the time, though, as it turned out, there was no need. It was well past eight thirty by that point, and there was no one waiting at the door. This made me so happy that I started singing in the street, pretty loudly, too. I got plenty of looks from passers-by, but what did I care for them? I wasn't afraid of them. I wasn't afraid of anyone of woman born—and even of the Son of God, all I asked was that he let me sleep a while. But that of course meant getting home first, which turned out to be quite a complicated business.

The problem was the trams. There were lots of trams in Pest that morning. If you wanted to go home, you had to select, from that multitude, the one that happened to be going where you wanted to go. The prospective passenger, in order to achieve this, had to be equipped with reason, decent eyesight and presence of mind, but also with a little luck—without which, of course, the whole enterprise was doomed—they'd manage to get through it. That was not the hard part. The problem with public transport was that at a certain point you had to get *off* the tram you had invested so much time and energy in getting on to, and what's more, you had to get off *at a specific stop*. There were lots of stops in Újpest on that morning, and the careless conductors would mostly only wake you at the terminus, spitting distance from the end of the earth, where even hedgehogs only went to sleep. In other words, you had to get off, and then get on again: and that seemed an impossible task. It was, I think, merely a happy coincidence that—despite all that—I managed to make it home.

The "folks" weren't home. I went into the room, where I faced a further set of difficulties. The shutters were closed and I couldn't find the light switch in the dark. It wasn't in its usual place, though I clearly remembered it being there the day before. This latest complication got me downhearted. I swore so hard that the light turned itself on in fright, which—what with everything else that had happened—surprised me not one bit. Besides, it wasn't entirely impossible that Manci had put it on, because Manci was home, as she almost always was at this time, and that did, after all, surprise me a little.

"Isn't it odd?" I shook my head.

Manci giggled infuriatingly.

"Well," she said, "looks like you've been at the bottle, dear."

"Got a problem with that?" I asked menacingly.

"On the contrary!" she assured me, and went back to bed. "Come on."

"What d'you want?" I asked suspiciously.

"Just the opposite of what you want, dear."

That was too complicated for me. All these complications!

"I don't understand," I muttered, "but I don't care."

"Well, then, come on."

I went, and threw myself down on the bed, but Manci was not satisfied.

"Take your clothes off," she said.

"Leave me alone," I growled. "I'm so sleepy!"

But Manci insisted I take my clothes off. I was fed up with these constant complications. I even thought I might take my clothes off, after all, but then I kept forgetting about the thing over and over again because meanwhile I would doze off. Finally, Manci got out of bed and started taking my clothes off for me.

"Excellent solution," I said, and snoozed on.

But Manci was insistent.

"Stand up," she said after a while. "I can't get your trousers off like this."

All right. I stood up. But then she said:

"Now sit down."

Suddenly my eyes were wide open. Nothing's easy today, is it? I thought.

Manci pulled down my trousers. I looked on in amusement.

"Hey, you're not blonde at all!" I said.

"You only just notice?" she giggled.

"I didn't understand before," I replied gravely. "But I understand now. None of us dare to be the way we are."

"I can't get your shirt off like this," she said. "Lift up your arms."

"Wait," I gestured. "I have to think something through. Yes. Of course." I examined her body attentively. "You see," I said as I guided my hand down her body the way the Schoolmaster had used to on the map when he was teaching us about mountains and rivers. "All this you can understand. You can understand you, Manci. If you go closer to you, then you're closer, and if you go far away, you're far away. You dye your hair, and it's easy to know why. Everything's plain and simple." I gave her cheeks a fatherly pat. "Maybe it's better if a woman's not clever," I said. "But then again," I wondered aloud, "who knows? Trees are also not clever, if you look at it that way, and yet we don't know a thing about them. What do you know about trees?"

Manci seemed annoyed by the trees.

"Don't ask such difficult questions," she said. "What am I? A scientist?"

"Scientist!" I waved dismissively. "They only know what they can see. Or what other people have seen before them, you know what I mean? But as to *why* things are the way they are, and how it all started, and

how it'll end... what do they know about that? Hey, leave me alone!"
I snapped, because she was pulling at my shirt again. "Where was I
again? Oh yes. That scientists only know what they can see. Well, there
it is, you see. What can a single person see, even the wisest person? Only
hieroglyphs, Manci, only hieroglyphs, and nothing else. Life's written
in hieroglyphs. Remember that, Manci, it's very important. Everything
you see, it's all hieroglyphs. Some you can decipher, some you can't,
and the scientists have a little breakthrough every now and then, but
a few years later it turns out that the text is incoherent anyway. Now I
know, now and then you do decipher a line or two, and start to get a
vague hint of what it's all about, but that's so little, Manci. So precious
little, and yet it's so much you can't even say it with words. It's more like
music—you feel the rhythm. You see? The rhythm, like with a line in a
poem. Yes!" I said, jumping up, "I think I'm finally on the right track.
You can feel that life wasn't written in prose. It has a strict metre, like a
classical poem, and it has unbreakable rules and laws. It's all a poem,
Manci, a great big poem! And the lines rhyme. D'you see?" I grabbed
her hand. "*They rhyme!*"

"All right," she said, with an unfathomable calm. "They rhyme."

"But with *what?*" I asked, getting caught up in the moment. "Don't
you get it? The other line is missing. It's missing the rhyme. The rhyme,
Manci!" I cried. "*Now* do you understand what I'm talking about?"

"Of course," she nodded. "Your mother told me you write poems.
Now be a good boy and lift up your arms. That's it. At last!" she sighed,
because she'd finally managed to get my shirt off. "Go on and lie down,
dear. Move over a bit, leave some room for me. That's better."

With that, she switched off the light and lay down beside me. It was
dark, it was quiet, it was unbearably hot, and it smelt of our bodies.
I was still thinking of The Great Poem. Manci, however, had something else in mind. The minutes passed. Suddenly, I noticed something
about myself.

It was a physical phenomenon, a well-known and not at all alarming phenomenon, but I observed it like a panicked researcher who has
just tested an experimental serum on himself and has realized—from
some apparently minor symptom—that something's gone wrong with

the experiment and the conclusion runs counter to the theory. Could my body really do it? I wondered in revulsion, and I fell to thinking the way only wise old scientists and young poets can. But I don't want her, I told myself, not even my body wants her. I'm disgusted by her, I'm thinking of someone else. So who *wants* me to want her? Is it "nature"? What does "nature" want? What does it want from us people? What does all this mean? Where is the corresponding rhyme?

"No!" I yelled at Manci and drew away in disgust.

Manci didn't pay much attention to such protestations, and it was fairly indifferently that she asked:

"Why not?"

"We can't," I said softly, but it seems there was something in my voice that shocked her.

She let me go.

"Hey," she asked me in a changed tone. "You ain't got some disease, do you?"

I was about to say "no", but then I remembered Gyula and I thought, if I had what he had, or at least *said* I did, then…

"Is that a yes?" Manci said, more as a statement than a question, and when I still did not respond, she snapped: "Tell me!"

"Yes," I finally spat out.

"The clap?"

"Yes," I consented.

Manci sat up.

"Her Excellency?" she asked mockingly.

"Fool!" I snapped and wanted to slap her. But the anger cleared the fug of alcohol from my head, and I was suddenly sober—frighteningly sober. "I caught it off one of the maids," I said quickly, hoarsely. "Works at the hotel."

"And what did Her Excellency have to say about it?"

The question hung in the air as if suspended on a wire. I didn't respond. I had been lying for months that she was my lover, and now, when it was finally true, I couldn't say a word about her. It was as if my blood, too, had drained away with my drunkenness, and I lay cold and lifeless on the bed, dying of shame.

"Manci," I said, "what I told you about that woman, it's... not a word of it is true. She really does live in the hotel, but... I can tell you now... I... don't even know her. I've never so much as spoken to her."

"You don't say!" Manci laughed. "You really think I swallowed all that? Come on, dear. If you'd made up some fallen lady or some old, rich crone... But the wife of a minister, a real lady..." She began to laugh once more. It came from the heart, without mockery or malice, the way you laugh at some innocent youthful misdemeanour. "I've heard it all before!" she shrugged, and her voice was almost maternal. "It's the only way some people can get off," she explained, and began recounting "cases" with the chilling detachment of which only doctors and prostitutes are capable.

I listened, appalled, my head woozy, and suddenly a word came to me: *stars*. She'd said something about the stars... but what? It had been so pretty.

Manci was telling me about a brothel in Kiskőrös, where...

I fell asleep.

I dreamt something terrible. Her Excellency had noticed that I had no underpants. It was in the bedroom; I was undressing hastily in my excitement. The wind outside was howling, the rain lashing at the windows. She was lying in bed and talking about the stars. I began to think I'd got it wrong and had imagined the whole thing, but when I tried to get into bed beside her, she pushed me away in disgust.

"Did you think I hadn't noticed?" she asked in that high, sing-song voice, and snatched up the receiver, eyes flashing. "Get out!" she screamed, "or I'll tell the Major!"

I pelted down the stairs, but spotted Elemér in the bend, and...

I woke with a start. The shutters were now half open; Manci must have opened them when she was dressing. I blinked sleepily in the half-light. Outside, it was still day, the late afternoon light glowed red on the window opposite, and the sky peered into the courtyard with bloodshot eyes. Manci must have been off somewhere in town, my parents weren't home yet, and the flat was empty and quiet—you could hear the dripping of the kitchen tap.

I sat up. There was a chair beside the bed; on it lay my shirt. Even its patches were patched and I had outgrown it so badly that it didn't come down to my navel. It was my only shirt. I looked at it and wondered, terrified, what would happen if one day I really did have to get undressed in front of her... one day? Perhaps tonight!

I jumped out of bed and started digging around in the wardrobe. My father had brand-new underclothes—I tried on a shirt and some underpants. Lately, we'd acquired a big, gold-framed mirror above the sink. My father had bought it from Márika and Árpád when they got down on their luck. Later, whenever I remembered that afternoon, I would always hold that mirror partly responsible for what happened. It started here, before it; as to what, exactly, I did not yet know. At the time, it was just a shirt and a pair of underpants. That's how the part of my youth which I still cannot think of without blushing began.

Don't get me wrong—I could see, even without looking in the mirror, that you could have got two of me into the shirt and the underpants. But in my eyes, the fact that I was wearing underpants at all was a big thing, and that my shirt did not stop at my navel. But something happened within me when I looked in the mirror. I was no longer seeing myself through my own eyes, but through hers. I could feel the sharp, critical gaze of the grey eyes, and could see that strange, wide mouth stretch into a mocking smile, and the thought that this could actually happen that evening made me completely lose my head. I swore to myself that come hell or high water, I would buy a shirt and underpants that evening. At first, I thought of asking my father for money, but then I realized it would be no good. Clothing shops closed at six, and it was now half past. I didn't know what to do. That's when I remembered the Constable.

It's not easy to explain just who the Constable was. When he had first come into the hotel, Elemér had glanced after him in shock and said, quietly and a little taken aback:

"But that's the Constable!"

"Who?" I asked.

"The Constable," he repeated. "That's what all the workers call him in Angyalföld."

"Why? Is he a detective?"

"No," he whispered. "He's a snitch. At least, he used to be. Whenever the workers asked for a pay rise in a factory, the management would get him in and he'd come and sniff out the 'instigators'. They were going to beat him to death a couple of years ago; that's when he vanished from Angyalföld. Now he's doing something else, I hear."

"What?"

"I don't know," said Elemér, because at that time, he really didn't know.

From then on, the Constable would come by the hotel twice a week. He was a thin, dark, gangly character who behaved as if he were some eminent and tremendously busy doctor. He would leap out of his rickety little car with an air of importance, sweep into the hotel in an ominous hurry, observing everything with a jumpy glance. There was a nervous tension in his very being—he walked with quick and hectic steps so that at first I refused to believe he had an artificial leg. He leant demonstratively on his stick, which legend had it, hid a sword. Márton apparently saw it once. He was always in a hurry, always slightly het up, and he burst into the hotel twice a week as if a patient were dying in one of the rooms, and only he could save them.

He made everyone call him "Doctor", though—as it later turned out in court—he had no right. He had only done three years of medical school when, instead of healing, the state started training him for something that was more closely aligned with its inclinations. He became an outstanding soldier, one of the first military pilots. After the loss of his left leg, he volunteered again for active service and kept on flying bombers with one leg, or rather with one artificial leg. He was on the front pages, his picture was in all the papers, he had a private audience with the King and a rather excitable poet wrote an ode in his honour: he became a national hero. He was all of twenty-two.

Three years later, peace broke out and national heroes were temporarily no longer in demand. His former classmates were by then rightfully calling themselves "Doctor"; most had even married and set up practices with their wives' dowries. But the national hero would have had to go back to being a student—and a rather impecunious student at that—his civvies faded and outgrown, eating in canteens and begging for grants and charity. Not to mention the fact that he would have had to study, study all the time so that—if he was lucky—and in three years' time he too found a rich wife—he could open a practice in one of the humbler side streets. This, of course, he didn't fancy at all—what national hero would? Though he did, obviously, want to be a doctor—otherwise, he wouldn't have had everyone call him that. There were a good many things to blame for the fact that his interventions in the human body were with the bayonet and not the scalpel, and to be fair—he was the least of them. He personally blamed the Communists and the Jews, which—on a human level—was also understandable, because it meant he once more had someone to stick his bayonet into and didn't have to feel useless. He became a *Freikorps* officer for Horthy and killed conscientiously and with great professionalism, but unlike my Deputy, had principles, and so got nowhere.

One day, they dissolved the *Freikorps*, his day in the sun was over, and he had to go back to his outgrown student civvies. Meanwhile, the country became wonderfully "consolidated". The Social Democrats he had been murdering for Horthy now extended to the same Horthy the "calloused hand of the workers", while the wealthy Jews were breathlessly telling the outside world that Horthy had mellowed and it was now OK to do business with him. They brought him British, French, Italian and even American capital, in return for which His Excellency the Anti-Semite appointed his pet Jews to positions of rank and honour. At the same time, he signed the most brutal "racial purity" laws, but those only affected the poorer Jews, about whom the rich Jews cared just as little as the rich Christians. The poor, whether they went to synagogue or church, only got poorer than before the war, while the rich only got richer. But there was peace and order in Hungary for whoever could put up with it—and whoever couldn't could go jump in the Danube. The number of suicides grew day by day, until in the end we held the record, beating the rest of the world hands down. To cut a long story short, the world "consolidated" all around the Constable.

Even his comrades from the death squads grew middle class eventually. They got jobs, families, accountants and doctors, and some even started getting bellies. Only the Constable stayed thin and true to the cause, and his eyes still burned with the old hatred. He hated everyone. The Whites for abandoning their principles, the Reds for not giving up theirs, the Jews for being Jews, and the Czechs, Serbs and Romanians for being Czech, Serb and Romanian. His only hope was the youth. He sought spiritual solace in the university youth movements. It was through them and with them that he wanted to fulfil his heroic dreams. But the youth were not at all heroic in nature. Their fathers had dreamt so much in the nightmarish dark of the last fifteen years that they were done with dreaming. These were weary, sober youths who dreamt only of a modest but secure position, and if they managed to secure one with the help of some well-placed uncle, immediately married—preferably someone with a dowry—and never came to another meeting again. But the Constable just kept on dreaming, his passion youthful, his temples greying. He joined every new right-wing party, organization and secret society and took part every time someone was beating up Jews or workers. He would turn up even at the impromptu and unforeseen fights, to join in, panting, at the last minute. Apparently, he always left word at home where he was, like his former classmates the real doctors, before running off to raise hell at the ring of a telephone, no matter where he was—in company, at the theatre or with his lover; God forbid he should miss out on a little National Rebirth.

At the same time, of course, he had to make a living. He made some money being a police informer for a time, but "consolidation" eventually put an end to that, too. The chastened unions now kept the workers so strictly in check that the factory owners no longer needed him. That's when he went freelance. He was received in a number of well-to-do homes, and could—on a friendly basis—buy up the clothes and even underclothes that ladies and gentlemen no longer wanted, for next to nothing. These he would then sell on, in attractively low instalments—but at all the higher price—to those for whom this was the only way to get hold of one or two nicer bits of clothing. He was primarily focused on waiters because he made the most profit on tailcoats; and thanks to his high-society connections, that really was his "speciality". He frequented only the finest establishments. He was always friendly with the management—unlike his clients, whom he always patronized, talking to them as if they were his subordinates. He would call waiters twenty years his senior "son", which—however strange it sounds—increased not only his standing but also his turnover, for the very finest places demanded the very height of servility from their staff, and they were impressed by his "aristocratic demeanour". He walked among them like a strict but kindly general ready to listen to the wishes of his troops and—if they were worthy—grant them. His former batman, who now served him in a general all-round capacity, carried the suitcases full of stock behind him like an aide-de-camp, and whenever the Constable spoke to him, he would snap immediately to attention. He would "look in" at the hotel twice a week, during lunchtime for the day shift and between eight and nine for the night shift, when the bar was still quiet. He really did only "look in", because he never spent more than fifteen minutes there. He negotiated with the speed of an express train, conveying to his clients the sense that as a national hero and future general, he had certain commitments to his country and couldn't go around wasting his precious time on rabble like them; and besides the whole thing was just a distraction to him anyway.

"It'll be war again soon, anyway," he would sometimes say, hopeful and confiding. "It really doesn't matter what one does till then. It's not worth starting anything really serious."

From the moment he first appeared at the hotel, other clothes merchants couldn't cross our threshold. He had the Jews to thank for that, for the Major, who—given the hotel's Jewish clientele—could hardly take part publicly in attacks on Jews, lived his passions vicariously, so to speak, through him. But our hotel wasn't the only place the Constable didn't have competition—he didn't brook it anywhere. There was always a Major in the management who took him under his wing for political reasons, or the opposite of the Major who, for political reasons also, was scared of him. It was a good, solid business and gave him a useful sideline as well. For in hotels and restaurants of that size, there was always something going on that the management was unlikely to approve of, and the Constable could sniff these things out like a bloodhound. Apparently, he was constantly sniffing around us as well, or at least so Elemér said.

437

As for Elemér, it goes without saying that he immediately instigated a boycott against the Constable. I was a keen supporter and I suspect that it was more on account of my fists than Elemér's world view that the boys didn't buy from him. I once smacked Gábor for buying a tie from him, and wouldn't let it rest till he'd taken it back.

This was the man I was going to turn to.

I recoiled, at first, from the thought, and was ashamed that it had even occurred to me. But since I could find no other solution, I eventually started bargaining with myself. I told myself this and that, that it was an emergency, and anyway, it was only a shirt and a pair of underpants; that hardly meant abandoning my principles. Besides, only the waiters on the night shift would know about it, and they never met the boys on the day shift, and even if they did, they're hardly going to talk about my shirt and underpants. As for the Constable, I'll pay him off quickly and that'll be that, once and for all.

What was I going to pay him with? Simple. I would just say I'd earned a little less at home—who was going to check?

It all seemed as simple now as it would have been unimaginable the day before. I always gave my mother everything I made, down to the last fillér, and I was a strict and careful bookkeeper. Whatever I received or consumed at home, I would immediately record in my "Owed to" column, not to mention the five pengős a month to "my mother for lodging". I have these notes in front of me now, and I can see I recorded even the thread with which she altered my father's suit for me. What's more, I also credited three hours' "wages" to her "account", at a much higher level than what her upper-class clients paid her. My mother had presumably long forgotten the promise I made her when I arrived and she had no idea that I was still clinging to it obstinately. I think she thought it a sort of childish enthusiasm from the beginning, but I took it deadly seriously always. I wanted to pay her back for every fillér, with cumulative interest to boot, and I had already pictured how wonderful it would be when one day I would lay out my accounts before her and say—humbly but manfully—"you see, Muther, I've kept my word". Yes, that had been my thinking up till now. Suddenly, it all seemed laughable and childish.

"Nonsense!" I mumbled.

It was late, I dressed quickly. Until now, I had thought I looked quite well in my father's altered suit, but looking in the mirror through *her* eyes, I felt pretty pathetic. What if she sees me on the street like this? I shuddered to think, and could once more feel her mocking gaze upon me. I decided to talk to my old man after all. He'd been promising me that new suit forever now, it was really time he made good on it. But the more I thought about it, the less I liked this solution. For what kind of suit would he buy me? Best-case scenario, he'd buy me the same as he used to buy himself. And, to be fair, his suits were quite nice, and were apparently made from English cloth, and were decently cut, but—who knows what that sort of thing depends on?—they still didn't quite seem to *cut it*. Or did I only think that because they were *his* suits? Maybe. But how was I to know? That blue suit the head waiter had bought from the Constable, on the other hand, still had the baronial crown embroidered into it. And if I could buy a shirt and a pair of trousers from him, why shouldn't I get a suit at the same time? What difference would that make? It was hardly going to change anything...

But the instalments wouldn't be so easy to manage. These "crowned" clothes cost a great deal. I couldn't just scrimp the payments from my wages—my mother would notice. I thought about that for a while, but then shrugged. She wouldn't have to notice. I would tell her myself. When the Major had taken exception to my shoes, she'd gone running to buy me a new pair, though we didn't have so much as a crust to eat at the time. Why couldn't I simply tell her he'd taken exception to my clothes? If she had the money for the theatre and silk I-don't-know-whats, then she was hardly going to die without my instalments. I was doing her a favour, anyway. Other parents supported their children. Only I was fool enough to hand over everything. It was ridiculous. And when you thought about it, one shirt and pair of underpants wasn't going to be enough. From now on, I would have to change my underwear daily, since I could never know when she was going to ring for me. Yes, I was going to buy *three* shirts and *three* pairs of underpants, and anyone who didn't like it could lump it. I'd need a tie as well—I'd almost forgotten. You can't wear a suit like that without a tie. And I didn't have any socks, either—unheard of!—not a single pair. I was still wearing footwraps like a filthy peasant, while she was flouncing around in silks and having a ball. The old man had even bought her a hat. Disgraceful. She's living high on my money. Just let her make a fuss—I'd give her a piece of my mind.

I was just gathering my things to go when I heard the front door open. I steeled myself for a frontal assault with my mother, but it wasn't her—it was my father. Before, I would have cut out my tongue rather than talk to him about this sort of thing, but now I seized the opportunity, knowing that with him, I'd have an easier time.

I wasn't wrong. The old man was incensed, and not because the Major had taken exception to his old suit, but that my mother dressed me in it. That she was only doing so because he hadn't bought me a new one never even occurred to him in his fury. He was honestly outraged, especially when it came to the money.

"You're still giving her your wages?" he said, clapping his hands together. "I don't understand your mother. What is she thinking? I can support my family myself, goddamn it. From now on, you do with your wages what you want, you hear? And if you don't have enough for something, don't let it bother you. You come see your old man, by God! D'you need cash?"

In actual fact, I didn't really need money, since I hadn't yet handed over my wages, but I still said to him, for the first time in my life:

"Well… if you could spare a little…"

He pulled out a ten pengő note. He pulled it out of his waistcoat pocket with two fingers the way other people pulled out a used tram ticket. He spat on it, and then stuck it to my forehead, the way the lords did with Gypsy musicians at balls.

"That'll do for tonight," he winked. "If she's a pretty piece, I can give you more."

And that was that—he didn't waste any more words; the matter, as far as he was concerned, was settled. Well, well, I thought, when I got to the street, you just have to be a little bit clever. Before, I hadn't even had two pengős twenty to buy my English language book, and now I had a crisp ten pengős in my pocket. Yes, you just needed a little cleverness was all, I nodded, like someone who's cracked the mysteries of life and the universe, and amazingly enough it didn't even occur to me that just yesterday I had looked down on this kind of cleverness.

I decided straight away to buy the English book on my way in, but by the time I reached Vilmos Császár út, I had changed my mind. Another time, I shrugged, the way clever boys do, the important thing right now was to have enough cash. From now on, I couldn't walk around without cash, things weren't like they were before. After all, this was a lady we were talking about, a Countess whom even Horthy's son had apparently courted. I was pleased with myself and the world as a whole. I was whistling as I walked into the hotel.

Needless to say, everyone in the bar wanted to know what had happened to me last night. I didn't lose my head, I was prepared for the questions and I lied smoothly enough to make even Franciska jealous.

"Nothing happened," I said, off-hand. "I served the champagne and went home."

"What about the Deputy?" the head waiter mocked.

"He was very gracious," I answered lightly. "Gave me a ten-pengő tip!"

With that, I produced the note my father had given me and stuck it under his nose.

"He must have been extremely drunk," the head waiter grumbled angrily, but left it at that.

All his threats of "seeing to me later" from the night before came to nothing; he moved on without a word and never mentioned the affair again. Well, well, I repeated to myself, you just need to be a little bit clever. I'll buy some handkerchiefs, too, three proper ones and one of those silk doodahs to have poking out of my top pocket. Then I set about devouring my dinner hungrily, had a glass of champagne, smoked a cigarette like a man well pleased with his work, and wandered up to the bar.

It was Friday, the Constable's day. He used to "drop in" on Mondays and Fridays with soldierly precision between eight and nine. It was now eight thirty. I decided to buy a hat as well. That was when Elemér entered.

My enthusiasm for shopping vanished. I stood before him as if I'd stolen the money I was going to spend directly from him and he was about to expose me. I didn't dare look him in the eye. I could feel myself blushing to my roots, and that made me even more embarrassed.

"What happened to you? Why didn't you wait for me this morning?"

"I didn't feel well," I mumbled, staring at my shoes like my mother.

"Are you sick?"

"No, I just…" I shrugged for want of anything better, "don't feel well."

Elemér gave me a searching look. Had he heard something already? flashed through me in fright. What could he have heard? He can't object to my having put one over on the Deputy—quite the contrary in fact! Or had Franciska been talking? I stole a glance at him, but the stiff, grey face gave nothing away. He drew a book out of his pocket.

"It's on syndicalism," he explained. "I don't agree with it, but—" His sentence was suddenly interrupted. I followed his gaze, and my knees began to tremble.

It was the Constable with his suitcases and "batman".

"Snitch!" Elemér whispered with a sour expression.

At that moment, it seemed inconceivable to me that I had ever meant to buy anything from the Constable. I'm a low, dirty pig, I thought, but at the same time I hated Elemér as if *he* were the low, dirty pig.

He signalled me to follow him into the corridor.

"Will you wait for me tomorrow?" he asked when we got there.

"I don't know yet," I shrugged.

"What do you mean, you don't know?"

He looked at me, surprised, and I, too, was a little surprised at myself.

"I went to the doctor this morning," I lied, "and—"

"Are you sick after all?" he interrupted impatiently.

"No," I said, getting into it, "I'm just exhausted from all these nights. Doctor told me to sleep more. So I can't meet you in the mornings for a while."

Elemér said nothing. There was an awkward silence. He was clearly waiting for something further, but I wasn't saying anything.

"You take care of yourself, then," he said finally, extending his hand, his expressionless face not letting on whether he was talking about my physical state or something completely different.

I stayed out in the corridor, pacing anxiously up and down. If he'd come a few minutes later, I thought with a shudder, then…

At that moment, the telephone rang. It rang in the kitchen and I could hear Iluci's voice.

"Yes, Your Ladyship, as you wish."

I forgot about Elemér completely. Was she talking to *her?*

No, it wasn't her. It was only some lady ordering a couple of martinis. Tonight, she'll order a bottle of champagne, I thought with a shudder, and the old, ragged, patched shirt seemed to burst into flames over my heart. What if I have to take my clothes off in front of her?

"Two martinis to 503!" Iluci called out the door.

"Two martinis to 503!" the barman repeated mechanically.

I suddenly turned around, rushed into the bar like a novice thief trying to fence something for the first time and went, my heart beating anxiously, up to the Constable.

That's how it all began.

2

As soon as the constable had left, I withdrew to the toilets and put on some gentleman's cast-off shirt and underpants. Well, well, I smiled, you just have to be a little bit clever. She could ring for me now! I could have undressed before a princess.

I examined myself in the mirror, satisfied. I liked the shirt, the underpants, I liked the world, and the life some gentleman had cast off; but somewhere deep inside me on the outskirts of reason, the secret police of guilt were tiptoeing after my thoughts, hot on their heels. My old shirt, which had served so faithfully during my seven lean years of poverty, I tore into pieces and cast into the toilet. I watched it flush away with the water like a murderer disposing of the evidence, convinced that no one—any longer—could prove a thing. I was seized by some wild, frenetic cheer. I was whistling when I went back to the bar. From then on, I whistled a lot.

The bar was still empty. I looked into the kitchen, had a glass of champagne and then ambled over to reception to see if *she* was home. She wasn't—her key was hanging under her room number. I went back to the kitchen and had another glass of champagne. For goodness' sake, I bet even Marx wore underpants!

"Forever young!" I said cheerfully to Iluci, too cheerful to know what to do with my happiness, and told her a dirty joke.

At last, the first guests arrived. The air soon filled with cigarette smoke, the band struck up their jazz, and the champagne started doing its thing inside my head. I calmed down. Champagne, jazz, smoke, the night—that all meant one thing: *her*. My fantasy, that crazy painter, coloured madly the random, skewed images of desire. In my mind, I was already in her bed; I could barely hear it when someone tried to talk to me. Every fifteen minutes I went out to check if her key was still hanging in reception, and about midnight, when

444

I discovered that it wasn't, I became so dizzy that the supervisor on duty asked me:

"Something the matter, son?"

"The air's not so good down here," I mumbled, and mopped the sweat from my brow.

My heart was beating like the village bell in a fire. She's home! She's home! I ran back to the bar and waited for her call. I was constantly hanging around the kitchen door, and when the phone rang downstairs, my heart skipped a beat. My imagination was in seventh heaven, as more genteel writers would say. The truth, however, is that my head was full of very earthly things indeed. I know it doesn't do to talk of such "prosaic" things when discussing love, but the fact remains that I was perpetually terrified of sweating through my shirt. I kept rushing to the bathroom to wash, but in vain—a few minutes later, I was sweating heavily once more. I had to keep rinsing my mouth, too, because the way God constructed man's mouth, even the thought of the sweetest, most heavenly delights make it sour. I awaited my miracles sweating heavily, bitter-mouthed, and constantly worried about my body odour from all the sweat, or the way my breath would smell; but at the same time, the lines of a nascent poem were humming within me, because poems and miracles are born not with fragrant scents and midwives, but amid secret sorrows, like a poor peasant child.

It was already one and she hadn't rung for me. The phone kept ringing in the kitchen, more and more frequently, as it usually did between one and two. This was "cognac hour", as the waiters jokingly called it, because it was the hour when gentlemen would apparently enquire in the back of the taxi home or during the last dance in some bar if "you wouldn't care, dear, to come and have a cognac back at mine?" The cognac was really flowing that night, but room 205 ordered no champagne.

By two, I was completely overwrought with excitement. The bar had started to empty out, people were ready to go home. There was only one smallish party left at one of the tables, and the waiters were starting to give them looks. I didn't know what to make of her silence. Was she angry that I'd become so forceful at the end? No, that can't be it, I told myself. If she really hadn't wanted "it" to happen, then why had she told me to take my clothes off, why had she invited me into her bed?

I hadn't given that much thought till now. I had told myself that women always play hard to get. But now that I was going over the previous night, I suddenly knew that this was more than that. I saw again the revulsion on her face, I felt her once more kick, bite and scratch me… Why, why, why? I asked myself, clueless. For she had done things even Manci would never have done; why was she so put off by "that"?

The more I thought about it, the less I understood. Would this be what the boys called a "perversion"? I'd heard plenty about "perversions" in the hotel, and had seen quite a few things through the keyholes, but this—or anything like it—never. It was only now that I understood the boys asking each other with a sheepish smile:

"Say, old boy, has it ever happened to you that…"

How I would have liked to ask! But who, who, who? Elemér was my only friend, and you couldn't talk to him about these sorts of things.

"You asleep?" the head waiter growled, because the guests were already making their way to the cloakroom, and I hadn't so much as moved. "Perhaps you'd be so kind as to get back to work!"

It was closing time. I went through the motions mechanically, then headed off down to the kitchen to watch the telephone till Iluci, too, closed up. I kept hoping, till the very last moment, that she'd call for me, but she didn't.

The telephone did not ring.

I was confused. Had Exfix come home?

No. Exfix was not home, as I established beyond a shadow of a doubt next day. He was in Geneva, at the League of Nations as a "government expert".

She didn't call me. Every night, I turned up at the hotel in a fresh shirt and underpants, and waited by the telephone in vain. The Constable, meanwhile, had delivered the new suit as well, and I had a necktie, handkerchief, socks and one of those silk whatsits. The only thing I didn't have is the reason I got all the rest. I was hardly eating, hardly sleeping—I was barely alive. I used to wake with a start after an hour or two of sleep and spend hours weeping alone, like a starving infant.

But one night, about a week after our night together, she came into the bar. She walked past me the way that mere mortals like myself cannot walk past even a dog. The only people capable of such perfect indifference are those whose ancestors have already spent three or four hundred years taking no account of "the staff", and never would until the day they beat them to death. I kid you not, she didn't so much as turn away—if only she had! That would still have held some message for me, something to remind me that I'm a person, too, a person who—for whatever reason—the other does not wish to acknowledge. She was with a big group and could have done it without attracting any attention—but no, why should she? She looked at me, and when I greeted her, she even nodded. Her gaze was neither "cold" nor "disdainful", the way you often hear; oh no, not at all. She smiled. She smiled the way queens smile at adoring crowds, and from that smile you couldn't so much as tell if she knew me or not. She was as impersonal as a lighthouse that projects its beam mechanically onto everything that comes within range and then sweeps on, high above the waves, stark and unapproachable; and as far as it's concerned the human race could drown out there in the dark—what was that to it?

They didn't stay long in the bar. I spied after them when they left; I saw her get into the lift alone and was seized by some desperate hope that perhaps I had imagined it all and tonight, she would call me. I couldn't accept the inevitable even after we'd closed. I sneaked back into the kitchen after everyone had left and watched the telephone till six in the morning. It was only then that I abandoned all hope.

The next night, however, the head waiter called me over.

"Um…" he croaked, a little flustered, "205 called for you. You're to take up a bottle of champagne."

She didn't say a word as to why she hadn't called for me, and when I asked her, she looked at me as if the champagne bottle were asking why she hadn't ordered it before.

"I don't really know," she said absently, as if she didn't like to veer too far from the matter in hand, and pointed a little impatiently at her glass. "Pour, would you, please?"

We drank, and everything turned out the same as last time. This time, too, she was in the living room when I came in, lying on the couch, smoking. The light was off; only the moon lit the room through the open balcony door. It was a warm, rich July night with a full moon, the sky was crammed with stars. She can't have been home long—her ermine cape was still hanging off the arm of one of the chairs, fallen half to the ground, the way she had cast it carelessly aside. She was wearing a silver-studded evening dress and nothing underneath. I had a chance, later, to establish that beyond all doubt, but only by eye. She didn't let me touch her, though she was drunk—perhaps even more drunk than last time. By dawn, she was full of such wild ideas that even the mere mention of them belongs more in a medical textbook, but she would not take off her dress. She only gave into my pleading when I was already half crazy with desire.

"On one condition," she said.

"What?"

She looked at me and was silent.

"You know."

"Yes," I nodded excitedly.

"You promise?"

"Yes."

I promised her everything before we went into the bedroom, but in the end I still couldn't keep my word. We once more ended up in a tussle and I had to force myself on her, in the strictest sense of the word. Afterwards, she went straight to sleep, and now here I was lying beside her open-eyed, hopelessly confused, and understanding just as little as before.

Outside, it was getting light. The birds struck up in the nearby park, the early-morning cargo barge hooted on the Danube.

She suddenly shifted.

"Get up!" she mumbled grumpily and pulled the covers higher.

"Are you angry?"

She didn't reply. There was silence, unbearable silence. Suddenly, I felt I couldn't stand the tension.

"Why is that you don't want *it*?" I whispered.

She didn't reply to that, either.

"For the love of God," I begged, "tell me!"

"I don't want it," she answered, terse and curt, "and if you're ever that forceful again…"

"I won't be!" I swore, and leant over her, imploring. "Are you angry?"

"Let me sleep!" she said and turned away.

That was how we left it. I was convinced, when I stepped out the door, that I would never cross that threshold again. But that night, the very same night, the head waiter called me and, hoarsely, with a strange, beetling look, he once more said:

"Take a bottle of champagne up to 205."

That night, I kept my promise, and everything was the way she wanted. But she didn't call me for six days after that, and by then I was so wild that I couldn't control myself. She threatened; I swore, once again; and from then on, that was how it went. For a while, I managed to restrain myself, and then I would once more break my promise. Then she would scratch and bite me all over, beside herself; I could barely control her. My body was constantly full of scars and there were often bloodstains on my shirt, like on a murderer's just after the deed.

The more I was with her, the less I understood her. She was revolted by what was, for me, the fulfilment, but when I tried to control myself, it seemed to get her even more het up. She wouldn't rest until I was completely wild, and later I got the impression that she enjoyed it when I stopped being a man and behaved with her more like an animal in heat. But then why did she threaten me afterwards? I asked myself—there being no one else to ask—since I never got a halfway decent answer out of her. She was always drunk when I went up; she never called for me sober. Afterwards, she went straight to sleep, and I already feared her waking.

She was unbearable when she awoke. She loathed me, herself, the whole world, and was full of revulsion and cruelty. Whenever I could, I sneaked out while she was asleep, but sometimes she started from her sleep and would chase me out of bed like a dog that had climbed in uninvited. There was so much disdain, anger and hatred in her eyes that more than once, on my way home, I said to myself: never again, never again! But when she didn't call for me, I would have been capable

449

of anything—in the very darkest sense of the word—even the deepest of humiliations.

The worst part was I never knew when she would call. There were times when I was with her every night for a week, and there were times she wouldn't call for two weeks in a row. I couldn't call her on the phone—she'd forbidden that right at the start, and the idea of just going up to see her or talking to her in the corridor or the lobby was, of course, out of the question. At those times, I used to pace up and down like a fever patient, my heart beat wildly, I had horrible visions. And if, after these nightmarish days, already afraid of more of them to come, I would ask her when I could come again, she would always just shrug.

"I don't know," she replied absently. Or she would say: "Maybe tonight. Maybe never."

I often felt she didn't even really consider me human, that I was to her like Cesar, or even less: a household object, and nothing more, that she could pick up and put down as and when she pleased.

My life consisted of waiting. By day for the night, by night for the call. Whatever happened between two meetings I lived in a sort of semi-dream, a narcosis, like an operation you just have to get through, somehow.

My nerves were completely shredded by the constant waiting. I became unbearably tense, quick to anger, impossible to be around. Sometimes I wouldn't say a word to anyone for days, and sometimes the words would pour out of me like some kind of emotional diarrhoea. Then I would talk for hours, yapping away at all and sundry. I became confused, rushed and distracted; I was totally unreliable. I didn't care a fig for my work; that I didn't get fired was only thanks to the midnight orders of champagne.

My head was like a rubbish bin. It was full of the flashy rags of vanity and, deep down at the bottom, under the dust and ash, there were scraps of thoughts, decaying feelings and half-buried convictions in a hopeless mess, mixed with the broken toys of desire.

I finally got hold of the English textbook that once meant Patsy, America and freedom, but now that I had it, I didn't get anywhere with it. Patsy had passed, like childhood; I never thought of America any more and found it impossible to study. I couldn't even read, and at that time, couldn't write. My only spiritual sustenance was the cinema and the radio. I spent all my spare time at the cinema and would always sit beside the radio at the hotel when I had nothing else to do. I didn't care about anything but *her*. I lived in a dreamlike state, whistled a lot, and was bored a great deal.

I became a hideous glutton. I got a taste for sweets, and my pockets were always full of treats and chocolate. I was constantly eating, and yet grew thinner by the day. I was frighteningly pale, there were dark circles beneath my eyes, and sometimes, at dawn, I would feel strange tremors in my heart.

I grew foppish and vain. I covered myself with perfumes and pomade, and indulged my body the way old ladies indulge their senile lapdogs. I lost all sense of proportion. I kept buying things, throwing money out of the window, though it failed to give me real pleasure.

I was tortured by some vague sense of guilt all the time. As soon as I reached the poorer parts of the city, I was seized by a strange, incomprehensible anxiety. I was ashamed of my fine new clothes and was as embarrassed in the shops there as if I'd killed someone, or worse, and was now spending their money, though I proved to myself clear as day that I had no reason to feel guilty. I was spending my own money, and it was nobody else's business. My mother didn't need my income. I was keeping up with the Constable's instalments, and if the others hadn't realized I'd broken the boycott till now, it wasn't likely that they'd realize in the future. As for the classless society… Well yes, there was that. I did still believe in it, just like before, only… was it my fault that they couldn't make it a reality? I can't change the world all by myself. You have to live somehow till the revolution comes, and why should I live badly, if I can live well? At this point, I would usually start whistling, softly, arrogantly, the way I'd seen upper-class gentlemen do it, but in vain—I couldn't whistle my anxiety away.

The soil, of which I was the rightful son, now seemed to slip from beneath my feet. I seemed to be walking a perpetual tightrope between Their Excellencies' suite and the Újpest slums. I belonged neither here nor there, or rather where I did belong I didn't want to belong, and where I wanted to belong, I did not belong. My soul was homeless, and in vain did I seek shelter for it. You couldn't talk seriously with the Countess. After a few minutes, she was seized by a strange anxiety; I could see she felt uncomfortable and then she would gesture me to stop, flustered and tense.

"Forget about all that. Let's drink."

It's not that she was stupid, far from it. She was clever, and not only with an animal intelligence. There was nothing catty about her, no; if I had to compare her to an animal, she was more like a leopard or a lion. But the truth is that, despite all her craziness, she was a clear-headed, well-read and surprisingly worldly person with a refined—a slightly over-refined—intelligence, independent and often original. Occasionally, towards dawn, when I thought she was already dead drunk, she would shed light on such dark corners of life with the occasional flare of a word or a casually dropped remark that I noticed them in awe and wonder.

Women like her are usually labelled "crazy", "sick" or—even more conveniently—"corrupted". But these are just words. Now I know that she was no more corrupted than the class to which she belonged and the age in which she lived. When I think back now to what the great and the good wrote and thought in those days, I'm surprised to see the extent to which her outlook matched theirs. This was that post-war "disillusioned" world view, the view of the "lost generation", the "*neue Sachlichkeit*", and various literary isms, the whole of whose so-called philosophy essentially consisted of those shrugging and dismissive waves of the hand with which peasants, in their own rougher but truer language, used to say: forget it, son, nothing lasts for ever and there's no use pissing in the wind. That was how the "disillusioned" thought; but when the wind turned, they turned with it, not rushing and randomly, but slowly and grindingly like a rusty weather wane, so no one would have anything on them. Because they were smart, cultured and enlightened, their clear-sightedness was not obscured by any kind of preconceptions—when it came to their own interests. They could see the writing on the wall, and the best of them even felt some remorse. They were like jaded, barren women who knew they had already eaten most of their bread and had only their past to look back on, a dubious past at that, and were therefore frantically searching—in a mood of abject *Torschlusspanik*—to bag a young man with a future. They slept in the soft beds of capitalism but they made fun of, and betrayed, them too—as one usually does with fat, rich husbands. They toyed with the idea of Marxism when that was the latest fashion, and something else when it was something else. Freudianism was their bible, it was this they used to explain everything, but deep down they didn't believe in anything except French cooking and American dollars, and after 1929 they didn't even believe in those. When the wind changed, they discovered "the little man", about whom they knew as much as Her Excellency knew about me, and were about as close. "Social conscience" was the buzzword of their literature at the time, and their theatres, too, paraded poverty—mostly to the people causing it, because no one else could very well afford the extortionate ticket prices. The people buying the tickets liked "social conscience" because at that time they were all smart, well read and enlightened, and because writers, despite all their "social conscience" were never too harsh on their audiences. Their works were obscure, like places for secret rendezvous, and no less profit-seeking. The rich consumed their "social" dramas and novels avidly, whose "bitter taste" was just as appetizing as the bitterness of the almonds on their delicate pastries and cakes. If *she* had had any talent for writing, she would no doubt have had a glittering career: audiences would have been fascinated by her.

I, too, was fascinated, no use denying it. I tried to imitate her, but at the same time there was some vague, unconscious resistance within me that I could not—and fundamentally did not want to try to—understand. I never quite believed her "truths", though I was always convinced that she was right, and if you like, she *was* right in the end, at least in the relative sense that everyone is right who drills down deep enough on their own little plot to supply all their needs for oil with which—in one way or another—they can then motor on all the way to the grave. It's just that I was a peasant, and peasants don't believe in truth. Peasants only believe in their survival instincts, and my survival instinct rejected her wisdom like good blood rejects poison.

As to why, I didn't know at the time—how could I have known? You have to have lived a great deal, been passionate and disillusioned and passionate again, before one day noting—quietly and humbly—that the famous "human spirit" is actually just like cheese: by the time it matures, it's already full of maggots. There's a certain kind of wisdom, and not the worst kind, either, that can live only on rot and putrefaction, like a maggot. This is a kind of wisdom which is "deeper", if you will, than the wisdom of the primitive productive classes but that it can no longer produce; it's impossible to live by any more and all you can do is die with it, slowly, by degrees, like the very world of which it was born.

Sometimes I'd spend weeks chewing over one of her comments, while the fact that they'd laid off another hundred and fifty workers in the Ganz factory, and that meant that almost everyone in our building was now jobless, didn't interest me a damn. The range of my curiosity, like a failing organ, shrank day by day; in the end, my universe became so small that it could fit, with all its planets and all its stars, in her bed, covered amply by her blanket. My thoughts were paralysed like stroke victims; they could no longer leave room 205.

I did sometimes feel that things couldn't go on like this. I was struck by sick foreboding, vague ill omens that something "terrible" would happen, and I can remember chilling nights when I would suddenly start from my dreams after those wild nights and look at her sleeping form with the frozen terror of someone terminally ill who, waking from a fever dream, grabs the mirror and sees only death in it.

One night, Elemér came to the bar. He acted like he didn't know any-thing, but he had always been a bad actor and I could see right away he knew everything.

I had long known that I'd become the subject of gossip. Sometimes when I went into the kitchen, conversations would be suddenly dropped, and I could feel oblique glances following me around; I knew people were whispering behind my back. In the first few days, this still upset me deeply, but later I got used to it like a camel to its hump, and in the end I no longer paid it any attention. But I was afraid of Elemér. I was afraid of him in the most serious and most ridiculous sense of the word. As to *why*, I didn't wonder too much—I simply convinced myself that I wasn't afraid of him at all. If he found out, he found out—what did I care? It was no skin off my nose, and he could go to hell. But that was the funniest thing about all this—it really was "no skin off my nose", and if he did find out then he'd find out, who cared; still, I was more afraid of him finding out than of the Devil himself, and though it was obvious that the rumours had reached him, too, I always tried to convince myself he didn't know anything. Now that he was here, standing in front of me, I could see he knew all, and all my tough posturing—telling myself I wasn't afraid of him—was in vain: I could feel the trembling in my knees.

It must have been around eight; there was no one in the bar yet. The moment made me flush with heat, and I was irritated by the thought that I might sweat through my shirt. I did my best to appear open, but kept talking nineteen to the dozen and hardly letting him get a word in edgeways. I was playing for time, just like we'd done in school when we thought the Schoolmaster might spring a test on us. I was hoping that someone would come in sooner or later or that they'd call me away and send me off somewhere, but no one came and no one called for me—we were alone, and there was no escape. There he was before me and, because he was so terrible an actor, even a blind man could see why he'd come. He was behaving like a bumbling small-town doctor the family had asked to pretend that he'd come by on a purely friendly visit because the patient was, unfortunately, far too stubborn to let themselves be examined, though it looked like there was something seriously wrong; please excuse them, doctor, they might not be all there any more. In the end, I had to admit that all this was in vain, and suddenly I switched to the very opposite of my loquaciousness: I didn't say a word.

Elemér treated me as if he were afraid that I really *was* not quite all there any more. He knew me, he knew I was difficult, and he was as cautious as a doctor in a sanatorium. He tried to "ingratiate himself" as they say, but he was far too direct a character and wasn't very good at small talk. He overshot the mark, as the boys would say when someone was being too nice. He talked embarrassingly overmuch and even tried to make some jokes so I could see how cheerful and unsuspecting he was, how he didn't know a thing, oh no, he just happened to be passing and thought he'd look in to chat a little about this and that, all perfectly innocent and above board.

"Feeling better?" he eventually asked, clearly trying to steer the conversation in the right direction.

But I wasn't going to play along. I told him I was, a little, thank you, and then relapsed into silence.

The conversation once more ran aground. I could see that Elemér was now out of ideas as to how he should drag the thing out of me.

"Oh yes!" he said, having thought of something at last, and his face cleared. "How did you like the book on syndicalism?"

But he was out of luck there, too. I told him I hadn't read it yet, I'd been very busy, I'd try to get to it tomorrow or the next day.

It went on like this for half an hour. Then the head waiter called for me from the kitchen, and Elemér of course knew that you couldn't keep the head waiter waiting. In the rush, he suddenly dropped his role and said straight out, with his usual directness:

"Look, I want a word with you. Would you wait for me tomorrow?"

I must have looked pretty alarmed because he quickly added, before I'd had a chance to respond:

"Just a little chat, you know. It's been a while since we talked."

I concurred.

"Some other time, perhaps. I'm very tired tonight."

"All right," he said, because there wasn't much else he *could* say. "Next time, then. I might try and look in at the end of the week."

But he didn't wait till the end of the week; he appeared just two days later. This discussion was even more awkward than the last. For want of anything else, he brought up the book on syndicalism once more, and I didn't dare admit I still hadn't read it. I "winged it" like a schoolboy who hasn't done his homework, making up this and that. Elemér, who would always interrupt me straight away when I got something wrong, now listened to me, nodding away, as if indulging a quiet eccentric. In the end, he asked me again if I would wait for him in the morning, and I again replied, "Some other time, tonight I'm very tired." Then Mr Saccharine walked in with an English guest and we, of course, had to cut our conversation short.

"Let's go down to the basement," Elemér said, and I could hardly say "some other time, tonight I'm very tired" to *that*.

I followed him anxiously. I knew what was coming, and I was afraid I was going to deny it. But as it happened, I didn't get the opportunity. Elemér said, quiet and determined:

"I don't want you to respond in any way to what I'm about to say."

There was no one in the basement, there was only silence and a faint subterranean smell. Thick, rusty pipes ran along the unplastered wall, as if we were wandering through the belly of the hotel, among the exposed bowels of the building. Elemér didn't say anything for several minutes. We walked side by side in silence in the yellowy half-light. Our steps echoed unnaturally under the bare cement vaults.

"You were doing well," he said at last. "*Very* well," he repeated with special emphasis, and then added, without looking at me: "But now you've lost your way."

There was silence, I listened to our reverberating footsteps. Elemér looked at me.

"Understand?"

"No," I replied curtly.

"I can understand you," he said quietly, turning away and adding awkwardly: "I'm your friend. You understand *that*, don't you?"

"Yes," I nodded.

"That's all it is," he said. "I'm your friend, and I can understand you. And you'll understand me too, we've always understood each other. What I want to say comes down to this: have no qualms—I'm not a prude, and I'm not a bourgeois. I don't preach. I'm a Socialist. We can talk calmly and practically, the way conscious proletarians should." He quickly added, because he had clearly noticed something in my face: "No, not now. When you feel ready. Then you can wait for me in the morning and we'll go for a walk in Buda. All right?"

"Yes," I nodded once more.

He pulled a book out of his pocket and told me to read it, and that we'd discuss it next time. Then he gave me his hand, as if nothing at all had happened, and left.

A number of sentences were underlined in pencil in the book.

Elemér's books always had a lot of sentences underlined in pencil, but this had one I know he'd underlined specially for me. He had underlined it twice and put three exclamation marks beside it. It was a quotation from Montesquieu. I still know it by heart and there's not much chance of me ever forgetting it. It went:

> All decent men have some memory in their lives that will make them blush to think of it in a contemplative hour.

I felt a strange lump in my stomach when we parted. It must have been half past nine, the night shift at the bar was ready for its guests, the jazz band was practising a new song. I put the book away, shrugged and began to whistle—softly, disdainfully, the way I'd seen the gentlemen do it. But the lump in my stomach just grew and grew.

By about ten o'clock, I felt sick. At first, I felt tiny, piercing cramps in my stomach, then constant, tearing pain. I'd never had stomach cramps like this before, though I'd lived, as you may remember, on the dog's dinner. I couldn't understand what had got into my stomach, because back then I was still writing poems about the Soul with a capital S, and I didn't know that it could also give you the most merciless cramps, and that it comes not in the fiery chariot of grand visions, but on foot, sweating profusely, by the back stairs, mostly when you least expect it. It had arrived now, and because I was refusing to acknowledge it, it was through severe cramps that it announced that it had arrived, that it was here, still alive and kicking; that it had come again, perhaps for the final time, and if I didn't listen to it now, it would once and for all give up on me.

Needless to say, I didn't listen to it at all. I was consumed by my stomach ache and by hating Elemér. I cursed him privately, wishing he'd go to the devil; why did he have to go sticking his nose into other people's business, the arrogant fool, why doesn't he mind his own damned business? But at two in the morning, when I was certain that she wasn't going to call me, I decided from one moment to the next to wait for him in the morning.

But that didn't happen, either. The more I thought about the conversation we would have, the more I came to see that… what, exactly?

I shrugged. What could I say to him, and what could he say to me? All he knew about women was what Bebel had written about them in *Women and Socialism*, and that wasn't going to help me very much. What else? Well yes, of course. He'd tell me to leave her, that I had lost my way, that there was only one path for a conscious proletarian, and so on and so on. I could almost hear his voice, almost see his gestures, and I knew that what he was going to say would be clever and convincing, as always, and I might even—in the end—promise him everything, but that when *she* called me, I would break all the promises I had made.

I did not wait for him the next day—nor any other day—but in my mind, I was always at that missed meeting and I lived in the world like someone guilty of a grave sin, a murder perhaps, about which no one but Elemér knew. In time, I began to think of him as a sinister blackmailer who abused my constrained position. I hated him for everything that was hateful in my life, and that hatred grew within me day after day like a cancerous tumour.

About two weeks later, one night when I was hanging around the kitchen, one of the junior wine waiters from the bar told me:

"Go upstairs. Elemér's waiting for you."

I answered without hesitation.

"I can't go now, I've got things to do."

But as I said it, I suddenly realized something. I knew that with this lie, I had hit upon the truth.

"Want him to wait for you?"

No, I was about to say, but suddenly stopped. I felt that something was about to be decided once and for all, without appeal, and I was unable to answer. Only sixteen-year-old poets can feel a moment so important and so flooded with symbolism as I felt this one to be. I looked at the wine waiter as if it had been Pontius Pilate himself standing before me, and he had asked: Who do you choose? Jesus or Barabbas?

"No, tell him not to," I replied, and suddenly felt deadly tired, like a murderer who—after denying everything for the longest time—finally cracks and confesses his crime.

I had chosen Barabbas.

3

ONE DAY, MY FATHER VANISHED.

It was a strange day, and it began strangely—I remember singing loudly all the way home. I was coming from *hers*, the Saturday moon was still high over the Danube, but the dawn had lit its fires behind the hills and Sunday was floating towards town with the reddish clouds. The streets, as always at such times, were overrun with lovers. Shadowy forms pressed together, swaying in the bluish gloaming as if blown by the wind, a strange wind from someplace else. You could hear nervous female giggling from the parks, cars with curtains drawn sped past on the abandoned *Ring*, kissing couples shimmied in doorways, and all this—beneath the reddish clouds—was like something from a poem.

There was a couple kissing in our doorway too. I had noticed them from afar as I was crossing the vacant plot, but it was only as I got closer that I realized it was my mother and father. They were both a little tipsy, but so charmingly and playfully so that after a few minutes, their contagious good mood had got to me too. They were waiting for Herr Hausmeister, because the gate was—of course—still locked, and Herr Hausmeister did not like to rush. My father gave the gate a rattle, accompanying it with an appropriate tune:

Darling, open up the door!

My mother was in no less good a mood, so she joined in softly, just at the perfect moment:

I won't, I won't, they'll hear next door!

And then the old man let loose his fine, deep baritone and sang:

If they hear, then let them hear—
They already know both far and near
That it's you alone I love
I love
You I'll be always
Thinking of.

The morning wind cartwheeled over the vacant plot, sweeping up the litter, carrying it along and stirring it on high; but under the reddish clouds, even that rubbish looked glorious—the world was so young, everything suited it.

"How is it," my father wondered, "that you can't help singing on mornings like this? I remember I was always in a foul mood if we had to stand watch at night, but when the sky went red like this, God knows why, but all of a sudden, I felt I had to sing."

Meanwhile, he'd mischievously kept his finger on the bell, occasionally adding the odd snatch of serenade:

Baby, open up the door!

Herr Hausmeister, at last, came shuffling out. His rumpled slippers resounded sleepily on the uneven stone floor, and his nightshirt and long trousers protruded from under his half-donned jacket. My father raffishly threw him a pengő.

"Forever young!" he called with great conviction and patted the sleepy Herr Hausmeister chummily on the behind.

Upstairs, he opened a bottle of red wine and we sat around the table, humming and drinking. They grew more cheerful with every glass, while I slowly—though I don't know why—grew more and more melancholy. I felt so old beside them, and youth seemed so unbearable. I wanted to tear it off me, the way people fleeing a fire will tear off their burning clothes, but I knew that I had locked the door and there was no escaping this fire. I'm going to burn up, I thought, as I sipped the wine.

My "folks" didn't notice that there was anything wrong with me—they were pretty caught up in each other. My father was humming:

I walked in the quiet forest glade
I saw a bird there in the shade
And a nest made just for two
How I fell in love with you

"You know when your old man learnt that song?" he asked, immediately answering his own question with a dreamy little sigh: "The night I first laid eyes on your mother."

"Yes, you've told us before," my mother chided, but you could see she was enjoying his forgetfulness.

My father laughed.

"Now look at her," he joked. "Old as the hills. You'd never know she was young and pretty once. But she was, oh how she was! Believe it or not, it wasn't a bit hard, fallin' for her."

"You never fell for no one in your life!" my mother answered back tipsily, because she always got cocky when she drank. "You didn't love me at all, did you?"

"As if you loved me, back then?"

"I asked you first."

"What d'you want me to say?" my father said, turning his wine glass round and round. I could see his thoughts were wandering far from the hearth. "Back then, I was just marvellin' at all you girls," he said. "I didn't have a clue about love!"

"And now you do?"

"Wish I didn't!"

"Why?"

"Because when you start clinging to one skirt, it means you're gettin' old."

My mother laughed harshly.

"Who's clinging to one skirt here?"

"This here man," my father said, slapping his hand to his heart. "Devil take it all!"

"Flatterer," grumbled my mother, all the while cramming herself with his ingratiating smile the way people cram a winter trunk with necessaries half an hour before their train departs.

"Why're you so quiet, eh?" asked my father. "Pinin' for your girl?"

"I ain't pinin'."

"Well, and don't you start!" he threatened. "I don't like it. Leave the long faces to the horses. Where's my wallet?" he said, flashing me a glance and pointing to his waistcoat, which he'd thrown on the bed when we got home.

"How much is in there?"

"Thirty pengős."

"Go live it up!" he said. "Never going to be young twice, are you?"

"You mad?" my mother yelled at him, deadly serious this time. "Is that what you want to teach the child?"

"He's no child. I just did the maths, and he's the same age you were when I met you."

My mother looked like she didn't want to believe it. I could see her counting in her head.

"Yes," she said quietly, and her eyes clouded over. "How strange," she sighed. "My God! My masters seemed so old then, though they can't have been older than we is now."

"And? If you don't want to get old, best go hang yourself. Well come on, then, you old maid, come to bed," he said, poking my mother gently in the ribs. "And don't you go lettin' yourself get all down in the dumps. So we're getting a bit worn, well, so what of it? That's the way it is, with boots the same as people. But anyone who leaves a lad like him to fill his boots ain't got worn down in vain, take my word for it—and take my word for it you can, I got it straight from the mouth of St Peter!"

He was so carefree, so calm and confident, that it was as if he really had sorted everything out with St Peter already; as if he'd sown, and reaped, and found his harvest good.

"G'night, son!" he said with a smile, putting his arm around my mother's waist the way he used to, and before he went out, looked over his shoulder and gave me a wink.

That was at dawn, around five in the morning. Around seven o'clock that evening, he left the house and didn't come back.

*

As to why, I had no idea. My mother didn't bring it up, and I didn't ask. We kept quiet about it, the way only peasants could.

Later, I would often think back to that final dawn. Did he already know he was going to go? Or did something happen between five in the morning and seven that night? What could have happened? What went on in the kitchen while I was asleep in the room? Or did he himself not have any inkling when he left home, and whatever happened only happened later? But what, what, *what* could have happened? Was it yet another woman? Or?…

I stopped there. I didn't dare take things any further. As if I care, anyway, I shrugged. It's their affair. What's it got to do with me? They don't exactly break themselves in half over me. I tried to drive the thought away, but it kept coming back like a ghost in a fairy tale, and kept me in a perpetual state of turmoil. My fingers shook whenever I opened the paper: I was looking for my father's name. Only now did I notice that from the very first moment I'd known him, I'd thought him capable of anything, both in the most abject and in the most noble sense, capable of the worst and the best deeds, but now—of course—it wasn't the best of deeds I was worried about. I thought of his shady, mysterious "deals", the incredible sums that had flowed through his fingers like water, and… No, I didn't dare go on. I shuddered. Is *that* why my mother was keeping so quiet?

Or did she, too, not know anything?

I noticed that she was avoiding me. In the early mornings, when I came home, she always pretended to be sleeping, but later, when I went to bed and was quiet in my little improvised bed, I often heard her crying in the kitchen. In the evening, when I woke up, she was generally out, and when she *was* home, she made sure she was never alone. Márika would be sitting in the kitchen with her in excited, *sotto voce* conference, and if I came in, they would fall awkwardly silent.

These were suffocating days. Our unspoken words seemed to have crept into every corner of the flat and took wing in the dark like bats, while I tossed and turned sleeplessly.

One evening, something strange happened. Around six thirty, I woke to find someone banging on the kitchen door. He must have been banging away for a while, because he was banging hard enough to set the glass rattling. I pulled on my trousers and rushed out to open the door.

A strange man entered, very het up. He was a huge, thickset man with a scar on his big bald head, and pockmarks and stubble on his rough, bony face. He kicked the door closed behind him, looked me up and down with his sharp, piggy eyes and, instead of a greeting, yelled at me:

"Why didn't you open the door?"

"I was asleep," I replied, frazzled.

"You Mishka's son?"

"Yes."

"Your mother not home?"

"No."

He pushed me aside and went into the room. He stopped, looked around, and then said, a little more quietly:

"I've brought a letter from your father."

"I see," I nodded, excited.

He produced the letter.

"Give it to your mother," he said, turned on his heel, and left without saying goodbye.

It was only then that I came to from my shock. I tore open the kitchen door and called after him:

"What should I say to mother, who called?"

He looked back, but did not respond. He hurried, silent, into the staircase and quickly vanished.

I looked at the crumpled envelope, heart thumping. Now we'll see, I thought, and quickly turned the key in the kitchen door. I went into the room and carefully opened the envelope along the gummed edges. The letter was no more than five or six lines in all; they were hurried, agitated lines, and you could tell they had been written in a hurry, on the fly—the letters skipped excitedly up and down within the crooked lines. There was no date or place, and the text itself did not shed any more light on where or when these lines had been written. They didn't shed much light on much of anything else, either, really, but there were two lines in it that set me terribly on edge. It said something like:

I still don't know anything. It may be that by the time these lines reach you I, too, will be home, but I also might never see either of you again.

I read and reread the letter, but was still none the wiser. Now I understood everything even less. So he does want to come home, and he might even *be* home soon, but… "*I also might never see either of you again.*" Why, why, why? What did all this mean?

I must have been lost in thought for a while, because when I looked at the clock, I was horrified to see that it was past seven thirty. I dressed hurriedly, gummed the envelope back down and placed it just inside the kitchen door before I left, so my mother would think someone had slipped it under the door when no one was home.

I couldn't get those two sentences out of my head. In the morning, when I got home, he might already be there, I thought, and from then on, I was always waiting for him. I would start from my sleep whenever someone walked past our window and turn, startled, in the street if I heard someone whistling behind my back.

I didn't want to think of him—and thought of nothing else. I had wild, scrambled dreams. Cars bristling with machine guns chased him through dark alleys as he climbed up belfries like a cat, or jumped easily and gracefully from a tall building and then sauntered casually off as if nothing had happened. It seems that even in my dreams I couldn't imagine any harm actually befalling him. Whole packs of people came at him, knives flashed, guns flared, but in the end he always came out on top. He always won, he always had the last laugh. He had his fine, strong teeth, he drank his wine, made up to my mother, and I could hear his raw, rich baritone sing that life was good, that it was good to be alive. Or, it would be morning and I could hear his cheery whistling from the kitchen as he shaved, half naked, before that scrap of mirror, and in my dream I was no longer angry about the naked woman tattooed on his chest, with the real hair—and not just on her head.

In my waking moments, however, I was not nearly so forgiving. I cursed him and God Almighty for lumbering me with a father like him. I thought of him with disdain and unflinching hatred, but at the same time, I missed him terribly. It was as if the spirit had gone out of our apartment since he was no longer with us. My mother, once more, kept meticulous order, everything gleamed with cleanliness; there was no one, any more, to make it untidy. It was the order and quiet of the cemetery. Sometimes, when I came into the empty flat, I almost had the feeling that no one lived there any more. The apartment was dead, its corners webbed up by the grey spiders of care, and our days hung in those webs like flies.

The memories of our brief "riches" quickly disappeared. The wardrobes emptied out, the flat grew bare, and even the gilt-framed mirror disappeared from above the sink. One morning, when I came sleepily home, I simply couldn't find our bedding. That, too, had gone, and I didn't ask where. I slept once more on the bare floor, because Manci was frightened of my "illness" and had asked me not to lie in her bed.

Only my father's clothes were left in the wardrobe. My mother didn't sell his things; she left everything just where it was. His ashtray, however, strangely disappeared. It was a worthless, battered little thing, without any value whatsoever. I didn't understand where it could have got to. But one evening, when I reached into my mother's drawer, I found it there, to my surprise. There was a half-smoked cigarette in it. Dappermishka's last cigarette? I don't know, I never found out. My mother, who was otherwise so compulsively tidy, kept this half-smoked cigarette in her drawer till the end. It lay there among her obsessively arranged boxes like a dead body someone just didn't want to bury.

Then one day, his clothes vanished, too. The flat was now like a bare tree in winter; the fish-faced pawnbroker wouldn't have given us ten pengős for it.

My mother was in a terrible state. She was drying out before my eyes like a plant whose roots have rotted away. She grew thin and wrinkled and started greying heavily. She aged almost overnight. She barely resembled that fetching young woman who'd sung along with Dappermishka under the reddening clouds... how long ago, exactly? A few weeks before. She let herself go, regressed to her peasant past, and became a spinsterish, burnt-out case. The transformation was as sudden, from one moment to the next, as that of the fields after a hailstorm. Her life was once more lying fallow, weeds seemed to have overgrown her soul. Only her eyes still reminded me of the old her—her deep-set, dark little peasant eyes, which were now forever red and swollen from crying.

I suspected—no, I think I knew—that she was starving. I had to have known, for I could see that there wasn't so much as dry bread in our kitchen. And yet I didn't give her any money.

Not because I didn't have it, either. Back in those days, I always had a few pengős in my pocket, and it wasn't that I begrudged her those. I was more afraid that if I gave her money once, I would have to give again, and that she would ask for more each time—until we were back to the way things had been before. And I was not having that. *She* often sent me out for this or that and, needless to say, the shops did not give me things for free. And, to be fair, she always told me to go ahead and take money out of her purse, but the problem was that… well… she told me that even when I hadn't spent any money on her.

It had begun that first morning. I was too drunk, at the time, to see what she was getting at, and later—when I was sober—I thought she'd just said it because she was drunk. But I soon realized that was not the case. The invitation was often repeated.

"My purse is over there," she would say casually, as if it were the most natural thing in the world. "Take some cash."

I was overcome with savage anger whenever she said it. I was always scared I'd end up hitting her. But I didn't dare say a word. I pretended not to have heard and gave her purse a wide berth. We never talked about it, and I still don't know whether she even noticed that I never once took money out of her purse. But since I didn't take money on those occasions, I couldn't take money on any other, and so I ended up paying for everything out of my own pocket.

That was why I didn't give my mother any money. The thought that I'd have to reach into *her* purse one day after all on account of my mother was more terrible to me than the knowledge that she was starving.

Yes, that's how I was by then. Once you breach that narrow barrier your conscience draws before your actions, there's no stopping—the tide drags you on. Only the first murder is a crime. The second, the third, the hundredth—those are merely consequences.

*

One evening, though, my mother did say something, after all. We were alone, it was about seven in the evening, and I was washing at the tap. My mother paced up and down beside me for a long while, arranging this and that, before all of a sudden saying:

"Could you give me a bit of money?"

My heart climbed into my throat.

"How much you need?"

She sighed.

"A lot. I can't make up the rent."

"You know I've got my instalments to pay."

"I know," she sighed again, "but it's very bad this time, son. Herr Hausmeister wants to throw us out."

How many times I'd heard that before, and yet the familiar words had not lost their menace. I glanced, involuntarily, at the lye bottle, and shuddered.

"He wants to throw us out?"

"Yeah," she nodded. "We're three months behind."

"How can that be?" I burst out. "Father ain't been gone three months... And he always had plenty of money..."

I fell silent. It was only now I remembered who I was talking about. There was silence. My mother stared, blanching, at her shoes.

"You know how forgetful he can get," she mumbled. "He forgot to pay, and Herr Hausmeister didn't tell him. He knew he was good for it, and besides, he was scared of him..." she burst into tears. "Now he don't have nothing to be scared of! Oh God, oh God, what we going to do?"

She slumped onto the footstool, buried her face in her apron, her whole body trembling with her sobbing. I watched her and felt like spitting in my own face.

"Couldn't you ask Father for it?" I asked helplessly.

My mother went red.

"You father's not in town," she said barely audibly.

"Where is he?" I blurted out.

My mother glanced away, swallowed, and said:

469

"Somewhere in the country."

"Couldn't you write him?"

"No."

I could have asked, of course, *why* she couldn't write to him, and a whole bunch of other things, but I was afraid that… she might answer me. I quickly stuck my head back underwater and didn't say a thing.

"Couldn't you ask that man to wait just a little with your instalments?"

"You mad?" I snapped so loud that even I was shocked. "That man is a friend of the Major's. It's not been two weeks since they fired a waiter for not paying."

That was true, but I was still lying. I could have tried, and frankly, I did have some little hope of succeeding. The Constable liked me. He used to chat to me, which he never did with anyone else; he used to take an interest in my affairs—he wanted to know all about me. Once, he'd said to the head waiter:

"This boy has more brains than three grown-ups."

You like that sort of thing at sixteen, of course you do; I liked it, too. And yet I was still repelled by him from that first moment on. There was some vague, inchoate fear floating around inside me—as to why, I never stopped to analyse. Back then, everything inside me, not just this, was so undefined. I was terrified of the light, and fled into the shadows—I didn't want to think about things. I was living like a newborn animal—I had only my instincts left. But they, whenever I got near the Constable, would say: careful, careful, careful!

"You could ask him," my mother insisted timidly. "What harm could it do? At worst, he'll say no, and there ain't no harm in that."

No, there was no harm in *that*; I was afraid of the opposite. I was scared he'd say *yes*, and…

"I ain't that desperate!" I yelled hysterically. "Not yet, not yet!"

My mother looked at me, shocked.

"What you talkin' about? I don't understand you."

I didn't quite understand myself, either. I looked on in alarm at what was happening to me. I felt a terrifying trembling in my heart and the blood went to my head.

"I won't hear of it!" I cried, and suddenly knew that I didn't only mean it for my mother.

No, I was not that desperate, not yet!

4

WE DID MANAGE TO MAKE it past the first again, somehow. As to how, I have no idea. I suspected that my mother was once more washing for Herr Hausmeister's "friends" for free, but I didn't know for sure. My mother didn't say a thing about it, and I didn't ask. We kept quiet once more.

I still didn't give my mother money, but I did take her home food every day. I bought the food in elegant stores downtown, but before I took it home, I would re-wrap it in newspaper so she'd think I was taking it out of my rations at the hotel, the way I'd done before. We didn't talk about that, either. I put the packet of food on the kitchen table at dawn, when I got home, then went into the room and went to bed. By the time I got up, the food was no longer there. That was the only way I had of knowing that my mother had eaten it—there were no other signs. When I got home, she was still asleep—or at least, pretending to be, and when I got up, she was already out.

I had, it seems, alienated her even further with my questions. She was now literally avoiding me. In the evening, when she heard me get up, she would sneak out of the apartment and go to Márika's. The only time she'd be home was when Árpád hadn't gone out, but then Márika would come over to ours.

"I don't want to breathe the same air as that toad," she would say, because that was how she was referring to her husband by then; the husband she had once been so in love with.

My father's disappearance had brought the roof crashing down on them, too. They had managed, till then, to get by somehow. The old man couldn't pass Márika without slipping her a pengő or two, and I suspect he would occasionally give her larger sums as well. That source had dried up, of course, and at the worst possible time. The cleaning firm where Márika had worked went bust, like so many other businesses servicing the middle classes. Horthy's fine, feudal society that had already sucked all the blood out of the peasants and the workers, now turned in its desperation to devouring itself; it started biting its own tail: the already weakened middle class. Engineers were now driving taxis, lawyers hawking this and that, civil servants selling vacuum cleaners door to door; there were even ladies who, having lost their husbands, sank so low as... keeping store.

But these were the exceptions. Most people decided to embezzle instead, or commit suicide rather than sink so low. The gentlemen of the middle classes looked down profoundly on anything other than office work. Whenever a middle-class woman opened a tobacco stand, the newspapers would devote several column inches to gasping at the fact, and the ladies and gentlemen of the readership would shake their heads sadly, wondering what the world was coming to.

They were already up to their ears in debt and moral decay, but they never let their petty prejudices slip an inch. At home, the owls of want hooted at them from every corner, but outside the house, they carried on with their showy lifestyles. "One has one's social obligations," they'd say. "One cannot live beneath one's station." But they had no problem with owing the starving cobbler money; and if the poor man ever snapped with impatience, they would call him a Communist and threaten to see he got his comeuppance.

Half the patrons of our bar were still from the middle classes, though few bars in town were more expensive. They didn't drink much, it's true, and whenever they could, they "forgot" to tip, but what they spent on Saturday night would have kept us comfortably for a week. As to where they got the money, that only came out later, in the court papers, or after the suicide of some "pillar of the community" or other. For the spate of suicides was increasingly widespread in society circles, too—there they used Veronal and Luminal which, I daresay, were more pleasant than drinking lye, but had the same effect nonetheless.

These days I know, of course, that even hardship is relative, like everything else in life; but back then, I must confess, whenever people talked about the suffering of the middle classes, it made me want to laugh. What they considered suffering was—for us out in Újpest—unimaginable luxury, even at the best of times. Every day, you read in the papers that some elegant couple had "chosen to take their own lives in the face of mounting financial difficulties" with the eternal refrain that "the maid had found them dead in their bedroom in the morning". But they could still afford a maid! I said to myself, failing to understand it all.

I thought of Mátyás's family who slept seven to a room because they had to rent out the kitchen. Their nocturnal lodger paid four pengős a month and those four pengős were the family's only steady income. When they got to eat, they ate whatever the children had managed to steal, since Mátyás didn't know how to steal; all he knew was how to work. He simply could not, however, get a job. This despite the fact that he was a big man, strong as an ox and good-hearted, like a big bear in a children's story. When I first came up to Budapest, he had been one of the best earners in the house. They had, rather extravagantly, lived in a bedsit *overlooking the street*, on the first floor.

Mátyás was a metalworker, outstanding and reliable at his job. He didn't drink, he didn't gamble, he didn't go chasing women. On Saturday night, he would take his wages straight home and never missed a mass on Sunday. But a year and a half ago he too was laid off, and in that year and half, Mátyás's coal-black hair turned white. He couldn't find work, neither could his wife, and his children were all of school age. They moved from the first floor down into the basement and no longer only went to mass on Sundays—they now had the leisure to do so on weekdays too. But the heavenly authorities were busy and left their daily prayers unanswered. They failed to assign the family any work, and no manna dropped through the basement window. And, the lilies of the field notwithstanding, their clothing wasn't seen to either. Mátyás knew that his pretty young wife occasionally slept with Herr Hausmeister for the rent; she, it seems, must have told him in advance, because Mátyás would always leave the house at such times—usually taking his five sons to church. Everyone in the building knew what went on at Mátyás's during mass. The children, true to habit, would go spy on Herr Hausmeister and watch the alarm clock to see "how long it lasted". In the end, Mátyás's sons were so afraid of what the other children said that they didn't dare show their faces.

They hid in the basement like hunted rats. What could Mátyás have felt about all that?

"It's easy for them," said the middle class when discussing the "lower orders"; it was one of their favourite phrases, and I heard it often. "They don't have needs."

That's how they thought about the "lower orders", and that's how they treated them. The judges, most of whom were middle class, were incredibly harsh with the poor. They showed even children no mercy if they stole bread when they were starving. "An example must be made"—that was the principle Their Honours crowed from the top of the dung heap that was the Hungarian justice system.

But how quickly all those ladies and gentlemen forgot their precious dignity when their own bread began running short. Then they complained that they were paid too little. Well, that may be true, but the "lower orders" still thought it a lot, because that little could have comfortably kept… two or three families of workers.

This "upper middle class" that dealt so brutally with the poor in the name of Christian principles, now—when it, too, got into trouble—let itself go far faster than the "lower orders" they so looked down on. The papers were full of their official scandals, embezzlement and fraud, even though when it came to "gentlemen" the papers tried to keep quiet as long as possible. At this point, almost everyone in Hungary was for sale—if not for money, then for a job, or directorship, or rank and status or political promises. Yes, when the chips were down, the gentlemen would do anything, and by this time, it wasn't just the gentlemen.

There was a rather elegant little bar near the hotel whose proprietress, interpreting correctly the spirit of the age, specialized exclusively in the buying and selling of well-bred ladies. She ran only the most exclusive society women and wouldn't touch anyone else—perhaps the occasional actress at most, if they'd made a name for themselves, but actresses had always been a case apart. We bellboys, too, so to speak, had our commercial ties with her. Whenever a rich foreigner made discreet enquiries of us, we would send them to her elegant little bar, which they would always find charming. I remember a British gentleman once saying:

"It's unique!" with an admiring click of his fingers.

And unique it was. Everything was done in the most exquisite taste; one part of the clientele didn't even know there was anything going on at all. Fanny, the proprietress, whom everyone called only by her first name, would occasionally conduct a lady, running late, to a table where a gentleman would be waiting, the way people generally did with ladies who'd arrived a little late. That was all there was to it, and what could be less objectionable than that? The conversation was polite and restrained; couples would talk theatre and books, the social whirl, have a couple of drinks, and then leave.

Nothing ever actually took place in the bar. Fanny was jealous of her reputation and would have no immoral goings-on in her establishment. Besides, she never kept her "goods" in stock—she worked only to order, like the finest tailors. Her place was frequented mostly by aristocrats, money men, politicians and captains of industry. Over a cocktail, they would discreetly enquire if Miss So-and-so was available yet. That's how they would ask—whether she was "available", because, being men of the world, they knew that a woman's virtue was like fruit: it had its time. Fanny would find out. She knew the city's orchards well and had excellent connections. The exclusive society women would rush to hers in their cars like firefighters to a blaze, all the while never hesitating to call the maid a whore if she got home after ten from her afternoon off, because needless to say they still kept maids and needless to say they still did not consider them people.

Oh yes, there was still always a maid and a dog in the household, and of the two, the dog had the better life. The maid couldn't eat what she herself had cooked for the family—she got special "servants' rations"; and as to what they were like—the less said, the better. In most households the maid had to get up at six, and if her employers decided to entertain till six in the morning, they had to stay up till six. They did not have days off, and had to make do with a Sunday afternoon instead; and they were still expected to be home before the gates were locked. Maids had to kiss their mistress's hand deferentially; in some places, their master's too. The older sons of the household would creep to their rooms at night, a fact tacitly acknowledged in most places, and there were even some households where the maid was more or less expected—during those testing times of the boys' growing pains—to serve the family in this way, too. A favourite bon mot about the servants was that they were the "paid enemy", and even after twenty years of service, people were convinced that the only reason their maid never stole was because she never had the opportunity. They locked all the cupboards as a precaution, including the larder, and if they *still* got suspicious, they would frisk their maids, to which by law—there was a special law for servants—they were entitled. Their wages, however, would not always be paid on time, and if a girl dared so much as open her mouth, there was hell to pay—they would immediately call her an idiot or a Communist, and if that didn't work, strike her. The middle class, which was so proud of its much-vaunted Christian values, regarded this behaviour as normal and was—what's more—absolutely convinced that their maids owed them a debt of gratitude.

Their masters had always looked on the peasants and the workers as a sort of domesticated animal that God had created for their service. They remembered the days of the Soviet Republic in the same way a coachman remembers a particularly wilful episode with his horse, and it never crossed their aristocratic minds to wonder whether it really was a coincidence that Communism had happened to come to *this* country in particular. They carried on taking no notice of the problems of the poor and carried on not learning from their own. Even now, when the capitalist elite had fleeced them for everything they were worth, they still stuck with them politically and voted exclusively for those who could best be relied upon to bleed the people white. They had always been the staunchest bastion of reactionary politics and now, in these unfortunate times, they turned even further to the right. They expected their salvation from some strangely Hungarian, gentrified version of Fascism and only had misgivings about Hitler (for a while) because his party was called the *Arbeiter-partei*: the Workers' Party. Later, when they established the Nazi Party in Hungary, they left that word out of the name, because after all, *that* wouldn't do—*that* was a bridge too far. Times may change, but God's immutable law did not, even under Hitler: a worker was still just a dog, while even in hell, a lord was still a lord.

*

477

The typesetter and his wife, however, were no lords. They were the "lower orders" who apparently had no needs—but strangely enough, they still clung to an odd desire to eat. Every morning, they would cycle into town, going from place to place to look for jobs, but their situation did not improve—they only wore out their tyres. One morning, they could no longer patch them, and since they couldn't afford new ones, and could no longer bear to starve, either, they had to sell the bicycle. They ate what they'd got for it in a matter of days, and then they were stuck, starving, with no money for the tram, three hours from the centre of town. Even sitting is no fun when you're starving, let alone traipsing six hours a day. But the typesetter still traipsed into town every day because the authorities in heaven, it seemed, had given even typesetters souls, and his soul clearly could not accept that it should be not the Lord in heaven, but the lords and ladies down here on earth that would make him shuffle loose this mortal coil. His soul wanted to live; it wanted to perpetuate itself in little Árpáds, but the gods, sadly, had forced it into a human form and that form couldn't take walking six hours a day on an empty stomach. To do *that*, it seems you have to have Dappermishka for a father and not a Salgótarján miner whose family inherited lung disease like counts inherited titles.

One morning, Árpád could not get out of bed. Márika sold what furniture was left, but that was only enough to feed her husband for a week. Then she had to sell the bed, and where there's no bed, there's nowhere to be bedridden. Árpád got up and dressed, but never went into town again. His trips had always been in vain, it's true, but he could still come home in the evening and tell his wife:

"Maybe tomorrow."

Now, there was nothing to say. He sat silent in the window day in, day out, in the place where the baby carriage had once sat, staring at the passers-by with such a glazed expression, he might as well have been blind.

The first time he vomited blood, Márika ran to my mother in tears. She must have felt terribly guilty; I could hear her blaming herself through the door. She ate more or less nothing for two whole weeks, cramming every available morsel into her sick husband. Márika was a

478

good soul, but the gods, unfortunately, had crammed her soul, too, into a human body, and the human body does strange things if it goes unfed for two weeks. On the third week, she called Árpád a lazy pig, burst into tears, felt horribly guilty and apologized; but a few days later was even meaner. Since she couldn't blame herself for her problems and, as a devout Catholic, could no more blame the Trinity, she blamed poor Árpád for want of anyone else. You have to blame *someone*.

I remember one exchange between them. On one of my days off, I visited Árpád and what I saw shocked me so much I couldn't speak for several minutes. It wasn't so much Árpád that shocked me, for I saw him every day in the window, but more the room, which I hadn't seen in months. It was completely empty. There was nothing but two battered suitcases in it and a raw wooden crate serving as a table. Only the lighter spots on the bare walls indicated where the gilt-framed mirror had hung, where had stood the bed, the wardrobe and the couch—those lighter spots stood out on the wall like tombstones in a bare crypt.

Márika noticed my shock and burst into tears.

"At least if we had a baby!" she sniffled. "If only we had a baby."

"Yes," muttered Árpád, "then he could be starving to death now right along with us."

That was what had occurred to me, too, but not Márika. Her eyes flashed at Árpád.

"At least I'd know what I was starving *for!*" she screamed, a frantic hatred in her eyes.

Árpád did not reply. What could he have said? He blinked, pale, behind his thick glasses which exaggerated his bloodshot eyes frightfully. He began to cough, pressing his handkerchief to his mouth, and before he put it away, sneaked a quick look. None of us said a thing—a nasty silence descended on the room.

Suddenly, Márika began sobbing loudly. Árpád went over to her, stroked her head shyly, awkwardly, and—as if in response to her silent self-recriminations—said:

"You're just hungry, that's all."

No, it couldn't have been easy, hating Árpád, but when God gives he gives with both hands, and eventually even gave Márika a reason to hate him. Árpád started going out at night. Rarely at first, then more often, and eventually every night. By that point, they were no longer on speaking terms—screaming terms, at most—and whenever Márika screamed "Where were you last night?" Árpád would just reply:

"I was busy."

"He won't tell me no more," Márika complained to my mother. "He just sits there in the window, all silent."

In the building, where everyone knew everything about everyone else, they knew about Árpád's mysterious wanderings, too. Previously he had been the most respectable young man in the building, the ideal with which unhappy wives reproached their husbands. They'd turned away from Márika some time before, because she'd become foul-mouthed and had quarrelled with half the building, but they liked Árpád and pitied him—and couldn't understand what was wrong with him. Was he drinking? No, no one ever saw him come home drunk, and besides, they knew he didn't like alcohol. Was it gambling, then? Not a chance. What did he have to gamble with? Did he have a lover? Well, yes, that was the most plausible version, it's true, but somehow no one wanted to believe it. Árpád?… Ah, nonsense, people would say dismissively. But then, where did he go all night?

"Maybe he's working?" I once suggested during the course of one of these conversations in the building, because I didn't want people to gossip about him even more.

"Nah, his wife would know," Rózsi replied, and of course there wasn't much I could say to that.

Then the one-eyed wheelwright took the pipe out of his mouth and said:

"Maybe he's got some work that's…"

He fell silent. He was a decent man and didn't want to cast aspersions. I could see he was sorry he'd said anything at all. But Rózsi, who would have sold her grandmother for a juicy piece of gossip, was all over it like a vulture.

"It could be," she enthused, suddenly officious. "He is a *printer* after all…"

And she looked at us as if to say, *you know*.

"Ah, nonsense," I said angrily, but I must confess, the suspicion took root in me too.

Their money's got to come from somewhere, I reflected, and even if they were starving, they still had to pay rent. But I soon found out that Árpád wasn't printing dirty pictures or counterfeit money—or doing anything at all, in fact, that would allow him to pay the rent.

One night, about six, I woke to the opening of the door and heard Márika's voice in the kitchen.

"I've figured out what that good-for-nothing's up to!" she said, full of excitement.

"Shh!" my mother chided, "Béla's still sleepin'."

Márika dropped her voice to a whisper, but whatever she said got my mother so excited that it was now she who forgot all about whispering.

"How d'you know *that*?" she asked aloud.

Márika was quiet for a moment, then said evasively:

"Somebody told me."

My mother didn't ask who: that sort of thing wasn't done in Újpest. If someone wanted to tell you something, they'd go ahead and tell you, and if not, why bother asking? I listened attentively.

"What d'you say to that, then?" I heard Márika say.

"I don't believe it."

"What d'you mean, you don't believe it?" Márika asked testily.

"I don't believe it," said my mother "Árpád was always a Social Democrat."

"*Was*," Márika said, emphasizing the past tense. "Now he keeps cursin' them, too. He says they sold out the proletariat to Horthy."

"Lots of people say that," replied my mother. "Men'll say anything if they've got too much time on their hands. It don't add up to anything. Not a bit of it. It's all gossip, just talk. But what d'you mean, he's doin' *underground work*?"

"He's turned Commernist. He's gone and joined the Commernists."

"Come off it, there ain't even a Commernist Party."

"That's why they're working underground."

"Then how could they have seen him?"

"They just did."

"They only saw him working for *a* party—I'll bet that's how all this started. But he must be working for the Social Democrat Party, always did. He always went to their meetings, I'll bet that's where he's going now."

"All night?"

"He'd come home late at night before, too, when they had a meeting. Now he ain't got the money to come in once the gates are locked, so how's he supposed to get home? Must sleep at a friend's."

"More like the Devil's!" snapped Márika. "He's gone and got mixed up with the Reds. I have it on good authority."

"Good authority!" grumbled my mother. "Good authority. I'm a good authority, too. And I say Árpád's always been a good man, and good men ain't Commernists."

"Then he ain't a good man."

"Stop saying that! Stop bein' so ungrateful to God, that gave you such a good man. Before, you was all over him, had nothing but kind words for him, and now you're always goin' on at him. Why? He's the same man now he always was. Árpád ain't changed, oh no, Mári, not a bit."

"Just me, eh?" Márika burst out. "It's all my fault, is it? Forever going on at poor Árpád, listenin' to gossip. D'you really think I made all this up? Well, if you must know," it slipped out of her, "Herr Hausmeister told me!"

"Herr Hausmeister?…"

My mother's tone was strange. There was suddenly silence in the kitchen.

"And how does that pockmarked Kraut know?" my mother asked after a while.

"He knows. He knows everythin'. Anything goin' on in Újpest, even the coppers come to him to ask. And it's good of him to tell me. The coppers would have paid for that kind of information. So you can call him a pockmarked Kraut all you like, he means well."

"Oh sure," my mother said pointedly. "He means well with all the ladies. And they treat him well in return. And what do they get?" My mother's voice suddenly changed. "Listen, Mári, is it true you went to the pictures with him?"

"Me?!" Márika cried. "Who told you that?"

"People."

"Don't you start!" Márika's voice faltered, and I could hear her crying. "All because I went to the pictures with him one time?"

My mother did not reply. Márika, too, was silent for a space, and then said:

"Goddamn the bloody Jews!"

As to what the Jews had to do with Herr Hausmeister and the pictures, my mother seemed to have just as little idea as me.

"What've they done to you?" she asked.

"It's all their fault!" sobbed Márika. "They're the ones that seduce these poor jobless folk. Look at what they're doing to 'em! In the end, they all finish up thieves or Commernists. And the bloody Jews get money for it from Moscow. Damn their eyes!" she screamed, and went on cursing the Jews for quite some time.

Herr Hausmeister's power grew in direct correlation with the misery in the house. There was still huge demand for flats on the outskirts of the city, and people lived huddled on top of one another in terrible rented tenements; when an apartment did become available, they wouldn't rent it to anyone who was jobless. The unemployed ended up on the streets when they got evicted, trying to make do as best they could. The older ones begged, the younger stole, and all of them sooner or later reached a point of starvation where they were capable of anything. Fourteen-year-old girls would go to the "Mauthner" for a square meal, sixteen-year-old boys would throw themselves on anyone halfway decently dressed walking the streets at night. The government looked on the jobless the way villagers do on the hungry wolves hanging around the edge of the village in midwinter. There was still no jobless assistance, only more and more police, and constant warnings to the populace to beware of beggars. In the end, no one dared open the door when they rang—they grew afraid of them and chased them away. They became the lepers of the capital, shunned by all. They fell through the branches of society like maggot-infested apples, to roll aimlessly in the streets for a while and then rot in the sewer. Their next abode was either prison, a brothel, the hospital or the cemetery, and whoever wanted to skip the intervening stations on the way to a pauper's grave drank lye when they got served their eviction notice.

Who got that letter depended entirely on Herr Hausmeister, and all the residents knew it. They were deadly afraid of him and were willing to give up what little was left of their dignity so they could stay in their miserable bed-sitting rooms and keep the family together somehow, despite everything. I suspect that by this time, it wasn't only Mátyás who left home when Herr Hausmeister wanted to talk about the rent, and I know—as everybody else did, too—that my mother wasn't the only one working for him for free.

But he never *made* anyone, oh no, far be it from him! He merely asked people for a friendly favour, that's all. He would say to the unemployed watchmaker:

"Jóska, you're not doing anything, why don't you fix this watch for me? Belongs to a friend of mine who ain't doing so well at the moment, so it would be a little friendly favour."

No one, of course, dared refuse these "little friendly favours". The watchmaker fixed the watch, the repairman fixed the radio, the tinsmith patched the bath, the upholsterer redid the couch, and the carpenter made the cribs and the coffins. Herr Hausmeister had a lot of "friends"; in the end, half the building was working for him. They knew full well, of course, that Herr Hausmeister pocketed the money for their work, but they also knew that there was such a thing as an eviction notice, and there wasn't a single person in their right mind who would have refused a little "friendly favour".

Only Old Gábor dared to, but he wasn't really in his right mind, poor man. This odd evangelist of the cheerful coffin was finally driven mad by his poverty. He'd always been a bit "funny" as people used to say of him, but previously you would hardly have noticed, when he wasn't talking about his happy coffins. It's true that he said some pretty crazy things about the Jews and in praise of the war, but no one really noticed that because they weren't all that much crazier than the headlines in the right-wing newspapers, whose authors were apparently sane. His obsessive tidiness, too, had deceived people. They admired his punctilious neatness, and needless to say it never occurred to them that that, too, was merely a symptom of his illness. They were in awe of his flat, which really was the neatest in the house. He was forever cleaning and repairing it. A single scratch on a piece of furniture had him running for his plane; he became agitated if he saw a speck of dust, and would berate the lodgers if they moved a chair from those four little red-white-and-green circles that marked the position of the individual legs on the floor. He was very particular about his appearance, too, and I've rarely seen a cleaner, neater, more handsome old man.

"He's a bit funny," the residents would say, but fundamentally they took him seriously, and they only realized he was actually crazy when he fell from his obsessive neatness into the other extreme.

One day, he told us he was retiring, and from then on, never washed. He was no longer willing to clean, either, and his flat became covered in spiders, insects and cockroaches, while he himself was filthy and went about in rags. He stopped shaving, too, and his wild prophet's beard ran all the way down to his chest, his hair hung to his shoulder, and his moustache drooped wetly into his mouth. His eyes grew empty and glazed and he dribbled constantly, like a baby. He nailed up his coffin in a big black box "so the competition didn't get sight of it" and that was the end of his professional life. He never picked up another plane or hammer, and from then on sat idle in front of his flat all day, forever watching the gate, as if expecting someone. On the rare occasions he went down into the courtyard for a walk, he would inform the neighbours where he was and even while he was walking round and round, would shout up to them more than once to see if anyone had called for him. He always walked beside the wall, slowly, carefully, almost pressing himself against it, and was painfully careful only to step on every third cobblestone. If he ever lost count, he would quickly go back and—much to the amusement of the children—start again from the beginning.

Sári, Böske and Borcsa still lived with him. He got enough from them to pay the rent, and didn't care about the rest. Áron the Sabbatarian fed him; he came twice a day bringing food. Áron was hardly rich, either—he got ten pengős a week as a watchman, but his friend nonetheless took it for granted that he fed him. It's not like he was grateful either—quite the opposite. He treated the Sabbatarian like a servant, grumbled and snapped at him, would take the food out of his mouth. Old Gábor ate a lot. He gobbled the half-chewed mouthfuls hurriedly, his face a reddish purple as he ate, his brow covered in sweat. He was the only person in the building to put on weight. He did so in a funny way—he was like a sponge soaking itself with water; he grew puffy and soft. He never talked to anyone—barely said a word to Áron—and whenever Herr Hausmeister passed him, he'd growl:

"You ought to greet your elders, even if you ain't our race!"

The only reason Herr Hausmeister didn't kick him out, I think, was that even he didn't dare cross the Sabbatarian. Anyone who can sue a big company and stop them tearing down the house could do plenty more, he must have thought. Besides. Old Gábor's behaviour did nothing to damage his reputation anyway. Quite the opposite: it proved you'd have to be crazy to pick a fight with Herr Hausmeister.

And Herr Hausmeister was far from crazy. His fortunes swelled like a pregnant sow, and the better he did, the stingier he got. He didn't even want to buy his wife milk, though the "consumptive" woman's days really were numbered. There wasn't much life left in her, but even that little was a little too much for Herr Hausmeister, it seems. He was clearly scared the milk would help. Before, he'd been merely waiting for her death like people hoping they'd win the lottery, but now he was certain it was imminent and that made him impatient, like the last half-hour of a train journey.

Once, when he wasn't home, she became unwell and one of the tenants called a doctor. The doctor told her to eat better, to drink at least a litre of milk a day and prescribed all sorts of medicines. Herr Hausmeister did, grudgingly, pay the doctor, but wouldn't hear of buying the drugs. This led to such a row that it brought half the house running outside their door.

"You ain't drivin' me into the grave!" shrieked the wife. "I'll outlive you yet, you filthy Kraut!"

"You won't outlive the lice on your head!" Herr Hausmeister replied gently, and from then on gave up putting milk in his coffee just so his wife wouldn't get any milk either.

But his wife outsmarted him. She was a nasty piece of work, too, and had been stealing from her husband for years. She had five hundred pengős saved, if I remember rightly—they found it stuffed in her mattress after she died. She started feeding herself from these secret funds. When her husband went out, she dragged herself to the door and asked one of the women passing by to do some shopping for her. Márika was the first one she decided to trust, and Márika did as she asked. The trouble was that when it came to bringing her the change, she'd deducted the price of two litres of milk, not one.

"Where's the other litre?" Herr Hausmeister's wife asked.

"Little Mózes had it," Márika replied, looking the woman in the eye calmly, with steady defiance.

Little Mózes was, by occupation, an infant. He must have been three or four months old at the time, and although he belonged to the "lower orders", he still demanded to be fed with milk. He was the locksmith's son, the same young locksmith whom legend had it had played cards all night with the watchman at the timber yard while his wife dragged home the wood they needed for Old Gábor to make their furniture with. But for this foresight, Little Mózes would have lain not in a crib but on the floor, because his parents had hardly grown richer since. The baby's grandiose name came from his father, who had inherited it from his father. But the biblical name didn't help Little Mózes much. His father, Big Mózes, couldn't bring forth water from a rock—despite the name—and besides, Little Mózes wouldn't have got far with that, even if he could. He insisted on milk and screamed when denied it. He couldn't have his mother's milk, because his mother's breasts had dried up from permanent starvation, and cow's milk cost money; and the locksmith's wife was hardly starving because she was well supplied with money. Little Mózes once screamed for twenty-four hours non-stop. His mother got to the point of wanting to strangle him. It was pure luck she didn't actually go through with it. Her husband had fled the house because he couldn't bear to listen to the baby's cries of hunger any more, but suddenly remembered—out on the street—that he had forgotten his keys, and went back. It was thanks to him that Little Mózes got to go on starving.

Little Mózes's mother, however strange this might sound, was a very good mother—she was crazy about her child. It was just that he cried day and night, and his mother knew full well it wasn't beer he was after—as for milk, there was none in the house and a mother who can't provide for her starving infant is capable of pretty much anything; if you don't believe me, try it.

Little Mózes's situation caused a great deal of excitement among the women in the house, especially the younger ones. There hadn't been a newborn in the house for a long time, but there were plenty of young women who'd been longing for a baby for years. Pregnancy, by that point, had become taboo for them and if one of them did become pregnant, she'd go running straight to Máli on the first floor, because Máli would do away with their embryos on credit. They knew they couldn't actually have babies, and that knowledge, it seems, made motherhood even more appealing to them. Máli would scrape the growth out of their bodies, but their souls seemed to go on being pregnant. They grew and grew through some indestructible instinct, swelled and hurt, like a young mother's breasts from which no baby sucks the milk. They had to give their pregnant souls to someone, and Little Mózes was the only baby in the building. He got all the love and tenderness that nature meant for his unborn companions. If his mother put him out on the walkway to get a little sun, the young women sprang forth from their dark bedsits like bears scenting spring. They gathered round the battered soapbox that served as a crib at the locksmith's as if waiting for something. The locksmith's wife, it seemed, knew what they were waiting for, because from time to time she would call out to one or other of the ladies:

"Well, why don't you pick him up? Can't you see the way he's lookin' at you?"

How those women were changed then! Their storm-tossed working-class faces suddenly grew beautiful, their hard lines softened, and their expressions grew sweet and warm, like mother's milk.

Sleep, baby, sleep
The stars above are bright,
And all the little sheep
Are coming home tonight.

Even their voices changed. They chirruped like birds, pecking heavily from the locksmith's wife's motherhood with their greedy beaks. They denied themselves their own milk—when they had milk to deny themselves—and took it to Little Mózes. It was only skimmed milk, of course, but they brought the watery grey slop as if it were holy water. They proceeded slowly, self-importantly along the walkway so the other residents, so the whole house, would see: Little Mózes was about to get some milk, and they were the ones that brought it him. They knelt before the soapbox and watched the baby snuffling and sucking down the watery milk as if it weren't a soapbox they were kneeling before at all, but the altar in church.

But Herr Hausmeister's wife was not one to kneel. She was stingy like her husband, and cared only for her own belly. She was forever cursing bitterly about Little Mózes, but Little Mózes didn't mind—it never spoilt his appetite. He drank his milk with gusto and Márika just laughed at the owl-faced woman's yapping.

"If you don't like it," she said, brimming with glee, "go tell your husband."

Herr Hausmeister's wife, needless to say, never did tell her husband, but the next day she tried her luck instead with Rózsi. She fared no better. Rózsi, too, took two litres out of her money instead of one, and when Herr Hausmeister's wife asked her where the other litre was, she too—like Márika—replied:

"Little Mózes had it."

That was how Little Mózes carried on living, and that was how the life of the house also carried on. The amazing thing about all this was that these miserable pariahs, forced to live like animals, who didn't always have enough for a crust of bread, still mostly managed to pay the rent. They may sometimes have run up several months of arrears, but—if they weren't evicted in the meanwhile—they would eventually scratch together the money somehow. How? I don't know. All I know is I was waking up more and more often to the sound of someone knocking on the kitchen door and a panting boy calling to my mother:

"The coppers are comin', miss!"

They knew that that didn't affect this particular Miss, or at least, it hadn't in the past, but just to be on the safe side, they knocked on her door, too—you never knew in today's world.

There were no professional thieves or burglars in the house. There were only workers, and they were almost all decent people; but even the most decent of people will have enough of decency when they've been watching their children starve for months. A crying child is stronger than the word of conscience. It's so loud that you have to run away from it, and people will run wherever they can. They were very modest in their stealing, when they had to steal, and mostly did it badly. They were hopeless thieves, and that was not all that made stealing hard for them. These unwilling amateurs dared only steal at night, but since the gates were locked at ten and only opened up again at five, Herr Hausmeister knew just who went out and who came in during those hours—and reported all that faithfully to the "coppers". If something happened in the neighbourhood, the coppers would come for those people first, and that made the prospect of these night-time escapades pretty unappealing.

That was how the basement window came into use. There was an old woman in the house whom everyone knew as Auntie Samu. She was known as that because her husband was known as Uncle Samu, and because she was a very mischievous old lady. She bent over her stick as if she was searching the floor for the final nail for her coffin, but in reality, she cared only for money, and was constantly coming up with clever little schemes. In winter, she would roast chestnuts outside Nyugati railway station, while in summer she sold fruit from a two-wheeled little cart, but all the while she did little "deals", the nature of which the other residents discussed only in a whisper. Once, she had Árpád write a letter for her to the Post Office Savings Bank, from which it turned out she had some two hundred pengős, but she still sent her blind husband out begging and only dared cook hot food when everyone else in the house was in bed, for fear that people would start talking about her "riches".

She lived in the basement, and it was easy enough to climb out onto the street through her window; one day, she decided to share this information, in case anyone was interested. From then on, anyone who wanted to sneak out at night would knock on Auntie Samu's door and the next morning, the coppers would be scratching their heads. Auntie Samu was a very religious woman, it's true, but she didn't give up her beauty sleep purely out of love for her neighbours. She took a fifty per cent cut—people had to hand off half of what they'd stolen on the way back in. The house, of course, knew who was going in and out through Auntie Samu's window, but there wasn't a policeman alive who could have dragged it out of them. They had their quarrels, it's true, but they stuck together against the upper classes like a family. Auntie Samu's business flourished and grew, until there was hardly a single resident who wasn't doing some kind of business with her.

Yes, Márika was right: in the end, they all turned into thieves or "Commernists", which had much the same result in Hungary. Both lots sooner or later ended up in jail, the only difference being that they only arrested thieves if they caught them stealing, whereas they arrested Commernists even if they weren't Commernists at all. Anyone who got drunk and sang "The Internationale" one time would find themselves charged with incitement, and more than one innocent person ended up in jail because someone with a grudge against them had denounced them as a Communist. But there were some people in the building for whom being a Commernist came in handy. Take, for example, Mátyás's story.

One night, Mátyás's five sons went out stealing coal. One of the neighbourhood children claimed they were delivering coal to the smelting plant at midnight, which sounded pretty far-fetched, but the five boys believed him nonetheless. They couldn't resist the temptation, because Auntie Samu would give you half a kilo of bread for a bucket of coal, and they hadn't eaten a thing all day. Plus, it was winter and bone-chillingly cold, so they could have done with a warm stove as well. But to steal coal you needed a cart, and there wasn't one anywhere to be found nearby. They waited till two in the morning, then numb with cold, hungry and hopeless, they headed home. And then something incredible happened.

The door to the corner bakery was standing wide open, not a soul inside. The wind blew the open door to and fro and carried the smell of bread out of the darkened store. It must have been about half past two and the boys were drowsy with exhaustion and hunger. It might have been that, or it might have been the religious upbringing Mátyás had given them, but Andris, the youngest, later swore in the dock at juvenile court that they thought there had been a miracle. But there was nothing miraculous in what had *actually* happened. The baker had gone across the road to a tavern and forgotten to lock the door. The bakery opened onto a courtyard, but you could also get out onto the street via the store, which is what the baker had done to save on money for the gate.

The children, of course, did not know any of that. It was a fine white evening in Advent, the sort you hear about in Christmas stories. It was snowing, there was no one on the street, the bakery door was wide open with all the freshly baked bread inside. The children went in, grabbed a two-kilo loaf each, and were about to make off when the door opened and in walked the baker. He relieved them of the bread and gave each one of them a smack. Then he locked them in the flour store and went back to the tavern to fetch the policeman.

The flour store was beside the bakery, and the bakery itself was full of freshly baking bread. The children hadn't had any bread all day, or indeed anything at all apart from the smack the baker had given them, and a child—under these circumstances—is capable of many things— almost anything, in fact. If you don't believe me, you can try this, too. I wasn't there, I don't know for sure how it happened, but what I do know is that when the baker came back with the policeman, Mátyás's devout Catholic children were belting out "The Internationale" in the flour store.

> *Arise ye workers from your slumber,*
> *Arise ye prisoners of want!*

The policeman, first and foremost, gave the children another hefty slap each, then grabbed the two eldest by the scruff of their necks and ordered the smaller ones to march ahead of them. And they did—right up to the third corner, where they were repairing the road (by day) and there were large piles of stone heaped beside the pavement. The three boys reached into one of the piles and, before the policeman could recover from his surprise, gave him a nice sharp bit of basalt to the head. He let the eldest go in fright and all five of them ran for it. They ran as fast as their legs could carry them, and even made it home—but that didn't help them much. The baker knew them because they'd used to buy their bread from him when they had money to buy it with, so they were arrested that same night. They locked them up in the reformatory in Aszód for "Communist behaviour" and "assaulting an agent of the law" though their years could hardly—if you added all their ages up—have exceeded those of the judge who sentenced them.

This was a great disgrace by middle-class standards, but Mátyás nonetheless went about the house as if he'd had an unexpected stroke of luck.

"Ain't they beating 'em?" my mother asked once, because everybody knew they beat the children in Aszód horribly.

"Oh they are, they are," Mátyás replied, "but they're feeding 'em, too."

"That's a piece of luck," my mother admitted. "They happy?"

"Happy? 'Course not!" Mátyás grumbled. "Little kids like that don't know what's good for 'em. The other day they sneaked me a letter full of complaints, makes your heart bleed to read it."

"On account of the beatings?"

"That too, but that ain't the main thing. They miss their freedom."

"'Course they do," nodded my mother. "That's the main thing, after all, freedom."

Mátyás took the cold pipe out of his mouth and spat heavily.

"Freedom!" he mumbled under his breath. "You got to have somethin' to eat first, love. The rest comes after."

The starving house huddled on the outskirts of the city like a dog whipped into a corner. It pulled its tail in, did Herr Hausmeister's bidding, and was at the beck and call of the upper classes. It didn't move, didn't make a sound, and didn't give anything away. It was only in the dark depths of its bedsits that it ground its teeth—out in the walkways, there was order and quiet. The house was quiet—so quiet it sometimes gave me a chill.

I have a frightening memory of that quiet. One night, not long before the elections, Herr Hausmeister made a speech to the residents. It was a campaign speech—a patriotic, rabidly nationalistic speech. For Herr Hausmeister, being an ethnic Swabian, was a rabid Hungarian nationalist—until Hitler came along and reminded him he was a German. His Hungarian nationalism included canvassing for the governing party—for a fee, of course. He proved, clear as day, that the Social Democrats were Jews, the Jews were Communists, and the Communists were murderers. Therefore, it was the duty of every self-respecting Christian Hungarian worker to vote for the governing party's candidate—another great Hungarian patriot of German extraction, about whom even the youngest children in the house knew that he was one of the dirtiest enemies the working class had.

But there was no way of telling that just by looking at the residents. The crowd corralled into the courtyard was as silent and still as a bunch of statues. They listened stiffly and impassively, their faces revealing nothing. Their minds were probably taken up with petty matters, such as where they could get hold of half a kilo of bread, while Herr Hausmeister was talking about big things. He was holding forth on the horrors of life under Bolshevism and the bloodthirsty Jewish ringmasters who'd locked up the cream of the nation's youth, among them the governing party candidate himself. This irrepressible firebrand had languished three weeks in a Bolshevik jail on nothing but bread and water.

A few of the crowd smiled at that. They smiled cautiously, in the cover of the person standing before them, so Herr Hausmeister didn't see a thing. He finished up his speech and went back to his flat, pleased with his work.

"Oh, the poor bourgeoisie," Mózes the locksmith sighed then, and that was the first and last time I heard the house laugh.

The laughter, too, started cautiously. Barely a sound came out of their mouths, they swallowed the ticklish temptation. But on the stairs, one of the ladies burst into hoots and suddenly no one could contain themselves any more. The laughter grew and swelled like a river in flood, and by the time it reached the upper floors, burst its banks completely, loudly inundating the walkways. Even now, the house expressed no opinion, only laughed, laughed, laughed. The hard left-wingers had gone out so they wouldn't have to take part in the meeting; it wasn't them laughing, and that was what was frightening. It wasn't politically motivated laughter, this, and it wasn't mocking. It came from somewhere deeper and it cut deeper too. It was frightening laughter.

"The poor bourgeoisie!" someone would sigh again, and the house, which had already begun to quieten, once again clutched its sides in hilarity.

They couldn't stop. Their laughter, which had started so cautiously, thirty minutes later had become mass hysteria. I have never seen or heard anything like it. The house, in the strictest sense of the word, had a giggling fit. People were swaying, panting for breath, slapping their thighs, grabbing each other for support, sweaty and red, as if they were about to have a fit. Their faces twisted, grew bestial, the veins in their necks stood out fit to pop, their eyes turned bloodshot.

Their laughter gave me goosebumps. I remembered old stories from when we were learning about the French Revolution and the Schoolmaster told us about how vicious the masses had been. Back then, I had felt nothing but disdain for the "French rabble", but now I pictured these familiar faces under the Jacobin hats and wondered about the kind of houses those people had lived in, and whether their children had had milk? And I wondered if Mátyás too, so devout, was capable of viciousness, and Árpád—quiet, clever Árpád—and Mózes, that good and gentle father? And the other fathers and mothers—could they, too, kill, steal, burn? I looked at the familiar faces as if I were seeing them for the first time and suddenly knew, knew with a terrifying certainty that yes, yes they could. All at once I knew that the day would come when they, too, would be the masses, and just as cruel as the masses always and everywhere, but at the same time, I also knew that no, no, no they weren't cruel, not Mátyás, nor Árpád, nor Mózes and the rest, and that was the first time I suspected, in a confused, vague and frightening way that sometimes the killer is the victim and the victim is the killer.

These potential killers were gentle folk; hardly any of them touched a drop. They were homebodies, generally—quiet and good-hearted. They liked to read their wives the paper of an evening or explain the way a steam engine worked to their children, play a few hands of cards with the family for beans instead of money, or play their harmonicas out on the open walkways. They liked pottering around fixing up the house, making repairs, hammering or drilling this and that. They liked sitting quietly in the windows in the evenings, and putting the world to rights with the neighbours over a pipeful of tobacco. Of course they argued as well, I don't deny it, but when the chips were down they would go and help even the people they'd been quarrelling with, any way they could.

It was more or less the house that kept the locksmith's baby. I often watched them dandling the child, and couldn't believe that these gentle, tender hands could kill. They were victims' hands, not killers'. Whatever good was left in their larders and their hearts they took to this child, and if it's true that the human heart is filled with hidden treasure, then Little Mózes could have given any maharajah a run for his money.

"Who knows?" Áron the Sabbatarian once said. "We might even be feeding our saviour in him."

Áron did sometimes say strange things like that, and no one took the slightest notice. The women smiled indulgently, but Áron was deadly serious.

"Don't laugh," he said to the women. "Someday these new slave masters, too, will be afflicted with plagues like Pharaoh, and then a poor little Mózes just like this one will arise to lead the slaves, and he'll take them out, just like that other Mózes did, and on that day, you'll see, the Red Sea will part again."

"'Course it won't, Áron dear," said the locksmith's wife with a dismissive wave. "Unnatural things like that don't happen in this day and age."

"Don't they?" The Sabbatarian looked at her. His thin, vellum-like nose was almost transparent in the blazing sun and his greying reddish mane looked as if it were ablaze. "I think it's far more unnatural," he said, "that you wanted to strangle the boy though you love him to death. Why did you want to strangle him? Because you couldn't give him any milk. Why couldn't you give him any milk? Is there no milk to be had? Read the papers! They're always moanin' there's far too much around, they don't know what to do with it! Or take little Rozi here. How she wants a baby, but she can't have one, 'cause her man can't get a job. Because there ain't no building work. Why ain't there? Is it because there's too many flats? I don't need to tell *you* there ain't—more than one of you are living seven to a room. Or is it because there's not enough wood to build with, or stone, or iron, or mortar? There's enough to plaster over the sea! Or is it 'cause they don't have the money to buy it with? There's so much money even the banks don't want it, they hardly give you any interest. If you want to hear unnatural things, my dear, you just have to read the papers. All the farmers are complaining there's too much wheat and you can't get rid of it, but none of *you* have bread to give your children. And if some boys go steal a loaf because they're starving, they go lock 'em up like they were murderers."

"Ain't that the truth," Mátyás's wife sighed, bursting into tears.

Her tears now infected the others just the same as the laughter had after Herr Hausmeister's speech. The women cried, every one of them cried. Mátyás's wife who was sleeping with Herr Hausmeister, the locksmith's wife who'd wanted to strangle her son, little Rozi who so desperately wanted a baby, and Máli, who did away with little babies on credit. Auntie Samu was crying too, who lived off fencing other people's stolen goods, and all the others cried, who went out stealing through her window. They were all mourning something that had been unjustly taken from them, and all of them could have been charged with taking something unjustly from someone else.

It was a fine summer's day. The sky was blue, the grass was green, the dogs were barking and the poor women cried. It was Sunday, but not many people went to church, because it's hard to walk on an empty stomach. Some of them didn't believe in religion anyway and some believed in a new, secular religion, while some believed in nothing at all. But now they all nonetheless believed in something, in the same thing, because a shared fate will give people a shared faith. And if someone just then had struck up "The Internationale", they would all have sung along; but perhaps they would all have sung along to a Fascist song too, because their minds were addled with suffering and hunger and because they were so desperate they no longer cared about anything; they didn't care what happened as long as something, anything, *anything* would just happen.

But nothing happened. It was Sunday and the dogs were barking in the scrapyard. No one sang, no one prayed. The walkways were shrouded in silence, the windows seemed to be yawning. The house was quiet, so quiet a chill ran down my spine.

5

I T WAS THESE QUIET PEOPLE WHO spoke in my poems. Their silence was my message. It had been their awakening I dreamt of during those long nights of my childhood, and my life hadn't rhymed since I'd forgotten those dreams. I didn't have anything to write about, and I didn't have anything to live for. Something had been crippled inside me. My thoughts could not escape *her* bed; my better self was snoring away and there was no one left to wake it. Elemér didn't come round any more, and with him went my conscience-pangs. I thought of them, when they came to mind in some anxious, lonely hour, the way a blind man might remember when his eyes still hurt. It didn't hurt any more; it didn't even hurt. I was blinded totally.

My conscience only stirred on those rare occasions when I bumped into my mother and saw the state she was in. I would then tell myself, again and again, that I would talk to the Constable, but the next time he came into the bar, the fear always overwhelmed me and I didn't dare say a thing. I found him repellent. I mostly used to slink out to the corridor so I wouldn't have to talk to him, but these days I didn't dare do even that, for I had noticed that he had his eye on me.

"You've been very busy lately," he called after me once tersely. "Where are you off to now?"

"I've got things to do," I replied awkwardly.

"Are they urgent?"

"N-no," I stuttered.

"Then come here," he said, gesturing me over. "Let's have a chat."

That was how he always began. He gestured me over, like a general gesturing to a private, drew me into a corner, sat me down, offered me a cigarette and said "Let's have a chat." I didn't know why he wanted to "chat" to me specifically, but I always got this heavy feeling when he looked at me with his yellow, blinking eyes, that *he* knew all too well.

He spun the threads of these conversations like a thin, irritable spider. I could feel he wanted to catch me in his web.

One night, when I was alone in the bar, he appeared unexpectedly. He came blowing in as always and his hurried, impatient steps echoed disconcertingly in the empty bar; his wooden leg made a strange, creaking sound.

"Are you alone?" he asked softly.

"Yes, sir," I said from atop the ladder, because I happened to be changing the light bulbs in the chandelier.

"Come down," he said in a strangled voice, glancing nervously at the door.

I climbed down.

"Where's the head waiter?" he asked.

"In the kitchen," I replied with growing nervousness—he'd come so close I could feel his breath.

"Get him to let you off," he said, whispering now. "Tell him you're not feeling well, or…" he gestured impatiently. "Tell him whatever you want."

In my fright, I dropped a light bulb, which crashed to pieces on the floor.

"Why should I tell him I—"

"You'll find out later," he cut me off impatiently. "Change into your civvies and wait for me in front of the Vigadó. And not a word to the others. Got it?"

"Yes, sir," I nodded anxiously, "but—"

"What do you mean, but? Get on with it, go!"

"The head waiter isn't going to believe I'm not feeling well."

"Don't worry about that. The Major knows all about it."

"About what?"

"Stop asking so many questions. Just be in front of the Vigadó in ten minutes."

I didn't have much time to wonder. The head waiter took his time giving me a piece of his mind, and then I had to change all my clothes, so by the time I reached the Vigadó, panting, the Constable was already waiting for me in his car.

"Get in," he said impatiently.

"Yes, sir."

I got in and the car sped off. I thought he would finally tell me what he wanted, but he didn't say a thing. He leant, silent, over the steering wheel, staring out at the street grimly and swearing softly whenever a car got out in front of him. He always seemed this angry and het up, even when he was bargaining over a tailcoat or a pair of trousers. His eyes were always in a blaze like a fever patient's and he drew his thin, cruel mouth shut so tight that his jaw was in a constant tremble. I had the feeling he was smouldering inside and that he could go off at any moment like a bomb.

He headed for Buda. The rickety little car panted across the bridge. It was a fine night—there was a warm fragrant breeze from the hills and the moon made silvery scales on the Danube. Where is he taking me? I wondered anxiously. What does this all mean? My mouth went dry, my heart was beating fast. I couldn't stand the silence any longer.

"Where are you taking me, sir?"

He didn't so much as glance at me.

"To dinner," he said, his voice curt and dry, and then relapsed into silence.

His answer stirred me up even more. To dinner!... So he doesn't want to tell me where we're going. Why not? What does he want from me? Where *are* we going?

The car headed uphill. I'd never been this way before. Crooked, dark, meandering streets wound before the speeding car, the wind howling in the draughty bends. There were few street lights and lots of cats, flat-footed little single-storey houses hobbling along up the hillside. The car rattled heavily in the dark, the cats meowed and the Constable kept swearing. There were no cars, no people up here; the streets were laden with the dark and silence—there wasn't even a policeman anywhere. These streets were uninhabited, they'd begun demolishing the houses. Vacant sites stood out darkly amid the abandoned yellow houses, the wind blowing creaky, abandoned doors open and shut and whistling through broken windows. My mind brought up horror stories and I was seized with childish fright. In one of the bends, something heavy bumped against my leg. I felt it—it was a large screwdriver. I might need that later, I thought with a shudder and squeezed it tight between my feet. But this proved to be an unnecessary precaution, at least for the moment.

We really did stop in front of a restaurant. The upper classes called these hidden little restaurants, so studiously whimsical, in the Buda hills "little inns", though they were neither little nor inns. They were furnished in a folksy, peasant style, it's true, but they charged enough for a dinner for a peasant, if it came down to it, to live on for a month. It was a one-storey whitewashed building with tiny, flower-filled windows. It looked like a modest village home, but there was a white-gloved doorman to greet the guests; he spoke fluent German with a monocled Prussian and greeted a party of Frenchmen with a hearty *bonsoir*. There was a whole row of cars lined up before the entrance and I was struck by the heady smell of perfume as Gypsy music filtered out from within.

We went in. The place was made to look like a peasant house inside as well, but it was a very upper-class peasant house—they must have spent a fortune making it look so homely. This was a rich kind of poverty, a wonderfully wealthy poverty—I thought of peasant houses in my village and felt I was being made fun of. The maître d', in tails, was making crêpes Suzette with mysterious gestures like an alchemist; there was French champagne and Russian caviar on the tables, while husks of corn hung off the crossbeams—it was all terribly folksy. The moustachioed, paunchy innkeeper was roasting something on a spit on an open fire in a sort of fireplace; his fat sausage fingers were adorned with rings and his face was grave and transcendent like someone sacrificing to his god, who knew full well that his clients, too, believed in none other. This was the only sizeable space—little rooms opened off it, where lovers could whisper together like conspirators huddled in dark corners.

The real action, though, was in the courtyard. Flower-bedecked tables stood beneath the ancient walnut trees with little nooks behind them, overgrown with vines in the murky semi-darkness. Most of these nooks were inhabited by couples, apparently unmarried; the Gypsy violinist would sidle up to play a sentimental tune beside the lady, the band accompanying him softly from the podium. The tables had candles in windproof holders, the moon bathed the walnut trees in liquid silver. The foreigners must have gushed, back home, about the charming, happy country they'd visited. When the violinist had finished his tune, he started going round the tables, collecting money in his hat; the foreigners must clearly have found this charming, too, and judging by their faces they didn't spend too much time wondering why someone who worked in such a fancy restaurant had to make his living begging for donations.

Everybody knew the Constable. The staff made a big fuss of him, but I seemed to see an uneasiness behind their soft, subservient smiles. They're afraid of him too, I thought.

He knew a lot of the guests, as well. He greeted people left and right, stopping occasionally at a table. He was on first-name terms with the gentlemen, but greeted them by their ranks.

"Hello, Your Honour... How are you, Your Lordship?... Nice to see you, General."

He did not greet them all alike. He apportioned his smile with as much punctilious care as a pharmacist his poison. His Honour got a little less than His Lordship, while the General got even more. But suddenly, he began to flicker like the candles on the table, dripping humility and awe:

"Your humble servant, Minister," he gushed, bowing deeply. Only Horthy himself could have elicited a bigger smile. "The former Minister of Defence," he whispered to me, and I could see him watching me out of the corner of his eye for the effect.

Why has he brought me here? I wondered. What does he want?

The waiters danced around him like dogs wagging their tails.

"Would you care for this table, Doctor? Or would you like something a little farther from the band?"

They got nothing of his smile; he didn't even deign to respond. He pinpointed a nook and was there like a shot.

We sat down. Three of the waiters came kowtowing—the head waiter, another waiter and the sommelier—but the Constable still took no notice. He was no longer in a hurry. He leant back in his chair, took out his monocle with a casual gesture, wiped it leisurely with his handkerchief and inserted it into his right eye; but instead of studying the menu, he turned his attention to the other guests. The head waiter, waiter and sommelier stood to attention before him. I didn't dare look at them—I was horribly ashamed.

The Constable's attention was caught by one of the tables; he grimaced bitterly. I followed his gaze but could see nothing special about the party by which he was so disgusted. They were elegant and clearly rich; their appearance and manner was no different to those of the other guests. But the Constable thought differently.

"What is this?" he snorted at the head waiter. "A synagogue?"

The company in question pretended not to have heard him, but a few minutes later they stood up and paid.

"At last!" the Constable said, nice and loud so they would hear, and laughed derisively.

I saw red. I felt as if *I* had been humiliated, and it was as if I could still hear that terrible chorus from behind the bushes: old Roz-ee's son, where's your faa-ther gone?... These Jewish ladies and gentlemen would probably have forbidden their children my company just like Sárika's parents, but my heart was now with them nonetheless. My hand made a fist, my heart thumped in outrage.

The Constable ordered; he didn't bother to ask me what I wanted. He had chosen a splendid meal—the problem was, I couldn't taste it at all. My stomach, it seems, was protesting against the good doctor's dinner and refused to get its juices flowing. My mouth was dry and all I wanted was a beer. I drank greedily and drained the enormous mug almost in one go. The Constable immediately ordered a second, and wanted to get me a third, but I was ready. I had observed in the hotel bar that gentlemen, when engaged in a negotiation, tried to get the other party drunk—and I had a suspicion this *was* a negotiation.

But of this the Constable gave no indication as yet. He spent the entire dinner staring at the women, making quiet, indecent comments and telling coarse, lewd anecdotes.

Suddenly he said:

"I hear you're lucky with the ladies."

"Me?" I muttered faintly, and felt myself blushing to my roots.

"Why, shure!" he said with a Jewish drawl, because he loved to affect a Jewish drawl. Then he winked at me: "I'm a little bit jealous myself, you know."

I was beginning to think that this strange dinner had something to do with room 205, but I soon realized it didn't. As to why he'd made that comment, I only understood much, much later.

After dinner, he called the waiter over.

"Is there a good peach *pálinka* in the house?"

"Yes, sir," the waiter said, clicking his heels. "We have a lovely twenty-five-year-old. Made in small vats in Kecskemét. I highly recommend it."

"All right," he nodded.

"Two glasses?"

"Bring the bottle," the Constable decreed. "Then leave us alone."

I could tell he wanted to get me drunk. He kept plying me with drink after drink, cracking jokes and telling stories, doing everything he could to distract my attention. I drank in moderation and only when I really had to, but despite all my precautions, I suddenly noticed that my head was fogging up. I was frightened. What if I do get drunk? I screwed up my courage.

"May I please have a coffee, Doctor?"

"Later," he said, and I, of course, knew why.

That sobered me up for a while. I watched him like a card sharp—I knew the stakes were high.

"Well, my boy," he asked suddenly, pulling his chair a little closer. "How does it feel to be in with the upper classes?"

"Ummm... fine," I stammered.

"Would you like to be part of it?"

What could I say to that? I replied:

"Who wouldn't, sir?"

"Well, this is your chance," he said mysteriously. "It's up to you whether you take it." He gave me a look full of meaning and paused, clearly for effect. "So," he said, "what do you say? This is your chance to really make your luck."

"How do you mean, Doctor?" I asked naively.

There was a brief silence. The Constable did not reply at once. He removed his monocle, rubbed it with his handkerchief and surveyed me thoroughly.

"How much do you know about me?"

Oh I know plenty about you! I thought, and replied haltingly:

"That… you were a hero during the war, Doctor."

"What do you mean, during the war?" he asked. "You think there isn't a war on now? Nineteen eighteen was merely the end of the first act—but the play is far from over. This is just an intermission, that's all. The audience is still out in the bar, but behind the scenes, they're already preparing the next act. Do you see what I mean?"

"Yes, sir."

Strange, I thought. Elemér says the same thing.

"Wars," he explained, "do not start when the cannon start booming, and don't end when they fall silent. What happens in between is the most important part. The rehearsals, get it? That's what determines if the play's going to be a success or a failure. The Jews have known that for some time. When we went out to fight in 1914, they'd already stealthily undermined the country so thoroughly, it was only a question of time before it collapsed. They're doing the same thing now. They're working underground, the Red moles. They leave the dirty work to the stupid goys, while they live high on the hog on Moscow's money and deck their wives with diamonds. Well, cheers! Here's to your health."

"Your health, Doctor."

He offered me a cigarette. We lit up.

"But there was a time," he said, "when that wasn't possible. After that Communist interlude, even the goys opened their eyes—or if they didn't, we took them out. Your older workers didn't forget that lesson, but the ones your age weren't even in school back then. Today's youth are easy pickings for the Jews. The outlook's not so rosy—our lads are disappointed and these kosher messiahs are selling them some Commie Promised Land. They buy their way in to the workers' youth organizations, and…" He looked up at me. "But I'm sure you know all about that."

"Me?" I started in fright. "Not at all, sir."

"Oh, come off it!" he snapped at me suspiciously. "You don't mean to tell me that you've never heard of the Workers' Youth Movement?"

"I've heard of it, sir, but… that's it. I didn't even know it was banned."

"That's just the thing—it isn't banned, and that's what makes it all the more dangerous. They can get the Communists straight away, but these people won't admit they're Communists. They belong to the Social Democratic Party and the Social Democratic Party is, for the moment—sadly—allowed to carry on freely. They melt into the crowd like needles in a haystack. Do you know how many young workers' heads they've turned?"

"No, sir."

"Thousands!" he hissed furiously. "Tens of thousands, possibly hundreds of thousands! What do you make of that?"

Like I'd tell you of all people! I thought, and said:

"It's disgraceful."

"That doesn't even begin to cover it!" he doubled down. "It's downright murder! Spiritual mass murder! Do you see now why I said before that there's still a war? Shouldn't every decent man do whatever he can to fight against all this?"

"Yes… of course…"

It was as if that was just what the Constable had been waiting for. He suddenly leant right over and put his hand on my shoulder.

"Do you want to join our fight?"

"Um…" I muttered, "sir, I… don't know…"

"What do you mean you don't know?"

"Wh… what could *I* do?"

"I'll tell you, my boy." He looked around to make sure nobody was listening. "Listen here," he whispered then, and his eyes flashed as if some warning light had gone off behind them. "If you breathe a word of what I'm about to tell you to anyone, even your own mother, I will personally beat your brains in with my bare hands. Got it?"

"Yes, sir."

"Well, then. Don't ever forget it." He smiled. "Let's get to it, then." He looked around once more, dropped his voice, and carried on: "Look, even the leading Social Democrats are up in arms about this movement.

But they're hardly heroes and they want to save their own skin. Most of them, I think, would happily give up the Communists, but they themselves don't know who they are. They're very cunning—even the police haven't managed to catch up with them yet. So the task has fallen to me. So," he looked at me, "are you going to help me?"

"Y-yes, but…"

"What do you mean, but?"

"But… I'm just a nobody, sir… a bellboy… a… um…"

"That's just how you can help. I can't get in with them, you see, but you can. Do you see what I'm getting at?"

"Yes, sir."

"Well then, that's settled. Put it there!"

His hand was like a toad—cold and clammy. I shuddered. What now? The question hammered away inside me. How am I going to get myself out of this?

The Constable patted my shoulder.

"I hope you know what an honour it is to have been chosen for this task."

What could I do? I nodded yes.

"And so you should," he assured me. "It's a great thing, truly great. If you do your job well, all sorts of doors will open for you. You can really make your luck." He lifted his glass. "Well, cheers. Long live the fatherland!"

"Cheers!"

If I asked him for a break on the instalments now, I thought, he'd be bound to give it to me. But just at that moment he turned suddenly towards me.

"Tell me," he asked, "how do they approach these lads?"

"I don't know, Doctor."

"What do you mean, you don't know? They must have approached you, too."

"No, sir."

The Constable furrowed his brows.

"How is that possible? You live in Újpest, in a working-class building, and I know," his voice suddenly changed, "I *know*," he repeated pointedly, "that they're active in the hotel, too. You must know them. They're your friends."

Elemér! I thought, petrified. I've got to warn Elemér!

I quickly said:

"I don't have friends, sir."

"How do you mean?"

"I just don't."

"What about before?"

"I had some before, but…"

"But you don't want to betray them, eh?" he interrupted, and guffawed harshly. "Well, why are you looking at me like that?" he asked. "It's a fine thing not to betray one's friends. I wouldn't want you to, anyway. We're both gentlemen, after all, or whatever. Well, cheers!"

"Cheers, Doctor."

My head was now all over the place and my stomach was up in arms.

"Have a cigarette," he encouraged me, extending his case. "And I'll explain what's going on. You're a bright lad, you'll get it right away. I'm looking for the ringleader, but in order to find him, I have to know his crowd. I have no problem, mark you, with the crowd. Those lads are just poor misguided sheep. I'm after the big game, my boy. Follow the stench to the Jew. I wouldn't touch a hair on the boys' heads. Understand?"

"Yes, sir."

"Then go ahead and tell me the names," he said casually, producing a notebook.

"What names, sir?"

"Oh for the love of…" he swore. "Don't play the fool with me, you're not smart enough. You know what I'm talking about. Tell me the names of the Communists."

"I don't know any Communists, sir."

"Is that right?" he looked at me menacingly. "You'd better stop playing around, I'm in no mood."

"I mean it, sir."

The Constable laughed.

"Oh I see!" he said, all friendly. "You're scared the boys will find out where the wind's blowing from. Don't you worry about that. It's all very simple. One day, we'll get the Jews, and that'll be that. The boys won't even know they were being watched. You don't doubt what I'm telling you?"

"No, sir."

"Well, then. Let's have the names."

"I don't know any Communists, sir."

The Constable slammed the notebook down on the table. His face went red.

"Tell me, boy, are you looking for a new job?"

"Not at all, sir, why do you ask?"

"Because let me assure you that if you lose this one, you'll never get another in this country again. Or haven't you heard of the blacklist?"

"I have, sir."

"Well, then. Use your head and start talking."

My fright sobered me up completely.

"Please understand, Doctor," I said, now hard and determined, "that I can't do without the money I make, but I don't know any Communists, I never have, and there's nothing more I can tell you."

There was now a longish silence. The Constable once more removed his monocle and rubbed it with his handkerchief. He never took his eyes off me meanwhile.

"Listen here," he said, unnervingly calm. "I don't know what you do and do not know. I can't get inside your head, but I swear to God I'll beat it to a pulp if you're lying to me." With that, he pulled out his wallet and took out a calling card. "Here's my address and telephone number. If you really don't know what I want to know then I recommend you find out, and fast, because otherwise there'll be trouble. Understand?"

"Yes, sir."

"All right, then, let's be off. Waiter! The bill."

I thought he'd finally cut me loose, but oh no.

"Get in," he said, in front of the restaurant.

He drove back over to Pest and I was shocked to find that we were heading to the outskirts. I didn't understand quite what the meaning of that could be, since I was certain he did not live in the poorer part of town.

"Where are we going, sir?"

"I'm taking you home," he mumbled without looking at me. "The tram doesn't run this late."

"How do you know where I live?"

"How?" he said, turning towards me suddenly with a twisted, nefarious smile. "I know a lot more about you than you think. And you'd better not forget it."

With that, he leant once more over the wheel and didn't say another word.

He stopped the car in front of the scrap metal yard.

"Get out here," he said. "The proles needn't know I brought you home."

"Yes, sir. Good night."

"Have a nice evening!" he replied sardonically and started the engine.

My mother was asleep by the time I got home, but Manci was still awake.

"What's wrong?" she asked.

"Nothing," I growled.

"You don't look so good." She shook her head and, dropping her voice to a whisper, asked: "You still got the clap?"

"Yes."

"Shame," she laughed. "I could have used a little something to help me sleep."

But she got to sleep without it anyway. In a matter of minutes she was snoring gently.

I undressed, lay down on the floor and gazed muzzily into the darkness. They're going to fire me, I thought, just now when my mother's in trouble. No job, no flat, nothing. We're going to starve to death in the street—that is if the Constable doesn't get me first. I could see my predicament clearly, and yet at the same time saw it the way an anaesthetized patient watches their operation. An astoundingly deep numbness came over me, an incredible, frightening emptiness.

"I deserve it," I mumbled aloud, shuddering at my own voice like a criminal being read the verdict.

I thought of Elemér. Now there's a man. But me? What good had I done in life, what had I created? Nothing. I'd just been tossed about this way and that like a rag—and I deserved it, because a rag was exactly what I was. I wasn't going to be much of a loss to anyone. Tomorrow, I'll warn Elemér, and then… who cares!

I spun into a hazy dream, but was awake again by five. What would Elemér say? That was my first thought, and I was pierced with fright. He'll find out that I'd broken the boycott, and… I almost cried. A terrible thought occurred to me—that Elemér would say: *I wonder why he picked you?* What could I say to that? He might end up thinking that… Oh damn it all! I swore. That's all I need! Didn't I have enough trouble already? Why do I have to talk to Elemér, anyway? What was I going to warn him of? Did the Constable say anything about him? No. Not even indirectly. So what was I worried about? The Constable was only after Communists. Elemér was a Social Democrat. Isn't that what he'd always said himself? Well, then. Why make such a fuss about it? The whole thing's ridiculous.

But I couldn't get to sleep. I got up to fetch a cigarette from my jacket pocket, but bumped into a chair in the dark and woke up Manci.

"What is it?" she mumbled sleepily. "Can't you sleep?"

"No. Could you give me a little *pálinka*?"

"Next to the sink. But don't use my glass."

"All right, all right," I grumbled. "So you'll catch it from someone else instead."

I drank till I was completely drunk and then I told myself, all full of swagger: it'll be all right in the end. It's never not been before. But from then on, I couldn't get to sleep without *pálinka*.

I took to the bottle.

6

I LIVED IN A SHADOWY STUPOR like fever patients and the quietly insane. I woke up each night with a hangover and went to sleep drunk in the morning. During the night, I kept going down to the kitchen for a drink—I was never fully sober. I didn't want to think. I could feel the noose around my neck; there was only one way out of it and I knew, with every drop of my blood I knew that I would never, never take it, no matter what. And I also knew, of course, that sooner rather than later, it would all come out and they would fire me from the hotel and blacklist me, and I would never get another job. They'd chase us out of the apartment, my mother would eventually drink lye, and sooner or later I would end up like all the other homeless people. What was there for me to think about? Whether it would be better to be a snitch or a convict? These were the two careers left open to me in my fair homeland, the country I was meant to stick with through thick and thin.

My every heartbeat said no, no, no, but who in Hungary gave a damn about a peasant boy's heart? What could I do? My life was in other people's hands. Someone had set a bomb ticking—had set the hours and the minutes on the timer so that it could go off at any moment, but I knew that there was nothing, nothing I could do. The Constable's threats haunted me even in my dreams, and I waited, helpless and terrified, to see what would happen.

This was just before the first of the month. The bare flat was like a tomb, waiting to receive its body. Sometimes I thought I could even smell that mixture of incense, flowers and body odour that I remembered from my days as an altar boy at village funerals, and the bottle of lye seemed to have grown and swelled beneath the sink.

One night, my mother started hanging around me as I was washing at the tap and I knew, of course, what she wanted. I didn't wait for her to come out with it.

"I have some money," I muttered, forcing my voice to stay neutral, and started fishing about in my pockets.

I gave her everything I had, down to the last fillér, but still had no more than six or seven pengős. My mother didn't say anything, just stood there staring at her shoes.

"Will we make it past the first?" I asked woozily.

My mother shrugged and sighed heavily.

"That's for Herr Hausmeister and God to decide."

That was all she said. My gaze fell, unconsciously, on the bottle of lye, and I shuddered.

I counted off the days like an old woman fingering her rosary. My heart would start beating faster on the tram home—I was constantly afraid of coming home to find her dead. Invisible highwaymen of dismay lay in wait for me at every corner, and the world was full of monsters. The Constable! My father! Elemér! And her, her! So many open wounds that stung whenever my thoughts brushed them. And not a soul on earth I could confide in.

I hadn't seen her in three weeks. She'd never made me wait this long before, and her timing couldn't have been worse. She was the only solid point in the obscure flux of these nightmarish days. She was the sin and she was its absolution, for everything—everything—was for her. It was for her that I had descended into this hell, and it was only through her, I felt, that I could make it out. If I could only talk to her! I thought. If I could only talk to her. I don't even know what I expected from that conversation, and I suspect I couldn't have said clearly even at the time. The longer I waited, the more significant, the more fateful it seemed, until in the end I was convinced that if only I could talk to her, everything would be resolved. But in vain. She did not call me.

One early morning when I left the hotel, I saw a short, stocky man in a bowler hat on the other side of the street. He was standing propped on his walking stick, apparently waiting for someone. I caught only a glimpse of him and didn't even realize that my eye had fixed his image like a camera. My mind only developed the negative days later, one terrifying night, without any warning. It was my day off and I was heading home on the tram. All at once, I got the uncomfortable feeling that someone was watching me. Then I seemed to spot him.

Was it really him? I could have sworn to it at first, but later I developed doubts. I've begun seeing things, I thought angrily, and tried to dismiss the thought. But when I got off, he got off too.

They're watching me! I realized, and ran, panting, through the dark, abandoned plots. I didn't dare look back for ages—I just ran, the sweat streaming off me. In the end, I did turn around, but by then, I couldn't see him anywhere.

From then on, I always had the feeling that he was following me. I shuddered whenever I heard footsteps behind me, and I was forever stopping in front of shop windows or pretending to retie my shoelaces so I could steal a backward glance. If I spotted a short, broad-shouldered, bowler-hatted man at the other end of the street, I would immediately turn off into the first side street and run, terrified. Or just the opposite: I would get after him to see if it really was him or not. It wasn't, but then ten minutes later I'd spot another bowler hat, a broad set of shoulders and a thick walking stick, and my knees would begin to tremble.

I was afraid, with a dark, inhuman fear. Like a savage beast in a trap, I wanted to howl in fear. I drank more and more each day, though I could no longer stand the smell of the stuff. I hated it, I was repulsed by it, but I still needed it, like a convulsive needs painkillers.

That was my mental state when one night, *she* came into the bar. At other times, I wouldn't have dared so much as look at her, but now I couldn't take my eyes off her. I wanted her to look at me, to feel what was going on inside me, to read the supplication in my eyes. She must, indeed, have felt something of that, because she looked away more quickly than usual.

She was with a big party; they drank a lot and laughed a lot. I just kept watching them from beside the telephones and did something in my desperation that I would never normally have considered. I wrote to her. If I remember rightly, what I wrote to her was:

I absolutely must talk to you. I beg you, please call for me.

I folded the paper up very small and, around midnight, when I helped her into her coat, I slipped it into her hand. She didn't so much as blink an eye. She kept chatting and laughing and then, without looking at me, left with the others. I watched her go and saw her get into the lift.

I waited. It was a long, long night, followed by a hell of a dawn.

She didn't phone. After closing, I went out onto the riverfront promenade and looked up at her windows from the other side of the street. It was still light in the living room. Maybe she has guests, I thought hopefully, and sneaked back into the kitchen. I sat for hours huddled in the darkness, because I didn't dare put on the lights lest they attract the night watchman. All in vain: the telephone did not ring.

At around four in the morning I went back out and looked up at her windows again. They were dark. I felt so helpless, I burst into tears. I slumped down on a bench, wracked with sobs.

The promenade was empty, the trams were no longer running; only the angry growl of the Danube was audible in the windy dawn. It was still quite dark. Down on the water, a moored rescue launch bobbed up and down, its lights casting greenish sparks onto the white crests of the waves. They'd introduced this sort of motorboat to help fish out suicides from the river; this was what they'd done instead of unemployment relief. There was a policeman sitting in the motorboat. From where I was, he looked like a big black doll. His head hung dozily down onto his chest, lolling from side to side with the boat. He was asleep—death was without its watchman.

She might not find out for weeks, I thought, looking up at her darkened windows. Then I thought, I should have been in school, where I belonged.

The wind was driving smoky clouds, the sooty moon galloped on above me. Suddenly, as if I'd lost my mind, I roared into the wind and darkness:

"I don't want to die! I don't want to die!"

Then I threw myself down on the bench and wept in helplessness.

The next night, when I went down to the kitchen to have dinner, Iluci drew me aside, agitated.

"Well, what's up?" she whispered. "Tell me! What happened?"

I looked at her in surprise.

"Who says anything happened?" I muttered. "Nothing happened."

Iluci was having none of it.

"Oh come on," she said, and nudged me with an elbow. "You can't pull the wool over my eyes! Then why is Franciska taking your place?"

"What?" I panted in disbelief. "What d'you say?"

"Didn't you know?" she asked, surprised.

"Know what?"

"You're being transferred to the day shift."

"And Franciska's taking my place?"

"That's right, and…"

"And?" I asked impatiently, but Iluci did not finish the sentence.

She took a long look at me, and her look seemed to have a note of pity in it.

"Tell me," she said in a strange voice, "do you really not know anything about all this?"

"No, I swear. Why, what have you heard?"

"No," she answered weakly, "I just thought…" She didn't finish that sentence either. "Strange," she said, shaking her head, "strange."

"What's strange?" I asked, getting more and more anxious.

"I don't know," she shrugged, and then repeated: "Strange."

I couldn't get anything else out of her.

I went up to the bar. It was still early; a woman was polishing the dance floor, the waiters were laying the tables. When I came in, the conversation stopped; only the tinkling of the cutlery and glasses could be heard in the sudden silence. I could feel them watching me. So it's true, I thought, and all I cared about now was my rep.

The head waiter called me over. He could never stand me, but since I'd been taking the champagne to room 205, he hadn't dared get out of line with me. He was a cowardly man, so he swallowed his anger, but he couldn't digest it. It hardened inside him like the stones in his gall bladder, and now it seemed he wanted to hit me over the head with it. His yellow face glittered with glee, and he grinned at me so hard his false teeth almost fell out.

"Well, dear boy," he said, relishing each word, "from the day after tomorrow…"

"… I'm on the day shift," I said, finishing his sentence for him, smiling as I did so.

The tetchy little man could not disguise his anger. He had been rehearsing for the role of Fate, and I had stolen his great speech. His liverish face now looked all green. He looked at me like a mouldy carp.

"How did you know?" he gulped.

"I just know," I said, still smiling.

"And you know who's taking your place?"

"Of course," I nodded. "Ferenc."

"And?" he asked with gloating hatred. "What do you say to it?"

"What am I supposed to say? I hope you'll be very pleased with him."

"Well, he's industrious, so they say," he grinned, glancing quickly at the others. "I hear he's particularly popular with the ladies."

Idiot! I thought. You trying to make me jealous with a queer?

"More like the gentlemen," I corrected him with knowing superiority, but no matter how well informed I was, none of it could reassure me.

I could feel that they all knew something here about which I knew nothing at all.

I got blind drunk that night; I have no idea how I got home. All I remember is that it was raining and I stood in front of the hotel for a long time after closing, looking at the five darkened windows on the second floor. The balcony door was open, the wind occasionally blowing out the familiar curtains, as if waving a shawl in the darkness, but not for me—not for me. I was weeping loudly. Then a policeman appeared in front of me. He said something, I said something in reply and then cleared quickly off into the side street. What happened after that, I have no idea.

I slept a day and a night. I did wake up around seven in the evening, as usual, but when I remembered I didn't have to go into the bar, that I never had to go in there again, and when that wasn't *all* I remembered, I started drinking once more. And then it was Monday morning.

The boys grew awkward and tense when I came into the changing room. They know, too, I thought anxiously, and tried to look unconcerned. I said hello, and asked them how they were, and they said hello and asked me how I was, and we chatted and blathered with nervous laughter and we knew that what we were talking about was not the subject at hand at all.

It had been almost a year since I'd left them, and a year is a long time at that age. They'd grown, got stronger and hairier—their long, simian arms protruded from the sleeves of their outgrown jackets. In some cases, even their voices had changed, growing as strange and unfamiliar as a ventriloquist doing Ali Pasha for the children. Other than that, things were still much the same—they still smuggled women, spied on people's bedrooms and took their "bit of skirt" to the "Mauthner", where:

"Oh ho ho, boys!"

Yes, everything was the same as before, and yet everything had changed. The "boys" were like twins of themselves: they were their own spitting images, and still somehow different. A lot of the old guard had gone, new boys taking their place. But they had adopted our habits and mannerisms so closely that there was something *terribly* familiar about their unfamiliarity. They're aping us, I thought angrily, when I noticed the extent to which they'd adopted our special, gently nurtured slang as their own, in which every collocation, every innuendo and rakish twist had its own special origin. We, the old guard, had assisted at the birth of all of these, but the new boys simply took them ready-made, fully grown and faded into clichés, and I looked upon the new lot as impostors and interlopers in just the same way the boys had looked on me three years before.

One of them, a big-mouthed, Gypsy-faced boy with curving eyes, they introduced by saying:

"He's Gyula."

Yes, we had a new Gyula now, too. When someone said "Gyula", they were no longer thinking of that kind, lanky, freckled teen we'd all thought of for years as a heartless womanizer and breaker of young girl's hearts, while secretly he dreamt of a fifteen-year-old virgin whom he was to betray—along with the happy Muses—one fragrant spring morning by severing his artery with a butcher's knife. His handsome young body had surely rotted away by now, and what a year ago all the "skirt" had been panting for was now a stinking, putrefied mass of hideousness. Now this new Gyula had come and killed his memory. There was nothing left of him. I had taken his place, and now my time was up, too. Was I to follow once more in his footsteps?… I started whistling, for fear of bursting into tears.

The new boys looked me over with interest. Their looks showed that they knew "all" about me, as I had once known about the *previous* András. They examined me with a sly mixture of revulsion and awe— for now I was the Legend, birthed on the straw of whispered words in this filthy, stuffy manger, beneath the ill-omened stars of their puberty. When *she* walked past them, they, too, undoubtedly tried to picture me, the way I had once tried to imagine the *previous* András; and now they must have been thinking that there was nothing so special about me after all. If I could do it, then why not them? That was something they'd spend a long time struggling over—they would grow grumpy, absent-minded and short-tempered; they would come in each morning with rings around their eyes, and if that red-haired lady ever did glide by them, they would flush hot as if a fiery wind blew from beneath her skirt.

They didn't even know my name was Béla.

I was introduced as "András".

That appellation had become completely natural in the bar. There, I had been András from the start, Their Excellencies' András, who took the champagne up to room 205 at night. But these boys from before had met me as Béla, and suddenly I wanted to cry when they, too, called me András.

I dressed wearily and with a headache. Usually, I would be undressing at this time. I had been sleeping through the day for a year, and now, when I was back once more among the babbling boys after what seemed like an eternity, everything that had happened in between seemed so chaotic and dreamlike, it was as if I'd been asleep that whole year, or drunk, and it was only now that I was waking up to the fact that… what? That I had lost my name. That I had lost myself.

These were uncanny moments. I hadn't looked in the mirror by day for a year and now, catching a glimpse of myself while combing my hair, I realized that it was not only my name that had died. No, this wasn't Béla at all. Looking back at me was a pale urban dandy with rings around his eyes, an empty-headed, vain, big-city pansy. András. Their Excellencies' András.

Where had Béla gone? A year ago, he was preparing for America; he had faith, and will. He worked, and studied, and when there was no other way, he'd scratch together the English he needed from the head porter's dictionary. His bags were full of dreams that would change the world, the bells of Easter and Resurrection rang in his heart, and poetry seemed to flow from him always and everywhere. Now, he was no more. I had buried him alive. He had rotted away, like Gyula.

I watched the door nervously. Elemér wasn't here yet, and I was expecting him as anxiously as if he were no less than my judge and jury—as if I was about to have to answer for everything I had done during the last year. I hadn't seen him for months—I'd been avoiding him like the plague. I'd even chased the thought of him out of my head, but in the devilish witches' bonfire of my subconscious, it was still he who stirred that murky, awful, amazing brew that is a seventeen-year-old boy's conscience. The less I thought about him, the more concerned I was with him. He swelled within me, developed a form of emotional elephantiasis, and slowly, imperceptibly, morphed into a symbolic monster riding its broomstick through the haunted nights of my teenagerhood. Now he was about to come, in the form of a hotel bellboy, and make me account for my sins.

"Hello, old son!"

It was Antal who joined me in front of the mirror, our resident expert on head-over-heels love, whom a year before I had found so ridiculous when he would start dreamily whispering, eyes gleaming, about Flóra, the third-floor chambermaid. Now he was the only one here I could take seriously. Maybe I could talk to him, I thought, I'm sure he'd understand. I moved closer and put my hand on his shoulder.

"How's Flóra?" I asked him softly.

Antal looked at me agape.

"That lousy tart? Dear oh dear, pal," he said, dismissing her with a wave of his hand, "where are the snows of yesteryear? Got a fag?"

"Sure."

We lit our cigarettes. There was a burst of laughter from one corner. We both looked over. Gyula, the new Gyula with the upturned eyes, was holding up a little pair of pink panties to show the boys.

"Greenhorns," Antal muttered dismissively. "I tell you, old man, these new boys aren't worth a damn. Oh yes," he added, taking a big puff of his cigarette, "they're not the same as back in our day."

"Yes," I said, and took a deep puff of my own cigarette. "Do you remember our Gyula?"

That's how I said it, *our* Gyula; Antal nodded sympathetically.

"Did you know his successor works in the boiler room here?"

I didn't understand.

"What do you mean *successor*?"

"I mean the fellow who married his fiancée."

"Katica?" I asked, far more loudly than I had intended. "Katica got married?"

"Yeah. Why're you so surprised?"

"I'm not surprised, it's just that…"

It's just that I had a picture of Katica before me, shaking with sobs in the dark, deserted park, sniffling—I could hear her thin, failing voice clearly—"Oh God, I think I'm goin' to go mad with all this!"

So she didn't go mad. She got married instead to a boiler man. Someone else now had Gyula's fiancée, the way someone else now had his locker, his uniform and even his name. It was the most natural thing in the world.

"What about Elemér?"

"What about him?" Antal shrugged. "He's still the same as always. Now it's this lot he's trying to induct into the mysteries of Socialism."

Yes, he must have found a new boy with whom to walk in Buda, I thought, and was seized by some wild, childish, stifling jealousy, though I would rather have gone straight to hell than to Buda with him.

"Does the Major still hate him?"

"Hate him!" Antal repeated somewhat testily. "For four years it's been all the higher-ups hate Pokerface like the plague, and now," he could hardly disguise his jealousy, "believe it or not, they had him standing in for the head porter last week! Does that make any sense to you?"

"No," I said, because it didn't. "So you mean he's still up there?"

"Oh yes," shrugged Antal, yawning as he combed his hair. "I hear that's where you're headed too."

"Reception?" I gasped.

"Yes," he nodded with equanimity, being so occupied with his hair he didn't notice my anxiety. "So you didn't know it was all over between me and Flóra, eh? Oh ho ho, old boy," he gave a low whistle, "I could tell you things about that filthy tart that…"

I didn't hear the rest. All I could think about was that from now on, I would have to spend all my time with Elemér, and the thought was unbearable. I quickly went up to the office in the hope that it was just hearsay, but there I found out it was anything but. They really had put me in reception, and half an hour later I was standing beside Elemér without the slightest hope of escape.

We were standing by the column nearest the door, the one the Major called "No. 1" in his decrees and orders of the day. For, being a dyed-in-the wool soldier, he had assigned numbers to each of the marble columns in the lobby, the way you numbered strategic outposts on a military map. Each column had its strategic purpose. No. 1 was for the "reservists", those boys who happened to be without a specific task. We had to stand in a perfectly straight line precisely a foot apart, wearing white gloves no matter what the season, in our regulation "kit", at regulation ease, with regulation smiles. Every time a guest or a higher-up came past, we had to snap to attention, nod, ratchet up the smile and click our heels together. We were forbidden to sit or talk, but we managed to get round the latter prohibition. We perfected the art of talking without moving our lips to such an extent that anyone more than ten feet away couldn't see a thing.

Elemér was on solitary sentry duty at No. 1 when I arrived.

"Hi," I whispered without moving my jaw.

"Hi," he whispered back.

We didn't look at each other; that was forbidden, too. We used to get round that prohibition, too, but in this instance, we both kept to it. There was a long pause. We stood in silence. Opposite where I was standing a fireplace stuck out of the wall; there was a clock on the mantelpiece. I watched the hypnotic swing of the pendulum and counted mechanically in my head, the way I used to do to get to sleep on uneasy nights. I must have been knee-deep in numbers when Elemér poked me in the ribs.

"Mussolini!" he whispered.

Attention, nod, ratcheted smile, heels. The Major walked past.

"Since when do you call him that?"

"Oh, it's been a while. Good, no?"

"Brilliant."

The conversation once more ran dry. The lobby was pleasantly cool, but I was soon nonetheless covered in beads of sweat. It must have been about nine. The early risers had already left, the late ones were still in bed. There were only four or five guests hanging around the lobby; the thick carpet swallowed the sound of their steps. Occasionally, a phone would ring, but then there was silence once more. The clock's pendulum swung with a maddening monotony. It felt like ants were crawling on my nerves.

I sneaked a glance at Elemér. He looked calm. His unflappable calm had always irritated me, but now I downright detested him for it. It was as if he were made of wood, I thought, wood and paper, stuffed with ideals. His head was full of printer's ink, and ink ran in his veins. He didn't cry and he didn't laugh. He had a heart of wood. He was invulnerable. Others suffered, worried, churned themselves up, while he just stood there calmly, pokerfaced, as if he'd found the philosopher's stone, as if nothing bad in life could ever touch him. The Major hated him, all his superiors did, and he knew it and didn't care a damn. As if he found it natural. He didn't pretend to feel sorry for himself and he didn't ask for any favours. And yet it was always him they called whenever a complex problem arose; he was the first bellboy ever to stand in for the head porter.

No, it just didn't make any sense, Antal was right. The other boys bent over backwards so the bigwigs would notice them, while he behaved with them like a vending machine. Money in, work out. He never had a kind word for them, never a smile. He took their orders with an icy, almost standoffish silence, but executed them just as quietly. He always found a solution even to the most intractable of problems, he knew everything, and knew how everything worked, though he wasn't the least bit interested in his job. How did he do it, then? What gave him the strength and perseverance, what gave him that unbearable, hideous calm? I hated him for his calm; I hated him so much I could have strangled him.

He spoke. He said:

"I thought about you a lot."

He said it neutrally, with no emphasis, the way someone else might say, it's raining, or the sun's out. It was a dispassionate, factual statement, but I knew that the sun really would be out if he said it was, and a shy little pleasure took flight within me.

"Me too," I said, so greedily I felt ashamed afterwards.

Attention, nod, ratcheted smile, heels. All new guests. Hardly a familiar face.

"What are the new boys like?" I asked, my mouth all dry.

"Oh," he said, "just like the old ones. There's one who's got his head screwed on. Working class, fifteen, thirsting for knowledge, full of zeal. Oh well," he added, his voice suddenly dipping. "I suppose they'll get to him, too."

Him too, I repeated to myself. *Him too.*

"What's his name?"

"The new boy's?"

"Yes."

"Laci."

"Is he interested," I swallowed hard, "in the movement?"

"Very."

"Are you teaching him?"

"Yes."

"So," I said, and swallowed hard again, "so you mean you're friends?"

"No," he said. "I don't make friends that easily. Did you make any friends?"

"No, me neither."

He looked at me. It was the first time he'd looked at me. I felt myself blush.

"I don't look so good, eh?" I said awkwardly. "It's all those nights… um… I haven't been feeling too good this past while."

The regulation smile faded from Elemér's lips.

"You'll get over it, Béla," he said simply and seriously, and I knew he wasn't talking about my exhaustion.

Suddenly, everything between us was as it had been before, when we'd walked the little winding streets of Buda together, putting the world to rights. We were back to the old tone, the old feeling; we were back wandering along under the flower-filled windows, our steps echoing gaily on the old cobblestones, with someone playing the piano in a little one-storey yellow house. "Für Elise"… One day, maybe we really will walk those streets again together, I thought, and everything will be fine.

We conversed quietly. It all seemed so simple for half an hour. And then the Constable's car pulled up to the main entrance.

Suddenly, I tensed up all over. What if he takes me aside, the way he did in the bar? Elemér would know right away that—

Attention, nod, ratcheted smile, heels.

No, the Constable did not take me aside. He came storming in as always, looked around hastily, playing the busy doctor. When he passed me, he handed me a suitcase and gestured for me to follow him. He walked ahead with quick, long steps, his wooden leg creaking strangely. I could feel Elemér watching me.

His batman followed us with two heavy suitcases.

"Go ahead," the Constable instructed him when we reached the staff area. The hound-faced man executed the order in silence. He never asked, he never talked, but I always had the feeling that he knew all.

We were near the kitchen. The steamy air was heavy with the smell of cooking, the rough oily walls sweating, and the bare, wire-clad light bulbs dewy with steam. The Constable stopped suddenly.

"Why didn't you call me?" he snapped at me quietly.

"I'm sorry, sir, but I haven't found out anything," I mumbled.

"I see!" That was all he said, but I could see the rest in his yellow eyes that never stopped blinking. He gave a me a dirty and suspicious look, his jaw working tensely under his taut skin. "I see," he repeated. "So what *have* you been up to, then?"

I shrugged innocently.

"I need some time, Doctor."

"I asked you what you've been up to!"

"I... um... I was observing."

"And?"

"And I haven't found out anything yet," I repeated, floundering.

"I see," he said once more, and suddenly raised his voice. "Well, just you watch out *I* don't find out something!"

My knees began to shake. I pictured the short, broad-shouldered, bowler-hatted man propped on his walking stick and waiting... for whom? What do they want from me? What right did this man have to threaten me? Why was I afraid of him? Elemér would probably say: I'm no stooge. Why didn't *I* say that? He'd find out sooner or later, anyway.

"I'm sorry, Doctor, I'll... I'll call you as soon as I know anything."

The "Doctor" did not reply. He just stood there looking at me and then snatched the suitcase out of my hand.

"You'd better watch out," he growled softly. Then he turned on his heels, and I was alone.

I don't know how long I stood there in the corridor—it must have been quite a while. All at once, I heard steps. It was only then I noticed I was smoking—I hadn't even realized I'd lit up. I quickly hid the cigarette in my hand and rushed into the bathroom.

I sucked the smoke in greedily. *You'd better watch out! You'd better watch out! You'd better watch out!...* These four words repeated themselves mechanically in my brain, like a broken record in my head. I couldn't think. I finished the cigarette and slinked back to No. 1 column.

"No sign of a tip, I suppose," Elemér whispered.

"Fat chance with him," I waved dismissively.

Elemér's face turned angry.

"Damn snitch!" he grumbled. "What right does he have to make us carry his suitcases, I'd like to know."

He spoke unsuspecting, and I could see he didn't know; but instead of feeling relieved, my heart grew heavy. I was unbelievably ashamed. What a filthy rag I am! I thought, disgusted, and suddenly felt that I could no longer be silent, that no matter what the consequences I would have to tell him everything, to the last detail, right now.

"Elemér!" I whispered in agitation.

He looked at me.

"Yes?"

"I want to tell you something."

I must have looked pretty upset, and I think Elemér could see straight away what the matter was. The clock's pendulum seemed to swing faster, and the air around us grew hot.

"Yes," he said, and now he, too, seemed agitated, "go on, Béla."

Just then, the bell pinged in reception for a boy.

"Elemér!" cried the head porter, and he of course had to go.

They sent him to the Customs Office. He only got back in the afternoon, and by the time we were together again, it was evening.

"What did you want to tell me?" he asked as soon as we were alone, but by then, the question was in vain.

The moment had passed, and I had come to my senses.

"Do you know," I said, with forced cheer, "I can't remember any more. Can't have been important."

Elemér gave me a strange look, but said nothing. He said nothing, the way only he could, and never mentioned anything about it again.

The days limped slowly, painfully on. Tuesday, Wednesday, Thursday… It had been almost a week since I'd slipped that desperate note into her hand, and nothing. She passed No. 1 column several times a day. I saw her and couldn't speak to her; I didn't even know if she'd noticed me.

I only spoke to her once, a few words, and that was thanks to Cesar. Whenever he saw me, he would yank his lead out of her hand and literally jump all over me. He put his two front paws up on my shoulders and licked me, whining and trembling, wherever he could reach. His excitement was contagious. If only I could walk him again, then I could go up to room 205 four times a day, and…

"Cesar!" she cried, but the dog paid her no attention.

In the end, I had to drag him over to her. It was noon, there were a lot of people coming and going all around. I stood there, desperate and beseeching, but what could I have said?

"May I take Cesar for a walk?" I asked innocently.

"No," she replied. "He's coming with me."

She was not unfriendly, but she wasn't friendly, either. She wasn't anything. She was a Countess talking to a bellboy, and at that moment it seemed unbelievable even to me that there was anything more between us than that.

After that, we had a few more of these short conversations. Twice a day, a boy went up to get Cesar and take him for his walk. The head porter would send whoever was available, but would somehow always forget about me. Whenever Cesar saw me, he would run right over, barking and snapping when they tried to drag him away. But in the end there was nothing he could do, either. We were just dogs, the both of us, and there was no use our complaining about our fate.

The days went by and nothing happened. My life was merely waiting, and sometimes, I no longer even knew what for. I got filthy drunk each night, but even so could sleep only three or four hours.

My nerves began to give in. Peasant boys weren't made for this. Just as strong, primitive tribes will often succumb to certain diseases that weaker and more dissolute peoples hardly even notice, a big, strong peasant boy could break under the emotional strain of something that effete city dandies would get over in a week or two. I, too, was on the high road to breaking point. I was all over the place and I was eating myself up inside. I wanted at any cost to understand something you can't understand with peasant logic, I saw mysteries where others saw only the most mundane facts, and it took me weeks and weeks to realize what everyone around me already knew.

It started with a box of Amneris. One evening at the end of June, the head porter said:

"Take a box of Amneris up to 302."

Room 302 was Franciska's German's room. He'd already been there when I joined the hotel, and he'd always been—for us—room 302.

Now, it was a young woman who opened the door. She didn't let me in, just stuck her hand out through the gap for the cigarettes. She was a pretty, attractive woman, and I could see that she was half naked. I didn't understand. Had the German switched to women?

"What's up with Franciska's fiancé?" I asked Antal right away, for he was on duty at No. 1 column when I got back to the lobby.

Antal looked at me slightly dumbfounded, then looked away again.

"He moved," he replied curtly.

"Back to Germany?"

"No, to the Hungária."

"The Hungária?" I asked, surprised. "Come on. He didn't ditch Franciska, did he?"

"Didn't you know?" he asked in an odd voice.

"No," I said, and I was suddenly seized by a strange anxiety. "Why?" I asked. "What happened?"

Antal blushed.

"Um… I don't know."

He hummed and hawed, growing more and more embarrassed. I kept asking him, but in vain—he ended up claiming he didn't know any more.

It was this lie that helped me realize the truth. It didn't come by degrees, built up on the basis of logical conclusions, but all at once, like a flash, devoid of all reason. Suddenly, I could hear Franciska's voice clearly telling me, casually, shrugging, up on Gellért Hill: "*Some people are born that way, and some people just do it. I just do it.*" I could even see the little gesture with which he accompanied his words, and the debauched little smile that appeared on his face. "*Why shouldn't I do it, if it's to my advantage?… Eventually, I'll get married, and…*"

That night, I couldn't sleep, even with the *pálinka*. I pictured *her* in the dark, lying naked in bed, with Franciska beside her. My tamest thought was to strangle them both tomorrow, but come the morning, my thoughts had gone to the other extreme. My previous assumption seemed completely impossible… Her and Franciska? It's ridiculous! I've gone mad, I thought, and all this is just some horrible figment of my diseased imagination. But then at night, I saw them in bed once more: as close and as clear as only the terrible magnifying lens of jealousy can present things when you're lying alone at night in the dark, thinking of a woman who is no longer alone.

One day, I decided I'd had enough of the uncertainty. It happened quite unexpectedly. I was telephoning for a guest when I happened to spot her through the glass of the booth. She was alone, and I saw her get in the lift. It was evening—I still remember clearly, it was a quarter to seven. I looked at the electric clock. In two minutes, she would be in her room, I thought, maximum three. I'll give her another two, that's five. Five times sixty is three hundred. I started counting.

Right then, I simply couldn't understand why I hadn't telephoned her before. She had forbidden me to, it's true, but this was something else, this was life or death, and she knew it—I'd told her so in my note. Two hundred and fifty-two, two hundred and fifty-three, two hundred and fifty-four... Yes, she's bound to understand.

But will she? Or should I leave it? Should I sleep on it?

The telephone rang for a long time. I was just about to hang up when she suddenly spoke:

"Hello. Who is it?"

"Béla," I said excitedly.

"Who?"

"Béla," I repeated, and that was when I remembered that she didn't even know my real name. "András," I corrected myself.

Her voice suddenly changed.

"What?!" she growled. "So it's false names now, is it?"

"Please, I..." I stuttered, "I... my..."

I couldn't finish the sentence.

"Didn't I tell you never to phone?" she screamed. "If you ever dare disturb me again, by telephone, or any other way, then..."

"Please... I beg you..."

"... then you've no one to blame but yourself for the consequences. Do you understand?"

"Please," I begged, "please just hear me out... I—"

"Understand?" she repeated, harsh and threatening, and then there was a soft click on the line.

It was over. The connection was broken. The receiver was silent and there was an eerie silence in me, too.

Over?

I replaced the receiver slowly, with particular care. I'm going to go up there, and…

No! No you won't, said my peasant common sense. You're going to go see the head porter and ask him to give you the evening off. Then you're going to go home and buy a bottle of *pálinka* on the way. Then you're going to sleep. You'll get this day over with. Otherwise, you really would go up there, and…

And?

And nothing. You're going to bed. This day is over.

I stepped out of the booth. I can't have been more than twenty paces away from the head porter, but I can still remember those twenty paces. There was some sort of unnatural hypersensitivity inside me, and yet it all seemed so dreamlike. I walked on the soft carpet like a man on quicksand who knows he could sink at any moment.

"What's the matter with you?" the head porter asked.

"I don't know, sir."

He looked at me strangely, and it seemed to me, for a long time. Then he said:

"Off you go."

I went. I went home. I bought a bottle of *pálinka* on the way.

But the day was far from over.

7

I COULD SEE FROM THE CORRIDOR that the light was on in the flat. It must have been around eight. The northern star was dozing sleepily over the courtyard, and there was a bluish obscurity hanging over the walkway. Old Gábor was sitting out in front of his apartment, drooling. Someone was playing the harmonica on the second floor.

I tried anxiously to guess who it could be at ours. Manci? My mother? There was no one in the kitchen. I opened the door into the room. Then I just stood there, completely speechless.

There was my father in the petroleum-scented half-light. The smoky lamp cast a jerky, uncertain light over him, his shadow shifting strangely on the wall. He was sitting at the table beside my mother, and I looked at him in shock. He'd gone grey. There were silver streaks in his coal-black hair, and it was as if it were something more than his hair that had gone grey. He was pale, all skin and bones. His Adam's apple protruded from his thin neck, and the baggy, almost pathetic clothes hung off his body. Dappermishka had grown worn. He'd aged, like my mother. The last time I'd seen them together, they were kissing in the gate under the crimson clouds, tipsy, carefree and young, singing in the morning wind, and my father had tossed the Hausmeister a whole pengő. All that seemed so unlikely now. Two faded, ageing people sat at the table beside a smoky lamp running out of petroleum.

My father smiled at me, and I tried to smile back.

"Good evenin'," I said hoarsely.

"Good evenin'," my mother said.

My father said nothing. He stood up, came over to me, and did something he'd never done before: he hugged me and kissed me. I could see his eyes grow moist and suddenly, I could no longer control my frayed nerves. I burst into tears. My mother, too, started crying, sniffling softly.

"Well, you two are a barrel of laughs," he said, forcing a chuckle.

My mother laughed, and I started laughing too. All three of us laughed.

Then there was an incomprehensible silence around me. I could see them looking at me, puzzled, and it was only then I realized that I was still laughing. I was making hoarse, inchoate noises, shaking with nasty, unhealthy laughter. I couldn't stop. I tried gritting my teeth together, but it still took several minutes for me to quieten down. I muttered something disingenuously, tried to laugh it off. I didn't know what to do with myself. I was still standing there the way I'd come in, with my hat still on, the bottle of *pálinka* in my hand.

"What's that?" my mother asked, clearly just to break the silence.

"*Pálinka*," I said awkwardly. "A… um… guest gave it me. Would you like some?" I asked my father.

"Thanks," he said, "but I don't touch the stuff any more."

We both stared at him, stupefied. There must have been something very wrong with Dappermishka if he didn't want his *pálinka*.

"You ill?" my mother asked him in fright.

My father laughed, this time for real.

"The hell I am!" he said. "I could drink anything, even the petroleum out of that lamp. It's just that I've come off the sauce, and I don't want to go back on it."

"A little drop won't hurt," my mother encouraged him, but Dappermishka had principles.

"I can't drink a little, my dear. I can't do anything by halves. It's all or nothing with me. It's my nature. Believe it or not, I've even given up cigarettes."

"Cigarettes, too?" my mother repeated, her eyes full of concern. "What's got into you, Mishka, dear?"

"Into me?" my father laughed again. "All it is, my love, is I want to be a decent, upstanding citizen from now on, and I can't do that by halves, either. Since I got ou—" he said, swallowing the end of the word when my mother cast an anxious glance at him, "so… um… anyway, for the last two months…"

I didn't hear much of all that followed: that half-word kept hammering away inside my head. Got out… So he'd been in prison.

Prison. That's impossible. Then he wouldn't have written to my mother that... what was it again? Oh yes.

It may be that by the time these lines reach you I, too, will be home, but I also might never see either of you again.

No, he couldn't have written that in prison. In prison, you know when you're going to be released. So why would he have thought he might never see us again?

What had happened to this man? Where had he been? What had he done? What had made his hair go white?

"Did I hear you right earlier?" my mother asked. "You've been um... for two months?..."

"Yes," my father nodded, "two months yesterday."

"Why didn't you come home?"

"Why?" he stared stiffly and shrugged. "I didn't want to show up like some beggar."

"Where were you?"

"Down... um... there, down there. I was looking for work. Only there ain't much work in the countryside, and I didn't want to come back to the city empty-handed."

"That's silly," my mother said. "Didn't you give us plenty when you had some to give?"

"It's easy to give when you've got enough. It's when you ain't got enough that separates the men from the boys. I wasn't born a beggar, my love. I slept in the forest instead."

"And? How did you get on?"

"Oh, I got on all right. *Moved* on, that is."

"I can see you found *some* work. Heavy work. You can tell, just lookin' at your clothes."

"That's right," my father smiled. "It was bad for them, and not much good for me."

"Oh dear," my mother gestured. "It's a dog's life, this. Ain't fit for humans."

She gave a deep sigh, but my father did not join her. He moved

534

cheerfully round beside her, and then said with a wink, in his old Dappermishka voice:

"I brought you something, though."

"You did?"

"That's right. You can't keep Dappermishka down. Couldn't get you no silk, so I got you some paper instead."

"What?"

"Some paper. Here, look."

With that, he produced a document, folded into four, from his pocket.

"What's this?" my mother asked.

"Papers, can't you see?"

"What kind of papers?"

"Official papers."

He made her drag each word out of him. You could see he was enjoying the act terribly.

"And what do them official papers say?" pressed my mother.

"What do they say? Let's see…" he said, unfolding the papers deliberately slowly. "It says here, it says…" his voice now became terribly *official*, "it says that Mihály T., forty-three years old, Roman Catholic, residing in Budapest, wishes to marry… Here, you read it!"

Even my mother's lips went pale as she read it. The papers trembled in her hand, her eyes were full of tears.

"Aw, don't cry," joked my father. "You ain't signed it yet. There's still time to change your mind."

My mother laughed, but the tears kept streaming from her eyes.

"Mishka," she stuttered, "you… you're a real… a real…" She couldn't find the words, no matter how hard she tried. "A real sailor," was all she managed in the end.

The lamp hissed heavily, it was almost dark in the room.

"Did you hear that?" my mother sniffled. "Did you hear that, Béla?"

"I heard," I said gruffly. "I ain't deaf."

"Come over here," she told me, "come read it yourself."

She handed me the document and waited for the effect. She waited in vain, I said nothing.

"Don't you get it?" she asked excitedly. "This here document says... it says..." her voice faltered with her tears, "that... that... from now on... you won't be illegitimate."

"Yes," I mumbled, "that's what it says."

I tried to pretend I didn't have anything much to do with the whole thing, but I really had to grit my teeth to stop myself from laughing or crying again. I thought of that night long ago when Piroshkamydear took her Istvány away from old Rozi's, with me just watching them walk, from afar, down the main road, the three of them, the half-pint mother on the left, the great big father on the right and the boy István in the middle, his parents each holding one of his hands. And the postcard that came a few days later, the postcard on which instead of István Cs., he wrote István K., and we bastard children read it over breakfast and all at once fell silent and didn't dare look at one another.

"Old Roz-ee's son, where's your faa-ther gone?"

I could hear the mocking cries that even now sometimes woke me from my sleep and in my mind I went and stood out in the middle of the high street to tell the village:

"You can shout all you want now! You can shout all you want!"

Mihály T., forty-three years old, Roman Catholic, Budapest resident, spent two months sleeping in the forest, but did not come home empty-handed. He was a gentleman at heart. He'd brought us a present.

And boy, did I repay him.

I still can't talk about this completely candidly, so I'll keep it brief. Let's get it over with. It happened the next evening. I was having my dinner when a waiter called in the door:

"András, go up to reception!"

I could see as soon as I got to the lobby that it was *her* standing at reception. My heart jumped into my mouth, expelling all the air.

It must have been half past seven. The people from reception were having their dinner. Elemér was standing in for one of the senior staff.

He was standing in front of the pigeon holes when I reached the desk, with his back to me—he did not see me straight away.

"Good evening, ma'am," I muttered nervously.

She nodded, but said nothing. Elemér took out a bunch of letters from the slot for 205, then turned and came over to the desk.

"Somebody wants you," he said when he saw me. "I think it's your father."

He pointed towards the entrance. There stood my father beneath the overbearing marble columns, gilded stucco and crystal chandeliers, and in this flood of pomp and light, he looked even more shabby and miserable. I tore my glance away and loudly, so *she* too would hear, said:

"That's not my father!"

That's how it happened. I have nothing to add.

"Come with me," I whispered to my father before he could say anything, and rushed out into the street.

My father scanned my face.

"They didn't make a fuss about me asking them to fetch you, did they?"

"Um… well…" I huffed, "they don't much like it. What brings you here?"

"I wanted to talk to the head porter. I thought maybe he could get me into the hotel, too."

My stomach started twitching.

"He's not in," I said, my mouth all dry, and though I knew he'd only gone to get his dinner, I quickly added: "I don't think he's coming back any time today."

"Would you ask him for me?" he asked, unsuspecting.

"I could," I mumbled.

"Tell him," my father cleared his throat anxiously, "that um… I'll do anything… the most menial task." He smiled wanly, avoiding my gaze. "Surprised, ain't you?"

"Why should I be surprised?"

"Well, that I… that it's come to this. Oh, well, never mind, damn the whole thing anyway. Your mother can't buy bread with pride." He looked out above me, as if he were scanning the sky. "You noticed how poorly she's lookin'?"

537

"Yes," I nodded, my stomach trembling.

"I don't like her cough at all. It's a nasty cough she's got."

"Yes," I nodded once more.

Then we just stood there in silence.

"Well, so long, then," he said at last, awkward and anxious, and left quickly, as if he were fleeing something.

I watched his crooked back recede in the night and thought: maybe he killed someone. And I loved him like never before, and felt as guilty as if *I* had killed someone.

I was gripped by a perverse fear. I didn't dare go back into the hotel. I felt I couldn't look Elemér in the eye. I wandered the side streets feverishly, like a murderer hiding from his judges.

It was very warm and unusually dark. Clouds steamed in the low, starless sky, and there was a heavy, suffocating humidity in the air. I didn't want to think. Just one glass, I told myself, and went into the first bar I found.

It was a grim little bar. There was a single bulb to light it, hanging above the cobwebbed gas lamp, half burned out and completely hopeless. A hunchbacked old man kept bar, a dirty cat purring about his legs—the solitary guest. I drained the *pálinka* standing, paid, and made to leave, but suddenly changed my mind.

"Another."

There was a tin clock above the old-fashioned bar mat, a fly perched on its minute hand. It was a quarter to eight. What could happen? I thought. They relieved me at eight. Elemér thought I was talking to my father, and by the time the head porter got back, the night-shift boys would have arrived.

"Another," I said.

I took myself off to a corner and drank non-stop till half past eight. Then I told myself: he must have gone home by now. I paid, got up and wandered, dizzily, out of the bar.

Outside, it was spotting with rain, but the heat hadn't eased. Big warm drops kept falling sleepily, as if the steam were making things sweat. I panted back to the hotel, my heart beating erratically. We had to "present" ourselves when we went off duty, but fortunately, the head porter was occupied with a guest and didn't bother so much as looking at me. I made it to the changing rooms without incident and began to change.

When I saw myself in the mirror, I was seized with a virulent hatred. I had never been as revolted by a human face as I was now by my own.

"Yuck!" I said aloud, spitting at the mirror.

I stumbled out, dazed. The basement was empty, I saw no one. But when I stepped out of the staff entrance, someone touched me on the shoulder in the darkness.

I shuddered. It was Elemér. He was standing in the doorway, looking at me.

"You been drinking?"

"Yeah. So?"

Elemér turned away. He was silent for a long time, then he said, without looking at me:

"That won't make things better."

"Do you have a better idea?" I asked him standoffishly.

He didn't reply. We stood in the spitting rain in silence.

"You going home?" he asked at last.

"Yes."

"I'll walk with you to Nyugati."

"What for?"

He didn't reply to that, either. We walked in silence for a while. Suddenly, he took my arm.

"Béla," he said, quiet and careful, "come back to your senses. Can't you see what's happened to you?"

"Let's say I can. So what?" I looked at him defiantly. "Stop beating around the bush. Say it and get it over with."

"Say what?"

"What you're thinking. That I'm rotten to the core."

Elemér now looked at me. His prematurely ageing cat's eyes were unusually gentle, and yet in some indefinable way still strict.

"I think," he said simply and calmly, "that the *society* is rotten to the core that lands an otherwise decent seventeen-year-old in this situation.

And that you feel so corrupt because you tried to get into that society, even though you knew full well what it was like. You can't be a half-hearted bourgeois, either, Béla. It's either or. You can't paddle around in the floodwaters and be in Noah's Ark at the same time. We are the Noahs of this age. We can't be mixing with them. Do you see? *We can't mix with them.* We have to lock ourselves in the Ark of our convictions, looking out at their world through its windows. Don't you remember what the Bible says about Noah? *Then the Lord shut him in.*"

He's talking like a Sunday School teacher, I thought angrily, and couldn't pay attention. Images kept swaying through my dizzy head, bleeding one into the other. *Her* at reception, the way she nodded, curt and distant, Franciska on Gellért Hill as he said, with that degenerate smile: *Why shouldn't I do it, if it's to my advantage?* And my father, who might have murdered someone, and my mother who was coughing nastily, and what if the Constable chooses to have me thrown out right now?

"In the society of the future," Elemér was explaining in a dry, stentorian tone, when I suddenly started screaming at him.

"Leave me alone with the society of the future!" I yelled. "We're living in 1930! Miklós Horthy is in the Royal Palace, the peasants can't make enough to eat working fourteen hours a day, and if I drop dead, the society of the future isn't going to resurrect me. Tell me what to do in *this* society! Or do you think a cancer patient will really suffer less if you can prove to him that in a hundred years' time there'll be a cure for cancer? You're always only concerned about society's problems. But go on and tell me, since you're so smart, what am I supposed to do about *my* problems?"

"They will cease along with this society," Elemér replied calmly. "Everything will change when society changes."

"The hell they will," I grumbled. "Human nature isn't going to change. They aren't going to start hanging women for not loving a man back and men are still going to eat their own hearts out. Or won't there *be* any love in the society of the future?"

Elemér did not reply.

"Not so wordy now, are you? Can't answer me that, can you?"

"Maybe I just don't want to."

"Why not?"

"Because I hate getting personal. You're talking about *love* in general, but I know you have someone specific in mind."

"So?" I snapped, ready to jump.

My anger now infected Elemér as well.

"For the love of God," he said, with unusual vehemence. "Do you still not see that you're mixing things up? Love! Oh please. A bourgeois woman used you, that's all. You were her András. She didn't even bother to remember your name. The day before yesterday it was a Dezső being András, yesterday a Béla, today it's a Franciska, and God knows who it'll be tomorrow. What does that have to do with love? This is all just a symptom, too, a symptom, nothing else. A rotten little piece of the so-called *Überbau* that Karl Marx says—"

"Karl Marx can go to hell."

Elemér stopped suddenly. I had never seen his grey, impassive face so angry.

"Aren't you ashamed?" he berated me quietly. "They might be torturing a comrade to death as we speak, now, at this very moment, because he dared stand up for Marx's ideas. He's dying for us, for you as well—yes, you! And you say Marx can go to hell and deny your own father for some rich whore. Do you know what Marx calls people like that? *Lumpenproletarier*. You're acting like a *Lumpenproletarier*."

"And you're acting like an old Jew rabbi!" I screamed in his face. "You want to explain life with Marx's kosher Talmud. Volume Three, page 458, paragraph 12: Love. What d'you know about love? It's like you're made of wood—wood and paper—stuffed with ideals. Your head's full of printer's ink and there's a Marxist gramophone where your heart should be. I hate you, d'you hear me? I always hated you. You and your Jewish Marxism can go to hell. Good night!"

A tram had just stopped in front of us, and I climbed, swaying, on board.

That was how it happened; I have nothing to add.

In the morning, when I came into the hotel, I could feel that something had happened. I thought of that eerie spring night when no one in the hotel said anything, and I only found out about Gyula's suicide hours later. That was when I had felt this inexplicable worry, this strange, undefined anxiety.

I felt an indefinable *lack*—I can't put it any other way. I observed keenly, but could detect no difference. The shift was moving soundlessly in its course, like some refined alien star to which earth's humdrum rules did not apply. There was no one in the basement. Silence and stale air, a dynamo humming monotonously in the distance, the walls reverberating in the yellow half-light.

I suddenly stopped. I knew what it was. It was the sound of the boys I was missing, that cheerful, familiar cacophony that you could usually hear at this time—between half past seven and half past eight—from far off in the basement. Now there was silence, an incomprehensible silence, and my steps echoed with unnatural loudness beneath the bare concrete vaults.

At first, I thought I was late. Had our clock stopped? I started running, but when I got into the changing room, I could see right away that our clock wasn't the problem. The boys were all there, every one, getting undressed, changing and washing as usual, but in stony silence.

I was watching them, stunned, when my heart skipped a beat. There was a short, broad-shouldered man in a bowler hat sitting in one of the corners, propped against the wall, reading the paper. He turned the pages absently, and it was so quiet you could hear the rustling of the pages.

"Copper!" Lajos whispered without moving his mouth. He stole a glance all round, then added breathlessly:

"He's come for Pokerface."

We can't have been more than ten feet from the "copper". Lajos was standing in front of his locker, the open door of which sheltered him from view. My locker was right next to his; I opened it mechanically. Lajos stepped back, took a quick look at the "copper", and then ducked back behind the door and gestured for me to come closer.

"Watch out!" he whispered. "He's tryin' to get Antal to tell him who's friends with Pokerface."

"I see," I whispered, and peeked out from behind the door.

Elemér's locker was at the other end of the room. He was sitting in front of it on the bench, undressing. He betrayed no sign of emotion. He was taking off his uniform as calmly as someone who has finished work in the evening, is getting ready to go home and wondering what there is for dinner.

I could see the bowler-hatted man watching him from behind his paper. He was a stocky man with a ruddy face and black moustache, a big pink plaster on the back of his neck, which was pudgy and strangely bare. He was again wearing that broad, double-breasted blue suit I had seen him in on the tram, his thick walking stick hanging off his arm. It's got a sword in it, I thought, it must have. Something happened inside me.

I had felt like this as a small child when I had stood up to the class, or when I threw the ink bottle in that gendarme's face. And later, squeezing the Deputy's hand, or when I stood in front of Franciska's loaded revolver. These are the moments in life that you simply can't explain. If I saw a short, broad-shouldered man in a bowler hat a hundred yards away on the street, I would turn off into the next side street and run, terrified. Now that he was sitting here ten paces from me, I felt no fear. There was only indignation and indescribable hate.

"Stop starin' at him!" Lajos whispered.

I didn't reply. I suddenly knew what I had to do. I closed my locker and turned around.

"Where you going?"

"Over to Elemér."

Lajos grabbed my sleeve.

"You mad?" he whispered. "He'll take you as well!"

"So what?" I said so loudly that it caught everyone's attention, and went over to Elemér.

The peasant in me always came out at times like this. I walked as if I'd had boots on my feet, with a knife tucked in the top. I could see the bowler-hatted man following me with his eyes, and this gave me a strange satisfaction.

I went over to Elemér and looked him in the eye.

"You were right," I said nice and loud, so everyone would hear. "You were right about everything, Elemér."

I will never forget Elemér's face at that moment. When I think back on it, I am always reminded of those naive paintings of ugly ascetic saints in rural churches. His thin, weather-beaten, working-class face grew even paler than usual and his prematurely aged cat's eyes seemed to reflect some kind of awkward emotion. The whole thing lasted no more than two or three seconds. Then, to my great surprise, he said:

"Where's that pengő, then?"

I had no idea what he was talking about.

"I told you when we bet you'd lose," he added almost cheerfully, and I suddenly understood.

That was him all over, that was Pokerface. He was still trying to protect me. And I had told him yesterday that there was a Marxist gramophone where his heart should be.

I could feel myself going red. I fished a pengő out of my pocket, fumbling, and handed it to him. Elemér dropped it, and I could see that it had been on purpose. I leant down after it, he leant down too, and when our heads touched, he whispered:

"Get out."

It was an order, and I executed it. I was suddenly standing in front of the changing room, without a clue what to do with myself. Opposite the changing room were the staff toilets. I went in, locked the door of the stall behind me, and lit up nervously. Thoughts came rushing through my head so fast that not a single one could make it out alive. They scampered one over the other, each trampling the last. Why am I just sitting here? I asked myself at once. What am I waiting for? Why don't I do something?

I jumped up. I'm going to go back in there, I thought, and… I had no idea what I was going to do. I wanted the "copper" to take me too, I wanted the devil to take the whole damned world.

I charged into the changing room, but Elemér and the "copper" were no longer there.

"Where are they?"

"They left."

"When?"

"Just now."

I ran out. I ran as fast as I could, galloping through the long, winding basement, but I couldn't see them anywhere.

Suddenly, I came up short. In one of the bends, I spotted the first window onto the street, and I could see Elemér through the dusty glass as the "copper" took him away in handcuffs. The police van, the Green Bertha as it was known in Újpest, was standing there in front of the window, with a crowd of curious onlookers gathered round. They must have been office workers and civil servants on the way to work, and the early risers among the upper classes on their way to ride or play tennis. You could see that they'd had a solid breakfast, a leisurely read of the paper, that their maids had said a respectful farewell when they'd left home, that they were—in a word—a "better class of people" who had as little to do with this handcuffed fellow citizen as a Zulu native or an Amazonian head-hunter they'd once seen in the newsreel at the pictures. They watched this little free entertainment with moderate interest, bustling and smiling, asking what was going on; a man with a monocle was shaking his head, and a woman in tennis clothes was laughing shrilly.

Elemér reacted to the curious looks with the complete indifference of a tree with a bunch of tourists gawping at it. It was a little tree, an ugly, bare tree, but it weathered the storm well. You could see that it had prepared thoroughly for winter and its storms, and it was now calm and unsurprised. He stepped into the police van like a civil servant into his office—a humble civil servant, decent to the soles of his feet, aware that he was doing nothing but his duty, expecting no reward.

The "copper" locked the door of the van behind him and the Green Bertha made off. It was only then I noticed that I'd removed my hat and was standing stiffly to attention, bareheaded, the way we did for our superiors.

8

ELEMÉR'S ARREST HAD A STRANGE IMPACT on me. Now that I come to try and write about it, I am overwhelmed by that oppressive confusion a pilot must feel when his plane hits a patch of turbulence. In great moments of excitement, there is always something unattainably dreamlike, and you relate to them—even later—as you do to dreams. Only if you try and talk, or in this case, write about them, do you notice that there are turbulent patches in between events that you cannot fly through using the cumbersome notions of rational thought. In the moment of action, the person doing it sees even the most appalling action as *natural.* They do it because they have to do it, but if they try to explain *why* they did it, they start humming and hawing or dissimulating. They think of Freud or the alignment of the stars, reaching desperately for the words to make themselves understood, and all the while they can feel that it's all in vain. The more words they try and use to get closer to the truth, the farther away they get, because they're trying to explain something in the language of waking consciousness that happened on the border between dreams and insanity. So I'm going to record this without any explanation: *I wanted to go to prison.*

The fuse just blew, there was a short circuit in my soul, and in the darkness, something happened for which there are no clear words. You must understand, I didn't want to *do* anything for which I might later go to prison, I simply wanted to go to prison, like Elemér. That's how it started; at the time, I wasn't thinking of anything else. The idea of killing someone only came to me days later.

One morning, Antal drew me aside in the changing room and took a pistol out of his pocket.

"Buy it off me?"

The question did not surprise me. The boys were constantly "wheeling-dealing" with each other and there was a roaring trade in pistols. We were all cadets, and the love of deadly weapons is inculcated early on in cadets. I was no exception—but where would I have got the money for a gun?

"I don't want it," I said curtly, and thought that would be that.

"Got a gun already?" Antal asked.

"No."

"Well, then," he said, "you'd better buy it quick, my friend, because you'll never get another one this cheap. I bought it for ten from someone in a spot, and now I'm in trouble myself. I'll give it to you for eight."

I knew about guns, and I could see right away that this one was worth twice that. It was a five-shot revolver, a serious, reliable weapon. I liked it, but I had no intention of buying it.

"What do I need a gun for?"

"You never know when you're going to need it. Take it for seven?"

"I don't have seven pengős."

Antal must have been trying to get rid of it for a while, and it seems he really was in a tough spot.

"I really need the money," he said. "If you pay cash, I'll give it to you for five."

"Five?" I asked in surprise.

"Yes. And I'll throw in twenty cartridges, too."

I didn't know what to do. I did have five pengős, but I had wanted to give four of them to my mother.

"I'd have to try it first," I said evasively.

Antal thought about it.

"If you lend me three pengős," he said at last, "I'll leave it with you till Monday and you can try it tomorrow on the range. All right?"

That was an offer I couldn't resist. We had cadet training on Sundays, and this was on a Saturday morning.

"All right," I nodded, and dug out the three pengős. "I'll give you my answer on Monday."

I pocketed the pistol, and at that moment something was set in motion within me. I can only put it that vaguely: *something was set in motion*. It was as if some poisonous stimulant had got into my blood—from then on, I couldn't calm down. My excitement seemed completely unreasonable, and yet simply kept on growing. I couldn't get to sleep for ages in the evenings; I would drink half a litre of *pálinka*, but still start again and again from my sleep.

The next morning, I was first out on the range. I went straight to the target and stopped at the ten-metre line. I looked around to check no one was watching and drew the pistol out of my pocket. Up till now, it had been just an object, but it suddenly came to life. When I loaded it and my finger touched the trigger, an indescribably great, almost perverse sense of security came over me. For the first time in my life, I didn't feel defenceless. If it came down to it, I too, could *do* something, and not just have other people do things to me. I could defend myself, therefore I was. I started humming loudly.

"*You'd better watch out!…*"

The Constable's threat had been terrifying me for weeks, but now when I thought of it, I suddenly laughed.

"You too!" I said aloud, and in my mind took aim at the dark, twisted man.

I could see his yellow, blinking eyes and told myself: right there, between the eyes!

The bullet drilled into the centre of the target with a great bang.

That was when I made up my mind.

Was I trying to take revenge for Elemér? Or for myself? Did I want to make amends for being the way that I was? I don't know. Probably all three played a part. But even so, the question remained, why wasn't it *her* I wanted to shoot? I have no answer to that, either. That was just the way it was.

I didn't think about the reasons, and didn't care about the consequences. The need for revenge is frighteningly similar to sexual desire, and sometimes I really did think about the moment of committing the act the way a lover will think about the night they can finally satisfy their desires. I did, occasionally, think about the short, broad-shouldered man in the bowler hat, the way lovers, too, sometimes thought of jealous husbands, but I was no more sober than those lovers. I was in love with this idea, obsessed with the feeling. After all my days of helplessness, I felt a strange liberation that at last, I too would finally *do* something and not die like a miserable worm, crushed by chance under an upper-class heel. I wasn't going to give up that easily—I was going to make them pay the price. And then the "coppers" could come and get me, and the devil could come and take the whole wide world!

Besides, he was bound to know by now that I didn't want to give up Elemér, and it was only a matter of hours or days before he made good on his threat. Well, let him try. The day they sacked me from the hotel, I'd shoot him like a dog.

This decision made me more or less calm. On Monday, I bought the gun, and waited.

For the moment, nothing happened. The Constable walked past me whenever he came to the hotel as if he'd never seen me in his life. He didn't rush me or threaten me like before. He was incomprehensibly, frighteningly silent.

I will never forget those silent meetings. I used to leave the pistol in the changing room, because I was afraid it would bulge through my tight uniform, but on the days I knew he'd be in, I always carried it with me. When I saw his car draw up outside the entrance, I would quickly reach into my pocket, pull up the safety, and wipe my sweaty palm unconsciously against my trousers, the way I always did at cadets before taking a shot. Right between the eyes!

The gun warmed through in my pocket. It was feverish, it ranted and raved. I knew that it could happen at any moment, and so every second was imbued with a special significance. There was a scary silence within me. My thoughts were all on tiptoes, a fog descended on my heart, and the world filled with mysterious signs. Once, I remember, I read the following word on a poster: *Beginning*, and shivered. Once, someone said: *Endless*, and my knees trembled. Images that previously I had never even noticed could now move me to tears. My mother as she stood before the tub washing, or as she went out to work with her bundle in her hand, adjusting her kerchief before she left. My father leaning down for something and then throwing back his soft, greying hair in the way only he did as he stood up. A cloud in the sky. A boat on the Danube. The wheelwright playing the harmonica on the second floor. I stored these images within me like someone taking their leave of a town and capturing a few final scenes on their way to the station. That was it, that's all. That little. That much.

I was saying goodbye. I had never been as gentle before as in these days when I was preparing for murder. I stopped drinking. I gave every penny I earned to my mother and took most of my food home, to boot. I went hungry a lot, but not like before. Back then, I had been hungry because I didn't have enough to eat. Now, it was a choice. I was fasting, like I had before Communion as a child.

I liked being at home. I would sit with my parents out on the walk-way or in the room, beside the rickety table. I smiled when they smiled, nodded as they talked. They didn't talk much. We had a lot of things to keep quiet about. Then, when we couldn't take the silence any more, one of us would say:

"Let's have a game of cards."

We still had the cards, the pawnbrokers wouldn't take them. Sometimes we'd play for hours without saying a word.

Now, if my mother brought home some washing, my father would join her beside the tub, and I helped too. All three of us would wash on these hot, sultry nights, suffocating in the steam and dizzy with the heat. Sometimes, we didn't have money for petroleum and the lamp overhead would go out while we worked. We laughed and kept on working. Our hands touched in the tub, and I would sometimes cry in the darkness. *My parents*, I thought, and the word was so heart-wrenching, it was as if no one had ever used it before me. My parents, and I, their son.

One night, when I was alone in the flat, I found the marriage licence. It was lying on one of the shelves in the wardrobe. It lacked the duty stamp because, of course, those cost money. The wedding would have cost money, too—not much, it's true—but we didn't even have that. Shame, I thought. The police would be sure to ask for my documents.

I went and sat in the window, staring out into the night. Shame, I thought. It's a shame about a lot of things. If I could have kept on in school, I'd be finishing next year. Nothing would have happened yet, and everything would still be before me. I would be learning, prepar-ing for life. I'd always been a good student, I would have stayed a good student. The Schoolmaster had always encouraged me by saying that if I got top grades for twelve years straight, they'd give me a free place at the university. Shame. It would have been nice. The world was full of wonders, and I did so want to see them. Shame, shame, shame. Not for me, but for the person I might have been.

Might… might… might.

One day, it would all be different—Elemér was right. But where would I be by then?

The salty tears ran down into my mouth, and I didn't bother wiping them away. The house was silent, the morning star winking red above the courtyard. Like a ruby, I thought, like a ruby in the mechanism of a watch, and at that thought, I trembled.

What a mechanism! What a piece of clockwork.

Who wound it, that it never stopped? What drove it, that it worked with such chilling perfection? We saw only a ruby up in the distance, a tiny cogwheel, an insignificant screw, but never the dial. It ticked on and on, day and night, right in front of your face, and yet you never knew what time it was.

All you knew—and that only in moments such as this—was that *it was all connected*. That every screw, wheel and spring served the *Work*, with merciless efficiency. That every screw had its place, every star had its orbit, and that you—yes, you too—had your own place and trajectory, like the stars, the fish and the plants, or the bird up on the rooftop that does nothing but sing and then fall down dead. You came for some purpose, you were sent to do something, and now you're standing there in the world like a small child their parents have sent next door with a message who, by the time they arrive, have forgotten why they were sent in the first place.

I should have expressed something. I should have expressed something!

There it was, in my heart, and I aborted it, like poor women did their babies. It was a simple poem, a fractured peasant poem, but it was my poem, and I should have been the one to write it. It might have been clumsy, and certainly wasn't clever, but it came from the soil like the wheat I'd reaped and reached for the sky like everything that grows out of the earth. The earth and the sky rang in a single rhyme within me, smelling of compost, like freshly turned soil, fragrant like the flower that grew out of it, simple like the expressions of the animals, and mysterious like the faces of the dead.

Yes, I suddenly knew. I understood for the first time what I had been born for, though I may not have been able to put it into words. I knew it in my blood and in my marrow, in my sinews, muscles, veins, in my guts, trembling with excitement, and in my skin, which got goosebumps at the thought. *I have to express this poem.* I had to express the poem—the rest didn't matter. Happiness? Who ever asked a cog in the mechanism if it's happy? Every cog has its function, and what are you worth if you don't fulfil your function? Go, sing your poem, you wretch, and leave at least something fine behind you, a line that might echo for a while, like the organ after mass when the priest has long since fallen silent.

9

O N ONE OF THESE OCCASIONS, when we were quietly playing cards, just the three of us, there was an unexpected knocking on the door. It was late, it must have been around eleven.

"Who can that be?" asked my mother, with an anxious twitch.

She'd been uneasy all night. I'd hardly got through the door when she suggested we play cards, and she hadn't said a word since.

"I'll go see," I said, and went out.

It was old Máli. She was a flat-chested, pot-bellied old woman, caked in dirt and full of honeyed words.

"Praise the Lord," she said with an ingratiating smile, because she was from near Szeged originally and there they praised the Lord even instead of saying "good evening".

She was devout, gossipy and unbelievably smelly—none of us could stand her. We never visited her, nor she us, though we'd lived in the same house since who knows when. I couldn't understand what she was doing here. My face must have shown it, because her first question after praising the Lord was:

"Come at a bad time?"

"No, why don't you come inside?"

"Is your mother home?"

"She is."

Old Máli and her smell came into the room. The devout woman praised the Lord on entering that as well, and then said to my mother:

"I hear you were looking for me, my dear. I only just got home."

My father gave my mother a look of shock and my mother went red.

"Um… ah… it was on account of the washin'," she scrambled with a forced smile, "you know."

But no, old Máli did not know. She was a cunning old vixen, and she wasn't deaf or anything, but you could see that she really didn't know.

"Washin'?" she repeated vaguely, looking in two directions at once, being wall-eyed.

"Don't you remember?" my mother wheedled in an odd tone. "Just the other day, you was saying that... um..." she gave the old woman a long look, "you wanted some washin' done."

Máli suddenly understood.

"Oh that's right, that's right, it went right out of my head!" she said, and gave a hideously throaty laugh. "Yes, that's right, the washin'. 'Course."

My father looked from one woman to the other. He looked unusually agitated, and I, too, grew concerned. I knew what the old woman lived off, all the children in the house knew. Surely my mother wasn't...

"If you want," my mother said, "I'll come down with you now and take a look. Then we can fix a price right away."

"All right," the old woman nodded with a cunning expression. "We can discuss it downstairs, dear. Praise the Lord."

And she was off, my mother in tow.

"Back in a minute," she said hastily, flustered, and was out the door.

My father didn't say anything and neither did I. The old woman was already shuffling along the walkway outside, but her smell still lingered. My father shuffled the cards distractedly, then smacked them suddenly down on the table, as if he'd caught someone sharping. He stood up angrily and hurried after my mother without a word.

I could see a storm brewing and fled into darkness to avoid it. I turned out the light, undressed, and went quickly to bed.

A few minutes later, I could hear the door opening outside. There was silence, they weren't talking. My mother came into the room, tiptoed to the table and took the lamp. She paused a moment in the door, then slowly, carefully, closed it behind her.

"He's asleep," she whispered.

My father didn't answer.

There was the scratching of a match and the light of the petroleum lamp filtered in through the cracks in the door. Someone opened up the collapsible bed, there were steps on the stone floor, a quiet rustling, the familiar sounds of people undressing. A little while later, the bed creaked, one of them had got in it. The other poked about a little while longer, then the light went out and there was silence.

The silence was so deep, I could hear the dripping of the tap clearly through the closed door. One-two… one-two. Two drops together, then silence, and then: one-two… one-two.

"Mishka!" my mother said at last.

"Yes?"

"Is you angry?"

My father did not reply.

"Could you have gone through with it?" he asked after a long time, and his voice was dark as the room. "Could you really have done it behind my back?"

"No, I swear!" my mother whispered. "I swear on the Virgin Mary!"

"Then why d'you go see the old woman?"

"I just wanted to talk to her."

"Didn't I tell you that filthy old woman wasn't to touch you as long as I live and breathe? So what the hell did you want to talk to her about?"

"I don't know. Just to ask her. After all, she is a midwife. I dare say a doctor would do it better… but when we ain't got the money?"

"You know we'll have it. Weren't you there when Rudi said he'd lend it to me?"

"Yes, but… that was a while ago, and… you ain't said nothing since, Mishka."

"What was I meant to do? I ain't some old fishwife to go running my mouth all day."

"When did you talk to him last?"

"Yesterday."

"And what did he say? Will we get it?"

"Yes."

"When?"

"When, when?" my father groaned. "Next week."

"Next week?" My mother's voice changed all of a sudden. "Well, that's all right, then. Mishka," she said, relieved. "Mishka, come on, don't be angry with me."

"As if I had any right to be angry!" my father snorted. "All I do is lie to you. I was lyin' just now."

There was a frightened silence.

"You mean we won't have the money next week?" my mother asked faintly.

"Oh, the money was there yesterday!" my father replied furiously. "He was rubbin' it under my nose, the bastard, like a whore's tits."

"But he didn't give it to you?"

"Oh he wanted to. Only I didn't take it."

"Why not?"

"'Cause I didn't want to."

"Why not?"

"Stop asking so many questions!" my father snapped. "Stop asking so many questions, damn it, 'cause I swear to God I'll get out of bed right now and go fetch that money from Rudi, and then God help the whole wretched world!"

My mother didn't dare ask any further questions. They both lay in silence, only the tap said anything. One-two… one-two…

It must have been another ten minutes before my father said anything. Then he was calm, frighteningly calm.

"I don't know what to do," he said. "I don't know what to do."

"Why?" whispered my mother. "What happened yesterday?"

"It wasn't yesterday, or rather… It's hard to explain. Something happened yesterday, too, only… how should I say… what happened yesterday started a long time ago. Back in America."

"Rudi was with you in America?"

"That bum? Not a bit of it. I didn't even know he was born back then. That was a long time ago, back when I was a sailor. What happened was, one day, we docked in New York, you know, what the people hereabouts call 'Nooyok'."

"Yes."

"Well, later that day, I'm walking down the street in Nooyok, when suddenly a car slows right down beside me. It was a fine car, with a fine gentleman inside. He looks at me, and looks at me, looks at me so hard his eyes almost pop out his head. Then he stops the car and right there, in the middle of the Nooyok street, calls out to me in Hungarian: Dappermishka? That's my name, I says. Don't you recognize me? he says. So I take a good look at his face, and then I cry: Dippymishka?"

My mother laughed.

"What?"

"Wait for it, wait for it, all in good time. So the story was we were at school together, and he was called Mishka, and so was I, and so the boys—to tell us apart—started calling him Dippymishka. 'Cause he was a bit dippy, you know, sort of slow and whatnot. People had no more regard for him than for a pair of socks."

"Weren't he the pig-herd's son?"

"That's right. You know him?"

"No, but they used to talk about him in the village, 'cause the story was he always sent his folks ten dollars at Christmas. They said he were a millionaire. Can you really become a millionaire out there drivin' someone around?"

"He wasn't nobody's driver. That was his own car. He had a ranch out there."

"A what?"

"A ranch. Land. That's what the Americans call it. He showed it to me and all, took me straight out to his ranch. Oh, you should have seen that!"

"He really became a millionaire?"

"No, he was no millionaire, Anna, he wasn't even rich. But he lived better than a lord does here. He had everything. Good, rich land that grew anything—cows, pigs, chickens, whatever you can think of. There was a fine little white house out on the ranch, with three rooms, like a vicarage. And you should have heard the way people talked to him. Like a count! Mister this, mister that…"

"What's that, 'mister'?"

"It's a mark of respect, like sir. And missus means madam."

"They called his wife madam?"

"Out there, they call everybody madam."

"Even washerwomen?"

"Even them."

"What a strange world," my mother sighed. "What a wonderful, strange world."

"Well… as for wonderful, it's not quite as wonderful as people here think it is. Because mister here or mister there, your bourgeois is still a bourgeois, and steps all over the poor. The only difference is that the bourgeois there have more money, so there's a little more that makes its way down to the working class. Only I didn't know that at the time, so Dippymishka's farm blew me away. I says to him: how did you make all this? Just the same, he says, as anyone. I worked. What d'you do? Same as at home. Peasant work. And you got this rich off that? Oh, I ain't rich, he says, I'm still making the payments on the ranch, 'cause I bought it on instalments. It don't bring much, but it keeps the family. 'Cause he had a family, too, see, I didn't tell you that. He married a Hungarian girl from out there, quite an eyeful. There were three pretty children running round the yard; I played catch with 'em all day, and then when it got dark, we took the cauldron out in the field, the way we used to when we were kids minding the animals. We made a goulash fit to make the angels weep. It was a good night, a very good night. There was a crescent moon in the sky; I still remember it, 'cause the moon there, when it's crescent, ain't the same as it is here for us, but the other way around. And that's where it happened, under that moon. We ate a lot, and drank a lot, and we were in a fine mood. And then I almost burst into tears."

"Why?"

"I don't know. Maybe it was the wind. It was a warm wind, a late-summer wind, bringing the smell of hay and soil at night. Hard to say it with words. You know, I was still a beardless youth when I escaped from the poverty at home. I'd been out on the sea ten years by then, wanderin' the world, lookin' for somethin', I didn't know what. And there, under that backwards crescent moon, with the wind bringin' the smell of the earth, I suddenly knew that was what I'd been looking for. A bit of land. And everything that goes with it. A wife, and children, harvestin'—a good, decent, peasant life. Believe it or not, when I was alone in bed, I could feel the salt water flowing down into my mouth. You'd laugh at that, wouldn't you?"

"No, why would I? 'Course I wouldn't. And, what happened next?"

"Nothin'. I went sailin' on. There were other cities, other seas, other worlds. Then the war broke out, and the peace, the revolution broke out, and the counter-revolution, everythin' broke out. There was so much trouble, always, that I didn't really have time to think on it, not till I got put away just now. There was nothing else to do *but* think on it there. I paced up and down in the cell and thought of that ranch. Then one night, when I couldn't get to sleep, I suddenly sat up on my bunk, and I said to myself, Dappermishka, I says, is there anythin' you can't do that Dippymishka can? Well, to cut a long story short, that night I swore to myself I'd get the price of the crossing together and take you all out to America, no matter what. I'll make you a missus and the boy a mister. We'll have him educated, and send him up to university so he can write poems like Sándor Petőfi. And we'll work for him, while we can; we'll get on with our land and animals, and when we get old, we'll sit in front of the house and look on that backwards crescent moon till our poet son comes and closes our eyes for good. That's what I was thinking."

The bed creaked. My father must have sat up.

"Anyway," he said, "that night I swore to myself I'd never do anythin' else that could land me in trouble. It was a strange night, a very strange night. I hardly closed my eyes, Anna, but I tell you, I still woke the next morning the way I used to before Communion when I was a boy, and I'd been to confession the day before. D'you know what I mean?"

"'Course I do. You repented of your sins."

"The hell I did! Why would I have repented? You don't get me, Anna. I say what Menyhért says, my comrade Menyhért, that in a world like ours you can only be two things. A revolutionary or a crook. Well, I wasn't born a revolutionary, but you can take my word for it, I wasn't born a crook, either. I was a decent man, long as they let me. If they hadn't taken away our sea, I'd be a sailor still. If they hadn't pulled the land out from under me, I'd have stayed a peasant till my dying day. I didn't care for factories, it's true, but I would have gone for factory work, too. There just weren't any jobs to be had. What could I do? Starve to death? Let Horthy starve. Who's to blame? The man that shoves someone into the sea, or the one that climbs on the other's back because he's drownin'? Those millions and millions of jobless were pushed into the sea, Anna. They're drowning, poor fellows, gaspin' for air. They keep on sufferin', puttin' up with it, and starving, and when they can't take it no more, they take a bite of someone else's bread. Then they lock 'em up. Well, when I saw that was how it was, I says to myself, Mishka, I says, if the poor man ends up in prison either way, it's better to know what for. I thought bigger than the others, that's why I wasn't put away before. And if I could have done it even bigger, I may never have been locked up at all. They might have made me a minister in the end, 'cause it's them that are the biggest crooks. I just wanted to tell you so you'd know: I ain't repented of nothing. I wanted to go straight on account of you. So I could take you out to America. I didn't want to get into trouble no more, and that was what landed me in it."

"How's that?"

"I'll tell you. I could tell right away when they picked me up, they didn't have no proof. So I was happy as Larry and just laughed at the whole thing. I liked it that they couldn't get one over on me. I played with them like a cat with a mouse. But when I thought about that plan with America, I suddenly lost all my cheer. I started to get scared. I was scared for that fine, decent little life of ours. I was scared they might cotton on to something. I'll tell you straight, I got in a real state. And then one day, as if it weren't enough, they brought in a lawyer in the cell next door, and more fool me, I started tapping away to him."

"What?"

"Tapping. That's how prisoners talk."

"The lawyer was a prisoner, too?"

"That's right. Exchange fraud."

"What's that?"

"He took money out of the country."

"Money he stole?"

"'Course not. His own."

"Since when's that a crime?"

"A crime, my dear, is whatever the Almighty says it is. Not the Almighty sittin' up there in heaven, but the one sitting in the Royal Palace. The one that has a man kill innocent men, women and children on his orders, and then makes them a member of parliament, with the country paying his wages. And whoever don't want to keep his money in a country where that murderer can do with it what he wants, they drag off to jail. That's the way it is, my love. So I start tapping with this lawyer, and that was the worst of it."

"Why?"

"'Cause I got curious. I asked him how much time I could get for what I done. 'Course, I didn't tell him it was me that done it, but just asked, you know, in general terms."

"And what did he say, how much?"

"One or two years."

"One or two *years*?" my mother gasped.

"If only that had been it! But then I asked about the past ones, too, 'cause I couldn't sleep at night, and everythin', everythin' I'd ever done wrong came back to me. Little things, you know, but it all adds up. And the lawyer just kept tappin' out the years, and I scratched it all up on the wall, and added it all up in the end. You know what it came to? Eighteen years."

"God help us."

"Quite. I'm forty-three now, I said to myself. Forty-three and eighteen is sixty-one. What can you do at sixty-one? So much for America. So much for life. At least the other prisoners knew what they had coming. They could count the days. They could say: that's one less. But I went to sleep each night not knowing if I'd wake up in your bed, or be lying there on that cold hard bunk at the age of sixty."

"God help us!" my mother sighed again, and I suddenly understood that mysterious letter, and a host of other things besides.

"In the end, I did still manage to outwit 'em," my father said, not without a touch of pride. "They couldn't pin nothin' on me. But it was strange, Anna, mighty strange, when I looked in the mirror for the first time after all that time. I thought my hair was black, and suddenly I see it's white. It turned my hair white. Oh well, I says, so what? So you've gone grey, Mishka, but you've learnt a thing or two as well. From now on, you won't get into no more trouble. You'll take the family to America and you'll all live decently, the way people should. I gave up drinking, I gave up smokin', and didn't touch the women or the cards. There ain't a job in the world I wouldn't have done. I would have gone digging out latrines, if that was what was needed. But it wasn't needed. And then I hear you're in the family way. Well, I says to myself, I'll have to go see Rudi after all. 'Cause I didn't tell you, but it was Rudi and me did what they picked me up for, and that crook's only got me to thank they didn't get him and all. What I asked him for wasn't what he owed me, oh no, but a tenth or a twentieth. But I didn't want to go see him, and I thought he might leave me in peace if I only asked for that little."

"But he didn't?"

"No he didn't. He promised me the money when you were there, but when I went to see him to ask when he was going to give it to me, he says: I'll give it you, Mishka, when you do another job with me."

"He denied he owed you the money?"

"Didn't even deny it. He just laughed. He says: if you don't like it, Mishka, go turn me in. That's what he says. He wouldn't have dared say that before. He knew I could bash his brains in with one hand tied behind my back. But his sort always knows when you won't put up a fight. And I wasn't going to. I was worried about our voyage. And now here I am. If I take his money, it all starts again from the beginning, and if I don't, you'll end up going to that old woman. As the Lord is my witness, I wanted to do the decent thing. But if you die of it, what use is decency to me? So I don't know what to do now, Anna. I don't know what to do."

My father fell silent. There was silence—a dark, thick silence. One-two... one-two... one-two... As if the tap were dripping louder now, as if the silence itself were dripping in the darkness.

At last, my mother spoke. She said:

"I'll keep it, Mishka."

My father did not reply.

"Why don't you say anything?" she asked.

"Ain't my place."

"Why not? You're its father."

"It's easy bein' a father. All I've had is happiness from my son. You're the one that suffered for him."

"That's why I think that, Mishka."

"What?"

"That it's worth it. It's worth the suffering. If eighteen years ago the pharmacists' assistant didn't bleed to death and the angel-makers didn't get the wind up about the gendarmes, there wouldn't be no Béla now."

"That's right," my father said in a strange, heavy voice. "And what a boy he is! He's goin' to beat Petőfi into a cocked hat. And I ain't just saying, that, Anna, I read up on this Petőfi on account of him."

"You did what?"

"Read up on him. You know, in prison you get books for good behaviour, so I went and read all of Petőfi's poems, cover to cover. Well, and the professor that compiled them poems was obsessed with how *humble* Petőfi's origins was. Because his father was a butcher. But goddamn it, at least a butcher has meat for his son. What did our son get? And just look at the fine poems he's writin' at fifteen!"

"That's right," my mother said, taking up the thread, "with no schoolin' and no bread. He had to steal the paper to write on from the hotel. Tell me, Mishka, that sort of thing, where's it come from?"

"I don't know where it comes from, Anna, but one thing's for sure: it don't come from the upper classes."

"Maybe it's from the Lord, Mishka. Or d'you still not believe in him?"

"Who knows? Sometimes when I look at the boy, I almost start believin'."

"Would you want another one like him?"

"Ain't for me to say," my father repeated stubbornly, quietly, but his voice almost burned with joy. "We'll go to America, the four of us."

"Oh, how good it'd be!" sighed my mother.

How good it would be! I sighed as well.

Shame, I thought. Shame, shame, shame. We just don't have any luck, this family. We only came together when it was already time to say goodbye.

10

A FEW DAYS LATER, ON A STIFLING late August night, something strange happened. It must have been around nine when I got home, but the house was very quiet, as if it had been well past midnight. I had a bad feeling as soon as I got to the gate, because when a working-class house is that quiet, it always spells trouble. Were the police raiding someone again? Had someone died?

I listened anxiously. Silence, darkness, not a soul about. My steps echoed eerily on the winding stone stairs as I stumbled up in the darkness.

At the first turn in the stairwell, something grabbed my attention. I thought I'd heard noises. I looked out onto the walkway. I couldn't believe what I saw there. In the dark, like a petrified collection of statues, stood a crowd of people completely still, leaning against the railings and staring up, silent, into the darkness, craning their necks towards the third floor.

Had something happened at ours? I started scrambling up the stairs. But when I got to the third, I saw that the centre of attention was actually Árpád and Márika's apartment.

I couldn't understand what they were staring at. Árpád was standing in front of the apartment, but there was nothing peculiar about him. He was standing there perfectly calmly, as if he'd just got home and knocked on the pane in the kitchen door. You couldn't have imagined a more prosaic scene. A resident comes home at night and knocks on the door. What was there to be staring at? I wanted to ask, but people were listening so gravely in the darkness I didn't dare make a sound.

Árpád now struck a match and held it to the keyhole. The key, it seems, must have been in the lock, because Árpád grew agitated.

"Márika!" he yelled, rattling the door, "you all right?"

That was when I noticed that the shutters on their windows were closed. In this heat, you didn't close the shutters even at night, let alone now when the air had barely cooled from the day. I shuddered. Had she committed suicide? Is that why everyone was staring? But then why don't they tell Árpád?

Then something unexpected happened. Árpád, as if he'd sensed the curious looks, suddenly turned around. When he spotted the crowd of onlookers, he turned and headed straight for the stairs.

That was even less comprehensible. A moment before, he'd been afraid that Márika had come to some harm, and now he was abandoning their door without a word. Why? After all, he could see they were all staring at him.

I rushed into our apartment to ask what had happened, but my parents weren't home yet. There was movement outside. Little groups formed, whispering in the darkness, but from our window, I couldn't hear what they were saying. I was just on the point of going back out when I noticed something strange. Someone had drawn the curtain carefully aside in Árpád and Márika's kitchen. I couldn't make out who in the darkness, but from then on, I didn't shift from our window.

Five minutes passed, then ten, fifteen, and nothing happened. I was just beginning to think I'd been seeing things before, when the door opposite suddenly sprang open.

There was a fearful silence. It was Herr Hausmeister who stepped out.

He filed past the residents slowly, strutting provocatively, the crowd parting to make way for him. No one said a word, no one moved from their spot; only their heads turned in the darkness to follow him. And in that silence, someone suddenly started laughing.

At first, Herr Hausmeister pretended not to have heard, but the laughter grew louder and he suddenly stopped.

"Who's that laughing?" he asked menacingly.

No one replied. The silence became even thicker, and the laughter louder. I had never heard laughter like it. It reminded you a little bit of an infant's cries or the whining of a dog, and yet it was still laughter—cheerless, ghostly laughter.

I went outside and could see that it was Old Gábor who was laughing. He looked like he might not even know what he was laughing at.

His face was serious, he was staring absently before him, the drool came dripping from his mouth.

Herr Hausmeister went up to him and yelled:

"What you laughing at?"

The coffin-maker did not reply. He just kept laughing that dreadful, crazy laugh, as if he hadn't heard the question, as if he hadn't even seen Herr Hausmeister, who now suddenly grabbed him by the lapels.

"Old fool!" he growled, and slapped him in the mouth so hard he laid the old man out.

He must have fallen very hard, because it took three people to lift him, and even they could barely manage it. But when he was back on his feet again, he acted as if nothing at all had happened. At other times, when Herr Hausmeister walked past him peaceably, he would always yell at him to say good day to his elders, but now, when he had treated him this way, he didn't say a word. His face was expressionless, his eyes vacant; he just carried on drooling.

Herr Hausmeister, for his part, withdrew like a wrathful god and turned into the staircase with slow, dignified steps. Then, like a crash of thunder from the sky, a man's voice broke the darkness and the silence.

"Shame!"

The word struck like lightning, setting the whole house on fire.

"Shame!" people chorused everywhere in the dark. "Shaaaaame!"

The chorus came from the basement, rising through the ground floor to all three upper floors as well. The house became a wild beast provoked, growling aggressively in its cage.

"Shaame!"

"Shaaame!"

"Shaaaaame!"

"Shut it!" yelled Herr Hausmeister from the courtyard. "Shut your faces or I'll call the police."

But the house did not "shut their faces".

"Shame!!" their disgust thundered ever louder. "Shaaame!"

It must have taken a good half-hour for the house to settle back down, but Herr Hausmeister did not call the police.

"He daren't stir the pot," said the one-eyed wheelwright. "Even a copper would smell a rat."

"That's just why he ain't going to let it drop," said Mózes the locksmith, and unfortunately, he was right.

But meanwhile, something else happened as well.

In the morning, I woke to hear my mother in the kitchen saying:

"Look, Mishka, they've put one of them flyers under the door again!"

I immediately jumped up and started to dress so I could go out into the kitchen and read it, because I knew my mother burned these flyers—they'd already got more than one tenant in trouble. The police had been out several times to search people's flats and had arrested everyone who'd had one, though it hadn't done them much good. They got only the stupid and the naive, because anyone who had any sense, and especially anyone with anything to hide, did not keep flyers around the house. The people they arrested didn't know anything, and the people who did know weren't on speaking terms with the police. Sometimes you'd wake to find another one of "those" flyers lying on the kitchen floor. Someone had shoved it under the door, but as to who, and when, no one knew. On these mornings, the house would wear a furtive smile. The residents would read them and then throw them in the stove, and when they were all burned up, they'd call across to the neighbours:

"Good, ain't it?"

As to what was good, they didn't say, and the neighbours never asked. They looked at each other the way peasants do in a drought when the sky starts clouding up above them. A storm's coming, people's expressions said, and the house listened and waited.

As soon as I'd pulled on my trousers, I rushed out into the kitchen. My mother shuddered when I opened the door.

"Scared of your own son now?" my father joked, laughing tensely.

"Give it here," I whispered, because you always lowered your voice unconsciously when talking about those flyers.

My mother went to the door and locked it. Then we all sat down on the edge of the bed and started reading. It wasn't printed like the rest, but typewritten and mimeographed. I could see straight away why. It read:

COMRADES!
PROLETARIAN BROTHERS!

Don't get bogged down in righteous indignation! The hausmeister's lording it over us is a symptom of the Fascist insanity that forces the working class in Hungary to live like dogs; and now they're trying to stifle our cries of pain with the arm of the law.

Fight the system, which cannot survive without inhuman hausmeisters, informers, assassins, exploiters and sadistic policemen. A rotting tree has to be cut down at the root; what use is it tearing off a single bad leaf?

Only a rabble can't see the wood for the trees. The class-conscious proletarian is organized to fight the systematic Fascist oppression and doesn't lose itself in pointless individual acts.

You're only assisting the enemy if you bring the police down on your necks with rash acts!

We are not here to destroy, but to build.

We want to build a unitary society and we're going to eradicate the roots of this sickness legally. The bloodsuckers must die—the small fry of these proletarian traitor-fleas along with the great leeches of the peasants and workers. They will all, to a man, be tried in proletarian courts and there will be no mercy for the merciless.

Think of that in the dark days of helplessness and desperation. Come together and light the way for your comrades stumbling in the dark; study and teach so you can be good soldiers of the proletarian struggle for freedom and worthy of the great task that history has assigned you.

Down with Fascism!

Workers of the world, unite!

My mother was already fetching the matches to burn the dangerous document, but my father read it over again carefully.

"It's quite something," he said pensively.

"What?" asked my mother.

"That they're darin' to take a stand. Do you know how much jail time you can get for this?"

"How much?"

"I knew a fellow got fifteen years."

"And they still keep doin' it."

"Why? Who pays them?"

My father smiled at the naivety of the question.

"They're working on credit, dear," he replied, but my mother still did not understand.

"Who for?" she asked seriously.

"For this one here," my father said, pointing to me, his smile gone. "Him and all the other poor children."

"They must be a fine lot," my mother said pensively. Then she took the flyer out of my father's hand and lit it.

The paper caught, illuminating, for a moment, the darkened little kitchen.

The flyers burned just like that all throughout the house. If a "copper" or a fairy godmother had peeked through the keyhole, they would have seen a little light in every flat.

The shutters were closed all day on Árpád and Márika's flat, and Márika did not venture out.

"I ought at least to go see how she is," said my mother, but couldn't quite bring herself to do so.

The house made Márika a pariah, and my mother knew that the same fate awaited her if she went over there. She was very fond of Árpád, she hated Herr Hausmeister profoundly, and Márika's infidelity made her very angry. In other words, she was in complete agreement with the rest of the house, but she still pitied Márika. She couldn't sit still all evening and kept bursting into tears.

Though it's not like they were even close any more. Márika—as I learnt that evening—had been "shacking up" with Herr Hausmeister for months, and my mother had cooled towards her. There wasn't any animosity, but Márika only came over if my mother invited her, and my mother only invited her if she had some food to spare or if she was washing at home. Then Márika would bring her laundry over, Herr Hausmeister being such a generous type that his sweetheart couldn't even afford soap.

"I don't know what to do!" complained my mother, "I don't know what to do."

"Do what you think is best, my dear," replied my father, but my mother didn't know what she thought best.

"The worst is when everybody's right," she said, then cried a bit and ended up not going over to Márika's.

The next day I had a day off. My mother was washing at home that morning, my father and me helping her. It was brutally hot. You could barely see for the steam in the narrow, windowless little kitchen, because we weren't allowed to open the door even on boiling days like these—don't ask me why. Herr Hausmeister had so decreed, and Herr Hausmeister worked in mysterious ways, as deities generally do.

My mother went over to the door every five minutes, wiped the condensation off the glass and peeked over at Márika's. Their shutters were still closed. Árpád had not come home and Márika still hadn't shown her face.

"It's been three days!" she said hoarsely, staring intensely at her shoes. Then she said quietly: "I'm goin' over there, come what may."

My father did not object, nor did he approve, but when my mother left, he went and stood outside the door so everyone could see that anyone who said anything about my mother would have him to reckon with.

My mother's going immediately caught the house's attention.

"Well, would you look at that!" a woman said nice and loud when my mother knocked on Márika's door. Then there was silence, a dangerous silence.

Márika did not answer my mother's knocking for a long time. I was beginning to think there really was something wrong with her when she finally opened the door. She looked terrible, you could hardly recognize her. She stood there in the crossfire of hostile looks like a sick, exhausted little animal that no longer has the strength to defend itself.

My mother ignored the house completely.

"We're doin' some washing," she said calmly and simply. "Come on over, Márika, bring your laundry."

"Th-thank you," Márika stuttered, swallowing heavily to suppress her tears.

My mother waited in front of the door while Márika went in to fetch the laundry, keeping her eyes peeled. By the time Márika set foot in the walkway, all the doors and windows had filled with curious faces. Their looks were dark and savage, ready to strike; but my father, as I say, was standing there in front of the door, and everyone in Újpest knew it wasn't a good idea to tangle with Dappermishka.

Nothing happened for the moment. My father closed the kitchen door and Márika started in on the washing without a word. My mother took three boiled potatoes and a decent portion of bread from the cupboard and handed them to Márika. That was our lunch, all three of us, but as we didn't belong to the upper classes, we held strange and I might even say seditious views on private property: we held that lunch belonged to whoever hadn't eaten for the longest time, and in this case, that honour unquestionably went to Márika. The poor thing can't have eaten anything for ages, because she didn't even bother to make the customary excuses, but simply started gobbling the food right away. She didn't even sit down, just turned away from us into the corner, her shoulders heaving silently with sobs as she ate. We pretended not to see her and just carried on washing. But all at once, she gave a small, inarticulate sound, and if my mother hadn't caught her at the last moment, she'd have fallen clean across the floor.

We had all starved enough in our time to know what that meant. We didn't need to consult each other for advice; we acted quickly, without words. My mother supported the semi-conscious Márika into the room, laid her down on Manci's bed, and pulled open her shirt. My father brought in the bucket and poured water into the washbasin and jug as I wet a cloth and took a clean towel from the wardrobe. Then we left the women to themselves, because we knew what was coming next.

Half an hour later, we were all four back by the tub, washing on. I was just about to pop down to the shop because we'd run out of starch, when I saw that Mózes was heading straight to our apartment.

"The police are coming!" he whispered breathlessly, running on to the next apartment.

My mother glanced quickly at Márika.

"Did you burn it?" she asked.

She didn't specify what, but Márika understood. She nodded yes, and we kept on washing. We were used to this kind of thing, and besides, we were convinced the police weren't coming to ours, anyway.

But a few minutes later there was a knock and the outlines of a police helmet appeared on the steamed-up glass of the kitchen door.

My father blanched when he saw it, but he was still the old Dappermishka. He winked mischievously, wiping his hands calmly; his steps were chillingly calm when he went outside. We didn't hear what he said to the policeman, for he'd closed the door behind him, but when he came back, we knew at once that there was trouble.

"Márika," he said, with barely disguised anxiety, "the officer would like a word with you."

The officer wore glasses, which immediately clouded up with steam, so he stopped in the door as if he'd gone suddenly blind. He was no spring chicken—a hefty, slightly paunchy man with a white moustache. He took off his spectacles and glanced myopically about. He had a good, simple peasant face, and it was easier to imagine him with a scythe than with the waxed document holder he now so officiously opened. He leafed through the documents, reading Márika's name off one.

"Which one of you is it?" he asked.

"Me," Márika said timidly.

The officer came closer. He was worryingly gentle—I'd never seen a policeman so gentle in my life. He said:

"Could you please come with me, miss?"

"Yes, sir," Márika nodded, drying her hands. But this gentleness on the part of the authorities made her, too, anxious, it seems, because all of a sudden, she stopped drying her hands and asked the policeman:

"Where you taking me, officer?"

"To identify a body," he replied neutrally, avoiding Márika's gaze.

"Who… whose… body?"

"That's what you have to tell us, miss."

"Why me, officer?"

"They say it's your husband."

There was a terrific silence. Márika, who otherwise cried so easily, now stared at the policeman completely dry-eyed and didn't say a word. You cry out with pain if someone steps on your corns, but if they shoot you through the heart, all you feel is a dull blow. Then you die.

Márika's face was like a death mask. It was so stiff it looked almost impassive—eerily, almost inhumanly impassive. A fly landed on her sweaty forehead, but her skin was so inured she didn't even twitch. Even now, when I think of those moments, I see that fly walking leisurely across her face, from her forehead to her nose, her nose down to her upper lip, and from there to the side of her mouth, into those happy dimples that back when Márika still laughed, would grow deep like a crater, but now looked as terrifying as an empty eye socket.

My mother cried softly.

"What happened to him, poor thing?" she asked the policeman, sniffling.

The old myopic policeman lifted the piece of paper to his eyes, and then said:

"Internal bleeding on the lungs."

"Was he in the hospital?"

"No. He died in the ambulance."

Márika listened to this exchange as if it had been in a foreign language and she hadn't understood a word.

By this time, a large crowd had gathered outside our door. You could hear excited chattering and a woman weeping loudly.

"Shall we go?" said the policeman, and made to leave.

Márika did not move. She stared in front of her as if she was going to fall asleep at any moment and could only keep her eyes open with a great effort. My mother went over to her and hugged her, crying.

"You'd better go," she said, and gave her a lingering kiss.

Márika went like a sleepwalker. Outside, people made way for her, their looks no longer hostile. They stood on both sides of the corridor as if there were someone with their finger pressed to their lips hushing them, someone of whose coming Mózes had not warned the house because he wore a cloak of darkness and no sword or gun, but who might be back tomorrow to knock on another door and to take another of their number, like the policeman.

When Márika reached their flat, she said:

"Oh."

That's how she said it, with no exclamation mark; it was short, dry, almost a statement of fact. You would have thought she'd just remembered a handkerchief she'd left in the apartment, or she had to go back and fetch her handbag and was about to ask the policeman for permission. But instead, she let out a blood-curdling scream. Her whole body began to shake and tremble, she kicked and screamed like a lunatic, and before the policeman could stop her, she'd thrown herself into the crowd.

"Kill me!" she screamed at the top of her lungs. "I'm a whore! Kill me!"

People tried to calm her, but in vain. Márika threw herself down on her knees before them, hands clasped together, and begged:

"Kill me! Kill me! Kill me!"

My mother knelt down beside her to comfort and quiet her, but nothing worked. Márika went on screaming and her hysteria gave her such strength that my mother, who could usually have carried her easily, was now unable to lift her.

At this point, it occurred to the gentle policeman that he was representing Authority. He leant down, jerked Márika up and, as befitting a person in Authority, yelled at her roughly.

"Get a move on, the devil take you!"

That had its effect. This was the voice of the Royal Hungarian Police: the master's voice that at once reminded Hungarian dogs of a thousand years of the whip, and had them snapping to attention even on their deathbeds.

"Y-yes, o-off-officer," Márika sobbed, slinking after the master, the way a good dog should.

That must have been around nine in the morning. At twelve—I remember they had just rung noon—Rózsi came in a state of excitement to pass on the news:

"Herr Hausmeister's coming with some Krauts!"

We looked at each other. That meant someone was getting evicted. No one in the building was willing to come and throw another tenant's things out into the street, and besides Herr Hausmeister didn't really trust Hungarians. He used to bring Swabians from Budakeszi for the occasion, two straw-haired, moon-faced giants with blue eyes who came and went in the house like executioners and couldn't look their fellow Hungarians in the eyes, not—I believe—out of racial hatred, but simply because they, too, were poor, and it's easier to hate than to feel ashamed.

"Who's gettin' evicted?" my mother asked.

"I don't know," said Rózsi, "they're jabberin' in German."

And on she ran, her hair flapping in the wind, to carry the fateful news on to the next flat.

We went into the room and positioned ourselves at the window, because Herr Hausmeister really was on his way with the two Swabians. They'd just passed the second floor.

"They're comin' to our floor!" my mother said, and she blanched to her roots.

The house, too, seemed to blanch. The tenants stared out of their apartments like prisoners from their cells when one of them is being taken off to be hanged.

Moments later, we all knew who Herr Hausmeister was putting out on the street. He stopped in front of Márika's apartment, opened the door with his key and gestured to his bodyguards. They went in. Herr Hausmeister opened the shutters that Márika hadn't dared open for three days because of him, and the Swabian boys threw the flat's "furnishings" out of the window. These, to be precise, consisted of two battered suitcases, a brown horsehair blanket and the rough-hewn empty wooden crate that served as their table. That was it. That was all the industrious little printer had left behind, a man who didn't drink, didn't gamble and didn't smoke, just worked from morning till night while they let him, dreaming of a child of his own and a more humane world.

"Oh damn it all!" my father burst out. "I never heard of such a thing!"

There was something in his eyes that really frightened me. I had never seen him like this. My mother looked at him, terrified.

"Mishka, dear," she whispered with a pleading look, "don't make trouble. You know he can put us out, too, if he wants."

"I know," my father growled darkly, grinding his teeth in impotent fury. "I know," he repeated slowly, hoarsely, and flashed a fiery gaze at my mother. "So I'm supposed to let him put that poor widow out on the street before she's even had a chance to bury her husband?"

"What can you do, Mishka? Ain't nothing you *can* do."

"We'll see about that!" he snapped. Adjusting his belt, he went out the door.

He walked slowly, with slow peasant steps, like someone with all the time in the world, but when the tenants saw him they all flooded out onto the corridors and the house fell so quiet, it was as if the whole building were holding its breath.

"What you up to?" he asked Herr Hausmeister so calmly that anyone who didn't know better would have thought he'd just come out into the corridor in boredom, to have a bit of a chat.

Herr Hausmeister, however, could not muster such self-control. He went red—his face looked like it had been pebble-dashed with white-wash, since his pockmarks remained white.

"Evictin' someone," he said with feigned indifference, imitating my father's manner. Meanwhile, however, he sneaked a sly glance at his Swabians, who immediately started circling, *zurucking*, as they said in Budakeszi, so they could get my father from behind if need be. At that, I too, pulled my belt up and went outside. The house had clearly expected nothing less, because they immediately made way and let me through, the way people make space for the speaker at a public meeting.

Then my father said, still calm:

"But you ain't even given her notice!"

"Ain't I?" laughed Herr Hausmeister. "They got their papers six months ago. I only kept 'em on out of kindness."

Márika hadn't told us that. I could see that it had come as a surprise to my father, too. He didn't say anything for a while.

"Did you know her husband died?"

"I know, I know," shrugged Herr Hausmeister. "But life goes on."

Then there was movement. Everybody turned around, and I followed their gaze. That was when I saw Márika standing there in front of her belongings that they'd thrown out of the window.

"Leave it, Mishka," she said with difficulty. "It don't matter now, anyway."

She gave a tired wave of her hand, then turned and headed for the staircase. My father turned his head after her.

"You're stayin' here," he said.

"Leave me be," Márika pleaded. "I don't ever want to look at that toad," she said, pointing at Herr Hausmeister.

"You're stayin' here!" my father repeated, because Márika had made to leave again.

"I'll be back later," she said. "Let me be for now." She started crying. "I… don't… want to see him…"

"All right, all right," my father reassured her. "Come back in half an hour. It'll all be taken care of."

"Heaven pay you for your kindness, Mishka," Márika sniffed. "Lord knows I can't."

With that she left, but she did not come back in half an hour. Nor did she come back in an hour—she never came back at all. We never even heard of her again, and to this day, I don't know what happened to her. But we had no idea of that at the time.

When Márika left, my father said to Herr Hausmeister:

"I want a word with you. Come in here for a minute," and pointed to Márika's flat.

"I'm busy," Herr Hausmeister replied curtly. "Some other time."

"I want a word with you *now*," my father said with menacing calm.

I suddenly understood why all of Újpest was frightened of him. He was terrifying as he stood there in front of Herr Hausmeister, though he still looked as calm, as spine-tinglingly calm as he had done in the morning when he went out to speak to the policeman.

"And when Dappermishka wants a word with someone," he said slowly, emphasizing more or less every syllable, "then that someone will either have a word with him or never open his mouth again. Got it?"

he screamed at Herr Hausmeister, and as if he'd sensed what the two Swabians were up to, spun suddenly round.

A knife flashed in Herr Hausmeister's hand. It was a long kitchen knife; I don't know where he produced it from—from among Márika's things or his own pocket. I don't know anything about what happened during those moments, because the two Swabians also produced pocket-knives, and I was whipping out my pistol and pointing it at them.

"Drop the knives!" I said, and gave them both a good smack in the mouth with the back of my left hand.

The Swabians obeyed and I kicked their knives down into the court-yard. The whole thing happened so quickly and so quietly that the people around me, who were watching my father's duel, didn't even notice.

It was only really at this point that I realized what was going on. My father had caught Herr Hausmeister's wrist, it's true, but he was no wallflower, and the blade kept dancing between my father's chest and his throat. I knew that Herr Hausmeister could stab him through the heart at any moment and also—of course—that I had but to take two steps and he would drop the knife the second he saw the gun. But I did not take those two steps.

Where I came from, duels have unwritten rules—precise, strict, peasant rules. I knew that if I pointed my pistol at Herr Hausmeister, my father would beat me senseless and never forgive the shame I had brought upon him. So I had to stand there, gun in hand, not doing a thing but watching the flashing blade of the kitchen knife now pointed directly at my father's chest.

Someone groaned beside me. I looked—it was my mother. She loved the man that another was now trying to kill more than she loved life itself and she was a strong-armed woman. If she'd grabbed Márika's frying pan then, Herr Hausmeister would have spent the rest of his life a cripple; but she was a peasant woman and she respected the unwritten rules—so she did not reach for the frying pan. She just stood there, white as a sheet, her lips trembling, rooted to the spot, watching her man.

There was a collective hiss. Herr Hausmeister took my father's legs out from under him so he almost fell onto the point of the knife. It was only at the last minute that he regained his balance, but then his anger redoubled his might. He twisted Herr Hausmeister's arm so hard he yelped in pain like a wounded animal. The knife fell out of his hand.

"Well, well," said my father with a smile, and slipped his left hand slowly into his pocket.

He pulled out a huge knife. It was a flick knife that produced a long, thin blade.

"You see," he said to Herr Hausmeister, "I've got one too. Only I don't use it. 'Cause when Dappermishka wants to stab, he stabs, and when he wants to talk, he talks. And now, I want to talk."

With that, he handed me the knife and let go of Herr Hausmeister, who followed him without protest, silent, head bowed.

They went into Márika's apartment. They were only in there for a few minutes, but when they came out, Herr Hausmeister told the Swabians:

"Take the things back in."

The Swabians did as they were told and then cleared off, along with Herr Hausmeister, without a word.

Never had those walls seen a miracle like this! The house was drunk with the idea that a tenant had triumphed over Herr Hausmeister, for whom nothing was sacred, not even their wives. They snatched my father onto their shoulders and carried him around the corridor in triumph.

"Long live Dappermishka!" the basement, the courtyard and all three floors chanted. "Long live!"

I, too, rejoiced. I rejoiced the way people do in stories. After all, good had triumphed over evil, I told myself, because I was seventeen and had no idea of the evils we would suffer later for this "triumph".

11

"ANDRÁS!" ONE OF THE OFFICE STAFF called into the heaving changing room. "The Major wants you."

"Right away," I called back, and was surprised at the calmness of my voice.

It was Sunday morning, 31st August 1930. So today's the day, I thought with numb, hollow surprise, feeling basically nothing. I took my uniform out of my locker and started dressing mechanically.

It worked out well, it being a Sunday. The Constable always came in on Sundays… at least I wouldn't have long to wait. I'll go upstairs, get my marching orders from the Major, and…

I looked at Lajos's watch. It was a quarter to eight. The Constable would definitely be in by eleven. Another three hours. A hundred and eighty minutes.

The changing room was crowded, the boys were gabbling loudly all around me. Antal was telling them about a "skirt" he'd taken to the Mauthner the night before, where…

"Oh ho ho, boys!"

The "boys" were listening to the filthy details, entranced, occasionally breaking into roars of laughter. If you only knew! I thought, and hiding behind my locker door so they wouldn't see me, quickly slipped the pistol into my pocket.

I waited a long time in the Major's anteroom. In the first fifteen minutes, I felt a strange angst, but then my exhausted nerves went limp and I was overcome with a sleepy dullness. I couldn't think about anything. I just stood there, shifting from one foot to the other, staring at the electric clock on the wall. The big black hands stood still for sixty seconds and then jumped forward again and again with a dull click. Another hundred and thirty-five minutes… a hundred and thirty-four… a hundred and thirty-three…

At length the green, padded door opened and the head porter gestured for me to enter.

Mussolini was engrossed in some papers and didn't even look up when I came in. His green, shrivelled toad's face was fixed, expressionless, on the documents, the monocle flashing menacingly on his small, yellow eyes. In front of him lay a large inkstand made from the shell of a hand grenade, on either side of which two semicircles of pencils and pens lay in strictly regimented order. There were a great many pens and pencils, grouped according to size and colour in painstaking symmetry. Old Gábor had been this devoted to symmetry in the first stage of his madness, when the house had still admired him for it, the way the liberal press had marvelled at *Il Duce* for making the Italian trains run on time. Everything was so symmetrical in this regimental sanctum it was as if the position of all the furniture, paintings and files had been set with a compass and ruler. You got the feeling that the whole room was standing to attention and would do an immediate about-turn if the Major ever gave the order.

But the Major wasn't saying anything. The Major was reading and did not acknowledge my presence. The office was as silent as a military graveyard; the only sound was the rustle of the papers whenever the great man turned a page. I stood there at attention before him, my hands on the piping of my trousers, as per regulation. The head porter, too, was standing to attention. All that was missing were some drums in the background.

It was a quarter past nine. There was an electric clock on the wall in here, too, but this one seemed to be slower. Another hundred and five minutes... a hundred and five minutes... still another hundred and five minutes...

Mussolini looked up at last.

"Well, how are we?" he asked, full of concern, treating me to a smile.

This was not, of course, what I was expecting. I stuttered in my agitation:

"F-f-fine... thank you, sir."

The Major scribbled something in the margin of his document and then, without looking up, said:

"I hear you won the shooting prize."

This was even more surprising. So he really *did* get reports from the trainers at cadet practice.

"Yes, sir."

"Very good, very good," he said with soldierly approval. "Bound to come in useful in life."

Much sooner than you think! I told myself, and the gun seemed to move in my pocket.

Then the great man interrupted his reading.

"I've called you here because…"

The telephone rang. It was some grandee or other; they arranged a rendezvous at the Officers' Club for the evening. That took up another five minutes.

"Right," he said absent-mindedly when he'd hung up. "Where was I? Oh yes," he recalled, "the head porter tells me that the night shift boy is ill. Could you take over from him tonight?"

The question came as such a surprise that I was simply lost for words. Is that why he'd called me in here?… No, it can't be.

"Well, why do you look so scared?" he asked. "Got other plans?"

"No… not at all. Yes, sir, I can, sir."

"Good," he nodded and started leafing through his papers once more. "In that case, you can go home and sleep a bit."

"Yes, sir," I replied, still waiting for him to fire me, but the Major smiled at me and indicated that I could go.

I simply couldn't understand what this meant; how could I have? The Constable had told me plainly that "The Major knows all about it", so he also knew that I hadn't turned in Elemér, and that… in short, he knew everything. And now, instead of firing me, he's asking me how I am, praising me for my skills as a cadet, and having me stand in for the lift boy on the night shift. Why?

What have they got planned for tonight?

Why was the Major suddenly so chatty? And why was the Constable so silent?

I knew that something had happened, something I would only find out about—yet again—afterwards, something that… but what? What could it be?

I went home but couldn't sleep at all. I waited for the evening, dazed and anxious.

Nothing happened till midnight. I stood there in front of the lift with nothing to do; sometimes there was no one for ten or fifteen minutes. Most of the guests had left after St Stephen's Day, and the hotel was mired in the dusty, diffuse boredom of the low season. The restaurant closed an hour earlier than in high season, and the lobby was deserted by eleven. At midnight, they turned off the big chandeliers; quiet and semi-darkness hovered over the lifts like in a sickroom. I shifted my weight sleepily from foot to foot, because we weren't allowed to sit down or walk around even at such times. The music came filtering through, but so faint and otherworldly that it seemed to be coming from another building, or another universe… I nodded off on my feet.

I woke with a start to find the door of the office opening. The duty manager stepped out of it, heading straight for me.

"András," he said. "Go up to 205 and tell Her Excellency that His Excellency's calling her from Geneva. We've been trying her for five minutes, but there's been no answer. It looks like she's taken the phone off the hook."

"She might be sleeping," I said, anxiously.

"Then wake her up," he said. "I'll cover the lift till then."

"Yes, sir."

My heart was in my mouth. Whether out of fear or joy, I couldn't have said exactly. The whole thing had happened so unexpectedly—a moment before, I'd been dozing. I'd been dozing alertly—I was alert and attentive as I dozed as only people on the night shift can be. Reality now seemed far more dreamlike. I was getting to see her at last, talk to her, tell her… what was it, again? I realized with horror that I didn't know. That I was no longer sure I wanted to talk to her at all. So much had happened since. In the last weeks, I'd grown so distant from room 205, and yet here I was standing once more before it. I heard myself knock.

Inside, a piano was playing, a gay cacophony could be heard. A woman's trilling laugh. Was it her?… A dubious sweetness washed over me. Hope?… Or only memories?

I kept knocking for some time, but no one answered. In the end, I opened the door. The suite was full of guests, dancing everywhere—even in the entrance hall. Strange faces wandered around me in the smoke and darkness, women's naked shoulders, flashes of dress shirts, gilt-embroidered dress uniforms, with—among them all—waiters holding trays above their heads like tightrope-walkers criss-crossing everywhere. They must have had a lot to drink; no one was quite sober. All about me, amidst dizzying clouds of perfume, couples danced, rubbing one against the other; in the crimson half-light of the bedroom, people started applauding for some unknown reason. Rippling laughter erupted somewhere as people whispered here and shouted over there, all this drowned out by the piano pouring out its rough, schmaltzy, artificially sensual dance music.

I couldn't find her in the enormous crowd. They were doing a tango, and the lights had already been dimmed for "mood lighting", but apparently not enough for some people's taste. A lamp went out, the darkness in the salon grew, the night seemed to lighten behind the open windows. It was an amazing image, quite absurd. The mercury-silver of the moonlit Danube, the winding golden garlands of the lamps scattered on the hillside opposite, the pale marble lattice of the Fisherman's Bastion, the greenish domes of the Royal Palace above, the sky, the stars; the whole moonlit landscape as it was framed in the windows and the way the couples danced and swayed before it… I'd only seen the like at the pictures—and I was quite overcome. Everyone simply danced around me, spinning and whirling, sweeping me up with them, stepping on my feet—a man snapped at me angrily, a woman laughed… At me? I felt like someone who'd wandered accidentally onto the stage instead of into the audience, with everyone now staring at them—someone who did not quite understand what was going on yet—but who was on the verge of realization; at which point laughter would erupt and scandal would ensue.

I spotted her at last. She was dancing in Exfix's room, right at the back, in a dark corner. She was dancing up a storm with a captain of the Hussars who, with his gold-embroidered sky-blue uniform, heart-throb thin moustache, medals for gallantry, spurs, and face off a tooth-powder advert, practically reeked of celluloid. Greta Garbo danced with such unlikely Hussars, but she did it in period costume in films set at least a hundred years ago, preferably in St Petersburg on a winter's night. The heart-throb must have had a lot to drink, because he was whispering away as they danced like fever patients, while she just laughed and laughed. Her copious loose hair flew all around her face, her breasts rocked as she whirled, occasionally flashing out from beneath the black satin. She was very beautiful and very drunk. I watched her, completely overcome. I could hardly speak.

"Your Excellency!"

She smiled when she saw me, and her smile made me weak at the knees. I knew that drunken smile of hers, oh Lord, how I knew it! It was full of memories for me, memories to make me go weak at the knees—the memories of bygone nights when she would leave the bar, tipsy, around dawn, and I could feel, I *knew* that when she gave me *that* smile, she'd be calling down for me in a minute or two.

"Oh is that you, András?" she said, and touched the tip of my nose playfully with her finger, like in the good old days. "Well, what news?"

"H-His Excellency is calling from Geneva."

"His Excellency?" she repeated absently, as if she didn't know who I was talking about and then, with a light and familiar gesture, she smoothed back her hair and added sleepily: "Tell him I'm not home yet."

"Should I have them put it through to my room?" the Captain asked softly, and smiled, his eyes full of meaning. "It could be important."

She did not reply at once. You could see that she was thinking, and that she was finding it hard. Meanwhile, she kept her eyes on me, kept looking at me, just looking, and looking… was it only because she was so drunk? Or?… I flushed hot.

She turned away a little from the Captain and came closer.

"When the guests have gone, I'll call," she said softly, with a smile, touching the tip of my nose with her finger.

I went out into the corridor as if I, too, had been drinking all night. *When the guests have gone… When the guests have gone…* Who would they get to stand in for me if she did telephone? Could it be Franciska?

"Did they speak?" the duty manager asked.

"No, sir," I replied. "Please tell him that Her Excellency is not yet home."

The duty manager nodded and was off back to the office. But he hadn't even closed the door behind him when a terrible thought occurred to me. Maybe that wasn't what I was meant to tell him at all. Could I have misunderstood her?

When the guests have gone, I'll call... Could she have meant she'd call Exfix? But then why would she have said it in a whisper? Could it be just that she was afraid her guests might overhear and misunderstand, thinking that she wanted to get rid of them? But then why did she look at me like that? Just because she was drunk? No!... Yes!... No!... Yes!...

By about half past one, I could no longer control myself. I went to the night porter and asked him to replace me for a few minutes.

"I have to step outside, sir," I said, the way we did on such occasions. But instead, I went down to the kitchen and wet my whistle thoroughly.

After that, I heard the "yes" more emphatically: yes, yes, yes, she would call for me!

Around two, her guests started drifting out, and at half past three the waiters followed them.

"They all gone?" I asked.

They said yes, and I thought: she must be getting undressed.

If a phone started ringing somewhere, my heart skipped a beat: now, now, now!... No, that's not it... Maybe she's having a bath first?...

Suddenly, the door to the bar sprang open, and I almost screamed for joy. It was Franciska, and he was heading straight for the lift. So I hadn't been wrong. She had telephoned for me. And now they were going to get Franciska to stand in for me—him of all people! How odd. But who else could they have got to stand in for me?

I pretended not to see him and looked the other way. I could hear his steps as he came towards me... he's about to stop right before me, and...

He didn't stop. He jumped in the lift.

"Second floor," he said quietly, a little hoarsely, and turned away.

I must have been very drunk by that time, because I didn't realize what had happened straight away. Mechanically, I closed the door and started the lift. We stood, silent and stiff, not looking at each other at all. The lift sped upwards. I was dizzy.

We'd passed the first floor when I caught sight of the champagne. He had a bottle of champagne in an ice bucket and four glasses on a tray… just like I used to. The blood rushed to my head—I was overcome with fury, and if something hadn't happened just at that moment, there's no question I would have been at him.

It was a small thing, a ridiculously little thing, but almost everything in life comes down to such ridiculous little things, and what's more, I was drunk. All that happened was that someone downstairs rang for the lift. We were on the second floor by then, and before I could recover from my surprise, Franciska had got out and the lift, I, and the whole world around me, went plummeting down. A couple were waiting on the ground floor. I took them up to the third, then the lift stopped once more on the ground floor, and everything that happened after that was, so to speak, pure automatism on the part of my hands and feet. I came and went like a worm someone had cut in two: my head and body were completely separate. It was as if the link between the two had simply ceased. I knew, and yet was completely unaware of, what I was doing: I was a trampled worm, headless, dragging itself hopelessly on.

I ran down to the bathroom, took the gun out of my locker, and put it in my pocket. Then my feet once more took control by themselves— basement, stairs, corridor, stairs—one foot after the other, onwards.

When I got back to the lobby, I was alarmed to see that the lift wasn't in its place on the ground floor. I was just thinking of taking the stairs when the lift suddenly appeared in front of me, and the night porter got out.

"You've got a bloody nerve," he said, red as a beetroot. "Where the hell have you been?"

"Sir, I…" I mumbled, "I… I…"

I couldn't say any more. I was overcome by dizziness, started sweating profusely, and a chilling tremble ran through my insides.

The porter looked at me with concern.

"What's the matter with you? You're white as a sheet. You haven't got the shits, have you?"

I said yes, that was it, I had the "shits". He softened a little.

"You could have said something!"

I agreed that yes, I could have said something. At that, he proceeded to tell me in great detail how, back at the front, he'd always get the shits before an attack, and how by the end, he could tell in advance when they were coming and could prepare.

"There's this powder," he explained. "A powder, you know, that stops it right away. Go get yourself some at a pharmacy on your way home."

I said yes, I would go and get myself some in a pharmacy on the way home. He finally left, and I was just about to get in the lift at last when he stopped suddenly and turned around.

"Oh yes," he said. "I almost forgot. Your father's here."

"My father?" I blanched. "What does he want?"

"I don't know. He's in front of the main entrance."

The main entrance... at three in the morning! I was suddenly completely sober. Tomorrow's the first! I realized, and remembered Herr Hausmeister's grimacing face as he dropped the knife in pain. The eviction notices would have come today...

"Can I have a word with him?" I asked, my mouth all dry.

"Yes," he replied, "but..."

He didn't finish the sentence, and I knew why. There was no way you could let a man as ragged as my father into the lobby of the hotel.

"You know what?" he said generously. "Go take my place at the entrance. I'll mind the lift till then."

"Yes, sir. Thank you for your kindness."

I hurried out. My father was pacing up and down in front of the hotel. I could see him from afar as I came down the steps, but he didn't notice me. He was staring at the pavement, as if he were looking for something, and only looked up when I came out onto the street. He kept blinking, as if he were just waking up, and his eyes were so fuzzy I thought at first that he was drunk.

I couldn't summon words, and he, too, struggled. He cleared his throat and tried to smile.

"I was just passing," he said, awkward and hoarse. "Thought I'd look in."

I remember, everything became clear to me in that moment. They'd got the notice, and my mother… my mother…

"Just passing?" I repeated dully.

"Yes," he nodded, and his face almost twisted with the forced smile. "I was… in the hospital," he mumbled and looked at me, adding quickly: "She's… out of the woods now."

As to who, he didn't say and I didn't ask. Anyone who'd actually grown up with their mother couldn't quite understand what I felt at that moment. Feelings ripen slowly in the gentle climate of a home, love for your mother just as slowly as the opposite: the knowledge that sooner or later, you're going to lose her. Most people discover in these moments with alarm and surprise the extent to which they are already subconsciously prepared for the loss of their mother, and how relatively easily they can withstand the blow. It was just the opposite with me. Until now, I couldn't even have said, hand on heart, that I really loved her. Vague, incipient and awkward feelings moved within me and it was only now, when there was trouble, that I realized what lay behind this timid pull: the immense intensity of my emotions. The abandoned little boy in whom savage loneliness had petrified all emotion now cried out inside a strapping, six-foot lad: Mother!… Mother!…

I couldn't speak for some time, and even then, I just asked:

"Did we get our notice?"

I might just as well have said: "Are we done for?"

My father nodded. I shivered.

"She drank the lye?"

"Not… too much," he said, slowly. "I got there in time… um…"

He took off his hat and wiped the sweat from his forehead. I stood there beside him, not saying a word. He, too, was silent. We were quiet together as only peasants know how.

It was still dark, there was no one on the street, the silvery tarmac mirroring the powerful moonlight. There was a breeze off the Danube, the faded leaves of wild chestnuts rustled on the pavement, and somewhere far off a ship's horn cried hoarsely.

"If I'd come a minute later," my father said at last, without finishing the sentence. He stared out into the distance and shook his head. "One minute," he said pensively to himself. "What's a minute? Lightin' up a cigarette. That was all that stood between her and death. Luckily, I saw right away she'd left the key in the lock when she locked herself in and ran straight to the window. That was locked too, I broke it with my fist. Look," he indicated: his hand was still covered in dried blood. He swallowed hard and stared once more at the pavement. "I'd never have thought it," he muttered, "that that timid little woman could want something as much as she wanted to die. For the first time in her life she was forceful, poor thing. She wouldn't let go of the bottle and wrestled with me though she could hardly stand on her feet. I carried her downstairs like a child, I ran down to the tavern to phone. There was a big crowd out on the street by the time we got out, then the ambulance came." He gave a wave of his hand. "Anyway, enough."

"What did the doctor say?"

"She'll feel lousy, he says, but won't come to no greater harm. The… baby's all right too," he added softly with a timid awkwardness, "because… um… we ain't had a chance to tell you yet, but… your mother's expectin'… I don't know how she could do such a thing." He looked at me. "Do you?"

I didn't reply. I stared at my shoes, the way my mother did. We were silent again for a space.

"They've given us till October first," my father grumbled, and came closer. "Son," he said, looking me straight in the eyes. "If we can't get the money together by then, it's all over, she'll do it again."

"She said so?"

"Not her. Her eyes. I saw it in her eyes, my boy… Do you get me?"

"'Course I do. How much do we owe?"

"Seventy-six for arrears, twenty for the rent. It's ridiculous!" he burst out angrily, his voice full of disdain. "Ninety-six pengős!… I could get that in half an hour if…" It was only then he noticed that he had said too much, because he suddenly fell quiet. "I'll explain all that to you, one of these days," he said, more quietly. "The important thing now is to get hold of that ninety-six pengős."

"We can't let it all fall apart over that!" I waded in. "There's three of us, damn it, all three of us working people. I'll bring home every last scrap they give me here for mother, the two of us'll manage somehow. It ain't so easy to starve to death, you know."

"That's right!" my father rallied, and it was as if he had once more grown younger. His fine grey eyes were full of life, full of daring, full of the Dappermishka spirit. "By God," he cried, "ninety-six pengős ain't the world! And I've got all sorts of schemes, let me tell you. Take the railway stations. People these days don't have the money for porters, but the old boys really can't carry their bags themselves any more, can they? If I get 'em in front of the entrance, 'cause of course they'll never let you inside, I'd be bound to get a few krajcárs together, wouldn't I?"

"'Course you would!" I encouraged him, and I, too, was awash with plans. "And I could go down the river after work and look out for the late ships. If I give half my pay to the longshoreman, he's bound to give me a few sacks to carry, ain't he? And I could try before work, and all. The merchant ships come in at dawn—"

"And then there's all them lah-di-dah drunks!" my father interrupted eagerly. "After midnight, when you can't get no other work anyway, I'll keep an eye out round here at the bars, and if there's one comes along, I'll open his car door for him and hold out my palm. Most of them give you somethin', they say, if you call 'em sir. Well, damn it all, I'll call 'em Your Grace! It's a good title, ain't it?"

It seemed a great idea, and I immediately had another that he was very keen on. Later, when I remembered these days, I could never understand how my father, who was a clever, experienced man, could believe in such silly ideas. These days, I know that you either believe in something or you drink lye, and if you believe, it makes very little difference in what. In life, as in a song, it's never about the words, but about how you sing them. Dappermishka often got the words wrong, but his tune was always right. Now and then he would ignore the people who wrote the lyrics and the laws, but he was always loyal to the spirit of the piece. All his cunning and idealism, his actions, intentions and thoughts all seemed to be written for a recurring theme which would break through at the end of every movement, saying live, live, live! and to hell with all the rest. No, he would never have drunk lye, and on that early morning I learnt that I wouldn't either. That was the first time I had felt, in an almost bodily sense, that my blood was his blood, and however much the words in our two lives may differ, the underlying tune was the same.

I had never felt anyone as close to me as I did him in those moments. The words poured out of us, flying from mouth to mouth like a well-thrown ball; our plans went back and forth, igniting each the other, entrancing us both. Live, live, live! That was the theme that marked our words, and we took even the most outlandish plans seriously—the way believers will take seriously the rituals of their religion. Because, beyond the words and the outward forms, they represent for them the core: Jesus, Jehovah, Buddha, or some stony-faced, bloodthirsty, gentle or debauched god—it was all life, life, life! We grew drunk on our words and believed in them so hard we couldn't even understand what we'd been so upset about before. Then all of a sudden, we found ourselves laughing.

"Well, by the holy-hairs-on-the-heads-of-the-heavenly-host!" my father cried, his fine, strong teeth flashing as he laughed. "If you and me put our heads together, brother, Beelzebub himself'll be shitting himself, ain't that right?"

"It is!"

"So should we put our heads together, then?"

"We damn well should!"

"Put it there!"

He squeezed my hand and I was so overcome with emotion I was afraid I'd cry; and that is something you can only fully understand if you feel your father's hand for the first time at fifteen, and for the last two years later. How much gentleness there was in that tough hand, how much that could never be put into words! There was a torrent of feelings within me, my eyes grew wet as a leaky roof. I turned away, but by then the rainclouds must have been gathering inside my father, too, because without any further ado he mumbled "so long" and left, just like that.

It was at that moment I decided. I wiped away my tears and ran after him.

"Father!"

"What is it?" he asked, flustered.

I took the gun out of my pocket and gave it to him. There was something richly symbolic in that gesture, and my father, it seems, understood it. He looked at me, surprised, but didn't ask any questions.

"Sell this," I said quietly. "It'll be a start."

"All right," he said without looking at me, and slipped the revolver in his pocket. "I'll be off," he muttered then. "I want to be up early in the morning. Evenin'."

"Evenin'," I muttered too, grabbing his hand.

It was the first time I had kissed his hand. I can still see the way he looked at me: I could never forget that face. He was trying to smile, but wasn't having any luck. In the end he turned and left without a word.

I watched him go, out on the street at dawn, and cried. It had been a long time since I'd been this happy.

I simply forgot all about her. I was calculating soberly how much I could put aside after paying my instalments when it suddenly occurred to me that I had almost killed the Constable not long before. There was nothing awful about the thought. It was simply unlikely; it had lost its charm, like a dream you remember while tying your shoelaces, after the first cigarette of the day, the sun outside shining. I suddenly awoke from something, realized something all at once.

An old memory was rattling around within me, the memory of an eerie November night when our priest went to say mass in a neighbouring parish and took us altar boys with him. It was a vicious autumn, fit to murder you, and I caught a nasty cold in my rags, lined as they were only with the wind. I didn't say anything to the priest because I was worried he wouldn't take me along; I climbed with the others onto the rickety peasant cart, shivering with fever. The village was sleeping by the time we got there. It was dark and foggy, with a howling wind. The cart sank to its axles in the autumn slush and we proceeded at a snail's pace. I stared out into the darkness, shuddering; I'd never seen a more dreadful village. Not a light, not a soul, just small houses huddled in the fog, and the darkness, and slush. I'd never seen such funny-shaped houses outside my dreams. Occasionally, a peeping face blinked whitely behind the tiny darkened windows, dubious shadows slipped past in the darkness, and when we reached the cemetery, I was horrified to see someone duck behind a headstone. The wind brought strange, moaning sounds. Something had *happened* in this village, and sometimes I clearly heard someone sharpening a knife. By the time we arrived, I was half insensible with fever and fear. The old lady with whom we were staying got some cinnamon mulled wine down me—no better cure for the cold has ever been devised. I woke free of fever and ran straight out of the house to get a look at this village out of a Gothic novel. The fog had lifted by then, the wind had calmed, and the horror-novel village was neither horror-inducing nor at all novelistic in the sleepy grey dawn of that autumn Sunday. It was a nothing-special little Trans-Danubian settlement, just the same as ours—the same as all the rest. *I woke up somewhere other than where I went to sleep; but it was the same place, nonetheless.*

The same thing seemed to have happened now. My situation hadn't changed, in much the same way as in that no-name little Trans-Danubian village, but it was still completely different than half an hour ago, because I was looking at it through different eyes. I had awoken something; I had realized something. I still knew there was a reason that the frog-faced Major had complimented me on my soldiering skills, and that the one-legged "Doctor" was up to no good. I still hated that blinking, thin, nervous spider who had me caught in his web, but killing him… what for? Should I really go and tell my mother, if they ever fired me from the hotel, that she should go ahead and drink the lye, because the game was all up anyway, and from now on I was going to go around shooting people up like the tough guys with the bloodshot eyes you saw at the pictures? No, no, I didn't have time for the pictures, prison and a broken heart. My mother's life hung on a matter of ninety-six pengős, and I had no right to think of anything else.

It was closing time. The guests were flooding out of the bar, the world transformed around me. Brightly lit cars appeared, uniformed chauffeurs clicked their heels. Silk rustled, jewels flashed, clouds of perfume hung in the air. Wealth was parading its fat behind, and I was looking at it as if I was seeing it for the first time. These people paid twenty pengős for a bottle of champagne, I thought, while bowing to them with my regulation smile, and my hand made a fist. *My mother's life is hanging on five bottles of champagne!* And was it just my mother? No. It was millions of people, millions, millions! My heart thumped with indignation.

"Goodbye, sir!" I said with a rictus smile to a fascist English Lord, and I knew that I had once and for all said goodbye to their world.

12

MY MOTHER SKIPPED FROM THE HOSPITAL. One night, when I got home with my father, we found her standing there beside the tub. She was washing, just as she had been a week before and a year before, as always. She was indifferent to our greetings and hardly looked up from the tub—she kept working the clothes with a fixed expression.

"I promised the newsagent I'd have it done for tomorrow," she said, and went on washing as if nothing had happened.

We, too, tried to pretend. We didn't ask how she was—we could see she was poorly, anyway. We removed our soaking clothes without a word and got stuck into the washing. It was an unpleasant, rainy night, the autumnal wind whistling in the chimney, lashing the windows with rain and rattling the rickety door as if it wanted to come in.

"Grim weather," I said, just for the sake of saying something.

"Aye," my mother nodded. "Autumn's coming on."

That was about all we had to say. My father started in on some chaotic tale of the high seas a little later, but when my mother poured the lye into the tub, he got all muddled.

"Where was I again?"

"Um…"

"Hm, where *was* you?"

None of us knew. There was a nasty silence. My mother leant well into the tub, her back wracked by soundless sobs.

"Autumn's early this year," my father said, as if he hadn't noticed, and looked at me flatly.

I knew what was coming next. He went over to the kitchen cupboard and took out the ginger tin where we kept the money.

"Look at this," he said loudly to my mother, sticking the tin box under her nose.

There were fifteen pengős in it. My mother looked at the tarnished silver coins as if she couldn't believe her eyes.

"D'you kill somebody?"

"We worked for it," my father said haughtily, and you could see he was pleased with the effect.

The fifteen pengős had their effect. My mother's face lightened with hope.

"My God," she sighed, "if we could keep this up!"

"Why couldn't we?" my father asked nonchalantly. "Manci owes us another five at the end of the month. That makes twenty. And today's only the fifth."

"You made fifteen pengős in five days?"

"We did."

That wasn't true. We got seven for the gun, and three more I had taken out of what I'd been saving up for my current instalment. My father had talked me into it.

"It'll sound better," he said. "She'll be happier this way."

"But what if I have to take it back?"

"Why would you? I'll have made it five times over by then."

He was completely convinced of that—which must have helped him feel better, but did not improve our situation one bit. If he was lucky, he made a pengő a day, which he had to put into the ginger tin each evening because my mother would count our funds at the end of each day.

"Tomorrow," he'd say, when we were alone, and then the next day, "tomorrow," he'd say again.

The days passed. My father tried everything—running around town from dawn some days, but in vain. There was no work to be had. There were crowds of the jobless hanging around outside the factories waiting, waiting for they knew not what. The management put up huge posters saying there were no vacancies, but they still came each morning and didn't shift from outside the gates till night. The ones who were homeless didn't have anywhere to go anyway, and the people who *did* still have somewhere to live couldn't bear to sit there watching their children starve. Outside the factory they could at least hope, hope that something would finally happen someday—that one of the workers would get his hand caught up in a machine, or get arrested by the police, or that the proletarian revolution would break out, or some philanthropic American millionaire would buy the plant.

My father's prospects were even more unrealistic. A metalworker could hope that there would, eventually, be some need for a metalworker and that for some mysterious reason he would be the one they'd pick out of all the multitude of unemployed metalworkers. But what could a sailor hope for? Every company, even the smallest workshop, office or shop, could choose from thousands upon thousands of skilled workers. The only people with a chance were the ones with long records of service, and even they were treated with suspicion without letters of recommendation, which were nigh on impossible to get, since people were primarily concerned with finding positions for their kith and kin.

I tried to find him something at the hotel. I talked to the head porter, abasing myself to him. I told him my mother was sick, that we were going to get evicted if he couldn't find a job, but the old porter just shrugged.

"Could be me in a year, you never know," he replied. "You know full well they're laying people off."

That was true, but the only people who make a living from the truth are judges. Two thirds of the rooms were empty, and I was glad if my tips covered my instalments. Every night, I hit the town, looking for extra work late into the night. Often, I would check which docks they'd be unloading during the day, then run straight there after work at the hotel. I would happily have handed over part of my earnings to the longshoreman or anyone else who got me work, but I wasn't the only one with that idea, and I was generally left empty-handed. Only once did I get work at the docks, and that was by accident. A dockworker I knew, whose wife had been in labour for two days, asked me to stand in for him while he went to see her in hospital. He promised me forty fillérs, but ended up giving me only half—having drunk the rest in his joy at the baby that had been born meanwhile.

I was out of luck. I criss-crossed the city, but in vain; the starving packs of jobless always beat me to it. They had all day and would start queuing for the evening shift early in the morning; and they didn't tolerate any "amateurs" like me in their ranks. I once got a hiding for going down to the docks early in the morning when the goods ship came in and offering to take an old merchant's goods down to the central market. It was no use telling them I desperately needed the money, the ragged men just shrugged.

"With fancy clothes like that?"

What could I have said? I stopped going to the docks.

But one day Lady Luck did nonetheless start flirting with me. It was only a brief dalliance, but at the time, I thought it would last for ever—or at least until we'd paid off the rent. I had Lajos to thank for my day in the sun, or rather the fact that Lajos was in love. He was in love with Eszter, the pretty little chambermaid from the second floor that Her Excellency had once slapped so hard she bled. Not all the guests were so hard on her. One of the attachés at the Italian embassy was just the opposite. He used to give her unusually large tips, and one night while making the bed, Eszter found out why. Lajos, who was waiting in the corridor for her, heard her scream, the result of which was that instead of Eszter, it was the attaché who ended up laid out on the bed. He couldn't get up for three days, but on the fourth he hobbled down to the office and Eszter and Lajos were both dismissed.

Lajos, as I found out, was engaged not only in courting Eszter, but also supporting a family. His father was unemployed, his three younger brothers were still in school, and his mother had been bedridden for years. Lajos never said a word about any of that. He was one of those Budapest working-class boys who had heard so much crying since their early childhood that all they could do was laugh. They lived in the jungle of the city like hungry foxes on the prowl, and Lajos was one of the most cunning. He was proud of his cunning. He would talk loud and dirty, all high and mighty, but at heart he was a sensitive lad—a fact of which he was ashamed, and something he hid like a physical deformity. We worked together for three years and had always been friendly, but had never met outside the hotel. He got thrown out in spring, and I didn't see him after that. But then one night, when I was trying my luck as a baggage porter in front of Keleti station, he suddenly called out to me:

"Well, well, what you doin' here?"

I was ashamed to tell him the truth, so I said:

"Weather's nice. Thought I'd come down and hang around a bit."

"In that case, we can have a bit of a catch-up," he replied. "Sit down, old son. I've still got another half an hour to wait."

"Who you waiting for?"

"Eszter."

"What train she on?"

"No train, she's havin' dinner."

"At the station?"

"That's right."

I didn't understand.

"Why there?"

Lajos grinned.

"'Cause there's nothing to eat at home."

"And they're handing the stuff out for free at the station, are they?"

"If you know what you're doin'," Lajos winked, and leant closer, grinning. "What a scheme, old pal!" he whispered, and showed me his fist. "There's a what-d'you-call-it," he told me, "one of those charity things. Bored old bourgeois bags determined to protect the virtue of single lady travellers. You know what I mean, old chum, you get the idea. As we speak, Eszter's playing the little lady travelling on her own. She's got an old suitcase, she goes into the old hags with that, playing the lost provincial maiden for 'em so you'd burst your sides laughing. She tells 'em someone made off with all her money on the train while she was sleeping... you get the rest. A bit of 'oh, dear', and 'you poor thing', and then the teary confession that she's hungry, 'oh madam, I ain't had a thing to eat since...' 'Course that don't require much acting on her part, 'cause the poor thing's been so hungry lately she'd eat the nails out of a horse's hoof. The old bags can see that, too, but the old bitches won't give her money, 'cause what good would that do a starvin' working-class girl, eh? Morals is the main thing... But Eszter's cryin' real tears by that point, and the old bags can't take it, so 'there, there', and off they go to the station buffet. She's been eating there for a week."

"Haven't they caught on?"

"How would they? Goes to a different station every day, at different times. This ain't my first time at the circus, old pal. I know exactly when the old bags change shifts. Thing is, they're only good for another four meals. Pretty neat, ain't it?"

"Grand," I replied.

We laughed. How we used to laugh at things like that! The laughter poured out of us like steam out of an overheated engine; we rocked to and fro, screaming with hilarity—we just couldn't stop. A fat old man looked at us and panted:

"It's good to be young, eh?"

"Piss off," Lajos said when the old man had gone, and spat.

It was a nice evening. The weather had turned summery again and a warm breeze was fluttering the girls' skirts, as the stars paraded up in the sky. We were sitting on the steps of the station, wishing that we, too, were old and fat.

"How's Eszter?" I asked.

Lajos shrugged.

"How would she be? Job zero, funds likewise, some fat butcher desperate to marry her, her old folks are up in arms about me, but otherwise we're fine. You?"

I shrugged.

"Much the same."

Lajos pulled a thin, crumpled cigarette from behind his ear.

"You got one?" he asked.

"No."

He broke it in two and gave half to me. We puffed away in silence.

"If only she weren't so pretty!" he said after a while. "They all keep on at her all the time—pretty girl like you could do a lot better—and who knows, old pal, maybe they're right. All the men are after her, people in cars stop her on the street, that butcher's promisin' her the moon, and this is how I take her out to dinner. How long is any woman goin' to put up with that?"

What could I say to that? I said nothing. Lajos threw his cigarette away.

"Oh no, my friend, it ain't good to be this mad about a woman. I can't stand the constant jealousy, it'll be the death of me; I'm a complete wreck. Want to hear something funny? Every night, I walk her home, and every mornin' the postman wakes her with a letter from me."

"You write to her every day?"

"Every day. Got to. Can't get no rest otherwise. What d'you make of that?"

"I get the letter," I said, "but not the stamp. How've you got money for all those stamps?"

"Don't use stamps."

"How's that?"

"Simple. I write my own address on the letter and put Eszti down as the sender. Get it?"

"No."

"God, you're green. If there ain't no stamp on a letter, the postman takes it back to the sender, and since Eszti's the sender, they take it back to her. Simple, no?"

We had a good laugh about that, too.

"Life's just a big con, my friend," Lajos mused. "And it don't do to be too fussy. These days, of the Ten Commandments only the eleventh is still valid: *survive*. If you're working class, you either learn that or starve to death. I'm startin' to learn. D'you know I found myself a job?"

"No. How?"

"That's a story in itself. I've got an uncle, see, a dreadful sort, stiffs his own mother, even though he's lousy with the stuff. He's the manager in a decent little bar and my mother begged him to take me on, but it looks like the old bird feels the same way about me as I do about him, 'cause he told her he hates me and I can go starve, 'cause I'd only end up on the gallows, anyway. Well, when she came and told me that, I upped and had a word with the old man. 'Clear off!' he screams. 'I ain't talkin' to you!' 'No need,' I says, 'I'll do the talking. D'you want to make fifty pengős a month? 'Course you do! Well then put me on the payroll and I'll give you all my wages.' He liked that all right, the bastard. 'But you're still an apprentice,' he says. 'Yes,' I tell him, 'but does the owner have to know? I'll sign the receipt saying I've collected my wages and keep whatever I get in tips.' And that's how it was, my friend. The old man makes fifty pengős a month off my back, while yours truly here gets thirty or thirty-five. Disgusting? You bet it is. Still, beats starving to death."

He carried on telling me about his old scoundrel of an uncle, but I only heard the half of it.

"Hey," I said suddenly. "Get your uncle to hire me. I'll give him my pay, too."

Lajos looked at me in surprise.

"You get kicked out and all?"

"No," I replied. "But I really need the cash."

Lajos knew what that meant and didn't ask any questions.

"I'll have a word," he said succinctly, and we said no more about it.

But he introduced me to his uncle that evening, and I got the job. During the day I worked at the hotel and in the bar at night. This blessed state lasted four days. Then the cloakroom woman, who wanted to bring her son in instead, reported me to the guild, and if the cunning old uncle hadn't hired some relative of the guild secretary's quickly, I'd have lost my job in the hotel to boot.

That was the end of my glory days. I couldn't find any extra work, and the tips at the hotel just kept drying up. In the end, I had to take back the three pengős out of the ginger tin to make my instalments. My mother realized that night. I didn't know what to say—in the end it was my father who came to the rescue.

"He'll put it back next week," he said with beatific calm, and gave my mother a knowing wink as if to say that there was an affair of the heart at hand, and my mother had best not get involved.

That would have been more or less enough to reassure my mother, but a few days later, there was more trouble over the ginger tin. One evening, when we were washing in the kitchen, a filthy old woman came round and without any ado said:

"I've come for Miss Manci's things."

My mother went as white as a sheet.

"She started renting a bed someplace else?" she asked, distraught, but the toothless old biddy shook her head.

"Oh, no, no," she shook her head. "No, it's her bed they'll be rentin' now."

"She get married?"

"No," she answered. "Not at all. She's had a bit of luck. They've taken her in a brothel."

So we lost that money, too. Manci still owed us a pengő or two and said she'd come by on Sunday to pay it—but my mother waited for her in vain. She didn't come and we never saw her again.

Her bed remained empty. People who worked wouldn't rent it because they thought the electricity too dear, and we wouldn't rent it to anyone without a job. Besides, it was still warm outside, and the poor, if they had any money, used it to buy food and slept on benches or in Népliget Park, under bushes. The Népliget back then led a double life, like gentlemen thieves in the pictures. During the day, it was full of jolly petit bourgeois, children, nurses, and ambling couples, while at night it was colonized by the homeless, and often even the police wouldn't dare go in there, because anything could happen in the darkness among the bushes. It was its own little world, a separate society. Entire families used to camp out among the bushes, generations of them, from grandparents to newborns. The quiet and the cicadas were interrupted by snoring, crying babies, copulating couples, the elderly groaning, the moaning of the sick, sudden angry shouts and the flash of blades. The ragged masses fought and made love, prayed, swore and did their wheeling-dealing. But in some of the bushes, there were serious political and literary debates to be heard, too—thin, nervous young men reading poetry to other thin, nervous young men; banned religious cults gathered around their long-haired, barefoot prophets, and beggars, thieves and burglars bought and sold "tips". Ominous deals were made there, the underworld did a roaring trade. The gold standard there was bread, and you could get anything for it there, *anything* in the nastiest sense of the word. Little girls would go from bush to bush at night, offering themselves to the men in thin, schoolgirl voices, men whose faces they could not even see in the dark.

"Got any bread?" they whispered, and the next day, they didn't even know who they'd slept with.

That was how children became whores, workers criminals, and desperate men murderers.

That was the fate awaiting us. That was the fate my mother wanted to kill herself to avoid, and that was why she got more and more desperate each day. Despite our best efforts, she slowly cottoned on to our well-intentioned ruse.

"While I were gone," she said, "you said you made three pengős a day. But now…" she pointed to the ginger tin and burst into tears.

My father kept insisting that we'd have the money by the first, but he could no longer convince my mother.

"How?" she kept repeating. "How?"

One night my father finally lost his patience.

"Don't you worry about that!" he snapped at her, banging the table. "I'll get it, come hell or high water."

My mother looked at him, het up as he was, in fright.

"Mishka," she said quietly. "D'you remember what you promised me?"

"I do," my father muttered, pacified.

"You still keepin' that promise?"

"I am."

But even that wasn't enough for her.

"You swear?"

"Yes."

"What on?"

"Whatever you want."

"My life?"

"Yes."

My father swore and miraculously kept his word. He didn't flinch from even the most inhuman work. He wore himself out, starved and went about in rags, but I still sometimes got the strange feeling that this, too, was a role that he was playing, like everything else in life. He couldn't take penury seriously—it was just a guest appearance as far as he was concerned, but nonetheless a role he tried to play as well as he could. He was playing a beggar but acted all the while as if he were negotiating for the part of a king, with only a few more minor details to clear up… He was more determined than ever and just as haughty—he didn't give an inch of the Dappermishka spirit. Funnily enough, he started to resemble those great, greying actors that young girls tend to dream about. He was handsome, he was charming, he was cheerful, and he was always up for a laugh. Sometimes, at night, when he'd come home, he'd be almost too tired to speak, but in the morning, I would always wake to find him whistling in the kitchen, and sometimes he'd reply to my good morning as if he'd won the lottery the night before.

"I've got a new idea!" he'd tell me, full of excitement. "Worth a fortune, my son, it's brilliant!"

He'd drop mysterious hints, smile meaningfully, and whenever my mother left the kitchen, he'd say:

"She won't have to go to work tomorrow, you'll see."

That was his dream. If he'd had his way, he would have had my mother lie in bed all day, eating and drinking and waiting for her son, because of the fact that his unborn child was a boy he was just as convinced as of the sure-fire success of his scheme.

"It'll all be settled by tonight," he said before he left home, and you could see he truly meant it.

And then it was the evening, and he'd come home and wouldn't say anything. He'd dig fifty or sixty fillérs out of his pockets, a pengő at most, silently and submissively drop it into the ginger tin, undress and climb into bed. At those times, he was like a schoolboy who'd done badly on a test and didn't dare look his parents in the eye. But a few days later, he'd have another brilliant idea, and one morning, he said again:

"It'll all be settled by tonight."

Sometimes he really did have brilliant ideas. The only problem was, they were impossible to execute. It would have taken a little money, a little time and a few connections, but we had neither time, nor money, nor connections. We had to get hold of the money by 30th September, and the contents of the ginger tin did not give much cause for hope.

"What we goin' to do?" I would ask my father when we were alone, but he always gave me the same answer:

"We'll have the money by the first."

"How?"

"Don't you worry about it."

He was still absolutely convinced that today or tomorrow he'd have an idea that would fix everything in one fell swoop.

"You have to keep trying till you succeed," he said, and kept on trying things out with the devotion of an alchemist.

One night, he came home beaming.

"I've got it!" he said, full of excitement. "This time I've really got it!"

"What?" my mother asked.

"The solution to joblessness," he announced studiously, with the pride of an inventor. "It's so simple," he said with a superior smile. "I don't know why I didn't think of it before. You just have to think scientific, that's all there is to it. Why can't the locksmith get a job? 'Cause there's too many locksmiths. Why can't the carpenter get a job? 'Cause there's too many carpenters. It's obvious, ain't it? Everybody knows. It's just that nobody thinks about the logical conclusion. Last night, when I realized, I got so excited I couldn't get a wink till morning. Then I ran straight to the city library to study the employment figures."

"The what?" asked my mother.

My father explained what the employment figures were, but that only added to my mother's surprise.

"What the hell did you go and study them for?"

"Don't you get it?" my father said. "I was looking for a field where there's a lack of skilled workmen."

"Is there any such thing in this day and age?"

"Yes there is. I didn't even have far to look. I found it right under 'D'. Go on, guess what it is."

We couldn't guess.

"Diver!" he announced triumphantly. "In Hungary, there's a shortage of divers."

"Ain't no one else noticed?"

My father laughed.

"Even if they have noticed, where's that got 'em? Your Budapest lot're a bunch of landlubbers. Ain't one of them knows a thing about diving." You could see he was amused by my mother's doubts. He scooped her up playfully and sat her in his lap. "Well, ma," he asked cannily, "what'd you say to that? Good, ain't it?"

"Yes," my mother answered dubiously, "but how're you going to get a diving job here in the city?"

"Already have," my father replied calmly. "Start tomorrow."

"You could've told us!"

"I'm telling you now, silly," my father laughed, shaking his head like a chess player who doesn't understand how their opponent could ever have doubted their victory once he'd made his fantastic gambit. "Thinking's the main thing," he explained with deep satisfaction. "Got to think scientific, you see, love."

"Yes," my mother replied happily, though you could see she didn't understand a thing.

The next evening, they called me to the telephone in the hotel. One of the managers at the shipyard informed me that my father had had an accident, and told me to come at once.

I raced desperately to the shipyard. I found my father in the first aid room; he was lying on a couch in a small white room that smelt of carbolic. He, too, was white, scarily white, with bloodied compresses and bits of cotton wool scattered around him. Apart from that, there were no signs of his accident.

"What happened?"

My father laughed, as always when he seemed scared.

"Nothing special," he said dispassionately, "my nose started bleedin' underwater, then my mouth, and my ears an' all, and that's all I remember. They tell me it was touch and go."

I listened to this cheerful account, horrified.

"Whose fault was it?"

"I don't know," he shrugged. "Doesn't matter. The bad thing is, they don't want to give me my day's wages."

This I couldn't understand at all.

"Why not?" I asked, incensed, but he just kept on shrugging.

"Scoundrels," he muttered.

No, I couldn't understand any of it. Eventually, a vague suspicion took root in me that he might have been somehow to blame. He can't have been diving for a long time, I thought, maybe he was out of practice. But since I didn't want to hurt his feelings, I kept skirting the issue.

"Father," I probed gingerly, "where were you last underwater?"

"Me?" he laughed. "In my mother's belly. Looks like I've lost the knack since."

But the experience must have made him think, because a few days later he said to my mother:

"This ain't right, Anna. You get three pengős for a big wash, and I'm lucky if I make one a day. Why don't you work from home? Then I could help you wash all day and I could make three times as much."

"I'd thought of that myself," my mother said. "But only people with no laundry room give you the clothes to wash at home."

"And if we were to do it cheaper? For, say, two pengős instead?"

"Two pengős?"

At first, my mother was horrified, but my father once more brought out his "scientific thinking" to prove, clear as day, that with greater turnover even a smaller profit margin would bring more return.

"I can try," my mother said at last, and did.

The idea worked—at least in so far as she brought home mountains of laundry. No one, I think, apart from us, was willing to do a big wash for two pengős; we soon realized why. Partly, the money went on electricity, and you needed a huge amount of wood to heat the water, as well as more soap and petroleum, none of which was free. They worked fourteen to fifteen hours a day and I, too, joined in in the evenings. We had to take it in turns working round the clock to put aside anything at all of the two pengős.

Meanwhile we went hungry. While my mother had gone out to wash, she'd got food as well as her three pengős, so she would at least get a square meal ten or fifteen times a month. Now all three of us were eating what I brought home from the hotel. And though my father and I kept fibbing that we'd already eaten in town, my mother would divide the food in three and wouldn't touch hers till we'd eaten all of ours. So all three of us went hungry.

That kind of life is no good for anyone, especially not a pregnant woman. She could barely keep the little she ate down as it was—she was sick three or four times a day, and since there was not much inside her, she threw up mostly bile. She was skin and bones and used to cough so hard she turned blue. Her womb was full of life, but her lungs were full of death; and she lingered somewhere between these two great eternal forces in the awful dullness of some liminal state. She no longer cried, no longer complained. She washed and she was silent. She would occasionally hiss with pain as she worked, reach for her back or her heart, her face distorted with agony. At those times, instead of resting, she would lock herself in the room and pray.

She became religious, frighteningly so. Before, she had only rarely gone to church, but now she'd go two or three times a week and take Communion every Sunday. Whenever she had a free moment, she'd retreat to a corner of the room to do her rosaries. Sometimes we even saw her lips move in prayer while she was washing. She hardly ever said anything any more in which Jesus or the saints didn't figure. Back in the village, the peasants were not much given to mysticism, and her Jesus was not much of a mystical figure, either. She talked about him the way a peasant child might talk about an uncle in America, who once, before their time, had lived in the village too, had been poor like them, a landless peasant or perhaps even a carpenter, but who now lived up among the clouds, on the hundredth floor—and if he was a good little boy, and always behaved, he might one day help him out or even send him tickets for a passage so he could go live with him in America. That was how she thought of Jesus, and whenever she talked about him to me, I had the impression she pictured him in tails or a Hungarian dress coat, like the lords and magnates in the illustrated magazines. Yes, there was no other way she could picture the Lord but as a lord, a very great lord, a greater lord even than Horthy himself, and the only thing mystical about the whole thing for her was that there *was* a lord greater than Horthy and that he would deign to speak to her and to take her part. The Lord was the only lord in Hungary who showed the slightest inclination to do so, and the only one who considered her—a washerwoman—just as much of a person as the newsagent or the Secretary of State's wife.

"Even though I barely gave a thought to him!" she would repeat guiltily, her eyes welling up.

My father kept pestering her to lie down and rest, telling her he could do the work all by himself, but in vain—my mother wouldn't leave the tub.

"Think of the baby," my father would plead. "You can't take much more of this."

My mother would reply:

"I can if the Lord wills it. And if he don't, it don't matter anyway."

Then she'd cross herself and go on with the washing.

One night, I was woken by my father shaking my shoulders.

"Get up, Béla," he said anxiously, "I don't know what's going on with your mother."

I had heard what he'd said but couldn't make sense of it at first. Starting from the deep, comatose sleep of the starving, my father's face was like an apparition as he leant over me with the petroleum lamp. I stared blearily at his huge, swollen shadow as it fluttered unsteadily on the ceiling above. I shivered with tiredness and cold.

"What's happened?" I mumbled.

"I don't know," he said hoarsely. "She ain't come home."

"What time is it?"

"Nearly two."

"What time'd she go?"

"This afternoon. She took the washing for the Captain's wife. Said she'd be home by eight."

I looked at the clock. I remember it was ten to two. I scrambled up. We stood there, confounded, the clock ticking in the darkness like the timer on a bomb.

"I don't know what to think any more," my father said and reached for his hat, very pale. "I'm going to go call the Captain."

"Wait," I said, pulling on my trousers. "I'll come with you."

We ran down to the tavern. It was the early hours of Sunday, the Gypsy violinist was still at it. Swollen-faced drunks tottered in the smoky fog of the bar, reeking of stale beer. A blonde girl was dancing on one of the tables. The owner, too, was drunk, clinched tightly with some beardless youth. When she saw us, she broke free of the boy awkwardly, though there was no need—my father hadn't even noticed.

We closed the door of the phone booth behind us and waited anxiously. The number didn't answer for several minutes. I was about to hang up and try again when I heard a soft click.

"Who is this?" asked a woman's sleepy voice.

I told her.

"Who?" she asked testily, "who?"

I put on my most ingratiating manner.

"Forgive the intrusion, madam, I know it's late," I said, "but we're terribly worried. My mother went to yours this afternoon and hasn't come home."

"How is that any of my concern?" the good lady screamed hysterically. "How dare you call me at this hour?"

"Begging your pardon, madam," I pleaded. "I just need a little information… please understand… it's about my mother—"

"The devil take your mother!" she interrupted, her voice choked with fury. "Waking people up at this hour! Riff-raff!"

With that, she slammed down the receiver and we were left, helpless, with the silent telephone.

"What do we do now?" I asked.

"Let's go down to the police station," my father grunted, cursing an assortment of the lady's extended family.

The police station wasn't far. It consisted of two dirty little rooms. There was no one in the first, so we went into the second.

"Ever heard of knocking?" a fat, bald, scarlet-faced police sergeant bellowed, clambering out of bed. "What do you think this is, an inn?"

My father knew what was expected of him when addressing the authorities.

"Sorry," he said with what was, for him, unusual deference. "We've come on an urgent matter, officer."

"What's this urgent matter, then?" the sergeant asked and, before my father could respond, went into the toilet. He left the door open, we could hear him pissing. "Well, go on, then!" he said. "You said it was urgent."

My father told him what had happened. The sergeant came back, buttoned up his trousers, yawned, sat down, lit a leisurely pipe, put on his spectacles and opened a large book. He started browsing through it.

"There's been no report," he said at last, officiously, and was back off to bed.

We stood there, in front of the desk, completely at a loss. We knew we had to go now, but had no idea where.

"What we supposed to do now, poor thing?" my father asked, helpless as a child despite his size.

"I don't know," I replied.

At that moment, either the Holy Spirit took hold of the sergeant, or he remembered his own wife, because he clambered out of bed, saying:

"Wait. I'll call headquarters."

He called them, but they had no more information. We ambled home, not knowing what to do. When we reached the tavern, my father said:

"Come on, let's call the ambulance people."

We went in, and I repeated my little speech.

"Please wait," said a voice.

We waited and waited. Suddenly, we were disconnected; we were out of money. My father swore.

"Maybe she's home by now," I said, trying to reassure him, and ran up to the apartment.

She wasn't home. I took some money out of the ginger tin and ran back down to the tavern to call the ambulance service again.

"Yes," replied a sleepy voice. "We took a woman by that name to the Rókus this evening."

"What happened to her?"

"I'm sorry," the voice said, "I can't give you any further information."

"Just tell me, is she alive?" I begged.

"Ask the hospital," he said, and hung up.

We ran out of the tavern. The trams weren't running yet, so we headed into town on foot. It was a warm, late-summer night of pure silver, the empty streets populated only by the crazy spirits of the moon, hunger and horror. We were going as fast as our legs could carry us and the pale, sleepwalking houses seemed to gallop alongside. We did the three-hour trip in two.

When we got to the hospital, they directed us to the duty doctor. The doctor on duty was handsome, and he was on the phone. With his carefully slicked-back gold-blond hair, his lilac silk tie, monocle, signet ring and *Junker* hound-dog charm, he looked more like a German film star than the duty doctor in a Hungarian public hospital. The way he was talking into the phone, too, with his soft, fluting staccatos, reminded you more of the leading men in cheap, sentimental German pictures.

"But, darling!" he was whispering as we fell, panting, into the room, and was not the least bit bothered by our arrival. There were some chairs near the door, and he gestured for us to sit down. Then he said "But, darling!" again.

She must have been an odd sort, this darling, a very timid sort, for she was apparently scared to see the doctor.

"But why not?" he probed in a suggestive baritone whisper. "What are you afraid of, dear? Didn't you say he wouldn't be home till the day after tomorrow?… Well, then?… So what if they see? What would they see? That you're going to the hospital. Do you know how many hundreds of people go to the hospital every day?… Oh please, how could you ask something like that? Why do you *think* people go to the hospital? You're visiting a girlfriend… all right, not a girlfriend, then. A maid, let's say, a faithful old maid, your old nurse, say… Come on, darling, don't be like that!…"

My father couldn't take any more. He jumped up and went over to the doctor.

"Just tell me if she's alive!" he begged, but the dandy doctor waved him off angrily.

"Excuse me one moment, darling," he whispered into the telephone. He put his hand over the receiver and his *Herrenvolk* eyes flashed menacingly at the ragged Magyar. "This isn't the village fair!" he snapped. "Wait your turn!" He was on the phone for a good quarter of an hour more.

My father started grinding his teeth listening to the doctor's sweet, fluting chatter, and kept wanting to get up to go at him.

"Use your head!" I whispered, gripping his hand. "Use your head!"

If I wasn't there, he might have strangled the man, and anyone who's been through a quarter of an hour like ours would not, I can tell you, feel a drop of sympathy for the doctor.

Darling finally gave in. The handsome doctor put down the phone and graciously agreed to hear my father out. Then he looked in a little book and told us in a tone of utter boredom that yes, my mother was here, the ambulance had brought her in that evening; she'd collapsed on Horthy Miklós út, and she was on such-and-such ward.

"She's alive!" my father muttered quietly, hoarsely, and his face went so soft with release after the prolonged tension, he looked like an old drunk. His expression was fixed and hollow, and it must have been a good two or three minutes before he asked:

"What happened?"

The doctor consulted the book once more.

"Miscarriage," he said absently.

I didn't understand the word. I stared dozily at the handsome doctor, who was rubbing his monocle with his handkerchief and, it seems, thinking of his darling, for a lascivious little smile was playing around his lips. The room was very silent, until my father broke the quiet and said:

"Your brother's died, Béla."

That's what he said—word for word. The doctor must have thought he was drunk, and at that point he wasn't altogether sober.

"He's died," he muttered again and again, nodding stiffly. "Is it any wonder?" He gave a wave of his hand as if to say that there was no use talking about it, but his mouth kept on moving, empty and silent.

"And mother? How's my mother?" I asked the doctor.

The handsome doctor turned his monocle this way and that pensively.

"Pardon?" he said, starting at the question. "Yes, of course," he said, coming to, and smiled politely. "The patient is in quite a serious condition."

"Could she die?"

"Yes."

My father turned, without a word, and headed for the door with large, heavy strides.

"Wait!" I called after him, because I wanted to talk to the doctor more, but he didn't stop. "Where you going?"

"To see your mother," he said, and kept going.

"What do you mean?" the doctor cried after him. "Going to see a patient at this hour? Come back tomorrow and get permission!"

My father didn't respond. He didn't even look back. He left the room without saying goodbye and slammed the door behind him.

He'd reached the stairs by the time I managed to catch up with him. He was charging upstairs, taking them three at a time.

"That ain't the exit!" I called after him, but he just kept going.

I rushed after him, blocking his way when we got upstairs—I could see he wanted to go into the ward.

"You know you can't!" I whispered. "For the love of God, don't make a scene!"

My father didn't even look at me. He pushed me aside without a word and opened the door. He suddenly froze in the open door, rooted to the spot.

An icy, fearful silence emanated from the bluish half-light of the massive ward, with its smell of carbolic. Nothing moved—there was just the occasional stifled groan here and there, but these served only to deepen the silence. My mother was in the fourth bed on the left. She was lying on her back, barely covered, stiff and immobile. She was sleeping. Her mouth was open like the dead, and her nose stood scarily white between the dark valleys of her open mouth and closed eyes. She was only eight or ten steps away, and yet I felt like she was very distant—as distant as happiness itself.

"Anna!" my father groaned, his voice failing, his eyes filled with tears.

The ward went blurry for me too.

"Muther!" I heard myself say, and shivered.

My mother didn't move, but suddenly, out of nowhere, a nurse appeared in front of us. She was a shrivelled, mean-eyed old woman with a heavy moustache beneath her long, thin nose.

"Who are you looking for?" she whispered angrily.

"My wife," father whispered back, pointing at my mother.

"Have you lost your mind?" the old woman sniffed. "Coming to see a patient at this hour? Get out!"

"In a minute," my father said, never taking his eyes off my mother, merely gesturing to the nurse to wait, he'd be going soon.

"Not in a minute," the nurse insisted, "now!"

She wanted to shut the door in our faces, but my father put his foot in the threshold, sending the old woman into a hysterical rage.

"What is the meaning of this impertinence?" she snapped at my father. "Get out of here before I have you thrown out!"

My father looked at her at last. He looked at her as if he'd just woken from his sleep.

"Who's goin' to throw me out?" he asked hoarsely, his suppressed bitterness boiling up out of him. "What do you take us for? Ain't we human? You'd best watch yourself, damn it, before I say something that'll blow that cross right off your chest."

The old woman flapped to the telephone, squawking loudly. I grabbed my father's arm.

"Come on," I begged, dragging him towards the stairs. "Come on, for the love of God!"

My father started to curse loud and strong. I suddenly heard my mother moaning from inside the ward.

"Mishka!" she groaned in her weak little voice. "Mishka, my dear!"

Luckily, my father didn't hear her, because he was still swearing loudly. The tears, meanwhile, kept flowing from his eyes, but he didn't even realize he was crying.

I was glad when we finally got out into the street, but my relief did not last long. At the second corner, he suddenly turned back.

"Wait," he said.

"Where you going?" I asked in alarm. "I'll come with you."

"I said wait!" he growled at me, brooking no opposition, and rushed back towards the hospital.

I didn't dare try and stop him, but when I saw him disappear behind the hospital building on the corner, I ran after him. I ran only as far as the corner—there, I froze. There was a large crucifix in front of the hospital chapel, and in front of that crucifix knelt my godless father. I looked away as if I'd caught him doing something dirty, and wandered back to the corner.

It was getting light. It was morning, Sunday morning; the bells of the Basilica were ringing for mass. Almost time for work, I thought.

13

THAT MORNING, I HAD TO DELIVER an unusual letter.

"It's confidential," said the Major. "You're to hand it to him personally."

"Yes, sir," I replied and went over to the desk to take the letter.

The Major did not hand it to me. He held on to it absently, and then suddenly looked at me.

"There's something I want to say to you. Close the door."

The door to the outer office was open, so I went and closed it. The Major lowered his voice.

"The others don't need to know where you're going," he said, giving me a strange, close look. "Understand?"

"Yes, Major."

"If anybody asks, tell them I've sent you to the railway station."

"Yes, Major."

There was a brief silence. The Major removed his monocle and started wiping it on his handkerchief.

"I hear you're a patriot," he said slowly and with particular emphasis, his toad's mouth curving into something resembling a smile.

"Yes, sir," I managed.

The Major was still smiling.

"Keep it that way," he encouraged me paternally, handed over the letter and added mysteriously: "You won't regret it."

I glanced at the envelope and my heart missed a beat. It was addressed to the Constable.

I didn't have much time to wonder, though. The Constable lived nearby, and barely minutes later I was outside his flat, on the third floor of a house in Aranykéz utca.

The hound-faced batman opened the door.

"Wait," he barked, before I could tell him what I wanted, and disappeared behind a door, cat-like, silent.

I looked around the darkened entrance hall anxiously. I'd heard a great deal about this flat—numerous stories circulated about it in the city. They said that during the heyday of the White Terror, when life was cheap but real estate all the more expensive, the previous owner had been dragged off to a *Freikorps* basement in the middle of the night, where the "Doctor" took him under his care—like so many other political patients—and, before removing him once and for all from the property ladder down here on earth, made him sign over the deeds, for he was a pedantic sort and hated disorder. The incident did not make great waves in Budapest—people discussed it the way they did moderately titillating theatrical gossip. A lot of things went on in the *Freikorps*'s basements at that time: in a slow news week, when there was nothing more interesting to print, even the foreign press would be horrified by them for a while. A British MP even raised the matter in parliament, where they heard him out politely and promptly moved on. But it's one thing to hear about this sort of thing in parliament, and another to think about it standing in the entrance hall of one of these apartments, especially if you happen to be neither British, nor a Lord, and are perfectly aware that no one would make the slightest noise if you happened to disappear without trace.

I could feel my knees shaking. This latest incident came, on top of the drama of the night before, on an empty stomach, and my belly was beginning to rebel. All the acid was starting to gnaw at my insides; my throat constricted and I was overcome with dizziness.

Hound-face was still in the other room. I listened like a pointing hunting-dog, but all I could hear was the gurgling of water from the bathroom, whose door opened into the entrance hall.

Eventually, the valet came back.

"The Doctor will be right with you," he said, without so much as looking at me, and retreated with his silent cat's tread to the kitchen.

The minutes passed slowly. Someone turned off the tap in the bathroom, there was silence. I could hear someone climbing into the bath. Later, I could hear humming. It was a deep, pleasant voice, a woman's voice. Who could that be? I wondered. The word at the hotel was that the Constable had been seeing the wife of a far-right member of parliament for years, but I had always had my doubts. She used to come to the bar with her husband; she wore her hair up in a bun, no make-up, and was the patroness of a League of Patriotic Women. Surely it couldn't be her?

It must have been a good quarter of an hour till the Constable appeared. He was wearing maroon brocaded silk pyjamas emblazoned with a five-pointed crown, for the Doctor was of noble blood, and—it seemed—afraid of forgetting it in his sleep. He stepped through the door with a smile, but when he heard the woman's voice, his face twitched angrily.

"Don't tell me you're still here?" he shouted angrily into the bathroom. "Didn't I tell you to go home?"

"Like this?"

The door opened wide to reveal the patroness of the League of Patriotic Women bare naked. When she spotted me, she screamed and slammed the door, but she can't have been too upset, because she was giggling as she called out from inside: "Hand me my clothes, Bunny."

Bunny did not reply. He headed for the living room, shaking his head, and gestured to me to follow him.

"Wait," he said when we got into the room, and headed for the bedroom.

In the bedroom, it was still night. The closed shutters watched over a stuffy, untidy mess of women's clothing. The Constable picked up the clothes grudgingly and took them to the bathroom.

There was a muffled exchange from outside. The door was closed, and I couldn't make out what they were saying. But suddenly, I pricked up my ears. They seemed to be talking about me. Or was I just imagining it?

No, there it was again! *Bellboy*—I heard that clearly. It was the woman who said it, but I didn't know in what context. I tiptoed to the door and started listening. I could only catch the odd, louder, word, but nonetheless, I slowly got the gist. The Constable, it seems, had told the woman to leave before I'd come, because he was expecting an official visitor, a state secretary from the Foreign Office. She had either not believed him and stayed on or simply lost track of time, and had only got suspicious when she saw me. As to what she was suspicious of, I couldn't make out. The long and the short of it was, she wasn't going to go.

"Where's this state secretary, then?" she kept repeating, agitated. "Where is he?"

"Do you want him to find you here?" the Constable snapped at her.

"Don't worry, he won't see me in the bathroom. I'm staying and waiting for him here."

"No you aren't."

"Because he's not coming, is he?" Her voice buckled with emotion. "Are you at it again?" she shouted. "What do you want with this boy?"

"Shh!" the Constable hissed at her. "Shut your mouth or I'll slap you!"

But she wouldn't stop shouting, and the Constable, it seems, made good on his threat. Suddenly, there was a tremendous scream. Then there was silence, an incomprehensible silence. I was listening with bated breath, but couldn't hear a thing.

Ten minutes must have gone by. Then a door opened, and another—whispering, footsteps—someone was approaching the room. I jumped away from the door and tried to look uninterested.

It was hound-face. He hurried silently across the room into the bedroom. He reappeared with a lady's hat and disappeared once more. Outside, another door opened and there was the unmistakable clicking of a woman's high heels. She had clearly come out of the bathroom, but now she was quiet, incomprehensibly so. There wasn't a single word said. The high heels clicked along the entrance hall, then the door closed behind them, and a minute later, the Constable appeared.

He was as calm as if nothing had happened. He took the letter, crumpled it absently into his pocket, went over to the bookshelf with a yawn and produced a bottle of *pálinka*. He poured himself a glass, drained it, and repeated the procedure twice in quick succession. Was he really such a book lover? Or had they belonged to the *previous* owner?

I was standing carefully to attention, my heart beating wildly. After the third glass, the Constable made a little noise from the back of his throat and shook himself like a wet dog. Then he lit a cigarette and turned to me.

"Sit down," he ordered.

I sat down. He remained standing. His face had gone red from the alcohol, his eyes were bloodshot. He examined me stiffly.

"Do you know why you're here?"

"The… the Major told me to deliver that letter," I said, because I couldn't think of anything better.

The Constable drew the letter from his pocket.

"Did you read it?"

"N-no," I mumbled. "Why would I?"

"Read it," he said, handing it to me.

I looked at him none the wiser—I had no idea what he wanted. The envelope was still sealed.

"Open it," he said.

I tore open the envelope and stared at the paper inside in disbelief. There was nothing on it.

The Constable grinned.

"Interesting, isn't it?"

There was something of the cheap thriller about it all. This letter, this flat, this war hero turned rag merchant… until now, I'd thought this sort of thing existed only in pulp novels, and the trouble is, so did everybody else. It was in secretive rooms like this, with anonymous characters like him, it was in this humble and clumsy way that the plot of Europe's historical thriller began, whose blood-thirsty authors—back in those days—elicited only laughter from their unsuspecting victims.

I was not laughing. I was frightened, like the whole world would be in a few years, and the Constable was clearly enjoying it.

"Tell me," he said in a strange, melodic tone, "do you remember what I told you in that little inn in Buda?"

"I do," I stuttered.

"All of it?"

"Yes, sir."

"What would happen to you if you failed to carry out my orders?"

"Yes, sir."

"Tell me what I said."

"I… I don't remember the words exactly sir."

"No?"

The Constable smiled. It was a gross, frightening smile, deforming his thin, cruel mouth.

"Then let me remind you," he said slowly, emphasizing each word separately, and coming so close I could smell the alcohol on his breath. "I said I'd beat your brains in."

This, too, he said with a smile, a heady and hopeful smile, as if already savouring the prospect.

"Isn't that right?"

"Yes, sir, that's right."

"Did you carry out my orders?"

"Please, Doctor, I—"

"Stop gibbering! Did you carry out my orders? Yes or no?"

"No, sir."

"So why do you think I *haven't* beaten your brains in? Why haven't I said anything? Why did I *wait*?"

I didn't reply. What could I have said? I was so dizzy I could barely keep my eyes open.

"Nothing to say?" he said with mock politeness, and smiled. "No matter. That time hasn't come yet, anyway. There's a couple of things I want to ask you first. Do me a favour and don't lie for once. Provided, that is," he added unctuously, flicking a bit of dust from my uniform, "you intend to leave here with your head still attached to your shoulders. Am I making myself clear?"

"Yes, sir."

"Good," he nodded, went back to the bookshelf and downed another little glass of *pálinka*. "Question one. Think about your answer carefully. Who knows about what I told you in that inn?"

"No one."

"Your parents?"

"No."

"Friends, lover?"

"No one, sir."

"What about Elemér?"

624

"Oh, not a chance," I blurted out in genuine protest. "He'd be the last to know."

The Constable scanned me.

"Why the last?"

"Because… I… um… never talked about you with him, sir."

"What did you talk about?"

"All sorts."

"Politics?"

"Ummm… sometimes."

"Then why didn't you tell me he was a Communist? That's question two."

"He told me he was a Social Democrat, sir."

"And you believed him?"

"Everybody did. He told the others the same thing."

"He wasn't as close to them as he was to you. Which reminds me, question three. Why did you deny being friends with him?"

"I don't have any friends, sir."

"Oh, the solitary sort, are we? Poor boy." He looked concerned, shook his head. "There's just one thing I don't understand. Somebody told me you used to hang around together every morning in Buda. Apparently, they were lying."

"No, sir. That… that's true."

"Really?" he said, astonished. "What an odd sort of solitary sort you are. You work all night and then at closing time, instead of going home, you stay in the hotel to meet up with someone in the morning who… is not your friend. Tell me, aren't you at all attached to that solitary little head of yours?"

"Sir… I—"

"Don't mumble!" he shouted.

"All I said, sir—"

"Leave it," he said, dismissing it with a wave of the hand. "Question four. Why didn't you join the Party if you two got on so well otherwise? Elemér must have tried to convince you."

"No, sir."

"No?"

"No."

"Strange," he said absently, and gave me a massive slap. "Your friend said just the opposite down at the police station."

Impossible! I thought. After all, it had been me who wanted to join the movement and Elemér who dissuaded me. If he'd hit me two minutes before, when I really had been lying, I would have understood, but now… *Why was it this answer in particular that made him angry?*

"Surprised?" he grinned. "Your friend admitted plenty more, too. Not right away, of course. It took quite a while. I can tell you now that was why I didn't say anything all this time. Your friend is a remarkably reticent fellow. He finds it exhausting, talking. Our little chat, for example, tired him out so much that he's going to need a little rest in hospital. Broken ribs and whatnot. Yes, my friend, that's what happens when you…"

I didn't hear the rest. Oxen and peasants can take a lot, but there is a limit, after all. The midnight hunt for my mother, the constant fear and anxiety, the weeks of starvation, and now this… The world went suddenly black before me.

It was hound-face who roused me, dousing me with water. It can't have been his first time with that sort of thing. The Constable was looking on dispassionately from an armchair, like a surgeon waiting to operate while his assistant does the prep work. When he saw that I was better, he gestured to the valet to leave, then stood up, had a little tot of *pálinka*, and came over to me.

"I hope that little fainting fit has brought you to your senses," he said more peaceably, and sat down opposite me. "Are you ready to talk honestly, at last?"

"Yes, sir," I groaned.

An unexpected twist followed. The Constable said:

"Elemér told us at the station that the reason you didn't join the Party was because you're a Fascist sympathizer. Is that true?"

Suddenly, it all made sense. That was Elemér for you, that was Pokerface all over. First, he lends me his clothes, then his heart and mind, and now here he was, sticking his neck out for me. I couldn't speak. I was on the verge of tears.

I nodded. I knew that I was doing what Elemér wanted me to do; I knew that he wanted it this way, and yet I was still indescribably ashamed of myself.

"Then why did you lie?" he asked. "You must have known you were hurting your own cause. Were you really so afraid for that rascal?"

I burst into tears. That "rascal" was now lying in a prison hospital, ribs broken, beaten to a pulp. I pictured his bandaged head on the hospital bed as he looked at me with his prematurely aged cat's eyes, shrugging, as always, when I tried to thank him for something, and saying: *"Ah, it's nothing! We working-class boys have to stick together, that's all!"*

The Constable leant forward and put his hand on my shoulder.

"Tell me the truth," he said. "That's the only thing that can help you now. Were you covering for him?"

"Yes," I sobbed.

"All right," he nodded. "I can sort of understand that, even. But why didn't you go and work for me within the Party if you really are a sympathizer? Did Elemér notice something? Did he threaten you?"

"No, sir."

"Who threatened you, then?"

"No one."

"In that case, I just don't understand you, my friend. And when I don't understand someone, there's trouble."

There was silence. All I could hear was my own sobbing.

"Stop weeping like an old maid!" he said. "Tell the truth, like a man."

I just kept on crying, I couldn't stop. I tried clenching my teeth, but in vain—I tried gathering all my strength, but it was no use. The tears flowed out of me like blood from a severed artery. In the end, the Constable lost his patience.

"Why don't you answer me? Do you want me to have you fired? Have you blacklisted? Make sure you never find another job in the entire country?" He snatched up the blank letter from the hotel off the table and waved it around in front of me, his eyes flashing. "I can write anything I like on this!"

I knew that was true, but nonetheless I wasn't scared. The same irrational, perverse desire came over me that had almost driven me to murder after they arrested Elemér: *I wanted to go to prison*. I longed for some earth-shaking cataclysm—the Flood, or fire and brimstone, or for a policeman to come and take me away, for the Devil to come and take the whole world away.

The Constable stood up.

"I hope you know," he said with an ominous smile, "that you're not leaving here until you come clean. So why are you being such a coward? Why don't you confront the truth?"

I don't know why it was this, specifically, that made me lose my head. Anything else would probably have had the same effect. I wasn't entirely responsible for my actions by this point.

"I am not a coward!" I screamed hysterically, jumping up and waving my hands. "I may be just a bloody peasant the upper classes can treat whatever way they want, but I won't have anybody calling me a coward, because… because… all right… it's true that I'm crying, but that's… that's only because… because… I'm weak with hunger… it's true… I'm not ashamed… we're working class… and… we've got nothing to eat… though… the three of us work like dogs… and my poor mother has worked herself half to death, and… the ambulance picked her up last night in the street… and they said… it was life-threatening… and then on top of that… you think I've nothing better to do than go around sniffing out secrets, when… when my poor mother's lying in the Rókus… and… and they're going to evict us come the first… and…"

I don't know what else I shouted in the state I was in. The surprising thing was that the Constable took it. He didn't shut me up—just the opposite. He nodded gravely to say he understood it all, but behind his yellow, blinking eyes prowled the hound, ears pricked, just waiting for the rabbit to bolt its hole.

I snapped back to my senses.

"Sorry," I muttered, and collapsed dizzily into the armchair. The room was spinning around me, I thought I was about to faint again.

The Constable sat down beside me.

"Why didn't you tell me all that before?" he asked. "We're both human. We're both Hungarians. Maybe I could help."

He watched me, waiting for the effect.

"Yes, sir," I mumbled, bathed in sweat.

The Constable leant closer.

"If you brought me some interesting information," he said, his voice slightly lowered, and smiled ingratiatingly, "then… I think… I could get you some money. Not a lot," he added carefully, "the police aren't exactly generous, but," he said, patting me encouragingly on the shoulder, "it would be enough to cover the rent, with a little left over for a crust of bread."

"Yes, sir," I said, because I could see he was waiting for an answer, but I thought: I'd rather starve!

The good Doctor, who was so adept at treating people's political illnesses, was not so skilled, it seems, in the art of psychology.

"Do we have a deal?" he asked, unsuspecting, and was so sure of himself, he was already extending his hand.

I took it, of course—what else could I do? Then he threatened me once more, purely as a formality, it seems, that he would beat my brains in if I didn't obey his orders, and started talking about more practical matters. He made me promise to join the Party within twenty-four hours, and that I would be a good little comrade. I would say what they wanted me to say and do what they told me to do. I would try to get lost in the crowd, but if it came time for action, I would be the bravest, ready for any sacrifice, and na-tu-ra-lly—that was how he said it, crunching the word like a dog a bone, na-tu-ra-lly, I would be the most radical of them all. His paternal advice extended to everything. He was astoundingly familiar with every nook and cranny of the young workers' movement, the financial situation of the various leaders, their principles, habits and even their weaknesses. He explained in excruciating detail how I was to ingratiate myself with each of them. He called my particular attention to the female comrades.

"In bed and in the bar, everybody talks too much," he explained with professional precision. "Trouble is, the bar's no use, because the little Commie saints are teetotal almost to a man. They've got *principles*, don't you know!" he laughed. "They only get drunk on words. But the female comrades, they like to… um… well, you know… and you can go and do your proletarian duty. Not such a bad deal, eh? Ha ha ha," he laughed, and I too, tried to laugh, yes, that's right, ha ha ha.

We were frightfully chummy now. Then the Constable looked me up and down and said, out of the blue:

"If you have any self-respect, a year from now you'll be wearing a *different* uniform."

I looked at him in surprise, which he evidently relished. He loved these unexpected twists. He inserted his monocle slowly and fussily, and smiled mysteriously.

"Tell me, what do you know about Hitler?"

I knew quite a lot. Elemér had talked often during our walks in Buda about National Socialism, and Elemér was a good teacher. The Constable could hardly contain himself. He was simply delighted with me.

"Very good," he said, patting me on the shoulder. "I can see you're serious about this. In a few weeks, we'll be setting up the National Socialist Party in Hungary, too, and if you're smart, you can have a great future in it. Ever heard of the *Hitler Jugend*?"

"Yes, sir."

"Then you know what I mean," he said confidentially. "We, too, will be organizing a youth movement like it. Not," he added proudly, "that we're copying Hitler, mind you. The truth is, Hitler's copying us. The *Hitler Jugend* is nothing more than our own Cadet Movement. In fact, National Socialism itself is nothing more than what we Hungarian counter-revolutionaries managed in 1919. Where was Hitler then? Where was Mussolini? The world was still dreaming Mr Wilson's democratic dream, and we smoked democracy, Socialism and the Jews out of the country under their very noses. We didn't give a damn about their peace treaty. We armed ourselves openly, and anyone who got out of line got a bullet in the head. Those were the days!" he mused lovingly. "We took on the world and won. Problem was, we won too easily. The French and the British, who'd put the wind up everyone so thoroughly, were licking Horthy's boots a year later, and the old lecher loved it. He stopped halfway and now we're slowly slipping back to where we started from." He waved bitterly. "We were teaching the world a lesson, and now our students are running rings around us. Take this Hitler, for example. He's not going to stop halfway—no, not him! Did you read what he said to the judge? He told him, right there in open court at his trial, that when he gets into power, *heads will roll.* That's the spirit, there's a real man for you. Today, the whole world's laughing at him, but I can see those laughing heads rolling—oh yes, my boy, I can see them roll already!" he said, and I believed him.

I must have looked very strange, because he suddenly fell silent.

"Why do you look so scared?" he asked, laughing. "You haven't been seduced by the priests as well, have you? I'm a good Christian, my boy, but Christianity was only great when the Church thought the way Hitler does. Or do you think heads didn't roll under the Inquisition?"

"Yes, sir," I replied obediently.

"Well then let's not kid ourselves," he said. "Whoever's not with me is against me, and whoever's against me, I'll bash his brains in. The weak keep gabbling on about equality—but the world belongs to the strong. There have always been masters to give orders and there will always be servants to obey them. The trouble is that these days the masters aren't masters and the servants aren't servants. Even the cattle are unionized, and every ass thinks he's smarter than his master. But we'll put an end to that, my boy. We're going to bring back the old order, and anyone who doesn't like it won't keep his head on his shoulders for long. Am I making myself clear?"

"Yes, sir," I said, with great conviction, because I felt he really couldn't be making himself any clearer.

He made me understand something that the world couldn't understand even years later, and he convinced me so thoroughly that by the time I left him, I no longer had any doubts. I knew what I had to do.

That very afternoon, I got hold of their address, and as soon as I got out of the hotel, I went to visit them. They lived in Angyalföld, not far from the edge of the world, where according to urban legend, not even "coppers" dared take their watches with them. The house was down a sloping alley, and I went all the way round it before I went in, because I was afraid that it was being watched. It was a dark, stiflingly hot night, the slanting, heavy drops of a rain shower battering the walls. There was no one in the alley, and the gate itself was deserted, too. I read the list of residents three times over, but couldn't find the name. I stood there before the battered list, speckled with fly droppings, confused. Had I got the wrong address? Had they moved?

I heard footsteps. A boy in a worker's hat, soaked to the skin, ran in from the street. He must have been an apprentice, about fifteen or sixteen. I asked whether he knew them.

"Yes," he said. "They live here."

"Where?"

"In the basement. Come on, I'll show you."

We cut across the darkened courtyard.

"Why isn't their name on the list?"

"On account of the bank," he replied. "Had 'em evicted."

"Then how can they still be living here?"

The boy laughed.

"Oh, you know, the way all us ordinary folk do," he said. "On the sly. One of the tenants let 'em have his woodshed in the basement, and the hausmeister don't say nothing, 'cause he gets to pocket what they're paying. Well, here we are," he said, pointing to the entrance to the basement, leaving me to my fate. "G'night."

"G'night."

The entranceway leading to the basement was so low I could only get through it doubled over. Cobwebs hung off the filthy walls, and the old, cracked stairs wobbled scarily beneath my feet. I struck a match, since it was pitch black, but there was a powerful draught coming from the basement that kept putting my matches out. By the time I got downstairs, there wasn't a single match left in my box.

I felt my way haltingly in the dark. It was a big, ancient basement, deep and damp. The earth had become so soft with the seeping ground-water that I couldn't hear the sound of my footsteps at all. The silence was unbearable. There was something constantly dripping from on high, and the walls were overgrown with slimy mould—I shuddered at their touch. I had the feeling I'd been wandering around down here for hours and would never make it out.

Suddenly, I stopped. I seemed to hear a child's cries. I headed in the direction of the sounds, but after a few steps, bumped into a wall. The corridor had come to an end, there was nowhere left to go. I felt about, helplessly. The crying hadn't come from here, before, but farther down, much farther. I kept listening for a long time, but heard nothing. Had I only imagined it?

I was ready to turn around when my hand felt a door. I pressed the handle, and it gave. I found myself in a long, narrow corridor, at the end of which there was a weak light. These were the tenants' wood stores—I recognized them at once. In our building, too, the wood stores were separated by such jerry-rigged, rickety wooden grilles, and they were just as devoid of firewood as these ones here. These were the crypts of working-class households, the burial grounds of martyred prams, unfortunate saucepans, skewered pillows and exhausted furniture.

The light was coming from the unit at the end. This, too, was a wood store like the others, but instead of discarded household items, it had five children lying on the floor, five sleeping boys wrapped up in rags. The youngest must have been around four, the eldest sixteen. They were lying in a row, packed tightly next to each other—otherwise, they wouldn't have fitted into the narrow unit. Next to them, on a crate, sat a stocky, broad-shouldered old man with a heavy moustache, rocking a sniffling little girl. The girl must have woken him from his sleep, because he was wearing neither shoes nor trousers, only a ragged, green-tinged black overcoat, from under which his long undershorts peeked out. The little girl gave the occasional cry in her sleep, the old man trying to calm her. He can't have heard me coming, because his head snapped up so sharply when I appeared out of the darkness, it was like he'd seen a ghost. That was when I saw he was missing an eye.

We looked at each other in alarm. The petroleum lamp flickered restlessly in the draught.

"I'm a friend of Elemér's," I whispered nervously.

"I'm his father," he replied with a sort of awkward grace, looking me over suspiciously. "What brings you here?"

I didn't know where to begin. The "plan" that had been born inside me back in the Constable's flat had consumed my mind so completely that such prosaic details had not even occurred to me. I thought I would come, and tell him, and that would be it. Now that I was standing here in front of the old man, I suddenly had doubts. Maybe he didn't know about it… or maybe he did… No, this was not how I'd imagined Elemér's father.

"I just came to ask," I said awkwardly, because I had to say *something*, "how,"—I tried to smile—"how is he?"

The old man did not reply. He just watched me stiffly out of his one eye. I knew what it meant when a working man looked at you like that. To try and gain his trust, I asked him:

"Is he still in hospital?"

"Hospital?" he repeated in astonishment, and his yellow, stubbly face took on a greenish tinge in horror. "Since when's he been in hospital? What's the matter with him?"

"I don't know," I replied, because I was afraid of telling him the truth, and that of course just made me look all the more suspicious.

He looked at me in shock.

"Then what makes you think he's in hospital?"

"That's what they told me."

"Who?"

"A… mutual acquaintance," I muttered, and I could feel myself blush.

Someone laughed derisively behind me. I turned. It was the oldest of the boys. He stood there in front of me, his legs spread and his hands in his pockets, his big black eyes almost overflowing with hate.

"What *mutual acquaintance*?" he asked, ready to jump.

"A friend of Elemér's," I lied, and I could feel myself blushing again. "A… um… mutual friend," I added quickly, to cover my discomfort. "A boy, who—"

"What's his name?" he interrupted. "I know all of Elemér's friends."

I was digging myself deeper into a hole. I said:

"Not this one."

"Is that right?…"

The boy looked me over disparagingly and laughed once more.

"Then I think I know who it is," he said. "Well, you go ahead and have a good look round, young master, so you can give him a detailed report. We're having a whale of a time. The money just keeps piling in from Moscow. Ain't it obvious?" he shouted, pointing at the ragged, skin-and-bones children who looked at me, terrified, from inside their appalling burrow. "Can't you see, young master? We're simply bursting with roubles!"

My gaze wandered to his right hand—I could see it shifting inside his trouser pocket. I knew he was holding a knife.

"Don't be stupid!" I shouted. "I'm your brother's best friend. Three years we worked together."

"Where?"

"In the hotel, of course."

"What's your name?"

I told him.

His face changed at once.

"That's a different matter, then," he muttered with a shy smile. "Why didn't you tell me right away? I'm Imre. Hi."

We shook hands. He was a tall, dark, handsome lad and bore not the slightest resemblance to his brother.

"Don't take it the wrong way, brother," he excused himself with a laugh. "They keep sending snitch after snitch after us—we can't even trust our own fleas any more. Anyway, pull up a pew," he gestured gran-diosely with a wink, pointing to a dirty soapbox. "A fine box that, first rate. Got that from Moscow too. Used to belong to Ivan the Terrible."

I laughed too. We were all three of us laughing. The four children crawled out of their burrow and stood there gaping at me like some sort of circus attraction.

"Shoo!" Imre waved at them. "Off you go to sleep, or I'll set Horthy on you. Go on, go on. Tomorrow's Monday, you've got school."

The boys went back to their places, but the little girl was startled awake by the laughter and started bawling and wailing. The old man rocked her like an infant, though she can't have been less than three. She was a thin child with rickets; only her belly looked frightfully swollen, like the bellies of all the children society keeps on starvation rations. Her big, swollen stomach trembled under her ragged little shirt, her grey, sick little face twisted with pain.

"What's the matter with her?" I asked.

"I don't know," the old man replied. "Could be she's upset her stomach."

"The hell she has," Imre whispered. "She's just hungry."

The little girl would not stop crying, but a quiet still fell over the wood store. A moment before, we'd been laughing, and now it seemed that that little girl was crying for us, crying for all of Angyalföld, and all of Újpest, too, for every working-class child. And China, far-off, unimaginable China, where tens of thousands of children were starving to death, now seemed no more than half an hour from Angyalföld.

"I've got a few fillérs," I muttered awkwardly, digging out the money.

"We ain't beggars!" the old man snapped at me. "No, we ain't beggars yet."

"Ah," Imre gave a wave of the hand. "What you putting on an act for with a friend? How much could you spare, brother?"

"I just need the tram fare," I said. "I can give you the rest."

"Jackpot!" he shouted, and pocketed the money happily. "That'll buy a whole loaf! I'll be off and get it before they lock the gate."

We looked at each other, and I suddenly knew it was him I had to talk to and not the father.

"I'll come with you," I said, and took my leave of the old man.

Outside, the rain had stopped and a warm wind was blowing through the alley. The raindrops were still glittering, a-tremble, on the leaves of the acacias, but the wind had almost dried the pavement and the sky was full of stars. I took Imre's arm and suddenly everything seemed so simple.

"Imre," I said calmly, without hesitation. "I came out to see you because—"

"Careful!" he whispered. "They're watching us from the house opposite. Ground floor, third window on the left. See it?"

"Yeah. Coppers?"

"That's right," he nodded. "Just keep walking. I know their habits. He'll turn up in a moment, follow us for a while, then walk past us slowly, turn into the side street and a few minutes later pop up again behind our backs. You can talk freely when he's in the other street. Slow down a bit," he said, poking me in the ribs. "Nice and slow. I'll walk you to the tram."

"All right."

We walked slowly side by side. The street was deserted, there was only the occasional drunk. Anyone sober had gone home already to save having to pay the hausmeister to open the gate, and you couldn't tell if the drunks were really drunks or not. The seedy denizens of the night sloped about the slums: informers, robbers, prostitutes and police-men, who—at this time—only dared show their faces round here in pairs. Our copper really did come out of the house. We could hear his footsteps clearly in the heavy silence.

"Were you wanting to talk about *that* with the old man, too?" Imre whispered.

I nodded yes.

"Thought as much," he said, and I could see he realized why I *didn't* talk to him about it in the end. "Poor old man!" he sighed. "He was a good comrade once. He's been a Party member for more than thirty years—the coppers knocked his eye out in the good old days before the war. Real hellraiser, so they say, always on the hard left. Now, he's nowhere. He did three years inside after the revolution, then he couldn't get a job anywhere any more. Ma died last year from consumption and the old man was left with six hungry children, and…" Imre drew up his eyebrows, and then gave a wave of his hand. "You know how it goes. Lost his edge. He don't know what to make of us any more. He's fifty-eight now and just sits in that wood store, talkin' about the good old days. When the coppers knocked his eye out for him. Hell of a thing, ain't it?"

The policeman's steps accelerated behind us.

"Is he comin'?" I asked.

Imre nodded.

"Turn this way so he don't see your face," he whispered, and started talking loudly about that afternoon's match.

The policeman walked slowly past us and turned into the side street. Imre winked at me.

"Now you can talk."

I felt his open gaze upon me, and had no trouble talking.

"I want to join an underground group," I said simply, not beating about the bush.

"Yes," he nodded. "I know."

I looked at him in surprise.

"You know?"

"I know," he repeated. "Elemér told me you'd come by sooner or later."

My throat went tight with pleasure. I had never been so proud—I had never been so humble. I won't let him down, I said to myself, I won't let them down! And I saw my father kneeling before that cross at dawn, and suddenly understood—beyond religion, beyond it all—that only someone who's fallen to their knees can truly rise.

"What are you?" Imre asked. "Social Democrat or Communist?"

"God knows," I said. "Don't know enough about it. Whoever's against *them* is a friend of mine, and whoever's with them is an enemy. That's what I know for sure."

Imre smiled. It was all so simple.

"Can you introduce me to the comrades?"

"Not yet," he replied. "You can see we're bein' watched."

"It's urgent."

"Why?"

"Because of the Constable. You know him?"

"Do I!" he said, his eyes flashing. "What about him?"

"He wants me to join the Party, and… you can guess the rest. Even promised me money this morning."

"That… really is urgent," he said pensively. "It's just that I don't know how…" He fell silent, then shrugged. "Whatever. I'll figure somethin' out. I'll introduce you in the next few days."

Footsteps sounded behind us once more. Imre glanced backwards cautiously, out of the corner of his eye.

"He's back," he whispered. "Vanish."

"Call me?"

"Yes. Go."

He pointed towards the bend in the street, where a tram flashed past.

"Is it going the right way?" I asked.

"Yes," he replied, and now I knew he was right.

I got to where I had to be.

14

THE NEXT AFTERNOON, THE DOCTOR told us flat out that there was nothing more to be done for my mother.

"Best to prepare for the worst," he said. "I doubt she'll make it through the night."

My mother made it. Barely two weeks later, one evening when my father and I were washing in the kitchen, the door suddenly opened, and there she was in the clouds of steam like an apparition. We could hardly believe our eyes. The day before, when we'd been to visit her in hospital, she'd been lying in bed and could barely sit up.

"What happened?" my father asked in alarm. "You ran away?"

"Not a bit of it," my mother said, with a wave of her hand.

"What you doing here, then?"

My mother's bloodless lips curled into a pitiful smile.

"I'm cured," she said, and gave a sharp laugh.

We thought she was joking. She could barely stand unaided.

My father looked at her, shaking his head.

"How could you do this, Anna?"

My mother started laughing once more, but this time she couldn't stop. A fit of coughing came over her, and she turned blue.

"Don't you get it?" she said, panting for breath. "Today, at rounds, the professor says I'm cured. I thought he were joking, too, to begin with, but then the nurse comes over and tells me to get up, 'cause they need the bed for someone else. So I guess I'm cured."

We didn't say anything. What was there to say? We had washing to do, so we washed. My mother went into the room to make the bed, but she didn't have the strength.

"Mishka, would you make the bed?" she called out, "I'm awful tired."

My father went in, and I carried on with the washing. We washed day and night, but we still hadn't managed to wash enough for that ninety-six pengős. It was 26th September already, and there was less than seventy pengős in the ginger tin. What would my mother say?... I listened anxiously, but the door to the room was closed, and the water for the washing was boiling volubly on the stove. I couldn't hear a thing.

A little while later, my father came back. He was on tiptoes, and he looked pretty pale.

"She's sleeping, poor thing," he whispered. "Her head'd hardly hit the bed, she was asleep."

"She didn't ask about the rent?"

"No, not *yet*." My father twisted his mouth bitterly. "But you can be sure she will tomorrow."

My mother didn't ask. She asked nothing, said nothing, and was silent—silent as those "cursed" fields on the abandoned outskirts of the village that the superstitious old women said bore an "unholy crop". In the morning, she clambered out of bed and dragged herself out to the tub, but when my father shooed her away, she did not protest. She went back to the room, sat down beside the table and stared at the tablecloth blankly. She would sit like that for hours, barely moving. Her rosary hung, gathering dust, on the black wooden crucifix above the bed; she didn't take it down, she didn't have any more use for it. She no longer prayed. She no longer had anything to say to God.

"Go to church," my father told her.

"No," she replied.

"Why not?"

"What for?"

The question dropped out of her mouth like a dead bird. My father and I looked at each other in downcast silence. An icy wind seemed to blow from the room; I shivered next to the steaming washtub.

The hours died slowly, agonizingly. It was my day off and, recently, I'd come to detest my days off. It had now been almost two weeks since I'd been to Angyalföld, but Imre had still not been in touch. I was full of uneasiness and forebodings and was constantly afraid that I wouldn't be at the hotel when he did, eventually, call me. I knew, of course, that he'd call again the next day, that it would just be a delay of a single day, but I found even that day too much to bear.

I found every moment too much. I was so impatient, it was as if I'd been sentenced to death, or I don't know what, and it was now from Imre that I expected news of a reprieve, though I knew that what I wanted from him had led plenty of people in Hungary to the gallows for real.

So why was I so impatient? Was I a "fanatic"? I don't know. I'm always suspicious of those kinds of words. I, too, wanted to live, like everyone else, to live well, if possible, and not at all "dangerously". The only people in awe of living dangerously are the ones bored for want of danger, and anyone born poor in Hungary had nothing to fear on that front. No, a working-class boy did not go hunting lions unless he had to. And I had to. There was no other way. I accepted the danger the way a pregnant woman accepts it, thinking of a new life and knowing there's no other way. I, too, was thinking of a new life that would emerge from this pregnancy and the thought filled me so completely that there was no room left within me for doubts or reservations or fear. The experience was almost physical, like a pregnant woman's—I could feel, yes, physically feel something move, come to life, and grow in the womb of the slums; that something was being born in Angyalföld, China and Újpest; it was being born everywhere, and I was drunk on the thought that I, too, would be part of this incredible struggle. Only a small part, it's true, one cell in the pregnant body, but I knew that even the smallest cell *lives* as long as it's part of the body, and even the greatest head will rot if it's cut off from it.

It was only now I came to understand why the poems had wilted within me and why I couldn't write even in the days of my prosperity, when loose change rang in my pockets and all was well at home. Now, nothing was well, and yet I still, after fourteen or fifteen hours of work, dizzy with hunger and exhaustion, had to reach for my pencil. The poems burst out of me almost completely finished, through some kind of immaculate conception, each affirming life: a hallelujah, amen and evoe. I was living in the heavy realities of a luxury hotel and a slum, and yet I was still above, or below, that in a floating, dreamlike state—outside all sense of place—that only lunatics and artists know. This was a kind of constant sober stupor, a waking *ecstasis*. The flat pastures of reality were flooded by a wonderful light and the old familiar image took on a new and unexpected depth—somehow, everything became simpler and more complicated, easier to understand and more mysterious. Hunger? Homelessness? Prison? Broken ribs? Death? I was no longer afraid of anything except that awful *what for* from my mother just now, and would have rushed head first into any kind of danger without thinking twice, if only I never had to say it myself.

I knew *what for*, I finally knew. I was preparing for it like a pregnant woman for the birth, and I gave myself over to my fate the way they give their newborn child the breast: here it is, take it, I'm yours, you're mine. I don't know what you're going to be like, I don't know how you'll treat me, but I accept you, I'll stand by you, and I'll be true to you—because that is all that you can do: that little. That much.

That was how I prepared for my task, for my fate. In the morning, I woke thinking it would be fulfilled today, and in the evening, *tomorrow, tomorrow*. And then one day they called me to the telephone, and it all happened completely differently.

It was a Monday, 29th September. It must have been two in the afternoon. I was getting out of the staff lift, coming back down from upstairs, when Boldizsár said, perfectly indifferently:

"You're wanted on the telephone."

I got so excited that, ignoring all the regulations, I ran head over heels for the booth. It was a woman's voice.

"Is that Béla?"

"Yes. Who's this?"

"That's not important," she replied softly, tensely. "Imre's been arrested."

My heart skipped a beat.

"Arrested?!"

"Over a week ago. I went to see him in jail today. He says hello."

"Didn't he say anything else?"

"No."

"Not when… when I can meet… with… um… with you?"

"You can't now, not for some time."

"Why not?" I asked, dim and childish. "Imre promised."

"Because you can't, get it into your head!" she replied, curt and impatient. "I have to go now."

"Wait!" I cried. "Hello?… Hello?"

There was a click, and the line went dead. At first, I tried to fool myself that we'd just been disconnected, but I waited in vain—the phone didn't ring again. I could see the electric clock through the window of the booth, could see its minute hand jumping every sixty seconds with nerve-shredding regularity. One minute, five minutes, ten. I was no longer fooling myself, I knew that it was all in vain, but still I just stood there in the booth and didn't budge.

What for?

The rent was due on 30th September. "Otherwise," ran the letter from the bank, "you will have to vacate the property by midnight."

That was all I thought about all day, of course, and that evening, when I got home from the hotel, I hadn't even got through the door when I asked:

"Well?"

My father laughed.

"Well what?"

He was sitting on the table, kicking his heels, and his brilliant, handsome teeth flashed as he laughed. I couldn't understand why he was so cheerful. Had something happened while I'd been out?

"Did you take care of it?"

"Ain't talked to the Schwab yet," he said, but he said it so cheerfully that I was mystified by the whole thing. "I didn't want to let your mother go down there alone," he explained easily, smiling. "And she said it would be better if I didn't go with her. So I thought you could go with her instead."

"All right," I nodded, giving my cheerful father an agitated look.

What had happened?

My mother said nothing, as usual. She was sitting at the table in her best dress; she sat there, poor thing, as if she was going to meet the King. She exuded some indefinable sense of occasion, purple spots of apprehension on her face. But my father looked so calm enthroned on the table, kicking his heels, that I was beginning to think he'd managed to get the money somehow after all.

"How much we got?" I asked.

"Seventy-four pengős," he said boldly, as if he had no idea that we had ninety-six to pay. "Why the long face?" he asked, and laughed once more. "You and your mother really are somethin'. You don't really think they're going to put us out on the street over twenty-two pengős, do you? You think the bank's that stupid? They know full well they won't get a fillér if they do. They ain't fool enough to throw seventy-four pengős down the drain."

I knew this easy tone was for the benefit of my mother, but it none-theless stoked a little dormant hope in me, too.

"That's true," I said, and smiled encouragingly at my mother. "Come on, then, let's get it over with."

My mother wasn't really up to the stairs yet. She kept getting out of breath, coughing and panting for air, blue in the face. Her heart can't have appreciated the three flights either; we had to stand in front of Herr Hausmeister's flat for a good while until it calmed. Then she drew herself up ramrod straight, like a soldier, knocked softly, humbly on the door, and even tried to go as far as smiling, just as a well-brought-up poor woman should.

"Come," called the all-powerful man, and in we went.

"Good evenin'," my mother said.

"Good evenin'," I said, too.

Herr Hausmeister didn't say anything. He just sat there behind a ledger on the table, counting like a grave deity totting up the sins of the mortals in preparation for imminent judgement.

We stood in the door and waited respectfully. Herr Hausmeister had really transformed his place since his wife had moved out to the cemetery. She hadn't even died yet when he was boasting in the tavern that he'd managed to wangle her a pauper's grave from the city authorities, and how he was going to do up the apartment with all the money he'd saved on the funeral, so that there would be nothing left to remind him of that "hideous cow". And there really was nothing left to remind him, that much is true. Everything in the apartment was new, and the whole thing had cost Herr Hausmeister less than a third-class funeral. It had all been done as "little friendly favours" by the craftsmen among the tenants who were good at their jobs but not at paying rent. Herr Hausmeister didn't so much as buy them a shot of *pálinka*—not even the Virgin Mary did he prize enough to actually pay money for her. Her picture, which now hung above his bed, he had extorted for nothing from Mátyás. Mátyás, being a religious man, had resisted parting with it for a long time, but eventually handed it over because what else could he do? Apparently, Herr Hausmeister was no longer interested in his wife.

He wasn't really interested in us, either. He just kept on counting and didn't so much as look at us. There was a suffocating silence in the room and a hideous smell of patchouli. Herr Hausmeister had taken to perfuming himself. He'd had something of a bouquet before, it's true, but that hadn't had anything to do with perfume. He, too, had changed, along with his place. He'd grown scented and alarmingly fancy. He'd been buying hand-me-downs from the upper classes hand over fist and used to go about on Sundays in black patent-leather shoes with spats, a silver-handled walking stick dangling from his arm. His politics had changed, too, but the only sign of that so far was that he had taken to wearing his moustache like his great fellow-countryman, Adolf Hitler. Officially, he still declared himself Hungarian, and at election time, he was still rabidly patriotic (for a fee, of course).

He finally looked up.

"What is it?"

The way he snorted those three short words at us was as if he'd been spitting in our eyes. But my mother just smiled at him very humbly.

"We've brought seventy-four pengős, Herr Hausmeister," she said, soft and agitated, and kept looking at the omnipotent man to see if the axe would fall or he'd show mercy.

He did neither. He was struggling with a cigar that wouldn't draw and his face was inscrutable, as the faces of deities generally are.

My mother screwed up her courage.

"You can see our good faith, Herr Hausmeister…"

"What good faith?" he asked drily.

"Well… we've brought seventy-four pengős," repeated my mother. "That's a lot of money, Herr Hausmeister."

Herr Hausmeister did not reply.

"For some," he commented evasively, and since my mother still hadn't shifted from the door, he barked at her impatiently: "Well, what you standing there for? Let's have it, then!"

My mother looked at me, as if for counsel, then stared down at her shoes before eventually going over to Herr Hausmeister and handing him the money. He counted it, but still refused to show his hand.

"Seventy-four pengős," he said neutrally. "I'll make you out a receipt."

"Thank you, Herr Hausmeister."

Herr Hausmeister went and took his receipt book out of the drawer of the sideboard, sitting imperiously back down at the table. There was silence; I could hear my mother's laboured breathing. Herr Hausmeister leant forward, dipped his pen in the ink, but before he started writing, looked at my mother.

"I hope you know what the law proscribes," he muttered under his Hitler moustache. "You can't take anything out of the apartment. We take possession tomorrow."

My mother, it seems, didn't quite understand, for she was still trying to smile.

"You doin' what tomorrow?"

"Taking possession. In light of the shortfall."

This time, she understood, poor thing. Her lips began to tremble.

"You… you throwing us out?"

"No," Herr Hausmeister grinned. "I'm going to move you in here with me. What did you think?"

My mother hardly dared say a word. She kept squeezing her handkerchief helplessly. She stood there in front of the great man like the personification of hopelessness.

"You wouldn't really do that to us, would you Herr Hausmeister?"

"Why wouldn't I?" he snapped. "You ain't exactly model tenants. It'll be good riddance to bad rubbish, far as I'm concerned."

My mother, poor thing, swallowed her tears, and the humiliation along with them.

"Herr Hausmeister," she pleaded. "I beg you, in the name of Our Lord…"

"Don't answer back!" he roared. "I've said what I said. If you ain't out of the flat by midnight, I'll have the police throw you out. Understand? And now shut up so I can make out the receipt."

With that, he leant fussily over the little book and started sketching out the letters slowly, awkwardly, his tongue sticking out of his mouth like a schoolboy.

The money was lying in front of us on the table. My mother just kept looking at it. What was going through her mind? The nights she'd worked for it? The days she'd starved for it? Horthy Miklós út, where she'd collapsed from exhaustion? The ambulance? The operating table? The baby it had killed? All of a sudden, she did something of which I would never have thought her capable. She swooped on the money like a hawk and ran for it.

"Thief!" Herr Hausmeister roared, running after her. "Thief! Stop her! She's taken the bank's money!"

In a matter of moments, curious onlookers crowded the entrance-way, but they were not about to stop my mother at all. Only Herr Hausmeister pursued her, and that not for very long. Suddenly, appearing from nowhere, there stood my father. Herr Hausmeister simply turned and sloped off back to his apartment. He only recovered his bravado when he already had the door half closed and felt completely secure again.

"Go ahead and take it, then!" he roared in impotent fury. "The police'll take it off you tomorrow anyhow. They'll take it all off you, the shirt off your backs and all! Bunch of dirty thieves! You're going to pay for this."

We were out on the street by the time he said it. My mother had run like crazy, but my father caught her in front of the gate and made a point of carrying on with her slowly, at a walk, to show everybody that we had nothing to run from.

My mother suddenly turned the corner.

"Where you going?" asked my father.

There was a gleam in my mother's eye.

"The grocer's."

"It's closed."

"Well, it's about to open again!" my mother replied in a strange, hoarse voice and gave a short laugh. "Because I'm about to go and spend seventy-four pengős there, seventy-four, you get me?!"

No, we didn't get her at all. Something had happened right under our noses that was incomprehensible and almost frightening. She started cackling like a madwoman, and simply couldn't stop.

"We're goin' to eat it all up, all them seventy-four pengős!" she guffawed. "And the upper class can eat the shit what comes out our rear ends tomorrow! They can go ahead and have *that*! They deserve it!" she cried, and just laughed, and laughed, and laughed.

It was horrible, her laugh, it still sometimes wakes me in the night. She was thirty-four back then. At six, she was already looking after the Count's geese, and from that day on she'd served the upper class faithfully. She liked order, hated "Commernism" and respected the laws of heaven and earth. Now all she could do was laugh. At those laws? Or at herself?

In the heart of Anna R., thirty-four, washerwoman, the revolution had begun.

Whatever there was edible at the grocer's, she bought, though there wasn't much, it's true. The grocer was a war cripple who'd got a lot of medals during the war but very little in the way of credit after. The poor man didn't even have an icebox, so in warm weather he could only keep as much fresh produce as he could sell in a day. He kept the tiniest little shop, the smallest I've ever seen, but there was no chance of going anywhere bigger because it was almost nine. This grocer of ours, for want of anywhere better, used to sleep in his shop, which must have been uncomfortable, but from our point of view was very convenient.

"If the police come knocking," he whispered even as he was letting us in the door, "say you're just here for a visit."

This was not how my mother had imagined this "visit". There she was with seventy-four pengős, and no matter how she tried, she couldn't spend more than ten.

"What do we do with the rest?" she asked when we came out of the shop, and she looked so careworn that my father had to laugh.

"You leave that to me, love!" he said. "You take the food home, and I'll go get a surprise to go with it."

Half an hour later, he was home, but the only surprise was that he hadn't bought anything.

"Where's the surprise?" asked my mother.

"On its way," he replied, and smiled suggestively.

"What kind of surprise is it?"

My father clicked his fingers.

"The kind, my love, they won't soon forget round these parts!"

He refused to reveal any more, no matter how hard we probed.

"Come on, let's eat," he said mysteriously, "'cause we won't have a chance later. There'll be plenty going on here before midnight."

With that, he rolled up his shirtsleeves as if he were getting down to hard work, and sat down at the table. My mother and I hadn't touched the food while he'd been out, because if a family starved together, it should eat together, too. Now we could finally start. My mother locked the door like a highway robber counting his loot, then joined us, and the feast began.

It was wonderful, and it was scary. We'd been going hungry for months, we didn't even remember the last time we'd been really full, and now here was this vast quantity of food; we could eat as much as we could stomach. The thought was intoxicating and I forgot about everything else, just like a drunk. I didn't think about what would happen at midnight—I didn't think about anything. This was how I'd felt back in prison, three years before, when I'd found the packet of food in my pocket, and as I ate, I hadn't even felt the pain, though the bruises from that blow with the rifle butt hurt like hell. Now, too, I was seized by that great, wonderful, reassuring feeling; after the unnerving ramblings of the chaotic and unreliable mind came the mercifully direct words of the body: I'm hungry! I'm hungry and I can eat! I can eat as much as I like. My stomach rejoiced, my teeth tore into the meat in utter transport, my jaw laboured passionately through its loving motions, and vast, sweeping, enticing juices splashed through me. My body was filled by simple flesh-and-blood reality, the sweet, strong security of pure animal being... for twenty or thirty minutes.

Then I was hit with the most terrific hangover. It's hard to explain to anyone who hasn't been through it. Your imagination is still tickled by all the food, but your palate and your stomach are not. You're full, but you won't acknowledge it—you don't *want* to acknowledge it. You keep eating, wolfing down the food, stuffing yourself. You're seized by a hysteria that's impossible to satisfy, the same one that drives infatuated lovers when—after much waiting—they can finally be together for a night, and everything is suddenly possible. You want more, and more, and more, you want that point of ecstasy people seek at the table and in bed in vain, that exists only in the tropical world of an overactive imagination and in the visions of the deranged.

My mother was the first to feel unwell. Her face turned suddenly yellow, her brow was filled with sweat and a sort of grin appeared around her mouth, because the poor thing was trying desperately to smile so we wouldn't notice what was wrong. Eventually she got up and went out to the lavatory. We pretended not to have noticed anything. My father made her drink some rye *pálinka* when she got back, and that—it seems—pacified her stomach, because she started eating again. I was next, and then finally my father. We ate, threw up, and ate again. We couldn't, we didn't want to stop.

Suddenly, we heard a strange commotion from the stairs.

"What's that?" my mother asked.

"I don't know," said my father, but you could see that he knew all too well.

He didn't let us look outside—he charged our glasses and made a toast.

"Forever young!" he cried.

"Forever young!" I cried, too.

My mother didn't say a thing, just turned away in silence. The noise grew louder outside, but in the room there was such a sense of quiet that I shivered.

Then a Gypsy band struck up outside our front door. They started off very softly at first, with a man singing *sotto voce*:

Darling, open up the door!

A woman's voice just as softly replied:

I won't, I won't, they'll hear next door!

And then my father put his arms around my mother and let loose his deep, full baritone:

If they hear, then let them hear—
They already know both far and near
That it's you alone I love
I love
You I'll be always
Thinking of.

It was well executed, and you could tell that my father was very pleased with himself.

"Come on in, then," he called out at last.

"We can't," replied a Gypsy voice, "iss shut."

"Oh, of course."

My father went and opened the door, laughing all the while. A ragged little Gypsy violinist tumbled into the kitchen.

He clicked his heels together smartly and drew his bow from under his arm like a soldier drawing his sword to present arms.

"Four Gypshies and a barrel of wine reportin' for duty, Shir!" he cried.

"And a hundred thousand onlookers!" my father rejoined with a laugh, because the walkway was by then crowded with people—the whole building had turned out for the show.

The Gypsies rolled the barrel through the door and my father called out to the masses:

"Grab a glass and form a queue!"

The Gypsies propped the barrel on a couple of kitchen stools and my father gave them each a glass of wine. It was nasty, sour wine, but wine nonetheless, an incredible amount of it—enough to get the whole house drunk. Back then, intoxication was cheap in Hungary—the ruling classes, like quack doctors, calming the convulsive misery of the people with palliatives rather than cures. Their intoxication came now from inside the barrel, and now from on top of it—they plied the people with wine and incitement, so they wouldn't sober up to the truth. The poor drunk went home and beat his wife, the people in uniform beat the "enemy", and they both only noticed afterwards that, oh dear, the people they'd beaten weren't the ones they'd meant to beat. "Forever young!" they'd been crying for centuries while the country slowly fell apart—and only very rarely because of anything the "enemy" had done. Here, peace was always more dangerous than war, because the bomb has yet to be invented that can do as much damage as poverty itself.

"Forever young!" cried the building, holding its glasses to the tap.

The band played and people got quickly drunk, because even a little is enough on an empty stomach. Even people who didn't care for it drank. It was a palliative for bitter wounds, and everyone there had some need of it. The devout Mátyás got drunk—who'd had even the Virgin taken from him—and so did his pretty wife, whom Herr Hausmeister no longer wanted. Little Rozi got drunk, who'd wanted a child so badly, as did old Máli, who killed babies on credit. Old Gábor got drunk, too, the coffin maker who'd have taken on the world to regain Hungary's lost territories, and even Áron the Sabbatarian got tipsy, though he believed only in the Kingdom of God. Mózes got drunk as well, who—despite his name—couldn't strike a rock and make the water flow, and so did his wife, who loved her Little Mózes so much she'd wanted to strangle him. Blind Samu got drunk and his seeing wife, and so did all the people who used to climb out through their window at night to go stealing, working for Herr Hausmeister for free by day. Everyone got drunk. The building was like a buzzing madhouse—no one was quite steady on their feet; even the walls, it seemed, were swaying.

Herr Hausmeister restrained himself for quite a long time. He was afraid of my father and must have reckoned that it would soon be midnight anyway, and then he'd finally be rid of this dangerous man. But the noise grew so great that he did, eventually, come poking out of his lair.

"Quiet!" he shouted, "or I'll call the police!"

That sobered up the drunken house a little. They quietened down for a few minutes, but then my father cried:

"What is this, a funeral?"

Áron tried to talk some sense into him, appealing to his better nature, telling him not to go bringing the police down on our necks—after all he knew full well that no one's affairs were quite in order, and if Herr Hausmeister got really angry, we'd get the worse of it.

"I'll go quiet him down a bit," said my father with an ominous smile, and was off.

I wanted to go after him, fearing there'd be trouble, but he was outside, and I was in, and the flat was so full of people that by the time I managed to make my way through the crowd, I could no longer see him anywhere. So I headed for the ground floor, but only got as far as the first. I heard terrific shouting from the courtyard.

I ran out onto the walkway to look. My father had got Herr Hausmeister down on the ground, tied his hands behind his back, and was stuffing his mouth with a rag. Then he tied his handkerchief over his eyes and, to shouts of joy from all three floors, dragged him up to the apartment.

The band played a drum roll as they entered, and a general hysteria came over the building. People were jumping about, dancing, shouting their heads off, clapping each other on the shoulder—they just didn't know what to do with themselves. My father jumped onto the table and dragged up Herr Hausmeister. He grabbed him by the neck, showing him off to the drunken crowd the way the criers used to show off the "cannibals" at the fair.

"Laydees and gentlemen!" he cried. "I give you the great cannibal chief, the amazin' savage who's stronger than us all. No illusions, ladies and gentlemen, this is the real thing. Come see for yourselves! This beast in human form can have your hides at any time. He makes men his slaves and women his concubines. He's stronger than the Devil, and more powerful than God. We all owe him somethin', and now, thanks to yours truly here, it's time to pay him back. Don't miss this once-in-a-lifetime opportunity! One blow per person, soldiers from the rank of sergeant down get two. Step right up, ladies and gentlemen, step right up! The entertainment has begun!"

That was all the wild crowd needed. All of them wanted to hit Herr

Hausmeister at once, but before they could get near him, my father jumped off the table and established order.

"Get in line, get in line!" he cried. "No favouritism here! This is a democracy!"

He got two people to hold Herr Hausmeister down and lined up the rest facing his backside.

Mátyás went first. He had spent a lifetime with a hammer, but I doubt he'd ever struck the anvil as hard as he now did Herr Hausmeister's backside. The building cheered his effort as the band played:

> *The Germans weep now in old Wien*
> *If only they had never been!*

"Cut it out!" my father yelled. "His being German ain't the problem, it's his heathen behaviour. The Germans ain't no worse than any other people—the problem, dear friends, is that sometimes they think they're *better*."

But his fine little speech did not have much effect. There was barracking from the back:

> *Never trust a German,*
> *Even if he sounds so certain!*

"That ain't how it goes," Mózes barked. "The way we sing it, it's different."
"How?"
"Out with it! Out with it!"

> *Workers, never trust the upper class*
> *Remember that they're talking out their arse!*
> *When there's trouble they make nice,*
> *and fetch the coppers so you pay the price!*
> *They'll let your children starve to death*
> *And as you're coughing out your final breath*
> *They'll cross themselves all holy*
> *And go to auction off your dead body!*

"Hear! hear!" they cried. "Hear! hear!"

The blows, meanwhile, resounded on Herr Hausmeister's backside. They'd have beaten the life out of him long before if my father hadn't been careful to make sure it was only his backside they could reach.

It was now old Áron's turn. Silence fell over the flat—everyone was curious to see what the Sabbatarian would do. He was no longer steady on his feet, either, and the alcohol seemed to have caught fire within him. His eyes were glowing, and his face burned with crimson patches—only his thin, transparent, vellum-like nose remained eerily white. He hiccoughed heavily, then leant down to Herr Hausmeister, who had his eyes still covered, and made the following, slightly slurred but nonetheless solemn speech:

"It's me, Áron, the Sabbatarian. Can you hear me, Herr Hausmeister? I'm not going to hit you, because I don't like people treatin' other people ill, but don't think it's because I'm on your side. I'm not on your side, you heathen, but on the Nazarene's. And I can tell you this is the kind of lesson they're going to teach the whole world if it don't turn to my Saviour in time."

"All right, all right," Mátyás's wife—thoroughly tipsy—said, shoving him aside. "Enough of the speeches, it's my turn."

With that, before my father could stop her, she flipped Herr Hausmeister round, quick as a flash, and kicked him where it most hurts a man. It must have been a hell of a kick because the big German fainted there and then, crashing to the floor.

"That's enough!" my father said. "He's got his deserts."

That was what saved Herr Hausmeister from being beaten to death, and meant that fifteen years later, as SS *Kommandant* of the concentration camp at B——, he could go on to murder innocents by the hundred. But now he was docile like anyone who's fainted, and a lot of people were starting to feel sorry for him. Áron and the one-eyed wheelwright picked him up off the floor and carried him out of the flat like a big sack.

"And now," my father called, "everyone go fetch your axes!"

I remember very clearly: no one asked why. They just went and fetched them. They would have fetched anything at that point, done anything. At that moment, they were capable of anything.

My father gathered the people with their axes around him.

"We've got ten minutes till midnight," he said. "In that time, I want you to shred every single thing in sight, so there ain't nothin' left for those dogs. I'd give you everything I got, friends, but they'd only come and take it off you again. This way, at least you get to burn it. Right, get to it!" he bellowed, and took such a whacking swing at the wardrobe with his axe that the rickety old thing fell to pieces there and then.

The drunken crowd had at the furniture and I could feel, I knew, as I watched their savage faces that they would have done the same to their fellow men if someone had told them to at that moment. They broke, and smashed, and devastated. There was finally something for all those unemployed men to do.

By midnight, the flat was empty. They'd rolled the barrel next door to Old Gábor's flat, and the people followed the wine.

Suddenly, I realized I was alone. I looked at the bare walls on which only a few light-coloured spots showed that the flat had ever had furniture and pictures in it, and—drunk as I was—I burst loudly into tears.

"What are you crying for?" I asked myself. "Was it all really so good?"

No, no it wasn't. It was more than that—three summers, three autumns, three winters. Creation, flood, heaven, hell: the first flush of youth. My father, whom I had first met here. My mother, who'd first cooked *székelygulyás* for me. Manci, who had taught me love and revulsion here, and something else besides, something vaguer that she herself was not conscious of. This was the door through which had stepped Patsy and joy, and it was here in this kitchen that my mother had drunk lye. This was where we'd played cards, drunk, sang, in that wild spring when the tooth fairy had had her birthday ever night. This was where we'd starved and revelled, sat up and dreamt, argued and made love. It was good. It was rough. It was life. We hounded each other, and worried for each other, we couldn't understand each other, but we loved each other—we were a family. And now it was over. They'd smashed something along with the furniture. Something had died that I could never again revive. I slumped against the bare wall and the salty tears flowed into my mouth; I shook with sobbing. And then I suddenly saw they'd forgotten something in the flat.

I shuddered. It was the bottle of lye. That was all that had survived the destruction, nothing else—only that. It hid beneath the water pipe, sinister and calculating, like a cunning beast, and as I looked at it blearily, it seemed almost to be baring its teeth. I swore loudly. Then I staggered out into the kitchen, picked up the bottle and threw it as hard as I could against the wall.

That sobered me up a little. I suddenly remembered my mother. Where was she? I had completely forgotten about her in all the commotion. Where was she? Where was she?

I ran out of the flat. The band was playing next door, and the drunken house was dancing and shouting for joy.

Where was my mother?

There was such a crowd at Old Gábor's that I couldn't get through the door. The window, too, was clogged with people wanting to see what was going on inside. It took me some time to make my way through the throng so I could finally get a look inside the apartment.

It was an eerie scene. Two enormous candles were burning in the middle of the room, with Old Gábor sitting under them in his coffin. He was waving a wine glass around above his head and kept singing at the top of his lungs:

> *If I die, I die*
> *Angels sing my lullaby*
> *If I croak, I croak*
> *The Devil take me in one stroke*

The band played and the couples, like madmen, were dancing the *csárdás* all around the coffin.

"Forever young!" they cried. "Forever young!"

The feet pounded, the candles flickered, and everything tottered and wobbled, dust flying everywhere.

"Forever young! Forever young!"

Out in the kitchen, people were banging saucepan lids in time to the music. Jóska, the watchmaker, was riding the wine barrel.

"Giddyap! Giddyap! Forever young!"

Skirts were flying, there was the smack of kisses, Rózsi even tore her shirt off.

"Forever young! Forever young!"

"Silence!" Áron bellowed, standing at the head of the coffin and lifting his thin arms to the sky in frenzy. "Can't you see, my brothers, that this is a funeral? On your knees! Reflect! This is the funeral for a whole world, a sinful and wicked world that…"

"Shut it!" Old Gábor yelled from inside his coffin. "Shut up, you damn saint!"

> *If I die, I die*
> *Angels sing my lullaby*
> *If I croak, I croak*
> *The Devil take me in one stroke*

I finally spotted my mother. She was dancing with my father, making merry like the rest, but when I saw her face I suddenly felt, I knew, that this merriness would end in tragedy. No, she would never go out into the Népliget with the homeless masses, not her. She was preparing to go somewhere different, somewhere quite different.

I was now completely sober. I had to do something, I told myself, I had to do something right away. Suddenly, I knew what.

The thought frightened me at first, but then I shrugged.

It doesn't matter.

None of it matters any more.

I've got to do it.

15

I SNEAKED IN THROUGH THE STAFF ENTRANCE. It must have been around three in the morning; the hotel was fast asleep. I slipped up to the second floor and stopped in front of the familiar door. The corridor was deserted, and there wasn't a sound from beyond the door, either. Was she asleep? Or…

I shuddered. It sounded like someone was walking around inside. Surely Exfix hadn't come back from Geneva? Or was she with someone else?

I listened intently. Nothing stirred now. It was so silent, I thought I could hear my heart thump.

What would I do if Exfix opened the door? Or if…

It doesn't matter.

None of it matters any more.

I knocked.

The echo in the corridor multiplied the sound frightfully. I waited in alarm. Nothing. Had she not heard? Or had she not wanted to hear?

Someone started coughing nearby. Had I woken her from her sleep? What if she came out and…

Let her come. Nothing mattered any more anyway. I knocked again.

Nothing. Nothing! The minutes passed and the empty corridor filled with alarming noises. Something buzzed, something rattled… but what?… and where? The silence was suffocating. Could I still be drunk?

I started banging on the door with my fists. A year before, on a chilly summer's evening, someone had banged on her door just like this. She'd just smiled. "He'll get tired eventually," she whispered, and then she'd gone on to whisper something else entirely—for we were lying in bed at the time, very drunk. Who was she whispering to now? I wondered. Was it Franciska?

Suddenly, I heard footsteps from the back stairs. I came out in a cold sweat. Who could that be at this hour? It couldn't be a guest. Only the staff used the back stairs. Was it the night watchman? Or the Major? I had bumped into him once before like this, near dawn. Only then, I'd been in my uniform and that man, for all his high morals, knew full well where I'd been. He hadn't asked. This time, he was bound to.

I didn't know what to do. The footsteps were approaching quickly. I grabbed the handle in panic. The door opened.

Inside, it was dark and quiet. I closed the door, quickly and silently, and listened, petrified. You could hear the footsteps even through the closed door. Fortunately, Cesar was not in the entrance hall. He must be asleep in Exfix's room, I thought, relieved. So the old man can't have come home after all.

Outside, silence fell, and I could no longer hear the steps. Had whoever it was stopped in front of the door? Or gone up to another floor?

I tiptoed to the door of the salon and peeked in through the keyhole. The light was on inside. In other words, she was home.

I knocked. No answer. Eventually, I went in.

The room was bathed in a greenish half-light, like in some thriller. Silence. Not a soul. Only the little green-shaded standing lamp was burning in a corner, night-time insects buzzing all around it. The wind blew in through the open balcony doors, the curtains billowed in the dusk.

Had she come home drunk? That's when she usually slept so deeply. Or was she awake? Were *they* awake?

It didn't matter. Nothing mattered any more. I headed for the bedroom.

The door was not quite closed. I peeped in through the crack. No one. The bed was empty, the bathroom dark. Was she out? Or...

I sneaked over to Exfix's room and listened for a long time at the closed door. There was some sort of gentle wheezing from inside. Cesar?... Of course it was. Who else could it have been? I was really starting to lose it.

I looked at the clock. Quarter past three. She should be home any minute now. What would she say when she came home and found me here? I'm so sorry, Your Excellency, for disturbing you at this hour. It's my mother, you see, and a matter of life and death, and... Rubbish!

What did she care about my mother's life? That was no good. It was silly and all over the place. I had to be simpler, more direct. After all, it was just a question of a loan. What was a hundred pengős to her? Five bottles of champagne. She'd paid two hundred and fifty for a dress she ended up giving to a maid. Here's two hundred and fifty pengős, Muther, we're bound to find somewhere to live with that.

I was dizzy, frighteningly so. All that wine, the food, the excitement, had gone to my head, and my bowels were constricting convulsively. I sank shivering into a chair with a cold chill.

Then I was no longer aware of anything. I thought I'd just nodded off for a couple of minutes, but when I looked at the clock, I was horrified to find it was a quarter to four. She might not even be coming home. And I was just sitting there and dozing, while my mother...

Oh my God, how could I have left her alone! I shouldn't have left her side all evening; I should have dragged her with me to town in the morning. A guest has promised us two hundred and fifty pengős, Muther. If you just wait for me outside the hotel, I'll bring it right down and then you can go and start looking for a flat. Yes, that's what I should have said, or rather...

I jumped up. It's not too late! If I ran straight home, I'd be bound to find her still at Old Gábor's. Off I ran.

I only got as far as the entrance hall. I heard *her* voice from outside. She was talking to a man, their steps approaching fast. She wasn't bringing someone home, was she?

I sneaked back and ran desperately from room to room. I didn't know where to hide. Under the bed? No, that was no good, it was very low. The wardrobe? Nah, she's bound to open that.

In the end I ran out onto the balcony and hid in the corner behind the deck chair. By that time, the front door was open, and you could hear her laughter from the hall. It was a strange laugh with tiny, hoarse, strained trills, the way she always laughed when she was drunk.

They headed straight for the balcony. They cast long shadows from the room as they passed by the window and then, suddenly, there she was in the balcony door.

"At last, a bit of fresh air," she said, and held her face to the wind. "What heat… phew!"

She leant unsteadily against the door frame, fanning herself, her head thrown back.

"Give me a cigarette," she called inside. "The box is on the table, see it?"

"Yes," replied the man, bringing the box.

I didn't want to believe my eyes. The "man" I had pictured as a gentleman in tails was actually a sixteen- or seventeen-year-old Gypsy boy, one of those unfortunate, ragged scamps who hung around outside the cabarets and bars all night and would play a few bars for the well-to-do as they rushed out to their cars, hoping for a few coins, till the police or a doorman moved them on. He was still clutching his violin under his arm, and you could tell he didn't understand what was going on. He was a handsome Gypsy lad, his face a dusky brown, fire in his eyes.

She looked at him with a sultry little half-smile.

"Have one yourself," she said in that high voice of hers, and stuck a cigarette in his mouth.

The Gypsy boy grinned, out of his depth, nonplussed.

"Missus," he whispered, "ain't there going to be trouble?"

Her Excellency laughed.

"What kind of trouble?"

"I dunno," he shrugged, "this is… such… such a… such a fancy hotel," he muttered, "and I thought, um… when you was asking me into that great fine car, that there was a dance and you wanted me to play for yous, and… and missus has had a lot to drink… and I don't want no trouble."

"Silly!" she said, and touched the tip of his nose playfully with her finger. "Give me a light."

The boy dug some matches out of his pocket nervously. She held her cigarette for him as if she were offering her mouth and as she leant forward, her breast touched the Gypsy boy. The match trembled in his hands, and his big black eyes caught flame with excitement. She blew her smoke into his face and laughed soundlessly.

"You're a handsome boy," she said, out of the blue, and drew the violin out from under his arm with a slow, dreamy motion, laying it down on the deck chair. "Come, let's have a drink," she whispered, and, taking him by the arm, took the boy inside.

My limbs were numb from squatting so long. Now that they'd finally gone inside, I moved, but so clumsily that I lost my balance and ended up shoving the deck chair.

"D'you hear that?" the Gypsy boy started.

"What?" she asked while—to judge from the noise—shaking a cocktail.

"There's somebody out there for sure," the lad whispered, terrified.

"Oh, pish!" she laughed. "It must be the balcony next door. Come on, let's have a drink. Cheers!"

"Your health."

I lay low in the dark like a frog playing dead. I was covered in sweat, hardly daring to breathe.

Inside, there was silence for a while. Then:

"Missus!"

"What is it?"

"There's somebody out there, sure as anything."

"Don't be silly."

"I swear!" the lad insisted. "Have a look."

I heard her get up and approach the balcony. My heart skipped a beat. I was sure she'd spot me, but she barely stuck her nose out the door.

"No," she said, "there's no one here."

With that, she went inside and locked the door.

It was a dark and stuffy night, lightning flashing in the sky above the Buda hills. A warm, humid wind whipped the textile shade covering the balcony, the Danube growling menacingly below.

Time passed. I had no idea what time it was. All I could hear through the closed door was the odd word here and there, the clinking of glasses, her laughter. All the while, I was picturing my mother slipping away from the dancers, spiriting Old Gábor's kitchen knife away beneath her blouse when no one was looking. Inside, they'd be dancing the *csárdás*, the Gypsies playing wildly, as suddenly the drunken house woke to a terrible scream. The wailing sirens of the ambulance, the clatter of the running policeman's sword, a crowd gathering, faces pale as they carry a black coffin down the stairs.

I was so helpless, I almost burst into tears. I had to get out of there. I had to go home before it was too late! But how, how?

About thirty or forty minutes must have gone by like this. Then the door sprang open and I was shocked to see the Gypsy boy come out on the balcony. Alone. Without *her*.

Inside, there was silence, deathly silence. The Gypsy boy kept moving about the balcony, all het up—he sat down, got up, couldn't stay still.

Where was she? What had happened? I was overcome by the terror of long-forgotten village nights, those nerve-wracking winter nights when the old women told us tales of bloodthirsty Gypsies as we shucked the corn. I was beginning to think that Her Excellency was lying dead on the floor inside when suddenly I heard her voice from within.

"Gazsi!" she cooed.

"Yes, missus."

"Come have a bath, too."

My stomach cramped up horribly. So she made everyone take a bath before. How proper.

The Gypsy went running. I could have a word with her while he was having his bath, I thought. I knew, of course, that it was hardly the best moment, but what could I do? It didn't matter. None of it mattered any more.

I crawled in from the balcony on all fours. There was no one in the salon. I crawled across the thick carpet noiselessly, listening, sniffing the air, like a beast in the wild. The bedroom door was open, and she was standing there in a dressing gown before the bed, her back to me. There was a light on on the night table, jewellery flashing underneath. Just one of those little trinkets could save my mother's life, I thought.

At this point, the water started gushing in the bathroom, splashing loudly. There was no chance of him overhearing me now, I told myself, and stood up slowly, carefully. She threw off her dressing gown and climbed naked into bed. By then, I was standing in the bedroom door. She screamed, terrified.

"Shh!" I hissed and was beside the bed in a single leap. "Quiet!" Fear sobered her up.

"What are you doing here?" she demanded quietly.

I was incapable of giving her an answer in my excitement, though I had been rehearsing feverishly what I was going to say to her since the moment I'd left home. God knows how many versions I'd come up with, but none of them now came to me. All I could say, awkward and stammering, was:

"Give me two hundred and fifty pengős."

She raised her head angrily but, it seems, thought better of it. Her voice was almost calm when she spoke.

"How much?"

"Two hundred and fifty," I repeated, slightly relieved. I'll take a taxi, I thought, that way it may not be too late.

She reached into the nightstand and slowly lifted her eyes to mine.

"Blackmail, is it?" she asked softly, hoarsely, a small, pearl-handled revolver flashing in her hands. "Well, you're barking up the wrong tree, you dirty peasant!" she whispered, aiming the pistol at me. "Clear off!"

"Please," I stammered, "please hear me out… I—"

"Clear off!" she repeated. "Get out of here before I shoot you like a dog."

I could see it was no use.

"So shoot me, then!" I cried. "I'm not leaving here till I get that money."

She had clearly not been expecting that. She hesitated for a moment or two, and then, quick as a cat, sprang to the other side of the bed and scrambled for the telephone. As she did so, I grabbed a diamond ring off the nightstand and was gone.

I didn't hear what she said, or if she'd made the call at all. I ran headlong down the back stairs and out of the staff entrance. There was a taxi just passing, so I clambered on and gave him the address of our pawnshop.

"Hurry!" I cried. "There's an extra pengő in it for you."

I had all of fifty fillérs. No matter, I thought. Maybe it's still not too late.

The car hurried through the deserted streets. We were in Újpest in half an hour.

"Wait for me," I said to the driver outside the pawnshop. "Back in a minute."

The gate was still locked. I leant on the bell impatiently. I must have been in a hell of a state because the sleepy old Hausmeister gave me a very suspicious look.

"Who for?"

"The pawnshop."

"Now? In the middle of night?"

"It's a family thing," I muttered. "It's urgent."

With that, I handed him the money and went in. I would have gone in if the way led over his dead body—by that time, nothing mattered to me any more.

I crossed the courtyard and rang the pawnbroker's bell. The fish-faced little old man shuffled to the door in his shirt and underpants. When he saw me, he was absolutely furious.

"How dare you wake me up at this hour?" he snapped at me in his high-pitched wail.

"It's urgent," I said, panting. "It's for a guest."

The old man stared at me with his bleary fish-eyes.

"A guest? What guest?"

"A guest at the hotel," I spat testily, and pulled the ring out of my pocket.

Fish-face looked at it, examined it, and his face suddenly changed. He gave me a flat look.

"Why's it so urgent?"

"They need the money."

"Hm," he muttered, with a crafty look, holding the diamond to the light.

"Please hurry," I said impatiently. "There's a taxi waiting."

The fish-eyes fixed their gaze on me.

"Taxi? So you're taking taxis now?"

I felt myself blush.

"The guest is paying for it."

666

"Hm," he muttered again, and then gestured for me to follow him.

He shuffled silently through a narrow entrance hall that smelt of onions and took me into the pawnshop through the back entrance. He put on the light, sat down, took out a magnifying glass and turned the ring this way and that beneath it.

"How much does the guest want for it?" he asked.

Today, I know that "the guest" would have wanted four or five thousand pengős for it, but at the time, I had no idea how much it was worth. So I tried to avoid answering.

"How much would you give them, sir?"

But sir did not take the bait.

"I asked how much the guest wants for it."

I thought it must be worth a hundred pengős, so I said:

"Two hundred."

"Two hundred?"

Fish-face gave an odd grin. I thought I'd asked too much.

"Oh all right," I said testily, "make it one fifty."

"I don't keep that much cash around at night," he replied, but instead of giving me back the ring, he took it and headed for the door.

"Where are you going?"

"I'm going to call my brother-in-law," he muttered. "He might be able to give me a loan."

I didn't like where this was going. If I'd listened to my instincts, I would have grabbed the ring back from him and run off. But where? I asked myself, where? The city was still sleeping, the pawnbrokers wouldn't open for hours, and by then it might be too late to save my mother, even with all of Darius's gold. Besides, Fish-face hadn't even waited for my answer, he'd just left. So what could I do? I shrugged. No matter. None of it mattered now.

The old man came back a few minutes later and gave me an encouraging smile.

"He'll be right here."

"With the money?"

"Yes."

And soon enough, the bell rang. The old man shuffled out to get the door and I looked at the clock, relieved. A quarter past five. They must still be dancing. I'll be home in ten minutes.

A portly policeman with a handlebar moustache appeared in the door.

"Come along, come along!" he snapped at me.

"Where?" I asked dimly.

"Don't answer back!" he roared. "Shut your trap and come along!"

"But, sir," I scrambled desperately, "I have to get home, I—"

"You won't be going home for a while," he growled, and headed straight for me, stinking of booze.

"But officer," I pleaded, backing away, "hear me out! My mother... my mother—"

There was a terrific blow, the policeman heaved me out, and the rest I can only remember like a chaotic dream. Curious faces. The hausmeister grumbling that he could "tell right away". The driver screaming for me to pay him. A search, swearing, blows upon blows. The policeman heaving me into the van. The van speeding along. The van stopping. The policeman heaving me out of the van, heaving me through a door. Steps, corridor, doors, faces, uniforms. Shoved into a room. A clock on the wall. The big hand touching eleven. Five to six. Inside, everyone's still dancing, doing the *csárdás*, the violinist's still playing, and suddenly the drunken house wakes to a terrible scream...

"What you crying for?" someone shouted. "Answer me, damn it, or I'll tear your head off!"

I started. A sleepy, moon-faced man sat opposite me, holding out Her Excellency's ring in my direction. I looked at him as if I really had only just woken up from a dream.

"What?"

"Don't what me, you little shit. Whose is this ring?"

I told him. The sleepy little man was suddenly so awake, it was as if I'd said the magic word. He was a poor, pathetic little detective, a servant of the Royal Hungarian State, and there was not a single servant of the Royal Hungarian State who wouldn't have liked to get to know Exfix. The poor man could hardly disguise his delight—he must already have been picturing himself being bumped up a pay grade. He wanted to know all about Their Excellencies, absolutely everything there was to know. Smacking his lips like a curious cow, he kept ruminating on completely irrelevant details while the clock on the wall just kept ticking and ticking. Six, six fifteen, six thirty… They'd be carrying out the coffin by now.

Finally, he called the hotel, but no matter how he insisted, they wouldn't connect him with Her Excellency. She had bigger fish to fry.

"What time does she usually get up?" he asked.

"Around eleven."

"So we'll talk more then," he said with an ominous smile, gesturing to the policeman to take me away. "Bring him back at eleven."

Eleven!… Jesus Christ!… Eleven!!

The policeman shoved me into a little cell that stank unbelievably, crammed full of Hungary's more modest class of criminal. There was an old woman in her seventies, grinding away at her rosary and mumbling, and there was a fifteen-year-old streetwalker talking about the practical and financial aspects of her trade with the dispassionate air of an accountant. There was a fancy bourgeois who, nose and trousers upturned, showed off his silk socks and superiority, and there was a half-naked ragged tramp covered all over in a black varnish of filth. There was a grave old worker, moustache flecked with grey, who just stood and watched this babbling mass in silence, and there was a loud-mouthed little hellraiser who'd pinched a couple of pengős out of another passenger's pocket on the tram and was now acting as if he'd robbed the central bank. They were small fry who'd taken the bait through hunger, while the great whites pored over the civil code and devoured half the country with the connivance of the government.

We were all waiting for questioning. The door would open from time to time, the policeman call out a name, and someone would make their way through the crowd and exit, pale. There was an appalling racket. Next to me, a young safecracker was arguing with two of his more senior colleagues. He was berating them for not moving with the times—you couldn't do things that way any more, he'd said so right from the start. A whiny young woman with greasy hair was breastfeeding a baby on her shrivelled chest, there was some sort of gambling going on in secret at the back, while the prophet of some banned religious sect kept quoting from the Bible and promising an imminent Flood. Then there was the hell of a fuss, because one of the drunks started throwing up—everyone tried to flee the tottering figure—some woman got a fit of hysterics in the melee. She started battering on the door, foaming at the mouth and screaming for them to let her out, she was suffocating. A policeman came in, whacked her round the head with his truncheon; she stopped screaming.

Slowly, it grew light. The light filtered through the window like sewage, a greyish-green. The safecracker fell asleep standing up and snored gently, propped against me.

Suddenly, I had the unpleasant feeling of being watched. I looked around. On the other side of the cell were three lads who looked like apprentices—I hadn't even noticed them in the general throng. When I turned to look at them, they snatched their gazes away, but from then on there was a vague, unsettling connection between us, though we didn't look at each other again. It was some link you couldn't put into words, an almost electric flow, like between antennas on the same wavelength. They were quiet, serious lads, the way you could be in your teens, especially if you'd been born working class in Hungary and they hadn't beaten the wonder out of you yet. I kept sneaking glances at them out of the corner of my eye, the way I used to do with guests in the hotel, and I occasionally saw that they, too, were looking at me. Later, they conferred in a whisper and one of them came over.

"Comrade?" he asked softly.

The word coursed through me like a wave of warmth.

"Yes," I nodded.

He gave me his hand, we smiled.

"When did they get you?"

"Just this morning, at dawn."

"Us too," he whispered. "We were distributing flyers. You doing underground work too?"

"No."

"What, then?"

I flushed hot all over. I'd never been so ashamed in my life.

"I… um… a ring," I muttered. "I needed the money, and…"

His face changed so suddenly, I couldn't even finish the sentence. The words stuck in my throat and stifled me—I couldn't talk any more. He didn't say anything, just stood there beside me for a while and then went back to his friends. I knew they were talking about me, and I didn't dare look.

I stood there like someone who's just been sentenced. Till then, I hadn't felt guilty, the way a soldier doesn't feel guilty if he's captured by the enemy. This was class war, and I was a soldier of the proletariat: at least, so I'd thought so far. All of a sudden, I woke up to the truth. A soldier of the proletariat?—big words, you stupid peasant, big words indeed. The reality was something smaller, more humble, something like these quiet, grave working-class boys who distributed flyers at night and put up with the humiliation, with prison, all the horrors, and went and did it again the next day. Yes, they were soldiers of the proletariat. They fought, they *did* something, but you… what had you done? Steal. They were in jail as prisoners of war, dragged from the trenches, but you… you were nothing but a common thief caught in the act, a run of the mill, pathetic, third-rate little crook. I despised myself, I despised them, I despised the whole world.

"Get off me!" I snapped at the safecracker and shoved him off me furiously.

Something had broken, I no longer knew what I was doing. The safecracker, of course, woken from his sleep, pushed back, and I punched him in the face so hard his nose began to bleed.

At that moment, the door opened and the policeman called out my name. Your turn next, moon-face! I thought to myself. You're going to get it, you're all going to get it. None of it mattered now anyway.

But moon-face greeted me, all smiles.

"Here, you little crook, you've got more luck than brains, know that?"

I didn't know what he was getting at, and scanned his grinning face suspiciously.

"Luck? What luck?"

"That Her Excellency doesn't want to get bogged down in a seedy little affair like this. She told me to turn you loose."

I couldn't believe my ears.

"You mean you're letting me go?"

"On one condition," he said. "If you promise never to set foot in that hotel again."

"Yes, sir," I muttered.

"Promise?"

"Promise."

"All right, then," he nodded. "You can go. But if you ever show your face in the hotel again, Her Excellency will have you arrested on the spot. Got it?"

"Yes, sir."

"Get out of here."

He didn't have to tell me twice. I got out of there all right, and went straight home.

The closer I got to the house, the slower I went, and the faster beat my heart. The neighbourhood was deserted and the house squatted like a lonely camel in the desert of vacant plots. There was a cart outside the gate, packed with elderly, frail, swaying furniture. Three ragged little boys were busying themselves about the cart while a man, clearly their father, carried the dining table through the gate. They were moving in. They were moving into our flat.

"Who're you after?" the smallest of the boys asked with the superior air of a resident. He must have been about five and consumptive.

I didn't reply. At that moment, I despised even this five-year-old. They were moving into our flat!

"I live here," declared the boy proudly. "Don't believe me?"

"Get lost," I growled at him, looking anxiously to the gate to see if Herr Hausmeister was around.

"I do live here, and all!" he insisted. "'Cause, you see," he added gleefully, "the tram took mother's leg off and they gave us three hundred pengős for it, so we're rich now and don't have to live out in the bushes no more. I'm sleepin' indoors tonight! Don't believe me?"

"I do," I mumbled, ashamed, still staring at the gate. "D'you know Herr Hausmeister?"

"The big puffy one?"

"Him. Go in and see if he's around. Don't say I sent you."

"As if," he said with a conspiratorial smile and a dismissive wave, and went running into the house. A minute later he was back, panting, and said: "He ain't there."

I sneaked up to the first floor and knocked on the Sabbatarian's door. He answered, dishevelled and bleary-eyed, but when he saw me, he grew disconcertingly alert. He kept glancing around anxiously, and his face grew pale beneath his ginger beard.

"Morning, Béla."

"Mornin', Áron."

That was all we said. Then there was a silence. He was clearly waiting for me to start, while I just looked at his strange, anxious face and didn't know where to begin.

"Have… have you been to the hospital?" he asked at last.

"Where?!"

"It's all right, calm down!" he blurted hurriedly. "She was still alive when they put her in the ambulance. I swear she was alive. I was standing right there beside her."

"What happened?"

"You mean you don't know?"

"No."

The Sabbatarian took a deep breath. Then he told me.

"She jumped."

"Off the third floor?"

"Yes."

"Jesus Christ!"

Áron took me by the arm, sat me down and ran out to fetch some water. When he got back, I was on my feet again.

"Is my father at the hospital?"

"No."

"Where is he, then?"

"I don't know. He skipped from the coppers."

"They wanted to get him?"

"Yes. Herr Hausmeister reported him. We were all still dancing when they burst in. The copper was almost face to face with your pa

673

when he flicked off the light. By the time we got it on again, he was nowhere to be seen."

"He doesn't know about mother?"

"No. That happened later. Suddenly, in all the commotion, there was this terrible scream, and…"

Áron did not finish the sentence. He stared straight ahead, shaking his thin, Christ-like face in silence. You could hear, from outside, Herr Hausmeister shouting. He was arguing with the new tenant for having scraped the wall with his furniture.

Áron looked at me.

"Do you have somewhere to sleep?"

"No."

"Well, you can't come here. Herr Hausmeister would get you too."

"I know."

There was silence once more. Áron went to the wardrobe, pulled open one of the drawers, and rummaged around. Then he came back and pressed two pengős into my hand.

"That's all I've got," he said quietly. "It's so hard these days. God bless, my boy."

"God bless, Áron," I muttered, but just stood there, not moving.

"You have to go," he said. "They won't let you in the hospital later."

So I went. My legs still worked, but my brain did not. I have no recollection of that journey. I don't know how I got to the hospital—I didn't know even at the time. But all of a sudden, there I was in the on-call doctor's room, the same one I had waited in so long one early morning with my father. This time, I didn't have long to wait.

"She bled out in the ambulance," the doctor told me. "You can go see her in the morgue, if you want."

"Yes, please," I nodded, and started laughing loudly, as if he'd made some terrifically funny joke.

Then I fainted.

16

WHEN I CAME TO, THE DOCTOR put a form in front of me. "Sign this."

"Yes, sir."

The form was a receipt for the "personal items of the deceased". I had to acknowledge that I had received them in good order and had no further claims.

The doctor handed me a tiny envelope containing the "personal items of the deceased". A thin little gold necklace, a battered little cross. My mother had got it from her mother, my grandmother from hers, and my great-grandmother from… who knows? It was an old cross, a lot of people had worn it. Now it was my turn. They'd left me their cross, and I had signed for it. Did I really have no further claim?

The doctor was getting impatient.

"Well?" he asked. "Everything in order?"

In order?… I didn't reply. I tramped out with the cross. The cross grew warm in my hand, my hand clenching into a fist. No, Doctor, nothing was in order. Nothing, nothing at all.

I looked at the better-dressed in the street as if they'd all, every last one of them, been my mortal enemies. There was my mother, lying dead inside, and out here the world belonged to her murderers. And I had no further claim?

I stared viciously out at the city. It was a fine, bright day. The sky was blue, the grass was green, the dogs barked, the poor starved, it was all so neat and tidy. Whoever could take it, took it, and whoever couldn't threw themselves off the third floor. Wealth paraded its fat backside, and the coppers' white-gloved hands never wandered far from their holsters. It was orderly and quiet in the city. The system moved along soundlessly in its preordained orbit, like some exclusive, alien firmament to whom the earth's prosaic laws did not apply.

I looked out at this neat, upper-class order and thought of that blossoming spring morning when Gyula had severed his artery with the pig knife. The hotel, too, was steeped in just that kind of neat, upper-class order. Most people didn't even know about Gyula, and the people who did never said a word, because anyone with any brains didn't go around sticking their nose into other people's business, and besides, why go looking for trouble with the big shots? They sneaked the bloodless corpse out of the back door and then went back to the guests, saying nothing. And they, too, were silent, even as the country bled to death.

I shivered—I must have had a fever. I swayed onto a bench, trembling with cold. Behind me, on a café terrace, a group were laughing uproariously. I heard a familiar voice and couldn't resist turning round. It was the Count from my village. Our gazes met, but the Count didn't recognize me. The Count wouldn't have recognized me even if I'd gone up to him, because the Count did not know his peasants. But I know you, I said to myself, I know you all right, you laughing Count. Berci died because you paid his father less for a week's work than you're about to spend on lunch. Berci walked barefoot to school in winter, and his stomach would rumble so loudly that when we wrote a test in class and it was quiet, you could hear it clearly. But you just keep on laughing—what was Berci's life to you? Your conscience is clear. You know there isn't a court in the land that would convict you. You're innocent, and you laugh. Just you keep laughing, then. I can see your laughing head on a spike. I can see the new György Dózsa leading his peasants in revolt to the castles of the Counts. When that moment came, heads would roll, and…

Hadn't I heard that somewhere before? Heads would roll… Who was it who'd said that? Wait a sec. The Constable? No. Or rather… yes. He was quoting Hitler. Was I really saying the same thing as Hitler?

There was a frightened silence within me. The Gypsy violinist in the café was playing "The Blue Danube". They wanted our heads and we wanted theirs. Good God, where would this end? Our hearts were ticking bombs, tomorrow they'd blow up the town, the country, the world perhaps, and this lot just sat there listening to the music, trying to digest their unbelievable apathy in three-four time. They're murderers and don't even know it. Or…

I couldn't keep my head up any more. It bobbed down onto my chest and my eyes closed. I woke to find a policeman shaking me by the shoulder.

"You can't sleep here!" he squawked. "If you want to sleep, go home."

"Home?…"

I laughed.

"What you laughing at?" he snapped.

"Nothing," I muttered, and slunk off silently.

My teeth were chattering with the fever. Where was I to go?… They'd chased me out of the apartment. They'd chased me out of the hotel, too, and the police wouldn't even tolerate me on a bench.

Is this how it was going to be from now on? Yes, it was going to be like this, and worse. At least until now I'd had a roof over my head, a job, a purpose, a home, and even when I went hungry, I went hungry with my parents. But now?… My mother was in the morgue, Elemér in prison, and my father who knows where. Where did I have to go? Who did I have to turn to? The Constable? Well, yes, at least he was keen. They'd formed the National Socialist Party not long ago, and I could go far there. Only he, too, would soon realize that he'd overestimated my capacity for betrayal, and then he'd have me blacklisted and I would never get another job again—even if there were jobs to be had.

What was there left for me? The Népliget, and crime, and slowly falling to pieces. What was it Menyhért had said? *In a world like ours, you can only be two things. A revolutionary or a crook.* If only they hadn't arrested Imre… If I could fight for something better, finer. But now? It was all so pointless. I was seventeen and had already been locked up twice. I had stolen, and very nearly killed someone. What was I waiting for? Wouldn't it be better if I threw myself off the third floor, too?

"No!" I said so loudly that people turned around in the street. "No, no, no!"

I was not a thief. I was not a killer. Why should I sentence myself to death? *They're* the killers, and I won't let them get rid of me the way they did troublesome witnesses. I'm going to live, I'm going to show

677

them, and I will be an accusation and a proof, and I will never shrink from the fight till the eyes of the world were finally open!

Don't carry on so! my peasant's common sense told me. What's all this about accusation and proof and fighting? When you get very sleepy, you'll go out to the park just the same, because a man has to sleep, and when you get very hungry, you'll steal too, because a man has to eat. And *you* want to change the world? Please. Don't be so childish.

Was I being childish?… Who knows? The apple has always fallen off the tree, since time immemorial, and people always thought it natural—until someone came along, a certain Isaac Newton, and asked: why does the apple have to fall off the tree? Don't be so childish, the sober and resigned told him, too. But today, what even the most serious and grown-up of physics teachers teaches is derived from Newton's childish question.

Well, dear fellows, I will not be resigned! Last night, you shook me out of the social tree and I should now, like a fallen apple, be rolling downhill like every other apple, to rot slowly in a ditch. But I'm a different kind of apple, ladies and gentlemen! I'm going to rebel against the tree and bite its rotten trunk and, if needs be, I'll claw out its roots tooth and nail. You're not going to get rid of me that easily. I'm not going out to the park to starve. I'm not going to steal. I'm not going to go to pieces.

What, then? asked my peasant's common sense, and there was a chilling silence. I stopped and stood stock-still for minutes. It was those few minutes that decided the rest of my life.

Suddenly, I heard my own voice. I said:

"Out, out of here!"

I must have said it aloud, because someone turned around to look at me and laughed. Go ahead and laugh, I said to myself. You're all so clever and so reasonable, you know everything, always looking at the facts. But I *believe* in something, and that's worth more. I'm not going to rot among you. I'm getting out of here, because my home is where the Elemérs of this world walk free and the killers are the ones in prison.

I walked faster and faster, scared I wouldn't catch up to my thoughts. I walked for hours like this, practically in a trance. The sky grew bitter meanwhile, a shower pelted the streets, but I just kept walking. My fever must have been through the roof. I was sweating buckets, I was on fire, and I was chattering with cold. I had the feeling that my feet were not quite on the pavement, but a centimetre or two above.

All at once, I found myself by the banks of the Danube. I stood there like a dripping tomcat in a storm, and stared, immobile, at the boat to Vienna. By tomorrow, it would be in Austria, and in Austria, there were other boats that went other places.

If only I could get on it!… If only it would take me out of here!…

I was struck by the raw, adventurous scent of the ship's fumes, and I was once more consumed by that old, shivering magic that would come to me as a boy on summer evenings when the smell of the train smoke would float over on the wind. Go, go, go! the old desire piped up once more. Escape the fate I'd been assigned. To go look for the Easter egg of happiness, that some mythical god had perhaps hidden for me somewhere too.

Words buzzed inside my fevered brain—strange, beguiling words, as if bees from another world were bringing me their sweet and bitter honey. I hadn't slept in thirty-six hours, hadn't eaten in twenty-four, I must have had a forty-degree fever, and instead of looking for a dry corner to hole up in like a sick dog, I just stood there in the wind and the rain and wrote a poem about the Easter eggs of happiness, that some playful god had hidden so that people had to keep on chasing and chasing them all the way to the grave.

I had forgotten about everything except the poem when something unexpected happened. It struck me with the force of a miracle, though it was a very everyday miracle indeed. A paper boy ran up onto the boat.

"*Nyolcórai, Kurír, Magyarország!*" he called, and the guards just let him by.

I started running. I was borne by the will to live, desire, desperation or something else, something more mysterious, for which there are no words. I took all my money, bought some papers in the street, and hightailed it back.

"*Nyolcórai, Kurír, Magyarország!*" I called too, and suddenly noticed I was on the boat.

I shouted myself hoarse hawking the papers, trying feverishly to explore. I ran down the narrow, darkened corridors not knowing where. It was the first time in my life that I'd been on board a "real" ship, and I didn't know what was where and what did what. I just kept trundling along, panting, heart thumping, along masses of stairs, corridors and decks, as if I really had been looking for the Easter egg of happiness. The boat seemed stunningly large, and yet I still couldn't find a tiny nook in it where I could hide from a hostile world.

The departure bell rang, and they chased everyone who wasn't travelling off. I ran around frantically, trying to slip through, but in the end was collared by a boatman.

"You deaf?" he hollered. "Can't you hear we're going? Get lost!"

"Yes, sir," I replied, but to myself, I said: "Fat chance."

As soon as he'd turned away, I turned too and ran like a rabbit from a hunter. Out, out of here! I cried inside. Out of here. I didn't have enough money in my pockets to get me to the next village, but it seems it's not only what's in your pockets that'll get you places. A wonderful feeling of certainty now came over me, that mysterious power and equilibrium of the soul that leads sleepwalkers safely along the edges of rooftops. It was a kind of sober drunkenness, some waking trance that I had only felt while writing poems. I knew now, too, that this was the moment, that I couldn't stop while I heard the music, that I had to find the rhyme of my life before the fever and the magic passed.

The third bell had gone when I reached the upper deck. I looked around. Not a soul. The slanting, heavy shower battered the deck loudly, and I had to keep holding on so I didn't get blown away by the wind. The anchor was already clanking its way up in the bow, the captain might reach the bridge at any moment, and I knew that I'd stick out a mile here on deck. I was heading for the stairs to go back down below when I noticed that one of the stacks wasn't smoking. My heart throbbed. I could see that it wasn't a real smokestack but had just been put there next to the real one to make things look symmetrical. I almost shouted with joy.

You might well smile. That night I, too, realized that many before me—rather too many, in fact—had discovered this little ruse of the shipbuilding industry, but at the time, I had no idea and climbed into the stack with the bliss of ignorance. It was narrower than I thought, I could barely squeeze in. I kept stretching my neck like a giraffe and panting for breath. A few minutes later, I had to pull my head in, too, because two hooded figures appeared on the bridge and the stack was right opposite them. But what did I care! I could hear the floor begin to vibrate beneath me. The siren sounded like a clamouring beast, and somewhere below someone struck up the "Rákóczi March". The ship was off, and I was on board.

I felt completely safe. After all that tension, my nerves relaxed completely and a heavy, dazed feeling of calm came over me. My fever rocked me slowly to sleep, and I slept safe for hours in the knowledge that no harm could come to me till Vienna.

I woke with a start because I couldn't breathe. Something heavy and large came tumbling down onto my head, blocking off the opening of the stack. My first instinct was to try and push it out, but I couldn't move inside the narrow stack, and when I remembered my situation, I no longer dared to, either. I could feel that there was some kind of bag above me, and though I didn't know much about merchant or other kinds of shipping, I knew enough to suspect that baggage wasn't usually stored in the smokestack. So who had put it there, and why?

Was there someone outside, watching over it?

I felt on the verge of suffocation, but I still did not dare move. I don't know how long I must have spent like this—every minute is sixty calvaries at times like this.

Suddenly, I heard footsteps.

"It's in here," a man's voice whispered just outside.

"Take it out," whispered back another. "Customs are bound to check in there. There's a place in the kitchen where…"

I didn't catch the rest. The bag and the two men disappeared. I gulped the fresh air greedily.

It was pitch black. The rain had stopped, but a damp wind that smelt of fish howled around the smokestack and the starless sky was black above me. Where were we?… By this point, I knew, of course, that I had to find a better hiding place before we reached the border. But how was I going to get out of here?

I peeked out cautiously. The captain was pacing the bridge with his hands behind his back. I yanked my head back in.

Minutes, or possibly hours, went by. Occasionally, I heard the captain's voice as he called a command into the speaking-tube, and then there was silence once more. Beneath me the Danube growled, above me the wind was howling, and I had no idea where we were, how long I'd slept, or what time it was.

Suddenly, the siren sounded and the boat slowed. Commands were barked, there was busy toing and froing, steps resounded on deck. We docked.

"Gönyű!" a voice called. "Border control!"

My heart stopped. I knew it was now or never. Either I got out of here and made it through the controls, or... I didn't even dare finish the thought. Their dragging me back from here and having to start all over again... no, no, no! I'd rather jump in the Danube, or tear open the border guard's throat, or...

My attention was captured by something. The deck went quiet. I listened carefully for a while, then peeped out of the opening of the stack. The bridge was empty. Slowly, carefully, I stuck my head out. Silence, darkness, not a soul about. I climbed out of the stack, but my feet hadn't even touched the ground when I heard voices from one of the steps.

I threw myself flat on my stomach. There were steps on the other side, too, so I crawled quickly, silently towards them. I only dared look back when I'd reached them. Uniformed shadows moved along the darkened deck.

I slipped down the stairs quietly. The stairs led to the bow, and I didn't meet anyone there. But the corridor was pretty crowded, and I was shocked to find that everyone who passed me stared at me.

I didn't understand what they were staring at. I fled their curious gazes, looking for a little corner in which to hide, but I happened into a bright, first-class saloon instead. There was a mirror on the wall opposite, and I reeled when I saw myself in it. My face was covered in

soot, my clothes were caked in mud, and my trousers had split, revealing the underpants below.

The first-class citizens on their plush crimson divans looked at me
with some astonishment.

"Excuse me," I muttered dimly and swooned out.

Outside, I could no longer control myself. I was seized with panic
and began to run. I ran down the first staircase I came across, fleeing
the light—down, down, as deep as I could go.

I found myself in the bowels of the ship, in a narrow, soot-encrusted,
badly lit little corridor. Somewhere nearby, generators hummed, and
you could feel the excited, burning breath of the boilers in the air.
The narrow metal planks reverberated under my feet, and the hot
steel handrail was throbbing in my hand as if I'd put my finger on
the ship's very pulse. No, there were no carpets and chandeliers and
monocles and apathy here. Down here reality, that good old reliable
reality, lay unveiled, birthing from its darkened womb heat, and light,
and power.

This was my world. I calmed down a bit. The machines clicked and
hummed, everything rattled, wrenched and thrummed, but in some
complicated way still seemed calm and quiet. I looked around. There
was nobody nearby. The workers must have been on break—you could
hear the clinking of plates from behind a door.

I tiptoed on. There was no one in the machine room. I could see,
when I went past it, that there was a water tap beside the door. I could
have a quick wash, I thought, and looked around carefully once more. I
couldn't see anyone; there was only the constant hum of the machinery.
I scurried over to the tap and poked my head under the water. At that
moment, the door opposite me opened.

A young machinist stood before me. He said something, but I didn't
understand what. He was speaking a foreign language. Of course! This
is an Austrian ship, I remembered, and my instinct was to flee. But then
the machinist smiled at me and threw me a towel.

I looked at him in surprise. Did he think I belonged here? No, he
can't possibly think that, he'd know the other workers, and besides, they
were all wearing uniforms. So why was he smiling?

I dried myself, hurried and nervous. The machinist just stood there before me, smiling. He had a good, simple face, a simple smile. What was going through his mind? I wondered. He could surely see I was in trouble. Was he thinking, like Elemér, that the working class has to stick together? Or was he just smiling like Fish-face was smiling, and would he, too, turn me over to the police in the end?

The machinist started talking again, but this time, I understood him, because his eyes, too, were speaking. He gave a quick, meaningful glance in the direction of the window in the corridor, and I followed his gaze with alarm. The Austrian border guards were coming down the passage.

The machinist pointed silently to a side door, and I was off.

"Thank you," I whispered, and he whispered something back.

I couldn't understand what he'd said, just as he couldn't understand what I'd said, but we still understood each other. It seems, I thought, it's not what language you're speaking that matters, but how you look at your fellow man.

The door opened into a coal store. Inside, two grimy, half-naked men were shovelling coal. They looked at me but said nothing and I ran on in the labyrinth of cargo holds, equipment stores and corridors.

I finally found the stairs. I ran up to where I'd come from, but almost ended up bumping into the Hungarian border guards.

I was in luck. This happened in the bow, where two parallel corridors met. I was at the end of the right-hand one when I happened to spot a customs man's trouser leg on the stairs as he was coming down off the deck. I sprang back just in time, and they turned into the other corridor. So they'd finished on deck, I told myself, and sneaked up the stairs.

There was no one on deck, and I climbed back into the smokestack. It was only then it occurred to me that the Austrians may not have searched the deck and were bound to find me here. I wanted to climb out, but it was too late. I heard the sound of footsteps. I could already see myself between the armed men as they dragged me off the boat, when all of a sudden the siren above me sounded.

"Cast off!" I heard the captain cry, and felt the boat moving.

I peered out. Slowly, almost imperceptibly, we were drifting away from the Hungarian coast. The quay commander saluted the ship, and then the lights in the tiny little border station went out.

It must have been midnight. Hungary was sleeping. Europe, too, was sleeping. The world was sleeping. They'd been sung to sleep by Briand and Kellogg's lullabies, sixty-two countries declaring formally that they would never again "resort to war". The Reverend Söderblom received the Nobel Peace Prize, the number of jobless grew and grew, people kept writing operettas about Hungary, and the world, unaware, hummed "The Blue Danube", which carried on washing the bloated corpses of its suicides down from the Black Forest to the Black Sea in three-four time.

The ship turned slowly in the night. I thought of the smiling machinist. He must be standing before a metal handle now, just waiting for the order to release the steam. Yes, down below, people were already working away, and one day, the ship would go where *they* told it to.

"Onwards!" the captain called from the bridge. "Full steam ahead!"

NEW YORK, 1947

BINOCULAR VISION

EDITH PEARLMAN

'A genius of the short story' Mark Lawson, *Guardian*

IN THE BEGINNING WAS THE SEA

TOMÁS GONZÁLEZ

'Smoothly intriguing narrative, with its touches of sinister,
Patricia Highsmith-like menace' *Irish Times*

BEWARE OF PITY

STEFAN ZWEIG

'Zweig's fictional masterpiece' *Guardian*

THE ENCOUNTER

PETRU POPESCU

'A book that suggests new ways of looking at the world
and our place within it' *Sunday Telegraph*

WAKE UP, SIR!

JONATHAN AMES

'The novel is extremely funny but it is also sad and
poignant, and almost incredibly clever' *Guardian*

THE WORLD OF YESTERDAY

STEFAN ZWEIG

'*The World of Yesterday* is one of the greatest memoirs of the twentieth
century, as perfect in its evocation of the world Zweig loved, as it is
in its portrayal of how that world was destroyed' David Hare

WAKING LIONS

AYELET GUNDAR-GOSHEN

'A literary thriller that is used as a vehicle to explore big
moral issues. I loved everything about it' *Daily Mail*

FOR A LITTLE WHILE

RICK BASS

'Bass is, hands down, a master of the short form, creating in a few pages
a natural world of mythic proportions' *New York Times Book Review*